VOLUME

USA	CANADA
1 teaspoon	5 ml
1 tablespoon	15 ml
1/4 cup	60 ml
1/3 cup	80 ml
1/2 cup	120 ml
2/3 cup	160 ml
3/4 cup	180 ml
1 cup	240 ml
1 pint	475 ml
1 quart	.95 liter
1 quart plus 1/4 cup	1 liter
1 gallon	3.8 liters

TEMP...

..., MULTIPLY b... , THEN DIVIDE BY 9

32°F	0°C
212°F	100°C
250°F	121°C
325°F	163°C
350°F	176°C
375°F	190°C
400°F	205°C
425°F	218°C
450°F	232°C

WEIGHT

USA	CANADA
1 ounce	28.3 grams
4 ounces	113 grams
8 ounces	227 grams
12 ounces	340.2 grams

PAN SIZE	APPROXIMATE VOLUME
2 1/2" by 1 1/2" muffin pan cup	1/2 cup
8 1/2" by 4 1/2" by 2 1/2" loaf pan	6 cups
9" by 5" by 3" loaf pan	8 cups
8" by 8" by 1 1/2" baking pan	6 cups
9" by 9" by 1 1/2" baking pan	8 cups
9" by 1" pie plate	4 cups
11" by 7" by 1 1/2" baking pan	8 cups
13" by 9" by 2" baking pan	15 cups
15 1/2" by 10 1/2" by 1" jelly roll pan	16 cups

MEASURING PANS

TO GET AN ACCURATE MEASUREMENT OF YOUR BAKEWARE, FOLLOW THE GUIDELINES BELOW

Pan Volume: Using a measuring cup, fill a baking pan to the rim with water, just short of overflowing. The number of cups needed to fill the pan equals the cup volume of the pan. If you have a pan with a removable bottom, substitute granulated sugar for water.

Pan Size: With a ruler, measure the length and width of a pan across its top from one inside edge to the opposite inside edge. Holding ruler perpendicular to pan, measure the depth of a pan on the inside of the pan from the bottom to the rim.

the Good Housekeeping cookbook

REVISED EDITION

Edited by Susan Westmoreland
Food Director, Good Housekeeping

1,039
recipes from
America's favorite
test kitchen

HEARST BOOKS
A division of Sterling Publishing Co., Inc.

New York / London
www.sterlingpublishing.com

Good Housekeeping

Editor in Chief: Rosemary Ellis
Food Director: Susan Westmoreland
Associate Food Director: Susan Deborah Goldsmith
Special Projects Director: Richard Eisenberg

The Good Housekeeping Cookbook

Culinary Consultant and Writer: Deborah Mintcheff
Copyeditors: Brenda Goldberg and Miriam Rubin
Proofreaders: Diane Boccadoro, Barbara Machtiger, Sydne Matus, Loisina Michel, Deri Reed, Carol Spier
Layout Designer: Laura Smyth
Illustrator: Alan Witschonke

Hearst Books

Publisher: Jacqueline Deval
Editorial Director: Marisa Bulzone
Project Editor: Maryanne Bannon
Art Director: Celia Fuller

Library of Congress Cataloging-in-Publication Data
The Good housekeeping cookbook : 1,039 recipes from America's favorite test kitchen / edited by Susan Westmoreland. — Rev. ed.
    p. cm.
  Includes index.
  ISBN-10: 1-58816-561-2
  ISBN-13: 978-1-58816-561-9
  1. Cookery, American. I. Westmoreland, Susan. II. Good Housekeeping (New York, N.Y.)
  TX715.G624 2007
  641.5973—dc22
                                    2007007273

10 9 8 7 6 5 4 3 2

Published by Hearst Books
A Division of Sterling Publishing Co., Inc.
387 Park Avenue South, New York, NY 10016

Good Housekeeping and Hearst Books are trademarks of Hearst Communications, Inc.

The Good Housekeeping Cookbook Seal guarantees that the recipes in this cookbook meet the strict standards of the Good Housekeeping Research Institute, a source of reliable information and a consumer advocate since 1900. Every recipe has been triple-tested for ease, reliability, and great taste.

www.goodhousekeeping.com

Distributed in Canada by Sterling Publishing
c/o Canadian Manda Group, 165 Dufferin Street
Toronto, Ontario, Canada M6K 3H6

Distributed in Australia by Capricorn Link (Australia) Pty. Ltd.
P.O. Box 704, Windsor, NSW 2756 Australia

For information about custom editions, special sales, premium and corporate purchases, please contact Sterling Special Sales Department at 800-805-5489 or specialsales@sterlingpub.com.

Manufactured in China

Sterling ISBN 13: 978-1-58816-561-9
ISBN 10: 1-58816-561-2

FOREWORD

Welcome to *The Good Housekeeping Cookbook*—my favorite of all our cookbooks. There's a good chance that you grew up eating *Good Housekeeping* recipes, just as I did. My mother kept *Good Housekeeping* on her night table for roughly half a century and frequently turned to it for great recipes that our whole family would enjoy. These days, I work closely with the experts in the Good Housekeeping Test Kitchen, and we make sure that the recipes—all triple-tested—continue to be delicious, easy to make, and easy to follow.

Growing up in the Deep South, I learned that creating a beautiful meal—even a simple one—can be one of life's greatest pleasures. This photo-filled cookbook will help you make dishes you've never tried and show you ways to add zest to some old favorites. You'll find more than 1,000 recipes ranging from classics like Susan's Meat Loaf and All-American Barbecued Chicken to international dishes such as Thai Chicken with Basil and Spaghetti all'Amatriciana to dazzling desserts including Orange Liqueur Soufflé and Banana Cream Pie. All the recipes have nutritional profiles, so you'll know how many calories and carbs are in them, as well as the amount of protein, sodium, cholesterol and fat (total *and* saturated).

Because grilling has become a more and more popular way to make dinner in a hurry (and to get your husband to help!), this edition includes two new chapters: Grilling and Quick & Easy Weeknight Meals. The Grilling chapter delivers useful tips from the Good Housekeeping Test Kitchen on how to get the best from your barbecue. Most of the recipes in the Quick & Easy chapter can be prepared and cooked within 30 minutes—great for you *and* your family.

This cookbook is also a handy reference for your kitchen shelves. No question is left unanswered, whether you are a beginner or have been cooking for years. You'll find reliable information on cooking techniques, safe food handling, and healthy eating. The book opens with an updated Basics chapter, introducing you to all you need to know to start cooking and serving tasty meals for family and friends. The Eating Well section has been newly researched and reviewed by a registered dietician, reflecting the latest research about nutrition. Every chapter begins with the fundamentals of its food category. For instance, in the Meat chapter, you'll learn about different grades of meat, what to look for when buying it, how to store it, and the various methods to prepare it. An illustrated chart depicts the most popular cuts, so you'll know exactly what to ask for when you go shopping.

The Good Housekeeping Cookbook, the latest in our long, venerable line, was created by Susan Westmoreland, our magazine's Food Director and the head of the famed Good Housekeeping Test Kitchen. While a trained chef who studied at cooking schools in the U.S. and abroad, Susan learned to cook where most of us did: in her mother's Italian kitchen. Named The James Beard Foundation's Editor of the Year in 2001, Susan is also a "real world" cook—she often tries out her latest *Good Housekeeping* recipes on her husband, Rip, and son, Lucio.

So from our kitchens to yours, happy cooking! I hope this book will give you years of delicious, healthy dining at home.

ROSEMARY ELLIS, EDITOR-IN-CHIEF

CONTENTS

1

BASICS

EQUIPMENT

A well-equipped kitchen is a must for cooking delicious meals. You can accomplish a lot with a good set of knives and a few well-chosen pots and pans. Just remember, you often get what you pay for. High-quality utensils, made from durable materials, last longer, so buy the best you can afford.

Stainless steel is easy to clean and not too heavy, but it isn't a very good conductor of heat; an aluminum or copper core is often added to improve its heat-conducting properties. By contrast, copper is an excellent conductor of heat and copper pots are gorgeous, but the pots must be polished and can be very heavy. Cast iron and aluminum are inexpensive and excellent heat conductors. Unfortunately, they react to acidic ingredients, such as tomatoes and wine, but they are also available enamel-coated.

ON THE STOVE

Here is a list of basic pots and pans that every kitchen should be equipped with:

Saucepan Three or four saucepans with lids, ranging from 1 to 4 quarts. They should be between 3½ to 4 inches deep, so you can stir without spilling food over the side.

Dutch oven These pots are ideal for braising roasts and stews on top of the stove as well as in the oven. A 5- to 6-quart Dutch oven is the most useful.

Skillets You'll need at least three sizes: small (8-inch), medium (9- to 10-inch), and large (12-inch).

Saucepot This wide, deep pot can be used for soups and stews. A 5-quart saucepot that has a tight-fitting lid is versatile.

Stockpot A tall, narrow, 6- to 8-quart stockpot can be called into action to cook many foods, including pasta, soups, stocks, lobster, and corn on the cob.

Basic cooking equipment: steamer, saucepans, grill pan, Dutch oven, thermometers, skillets, double boiler

Double boiler A saucepan topped with another covered saucepan; food is gently cooked in the top pan by water simmering in the bottom pan.

Grill pan This ridged skillet acts as a stovetop grill. Food can be cooked with little or no added fat; the ridges allow any rendered fat to drip away as the food cooks.

Griddle This flat metal pan can be heated on top of the stove to cook pancakes, French toast, cheese sandwiches, and bacon. Electric models (some have nonstick surfaces) are also available.

IN THE OVEN

Some of the most popular materials for bakeware include enameled cast iron (easy to clean and a good heat conductor), enameled steel (a reasonably priced, lightweight choice for roasting pans), stainless steel (moderately heavy and durable), aluminum (often laminated to create a nonstick surface), heat-resistant glass (a popular, inexpensive choice), and glass-ceramic (which can go from oven to freezer). Earthenware and stoneware are good for long, slow baking, like stews or beans.

Cake pans that have a dull heat-absorbing finish, such as aluminum, produce the best cakes. Avoid shiny metals, such as stainless steel, which reflect the heat, and dark metal pans, which absorb heat too quickly. When it comes to baking bread, choose heavy aluminum or dark metal pans for the best texture and a well-browned crust.

How to Measure a Pan

To measure a baking dish or pan, measure across the top of the dish from inside edge to inside edge. Measure the depth on the inside of the dish from the bottom to the rim.

Essential Bakeware Roundup

Baking dish A large, fairly shallow oval or rectangular dish with sides about 2 inches high; usually glass or ceramic. It's good to have a variety of sizes, but 10" by 15", 13" by 9", and 11" by 7" are the most commonly used.

Baking pan Similar to a baking dish but made of metal; the sides are 1½ to 2 inches high. You'll want an 8-inch square, a 9-inch square, and a 13" by 9" pan.

Basic baking and roasting pans: metal loaf pan, oval baking dish, jelly-roll pan, cookie sheet, roasting pan and rack, round cake pan, square baking pan, springform pan

Bundt pan Sometimes called a fluted tube pan. A 10-inch, 12-cup size is good for most needs.

Cake pan Layer cakes are usually baked in 8- or 9-inch round pans (you'll need two or three of each); baking pans are used for rectangular and square cakes.

Casserole Round, oval, square, or rectangular, this lidded dish can be glass, ceramic, or enameled metal.

Cookie sheets For the best air circulation and for even browning, choose shiny, heavy metal cookie sheets with one or two slightly raised sides. Double-thick insulated pans protect against overbrowning. Nonstick surfaces are another option.

Custard cups Purchase glass cups or ceramic ramekins with a 6-ounce capacity.

Jelly-roll pan Use a standard aluminum 15½" by 10½" pan for jelly-roll cakes.

Loaf pan Standard sizes are 9" by 5" and 8½" by 4½". There is a substantial volume difference between the two.

Muffin tins To bake muffins and cupcakes, use standard 2½" by 1¼" muffin-pan cups; 1¾" by 1" mini muffin-pan cups are nice to have too.

The recipes in this book have been perfected for use at sea level. At higher altitudes, adjustments in the cooking time, temperature, and ingredients could be necessary.

At sea level, water boils at 212°F. With each additional 500 feet of altitude, the boiling point drops 1°F. Even though the boiling point is lower, it takes longer to generate the heat required to cook food. Therefore, at high altitudes, foods boiled in water (such as pasta and beans) will take longer to come to a boil and will require longer cooking times than our recipes suggest. The processing times for canning foods and the blanching times for freezing vegetables will vary, too.

At high altitudes, cake recipes may need slight adjustments in the proportions of flour, leavening, liquid, eggs, etc. These adjustments will vary from recipe to recipe, and no set guidelines can be given. Many cake mixes now carry special directions on the label for high-altitude preparation.

High altitudes can also affect the rising of doughs and batters, deep-frying, candy making, and other aspects of food preparation. For complete information and special recipes for your area, call or write to the home agent at your county cooperative extension office or to the home economics department of your local utility company or state university.

Pie plate The standard size is 9" by 1"; deep-dish pie plates are 9½" by 1½" or 9½" by 2". Glass, dark metal, and aluminum pans yield crisp, nicely browned piecrusts.

Roasting pan A large deep pan typically made of stainless steel, enameled steel, or aluminum. A rectangular roasting pan with a rack is the most useful.

Springform pan 9" by 3" and 10" by 2½" are the ones most often called for.

Tart pan A shallow metal pan with fluted sides and a removable bottom that comes in many shapes and sizes: 9" by 1" and 11" by 1" round pans are the most common.

Tube pan Comes in 9- and 10-inch diameters.

UTENSIL CENTRAL

In addition to pots and pans, every kitchen needs other helpful tools. Here are some we find indispensable:

Bristle brushes Use one for cleaning pots and one for scrubbing vegetables.

Colander Choose a large colander with a stable footed base; the more holes it has, the more quickly food can drain.

Cooling racks If you bake a lot of cookies, you should have at least two large wire racks. Bakers who like to make layer cakes should have three or four small round racks.

Corkscrew A tool used to remove the corks from wine bottles. They are available at most kitchenware stores in a range of prices.

Cutting boards Plastic boards are lightweight and easy to clean in the dishwasher, but wooden boards are extremely durable and don't attract or retain any more bacteria than plastic ones.

Grater This flat or box-shaped tool can grate (small holes), shred (large holes), or slice (large slots). We love Microplane® graters for their sharpness and ease of use.

Measuring cups For liquids, use clear glass or plastic cups with pouring spouts. It's useful to have two sizes: a 1-cup measure for smaller amounts and a 2- or 4-cup measure for larger amounts. To measure dry ingredients accurately, use metal or plastic cups that come in nested sets of ¼ cup, ⅓ cup, ½ cup, and 1 cup.

Measuring spoons Come in nesting sets; stainless-steel spoons are the most durable. Most sets include ¼ teaspoon, ½ teaspoon, 1 teaspoon, and 1 tablespoon.

Mixing bowls Stainless-steel bowls are the most versatile because they react quickly to changes in temperature. Glass or ceramic bowls work well to insulate rising yeast dough.

Rolling pins Heavy pins, either hardwood or marble, work best for rolling out dough.

Sieve/strainer A wire sieve can be used to sift ingredients or strain liquids. Buy a few sizes with different mesh gauges.

Spatulas To turn food, use heatproof or metal spatulas (pancake turners). Rubber spatulas are used for mixing and folding; they're not heatproof. Silicon spatulas are heatproof. And a long, narrow metal spatula is a must for frosting cakes.

Thermometers Meat thermometers are vital when roasting meats and poultry, and many options are available. Instant-read thermometers, which register up to 220°F, are very accurate. Probe-type thermometers give a digital reading on a unit that is placed outside the oven. Candy thermometers register temperatures up to 400°F and can be used for candy making and deep-frying. An oven thermometer is the best way to accurately check the temperature of an oven, because control dials and thermostats are notoriously inaccurate. Optional, but nice to have, are freezer and refrigerator thermometers.

Tongs Spring-action tongs are the best for picking up foods and for turning meats without piercing them.

Vegetable peeler Swivel-blade peelers remove less peel than fixed-blade peelers; they conform to the shape of the food.

Whisk Use the right whisk for the job. A medium-size whisk is good for sauces, vinaigrettes, and batters. Flat paddle-shaped whisks are perfect for getting into the corners of roasting pans when making pan gravies. Large balloon-shaped whisks are ideal for beating air into heavy cream or egg whites.

Nice-to-Have Extras

Adjustable-blade slicer Use to slice, cut into matchstick strips, and waffle-cut. Adjustable-blade slicers range from the classic and pricey metal mandoline to lightweight plastic models that do a great job for much less money.

Apple corer This cylindrical tool neatly cores whole apples as well as pears. Buy the largest size because it will easily remove all the core.

Egg beater This hand-powered mixer can also be used for whipping cream. It's low-tech but useful.

Ice-cream maker Available in manual and electric models; some have insulated liners that must be frozen overnight.

Juicer Use for extracting fruit and vegetable juices. One of the most practical models is a simple ridged cone that easily juices citrus fruits. Small electric versions are great when you need a large quantity of juice.

Kitchen scissors For cutting kitchen string, snipping fresh herbs, and trimming artichoke leaves. Shears, which are larger and spring-loaded, make cutting up poultry simple. Buy sturdy models made of stainless steel.

Melon baller Besides scooping perfect globes of melon (and potatoes), this tool neatly cores halved apples and pears.

Mortar and pestle Use for grinding spices and herbs. You crush with the pestle (the batlike tool) in the mortar (the bowl).

Pastry bag For decorating cakes and pies, forming spritz cookies, and creating beautifully shaped pastries. Disposable plastic pastry bags don't retain odors and flavors as plastic-lined canvas bags do.

Pastry blender This tool's metal wires easily cut cold fat into flour for tart dough, pastry dough, biscuits, and scones.

Pastry brush Use to brush dough with melted butter or beaten egg and to apply glazes; also great for dusting excess flour from dough. When buying, look for well-anchored natural bristle brushes in widths of 1 to 1½ inches.

Potato masher Perfect for cooked potatoes and other root vegetables and for turning cooked beans into a chunky puree.

Ruler Keep a ruler in the kitchen for measuring pans and pastry shapes as well as for other tasks.

Salad spinner Uses centrifugal force to dry greens, preventing dressed salads from getting watered down.

Skewers A must for kabobs. Always soak wooden and bamboo skewers in water for 30 minutes before using to prevent them from burning on the grill.

Steamer The collapsible metal style easily fits into various-sized pots and pans. There is also a version that consists of a saucepan with a perforated bowllike insert that allows the steam to penetrate. Bamboo steamers fit into woks.

Zester Pulled across the peel of citrus fruit, it removes the colorful, flavorful outer layer, leaving the bitter pith behind.

Sharpening Up on Knives

The importance of good knives cannot be overemphasized. Poorly made knives make cutting and chopping tiresome work, while good knives will enable you to whip through these jobs with ease. If you take good care of your fine knives, they'll last a lifetime.

High-carbon stainless steel, an alloy that contains a large proportion of carbon, makes excellent knives that sharpen well. Some cooks prefer carbon-steel knives because they hold a very sharp edge, but they also corrode and stain easily. Knives that purport to never need sharpening have two drawbacks: The blades are finely serrated, so their ridges can tear food instead of cutting it. When the knives eventually do need sharpening, it isn't possible.

Before buying a knife, hold it in your hand to see if it feels comfortable. The best knives are made of a solid piece of metal (called the tang) that goes all the way through the handle. The extra weight of the tang gives a knife better balance.

Using the proper knife for each kitchen chore is more efficient and will make the job easier, ultimately saving you time in preparation. These knives should be in every well-run kitchen:
• Chef's knife (for slicing, chopping, and mincing)
• Paring knife (for fruits and vegetables)
• Long serrated knife (for slicing breads, cakes, and thin-skinned fruits and vegetables)
• Carving knife (for slicing meats). It often comes in a set with a carving fork.

Basic measuring cups and spoons: 1-, 2-, and 4-cup glass measuring cups, set of dry measuring cups, set of measuring spoons

• Thin-bladed boning knife (for trimming fat and cutting poultry and meat)
• Slicing knife (for cutting thin slices of meat). It has a scalloped edge and a round tip, so you won't poke a hole in the roast
• Heavy cleaver (for cutting up poultry)

COOKING BASICS

If you master just a few fundamental cooking skills, you will be assured success in the kitchen. Measuring ingredients may be a simple task, but if performed carelessly, it may mean the difference between success and failure. Learn how to chop, slice, and cut properly and your meal preparation time will be reduced. And remember, as with other skills, practice makes perfect.

MEASURING BASICS

Measure ingredients carefully, and you'll get consistent results each time you prepare a recipe. Every kitchen needs liquid measuring cups, dry measuring cups, and measuring spoons.
• For liquids, use clear glass measuring cups with pouring spouts. Place the cup on a level surface and add the desired amount of liquid; bend down to check the accuracy of the measure at eye level (do not lift up the cup).
• For dry ingredients, use standard-size metal or plastic cups that can be leveled off.
• Nesting sets of graduated measuring spoons are used to measure both liquid and dry ingredients.

We use the "spoon-and-sweep" method for measuring dry ingredients such as flour, sugar, and cocoa. To measure flour, for example, stir it with a fork or whisk to aerate it (flour tends to pack down during storage). Lightly spoon the flour into a dry measuring cup to overflowing, then level it off with the straight edge of a knife or narrow metal spatula: Don't pack the flour or shake the cup. If a recipe calls for 1 cup sifted flour, sift the flour, then spoon it into the cup. If you need 1 cup flour, sifted, measure the flour and then sift. Do not "dip and sweep" (use the measuring cup to scoop the flour); it packs too much flour into the cup.

Butter and margarine come in premarked sticks, so there's no need to use a measuring cup. Use the markings on the wrapper to measure the desired amount, then cut it off. One 4-ounce (¼ pound) stick of butter or margarine equals 8 tablespoons or ½ cup.

Ingredients such as vegetable shortening, butter, and brown sugar, should be firmly packed (pressed) into dry measuring cups or spoons and then leveled off.

Before measuring sticky ingredients, such as corn syrup or molasses, coat the measuring cup or spoon with vegetable oil or nonstick cooking spray, so the item can slide out easily.

If you have any doubts about the volume of a baking dish or casserole, pour a measured amount of water into the dish, right up to the top. Or double-check a baking pan's dimensions with a ruler; even a 1-inch difference can affect your baking success.

CUTTING BASICS

For the best results, use a chef's knife, and sharpen it on a steel before each use. To prevent the cutting board from slipping, place a damp towel underneath. Hold the  knife handle in your right hand near the blade. Your thumb should be on the left side of the handle and your fingers close together and wrapped around the other side of the handle.

In this book, we coarsely chop, slice, cube, cut into matchstick strips, finely chop, and mince. Here's how:

Coarsely chop To cut food into ½- to ¾-inch irregular pieces: When chopping, the tip of the knife remains on the cutting board; the knife handle is raised and lowered in a rocking motion while the knife is moved from left to right. If necessary, tuck under the fingers of your left hand and carefully push the food toward the blade.

Chop To cut food into small irregular pieces about the size of peas: Roughly cut up the food, then move the knife through the food until you have the desired size.

Finely chop To chop food into very small irregular pieces, less than ¼ inch.

Mince To cut into tiny irregular pieces, less than ⅛ inch. We use this term only for ginger.

Cube To cut into ½-inch blocks: First cut the food lengthwise into ½-inch-thick slices. Stack the slices and cut into ½-inch-wide sticks. Then cut crosswise into ½-inch cubes.

Matchstick strips First, cut the food into slices 2 inches long and ⅛ inch thick. Stack the slices; cut lengthwise into ⅛-inch-wide sticks.

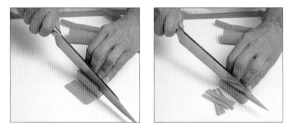

FOOD SAFETY AND STORAGE

Use these guidelines to help keep the food in your kitchen wholesome and safe to eat.

RULES OF FOOD SAFETY

Keep It Clean

Good old-fashioned cleanliness is the best safeguard against harmful bacteria. Keep a clean kitchen. Always wash and dry your hands before handling food. Frequently wash kitchen towels, dishcloths, and sponges. Rinse fruits and vegetables thoroughly before eating. Sterilize cutting boards once a week in a solution of 1 tablespoon bleach per 1 gallon water.

Avoid Cross-Contamination

Don't put cooked meat (or any ready-to-eat food) on a plate that has been in contact with raw meat, poultry, or fish. It's a good idea to have several cutting boards: one for raw meats, poultry, and fish; one for vegetables and cheese; and perhaps a third for fruits, nuts, and chocolate.

Cook It Right

To kill harmful bacteria that may be present in raw eggs, fish, poultry, and meat, it's essential to cook these foods thoroughly. The United States Department of Agriculture recommends cooking them to at least 160°F. At this temperature, however, food (especially meat) may be cooked beyond your preference. If you cook it less, some risk is involved, so the choice is ultimately a personal one. An instant-read thermometer is the easiest way to check for doneness. To check visually, follow these guidelines: Cook red meat to at least medium-rare, pork until the juices run clear and the meat retains just a trace of pink, poultry until the juices run clear, fish just until opaque throughout, and egg yolks and whites until thickened and set. Always cook ground meat until no pink remains. When cooking egg-based sauces, be sure the final temperature is no lower than 160°F.

Keep Hot Foods Hot and Cold Foods Cold

The safe zones for storing food are below 40°F and above 140°F. Keep food below or above these temperatures, and you'll discourage bacterial growth (bacteria love a moist, warm environment). Don't leave food out at room temperature for longer than two hours. In hot weather, protein foods such as chicken, egg salad, or any food containing mayonnaise should not be left out of the refrigerator for more than one hour. It's also unwise to cook food in stages. For example, don't partially cook fish, poultry, or meat, then return to it later to finish cooking. Even when food is stored in the refrigerator between the cooking stages, safe temperatures may not be maintained and bacteria could develop.

Treat Leftovers with Respect

Refrigerate leftovers as soon as possible. Divide large amounts among smaller containers for quicker cooling. Date all leftovers so you know how long you've had them. If you have any doubt about a food's freshness, throw it out.

REFRIGERATOR KNOW-HOW

Don't take your refrigerator for granted. Help it do its job by following a few simple rules:

Be sure the temperature of your refrigerator remains between 33° and 40°F; use a refrigerator thermometer for extra insurance. To prevent spoilage, store foods on a

HOW LONG WILL IT KEEP?

Foods frozen for longer than the recommended times aren't harmful—they just won't be at their peak flavor and texture.

FOOD	TIME IN FREEZER (0°F)
Milk	3 months
Butter	6 to 9 months
Cheese, hard (Cheddar, Swiss)	6 months
Cheese, soft (Brie, Bel Paese)	6 months
Cream, half-and-half	4 months
Sour cream	don't feeze
Eggs (raw yolks, whites)	1 year
Frankfurters (opened or unopened packages)	1 to 2 months
Luncheon meats (opened or unopened packages)	1 to 2 months
Bacon	1 month
Sausage, raw, links or patties	1 to 2 months
Ham, fully cooked (whole, half, slices)	1 to 2 months
Ground or stew meat	3 to 4 months
Steaks	6 to 12 months
Chops	3 to 6 months
Roasts	4 to 12 months
Chicken or turkey, whole	1 year
Chicken or turkey, pieces	9 months
Casseroles, cooked, poultry	4 to 6 months
Casseroles, cooked, meat	2 to 3 months
Soups and stews	2 to 3 months
Fish, lean (cod, flounder, haddock)	6 months
Fish, fatty (bluefish, mackerel, salmon)	2 to 3 months
Fish, cooked	4 to 6 months
Fish, smoked	2 months in vacuum pack
Shrimp, scallops, squid, shucked clams, mussels, oysters	3 to 6 months
Pizza	1 to 2 months
Breads and rolls, yeast	3 to 6 month
Breads, quick	2 to 3 months
Cakes, unfrosted	3 months
Cheesecakes	2 to 3 months
Cookies, baked	3 months
Cookie dough, raw	2 to 3 months
Pies, fruit, unbaked	8 months
Pies, custard or meringue-topped	don't freeze
Piecrust, raw	2 to 3 months
Nuts, salted	6 to 8 months
Nuts, unsalted	9 to 12 months

rotating basis: Place newly stored items at the back of the shelves and move older items to the front.

Store meat, fish, and poultry on a plate to catch any drips; if you don't plan to cook them within two days, freeze them immediately. Never store eggs in the open egg compartment in the refrigerator door; it's too warm. Eggs should be kept in their original container to prevent them from absorbing the odors of other foods. For this same reason, store cheese, cream, milk, yogurt, margarine, and butter tightly closed in their containers or packaging or wrap airtight.

PANTRY STORAGE

Unless otherwise noted, these pantry staples fare best in a cool, dry place. For more information on ingredients such as flour, pasta, and grains, see the specific chapter introductions.

Baking powder Once opened, it will keep for up to six months. To test its effectiveness, add ½ teaspoon to ½ cup warm water; it should bubble vigorously.

Bread crumbs Store dried bread crumbs for up to six months or, for better flavor, refrigerate for up to two years.

Honey Lasts indefinitely; if it crystallizes, remove the lid and place the jar in a bowl of hot water. Stir until the crystals dissolve.

Hot pepper sauce Refrigerate after opening.

Olive oil Keep in a cool, dark place for up to six months. Don't buy more than you can use; it can turn rancid, especially if stored in a warm place.

Pancake syrup It will keep for up to nine months (if stored longer, the syrup will thin and the flavor will weaken).

Peanut butter Unopened it will hold for a year in your cupboard. Refrigerate after opening to keep it from becoming rancid.

Soy sauce Unopened it will keep for one year. Once opened, refrigerate to keep for an additional year.

Spices and dried herbs Store in opaque containers in a cool, dark place (not near the stove) for up to one year. After that, herbs and spices begin to lose their flavor. It's a good idea to write the date of purchase on the label. Sniff before using: If the aroma is weak, discard and buy a new supply.

Vegetable oil Store in a cool, dark place for up to six months.

Vinegar Unopened it will keep indefinitely. The sediment that sometimes appears is harmless; strain off the vinegar, if you wish. Once opened store for up to six months. Vinegar with added flavorings, such as herbs, should be strained into a clean bottle as soon as the vinegar level drops below the top of the ingredients.

STORING FRESH HERBS

Most fresh herbs are highly perishable, so buy them in small quantities. To store for a few days, immerse the roots or stems in 2 inches of water. Cover with a plastic bag; refrigerate.

To dry fresh herbs (this works best with sturdy herbs like rosemary and thyme), rinse lightly and pat dry with paper towels. Hang them upside down, in bunches, in a dry, dark place. When the leaves become brittle (it typically takes from a few days up to one week), pick them off and discard the stems. Store the dried leaves in a tightly covered opaque container in a cool, dry place.

To freeze herbs, rinse lightly, pat dry, and remove the stems. Place them in plastic containers or heavy-duty zip-tight plastic bags. When frozen, herbs darken, but their flavor remains. There's no need to thaw frozen herbs; add them directly to the pot. Or place a few herbs (leaves only) in each section of an ice cube tray. Add enough water to cover; freeze. Unmold and store the cubes in heavy-duty zip-tight plastic bags. Add the cubes to simmering soups, sauces, or stews.

TAKING FOOD ON THE ROAD

Whenever food is removed from the refrigerator, it can easily warm to temperatures that encourage bacterial growth. But with some planning, you can avoid potential problems.

For picnics, use two small coolers rather than one large one. Use one cooler for nonperishables, such as fruit and beverages, and the other for perishable items, such as meats, poultry, salads, and cheese. Remember: A cooler cannot make foods colder than they already are, so chill foods thoroughly before placing them in the cooler. To preserve the chill, don't open the lid for longer or more often than necessary.

Double-wrap meat and poultry in zip-tight plastic bags so the juices don't leak out and contaminate other foods. Pack perishable items, like meat, next to the ice packs. Delicate items, such as green salads and slaws, should be stored away from the ice to prevent freezing.

Thermal carrying bags are the most convenient way to transport hot foods, but a cooler can also maintain the temperature of hot foods for a few hours. If you are bringing a hot dish to a party, heat it until piping hot. Wrap the covered dish in a thick layer of newspaper to insulate it and keep the heat in, then place in a cooler that isn't much bigger than the dish.

EATING WELL

The message is simple: Eat well to stay well. The good news is that you don't need a graduate degree in nutrition to eat healthfully on a daily basis. What follows are some guidelines and information to help you make informed decisions about what you and your family should eat to maintain a balanced diet.

DIETARY GUIDELINES FOR AMERICANS

- Consume a variety of nutrient-dense foods and beverages within the basic food groups. Choose foods that limit your intake of saturated and trans fats, cholesterol, added sugars, salt, and alcohol.

USING THE NUTRITIONAL VALUES IN THIS BOOK

At the bottom of each recipe, you'll find nutritional information. To aid you in using this information, see "Nutrients: The Big Three" (page 16) and "Understanding Food Labels" (right) for the recommended daily nutrient levels. Aim to balance higher-fat recipes with leaner accompaniments. For example, serve lasagna with a green salad tossed with lowfat dressing, skim milk, and fresh fruit for dessert.

- Our nutritional calculations do not include any optional ingredients or garnishes.
- When alternative ingredients are given (such as margarine), our calculations are based on the first item listed.
- Unless otherwise noted, whole milk has been used.

UNDERSTANDING FOOD LABELS

Food labels help you make informed choices about the foods to include in your diet.

The Percent Daily Values reflect the percentage of the recommended daily amount of a nutrient in a serving (based on 2,000 calories daily). You can "budget" your intake of nutrients by adding up these percentages. For example, the label below shows a food containing 13 percent of the daily value for fat. If the next food you eat has a 10 percent daily value for fat, you've already had 23 percent of your total fat allowance for the day. When it comes to fat, saturated fat, sodium, and cholesterol, try to keep the daily values below 100 percent. Aim for 100 percent of fiber, vitamins A and C, calcium, and iron . (Other vitamins and minerals may also appear on labels.)

The Daily Values footnote includes a chart that shows some Daily Values for diets containing 2,000 and 2,500 calories. Your own daily values may be higher or lower.

Food labels are required to have an ingredients list. The ingredients are listed in descending order according to their weight. This enables you to easily discern which food products contain larger amounts of ingredients that are healthful.

Nutrition Facts

Serving Size 2 pieces (29g)
Servings Per Container 15

Amount Per Serving	
Calories 150	Calories from Fat 80

	% Daily Value*
Total Fat 8g	**13%**
Saturated Fat 5g	**27%**
Cholesterol 25mg	**8%**
Sodium 115mg	**5%**
Total Carbohydrate 18g	**6%**
Dietary Fiber 0g	**0%**
Sugars 6g	
Protein 2g	

Vitamin A 0%	•	Vitamin C 0%
Calcium 2%	•	Iron 2%

* Percent Daily Values are based on a 2,000 calorie diet.

- Engage in regular physical activity and reduce sedentary activities to promote health, psychological well-being, and a healthy body weight.
- Consume 2 cups of fruit and 2½ cups of vegetables (dark green and orange-colored vegetables, legumes, and starchy vegetables) each day for a 2,000-calorie diet, adjusting the amount as needed.
- Consume three or more 1-ounce-equivalent servings of whole grains each day.
- Consume 3 cups of fat-free or low-fat milk or equivalent dairy products per day.
- Derive less than 10 percent of your calories from saturated fat and less than 300mg of cholesterol per day. Avoid trans fats.
- Keep your total fat intake between 20 and 35 percent of your calories, with most fats coming from polyunsaturated and monounsaturated sources, such as fish, nuts, and vegetable oils.
- Choose fiber-rich fruits, vegetables, and whole grains each day.
- Consume less than 2,300mg (about 1 teaspoon) of sodium each day.
- Women who choose to drink alcohol should limit themselves to one drink per day; men should limit themselves to no more than two drinks per day.

For the complete recommendations, go to www.healthierus.gov/dieteryguidelines.

NUTRIENTS: THE BIG THREE

Our bodies need three essential nutrients: carbohydrates, proteins, and fats.

Carbohydrates The right kind of carbohydrates is the mainstay of a well-balanced diet. "Good" carbohydrates include fruits, vegetables, and whole grains. Carbohydrates come in many forms. They can be made up of dietary fiber, starch, or sugar. Diets rich in dietary fiber have been shown to have a reduced risk of coronary heart disease, among other benefits, and research indicates that whole-grain eaters are thinner than people who eat few whole-grain foods. Fiber, which is found in the bran layer of some grains, including whole wheat, is credited with some of the health benefits of whole grains. When whole wheat is processed to make white flour, the healthful bran layer is removed,

along with the disease-fighting antioxidants in the bran. The latest government recommendations are that at least half of your grains should be whole grain (see "How to Spot a Whole Grain").

The starch and sugar in carbohydrates supply the body with the energy it needs for normal body functions, including brain functions, heartbeat, breathing, and digestion, as well as for exercise such as walking, running, and cycling. When carbohydrates are digested, they become blood sugar (glucose), which is then used as fuel in our bodies. In general, the less sugar you eat the better. This doesn't, however, include the naturally occurring sugar in fruit, milk, or yogurt. You need to limit the *added* sugar that comes from sweeteners, including white sugar, brown sugar, honey, maple syrup, high-fructose corn syrup, dextrose, sucrose, fruit juice concentrate, and other sweeteners. Remember that starch is an important part of a balanced diet. Look for good carbs, such as whole-wheat pasta, whole-grain polenta, buckwheat, and oatmeal.

Unfortunately, it is not always easy to tell if a product is a whole-grain–rich food. So here are some clues:
- Look for the word *whole* in the ingredients list.
- See where the whole grain falls in the list of ingredients. Remember that ingredients are listed in order of their weight: If a whole grain is listed first and is the only grain, there is a lot of whole grain in the product. If the first ingredient is *wheat flour* (which is really white flour), followed by some sort of sweetener, then *whole-wheat flour* is not the dominant grain.
- Check the amount of dietary fiber. In general, 100-percent whole-grain products should have at least 2 grams of fiber per ounce (29 grams) or per 80 calories; crackers at least 3 grams fiber per ounce; pasta at least 5 grams of fiber per 2 ounces dried. *For more information, go to* www.wholegrainscouncil.org.

Proteins The body needs protein to produce new body tissue. They are also a great weight-loss friend, as protein helps keep you feeling full for hours after eating. Too much protein, however, is unhealthy; it can stress the kidneys, and if it comes from fatty meat, it is also filling you with saturated fat. Beef, chicken, fish, pork, lamb, and other meats and tofu and other soy products are the richest sources of protein. Beans (black, pinto, etc.), lentils, cheese, milk, and yogurt are the next highest. A small amount of protein can also be found in grains, bread, and other starches and in vegetables. Ideally, your plate should look like this: half-filled with vegetables or fruits, a quarter with starches, and another quarter with protein-rich foods (and a little fat).

Fats The government guideline for fat consumption is 20 to 35 percent of your total daily calories, which is a wide range. Much more important than the total fat is the amount of saturated and trans fat in your diet. Here's what you need to know about these fats:

When an excess of saturated fat is consumed, it raises your blood cholesterol level, increasing your risk of heart disease and stroke. Saturated fat is found naturally in foods, but it is especially concentrated in fatty animal-based foods, such as butter and chicken skin and in some oils, such as palm and coconut. Even "good" oils like olive and canola contain a little saturated fat, so you can't avoid it entirely. For a heart-healthy diet you should derive less than 10 percent of your total calories from saturated fat, which is a maximum of 15 grams of saturated fat daily, based on a 1,500-calorie diet.

Even worse than saturated fat is trans fat, which not only raises the LDL ("bad cholesterol") but also lowers the HDL ("good cholesterol"). It is formed by a process called hydrogenation, which turns oils into semisolids like margarine and shortening. On the ingredients list these oils appear as partially hydrogenated oils or shortening and are reflected in the trans fat total on the Nutrition Facts label. It is important to keep your intake of trans fat low. Here are some tips:

- Use canola or olive oil whenever possible.
- Limit—or avoid—processed foods made with partially hydrogenated oils, or with oils high in saturated fat (palm, palm kernel, coconut) or with butter.
- Use "0 trans" or "trans fat-free" margarine.

HOW TO INTERPRET PACKAGE INFORMATION

While the Nutrition Facts label can tell you a lot about a food, you need to check the ingredients list to see what you're really eating. Is your breakfast cereal made with whole grains or does your favorite salad dressing contain oil that is high in saturated fat, for example.

By law, ingredients lists must be ordered by weight. The heaviest ingredient goes first, followed by the next heaviest, and so on. It is not a good sign if sugar is the first ingredient in a cereal or when bad fats like partially hydrogenated soybean and cottonseed oils are the third ingredient listed on a can of biscuit dough.

HOW TO SPOT A WHOLE GRAIN

To help you when shopping for whole grains, here are the words you should look for in the ingredients list:

It's a whole grain if it's called:
Brown (also black, red, purple) rice
Buckwheat
Bulgur (cracked wheat)
Millet
Quinoa
Sorghum
Triticale
Whole-grain corn
Whole oats and oatmeal
Whole rye
Whole spelt
Whole wheat
Wild rice

It's not a whole grain if it's called:
Corn flour or cornmeal
Enriched flour
Multigrain (this means various grains, not necessarily whole)
Pumpernickel
Rice or rice flour
Rye flour or rye
Stone-ground wheat (it needs to say "stone-ground *whole wheat*")
Unbleached wheat flour
Wheat or wheat flour
Wheat germ (not a whole grain but very good for you)
Whole barley (pearl barley; not a whole grain but very good for you)

Below is a list of common phrases found on many food packages:

Cholesterol free or No cholesterol Don't be fooled by the words *No cholesterol* written across the label of a jar of peanut butter or bottle of canola oil. If you turn to the Nutrition Facts label, you'll see that no brand of either food has cholesterol—and never did! Only foods of animal origin contain cholesterol. But manufacturers hope you don't know that.

Light This word is used to describe fat content, taste, or color. If the manufacturer is describing the fat content as "light," the product has at least 50 percent less fat than the original. The label must also say "50% less fat than our regular product." "Light" olive oil, on the other hand, describes the oil's color. The oil is as caloric as regular olive oil but has been processed to remove some of its flavor. A muffin mix can say "light and fluffy" as a way to describe its texture or consistency.

Lowfat or Fat free Lowfat products must contain 3 grams or less fat per serving and fat-free products must have less than 0.5 grams of fat per serving. But check the number of calories—that number could be very high. It is easy to gain lots of weight eating fat-free cookies because they are loaded with sugar.

Low sodium or Light in sodium This means that the sodium was cut by at least 50 percent over the original product. Be careful when using a "low" version of a super-high-sodium food such as soy sauce or soup. You can still end up consuming a lot of sodium. Check the numbers on the Nutrition Facts label.

Sugar-free, No added sugars, Without added sugars A sugar-free chocolate candy may not contain a speck of sugar, but it's still got plenty of fat and calories. Be sure to check out the Nutrition Facts label to know how many calories and grams of saturated fat you're consuming.

Sweetened with fruit juice, Fruit juice sweetener, or Fruit juice concentrate These sweeteners are made by reducing fruit juice—usually grape juice—into a sticky sweetener. These sweeteners are not nutritious; they are just like sugar.

KEEP IT LIGHT

In general, animal products are higher in fat than plant foods, but it's not necessary to cut out all meat and dairy products to keep your fat intake reasonable. Low-fat dairy foods, lean and well-trimmed meat, and skinless poultry provide the same amounts of vitamins and minerals as their fattier counterparts. Skinless poultry, fish, dry beans, and split peas are the "slimmest" foods in this category. By removing the skin from poultry, you reduce the fat by almost one half. Most seafood is low in fat and also contains beneficial omega-3 oils, which have been linked to lowering blood cholesterol. Dry beans also provide the body with fiber, which is necessary for digestion.

You can enjoy red meat if you choose lean cuts and trim away all the visible fat (marbled fat cannot be trimmed away). Here are some good choices:

- Beef eye round, top round, tenderloin, top sirloin, flank steak, top loin, ground beef. Choose ground sirloin; it's 90 to 93 percent lean.
- Veal cutlets (from the leg) and loin chops
- Pork tenderloin, boneless top loin roast, loin chops, and boneless sirloin chops
- Lamb, boneless leg (shank portions), loin roast, loin chops, leg cubes for kabobs

Trimming the Fat

Here are some suggestions to make trimming excess fat from your diet easier:

- Choose lean cuts of meat and trim off all the visible fat before cooking. Remove skin from poultry before or after cooking.
- Broil meat on a rack so the fat can drip away.
- Substitute ground chicken or ground turkey for ground beef. Look for ground turkey breast or chicken breast; otherwise, it may contain skin and therefore have as much fat as ground beef.
- Substitute protein-packed dried legumes, like beans and lentils, for meat in casseroles.
- Chill soups and stews overnight so you can remove all the hardened fat from the surface.
- Be skimpy with fat. Use nonstick pans and nonstick cooking spray, or "sauté" in a small amount of broth or water. Don't just pour oil into a skillet; it's easy to add too much. Measure or use a pastry brush to coat pans with a thin layer of oil. When baking, coat pans

with a spritz of nonstick cooking spray instead of oils or fats. (Kitchenware shops now carry oil sprayers you can fill with your favorite oil.)

- Experiment with lowfat or skim milk, lowfat sour cream and cheese, and nonfat yogurt: they provide the same amounts of calcium and protein as the whole-milk varieties but with less fat or none at all.
- When making dips, substitute nonfat plain yogurt for sour cream.
- Use fresh herbs and zesty seasonings liberally.
- Choose angel food cake instead of pound cake, especially when making cake-based desserts like trifle.
- To reduce fat and cholesterol, you can substitute 2 egg whites for 1 whole egg in recipes, but don't substitute egg whites for all the whole eggs when baking; the dessert will have better texture and flavor if you retain a yolk or two.
- Replace sour cream with buttermilk or yogurt in recipes for baked goods.

ENTERTAINING

Everyone loves a party, but the trick is to ensure that the cook has a good time, too. Whether you're planning a casual backyard barbecue, an elegant dinner, or a holiday buffet, a few simple strategies will guarantee you stress-free entertaining.

THINK AHEAD

- All good parties are well organized. Start with a few lists: a guest list, a menu, a shopping list, and a menu preparation timetable.
- Invite guests two to three weeks ahead. Depending on the event you may want to specify the appropriate dress, the type of food that will be served, and the expected duration of the party.
- Simplicity is the key to a successful menu, especially when you're expecting a large number of guests. The majority of the dishes should be those you've cooked and enjoyed in the past. Take advantage of dishes that taste even better when made ahead. It's also smart to include some dishes that freeze well.
- Look for food preparation time-savers. For example, if you're making a shrimp dish, purchase peeled, deveined shrimp instead of cleaning them yourself.

- Let the menu reflect the time of year. Use seasonal fruits and vegetables whenever possible. They will be at their peak of flavor and reasonably priced.
- Be sure you have a well-stocked bar with plenty of choices for nondrinkers. And keep lots of ice on hand—even more than you think you'll need.
- At least one week before the party, check your supply of chairs, glasses, serving dishes, and utensils. Consider the space needed to enable guests to circulate easily and, if necessary, shift or remove furniture.

BUFFET BASICS

Buffets are great for carefree entertaining; just put out the food and keep the bowls and platters full. But don't leave food out at room temperature for longer than two hours, and be sure to replenish the table with fresh platters you've prepared in advance.

- One of the easiest ways to entertain is to create a menu of room-temperature dishes. Hot buffets, on the other hand, should have one centerpiece dish with simple side dishes.
- Keep desserts simple; cakes and cookies that can be eaten out of hand, for example.
- Avoid traffic jams at the buffet table. If possible, place the table in the center of the room, so guests can serve themselves from both sides of the table. Provide two serving utensils for each bowl or tray. Bundle the forks and napkins together and place at both ends of the buffet.

DINNER-PARTY STRATEGIES

When planning the menu for a dinner party, it is important that the flavors, colors, textures, and richness of the food be well balanced. Follow a creamy soup with a simple roast, and avoid repeating ingredients and flavors. Also, consider the amount of time you'll need to spend in the kitchen. Soups, stews, casseroles, mousses, sorbets, and baked goods can be made ahead. Try not to have more than two dishes that require your last-minute attention.

Formal table setting: dinner plate, salad plate, bread plate, salad fork, dinner fork, soup spoon, dinner knife, dessert fork, dessert spoon, butter knife, white wine glass, red wine glass, water glass

SETTING A PROPER TABLE

There is a proper way to set a table. To begin, place a dinner plate at each setting. If serving soup, place the soup bowls on top of the salad plates. Set the bread plates to the left of the dinner plates above the forks. Napkins go either to the left of the forks or in the center of the dinner plates

Flatware is arranged in a common-sense way, in the order used, beginning farther away from the plate. Forks are placed on the left, while knives (cutting edge facing the plate) and spoons are on the right. If you are serving soup, the soup spoons are placed to the right of the knives. If you are serving salad, the salad forks are set to the left of the dinner forks. Butter knives may be placed right on the butter plates.

If you have enough flatware and room on the table, the dessert forks and spoons can be placed above the dinner plates (see photo above). Otherwise, set out the dessert flatware with the dessert. And don't forget to provide teaspoons for coffee or tea.

• If serving only one wine, place the wineglasses slightly above the dinner knives and set the water glasses to their left. If also serving wine to accompany the first course, place those glasses to the right of the primary wineglasses.

WINE

When choosing a beverage to complement a meal, there's no reason to restrict yourself to wine. Although wine can be suave and elegant or simple and refreshing, when food is spicy or very robust it can overwhelm or compete with a wine unless you choose very carefully. What follows is all you need to know to get you started choosing, serving, and enjoying wine with ease.

KNOW YOUR WINES

There are two kinds of wine: red (which includes rosé) and white. Wine is described primarily by its relative sweetness. A dry wine lacks natural sugars (but it still can be perceived as fruity), a semidry wine generally tastes sweet, and a sweet wine is very sweet.

White wines range from very dry (Manzanilla sherry) to very sweet (Tokay), while red wines are usually dry (except for some kosher-type wines). In general, wines are named either for the predominant grape used in production (cabernet sauvignon) or for the region of production (Chianti). A wine is judged by three basic components: its color, aroma (bouquet), and taste. White wines range in color from pale yellow-green to straw yellow to deep gold, whereas red wines range from purplish red to ruby red.

What is a good wine? Any wine you enjoy drinking. Let your eyes, nose, and mouth be your guides.

White Wines

Chardonnay One of the most popular wines, chardonnay is produced the world over. Most chardonnays are buttery, fruity, and fairly dry; they are often aged in oak. Chardonnays that have been aged in small oak barrels (sometimes new ones) are often characterized as being "oaky," a quality that can mask a wine's lovely fruity qualities. Serve with summer foods, such as grilled salmon or chicken, as well as with roasted chicken or fish.

Gewürztraminer A specialty of Alsace, France, although it's produced in other countries as well. It is a spicy wine that can be dry or semisweet. If dry, serve with fish, poultry, or spicy foods. If sweet, serve with fruit desserts.

Riesling This wine has a floral fragrance with hints of honey. Late-harvest Riesling is produced from super-ripe grapes that are intensely sweet, making it one of the world's most delicious wines. German Rieslings are much sweeter than Alsatian Rieslings. They are excellent with Chinese food, lightly spiced food, and roast chicken. Alsatian Rieslings are ideal summertime wines.

Sauvignon Blanc A refreshing, clean-flavored wine with a grassy, herbaceous aroma. It is sometimes labeled *fumé blanc*. Serve with poultry, fish, or shellfish.

Red Wines

Beaujolais A pleasant, light-bodied, fruity French wine that goes well with meats and poultry.

Beaujolais Nouveau A light, fruity wine that is seven to nine weeks old and is released for sale on the third Thursday of November. It is an ideal wine to serve at Thanksgiving.

Bordeaux Some of the greatest wines in the world are from the Bordeaux region in France. These wines are rich and fragrant and known for their ability to age well. Roast goose, lamb, and other red meats are the perfect partners.

Burgundy Wines from the Burgundy region of France are elegant, highly prized, and among the most expensive in the world. Burgundys, made from 100 percent pinot noir grapes, are lighter in body and color than some other red wines. They bear no resemblance to the typical California Burgundy. Enjoy with salmon, red meat, pork, poultry, and game.

Cabernet Sauvignon Produced in many countries, this well-known wine is full-bodied and can be complex, with hints of spice and ripe fruit. It complements hearty meats, poultry, and stews.

Chianti One of the most famous Italian wines, true Chianti is Tuscan. This sturdy, dry wine goes nicely with tomato-based pasta dishes, steaks, hamburgers, and pizza.

Merlot Rich, fragrant, and smooth bodied, this wine is easy to like. Serve with robust foods such as lamb, sausages, stews, braises, and Cornish hens.

Pinot Noir This intensely flavored wine is now produced in Oregon and California—often with great success. The wine can be light or full bodied. It goes with almost any food but is especially good with salmon, poultry, pork, veal, ham, and cheese.

Zinfandel Originally grown in Europe, "zin" has become a uniquely California wine. It has a spicy, fruity, slight raspberry flavor. It can stand up to hearty foods, such as steaks, lamb, veal chops, game birds, and hamburgers.

Other Wines

Madeira, Sherry, and Port These are wines that have been fortified with a spirit (usually brandy) to increase their alcohol content. They are usually enjoyed after a meal, although dry sherry is often sipped before dinner as an apéritif.

Rosé This light-bodied wine is made from red grapes: The grape skins are left on just long enough to produce the desired pink color. (Inexpensive rosés are often tinted.) Serve well chilled, before dinner or with lighter foods.

Sparkling Wine These bubbly wines range from slightly sweet to dry. Champagne is the most famous (even though we often use the term to mean any sparkling wine). True champagne is produced only in the Champagne region of France by the traditional *méthode champenoise,* but other countries also make fine sparklers, too. Sparkling wines go with every food, including dessert.

SERVING WINE

Serving wine at the proper temperature helps to bring out all its flavor. Red wine is often served too warm, while white wine is often served too cold, which makes it difficult to fully appreciate them. Red wine should be served at cool room temperature. If it's too warm, place it in a bucket of ice water for five minutes. Some young and fruity reds, such as Beaujolais, are best when slightly chilled. White wines and sparkling wines should be served well chilled but not so cold that their delicious flavors are hidden. To quick-chill white or sparkling wine, submerge the bottle in a bucket or pot filled with half ice and half water. Or wrap the bottle in several thicknesses of wet paper towels and place in the freezer for 20 to 30 minutes or until chilled. (Check to make sure the wine doesn't freeze.)

Wine is traditionally served in stemmed glasses: The large flat base allows you to swirl the wine, which helps release its aroma and flavor. When drinking wine, hold the glass by the stem. This is especially important with chilled wines; it prevents the heat from your hand from warming the wine. Glasses should be filled one-half to two-thirds full to leave enough room for swirling.

Exposing wine to air lets it "breathe" and release its flavor, but simply uncorking the bottle doesn't do much—the wine needs to be poured. If you wish, decant it (pour it into a decanter) before serving. (If decanting an aged wine, leave any sediment in the bottle.)

PAIRING WINE WITH FOOD

There really aren't any strict rules when it comes to pairing wine with food, but try to match the intensity of the flavors. For example, serve a light wine with a delicate entrée and a robust wine with a full-flavored dish. Gewürztraminer is a good match for gingery Asian dishes, while zinfandel can stand up to the spicy flavors of Mexican food. An easy way to pair wine with food is to serve a wine from the same region or country as the recipe you are preparing. For example, a paella is best enjoyed with a Spanish wine, while pasta with tomato sauce is ideally matched with an Italian red wine.

Here are a few rules of thumb: Red wines go well with meats, roast chicken, salmon, tomato-based pasta dishes, and hard cheeses (like Parmesan). White wines are a good match for delicately flavored fish, skillet poultry dishes, vegetable dishes, cheese-based pasta dishes, and soft and semisoft cheeses.

COOKING TERMS GLOSSARY

Al dente Italian for "to the tooth," describes perfectly cooked pasta: just tender and with a slight resistance.

Baste To spoon or brush a liquid over food to keep it moist during cooking. The liquid can be a sauce, marinade, broth, melted butter, or pan juices.

Beat To briskly mix or stir a mixture with a spoon, whisk, fork, or electric mixer.

Blanch To cook food (usually fruits or vegetables) briefly in boiling water, then plunge into ice water to stop the cooking. It locks in the color, texture, and flavor. Blanching is used to loosen tomato and peach skins (for peeling) and to mellow the saltiness or bitterness of certain foods.

Blend To mix ingredients until smooth or completely combined.

Blind bake To bake a piecrust before it's filled. To prevent the dough from puffing up during baking, the pastry dough is lined with foil and filled with pie weights or dry beans; they are removed shortly before the end of the baking time to allow the crust to color.

Boil To heat a liquid until bubbles break vigorously on the surface (water boils at 212°F). It also means to cook food, such as pasta or potatoes, in a boiling liquid.

Braise To cook food by first browning it in fat, then covered, on top of the stove or in the oven, in a small amount of liquid. This slow method tenderizes tough cuts of meat by breaking down their fibers and develops their flavor.

Broth A thin, clear liquid produced by simmering in water vegetables, poultry, meat, or fish (on the bone). Broth is used as a base for soups, stews, sauces, and many other dishes. Canned broth is a convenient substitute for homemade.

Brown To cook over high heat, usually on top of the stove, to brown food.

Butterfly To split food, such as shrimp or boneless leg of lamb, horizontally, cutting almost all the way through, then opening it up (like a book) to form a butterfly shape. It exposes a more uniform surface area so food cooks evenly and quickly.

Caramelize To heat sugar until it becomes syrupy and golden to deep amber in color. Sugar-topped desserts like crème brûlée are caramelized under the broiler or with a propane torch. Onions become caramelized when slowly cooked until golden brown and very tender.

Core To remove the seeds or tough woody centers from fruits such as apples, pears, and pineapple and from vegetables such as cabbage and fennel.

Cream To beat butter, margarine, or other fat until it's creamy looking or with sugar until it's fluffy and light. This technique beats in air, creating light-textured baked goods.

Crimp To decoratively pinch or press the edges of a single piecrust or to seal the edges of a double-crusted pie so the filling doesn't seep out during baking.

Curdle To coagulate or separate into solids and liquids. Egg- and milk-based mixtures can curdle if heated too quickly, overcooked, or combined with an acid, such as lemon juice.

Cut in To work a solid fat, such as shortening, butter, or margarine, into dry ingredients using a pastry blender or two knives scissor-fashion until the pieces are the desired size.

Deglaze To scrape up the flavorful browned bits from the bottom of a skillet or roasting pan in which meat or poultry has been cooked by adding water, wine, or broth and stirring while gently heating.

Devein To remove the dark intestinal vein of shrimp. The shrimp is first peeled, then a lengthwise slit is made along the back, exposing the vein so that it can be removed.

Dollop A spoonful of soft food, such as pesto, yogurt, whipped cream, or crème fraîche.

Dot To scatter bits of butter or margarine over a pie filling, casserole, or other dish before baking. It adds richness and flavor and helps promote browning.

Dredge To lightly coat with flour, cornmeal, or bread crumbs. Meats and fish are dredged before cooking to create a crisp, browned exterior.

Drippings The melted fat and juices that collect in a pan when meat or poultry is cooked. Drippings form the base for gravies and pan sauces.

Drizzle To pour melted butter, oil, syrup, melted chocolate, or other liquid back and forth over food in a fine stream.

Dust To coat lightly with flour (greased baking pans) or with confectioners' sugar or cocoa (cakes and pastries) or another powdery ingredient.

Emulsify To bind liquids that usually can't blend easily, such as oil and vinegar. The trick is to slowly add one liquid, usually the oil, to the other while mixing vigorously. Natural emulsifiers, such as egg yolks or mustard, are often added to vinaigrettes or sauces to emulsify them for a longer period.

Ferment To bring about a chemical change in foods and beverages that is caused by enzymes in bacteria or yeasts. Beer, wine, yogurt, buttermilk, vinegar, cheese, and yeast breads all get their distinctive flavors from fermentation.

Flour As a verb, means to coat food, a surface, or a baking pan with flour.

Fold To combine a light mixture (such as beaten egg whites, whipped cream, or sifted flour) with a heavier mixture (such as a cake batter or the base of a soufflé) without deflating either. A rubber spatula is the best tool to use for folding.

Fork-tender A degree of doneness for cooked vegetables and meats. When the food is pierced with a fork, there is only a very slight resistance.

Glaze To coat food by brushing with melted jelly, jam, or barbecue sauce or to brush piecrust with milk or beaten egg before baking.

Grill To cook food directly or indirectly over a source of heat (usually charcoal, briquettes, or gas) or in a special ridged pan.

Julienne To cut food, especially vegetables, into thin, uniform matchstick strips about 2 inches long.

Knead To work dough until it's smooth and elastic, either by pressing and folding with the heel of the hand or by working it in a heavy-duty electric mixer with a dough hook. Kneading develops the gluten in flour, an elastic protein that gives yeast breads their structure.

Leavening An agent that causes dough or batter to rise. Common leaveners include baking powder, baking soda, and yeast. Natural leaveners are air (when beaten into eggs) and steam (in popovers, éclairs, and cream puffs).

Marinate To flavor and/or tenderize a food by letting it sit in a liquid (such as lemon juice, wine, or yogurt) and, often, oil, herbs, or spices. When a marinade contains an acid, the marinating should be done in a nonreactive container.

Panfry To cook food in a small amount of fat in a skillet until browned and cooked through.

Parboil To partially cook food in boiling water. Carrots are often parboiled before they're added to other foods that take less time to cook.

Pare To cut away the skin or rind of a fruit or vegetable. A vegetable peeler or paring knife (a small knife with a 3- to 4-inch blade) is usually used.

Pasteurize To kill the bacteria in milk, fruit juices, or other liquids by heating to a moderately high temperature, then rapidly cooling it. All milk sold in the U.S. is pasteurized. Ultrapasteurized (UHT) milk is subjected to very high temperatures—about 300°F—and vacuum-packed for extended storage. It will keep without refrigeration for up to six months but must be refrigerated once it's opened. Ultrapasteurized cream is not vacuum-packed; it must be refrigerated.

Pinch The amount of a powdery ingredient, such as salt, pepper, or a spice, you can hold between your thumb and forefinger; about 1/16 teaspoon.

Pipe To force a food, such as frosting, whipped cream, or mashed potatoes, through a pastry bag fitted with a pastry tip in a decorative manner or to shape meringues or éclairs. You can also use a plastic bag with a corner snipped off.

Poach To cook food in a gently simmering (barely moving) liquid: The amount and type of liquid will depend on the food being poached.

Pound To flatten to a uniform thickness using a meat mallet, meat pounder, or rolling pin. Meat and poultry is pounded to ensure even cooking. Pounding also tenderizes tough meats by breaking up hard-to-chew connective tissue.

Preheat To bring an oven or broiler to the desired temperature before cooking food.

Prick To pierce a food, such as a piecrust or a potato, usually with a fork, to prevent it from puffing up or bursting during cooking/baking.

Proof To dissolve yeast in a measured amount of warm water (105° to 115°F), sometimes with a small amount of sugar and then set it aside until foamy to make sure that it is "active."

Punch down To deflate yeast dough after it has risen fully. It is not necessary to literally "punch" down the dough; it needs only to be gently deflated.

Puree To mash or grind food until completely smooth, usually in a food processor, blender, sieve, or food mill.

Reduce To rapidly boil a liquid, such as a sauce, wine, or stock, until it has reduced in volume in order to concentrate the flavor.

Render To slowly cook animal fat or skin until the fat separates from its connective tissue. It is strained before being used. The crisp brown bits left in the pan are called cracklings.

Roast To cook in an uncovered pan in the oven by dry heat. Roasted food develops a well-browned exterior. Tender cuts of meat, poultry, and fish are suitable for roasting, as are many vegetables.

Rolling boil A full constant boil that cannot be stirred down.

Sauté To cook food quickly in a small amount of hot fat in a skillet; the term derives from the French word *sauter* ("to jump").

Scald To heat a liquid, such as cream or milk, just until tiny bubbles appear around the edge of the pan.

Score To make shallow cuts (usually parallel or crisscross) in the surface of food before cooking. This is done mainly to facilitate flavor absorption, as in marinated meats, chicken, and fish, but sometimes also for decorative purposes on hams. The tops of breads are often scored to enable them to rise (during baking) without bursting.

Sear To brown meat, fish, or poultry quickly by placing over very high heat.

Shave To cut wide, paper-thin slices of food, such as Parmesan cheese or chocolate.

Shred To cut, tear, or grate food into narrow strips or pieces.

Shuck To remove the shells of oysters, mussels, scallops, or clams.

Sift To press ingredients, such as flour or confectioners' sugar, through a sifter or sieve. Sifting incorporates air and removes lumps, which helps ingredients to combine more easily.

Simmer To cook food in a liquid over low heat (at about 185°F). A few small bubbles should be visible on the surface.

Skim To remove fat or froth from the surface of a liquid, such as broth, boiling jelly, or soup. A skimmer, a long-handled metal utensil with a flat mesh disk or perforated bowl at one end, is the ideal tool for the job.

Soft peaks When cream or egg whites are beaten until they stand in peaks that bend over at the top when the beaters are lifted

Steam To cook food, covered, over a small amount of boiling water. The food is usually set on a rack or in a basket. Since it's not immersed in water, the food retains more of its nutrients, color, and flavor than it would with other cooking methods.

Stiff peaks When cream or egg whites are beaten until they stand in firm peaks that hold their shape when the beaters are lifted.

Stir-fry To cook pieces of food quickly in a small amount of oil over high heat, stirring and tossing almost constantly. Stir-frying is used in Asian cooking; a wok is the traditional pan, although a large skillet will do just as well.

Temper To warm food gently before adding it to a hot mixture so it doesn't separate or curdle.

Tender-crisp The ideal degree of doneness for

many fresh vegetables: They're tender but still retain some of their crunch.

Toast To brown bread, croutons, whole spices, or nuts in a dry skillet or in the oven. Toasting enhances the flavor of nuts and facilitates removal of the skin from hazelnuts.

Toss To lift and drop pieces of food quickly and gently with two utensils, usually to coat them with a sauce (as for pasta) or a dressing (as for salad).

Whip To beat an ingredient (especially heavy or whipping cream) or mixture rapidly to incorporate air and increase volume. You can use a whisk, egg beater, or electric mixer.

Whisk To beat ingredients (such as heavy or whipping cream, eggs, salad dressings, or sauces) with a fork or whisk to mix, blend, or incorporate air.

Zest To remove the flavorful colored part of citrus skin. Use the fine holes of a grater, a zester, or a vegetable peeler, avoiding the bitter white pith underneath.

INGREDIENTS GLOSSARY

Almond paste A firm but pliable confection made of ground almonds and confectioners' sugar mixed with glucose, corn syrup, or egg white. Available in cans or tubes, almond paste is similar to *marzipan*, which is sweeter and softer. If almond paste seems hard, microwave on High for a few seconds to soften.

Amaretti cookies Crisp, round almond-flavored Italian cookies, found at Italian grocers and specialty food stores. They often come tissue-wrapped in pairs and packed into pretty tin boxes.

Calvados An apple brandy made in the Normandy region of France. Applejack is a good substitute.

Capers The flower buds of a bush native to parts of the Mediterranean and Asia. They are usually dried and then pickled in a vinegar brine. Also available at specialty food stores are capers packed in salt, which have a purer flavor. Capers should be rinsed under cold water and drained before using.

Chili powder A blend of ground dried mild chiles and ingredients such as cumin and garlic powder. Ground dried chiles without added seasonings are also available and sometimes labeled chile powder.

Chipotles en adobo Dried, smoked red jalapeño peppers canned in a thick chile purée called *adobo*.

Handle these chiles and their sauce with care; they are very hot and can easily burn your skin. Leftover *chipotles en adobo* can be frozen. Freeze individual chiles with some sauce on a waxed paper–lined cookie sheet until firm, then remove from the waxed paper and store in a heavy-duty zip-tight plastic bag for up to three months. *Chipotles en adobo* can be found in Latino markets and many supermarkets.

Chorizo A spicy pork sausage seasoned with chiles and garlic. Spanish-style chorizo is a firm, smoked link sausage. Do not substitute Mexican-style fresh chorizo.

Cilantro A pungent green herb, popular in Asian and Latino cooking; sometimes called fresh coriander or Chinese parsley. It is often sold with the roots still attached; the roots are sometimes chopped and used as a seasoning.

Cinnamon sticks Used to garnish hot beverages. They can also be simmered in a liquid to release their warm, spicy flavor.

Coconut milk An unsweetened infusion of shredded coconut meat and water that is strained and canned. It is not interchangeable with cream of coconut, which is rich, sweet, and used in desserts and tropical mixed drinks.

Cornichons Tiny gherkinlike cucumbers that are pickled in a tart brine. Small dill pickles are an acceptable substitute if the cornichons are to be chopped and used in a sauce.

Crab boil A mix of herbs and spices (such as mustard seeds, whole allspice, peppercorns, bay leaves, and dried chiles) that is sometimes added to the water in which crab, shrimp, or lobster is cooked.

Curry powder Widely used in Indian cooking, the blend of spices and heat intensity can greatly vary. A typical curry powder can contain up to twenty different spices, including turmeric, cardamom, red chiles, black pepper, and cumin. Madras-style curry powder, available in supermarkets, is a reliable moderately spicy blend.

Durum A hard wheat that is ground to make semolina flour, which is used for pasta.

Espresso coffee powder, instant Available at Italian grocers and many supermarkets, it is a convenient way to add rich, deep-roasted coffee flavor to food and beverages.

Fish sauce An integral flavoring in Southeast Asian cooking, it is made from fermented fish. Also known as *nam pla* (Thai) and *nuoc nam* (Vietnam); the Philippine version, *pastis,* has a much milder flavor. Store at cool room temperature in a dark place; it will keep for about one year.

Five-spice powder A favorite seasoning in Chinese cooking; it is usually a blend of equal parts cinnamon, cloves, fennel, star anise, and Szechwan peppercorns.

Hoisin sauce This sweet, thick sauce is made from a base of soybeans. Refrigerate after opening. Often used in Chinese barbecue sauces for chicken and ribs.

Juniper berries Fragrant dried blue-black berries that are used as a seasoning and the main flavoring in gin. They can usually be found in spice shops and specialty food stores. If unavailable, stir 1 to 2 tablespoons of gin into the finished dish during the last five minutes of cooking.

Kirsch Also called *kirschwasser* (German for "cherry water"), a clear brandy distilled from cherry juice and pits. (This type of clear spirit made from fruit is called *eau-de-vie.*) Often used to flavor fondues and desserts.

Mango chutney A sweet and spicy condiment that is often served with curries. Major Grey's is made in the British style, slightly sweeter than Indian chutneys.

Maple syrup, pure Maple sap that has been boiled down until syrupy. It has a delicious subtle flavor that is incomparable. Maple-flavored syrup is made from a liquid such as corn syrup mixed with a small amount of pure maple syrup. Pancake syrup is corn syrup with natural or artificial maple extract added.

Marsala A fortified wine, originally from Sicily but also produced in California; available sweet (best for desserts) and dry (use in savory dishes).

Miso A highly concentrated fermented soybean paste made from a combination of soybeans and grain that is widely used in Japanese cooking and made in different strengths. *Red miso* has the strongest flavor; *golden* is fairly mild; and *white miso* is mellow and slightly sweet. Look for miso in natural food stores and Asian markets.

Molasses A by-product of sugar refining, molasses is the liquid that remains after the sugar crystals are extracted. Molasses can be sulphured or unsulphured. Light molasses is from the first boiling (refining) and has a mild flavor. Dark molasses is from the second boiling and is darker and less sweet. Blackstrap molasses, from the third boiling, is bitter.

Mustard, Dijon This prepared mustard gets its distinctive flavor from a special blend of mustard seeds and white wine. There are many different brands, with varying heat levels, so when you find a brand you like, stick with it.

Olives The fruit of the olive tree is naturally very bitter and must be processed to make it edible. There are many olive varieties, and the finished product depends on the ripeness of the fruit and the type of processing. While each has a particular flavor, many are interchangeable. Black olives include the tiny Niçoise, the gray-black Gaeta, the vinegar-cured Kalamata (also available pitted), and the pleasantly bitter, wrinkled, oil-cured Moroccan. Picholine and manzanilla are two popular green olives. To remove the pits from olives, use an olive or cherry pitter. Or put the olives on a work surface, place the flat side of a large knife on top of one olive, and press down to lightly crush the olive; remove the pit.

Olive oil Pressing tree-ripened olives produces the prized liquid we know as olive oil. Its flavor, color, and fragrance depend on the region of origin and the quality of the harvest. In general, extra-virgin olive oil, from the first pressing, is full-flavored, bright green to green-gold in color, and best used on salads or other dishes where its taste can be most appreciated. Regular olive oil (sometimes called pure olive oil) is from a subsequent pressing and has a milder but still distinctive fruity flavor; it's a good cooking oil. "Light" olive oil has been specially treated to remove much of the characteristic olive taste; it is not lower in fat.

Old Bay seasoning An aromatic, somewhat hot blend of ground spices that is popular with cooks in the Chesapeake Bay area, especially for seafood dishes.

Pancetta An unsmoked bacon that is rolled into a cylinder and sliced to order. It is used in Italian dishes. Pancetta is available at Italian delicatessens, specialty food stores, and some supermarkets. Substitute regular smoked bacon, if necessary.

Pepper The world's most popular spice, peppercorns are the dried berries of a perennial vine. They come in three colors: black, white, and green. Black pepper is picked just before the berry ripens; the skin turns black when dried. White pepper is the ripened berry with the skin removed; it has a milder flavor than black pepper. Green peppercorns are soft, underripe berries, usually preserved in brine. Freshly ground pepper has an incomparable flavor, so it's worth the investment to purchase a good-quality pepper mill (grinder). Some recipes call for coarse-cracked pepper (also called butcher's grind), but it's just as easy to crush your own peppercorns in a mortar with a pestle or on a work surface with a heavy skillet.

Pine nuts From the pinecones of certain pine trees, these small, elongated ivory-colored nuts are sometimes called *pignoli* or *piñon.* They turn rancid easily; store in the refrigerator for up to three months or freeze for up to nine months.

Porcini mushrooms, dried These members of *Boletus edulis* are imported from Italy and have a rich, earthy flavor; the French variety, called *cèpes,* are more expensive. They must be rehydrated in hot water before use. After soaking, rinse them under cold running water to remove any grit. Use the flavorful soaking liquid to add extra mushroom flavor. Available in specialty food stores and Italian markets.

Prosciutto A cured, aged, air-dried ham with a firm texture and delicious salty flavor. Imported Italian prosciutto, available at quality grocers and butchers, has a milder flavor than the domestic variety.

Salt There are so many kinds of salt available, it's easy to take this familiar ingredient for granted. Each has a different level of saltiness, so it's helpful to understand the differences. We tested our recipes with fine-grained table salt, which has additives that keep it free flowing. Iodized salt is table salt that has been treated with iodine (which helps prevent hyperthyroidism). Kosher salt has no additives. Some cooks prefer it for its mild flavor and its coarse texture, which makes it easy to pick up for sprinkling. Sea salt is also less salty than common table salt. If you use kosher or sea salt in your cooking, you will need a larger quantity. Grayish rock salt is not a food-quality salt but is used in old-fashioned ice-cream makers and as a bed upon which to bake and serve stuffed oysters and clams.

Savoiardi Long, crisp, Italian-style ladyfingers that are usually layered with a moist filling to soften them, as in tiramisù.

Semolina A coarse, sandlike grind of durum wheat used to make pasta and some breads.

Sesame oil, Asian Dark brown-orange in color, this oil is pressed from roasted sesame seeds. It is generally used as a seasoning, not a cooking oil.

Soy sauce Made from fermented soybeans and roasted wheat or barley, this dark, salty sauce is indispensable in Asian cooking. There are many different versions, and some can be quite salty. Use a reliable Japanese brand.

Star anise A star-shaped spice with eight points, each containing a seed. Often used in Chinese cooking, it has a delicate licorice flavor.

Tapenade A French olive paste seasoned with anchovies, herbs, and garlic and used as a condiment. The Italian version is called *olivada.*

Tahini Sesame seeds ground into a thick paste; stir well to incorporate the oil that rises to the top. Available at natural food stores and most supermarkets.

Tomatoes, dried Often referred to as "sun-dried" tomatoes but rarely dried in the sun anymore, these intensely flavored dehydrated tomatoes are processed by more commercial methods. They can be purchased loose packed or packed with oil in a jar. Loose-packed dried tomatoes should be soaked in boiling water to cover until softened, then drained.

Vinegar Bacterial activity can turn some liquids into vinegar; *vin aigre* means "sour wine." *Cider vinegar,* made from apple juice, is a popular vinegar. *Distilled white vinegar* has a strong flavor but is preferred for pickling because it doesn't darken food. Red and white wines are also made into vinegars. The more expensive vinegars are produced by an ancient process that slowly turns the wine sour, instead of by inoculating them with fast-acting bacteria. *Tarragon vinegar* is white wine that has been infused with tarragon. *Balsamic vinegar* is made from semidry Trebbiano grapes, so the resulting vinegar has a sweet note. Most supermarket varieties are tasty, but they aren't true balsamic vinegars, which are aged for years in wood caskets and are quite expensive. *Malt vinegar,* a British favorite, is a mild vinegar made from malted barley.

Wonton wrappers Delicate thin squares of wheat noodles, they can be stuffed to make wontons or other dumplings or ravioli. Look for them in the refrigerated section of the supermarket or at Asian grocery stores. Wrap leftover wrappers in plastic wrap and heavy-duty foil and freeze for up to one month.

2

APPETIZERS

Appetizers serve two important roles: They whet one's appetite and set the tone for the meal that follows. A stylish sit-down dinner calls for elegant appetizers that look and taste special, while dips and chips are perfect for a backyard barbecue. At a cocktail party, on the other hand, the hors d'oeuvres *are* the meal, so you'll need to offer a tempting selection. But some of our favorite appetizers are simply snacks, nibbles, and munchies that are meant to be served without ceremony and simply enjoyed.

HOW TO MANAGE THE MENU

- Prepare appetizers in advance whenever possible.
- Serve only one or two appetizers that require last-minute attention.
- For appetizers that require last-minute assembling, prepare the separate components ahead of time and chill until serving time.
- Plan on only one or two hot appetizers unless you have more than one oven.
- Be sure to serve some appetizers that are work-free, such as nuts or cheese.
- Figure on about ten to twelve appetizers per person if no meal follows. Otherwise, allow five or six pieces.

DO-AHEAD STRATEGIES

Vegetables for crudités can be prepared up to one day ahead. Wrap radishes, cherry tomatoes, cucumber, and celery in damp paper towels and refrigerate in plastic bags. Cut up asparagus, broccoli, green beans, and

cauliflower and boil until tender-crisp. Drain, rinse under cold water, and pat dry. Refrigerate as above.

Dips and spreads can often be made up to several days ahead and refrigerated.

Pâtés and terrines taste best if made one to two days ahead. Meat pâtés can be frozen for up to two months. Defrost overnight in the refrigerator.

Pastry appetizers can be frozen, raw or baked, for up to one month. Layer them in baking pans, separating the layers with waxed paper, then double wrap in foil. Arrange baked pastries on cookie sheets and reheat at 350°F for about 10 minutes. Bake frozen raw pastries as the recipe directs, allowing extra baking time.

Tea sandwiches make excellent appetizers. Make them up to four hours ahead and arrange in jelly-roll pans. Separate the layers with damp paper towels, cover securely with plastic wrap, and refrigerate.

TIPS FOR SERVING WITH STYLE

Be thoughtful. Appetizers should be easy to handle without being messy, easy to eat without utensils, and require no more than a couple of bites.

Make it pretty. Arrange cut-up vegetables on a tray or in a large basket lined with plastic wrap and covered with leafy salad greens.

Be creative. Serve dips and spreads in hollowed-out loaves of bread or cabbages.

Be dramatic. Add height by placing platters on inverted baking dishes covered with colored napkins.

Make it flavorful. Remove cold appetizers from the refrigerator about thirty minutes before serving.

Perfect Guacamole

Roasted Red Pepper Dip

Fresh roasted red peppers are what make this dip special, so don't substitute the ones that come in a jar. Roasting peppers is easy to do. If you've never done it, this is the perfect opportunity. Once you've tasted them, you'll wonder why you waited so long.

Prep: 45 minutes

- 4 red peppers, roasted (page 360)
- ½ teaspoon ground cumin
- ½ cup walnuts, toasted
- 2 slices firm white bread, torn into pieces
- 2 tablespoons raspberry or balsamic vinegar
- 1 tablespoon olive oil
- ½ teaspoon salt
- ⅛ teaspoon ground red pepper (cayenne)
  toasted pita bread wedges

1. Cut roasted peppers into large pieces. In small skillet, toast cumin over low heat, stirring constantly, until very fragrant, 1 to 2 minutes.

2. In food processor with knife blade attached, process walnuts until ground. Add roasted peppers, cumin, bread, vinegar, oil, salt, and ground red pepper; puree until smooth. Transfer to bowl. If not serving right away, cover and refrigerate up to 4 hours. Serve with toasted pita bread wedges. Makes about 2 cups.

Each tablespoon: About 23 calories, 0g protein, 2g carbohydrate, 2g total fat (0g saturated), 0mg cholesterol, 46mg sodium.

Roasted Red Pepper Dip

Roasted Eggplant Dip with Herbs

The fresh flavors of lemon and mint are a perfect match for the baked eggplant in this Mediterranean-style dip.

Prep: 15 minutes plus cooling and draining
Roast: 1 hour

- 2 small eggplants (1 pound each)
- 2 garlic cloves, thinly sliced
- 2 tablespoons olive oil
- 4 teaspoons fresh lemon juice
- 1 teaspoon salt
- ¼ teaspoon ground black pepper
- 2 tablespoons chopped fresh parsley
- 2 tablespoons chopped fresh mint
  toasted pita bread wedges

1. Preheat oven to 400°F. With knife, cut slits all over eggplants; insert garlic slices in slits. Place eggplants in jelly-roll pan and roast until collapsed and tender, about 1 hour.

2. When cool enough to handle, cut eggplants in half. Scoop out flesh and place in colander set over bowl; discard skin. Let drain 10 minutes.

3. Transfer eggplant to food processor with knife blade attached. Add oil, lemon juice, salt, and pepper; pulse to coarsely chop. Add parsley and mint, pulsing to combine. Spoon into bowl; cover and refrigerate up to 4 hours. Serve with toasted pita bread wedges. Makes about 2 cups.

Each tablespoon: About 14 calories, 0g protein, 2g carbohydrate, 1g total fat (0g saturated), 0mg cholesterol, 74mg sodium.

Baba Ganoush

Prepare as directed above. Omit parsley and mint. Stir in ½ **teaspoon ground cumin, ¼ cup tahini (sesame seed paste)** and ½ **cup lowfat plain yogurt.**

Artichoke Dip

Serve this simple dip along with crisp toasted wedges of pita bread. An assortment of olives and cherry tomatoes makes a tasty accompaniment.

Prep: 10 minutes

- 1 lemon
- 1 can (13.75 ounces) artichoke hearts, drained
- ¼ cup light mayonnaise
- ¼ cup freshly grated Parmesan cheese
- 2 tablespoons olive oil

1. From lemon, grate ½ teaspoon peel and squeeze 2 teaspoons juice.

2. In food processor with knife blade attached, puree lemon peel and juice, artichoke hearts, Parmesan, and oil until smooth. Transfer to serving bowl. If not serving right away, cover and refrigerate up to 3 days. Makes about 1¼ cups.

Each tablespoon: About 30 calories, 1g protein, 1g carbohydrate, 3g total fat (1g saturated), 2mg cholesterol, 70mg sodium.

Artichoke Dip

Tzatziki

In Greece, this is served as a dip with pita bread or as a cold sauce to accompany grilled fish or chicken.

Prep: 20 minutes plus overnight to drain, plus chilling

- 2 cups (16 ounces) plain lowfat yogurt
- ½ English (seedless) cucumber, not peeled, seeded and finely chopped, plus a few very thin slices
- 1½ teaspoons salt
- 1 to 2 garlic cloves, chopped
- 1 tablespoon chopped fresh mint or dill plus additional sprigs
- 1 tablespoon extra-virgin olive oil
- ½ teaspoon red wine vinegar
- ¼ teaspoon ground black pepper

1. Spoon yogurt into sieve lined with cheesecloth or coffee filter set over bowl; cover and refrigerate overnight. Transfer drained yogurt to medium bowl and discard liquid.

2. Meanwhile, in colander set over bowl, toss chopped cucumber with 1 teaspoon salt. Let drain at least 1 hour at room temperature, or cover and refrigerate up to 8 hours. In batches, wrap chopped cucumber in kitchen towel and squeeze to remove as much liquid as possible. Pat dry with paper towels, then add to bowl with yogurt.

3. With flat side of chef's knife, mash garlic to a paste with remaining ½ teaspoon salt. Add garlic, chopped mint, oil, vinegar, and pepper to yogurt and stir to combine. Cover and refrigerate at least 2 or up to 4 hours. Serve chilled or at room temperature, topped with cucumber slices and mint sprigs. Makes about 1¼ cups.

Each tablespoon: About 17 calories, 1g protein, 1g carbohydrate, 1g total fat (0g saturated), 1mg cholesterol, 182mg sodium.

Herbed Yogurt-Cheese Dip

Prepare yogurt as in Step 1. Stir in **1 garlic clove,** crushed with garlic press, **¾ cup chopped fresh basil, 1 tablespoon olive oil,** and **½ teaspoon salt.** Serve with crackers or cut-up vegetables. Makes about 1 cup.

Hummus

Middle Eastern dips, such as hummus, once seemed exotic, but now they're familiar old friends. Tahini is readily available at health food stores and supermarkets.

Prep: 15 minutes plus chilling

- 4 garlic cloves, peeled
- 1 large lemon
- 1 can (15 to 19 ounces) garbanzo beans, rinsed and drained
- 2 tablespoons tahini (sesame seed paste, page 27)
- 3 tablespoons olive oil
- 2 tablespoons water
- ½ teaspoon salt
- ⅛ teaspoon ground red pepper (cayenne)
- ½ teaspoon paprika
- 2 tablespoons chopped fresh cilantro (optional)
  pita bread wedges
  olives

1. In 1-quart saucepan, heat *2 cups water* to boiling over high heat. Add garlic and cook 3 minutes to blanch; drain.

2. From lemon, grate 1 teaspoon peel and squeeze 3 tablespoons juice. In food processor with knife blade attached, combine beans, tahini, garlic, lemon peel and juice, oil, water, salt, and ground red pepper. Puree until smooth. Transfer to platter; cover and refrigerate up to 4 hours. To serve, sprinkle with paprika and cilantro, if using. Serve with pita bread wedges and olives. Makes 2 cups.

Each tablespoon: About 28 calories, 1g protein, 2g carbohydrate, 2g total fat (0g saturated), 0mg cholesterol, 54mg sodium.

Perfect Guacamole
(Pictured on page 28)

Our favorite avocados for guacamole are the varieties with thick, pebbly, green skin such as Hass, Pinkerton, and Reed. While guacamole is usually served as a dip, it is also a great accompaniment for fajitas or tacos.

Prep: 15 minutes

- 1 jalapeño chile, seeded and finely chopped
- ⅓ cup loosely packed fresh cilantro leaves, chopped
- ¼ cup finely chopped sweet onion such as Vidalia or Maui
- ½ teaspoon salt
- 2 ripe avocados
- 1 plum tomato
  plain tortilla chips

1. In mortar, combine jalapeño, cilantro, onion, and salt; with pestle, grind until mixture becomes juicy and thick (onion can still be slightly chunky).

2. Cut each avocado lengthwise in half around seed. Twist halves in opposite directions to separate. Slip spoon between pit and fruit and work pit out. With spoon, scoop fruit from peel onto cutting board.

3. Cut tomato crosswise in half. Squeeze halves to remove seeds and juice. Coarsely chop tomato.

4. If mortar is large enough, add avocado and chopped tomato to onion mixture in mortar. (If mortar is small, combine avocado, tomato, and onion mixture in bowl.) Mash slightly with pestle or spoon until mixture is blended but still somewhat chunky.

5. Guacamole is best when served as soon as it's made. If not serving right away, press plastic wrap directly onto surface of guacamole to prevent discoloration and refrigerate up to 1 hour. Serve with chips. Makes about 1¾ cups.

Each tablespoon: About 25 calories, 0g protein, 1g carbohydrate, 2g total fat (0g saturated), 0mg cholesterol, 45mg sodium.

Warm Layered Bean Dip

This colorful dip is always a hit. The pinto bean, Jack cheese, and salsa layers can be assembled several hours in advance, then baked just before serving.

Prep: 35 minutes   Bake: 12 minutes

- 2 garlic cloves, peeled
- 1 can (15 to 19 ounces) pinto beans, rinsed and drained
- 2 green onions, finely chopped
- 1 tablespoon tomato paste
- 1 tablespoon water
- 4 ounces Monterey Jack cheese, shredded (1 cup)
- 1 cup mild to medium salsa
- 2 avocados, each cut in half, pitted, and peeled
- ¼ cup chopped fresh cilantro
- 3 tablespoons finely chopped red onion
- 2 tablespoons fresh lime juice
- ½ teaspoon salt
- 1 cup sour cream
- tortilla chips

1. Preheat oven to 350°F. In 1-quart saucepan, heat *2 cups water* to boiling over high heat. Add garlic and cook 3 minutes to blanch; drain. With flat side of chef's knife, mash garlic; transfer to medium bowl and add beans, half of green onions, tomato paste, and water. Mash until well combined but still slightly chunky. Spread in bottom of 9-inch glass pie plate.

2. Sprinkle cheese over bean mixture, then spread salsa on top. Bake until piping hot, about 12 minutes.

3. Meanwhile, in medium bowl, mash avocados just until slightly chunky. Stir in cilantro, red onion, lime juice, and salt. Spoon avocado mixture over hot dip mixture and spread sour cream on top. Sprinkle with remaining green onions. Serve with tortilla chips. Makes about 5½ cups.

Each tablespoon: About 22 calories, 1g protein, 1g carbohydrate, 2g total fat (1g saturated), 3mg cholesterol, 61mg sodium.

Easy Aïoli

Aïoli (ay-OH-lee), a garlic mayonnaise from Provence, is the classic condiment for Bouillabaisse (page 64). It's wonderful as a dip for vegetables and as a sauce for fish or lamb.

Prep: 5 minutes plus cooling
Cook: 20 minutes

- 1⅛ teaspoons salt
- 1 head garlic, separated into cloves
- ½ cup mayonnaise
- 2 teaspoons fresh lemon juice
- ½ teaspoon Dijon mustard
- ⅛ teaspoon ground red pepper (cayenne)
- ¼ cup extra-virgin olive oil

1. In 2-quart saucepan, combine *4 cups water* and 1 teaspoon salt; heat to boiling over high heat. Add garlic and boil until garlic has softened, about 20 minutes. Drain. When cool enough to handle, squeeze soft garlic from each clove into small bowl.

2. In blender, puree garlic, mayonnaise, lemon juice, mustard, remaining ⅛ teaspoon salt, and ground red pepper until smooth. With blender running, through hole in cover, add oil in slow, steady stream until mixture is thickened. Transfer to bowl; cover and refrigerate up to 4 hours. Makes about ¾ cup.

Each tablespoon: About 112 calories, 0g protein, 2g carbohydrate, 12g total fat (2g saturated), 5mg cholesterol, 276mg sodium.

MEZE

Test Kitchen Tip Meze, little savory dishes to be nibbled before a meal or with drinks, are a tradition in Greece, Turkey, and the Middle East. Try any of the following with pita or French bread, along with feta cheese chunks, olives, radishes, sliced cucumbers, or tomato wedges: Roasted Red Pepper Dip, Tzatziki, or Hummus.

Tapenade

This Provençal olive spread can be enjoyed on crisp bread or crackers or as a condiment for fish or chicken.

Prep: 20 minutes

- 2 garlic cloves, peeled
- 1½ cups Gaeta or Kalamata olives, pitted
- ½ cup pimiento-stuffed olives
- 1 tablespoon olive oil
- 1 teaspoon fennel seeds
- 1 teaspoon freshly grated orange peel

1. In 1-quart saucepan, heat *2 cups water* to boiling over high heat. Add garlic and cook 3 minutes to blanch; drain.

2. In food processor with knife blade attached, combine olives, oil, fennel seeds, orange peel, and garlic; process until chopped. Transfer to bowl; cover and refrigerate up 3 days. Makes about 1¼ cups.

Each tablespoon: About 41 calories, 0g protein, 2g carbohydrate, 4g total fat (0g saturated), 0mg cholesterol, 264mg sodium.

Marinated Mixed Olives

This assortment of olives is an inviting addition to any antipasto tray. If you have an orange on hand, mix its peel with—or use instead of—the lemon peel.

Prep: 10 minutes plus standing and marinating
Cook: 5 minutes

- ¼ cup extra-virgin olive oil
- 2 teaspoons fennel seeds, crushed
- 4 small bay leaves
- 2 pounds assorted Mediterranean olives, such as Niçoise, picholine, or Kalamata
- 6 strips (3" by 1" each) lemon peel
- 4 garlic cloves, crushed with side of chef's knife

1. In 1-quart saucepan, heat oil, fennel seeds, and bay leaves over medium heat until hot but not smoking. Remove saucepan from heat; let stand 10 minutes.

2. In large bowl, combine olives, lemon peel, garlic, and oil mixture. Cover and refrigerate, stirring occasionally, at least 24 hours or up to several days to blend flavors. Store in refrigerator up to 1 month. Drain to serve. Makes about 6 cups.

Each ¼ cup: About 107 calories, 1g protein, 3g carbohydrate, 10g total fat (1g saturated), 0mg cholesterol, 680mg sodium.

Sweet and Spicy Nuts

Packaged in pretty jars or cellophane bags, these treats are a perfect hostess gift.

Prep: 15 minutes plus cooling
Bake: 25 minutes

- 1 cup sugar
- 2 teaspoons salt
- 1 teaspoon ground cumin
- 1 teaspoon ground cinnamon
- 1 teaspoon coarsely ground black pepper
- ½ teaspoon ground red pepper (cayenne)
- 1 large egg white
- 6 cups raw unsalted nuts, such as walnuts, pecans, natural almonds, and/or cashews

1. Preheat oven to 325°F. Grease two 15½" by 10½" jelly-roll pans.

2. In small bowl, combine sugar, salt, cumin, cinnamon, black pepper, and red pepper; stir until blended. In large bowl, with wire whisk, beat egg white until foamy. Add nuts to egg white; stir to coat evenly. Add sugar mixture; toss until nuts are thoroughly coated.

3. Divide nut mixture between prepared jelly-roll pans, spreading evenly. Bake, stirring twice during baking, until golden brown and dry, 25 to 27 minutes. With slotted spoon, transfer nuts to waxed paper; spread in single layer. Cool. Store in airtight container at room temperature up to 1 month. Makes about 8 cups.

Each ¼ cup: About 165 calories, 4g protein, 11g carbohydrate, 12g total fat (2g saturated), 0mg cholesterol, 150mg sodium.

Smoked Trout Pâté

This smoky spread is easily prepared in a food processor.

Prep: 25 minutes

- 3 whole smoked trout (1¼ pounds total)
- 1 container (8 ounces) whipped cream cheese
- ¼ cup lowfat mayonnaise dressing
- 3 tablespoons fresh lemon juice
- ⅛ teaspoon ground black pepper
- 1 tablespoon finely chopped fresh chives
  or green onion
  cucumber slices and assorted crackers

1. Cut head and tail from each trout; discard along with skin and bones. In food processor with knife blade attached, puree trout, cream cheese, mayonnaise dressing, lemon juice, and pepper until smooth.

2. Spoon trout mixture into medium bowl; stir in chives. Cover and refrigerate up to overnight if not serving right away. Before serving, let stand 15 minutes at room temperature to soften. Serve with cucumber slices and crackers. Makes about 3 cups.

Each tablespoon: About 32 calories, 2g protein, 1g carbohydrate, 2g total fat (1g saturated), 7mg cholesterol, 101mg sodium.

CREAM CHEESE TO THE RESCUE

Test Kitchen Tip

Unexpected guests? For an almost-instant spread, place an 8-ounce block of cream cheese on a serving platter and spread generously with hot pepper jelly, mango chutney, olive paste (olivada), or salsa. Or, in a food processor with the knife blade attached, puree cream cheese with marinated dried tomatoes, roasted peppers, pickled jalapeño chiles, prepared horseradish, or grated onion; season with coarsely ground pepper. (If you wish, thin the spread with milk to make a dip.) No crackers? Toast some bread and cut into triangles.

Salmon Pâté

Prepare as directed (left) but substitute **1 can (15½ ounces) salmon,** drained and large pieces of cartilage removed, for smoked trout.

Chicken Liver Pâté

This exquisite silky-smooth pâté is seasoned the traditional way—with thyme and brandy. For the best flavor, refrigerate at least three hours before serving.

Prep: 25 minutes plus chilling
Cook: 20 minutes

- 2 tablespoons butter or margarine
- 1 small onion, finely chopped
- 1 garlic clove, finely chopped
- 1 pound chicken livers, trimmed
- 2 tablespoons brandy
- ½ cup heavy or whipping cream
- ½ teaspoon salt
- ¼ teaspoon dried thyme
- ¼ teaspoon ground black pepper
  assorted crackers, toast, or thinly sliced apples

1. In 10-inch skillet, melt butter over medium-high heat. Add onion and cook, stirring frequently, until tender and golden, about 10 minutes. Stir in garlic and chicken livers and cook until livers are lightly browned but still pink inside, about 5 minutes. Stir in brandy; cook 5 minutes.

2. In blender or in food processor with knife blade attached, puree chicken-liver mixture, cream, salt, thyme, and pepper until smooth, stopping blender occasionally and scraping down side with rubber spatula.

3. Spoon mixture into small bowl; cover and refrigerate at least 3 hours or up to overnight. Let stand 30 minutes at room temperature before serving. Serve with crackers, toast, or apples. Makes about 1½ cups.

Each tablespoon: About 54 calories, 4g protein, 1g carbohydrate, 4g total fat (2g saturated), 92mg cholesterol, 75mg sodium.

Tomato and Ricotta Salata Bruschetta

Bruschetta is toasted Italian bread that is rubbed with garlic and drizzled with olive oil. It's often topped with savory ingredients to make a simple appetizer. Here we use ripe tomatoes and ricotta salata, a lightly salted pressed sheep's milk cheese. Ricotta salata can be found at Italian markets and specialty food stores.

Prep: 25 minutes

- 1 loaf (8 ounces) Italian bread, cut on diagonal into ½-inch-thick slices
- 8 garlic cloves, each cut in half
- 1 pound ripe plum tomatoes (6 medium), seeded and cut into ½-inch pieces
- 1 tablespoon finely chopped red onion
- 1 tablespoon chopped fresh basil
- 4 ounces ricotta salata, feta, or goat cheese, cut into ½-inch pieces
- 2 tablespoons extra-virgin olive oil
- 2 teaspoons balsamic vinegar
- ¼ teaspoon salt
- ¼ teaspoon coarsely ground black pepper

1. Preheat oven to 400°F. Place bread slices on cookie sheet and bake until lightly toasted, about 5 minutes. Rub one side of each toast slice with cut side of garlic.

2. Meanwhile, in bowl, gently toss tomatoes, onion, basil, cheese, oil, vinegar, salt, and pepper until combined.

3. To serve, spoon tomato mixture on garlic-rubbed side of toast slices. Makes 16 bruschetta.

Each bruschetta: About 79 calories, 2g protein, 9g carbohydrate, 4g total fat (1g saturated), 6mg cholesterol, 236mg sodium.

Tuscan White-Bean Bruschetta

Prepare toast as directed (left) but prepare topping as follows: In bowl, with fork, lightly mash **1 can (15½ to 19 ounces) white kidney beans (cannellini),** rinsed and drained, with **1 tablespoon fresh lemon juice.** Stir in **1 tablespoon olive oil, 2 teaspoons chopped fresh parsley, 1 teaspoon minced fresh sage, ¼ teaspoon salt,** and **⅛ teaspoon coarsely ground black pepper.** Just before serving, spoon mixture over garlic-rubbed side of toast slices. Sprinkle with **1 teaspoon chopped fresh parsley.** Makes 16 bruschetta.

Each bruschetta: About 33 calories, 2g protein, 4g carbohydrate, 1g total fat (0g saturated), 0mg cholesterol, 77mg sodium.

Poker Chips

Save on cleanup by lining the cookie sheets with heavy-duty foil or parchment paper.

Prep: 10 minutes plus cooling   Bake: 8 minutes

- ½ cup olive oil
- 1 tablespoon freshly grated Parmesan or Romano cheese
- 1 tablespoon chili powder
- 1 teaspoon ground cumin
- 1 package (12 ounces) white or whole-wheat pitas

1. Preheat oven to 425°F. In cup, with fork, mix oil, Parmesan, chili powder, and cumin.

2. With knife or kitchen shears, carefully split each pita. Brush insides of pita halves lightly with oil mixture. Cut each half into 8 wedges.

3. Transfer pita wedges to two ungreased cookie sheets (wedges can overlap slightly). Place cookie sheets on two oven racks and bake pita chips until edges are golden, 8 to 10 minutes. Watch carefully, as they can burn quickly.

4. Transfer cookie sheets to wire racks and cool completely. Store chips in airtight container up to 1 week. Makes 8 dozen chips.

Each chip: About 20 calories, 0g protein, 2g carbohydrate, 1g total fat (0g saturated), 0mg cholesterol, 20mg sodium.

Easy Spicy Cheese Straws

Called *paillettes* (little straws) in French, these twisted strips of pastry are perfect with cocktails or wine. Feel free to substitute your favorite hard grating cheese for the Cheddar. Parmesan and Asiago are good choices. Frozen puff pastry makes preparation a breeze.

Prep: 30 minutes Bake: 20 minutes per batch

- 1 tablespoon paprika
- ½ teaspoon dried thyme
- ¼ to ½ teaspoon ground red pepper (cayenne)
- ¼ teaspoon salt
- 1 package (17¼ ounces) frozen puff-pastry sheets, thawed
- 1 large egg white, lightly beaten
- 8 ounces sharp Cheddar cheese, shredded (2 cups)

1. Grease two large cookie sheets. In small bowl, combine paprika, thyme, ground red pepper, and salt.

2. Unfold 1 puff-pastry sheet. On lightly floured surface, with floured rolling pin, roll pastry into 14-inch square. Lightly brush with egg white. Sprinkle half of paprika mixture on pastry. Sprinkle half of Cheddar on half of pastry. Fold pastry over to cover cheese, forming rectangle. With rolling pin, lightly roll over pastry to seal layers together. With pizza wheel or knife, cut pastry crosswise into ½-inch-wide strips.

3. Preheat oven to 375°F. Place strips ½ inch apart on prepared cookie sheets, twisting each strip twice to form spiral and pressing ends against cookie sheet to prevent strips from uncurling. Bake cheese straws until golden, 20 to 22 minutes. With spatula, carefully transfer to wire racks to cool.

4. Repeat with remaining puff-pastry sheet, egg white, paprika mixture, and cheese. Store in airtight container up to 1 week. Makes about 48 cheese straws.

Each straw: About 78 calories, 2g protein, 5g carbohydrate, 5g total fat (2g saturated), 5mg cholesterol, 68mg sodium.

Chorizo and Black Bean Nachos

These are serious nachos for chile lovers. Be sure to use fully cooked chorizo links, not soft bulk-style chorizo.

Prep: 20 minutes Bake: 5 minutes per batch

- 36 unbroken large tortilla chips
- 3 large ripe plum tomatoes, cut into ¼-inch pieces
- ⅓ cup chopped fresh cilantro
- ¼ teaspoon salt
- 1 tablespoon vegetable oil
- 1 fully cooked chorizo sausage (3 ounces), finely chopped, or ¾ cup finely chopped pepperoni (3 ounces)
- 1 medium onion, finely chopped
- 1 garlic clove, finely chopped
- ½ teaspoon ground cumin
- 1 can (15 to 19 ounces) black beans, rinsed and drained
- 4 ounces Monterey Jack cheese, shredded (1 cup)
- 2 pickled jalapeño chiles, very thinly sliced

1. Preheat oven to 400°F. Arrange as many tortilla chips as will fit in single layer on two ungreased large cookie sheets. In small bowl, combine tomatoes, cilantro, and salt.

2. In 10-inch skillet, heat oil over medium heat. Add chorizo, onion, garlic, and cumin; cook, stirring, until onion is tender, about 5 minutes. Stir in beans and heat through.

3. Place 1 tablespoon bean mixture on each tortilla chip. Sprinkle cheese over beans and top each nacho with 1 slice jalapeño. Bake until cheese begins to melt, about 5 minutes.

4. Spoon about 1 teaspoon tomato mixture on each nacho. Transfer nachos to platter. Makes 36 nachos.

Each nacho: About 51 calories, 2g protein, 4g carbohydrate, 3g total fat (1g saturated), 5mg cholesterol, 112mg sodium.

Savory Blue Cheese, Walnut, and Date Rugelach

Filling rich cream cheese dough with a mixture of blue cheese, walnuts, and dates turns rugelach into delicious appetizer pastries that go perfectly with a glass of red or white wine. They take a bit of time to prepare, but the filling and dough can be made ahead, if you like.

Prep: 40 minutes plus chilling and cooling
Bake: 30 minutes

- 1 cup butter or margarine (2 sticks), softened
- 1 package (8 ounces) cream cheese, softened
- 2 cups all-purpose flour
- ½ teaspoon salt
- 1½ cups walnuts
- 4 ounces blue cheese, cut into small pieces
- 48 pitted dates (about 12 ounces)
- 1 large egg white
- 1 teaspoon water

1. Prepare dough: In large bowl, with mixer at medium speed, beat butter and cream cheese until creamy, occasionally scraping bowl with rubber spatula. Reduce speed to low; gradually beat in flour and salt just until blended, occasionally scraping bowl.

2. Divide dough into 4 equal pieces; shape each into a disk. Wrap each disk in plastic wrap and refrigerate until dough is firm enough to roll, at least 4 hours or overnight. (Or place dough in freezer 1 hour if using butter, 1 hour 30 minutes if using margarine.)

3. In food processor with knife blade attached, process ½ cup walnuts until finely chopped; transfer to small bowl and reserve. In same food processor bowl, process blue cheese and remaining 1 cup walnuts just until a coarse mixture forms.

4. Preheat oven to 350°F. Line two large cookie sheets with foil; grease foil.

5. On lightly floured surface, with floured rolling pin, roll one disk of dough into 10-inch round. (If dough is too cold to roll, let stand 5 to 10 minutes at room temperature to soften slightly.) With pastry wheel or knife, cut dough into 12 equal wedges (do not separate). Beginning 1 inch from edge, sprinkle ½ cup blue-cheese mixture in 2-inch-wide ring,

leaving dough in center exposed. Place 1 whole date horizontally on wide curved end of each wedge. Starting at wide end, roll up each wedge, jelly-roll fashion. Place rugelach, point side down, 1 inch apart, on cookie sheet. Repeat with remaining dough (one disk at a time), blue-cheese mixture, and dates.

6. In small bowl, lightly beat egg white with water. With pastry brush, brush rugelach with egg-white mixture and sprinkle evenly with reserved walnuts.

7. Bake until golden, 30 to 35 minutes, rotating sheets between upper and lower racks halfway through baking. With wide spatula, immediately transfer rugelach to wire racks to cool. Store in airtight container up to 3 days, or in freezer up to 3 months. Makes 48 appetizers.

Each appetizer: about 125 calories, 2g protein, 10g carbohydrate, 9g total fat (4g saturated), 18mg cholesterol, 115mg sodium.

Quick Quesadillas

Serve as an accompaniment to Spicy Black Bean Soup (page 49) or as the first course for a Southwest-themed barbecue.

Prep: 10 minutes   Bake: 5 minutes

- 8 (7- to 8-inch) flour tortillas
- 1 jar (7 ounces) roasted red peppers, drained and thinly sliced
- 2 small green onions, thinly sliced
- 1 ounce Pepper Jack cheese, shredded (¼ cup)
- ¾ cup loosely packed fresh cilantro leaves

1. Preheat oven to 400°F. Place 4 tortillas on large cookie sheet. Sprinkle one-fourth of roasted peppers, green onions, cheese, and cilantro on each tortilla; top with remaining tortillas to make 4 quesadillas.

2. Bake quesadillas until heated through, about 5 minutes. Cut each quesadilla into 8 wedges. Serve warm. Makes 32 appetizers.

Each wedge: About 34 calories, 1g protein, 5g carbohydrate, 1g total fat (0g saturated), 1mg cholesterol, 56mg sodium.

Mini Gougères

In French bistros, diners are often presented with a small napkin-lined basket or plate filled with these cheese puffs known as *gougères*. Once you become familar with making the *choux* paste (batter), these puffs are sure to become part of your repertoire.

Prep: 20 minutes   Bake: 30 minutes

- 6 ounces Gruyère or Swiss cheese
- 1 cup water
- 6 tablespoons butter or margarine, cut up
- 1½ teaspoons Dijon mustard
- ½ teaspoon hot pepper sauce
- ¼ teaspoon salt
- 1 cup all-purpose flour
- 4 large eggs

1. Preheat oven to 400°F. Grease and flour two large cookie sheets. Shred Gruyère to equal 1 cup; finely dice remaining cheese.

2. In 3-quart saucepan, heat water, butter, mustard, hot pepper sauce, and salt to boiling. Remove saucepan from heat. With wooden spoon, vigorously stir in flour all at once until mixture forms ball and leaves side of pan.

3. Add eggs, one at a time, beating well after each addition, until batter is smooth and satinlike. Stir in shredded and diced cheese. Drop batter by rounded teaspoons, about 2 inches apart, onto prepared cookie sheets.

4. Bake 30 to 35 minutes, rotating sheets between upper and lower racks halfway through baking, until deep golden. Transfer puffs to wire racks to cool. Serve warm or at room temperature. Makes about 48 puffs.

Each puff: About 60 calories, 3g protein, 3g carbohydrate, 4g total fat (2g saturated), 34mg cholesterol, 65mg sodium.

Cheddar Curry Puffs

Prepare gougères as directed above, but use **Cheddar cheese** in place of Gruyere cheese. Add **2 teaspoons curry powder, ½ teaspoon ground coriander,** and **½ teaspoon ground cumin** to water mixture in Step 2. Makes about 48 puffs.

Mini Remoulade Crab Cakes

Crab cakes are a universal favorite. These luscious morsels can be prepared up to several hours ahead and refrigerated. Reheat just before serving.

Prep: 25 minutes   Bake: 20 minutes

- 2 tablespoons butter or margarine
- 1 small onion, finely chopped
- ½ red pepper, finely chopped
- 1 stalk celery, finely chopped
- ¼ cup light mayonnaise
- 1 tablespoon sour cream
- 2 teaspoons grainy Dijon mustard
- ½ teaspoon freshly grated lemon peel
- ¼ teaspoon salt
- ⅛ teaspoon ground red pepper (cayenne)
- 1 pound lump crabmeat, picked over
- 1 cup fresh bread crumbs (about 2 slices bread)
  Lemon Sauce (below)

1. In 10-inch skillet, melt butter over medium heat. Add onion, red pepper, and celery. Cook, stirring frequently, until vegetables are tender, about 10 minutes. Let cool.

2. In large bowl, stir mayonnaise, sour cream, mustard, lemon peel, salt, and ground red pepper until blended; stir in crabmeat and bread crumbs just until mixed. Cover and refrigerate 30 minutes.

3. Meanwhile, prepare Lemon Sauce.

4. Preheat oven to 400°F. Lightly grease two cookie sheets. Drop level tablespoons crab mixture, pressing lightly, on prepared cookie sheets. Bake until golden brown, about 15 minutes. Top each crab cake with about ½ teaspoon lemon sauce. Serve hot. Makes about 50 mini crab cakes.

Lemon Sauce

In small bowl, stir together ¼ **cup light mayonnaise,** ¼ **cup sour cream, 1 teaspoon freshly grated lemon peel, 1 tablespoon fresh lemon juice, pinch salt,** and **pinch ground red pepper (cayenne)** until blended. Makes about ½ cup.

Each crab cake with sauce: About 28 calories, 2g protein, 1g carbohydrate, 2g fat (1g saturated), 12mg cholesterol, 71mg sodium.

Main-Dish Crab Cakes

Prepare crab cakes (left) but divide crab mixture into 8 portions, about ½ cup each, and shape each into a 3-inch cake. Place on greased cookie sheet. Bake until golden brown, about 20 minutes, gently turning cake over with spatula halfway through baking. Serve with Lemon Sauce (opposite), if desired.

Each crab cake: About 138 calories, 12g protein, 5g carbohydrate, 7g fat (3g saturated), 68mg cholesterol, 366mg sodium.

Prosciutto-Wrapped Asparagus

Delicate, succulent asparagus is the perfect foil for salty prosciutto. You can assemble these early in the day and bake them at the very last minute.

Prep: 25 minutes	Bake: 10 minutes

- 24 thick asparagus spears, trimmed and peeled
- 12 thin slices prosciutto (5 ounces)
- ½ cup freshly grated Parmesan cheese
- ¼ teaspoon coarsely ground black pepper

1. In 5-quart Dutch oven, heat *3 quarts water* to boiling over high heat. Add asparagus; cook 3 minutes to blanch. Drain; rinse with cold running water. Pat dry with paper towels.

2. Preheat oven to 450°F. Working in batches, spread out prosciutto on cutting board; cut each slice lengthwise in half and separate slightly. Evenly sprinkle 1 teaspoon Parmesan on each prosciutto strip. Place 1 asparagus spear at end of 1 strip; wrap prosciutto in spiral along length of asparagus (don't cover asparagus tip). Transfer to jelly-roll pan. Repeat with remaining prosciutto, Parmesan, and asparagus. Sprinkle with pepper. If not serving right away, cover and refrigerate up to 6 hours.

3. Bake prosciutto-wrapped asparagus 10 minutes. Transfer to paper towels to drain. Arrange on platter and serve warm. Makes 24 appetizers.

Each appetizer: About 28 calories, 3g protein, 1g carbohydrate, 2g total fat (1g saturated), 6mg cholesterol, 148mg sodium.

Buffalo-Style Chicken Wings

Here's a broiled version of one of America's favorite appetizers. Serve with plenty of napkins!

Prep: 15 minutes	Broil: 20 minutes

- 4 ounces blue cheese, crumbled (1 cup)
- ½ cup sour cream
- ¼ cup mayonnaise
- ¼ cup milk
- ¼ cup chopped fresh parsley
- 1 tablespoon fresh lemon juice
- ½ teaspoon salt
- 3 pounds chicken wings (18 wings), tips discarded, if desired
- 3 tablespoons butter or margarine
- ¼ cup hot pepper sauce
- 1 medium bunch celery, cut into sticks

1. Preheat broiler. In medium bowl, combine blue cheese, sour cream, mayonnaise, milk, parsley, lemon juice, and ¼ teaspoon salt. Cover and refrigerate.

2. Arrange chicken wings on rack in broiling pan; sprinkle with remaining ¼ teaspoon salt. Broil 5 inches from heat source 10 minutes. Turn wings and broil until golden, 10 to 15 minutes longer.

3. Meanwhile, in small saucepan, melt butter with hot pepper sauce over low heat, stirring occasionally; keep hot.

4. In large bowl, toss wings with seasoned butter to coat all sides. Arrange chicken wings and celery on platter along with blue-cheese sauce and serve. Makes 18 appetizers.

Each appetizer (without wing tip): About 169 calories, 10g protein, 3g carbohydrate, 13g total fat (5g saturated), 39mg cholesterol, 349mg sodium.

Chinese Dumplings

Steamed dumplings are fun to make at home. Have them for brunch; it's the way the Chinese enjoy them.

Prep: 45 minutes   Cook: 10 minutes

- 2 cups packed sliced Napa cabbage (Chinese cabbage)
- 8 ounces ground pork
- 1 green onion, finely chopped
- 1½ teaspoons minced, peeled fresh ginger
- 2 tablespoons soy sauce
- 1 tablespoon dry sherry
- 2 teaspoons cornstarch
- 36 wonton wrappers (9 ounces)
- 1 large egg white, beaten
- Soy Dipping Sauce (opposite)

1. Prepare filling: In 2-quart saucepan, heat *1 inch water* to boiling over high heat. Add cabbage and heat to boiling. Cook 1 minute; drain. Immediately rinse with cold running water to stop cooking. With hands, squeeze out as much water from cabbage as possible. Finely chop cabbage. Squeeze out any remaining water from cabbage; place in medium bowl. Stir in pork, green onion, ginger, soy sauce, sherry, and cornstarch until well blended.

2. Arrange half of wonton wrappers on waxed paper. With pastry brush, brush each wrapper lightly with egg white. Spoon 1 rounded teaspoon filling into center of each wrapper. Bring two op-  posite corners of each wonton wrapper together over filling; pinch and pleat edges together to seal in filling. Repeat with remaining wrappers, egg white, and filling.

3. In deep nonstick 12-inch skillet, heat *½ inch water* to boiling over high heat. Place all dumplings, pleated edges up, in one layer in skillet. With spatula, move dumplings gently to prevent them from sticking to bottom of skillet; heat to boiling. Reduce heat; cover and simmer until dumplings are cooked through, about 5 minutes.

4. Meanwhile, prepare Soy Dipping Sauce.

5. With slotted spoon, transfer dumplings to platter. Serve with dipping sauce. Makes 36 dumplings.

Each dumpling without sauce: About 40 calories, 2g protein, 5g carbohydrate, 1g total fat (1g saturated), 5g cholesterol, 103g sodium.

Soy Dipping Sauce

In small serving bowl, stir **¼ cup soy sauce, ¼ cup seasoned rice vinegar or white wine vinegar,** and **2 tablespoons peeled fresh ginger,** cut into very thin slivers, until blended. Makes about ½ cup.

Each teaspoon: About 4 calories, 0g protein, 1g carbohydrate, 0g total fat (0g saturated), 0mg cholesterol, 221mg sodium.

Chinese Dumplings

Shrimp Cocktail

Everyone loves to dip shrimp into sauce; it's fun and it's tasty. So here are two sauces that are very different but equally delicious.

Prep: 25 minutes plus chilling
Cook: 17 minutes

1	lemon, thinly sliced
4	bay leaves
20	whole black peppercorns
10	whole allspice berries
2	teaspoons salt
24	extra-large shrimp (1 pound), shelled and deveined (page 193)
	Southwestern-Style Cocktail Sauce (below)
	Mustard Dipping Sauce (right)
12	small romaine lettuce leaves
24	(7-inch) bamboo skewers

1. In 5-quart Dutch oven, combine *2 quarts water,* lemon, bay leaves, peppercorns, allspice berries, and salt; heat to boiling. Cover and boil 15 minutes.

2. Add shrimp and cook just until opaque through-out, 1 to 2 minutes. Drain and rinse with cold running water to stop cooking. Cover and refrigerate shrimp up to 24 hours.

3. Prepare Southwestern-Style Cocktail Sauce and/or Mustard Dipping Sauce.

4. Just before serving, place bowls of sauces in center of platter; arrange romaine leaves around bowls, leaf tips facing out. Thread each shrimp on a bamboo skewer and arrange skewers on romaine. Makes 8 first-course servings.

Each serving without sauce: About 51 calories, 10g protein, 1g carbohydrate, 1g total fat (0g saturated), 70mg cholesterol, 141mg sodium.

Southwestern-Style Cocktail Sauce

In bowl, stir **1 cup bottled cocktail sauce, 2 tablespoons chopped fresh cilantro, 2 teaspoons minced jalapeño chile,** and **2 teaspoons fresh lime juice** until well combined. Cover and refrigerate up to 24 hours. Makes about 1 cup.

Each tablespoon: About 18 calories, 0g protein, 4g carbohydrate, 0g total fat (0g saturated), 0mg cholesterol, 191mg sodium.

Mustard Dipping Sauce

In small serving bowl, stir **1 cup reduced-fat sour cream, 3 tablespoons grainy Dijon mustard, 3 tablespoons chopped fresh parsley, 1/4 teaspoon freshly grated lemon peel, 1/4 teaspoon salt,** and **1/8 teaspoon coarsely ground black pepper** until well combined. Cover and refrigerate up to 24 hours. Makes about 1 cup.

Each tablespoon: About 28 calories, 1g protein, 1g carbohydrate, 2g total fat (1g saturated), 5mg cholesterol, 111mg sodium.

Prosciutto with Melon

The marriage of sweet ripe melon and salty prosciutto is a classic combination. Imported prosciutto di Parma, available at Italian grocers and specialty food markets, is much milder than the domestic varieties of this ham. It's worth seeking out.

Prep: 10 minutes

1	small honeydew melon or 1 medium cantaloupe, chilled
4	ounces prosciutto, thinly sliced
	freshly ground black pepper

1. Cut melon in half through stem end and remove seeds. Cut each half into 4 wedges; cut off rind.

2. Arrange 2 melon wedges on each of four plates; arrange prosciutto to side of melon. Sprinkle pepper on each serving. Makes 4 first-course servings.

Each serving: About 150 calories, 9g protein, 22g carbohydrate, 4g total fat (1g saturated), 23mg cholesterol, 548mg sodium.

Prosciutto with Other Fruit

Prepare as directed but substitute **8 large green or black figs,** each cut in half, or **2 medium papayas,** peeled, seeded, and sliced, for melon.

3

SOUPS, STEWS & CHILIS

Soups, stews, and chilis are the very essence of one-pot cooking, and, as you would expect, have a lot in common. They are all made in one pot, they taste even better a day or so later, and they are as easy to cook up in small amounts as in large potfuls. Even better, they make almost a complete meal. Begin with a crisp green salad, add some fresh bread alongside, and dinner is served. How easy is that?

In this chapter, you will find recipes from all corners of the globe, including Vietnamese Noodle Soup (page 58), Gazpacho with Cilantro Cream (page 51), Moroccan Vegetable Stew (page 68), Hungarian Pork Goulash (page 76), Provençal Beef Stew (page 69), and Pasta e Fagiole with Sausage (page 60).

SOUP

Soups are infinite in variety and for that very reason exceptionally versatile. A soup can be a light and elegant first course, a substantial rib-sticking meal-in-a-pot, or a refreshing cooler on a summer's day. It can be a crystal-clear golden liquid, a silky smooth and creamy puree, or thick with vegetables, noodles, and a protein, such as chicken or beef. Some soups are always served cold, like gazpacho, and some are always served hot, such as spit pea soup. And others are so versatile that they are just as delicious hot, cold, or at room temperature. Whatever your preference, there is a soup to suit your taste.

STEW

Warming, hearty, and always satisfying, stews are perfect cold-weather food. Stews can be made with chicken, pork, beef, veal, or fish that has been cut into small pieces or hearty chunks. And while some stews are laden with a variety of vegetables, others contain only one or two. The liquid can be as varied as the ingredients themselves: water, broth, tomato juice, and wine, or a combination can all work in a stew. Served up in large shallow bowls with hunks of bread for sopping up all the flavorful juices, a stew is comfort food of the first order.

CHILI

Just who cooked up the first chili is in dispute, but many chili aficionados believe credit must go to the Texas trail cooks who fed the cowboys while "winning the West." In fact, by 1880 eating a "bowl of red" was commonplace in cities like San Antonio. In this chapter we offer a tasty variety of all-American chilis. Some are made with chunks of beef, others with ground beef, and one is made with tasty pieces of pork. Our Cincinnati Chili (page 77) gets served up on a bed of spaghetti, while the New Mexican Green Chili (page 76) is a bold pot of pork shoulder chunks, onions, jalapeños, cumin, cayenne, fresh tomatillos, and poblanos that speaks of the best of the Southwest.

French Onion Soup

Onions, slowly cooked until deep brown and cara-melized, give this classic its distinctive flavor. Great for a party, this recipe is easily doubled; simply cook the onions in two skillets.

Prep: 10 minutes   Cook/Bake: 2 hours

- 4 tablespoons butter or margarine
- 6 medium onions, thinly sliced
- ¼ teaspoon salt
- 4 cups water
- 1 can (14½ ounces) beef broth or
  1¾ cups Brown Beef Stock (page 61)
- ¼ teaspoon dried thyme
- 4 diagonal slices (½ inch thick) French bread
- 4 ounces Gruyère or Swiss cheese, shredded
  (1 cup)

1. In nonstick 12-inch skillet, melt butter over medium-low heat. Add onions and salt and cook, stir-ring occasionally, until onions are very tender and begin to caramelize, about 45 minutes. Reduce heat to low and cook, stirring fre-quently, until onions are deep golden brown, about 15 minutes longer.

2. Transfer onions to 5-quart Dutch oven. Add ½ cup water to same skillet and heat to boiling, stirring until browned bits are loosened from bottom of skillet. Add to onions in Dutch oven. Add remaining 3½ cups water, broth, and thyme to onions and heat to boiling over high heat. Reduce heat and simmer 30 minutes.

3. Preheat oven to 450°F. Arrange bread slices on cookie sheet and bake until lightly toasted, about 5 minutes. Place four ovenproof bowls in jelly-roll pan for easier handling. Spoon soup evenly into bowls and top with toasted bread, slightly pressing bread into soup. Sprinkle Gruyère evenly on top. Bake until cheese has melted and begins to brown, 12 to 15 min-utes. Makes about 5 cups or 4 first-course servings.

Each serving: About 402 calories, 15g protein, 37g carbohydrate, 22g total fat (13g saturated), 64mg cholesterol, 887mg sodium.

Butternut-Apple Soup

Nothing can match a pureed vegetable and cream soup for texture and this subtly sweet combination of squash and apples just proves the point.

Prep: 15 minutes   Cook: 40 to 45 minutes

- 2 tablespoons vegetable oil
- 1 small onion, chopped
- 2 medium butternut squash (1¾ pounds each),
  peeled, seeded, and cut into ¾-inch pieces
- ¾ pound Golden Delicious apples (2 medium),
  peeled, cored, and coarsely chopped
- 1 can (14½ ounces) vegetable broth or
  1¾ cups Vegetable Broth (page 61)
- 1½ cups water
- 1 teaspoon freshly chopped fresh thyme or
  ¼ teaspoon dried thyme
- 1 teaspoon salt
- ⅛ teaspoon coarsely ground black pepper
- 1 cup half-and-half or light cream

1. In 4-quart saucepan, heat oil over medium heat. Add onion and cook until tender and golden, about 10 minutes. Stir in squash, apples, broth, water, thyme, salt, and pepper; heat to boiling over high heat. Reduce heat to low; cover and simmer, stirring often, until squash is very tender, 20 to 25 minutes.

2. Spoon one-third of squash mixture into blender; cover, with center part of cover removed to let steam escape, and puree until smooth. Pour puree into bowl. Repeat with remaining mixture.

3. Return puree to saucepan; stir in half-and-half. Heat through over medium heat, stirring occasionally (do not boil). Makes about 9 cups or 8 first-course servings.

Each serving: About 175 calories, 3g protein, 28g carbohydrate, 7mg total fat (3mg saturated), 11mg cholesterol, 525mg sodium.

Spicy Curried Carrot Soup

Prepare as directed but substitute **2 pounds carrots,** peeled and cut into 2-inch pieces, for squash. Increase broth to 2 cans. In Step 1, omit thyme and **add 2 tea-spoons curry powder,** and **2 teaspoons grated fresh ginger.** Omit half-and-half. Makes about 8 cups or 8 first-course servings.

Butternut-Apple Soup

Cream of Asparagus Soup

For the most flavor, choose the thickest asparagus you can find for this creamy soup. If you wish, garnish each serving with a sprinkling of snipped fresh chives or chopped tarragon or parsley.

Prep: 10 minutes   Cook: 25 to 30 minutes

- 2 tablespoons butter or margarine
- 1 medium onion, chopped
- 12 ounces asparagus, trimmed and cut into
    1-inch pieces (3 cups)
- 3 tablespoons all-purpose flour
- ¼ teaspoon salt
- ⅛ teaspoon ground black pepper
- 1 can (14½ ounces) chicken or vegetable broth or
    1¾ cups Chicken Broth (page 62) or
    Vegetable Broth (page 61)
- 1 cup half-and-half or light cream

1. In 3-quart saucepan, melt butter over medium heat; add onion and cook, stirring frequently, until tender and golden, about 10 minutes. Add asparagus; cook 1 minute.

2. Stir in flour, salt, and pepper until blended. Gradually stir in broth; heat to boiling, stirring constantly. Reduce heat; cover and simmer until asparagus is tender, 5 to 10 minutes.

3. Spoon half of mixture into blender; cover, with center part of cover removed to let steam escape, and puree until smooth. Pour into bowl. Repeat with remaining mixture.

4. Return puree to saucepan; stir in half-and-half. Heat through (do not boil). Serve soup hot, or cover and refrigerate to serve chilled later. If chilled soup is too thick, stir in some milk. Makes about 5 cups or 4 first-course servings.

Each serving: About 194 calories, 6g protein, 14g carbohydrate, 14g total fat (8g saturated), 38mg cholesterol, 657mg sodium.

Cream of Cauliflower or Broccoli Soup

Prepare as directed above but substitute **3 cups small cauliflower or broccoli flowerets** for asparagus. Use **1¼ cups half-and-half or light cream** and add **dash of ground red pepper**. If desired, stir in **4 ounces sharp Cheddar cheese,** shredded (1 cup) and **½ teaspoon Dijon mustard** when heating through. Makes about 5 cups or 4 first-course servings.

Cream of Mushroom Soup

Prepare as directed above but substitute **1 pound mushrooms,** trimmed and sliced for asparagus. Makes about 4½ cups or 4 first-course servings.

Quick Cream of Broccoli Soup

Frozen vegetables are picked and processed so quickly they often retain more nutrients than fresh ones. Many frozen vegetables are easily transformed into a satisfying soup. If broccoli is not one of your favorites, try one of the variations.

Prep: 5 minutes   Cook: 20 minutes

- 1 tablespoon butter or margarine
- 1 medium onion, chopped
- 1 package (10 ounces) frozen chopped broccoli
- 1 can (14½ ounces) chicken broth or 1¾ cups Chicken Broth (page 62)
- ¼ teaspoon dried thyme
- ⅛ teaspoon salt
- ⅛ teaspoon ground black pepper
  pinch ground nutmeg
  pinch ground red pepper (cayenne; optional)
- 1½ cups milk
- 2 teaspoons fresh lemon juice

1. In 3-quart saucepan, melt butter over medium heat. Add onion and cook, stirring occasionally, until tender, about 5 minutes. Add frozen broccoli, broth, thyme, salt, pepper, nutmeg, and ground red pepper, if using; heat to boiling over high heat. Reduce heat and simmer 10 minutes.

2. Spoon half of mixture into blender; cover, with center part of cover removed to let steam escape, and puree until smooth. Pour into bowl. Repeat with remaining mixture.

3. Return puree to saucepan; stir in milk. Heat through, stirring often (do not boil). Remove from heat and stir in lemon juice. Makes about 3¾ cups or 4 first-course servings.

Each serving: About 130 calories, 6g protein, 12g carbohydrate, 7g total fat (4g saturated), 21mg cholesterol, 594mg sodium.

Quick Cream of Corn Soup

Prepare as directed above but substitute **1 package (10 ounces) frozen whole-kernel corn** for broccoli; if you like, add **¾ teaspoon chili powder** after cooking onion and cook 30 seconds before adding broth.

Quick Cream of Pea Soup

Prepare as directed (left) but substitute **1 package (10 ounces) frozen peas** for broccoli; if you like, add ¼ **teaspoon dried mint leaves** with broth.

Quick Cream of Asparagus Soup

Prepare as directed (left) but substitute **1 package (10 ounces) frozen asparagus** for broccoli; if you like, add ¼ **teaspoon dried tarragon** with broth.

Caldo Verde

In Portugal, this delicious soup gets its rich green color from finely shredded Galician cabbage, which is sold in the outdoor markets there. Kale, readily available in supermarkets, makes a fine substitute. If you like, sprinkle the soup with ½ cup finely chopped fully cooked spicy smoked sausage, such as linguiça or chorizo.

Prep: 15 minutes   Cook: 40 to 45 minutes

- 2 tablespoons olive oil
- 1 large onion (12 ounces), chopped
- 3 garlic cloves, finely chopped
- 2½ pounds all-purpose potatoes (8 medium), peeled and cut into 2-inch pieces
- 2 cans (14½ ounces each) chicken broth or 3½ cups Chicken Broth (page 62)
- 3 cups water
- 1 teaspoon salt
- ¼ teaspoon coarsely ground black pepper
- 1 pound kale, tough stems and veins trimmed and leaves very thinly sliced

1. In 5-quart Dutch oven, heat oil over medium heat. Add onion and garlic; cook until onion is golden, about 10 minutes. Add potatoes, broth, water, salt, and pepper; heat to boiling over high heat. Reduce heat; cover and simmer until potatoes are tender, about 20 minutes.

2. Mash potatoes in broth, keeping potatoes lumpy.

3. Stir in kale; simmer, uncovered, until kale is tender, 5 to 8 minutes. Makes about 10 cups or 5 main-dish servings.

Each serving: About 251 calories, 7g protein, 41g carbohydrate, 7g total fat (1g saturated), 0mg cholesterol, 1,187mg sodium.

Spicy Black Bean Soup

Canned beans make this soup a snap to prepare, and the right blend of spices gives it a Tex-Mex wallop of flavor.

Prep: 10 minutes   Cook: 30 minutes

- 1 tablespoon vegetable oil
- 1 medium onion, chopped
- 2 garlic cloves, finely chopped
- 2 teaspoons chili powder
- 1 teaspoon ground cumin
- ¼ teaspoon crushed red pepper
- 2 cans (15 to 19 ounces each) black beans, rinsed and drained
- 2 cups water
- 1 can (14½ ounces) chicken broth or 1¾ cups Chicken Broth (page 62)
- ¼ cup coarsely chopped fresh cilantro lime wedges

1. In 3-quart saucepan, heat oil over medium heat. Add onion and cook, stirring occasionally, until tender, 5 to 8 minutes. Stir in garlic, chili powder, cumin, and crushed red pepper; cook 30 seconds. Stir in beans, water, and broth; heat to boiling over high heat. Reduce heat and simmer 15 minutes.

2. Spoon one-third of mixture into blender; cover, with center part of cover removed to let steam escape, and puree until smooth. Pour puree into bowl. Repeat with remaining mixture. Sprinkle with cilantro and serve with wedges of lime. Makes about 6⅔ cups or 6 first-course servings.

Each serving: About 137 calories, 7g protein, 19g carbohydrate, 4g total fat (0g saturated), 0mg cholesterol, 563mg sodium.

Vegetable Chowder

If you have your own vegetable garden or if you live near a farmers' market, you will want to make this luscious soup to take advantage of the fresh summer produce.

Prep: 15 minutes   Cook: 30 minutes

- 2 tablespoons olive oil
- 1 large onion (12 ounces), chopped
- 3 cups water
- 3 medium zucchini and/or yellow summer squashes (about 8 ounces each), coarsely chopped
- 2 red and/or yellow peppers, coarsely chopped
- 3 large ripe tomatoes (2 pounds), coarsely chopped
- 3 large garlic cloves, crushed with garlic press
- ½ teaspoon fennel seeds
- 2 teaspoons salt
- ¼ teaspoon ground black pepper sliced fresh basil leaves for garnish

1. In 5-quart saucepot or Dutch oven, heat oil over medium-high heat. Add onion and cook until tender and lightly browned, about 10 minutes. Add water, zucchini and/or yellow squashes, peppers, tomatoes, garlic, fennel seeds, salt, and black pepper; heat to boiling. Reduce heat to medium and cook, uncovered, until vegetables are tender, about 20 minutes.

2. Spoon one-third of the mixture into blender; cover, with center part of cover removed to let steam escape, and puree until smooth. Pour puree into bowl. Repeat with remaining mixture.

3. To serve hot, return soup to same clean saucepot and heat through. To serve cold, cover and refrigerate at least 4 hours. Garnish with sliced basil. Makes about 9 cups or 6 main-dish servings.

Each serving: About 120 calories, 4g protein, 18g carbohydrate, 5g total fat (1g saturated), 0mg cholesterol, 795mg sodium.

Summertime Corn Chowder

A basket of warm Buttermilk Biscuits (page 447) and thickly sliced ham are all that's needed to complete the menu for a real summertime treat.

Prep: 25 minutes   Cook: 35 to 40 minutes

- 6 medium ears corn, husks and silk removed
- 4 slices bacon, cut into ½-inch pieces
- 1 medium red onion, chopped
- 1 jalapeño chile, seeded and finely chopped
- 1 garlic clove, finely chopped
- 2 tablespoons all-purpose flour
- ½ teaspoon salt
- ⅛ teaspoon ground black pepper
- 1 pound red potatoes (6 medium), cut into ½-inch pieces
- 2 cans (14½ ounces each) chicken broth or 3½ cups Chicken Broth (page 62)
- 2 cups half-and-half or light cream
- 2 small ripe tomatoes (8 ounces), peeled, seeded, and chopped thinly sliced basil leaves

1. Cut kernels from corncobs (about 3 cups), reserving 3 corncobs; discard remaining corncobs.

2. In 5-quart Dutch oven, cook bacon over medium heat until browned. With slotted spoon, transfer bacon to paper towels to drain; crumble.

3. To bacon drippings in Dutch oven, add onion and jalapeño and cook, stirring, until onion is tender, about 5 minutes. Add garlic; cook 1 minute longer. Stir in flour, salt, and pepper; cook, stirring, 1 minute.

4. Stir in potatoes, reserved corncobs, broth, and half-and-half; heat to boiling over high heat. Reduce heat; cover and simmer until potatoes are tender, 10 to 15 minutes.

5. Discard corncobs; stir in reserved corn kernels and heat through. Transfer chowder to warm tureen. Stir in tomatoes and sprinkle with bacon and basil. Makes about 9½ cups or 8 first-course servings.

Each serving: About 272 calories, 7g protein, 29g carbohydrate, 15g total fat (7g saturated), 30mg cholesterol, 693mg sodium.

Summertime Corn Chowder

Vichyssoise

This elegant soup, traditionally served cold, is just as delicious hot (just call it cream of potato and leek soup). Either way, serve it in small cups, and be sure to garnish with a generous sprinkling of snipped fresh chives.

Prep: 20 minutes plus chilling   Cook: 55 minutes

- 4 medium leeks (1¼ pounds)
- 2 tablespoons butter or margarine
- 1 pound all-purpose potatoes (3 medium), peeled and thinly sliced
- 2 cans (14½ ounces each) chicken broth or 3½ cups Chicken Broth (page 62)
- ½ cup water
- 1 teaspoon salt
- ¼ teaspoon ground black pepper
- 1 cup milk
- ½ cup heavy or whipping cream

1. Cut off roots and trim dark green tops from leeks; cut each leek lengthwise in half. Cut enough of white and pale green parts crosswise into ¼-inch pieces to equal 4½ cups. (Reserve any leftover leeks for another use.) Rinse leeks in large bowl of cold water, swishing to remove sand; transfer to colander to drain, leaving sand in bottom of bowl.

2. In 4-quart saucepan, melt butter over medium heat; add leeks and cook, stirring occasionally, 8 to 10 minutes. Add potatoes, broth, water, salt, and pepper; heat to boiling over high heat. Reduce heat; cover and simmer 30 minutes.

3. Spoon half of mixture into blender; cover, with center part of cover removed to let steam escape, and puree until smooth. Pour into bowl. Repeat with remaining mixture.

4. Stir milk and cream into puree. To serve hot, return soup to same clean saucepan and heat through over low heat (do not boil). To serve cold, cover and refrigerate at least 4 hours or until very cold. Makes about 8 cups or 8 first-course servings.

Each serving: About 161 calories, 4g protein, 14g carbohydrate, 10g total fat (6g saturated), 32mg cholesterol, 778mg sodium.

Gazpacho with Cilantro Cream

Recipes for this full-flavored, uncooked tomato-based soup abound. Ours is topped with a dollop of cilantro-spiked sour cream, a tasty combination.

Prep: 30 minutes plus chilling

- 2 medium cucumbers (8 ounces each), peeled
- 1 yellow pepper
- ¼ small red onion
- 2 pounds ripe tomatoes (5 medium), peeled, seeded, and chopped
- ½ to 1 small jalapeño chile, seeded
- 3 tablespoons fresh lime juice
- 2 tablespoons extra-virgin olive oil
- ¾ plus ⅛ teaspoon salt
- ¼ cup reduced-fat sour cream or plain lowfat yogurt
- 1 tablespoon milk
- 4 teaspoons chopped fresh cilantro

1. Chop half of 1 cucumber, half of yellow pepper, and all of onion into ¼-inch pieces; set aside. Cut remaining cucumbers and yellow pepper into large pieces.

2. In blender or in food processor with knife blade attached, puree large pieces of cucumber and yellow pepper, tomatoes, jalapeño, lime juice, oil, and ¾ teaspoon salt until smooth. Pour puree into bowl; add cut-up cucumber, yellow pepper, and onion. Cover and refrigerate until well chilled, at least 6 hours or up to overnight.

3. Prepare cilantro cream: In small bowl, stir sour cream, milk, cilantro, and remaining ⅛ teaspoon salt until smooth. Cover and refrigerate.

4. To serve, top soup with dollops of cilantro cream. Makes about 5 cups or 4 first-course servings.

Each serving: About 156 calories, 4g protein, 17g carbohydrate, 10g total fat (2g saturated), 6mg cholesterol, 545mg sodium.

Cool Cucumber Soup

Cool Cucumber Soup

Homemade curry oil adds a taste of the tropics to this summer favorite.

Prep: 25 minutes plus chilling   Cook: 3 minutes

2 **English (seedless) cucumbers (about 12 ounces each), peeled**
1 **small garlic clove, crushed with garlic press**
2 **cups (16 ounces) plain lowfat yogurt**
½ **cup lowfat (1%) milk**
1 **tablespoon fresh lemon juice**
1¼ **teaspoons salt**
2 **tablespoons olive oil**
½ **teaspoon curry powder**
½ **teaspoon ground cumin**
¼ **teaspoon crushed red pepper**
1 **small tomato, chopped**
1 **tablespoon sliced fresh mint leaves**

1. Prepare soup: Cut enough cucumber into ¼-inch pieces to equal ½ cup; reserve for garnish. Cut remaining cucumbers into 2-inch pieces. In food processor with knife blade attached or in blender, puree large cucumber pieces, garlic, yogurt, milk, lemon juice, and salt until almost smooth. Pour mixture into medium bowl; cover and refrigerate until cold, at least 2 hours.

2. Meanwhile, prepare curry oil: In small saucepan, heat oil over low heat. Stir in curry powder, cumin, and crushed red pepper; cook until fragrant and oil is hot, about 3 minutes. Remove saucepan from heat; strain curry oil through sieve into cup.

3. Prepare garnish: In small bowl, combine tomato and reserved cucumber.

4. To serve, stir soup and ladle into bowls. Garnish each with spoonful of cucumber mixture; sprinkle with mint and drizzle with curry oil. Makes about 4 cups or 4 first-course servings.

Each serving: About 170 calories, 8g protein, 15g carbohydrate, 9g total fat (2g saturated), 8mg cholesterol, 830mg sodium.

Split Pea Soup with Ham

This hearty old-fashioned favorite is a perfect pick-me-up on a cold blustery day.

Prep: 10 minutes	Cook: 1 hour 15 minutes

- 2 tablespoons vegetable oil
- 2 white turnips (6 ounces each), peeled and chopped (optional)
- 2 carrots, peeled and finely chopped
- 2 stalks celery, finely chopped
- 1 medium onion, finely chopped
- 1 package (16 ounces) dry split peas, rinsed and picked through
- 2 smoked ham hocks (1½ pounds)
- 8 cups water
- 1 bay leaf
- 1 teaspoon salt
- ¼ teaspoon ground allspice

1. In 5-quart Dutch oven, heat oil over medium-high heat. Add turnips, if using, carrots, celery, and onion; cook, stirring frequently, until carrots are tender-crisp, about 10 minutes. Add split peas, ham hocks, water, bay leaf, salt, and allspice; heat to boiling over high heat. Reduce heat; cover and simmer 45 minutes.

2. Discard bay leaf. Transfer ham hocks to cutting board; discard skin and bones. Finely chop meat. Return meat to soup. Heat through. Makes 11 cups or 6 main-dish servings.

Each serving: About 343 calories, 21g protein, 52g carbohydrate, 7g total fat (1g saturated), 3mg cholesterol, 1,174mg sodium.

German Lentil Soup

Prepare as above, but omit turnips. Substitute **1 pound lentils,** rinsed and picked over, for peas, and substitute ½ **teaspoon thyme** for allspice.

Curried Lentil Soup

Based on an Indian classic, this thick and hearty soup is bound to become a staple in your soup repertoire. Lentils, unlike other dried legumes, don't require pre-soaking, so this can be prepared in less time than most other bean soups.

Prep: 30 minutes	Cook: 1 hour

- 2 tablespoons olive oil
- 4 carrots, peeled and finely chopped
- 2 large stalks celery, finely chopped
- 1 large onion (12 ounces), finely chopped
- 1 medium Granny Smith apple, peeled, cored, and finely chopped
- 1 tablespoon grated, peeled fresh ginger
- 1 large garlic clove, crushed with garlic press
- 2 teaspoons curry powder
- ¾ teaspoon ground cumin
- ¾ teaspoon ground coriander
- 1 package (16 ounces) lentils, rinsed and picked through
- 5 cups water
- 2 cans (14½ ounces each) vegetable or chicken broth or 3½ cups Vegetable Broth (page 61) or Chicken Broth (page 62)
- ¼ cup chopped fresh cilantro
- ½ teaspoon salt
  plain lowfat yogurt

1. In 5-quart Dutch oven, heat oil over medium-high heat. Add carrots, celery, onion, and apple; cook, stirring occasionally, until lightly browned, 10 to 15 minutes.

2. Add ginger, garlic, curry powder, cumin, and coriander; cook, stirring, 1 minute.

3. Add lentils, water, and broth; heat to boiling over high heat. Reduce heat; cover and simmer, stirring occasionally, until lentils are tender, 45 to 55 minutes. Stir in cilantro and salt. To serve, top soup with dollops of yogurt. Makes about 10 cups or 5 main-dish servings.

Each serving without yogurt: About 434 calories, 27g protein, 69g carbohydrate, 7g total fat (1g saturated), 0mg cholesterol, 966mg sodium.

Minestrone with Pesto

Freshly made pesto adds body and richness to this soup. During the summer, when basil is plentiful and well priced, make up a double or triple batch of our home-made pesto. Pack it into a jar, top it off with a thin layer of olive oil to keep it nice and green, then put the lid on. Refrigerate for up to several months.

Prep: 20 minutes plus soaking beans   **Cook:** 1 hour

- 8 ounces dry Great Northern beans (1⅓ cups), soaked and drained (page 243)
- 2 tablespoons olive oil
- 3 carrots, peeled and cut into ¼-inch-thick slices
- 2 stalks celery, cut into ¼-inch-thick slices
- 1 large onion (12 ounces), finely chopped
- 2 ounces pancetta or bacon, finely chopped
- 1 pound all-purpose potatoes (3 medium), peeled and chopped
- 2 medium zucchini (8 ounces each), each cut lengthwise into quarters, then crosswise into ¼-inch-thick slices
- ½ medium head savoy cabbage (1 pound), thinly sliced
- 1 large garlic clove, crushed with garlic press
- 1 can (14½ ounces) diced tomatoes
- 2 cans (14½ ounces each) chicken broth or 3½ cups Chicken Broth (page 62)
- 1 cup water
  Pesto (right) or ½ cup store-bought pesto
- ½ teaspoon salt

1. In 4-quart saucepan, combine beans and enough *water to cover by 2 inches;* heat to boiling over high heat. Reduce heat; cover and simmer, stirring occasionally, until beans are tender, 40 minutes to 1 hour. Drain beans.

2. Meanwhile, in nonreactive 5-quart Dutch oven, heat oil over medium-high heat. Add carrots, celery, onion, and pancetta; cook, stirring occasionally, until onions begin to brown, about 10 minutes. Add potatoes, zucchini, cabbage, and garlic; cook, stirring constantly, until cabbage has wilted. Add tomatoes with their juice, broth, and water; heat to boiling over high heat. Reduce heat; cover and simmer until vegetables are tender, about 30 minutes.

3. Meanwhile, prepare pesto.

4. In blender or in food processor with knife blade attached, puree ½ cup beans with 1 cup soup mixture until smooth. Stir puree, remaining beans, and salt into soup; heat to boiling. Reduce heat; cover and simmer 10 minutes. Garnish with dollops of pesto. Makes about 13 cups or 6 main-dish servings.

Pesto

In blender, puree ⅔ **cup packed fresh basil leaves,** ¼ **cup freshly grated Parmesan cheese,** ¼ **cup olive oil, 1 tablespoon water,** and ¼ **teaspoon salt** until smooth.

Each serving with pesto: About 444 calories, 18g protein, 53g carbohydrate, 20g total fat (4g saturated), 9mg cholesterol, 1,204mg sodium.

Quick Minestrone

Prepare as directed (left) omitting Step 1 and use **2 cans (15 to 19 ounces each) Great Northern beans,** rinsed and drained, for soaked beans. Add beans with tomatoes.

SOUP SAVVY

Test Kitchen Tip

Here are some of the most popular types of soups:

Bisque A classic French soup with a rich, creamy texture. It is usually made from shellfish and thickened with rice.

Broth A flavorful liquid made from simmered meat, fish, or poultry and/or vegetables.

Chowder Hearty and chunky, this soup is chock-full of fish, shellfish, and/or vegetables. Clam chowder has been popular in New England since colonial times.

Consommé Broth that has been clarified into a crystal-clear liquid.

Gumbo One of the signature dishes of Cajun cooking, gumbo is a thick soup that can contain chicken, duck, seafood, or ham and vegetables such as tomatoes, onion, bell peppers, and celery. It is thickened with a roux (a browned butter and flour mixture), okra, and/or filé (ground sassafras leaves) and is served over white rice.

Stock Similar to broth but made from bones, often roasted, that are simmered with water and/or vegetables.

Classic Black Bean Soup

True to the classic, we flavor this soup with ham and dry sherry.

Prep: 20 minutes plus soaking beans
Cook: 2 hours 30 minutes

3	tablespoons olive oil
3	large carrots, peeled and chopped
3	medium onions, chopped
3	stalks celery with leaves, chopped
4	garlic cloves, peeled
2	bay leaves
½	teaspoon dried thyme
1	pound dry black beans, soaked and drained (page 243)
2	smoked ham hocks (1½ pounds)
10	cups water
1	teaspoon coarsely ground black pepper
½	cup chopped fresh parsley
3	tablespoons dry sherry
2	teaspoons salt
12	paper-thin lemon slices

1. In 5-quart Dutch oven, heat oil over medium heat. Add carrots, onions, and celery and cook, stirring occasionally, until vegetables are tender, about 10 minutes. Add garlic, bay leaves, and thyme; cook 1 minute.

2. Add beans, ham hocks, water, and pepper to Dutch oven; heat to boiling over high heat. Reduce heat and simmer until beans are very tender, about 2 hours. Discard ham hocks and bay leaves.

3. Spoon one-fourth of bean mixture into blender; cover, with center part of cover removed to let steam escape, and puree until very smooth. Pour puree into bowl. Repeat with remaining mixture. Return puree to Dutch oven and stir in all but 2 tablespoons parsley, sherry, and salt. Cook 5 minutes.

4. To serve, ladle soup into bowls, garnish with lemon slices, and sprinkle with remaining parsley. Makes about 13 cups or 12 first-course servings.

Each serving: About 207 calories, 10g protein, 32g carbohydrate, 5g total fat (1g saturated), 2mg cholesterol, 788mg sodium.

Pasta e Piselli

Here is a quick weeknight version of *pasta e fagiole*. In season, use fresh peas (*piselli*). Cook them in the broth until tender before adding the pasta.

Prep: 10 minutes plus cooking pasta **Cook: 20 minutes**

2	tablespoons olive oil
3	garlic cloves, crushed with side of chef's knife
1	can (14½ ounces) diced tomatoes
2	cans (14½ ounces each) chicken broth or 3½ cups Chicken Broth (page 62)
½	cup water
¼	cup loosely packed fresh basil leaves, coarsely chopped
8	ounces mixed pasta, such as penne, bow ties, or elbow macaroni (2 cups), cooked as label directs
1	package (10 ounces) frozen peas, thawed freshly grated Parmesan cheese

1. In nonreactive 4-quart saucepan, heat oil over medium heat. Add garlic; cook, stirring frequently, until golden, about 2 minutes.

2. Add tomatoes with their juice, broth, water, and basil; heat to boiling. Reduce heat; cover and simmer 5 minutes. Discard garlic.

3. Stir in pasta and peas; heat through. Serve with grated Parmesan. Makes about 10 cups or 5 main-dish servings.

Each serving without Parmesan: About 317 calories, 12g protein, 51g carbohydrate, 8g total fat (1g saturated), 0mg cholesterol, 1,044mg sodium.

South-of-the-Border Chicken Soup

(Pictured on page 44)

We give this rich homemade soup a Latin accent with lime and cilantro, and serve it with chunks of buttery avocado and crisp tortilla chips.

Prep: 25 minutes   Cook: 1 hour

- 8 medium all-purpose potatoes (2½ pounds)
- 1 chicken (4 pounds), cut into 8 pieces
- 3 large stalks celery, each cut into thirds
- 3 carrots, peeled and each cut into thirds
- 2 medium onions, not peeled, each cut into quarters
- 10 cups water
- 10 sprigs plus ¼ cup chopped fresh cilantro
- 2 bay leaves
- 1 teaspoon whole black peppercorns
- 1 can (15¼ to 16 ounces) whole-kernel corn, drained
- 2 teaspoons salt
- ¼ cup fresh lime juice (about 2 large limes)
- 2 ripe medium avocados, cut into ½-inch pieces
   tortilla chips
   lime wedges

1. Peel 3 potatoes. In 8-quart Dutch oven, combine chicken, peeled potatoes, celery, carrots, onions, water, cilantro sprigs, bay leaves, and peppercorns; heat to boiling over high heat. Reduce heat; cover and simmer until chicken loses its pink color throughout and vegetables are tender, 35 to 45 minutes. Transfer chicken and potatoes to separate bowls.

2. Strain broth through sieve into large bowl; discard vegetables. Skim and discard fat from broth; return broth to same clean Dutch oven. Mash cooked potatoes with 1 cup broth; stir mashed-potato mixture into broth in Dutch oven.

3. Peel and chop remaining 5 potatoes. Add potatoes to broth; heat to boiling over high heat. Reduce heat; cover and simmer until potatoes are tender, about 10 minutes.

4. Meanwhile, discard skin and bones from chicken; cut chicken into bite-size pieces. Stir chicken, corn, and salt into broth; heat through.

5. Just before serving, stir lime juice and chopped cilantro into soup. Serve with avocado, tortilla chips, and lime wedges. Makes about 16 cups or 8 main-dish servings.

Each serving without garnishes: About 344 calories, 28g protein, 34g carbohydrate, 12g total fat (2g saturated), 76mg cholesterol, 772mg sodium.

Hearty Mushroom-Barley Soup

A real rib-sticker. Get a head start by cooking the barley the day before, then cool and refrigerate until needed.

Prep: 20 minutes   Cook: 1 hour

- ¾ cup pearl barley
- 8 cups water
- 2 tablespoons olive oil
- 3 stalks celery, cut into ¼-inch-thick slices
- 1 large onion (12 ounces), chopped
- 1½ pounds mushrooms, trimmed and thickly sliced
- 2 tablespoons tomato paste
- 5 carrots, peeled and each cut lengthwise in half, then crosswise into ¼-inch-thick slices
- 2 cans (14½ ounces each) beef broth or 3½ cups Brown Beef Stock (page 61)
- ¼ cup dry sherry
- 1½ teaspoons salt

1. In 3-quart saucepan, combine barley and 4 cups water; heat to boiling over high heat. Reduce heat; cover and simmer 30 minutes. Drain.

2. Meanwhile, in 5-quart Dutch oven, heat oil over medium-high heat. Add celery and onion; cook, stirring, until golden, about 10 minutes. Increase heat to high; add mushrooms and cook, stirring occasionally, until liquid has evaporated and mushrooms are lightly browned, 10 to 12 minutes.

3. Reduce heat to medium-high; add tomato paste and cook, stirring, 2 minutes. Add barley, carrots, broth, sherry, salt, and remaining 4 cups water; heat to boiling. Reduce heat; cover and simmer until carrots and barley are tender, 20 to 25 minutes. Makes about 12 cups or 10 first-course servings.

Each serving: About 133 calories, 5g protein, 21g carbohydrate, 4g total fat (1g saturated), 1mg cholesterol, 684mg sodium.

Vietnamese Noodle Soup

Although Vietnamese soup is traditionally served with thinly sliced beef, our variation uses chicken. The flat, wide rice noodles (*bahn pho*) can be purchased in the Asian section of some grocery stores or in Asian markets.

Prep: 20 minutes   Cook: 25 minutes

- 4 ounces flat dried rice noodles or linguine
- 3 green onions, thinly sliced on diagonal
- 2 garlic cloves, peeled
- 6 basil sprigs
- 6 sprigs plus 2 tablespoons chopped fresh cilantro
- 4 cans (14½ ounces each) low-sodium chicken broth or 7 cups Chicken Broth (page 62)
- 1 teaspoon coriander seeds
- 1 cinnamon stick (3 inches)
- 2 large skinless, boneless chicken breast halves (1 pound)
- 4 medium mushrooms, trimmed and sliced
  mint sprigs
  lime wedges (optional)

1. In large bowl, soak rice noodles in enough *warm water to cover* 20 minutes, or cook linguine as label directs. Drain.

2. Meanwhile, in 3-quart saucepan, combine one-third of green onions, garlic, basil and cilantro sprigs, broth, coriander seeds, and cinnamon stick; heat to boiling over high heat. Reduce heat; cover and simmer 10 minutes. Strain through sieve set over bowl; discard solids. Return broth to saucepan.

3. Cut chicken breast halves on diagonal into thin strips. Stir chicken, drained noodles, mushrooms, and remaining green onions into broth; heat to boiling over high heat. Reduce heat; cover and simmer until chicken loses its pink color throughout, about 3 minutes. Sprinkle with chopped cilantro and top with mint sprigs. Serve with lime wedges, if you like. Makes about 9 cups or 4 main-dish servings.

Each serving: About 269 calories, 30g protein, 27g carbohydrate, 2g total fat (0g saturated), 66mg cholesterol, 1,107mg sodium.

Turkey Soup

What's the Friday after Thanksgiving without turkey soup? Use your favorite vegetables to personalize the recipe.

Prep: 15 minutes plus overnight to chill   Cook: 5 hours

- 6 carrots, peeled
- 3 stalks celery
  roasted turkey carcass, plus 2 cups cooked turkey meat, finely chopped
- 2 medium onions, each cut into quarters
- 5 parsley sprigs
- 1 garlic clove, peeled
- ¼ teaspoon dried thyme
- ½ bay leaf
  6 quarts water
- 1¼ teaspoons salt
- 1 cup regular long-grain rice, cooked as label directs
- 2 tablespoons fresh lemon juice or 1 tablespoon dry sherry

1. Cut 2 carrots and 1 stalk celery into 2-inch pieces. In 12-quart stockpot, combine turkey carcass, carrot and celery pieces, onions, parsley sprigs, garlic, thyme, bay leaf, and 6 quarts water or enough water to cover; heat to boiling over high heat. Skim foam from surface. Reduce heat and simmer, skimming occasionally, 4 hours.

2. Strain broth through colander set over large bowl; discard solids. Strain again through sieve into several containers; cool. Cover and refrigerate overnight.

3. Remove and discard fat from surface of broth; measure broth and pour into 5-quart saucepot. If necessary, boil broth over high heat until reduced to 10 cups to concentrate flavor.

4. Cut remaining 4 carrots and remaining 2 stalks celery into ½-inch pieces; add to broth with salt. Heat soup to boiling. Reduce heat and simmer until vegetables are tender, about 15 minutes. Stir in cooked rice and turkey; heat through, about 5 minutes. Remove from heat and stir in lemon juice. Makes about 13 cups or 12 first-course servings.

Each serving: About 113 calories, 10g protein, 12g carbohydrate, 2g total fat (1g saturated), 21mg cholesterol, 355mg sodium.

Beef-Vegetable Soup

An old-fashioned crowd-pleaser, this soup can be made a day ahead, but for the most vibrant color, stir in the peas just before serving. You'll have plenty of soup here—the leftovers freeze well.

Prep: 30 minutes plus soaking beans
Cook: 1 hour 45 minutes

- 1 tablespoon vegetable oil
- 2 pounds bone-in beef shank cross cuts, each 2 inches thick, trimmed
- 2 medium onions, chopped
- 3 garlic cloves, finely chopped
- 1/8 teaspoon ground cloves
- 4 large carrots, peeled and chopped
- 2 stalks celery, chopped
- 1/2 small head green cabbage (8 ounces), cored and chopped (5 cups)
- 4 cups water
- 1 can (14 1/2 ounces) beef broth or 1 3/4 cups Brown Beef Stock (page 61)
- 2 teaspoons salt
- 1/2 teaspoon dried thyme
- 1/2 teaspoon ground black pepper
- 8 ounces dry large lima beans (1 1/4 cups), soaked and drained (page 243)
- 1 pound all-purpose potatoes (3 medium), peeled and cut into 1-inch pieces
- 1 can (14 to 16 ounces) tomatoes, chopped
- 1 cup frozen whole-kernel corn
- 1 cup frozen peas
- 1/4 cup chopped fresh parsley

1. In nonreactive 8-quart saucepot, heat oil over medium-high heat until very hot. Add beef, in batches, and cook until well browned, transferring meat to bowl as it is browned. Reduce heat to medium; add onions and cook, stirring, until tender, about 5 minutes. Stir in garlic and cloves and cook 30 seconds. Return beef to saucepot; add carrots, celery, cabbage, water, broth, salt, thyme, and pepper; heat to boiling. Reduce heat; cover and simmer until beef is tender, about 1 hour.

2. Meanwhile, in 4-quart saucepan, combine beans and enough *water to cover by 2 inches;* heat to boiling over high heat. Reduce heat; cover and simmer until beans are just tender, about 30 minutes; drain.

3. Add potatoes and beans to saucepot; heat to boiling. Cover and simmer 5 minutes. Stir in tomatoes with their juice; cover and simmer until potatoes are tender, about 10 minutes longer.

4. With slotted spoon, transfer beef to cutting board. Cut beef into 1/2-inch pieces, discarding bones and gristle. Return beef to saucepot and add frozen corn and peas; heat through. Spoon into bowls and sprinkle with parsley. Makes about 15 1/2 cups or 8 main-dish servings.

Each serving: About 278 calories, 24g protein, 35g carbohydrate, 6g total fat (1g saturated), 30mg cholesterol, 955mg sodium.

STORING SOUPS AND STOCK

Test Kitchen Tip

- Soup and stock should be quickly cooled before storing in the refrigerator or freezer. To cool down a pot of soup or stock, place the pot in a sink filled with ice water and let stand, stirring until tepid. Or pour the soup into small containers and cool for thirty minutes, then refrigerate.

- Stocks and most soups freeze well in airtight containers for up to three months. Be sure to leave at least 1/2 inch of headspace to allow for expansion. Freezing may diminish some of a soup's flavor, so be sure to taste the soup and adjust the seasoning before serving.

- Soup enriched with cream, yogurt, or eggs cannot be frozen because it will curdle when reheated; the soup base can be frozen, however. Prepare the soup just up to the point of adding the cream, yogurt, or eggs. Freeze like any other soup, then thaw and reheat, adding the enrichment at the last minute—just long enough to heat through. Do not allow the soup to boil, or it may curdle.

Pasta e Fagioli with Sausage

Pasta e fagioli, Italian pasta and bean soup, becomes a meal-in-a-pot with the addition of sweet sausage and fresh spinach. Using canned beans speeds up cooking.

Prep: 15 minutes   Cook: 1 hour

- 1 pound sweet Italian-sausage links, casings removed
- 1 tablespoon olive oil
- 2 medium onions, chopped
- 2 garlic cloves, crushed with garlic press
- 1 can (28 ounces) plum tomatoes
- 2 cans (14½ ounces each) chicken broth or 3½ cups Chicken Broth (page 62)
- 2 cups water
- 3 cans (15 to 19 ounces) Great Northern or white kidney (cannellini) beans, rinsed and drained (page 243)
- 6 ounces ditalini or tubetti pasta (1 rounded cup)
- 5 ounces spinach, washed and dried very well, tough stems trimmed, and leaves cut into 1-inch-wide strips
  freshly grated Parmesan cheese (optional)

1. Heat nonreactive 5-quart Dutch oven over medium-high heat until very hot. Add sausage and cook until well browned, breaking up sausage with side of spoon. Transfer sausage to bowl.

2. Reduce heat to medium; add oil to Dutch oven. Add onions and cook until tender and golden, about 10 minutes. Add garlic; cook 1 minute. Add tomatoes with their juice, breaking them up with side of spoon.

3. Add broth and water; heat to boiling over high heat. Reduce heat; cover and simmer 15 minutes. Add beans and heat to boiling; cover and simmer 15 minutes longer. Add sausage and heat through.

4. Meanwhile, in 4-quart saucepan, cook pasta as label directs, but do not add salt to water; drain.

5. Just before serving, stir spinach and cooked pasta into soup. Serve with Parmesan, if you like. Makes about 16 cups or 8 main-dish servings.

Each serving: About 558 calories, 28g protein, 65g carbohydrate, 22g total fat (7g saturated), 43mg cholesterol, 1,432mg sodium.

Pasta e Fagioli with Sausage

GARNISHING SOUP

Test Kitchen Tip

As delicious as soup is, almost any bowl of soup will be enhanced by an added splash of color or a bit of extra flavor. Chopped fresh herbs are the simplest of all garnishes. Choose an herb that complements the soup's flavor and color. For the best results, chop or snip fresh herbs just before using. Pureed soups can accommodate other kinds of garnishes. The smooth texture of a pureed bean or tomato soup calls out for a sprinkling of grated Parmesan cheese or crumbled bacon. Pureed vegetable soups are often topped with a drizzle of heavy cream.

Vegetable Broth

The optional fennel and parsnip add a natural sweetness to the flavor. For an Asian-flavored broth, add minced lemongrass, minced fresh ginger, or chopped fresh cilantro.

Prep: 25 minutes   Cook: 2 hours

- 4 large leeks
- 2 to 4 garlic cloves, not peeled
- 13 cups water
  - salt
- 1 large all-purpose potato, peeled, cut lengthwise in half, and thinly sliced
- 1 small fennel bulb, trimmed and chopped (optional)
- 3 parsnips, peeled and thinly sliced (optional)
- 2 large carrots, peeled and thinly sliced
- 3 stalks celery with leaves, thinly sliced
- 4 ounces mushrooms, trimmed and thinly sliced
- 10 parsley sprigs
- 4 thyme sprigs
- 2 bay leaves
- 1 teaspoon whole black peppercorns
  - ground black pepper

1. Cut off roots and trim dark green tops from leeks; thinly slice leeks. Rinse leeks in large bowl of cold water, swishing to remove sand; transfer to colander to drain, leaving sand in bottom of bowl.

2. In 6-quart saucepot, combine leeks, garlic, 1 cup water, and pinch salt; heat to boiling. Reduce heat to medium; cover and cook until leeks are tender, about 15 minutes.

3. Add potato, fennel if using, parsnips if using, carrots, celery, mushrooms, parsley and thyme sprigs, bay leaves, peppercorns, and remaining 12 cups water. Heat to boiling; reduce heat and simmer, uncovered, at least 1 hour 30 minutes.

4. Taste and continue cooking if flavor is not concentrated enough. Season with salt and pepper to taste. Strain broth through fine-mesh sieve into containers, pressing on solids with back of wooden spoon to extract liquid; cool. Cover and refrigerate to use within 3 days, or freeze up to 4 months. Makes about 6 cups.

Each cup: About 19 calories, 1g protein, 4g carbohydrate, 0g total fat (0g saturated), 0mg cholesterol, 9mg sodium.

Brown Beef Stock

For a richer, meatier flavor, use four pounds of beef bones and one pound of oxtails.

Prep: 5 minutes   Cook: 7 hours 30 minutes

- 5 pounds beef bones, cut into 3-inch pieces
- 2 medium onions, each cut in half
- 3 carrots, peeled and each cut in half
- 2 stalks celery, each cut in half
- 13 cups water
- 1 small bunch parsley
- 1 bay leaf
- ½ teaspoon dried thyme

1. Preheat oven to 450°F. Spread beef bones, onions, carrots, and celery in large roasting pan (17½" by 11½"). Roast, stirring every 15 minutes, until well browned, about 1 hour.

2. With tongs, transfer browned bones and vegetables to 6-quart saucepot. Carefully pour off fat from roasting pan. Add 1 cup water to roasting pan and heat to boiling, stirring until browned bits are loosened from bottom of pan; add to pot. Add remaining 12 cups water, parsley, bay leaf, and thyme to pot. Heat to boiling over high heat, skimming foam from surface. Reduce heat and simmer, skimming foam occasionally, 6 hours.

3. Strain broth through colander into large bowl; discard solids. Strain again through fine-mesh sieve into containers. Cool. Cover and refrigerate to use within 3 days, or freeze up to 4 months.

4. To use, skim and discard fat from surface of stock. Makes about 5 cups.

Each cup: About 39 calories, 5g protein, 5g carbohydrate, 0g total fat (0g saturated), 0mg cholesterol, 73mg sodium.

Chicken Broth

Nothing beats the flavor of homemade chicken broth. Make it in large batches and freeze in sturdy containers for up to four months. Our recipe has an added bonus: The cooked chicken can be used in casseroles and salads.

Prep: 10 minutes plus cooling
Cook: 4 hours 30 minutes

1	chicken (3 to 3½ pounds), including neck (giblets reserved for another use)
2	carrots, peeled and cut into 2-inch pieces
1	stalk celery, cut into 2-inch pieces
1	medium onion, cut into quarters
5	parsley sprigs
1	garlic clove
½	teaspoon dried thyme
½	bay leaf
	3 quarts water

1. In 6-quart saucepot, combine chicken, chicken neck, carrots, celery, onion, parsley, garlic, thyme, bay leaf, and 3 quarts water or enough water to cover; heat to boiling over high heat. Skim foam from surface. Reduce heat and simmer 1 hour, turning chicken once and skimming.

2. Remove from heat; transfer chicken to large bowl. When cool enough to handle, remove skin and bones from chicken. (Reserve chicken for another use.) Return skin and bones to Dutch oven and heat to boiling. Skim foam; reduce heat and simmer 3 hours.

3. Strain broth through colander into large bowl; discard solids. Strain again through sieve into containers; cool. Cover and refrigerate to use within 3 days, or freeze up to 4 months.

4. To use, skim and discard fat from surface of broth. Makes about 5 cups.

Each cup: About 36 calories, 3g protein, 4g carbohydrate, 1g total fat (1g saturated), 3mg cholesterol, 91mg sodium.

Pressure Cooker Chicken Broth

In 6-quart pressure cooker, place all ingredients for Chicken Broth but use only **4 cups water.** Following manufacturer's directions, cover pressure cooker and bring up to high pressure (15 pounds). Cook 15 minutes. Remove cooker from heat and allow pressure to drop 5 minutes, then follow manufacturer's directions for quick release of pressure. Strain broth through colander into large bowl; discard solids. Strain again through sieve into containers; cool. Meanwhile, remove skin and bones from chicken; discard. (Reserve chicken for another use.) Cover broth and refrigerate to use within 3 days, or freeze up to 4 months. To use, skim and discard fat from surface of broth. Makes about 5½ cups or 6 first-course servings.

BROTH

Test Kitchen Tip
Homemade stock is a wonderful ingredient to have on hand, but don't underestimate the convenience and quality of canned broth. Supermarkets carry an assortment of canned broths, including chicken, beef, and vegetable, not to mention reduced-sodium, no-salt-added, and fat-free.

Chicken broth is used a lot in our test kitchens, but we sometimes dilute one 14½-ounce can of broth with ¾ cup water. This step is entirely optional, but we think it softens the intense flavor of canned broth.

Low-sodium and no-salt-added broths are recommended in recipes when regular canned broth would oversalt the finished dish. This is especially true in dishes where the cooking liquid evaporates substantially. When using homemade broth or stock, add salt to taste.

Fat-free broth is healthful, but it's just as easy to remove the fat from canned broth yourself. Freeze the unopened can of broth for one or two hours to solidify the thin layer of surface fat. Open the can, lift off the fat, and discard.

Bouillon cubes and powders don't have as natural a flavor as homemade or canned broths, so while cubes and powders are convenient, broth has the flavor edge.

Lobster Bisque

When you serve lobster, save the shells and cooking liquid and make this splendid soup the next day.

Prep: 15 minutes   Cook: 1 hour 15 minutes

- 2 tablespoons butter or margarine
- 1 medium onion, chopped
- 1 carrot, peeled and chopped
- 1 stalk celery, chopped
- 1 garlic clove, finely chopped
- 3 tablespoons tomato paste
  leftover shells and heads from 4 steamed lobsters
- 2 tablespoons cognac or brandy
- 6 cups water
- 2 bottles (8 ounces each) clam juice or 2 cups cooking liquid from steaming lobsters
- 3 parsley sprigs
- ⅛ teaspoon dried thyme
  pinch ground nutmeg
  pinch ground red pepper (cayenne)
- 3 tablespoons all-purpose flour
- ¾ cup heavy or whipping cream

1. In 12-quart nonreactive stockpot, melt butter over medium heat. Add onion, carrot, celery, and garlic and cook until onion is tender, about 5 minutes. Stir in tomato paste.

2. Increase heat to high and add lobster shells; cook, stirring occasionally, 5 minutes. Stir in cognac and cook until liquid has evaporated. Add water, clam juice, parsley, thyme, nutmeg, and ground red pepper; heat to boiling. Reduce heat; cover and simmer 30 minutes.

3. Strain soup through sieve into 4-quart saucepan; discard solids. Heat to boiling over high heat; boil until reduced to 5 cups, 10 to 15 minutes.

4. In small bowl, with wire whisk, whisk flour into cream until blended and smooth. Gradually whisk cream mixture into soup; heat just to boiling, whisking constantly. Reduce heat and simmer 2 minutes. Makes about 5½ cups or 4 first-course servings.

Each serving: About 258 calories, 3g protein, 12g carbohydrate, 22g total fat (14g saturated), 77mg cholesterol, 441mg sodium.

Manhattan Clam Chowder

Chowder clams are flavorful but tough and must be chopped after cooking. Substitute cherrystone clams, if you like; there's no need to chop them.

Prep: 30 minutes plus cooling   Cook: 50 minutes

- 5 cups water
- 3 dozen chowder or cherrystone clams, scrubbed (page 186)
- 5 slices bacon, finely chopped
- 1 large onion (12 ounces), finely chopped
- 2 large carrots, peeled and finely chopped
- 2 stalks celery, finely chopped
- 1 pound all-purpose potatoes (3 medium), peeled and finely chopped
- ½ bay leaf
- 1¼ teaspoons dried thyme
- ¼ teaspoon ground black pepper
- 1 can (28 ounces) plum tomatoes
- 2 tablespoons chopped fresh parsley
- ¾ teaspoon salt

1. In nonreactive 8-quart saucepot, heat 1 cup water to boiling over high heat. Add clams; heat to boiling. Reduce heat; cover and simmer until clams open, 5 to 10 minutes, transferring clams to bowl as they open. Discard any clams that have not opened.

2. When cool enough to handle, remove clams from their shells and coarsely chop. Strain clam broth through sieve lined with paper towels into bowl.

3. In same clean saucepot, cook bacon over medium heat until browned; add onion and cook until tender, 5 minutes. Add carrots and celery; cook 5 minutes.

4. Add clam broth to bacon mixture in saucepot. Add potatoes, remaining 4 cups water, bay leaf, thyme, and pepper; heat to boiling. Reduce heat; cover and simmer 10 minutes. Add tomatoes with their liquid, breaking them up with side of spoon, and simmer 10 minutes longer.

5. Stir in chopped clams and heat through. Discard bay leaf and sprinkle with parsley. Taste for seasoning; add salt as needed. Makes about 12 cups or 12 first-course servings.

Each serving: About 117 calories, 5g protein, 12g carbohydrate, 6g total fat (2g saturated), 12mg cholesterol, 342mg sodium.

Bouillabaisse

Ask Provençal cooks how to make bouillabaisse and you'll get a different and passionate response each time. When preparing this classic fisherman's stew, use at least three different kinds of fish with textures ranging from firm to flaky; add the most fragile fish to the pot last. Serve with bread toasts and generous dollops of the aïoli. C'est magnifique!

Prep: 1 hour   Cook: 1 hour

- 3   leeks (1 pound)
- 2   tablespoons olive oil
- 1   large fennel bulb (1½ pounds), trimmed and thinly sliced
- 1   medium onion, chopped
- 2   garlic cloves, finely chopped
      pinch ground red pepper (cayenne)
- 1   cup dry white wine
- 2   bottles (8 ounces each) clam juice
- 1   can (14 to 16 ounces) tomatoes
- 1   cup water
- 3   strips (3" by 1" each) orange peel
- ½   bay leaf
- ¾   teaspoon salt
- ¼   teaspoon dried thyme
- ⅛   teaspoon ground black pepper
      Easy Aïoli (page 33)
- 1   pound monkfish, dark membrane removed, cut into 1-inch pieces
- 1   dozen medium mussels, scrubbed and debearded (page 187)
- 1   pound cod fillet, cut into 1-inch pieces
- 1   pound medium shrimp, shelled and deveined (page 193)
- 2   tablespoons chopped fresh parsley
- 1   loaf French bread, thinly sliced and lightly toasted

1. Cut off roots and trim dark green tops from leeks; cut each leek lengthwise in half, then crosswise into thin slices. Rinse leeks in large bowl of cold water, swishing to remove sand; transfer to colander to drain, leaving sand in bottom of bowl.

2. In nonreactive 5-quart Dutch oven, heat oil over medium heat. Stir in leeks, fennel, and onion; cook, stirring occasionally, until vegetables are tender, about 15 minutes. Add garlic and ground red pepper and cook 30 seconds.

3. Add wine and heat to boiling; boil 1 minute. Stir in clam juice, tomatoes with their juice, water, orange peel, bay leaf, salt, thyme, and black pepper, breaking up tomatoes with side of spoon; heat to boiling. Reduce heat and simmer 20 minutes. Discard bay leaf.

4. Meanwhile, prepare Easy Aïoli.

5. Increase heat to medium-high. Stir in monkfish; cover and cook 3 minutes. Stir in mussels; cover and cook 1 minute. Stir in cod and shrimp; cover and cook until mussels open and fish and shrimp are just opaque throughout, 2 to 3 minutes longer. Discard any mussels that have not opened.

6. To serve, ladle bouillabaisse into large shallow soup bowls; sprinkle with parsley. Spoon aïoli onto toasted French bread and float in bouillabaisse. Makes 11 cups or 6 main-dish servings.

Each serving without toast or Easy Aïoli: About 312 calories, 42g protein, 17g carbohydrate, 8g total fat (1g saturated), 149mg cholesterol, 835mg sodium.

A BRIEF HISTORY OF CHOWDER

Test Kitchen Tip

In the 16th and 17th centuries, fish chowder was enjoyed by the French as well as by the native Americans. In America, by 1751, recipes for fish chowder began to appear in newspapers. Many were prepared by "layering chowder ingredients." Each ingredient was placed in a pot in a layer of uniform thickness, then slowly cooked. By the mid-18th century, chowder was a mainstay throughout the Northeast. Clams and other shellfish were added to chowders largely because of their great availability, as all one had to do along the shore was to dig them up. When the 1896 edition of the *Boston Cooking School Cookbook* contained three recipes for chowder, it was clear that chowder was here to stay.

New England Clam Chowder

Clam chowder, New England's signature seafood dish, derives its name from *chaudière,* the French word for "cauldron." The saltiness of clams and salt pork varies; taste the soup before serving and season if needed.

Prep: 25 minutes plus cooling   Cook: 45 minutes

1	cup water
1½	dozen large littleneck clams (about 4 pounds), scrubbed (page 186)
3	slices bacon, chopped
1	medium onion, finely chopped
1	tablespoon all-purpose flour
¼	teaspoon ground black pepper
1	pound all-purpose potatoes, (3 medium), peeled and chopped
2	cups half-and-half
1	cup milk
¾	teaspoon salt or to taste

1. In a 5- to 6-quart saucepot, heat water to boiling over high heat. Add clams; heat to boiling. Reduce heat slightly; cover and simmer until clams open, 5 to 10 minutes. Transfer clams to a bowl as they open. Discard any clams that have not opened.

2. When cool enough to handle, remove clams from their shells and coarsely chop. Discard shells. Strain clam broth through sieve lined with paper towels into measuring cup; if necessary add enough *water* to equal 2 cups.

3. In same clean saucepot, cook bacon over medium heat until lightly browned. With slotted spoon, remove bacon to paper towels. Add onion to drippings in pot; cook, stirring occasionally, until tender, about 5 minutes. Stir in flour and pepper until blended; cook 1 minute. Gradually stir in clam broth until smooth. Add potatoes; heat to boiling. Reduce heat; cover and simmer until potatoes are tender, about 15 minutes.

4. Stir in half-and-half, milk, and chopped clams; heat through (do not boil). Stir in bacon. Taste for seasoning; add salt as needed. Makes about 6 cups.

Each cup: About 371g calories, 18g protein, 24g carbohydrates, 22g total fat (11g saturated), 77mg cholesterol, 534mg sodium.

Yankee Cod Chowder

Prepare as directed (left) omitting water and clams. Follow Step 3 through stirring in flour and pepper and cooking for 1 minute. Stir in **3 bottles (8 ounces each) of clam broth** until smooth. Add potatoes and cook as directed. Add **1 pound cod fillet,** cut into 1½-inch pieces, to pot. Cover and simmer until fish is just opaque throughout, 2 to 5 minutes. Stir in half-and-half; omit milk. Heat through (do not boil). Stir in bacon. Taste for seasoning; add salt as needed. Makes about 8½ cups.

Each cup: About 259 calories, 14g protein, 15g carbohydrates, 16g total fat (7g saturated), 56mg cholesterol, 590mg sodium.

Oyster-Corn Chowder

Prepare as directed (left) omitting water and clams. Drain **1 pint shucked oysters,** reserving the liquid in a bowl. Follow Step 3 through stirring in flour and pepper and cooking for 1 minute. Stir in **2 bottles (8 ounces each) of clam broth** until smooth. Add potatoes and cook as directed. Stir in half-and-half; omit milk. Stir in oyster liquid and **2 cups fresh corn kernels** (from 3 to 4 ears corn). Heat just to a simmer over medium heat. Stir in oysters and cook, stirring frequently, until oysters' edges curl and centers are firm, 3 to 4 minutes. Stir in bacon. Taste for seasoning; add salt as needed. Makes 8 cups.

Each cup: About 284 calories, 8g protein, 27g carbohydrates, 17g total fat (8g saturated), 54mg cholesterol, 634mg sodium.

Andouille-Shrimp Gumbo

This is one of the best gumbos around. Chock full of chicken, andouille sausage, shrimp, rice, and vegetables, including the holy trinity of onion, green pepper, and celery, this is perfect party food.

Prep: 30 minutes   Cook: 1 hour 10 minutes

⅓ cup plus 1 tablespoon vegetable oil
½ cup all-purpose flour
2 celery stalks, chopped
2 garlic cloves, minced
1 medium green pepper, chopped
1 medium onion, chopped
2 cans (14½ ounces each) chicken broth or 3½ cups Chicken Broth (page 62)
1 can (14½ ounces) stewed tomatoes
1 pound skinless, boneless chicken thighs, cut into thin strips
½ pound andouille or chorizo sausage, cut into ¼-inch-thick slices
6 ounces okra, cut into ½-inch-thick slices
1 cup loosely packed fresh parsley leaves, chopped
1 tablespoon minced fresh thyme leaves
1 tablespoon minced fresh sage leaves
¾ teaspoon salt
½ teaspoon coarsely ground black pepper
4 cups water
1 pound medium shrimp, shelled and deveined (page 193), with tail part of shell left on
1 cup long-grain white rice, cooked as label directs

1. In 6-quart saucepot, heat ⅓ cup oil over medium-low heat until hot. Gradually stir in flour until blended and cook, stirring, until mixture is dark brown, about 15 minutes.

2. Meanwhile, in nonstick 12-inch skillet, heat remaining 1 tablespoon oil over medium heat until hot. Add celery, garlic, green pepper, and onion and cook, stirring occasionally, until vegetables are tender.

3. When flour mixture is ready, gradually stir in broth until blended and smooth. Add stewed tomatoes, chicken, andouille, okra, parsley, thyme, sage, salt, black pepper, cooked vegetables, and water; heat to boiling over high heat. Reduce heat to low; simmer, uncovered, 40 minutes.

4. Skim off fat and discard. Add shrimp and cook, uncovered, until shrimp turn opaque throughout, about 5 minutes longer.

5. Ladle gumbo into large bowls. Top with a scoop of hot rice. Makes about 11 cups or 6 main-dish servings.

Each serving: About 525 calories, 40g protein, 46g carbohydrate, 19g total fat (6g saturated), 169mg cholesterol, 1,515mg sodium.

Mussels in Saffron-Tomato Broth

Serve steaming bowls of these mussels with hunks of country-style bread to sop up all of the savory juices.

Prep: 20 minutes   Cook: 30 minutes

3 tablespoons olive oil
2 garlic cloves, crushed with side of chef's knife
1 small bay leaf
½ teaspoon loosely packed saffron threads
⅛ to ¼ teaspoon crushed red pepper
1 can (14½ ounces) diced tomatoes
1 bottle (8 ounces) clam juice
½ cup dry white wine
5 dozen medium mussels, scrubbed and debearded (page 187)

1. In nonreactive 8-quart saucepot, heat oil over medium heat. Add garlic and cook until golden. Add bay leaf, saffron, and crushed red pepper; cook, stirring, 1 minute.

2. Add tomatoes with their liquid, clam juice, and wine; heat to boiling over high heat. Reduce heat; cover and simmer 20 minutes.

3. Add mussels; heat to boiling over high heat. Reduce heat to medium; cover and simmer until mussels open, about 5 minutes, transferring mussels to bowl as they open. Discard bay leaf and any mussels that have not opened. To serve, transfer mussels and broth to large soup bowls. Makes 4 main-dish servings.

Each serving: About 219 calories, 16g protein, 10g carbohydrate, 13g total fat (2g saturated), 34mg cholesterol, 642mg sodium.

Moroccan Vegetable Stew

Spiced with cinnamon and crushed pepper, sweetened with dried plums, and served over couscous, this typical Moroccan stew (called a *tagine*) is as rich and satisfying as any meat dish.

Prep: 15 minutes   Cook: 40 minutes

- 1 tablespoon olive oil
- 1 medium butternut squash (about 2 pounds), peeled and cut into 1-inch pieces
- 2 carrots, peeled and cut into ¼-inch-thick slices
- 1 medium onion, chopped
- 1 can (15 to 19 ounces) garbanzo beans, rinsed and drained
- 1 can (14½ ounces) stewed tomatoes
- ½ cup pitted prunes, chopped
- ½ teaspoon ground cinnamon
- ½ teaspoon salt
- ⅛ to ¼ teaspoon crushed red pepper
- 1½ cups water
- 1 cup couscous (Moroccan pasta)
- 1¼ cups vegetable or chicken broth
- 2 tablespoons chopped fresh cilantro or parsley

1. In nonstick 12-inch skillet, heat oil over medium-high heat. Add squash, carrots, and onion and cook, stirring frequently, until onion is tender and golden, about 10 minutes.

2. Stir in garbanzo beans, tomatoes, prunes, cinnamon, salt, crushed red pepper, and water; heat to boiling. Reduce heat; cover and simmer until all vegetables are tender, about 30 minutes.

3. Meanwhile, prepare couscous as label directs, but use broth in place of water.

4. To serve, stir cilantro into stew and spoon over couscous. Makes 4 main-dish servings.

Each serving: About 474 calories, 14g protein, 95g carbohydrate, 6g total fat (1g saturated), 0mg cholesterol, 1,022mg sodium.

Chicken Bouillabaisse

Serve in oversized soup bowls with a dollop of garlic mayonnaise (see Easy Aïoli, page 33) and thickly sliced French bread toasts.

Prep: 1 hour   Bake: 30 minutes

- 1 tablespoon olive oil
- 8 large bone-in chicken thighs (2½ pounds), skin and fat removed
- 2 large carrots, peeled and finely chopped
- 1 medium onion, finely chopped
- 1 large fennel bulb (1½ pounds), cut into ¼-inch-thick slices
- ½ cup water
- 3 garlic cloves, finely chopped
- 1 can (14½ ounces) diced tomatoes
- 1 can (14½ ounces) chicken broth or 1¾ cups Chicken Broth (page 62)
- ½ cup dry white wine
- 2 tablespoons anisette (anise-flavored liqueur; optional)
- ¼ teaspoon dried thyme
- ¼ teaspoon salt
- ⅛ teaspoon ground red pepper (cayenne)
- 1 bay leaf
  pinch saffron threads

1. In 5-quart Dutch oven, heat oil over medium-high heat until very hot. Add chicken, in batches, and cook until golden brown, about 5 minutes per side, using slotted spoon to transfer chicken pieces to bowl as they are browned.

2. Add carrots and onion to Dutch oven and cook over medium heat, stirring occasionally, until tender and golden, about 10 minutes. Transfer mixture to bowl with chicken.

3. Preheat oven to 350°F. Add fennel and water to Dutch oven, stirring until browned bits are loosened from bottom of pot. Cook over medium heat, stirring occasionally, until fennel is tender and browned, about 7 minutes. Add garlic and cook 3 minutes.

4. Return chicken and carrot mixture to Dutch oven. Add tomatoes with their juice, broth, wine, anisette, if using, thyme, salt, ground red pepper, bay leaf, and saffron; heat to boiling. Cover and bake until juices run clear when thickest part of chicken is pierced with tip of knife, about 30 minutes. Discard bay leaf. Makes 4 main-dish servings.

Each serving: About 317 calories, 36g protein, 18g carbohydrate, 11g total fat (2g saturated), 135mg cholesterol, 1,036mg sodium.

Provençal Beef Stew (Daube)

In southern France, food is often flavored with garden-fresh tomatoes, olives, garlic, fresh orange peel, and a variety of herbs, including lavender. We suggest serving our robust Provençal-inspired stew with boiled potatoes and lots of crusty bread for soaking up all of the delicious sauce.

Prep: 15 minutes   Cook: 2 hours 30 minutes

2	**pounds lean boneless beef chuck, trimmed and cut into 2-inch pieces**
4	**teaspoons olive oil**
1	**large onion (12 ounces), chopped**
2	**carrots, peeled and chopped**
2	**garlic cloves, finely chopped**
1	**can (14 to 16 ounces) tomatoes**
2	**cups dry red wine**
4	**strips (3" by ¾" each) orange peel**
3	**whole cloves**
1	**teaspoon salt**
¼	**teaspoon ground black pepper**
¼	**teaspoon dried thyme**
1	**bay leaf**
2	**tablespoons chopped fresh parsley**

1. Pat beef dry with paper towels. In nonreactive 5-quart Dutch oven, heat 2 teaspoons oil over medium-high heat until very hot. Add half of beef and cook until well browned, using slotted spoon to transfer meat to bowl as it is browned. Repeat with remaining 2 teaspoons oil and remaining beef.

2. Reduce heat to medium. Add onion and carrots to Dutch oven and cook, stirring occasionally, until tender, about 5 minutes. Stir in garlic and cook until very fragrant, about 30 seconds. Stir in tomatoes with their juice, breaking them up with side of spoon. Add wine, orange peel, cloves, salt, pepper, thyme, bay leaf, and beef; heat to boiling over high heat.

3. Reduce heat; cover and simmer 2 hours to 2 hours 30 minutes, until meat is very tender. With slotted spoon, transfer meat to serving bowl and keep warm. Skim and discard fat from stew liquid.

4. Increase heat to medium-high and boil liquid 10 minutes to concentrate flavors. Discard bay leaf and spoon liquid over meat. Sprinkle with parsley. Makes 6 main-dish servings.

Each serving: About 292 calories, 30g protein, 11g carbohydrate, 14g total fat (4g saturated), 95mg cholesterol, 601mg sodium.

STEW SAVVY

A few simple steps are the keys to success when making stew.

- Always use a heavy pot, such as a Dutch oven, which promotes even cooking.
- When browning meat or vegetables, first pat them dry. Always add meat to the hot oil without crowding the pan, so that it browns rather than steams. Give meat or vegetables a chance to brown before turning, which will create browned bits on the bottom of the pan that will add rich flavor.
- Add enough liquid to cover or almost cover the ingredients.
- Cook stews slowly on top of the stove over low heat to tenderize the meat.
- Quicker-cooking ingredients, such as potatoes and peas, are usually added near the end of the cooking time, so they don't get overcooked.

Boeuf Bourguignon

This classic French dish has become an American fixture. Begin with a salad of mixed baby greens dressed with a light vinaigrette and end with chocolate mousse topped with whipped cream—typical bistro fare.

Prep: 30 minutes   Cook: 2 hours 45 minutes

- 2 slices bacon, chopped
- 2 pounds lean boneless beef chuck, trimmed and cut into 1½-inch pieces
- 2 teaspoons vegetable oil
- 1 large onion (12 ounces), chopped
- 2 carrots, peeled and chopped
- 2 garlic cloves, finely chopped
- 2 tablespoons all-purpose flour
- 2 teaspoons tomato paste
- 2 cups dry red wine such as Pinot Noir
- ½ bay leaf
- 1 teaspoon plus pinch salt
- ¼ teaspoon plus pinch ground black pepper
- 1 pound small white onions, peeled
- 3 tablespoons butter or margarine
- 1 teaspoon sugar
- 1 cup water
- 1 pound mushrooms, trimmed and cut into quarters if large

1. In nonreactive 5-quart Dutch oven, cook bacon over medium heat until just beginning to brown. With slotted spoon, transfer bacon to medium bowl.

2. Pat beef dry with paper towels. Add 1 teaspoon oil to Dutch oven and increase heat to medium-high. Add beef, in batches, to bacon drippings and cook until well browned, using slotted spoon to transfer beef as it is browned to bowl with bacon. Add remaining 1 teaspoon oil if necessary.

3. Reduce heat to medium. Add chopped onion, carrots, and garlic to Dutch oven; cook until onion and carrots are tender, about 8 minutes. Stir in flour; cook 1 minute. Stir in tomato paste; cook 1 minute. Add wine, bay leaf, 1 teaspoon salt, and ¼ teaspoon pepper, stirring until browned bits are loosened from bottom of oven.

4. Return beef and bacon to Dutch oven; heat to boiling. Reduce heat; cover and simmer until beef is very tender, about 1 hour 30 minutes. Remove bay leaf. Skim and discard fat.

5. Meanwhile, in 10-inch skillet, combine small white onions, 1 tablespoon butter, sugar, and water; heat to boiling. Reduce heat; cover and simmer until onions are just tender, about 10 minutes. Remove cover and cook over medium-high heat, swirling pan occasionally, until water has evaporated and onions are golden. Transfer to bowl; keep warm.

6. In same skillet, melt remaining 2 tablespoons butter over medium-high heat. Add mushrooms and remaining pinch each salt and pepper; cook, stirring, until mushrooms are tender and liquid has evaporated. Stir onions and mushrooms into stew. Makes 6 main-dish servings.

Each serving: About 415 calories, 33g protein, 20g carbohydrate, 23g total fat (9g saturated), 116mg cholesterol, 261mg sodium.

A GLOSSARY OF MEAT STEW

 Test Kitchen Tip Meat stews are enjoyed around the world. Here are some of the most famous:

Beef Bourguignon This French beef stew is flavored with onions, mushrooms, and bacon.

Beef Carbonnade A Belgian stew that contains dark beer and caramelized onions.

Blanquette de Veau A rich, creamy veal stew, so named because the meat is not browned.

Daube In France, daubes are often baked in a pot known as a *daubière*.

Goulash Called *gulyás* in its native Hungary, this stew is flavored with paprika.

Navarin A French stew made with lamb and usually onions, potatoes, turnips, and herbs.

Stifado A Greek stew prepared with lamb or beef, flavored with tomatoes and oregano, and baked in a casserole.

Veal and Mushroom Stew

In this recipe, the veal is slowly simmered with mushrooms and a touch of sweet Marsala wine until tender. Peas are added for their subtle sweetness and color.

Prep: 30 minutes   Bake: 1 hour

- 1½ pounds boneless veal shoulder, cut into 1½-inch pieces
- ¾ teaspoon salt
- ¼ teaspoon ground black pepper
- 3 tablespoons vegetable oil
- 1 pound white mushrooms, trimmed and cut in half
- ¼ pound shiitake mushrooms, stems removed
- ½ cup water
- ⅓ cup dry Marsala wine
- 1 package (10 ounces) frozen peas, thawed

1. Preheat oven to 350°F. Pat veal dry with paper towels. Sprinkle veal with salt and pepper. In nonreactive 5-quart Dutch oven, heat 2 tablespoons oil over medium-high heat until very hot. Add half of veal and cook until browned, using slotted spoon to transfer meat to bowl as it is browned. Repeat with remaining veal (without additional oil).

2. In Dutch oven, heat remaining 1 tablespoon oil over medium-high heat. Add white and shiitake mushrooms and cook, stirring occasionally, until lightly browned.

3. Return veal to Dutch oven; stir in water and Marsala, stirring until browned bits are loosened from bottom of pan. Heat veal mixture to boiling.

4. Cover Dutch oven and bake, stirring occasionally, until veal is tender, 1 hour to 1 hour 15 minutes. Stir in peas and heat through. Makes 6 main-dish servings.

Each serving: About 249 calories, 26g protein, 12g carbohydrate, 11g total fat (2g saturated), 94mg cholesterol, 448mg sodium.

Creamy Veal Stew

Known in France as *Blanquette de Veau*, this velvety stew is perfect just the way it is. It can, however, be accented with 2 tablespoons chopped fresh tarragon and 2 tablespoons fresh lemon juice, stirred in with the cream.

Prep: 35 minutes   Bake: 1 hour 15 minutes

- 2 pounds boneless veal shoulder, cut into 1½-inch pieces
- ¼ cup all-purpose flour
- 1 teaspoon salt
- ¼ teaspoon ground black pepper
- 2 tablespoons plus 2 teaspoons vegetable oil
- 1 cup dry white wine
- 2 medium onions, chopped
- 1 cup chicken broth
- 1 bay leaf
- ¼ teaspoon dried thyme
- ¼ cup heavy or whipping cream

1. Preheat oven to 350°F. Pat veal dry with paper towels. On waxed paper, combine flour, salt, and pepper. Coat veal with seasoned flour, shaking off excess.

2. In nonstick 12-inch skillet, heat 1 tablespoon oil over medium-high heat until very hot. Add half of veal and cook until browned, using slotted spoon to transfer meat to bowl as it is browned. Repeat with 1 tablespoon oil and remaining veal. Add wine to skillet and heat to boiling, stirring until browned bits are loosened from bottom of skillet; remove from heat.

3. In nonreactive 5-quart Dutch oven, heat remaining 2 teaspoons oil over medium heat. Add onions and cook until tender, about 5 minutes. Stir in veal, broth, bay leaf, thyme, and pan-juice mixture from skillet. Heat to boiling; cover and bake until veal is tender, about 1 hour 15 minutes. Discard bay leaf; stir in heavy cream. Makes 6 main-dish servings.

Each serving: About 285 calories, 31g protein, 10g carbohydrate, 13g total fat (4g saturated), 139mg cholesterol, 696mg sodium.

Moroccan-Style Lamb with Couscous

This sweet but slightly spicy stew is served on a bed of couscous, grain-shaped semolina pasta.

Prep: 20 minutes   Cook: 1 hour 45 minutes

- 2 pounds boneless lamb shoulder, trimmed and cut into 1¼-inch pieces
- 2 tablespoons olive oil
- 2 garlic cloves, finely chopped
- 1½ teaspoons ground cumin
- 1½ teaspoons ground coriander
- 1 large onion (12 ounces), cut into 8 wedges
- 1 can (14½ to 16 ounces) stewed tomatoes
- 1 cinnamon stick (3 inches)
- 1¼ teaspoons salt
- ¼ teaspoon ground red pepper (cayenne)
- 1 cup water
- 2 pounds sweet potatoes (3 large), peeled and cut into 2-inch pieces
- 2 cups couscous (Moroccan pasta)
- 1 can (15 to 19 ounces) garbanzo beans, rinsed and drained
- 1 cup dark seedless raisins
- ¼ cup chopped fresh cilantro

1. Pat lamb dry with paper towels. In nonreactive 5-quart Dutch oven, heat 1 tablespoon oil over medium-high heat until very hot. Add half of lamb and cook until browned, using slotted spoon to transfer meat to bowl as it is browned. Repeat with remaining 1 tablespoon oil and remaining lamb.

2. To drippings in Dutch oven, add garlic, cumin, and coriander; cook 30 seconds. Return lamb to Dutch oven. Stir in onion, tomatoes, cinnamon stick, salt, ground red pepper, and water; heat to boiling over high heat. Reduce heat; cover and simmer, stirring occasionally, 45 minutes. Stir in sweet potatoes; cover and simmer 30 minutes longer.

3. Meanwhile, prepare couscous as label directs.

4. Add garbanzo beans and raisins to Dutch oven. Cover and cook, stirring once or twice, until lamb and vegetables are tender, about 5 minutes longer.

5. Just before serving, stir in cilantro. Serve lamb stew on couscous. Makes 8 main-dish servings.

Each serving: About 570 calories, 33g protein, 81g carbohydrate, 13g total fat (3g saturated), 75mg cholesterol, 651mg sodium.

Lamb Navarin

Celebrate spring with this vegetable-laden classic French *ragoût*.

Prep: 20 minutes   Cook: 2 hours

- 3 pounds boneless lamb shoulder, trimmed and cut into 1-inch pieces
- 2 tablespoons butter or margarine
- 2 small onions, each cut into quarters, then crosswise into slices
- 1½ cups dry white wine
- 1½ cups chicken broth
- 1 cup water
- 6 sprigs plus 2 tablespoons chopped fresh parsley
- 2 thyme sprigs or ¼ teaspoon dried thyme
- 2 bay leaves
- 4 garlic cloves, finely chopped
- ½ teaspoon salt
- ¼ teaspoon ground black pepper
- 8 ounces peeled baby carrots (1⅓ cups)
- 2 small turnips (4 ounces each), peeled and cut into ¾-inch pieces
- 8 ounces pearl onions, peeled (1 cup)
- 1½ pounds asparagus, trimmed and cut into 2-inch lengths
- 2 teaspoons sugar

1. Pat lamb dry with paper towels. In nonreactive 5-quart Dutch oven, melt butter over medium heat. Cook lamb, in batches, until well browned, using slotted spoon to transfer meat to bowl as it is browned. Add onions to Dutch oven and cook, stirring, until tender, about 5 minutes. Add wine, broth, water, parsley sprigs, thyme sprigs, bay leaves, and lamb to pot; heat to boiling over high heat. Reduce heat; cover and simmer 15 minutes. Add garlic, salt, and pepper and simmer 30 minutes longer.

2. Add carrots, turnips, and pearl onions to Dutch oven; partially cover and cook until lamb is tender, about 30 minutes longer. Stir in asparagus and cook until vegetables are tender, 5 to 10 minutes longer.

3. With slotted spoon, transfer meat and vegetables to deep dish and keep warm. Boil stew liquid over medium-high heat until it has reduced and thickened, about 10 minutes.

4. Discard parsley and thyme sprigs and bay leaves. Stir in sugar. Taste for seasoning; add salt as needed. Spoon stew liquid over meat and vegetables and sprinkle with parsley. Makes 8 main-dish servings.

Each serving: About 312 calories, 39g protein, 14g carbohydrate, 11g total fat (5g saturated), 117mg cholesterol, 500mg sodium.

Country Borscht Stew

Unlike cold beet borscht, this hearty richly flavored version is loaded with cabbage, carrots, parsnips, and succulent beef short ribs. Served hot, it is sure to warm you on even the coldest of winter days.

Prep: 1 hour 15 minutes	Bake: 2 hours

- 2 bunches beets (1¾ pounds without tops)
- 1 medium head red cabbage (about 2¾ pounds)
- 5 pounds beef chuck short ribs
- 1 pound carrots, peeled and each cut lengthwise in half, then crosswise into 1-inch-thick pieces
- 1 pound parsnips, peeled and each cut lengthwise in half, then crosswise into 1-inch-thick pieces
- 1 large onion (12 ounces), cut into 1-inch pieces
- 2 teaspoons salt
- 1 teaspoon caraway seeds, crushed
- ¼ teaspoon ground cloves
- 1 carton (32 ounces) chicken broth or 4 cups Chicken Broth (page 62)
- 2 bay leaves
- ½ cup loosely packed fresh dill sprigs, chopped sour cream (optional)

1. Trim tops, if any, from beets. Peel and shred beets (you should have about 6½ cups shredded beets). Cut cabbage into quarters; remove and discard core. Cut cabbage into ½-inch slices.

2. Heat 8-quart Dutch oven over medium-high heat until hot. Pat beef ribs dry with paper towels. Add beef in batches and cook until well browned on all sides, 5 to 6 minutes per batch, using tongs to transfer meat to medium bowl as it is browned. (You may need

to reduce heat to medium if fat in Dutch oven begins to smoke.) Preheat oven to 325°F.

3. Reduce heat to medium. Discard all but ¼ cup drippings in Dutch oven. Add carrots, parsnips, onion, salt, caraway seeds, and cloves; cook, stirring occasionally, until vegetables are golden, about 10 minutes. Add cabbage and cook, stirring frequently, until wilted, about 10 minutes.

4. Return meat with its juices to Dutch oven; stir in broth, bay leaves, and beets. Heat to boiling over high heat, stirring until browned bits are loosened from bottom of Dutch oven. Cover and bake until meat is fork-tender, 2 hours to 2 hours 15 minutes.

5. Remove stew from oven. With tongs, transfer short-rib meat and bones to large bowl to cool slightly. Discard bay leaves. Skim and discard fat. When short ribs are cool enough to handle, cut meat into 1-inch pieces; discard bones and fat.

6. Return meat to Dutch oven. Heat over medium heat until hot. Stir in dill. To serve, ladle borscht into shallow soup bowls and top with sour cream, if you like. Makes about 16 cups or 12 main-dish servings.

Each serving: About 525 calories, 22g protein, 22g carbohydrate, 39g total fat (16g saturated), 82mg cholesterol, 830mg sodium.

Country Borscht Stew

Five-Spice Braised Pork and Cabbage

In this dish, a generous amount of five-spice powder adds a lot of exotic flavor with very little effort. The powder, found in supermarkets, usually consists of equal parts of cinnamon, cloves, fennel seeds, star anise, and Szechuan peppercorns.

Prep: 1 hour   Bake: 1 hour 30 minutes

- 4 pounds boneless pork shoulder, trimmed and cut into 2-inch pieces
- 2 tablespoons brown sugar
- 1 tablespoon Chinese five-spice powder
- 1 tablespoon vegetable oil
- 1 teaspoon grated fresh orange peel
- ¾ teaspoon salt
- 1 medium head green cabbage (about 2½ pounds)
- 1 large onion (12 ounces), cut in half, then sliced crosswise
- 1 piece (3 inches) peeled fresh ginger, cut into slivers
- 1 can (14½ ounces) chicken broth or 1¾ cups Chicken Broth (page 62)
- ¼ cup soy sauce
- 2 tablespoons seasoned rice vinegar or cider vinegar
  long-grain white rice (optional)
- ¼ cup cornstarch
- 3 tablespoons water

1. Pat pork dry with paper towels. In large bowl, toss pork with brown sugar, five-spice powder, oil, orange peel, and salt until evenly coated. Set aside.

2. Remove tough outer leaves from cabbage. Cut cabbage into 4 wedges; remove and discard core. Cut cabbage into 2-inch pieces. Set aside.

3. Heat 6- to 8-quart Dutch oven over medium-high heat until hot. Add pork, in batches, and cook until well browned, 4 to 7 minutes, adding more oil if necessary, and transferring pork with slotted spoon to medium bowl as it is browned. (You may need to reduce heat to medium if oil begins to smoke.) Preheat oven to 325°F.

4. Reduce heat to medium. To fat remaining in Dutch oven, add onion and ginger, and cook, stirring frequently, until tender, about 5 minutes. Add cabbage and cook, stirring frequently, until cabbage wilts, 6 to 8 minutes. Add broth, soy sauce, and vinegar, and stir until browned bits are loosened from bottom of Dutch oven. Return pork with its juices to Dutch oven; heat to boiling.

5. Cover and bake until meat is fork-tender, about 1 hour 30 minutes.

6. About 30 minutes before serving, prepare rice, if you like.

7. Skim and discard fat from stew. In cup, combine cornstarch and water. Heat stew to boiling over medium heat. Stir in cornstarch mixture; heat to boiling. Boil until stew thickens slightly, about 1 minute. Serve with rice, if you like. Makes about 11 cups or 8 main-dish servings.

Each serving: About 455 calories, 49g protein, 19g carbohydrate, 20g total fat (6g saturated), 162mg cholesterol, 1,210mg sodium.

Mole Chili con Carne

From the word *molli*, which means "concoction," comes *mole*, a favorite sauce in Mexico that is probably prepared in as many ways as there are cooks who make it. Mole is a rich-tasting, reddish brown sauce, one of whose unlikely ingredients—chocolate—contributes body without making the sauce sweet.

Prep: 1 hour 10 minutes   Bake: 1 hour 45 minutes

- 2 pounds boneless pork shoulder, trimmed and cut into 1-inch pieces
- 2 pounds boneless beef chuck, trimmed and cut into 1-inch pieces
- 2 teaspoons vegetable oil
- 6 garlic cloves, crushed with press
- 2 medium onions, chopped
- 1 tablespoon ground coriander
- 1 tablespoon ground cumin
- 1 tablespoon paprika
- 1½ teaspoons chipotle chile powder
- ½ teaspoon ground cinnamon
- 3 cans (15 to 19 ounces each) pink beans and/or red kidney beans

- 1 can (28 ounces) diced tomatoes
- 1 cup water
- 2 squares (2 ounces) unsweetened chocolate, chopped
- 1½ teaspoons salt
  warm corn tortillas (optional)

1. Pat pork and beef dry with paper towels. In 6- to 8-quart Dutch oven, heat oil over medium-high heat until very hot. Add meat in batches and cook until well browned, 5 to 6 minutes, adding more oil if necessary and using slotted spoon to transfer meat to medium bowl as it is browned. (You may need to reduce heat to medium if oil in Dutch oven begins to smoke.) Preheat oven to 325°F.

2. Reduce heat to medium. Add garlic, onions, coriander, cumin, paprika, chipotle chili powder, and cinnamon to drippings in Dutch oven, and cook, stirring frequently, until onion is tender, about 5 minutes.

3. Return meat with its juices to Dutch oven. Stir in beans with their liquid, tomatoes with their juice, water, chocolate, and salt; heat to boiling over high heat, stirring until browned bits are loosened from bottom of Dutch oven.

4. Cover and bake until meat is fork-tender, 1 hour and 45 minutes to 2 hours. Skim and discard any fat. Spoon chili into bowls and serve with tortillas, if you like. Makes about 15 cups or 10 main-dish servings.

Each serving: About 525 calories, 55g protein, 34g carbohydrate, 19g total fat (7g saturated), 146mg cholesterol, 1,335mg sodium.

Mole Chili con Carne

Hungarian Pork Goulash

Old-world recipes for goulash often include sauerkraut. Look for plastic bags of fresh sauerkraut in the refrigerated section of the supermarket. Do not use the canned variety; it's too sour. Serve with egg noodles to sop up all the delectable sauce.

Prep: 20 minutes   Bake: 1 hour 30 minutes

- 2 tablespoons vegetable oil
- 2 large onions (12 ounces each), chopped
- 1 garlic clove, finely chopped
- ¼ cup paprika, preferably sweet Hungarian
- 2 pounds boneless pork shoulder blade roast (fresh pork butt), trimmed and cut into 1½-inch pieces
- 1 bag (16 ounces) sauerkraut, rinsed and drained
- 1 can (14½ ounces) diced tomatoes
- 1 can (14½ ounces) beef broth or 1¾ cups Brown Beef Stock (page 61)
- ½ teaspoon salt
- ¼ teaspoon ground black pepper
- 1 container (8 ounces) sour cream

1. Preheat oven to 325°F. In nonreactive 5-quart Dutch oven, heat oil over medium heat. Add onions and cook, stirring frequently, 10 minutes. Stir in garlic; cook until onions are very tender, about 5 minutes longer.

2. Add paprika to onions, stirring well; cook 1 minute. Add pork, sauerkraut, tomatoes with their juice, broth, salt, and pepper; heat to boiling over high heat. Cover and bake until pork is tender, about 1 hour 30 minutes.

3. Remove stew from oven. Stir in sour cream. Heat through over medium heat (do not boil). Makes 6 main-dish servings.

Each serving: About 450 calories, 33g protein, 17g carbohydrate, 28g total fat (11g saturated), 120mg cholesterol, 1,135mg sodium.

New Mexican Green Chili

At New Mexico's chile stands, green chiles are as popular as red ones. Tomatillos, which resemble small, hard green tomatoes and are covered with papery husks, are sold fresh and canned. Dark green poblano chiles are sometimes called fresh ancho chiles, but don't confuse them with dried anchos.

Prep: 30 minutes   Bake: 2 hours 30 minutes

- 1 bunch cilantro
- 3 garlic cloves, finely chopped
- 1½ teaspoons salt
- 2 pounds boneless pork shoulder, trimmed and cut into ¾-inch pieces
- 2 medium onions, chopped
- 3 serrano or jalapeño chiles, seeded and finely chopped
- 1 teaspoon ground cumin
- ¼ teaspoon ground red pepper (cayenne)
- 2 pounds tomatillos, husked, rinsed, and cut into quarters
- 4 poblano chiles or 2 green peppers, roasted (page 360), seeded, and cut into 1-inch pieces
- 1 can (15¼ to 16 ounces) whole-kernel corn, drained
  sour cream (optional)
  warm flour tortillas (optional)

1. Preheat oven to 325°F. Chop enough cilantro leaves and stems to equal ¼ cup; chop and reserve another ¼ cup cilantro leaves for garnish. With side of chef's knife, mash garlic and salt to paste; transfer to 5-quart Dutch oven. Add pork, onions, serranos, cilantro leaves and stems, cumin, and ground red pepper; toss to combine. Cover and bake 1 hour.

2. Stir in tomatillos and roasted poblanos. Cover and bake until pork is very tender, 1 hour 30 minutes to 2 hours longer.

3. Skim and discard fat. Stir in corn and heat through. Sprinkle with reserved cilantro and serve with sour cream and tortillas, if you like. Makes 6 main-dish servings.

Each serving: About 378 calories, 34g protein, 27g carbohydrate, 16g total fat (5g saturated), 103mg cholesterol, 802mg sodium.

Cincinnati Chili

This dish is served many ways all over Cincinnati. A "three-way" is over spaghetti with shredded Cheddar on top. Add chopped onion, and it becomes a "four-way." For a "five-way," add cooked red kidney beans.

Prep: 25 minutes   Cook: 3 hours

- 2 teaspoons vegetable oil
- 2 medium onions, chopped
- 2 teaspoons finely chopped garlic
- 2 pounds ground beef chuck
- 2 tablespoons chili powder
- 1 tablespoon ground cumin
- 1 teaspoon ground cinnamon
- 1 teaspoon salt
- ½ teaspoon dried oregano
- ½ teaspoon ground red pepper (cayenne)
- 2 cans (16 ounces each) tomatoes
- 1 can (14½ ounces) beef broth or 1¾ cups Brown Beef Stock (page 61)
- 1½ cups water
- ½ square (½ ounce) unsweetened chocolate, chopped
- 1 package (16 ounces) spaghetti or linguine

1. In nonreactive 5-quart Dutch oven, heat oil over medium heat. Add onions and cook, stirring occasionally, until tender, about 5 minutes. Transfer to small bowl; set aside. Add garlic to Dutch oven; cook 1 minute longer. Transfer to bowl with onions.

2. In same Dutch oven, cook ground beef over high heat, breaking up meat with side of spoon, until meat is browned. Discard fat. Stir in chili powder, cumin, cinnamon, salt, oregano, and ground red pepper; cook 1 minute longer.

3. Add tomatoes with their juice to Dutch oven, breaking them up with side of spoon. Stir in broth, water, chocolate, browned beef, and onion-garlic mixture; heat to boiling. Reduce heat; cover and simmer 2 hours 30 minutes. Remove cover and simmer until thickened, about 30 minutes longer.

4. Meanwhile, cook pasta as label directs. Drain. Serve chili over pasta. Makes 8 main-dish servings.

Each serving without spaghetti: About 270 calories, 26g protein, 12g carbohydrate, 14g total fat (5g saturated), 71mg cholesterol, 756mg sodium.

Two-Alarm Chili

If you like really hot chili, increase the pickled jalapeño and ground red pepper to your taste. Here cocoa is the secret ingredient that balances the seasonings.

Prep: 20 minutes   Cook: 35 minutes

- 1 tablespoon olive oil
- 1 medium onion, chopped
- 2 garlic cloves, finely chopped
- 2 green peppers, chopped
- 2 pounds ground beef chuck
- 3 pickled jalapeño chiles, seeded and finely chopped (2 tablespoons)
- 3 tablespoons chili powder
- 2 teaspoons unsweetened cocoa
- 1¼ teaspoons salt
- ¾ teaspoon ground coriander
- ½ teaspoon dried oregano
- ¼ teaspoon ground red pepper (cayenne)
- 1 can (14 to 16 ounces) tomatoes, chopped

1. In nonstick 12-inch skillet, heat oil over medium heat. Add onion and garlic and cook, stirring occasionally, until onion is tender, about 5 minutes. Add green peppers and cook, stirring, until tender-crisp, about 5 minutes longer.

2. Add ground beef and cook, breaking up meat with side of spoon, until meat is no longer pink. Stir in pickled jalapeños, chili powder, cocoa, salt, coriander, oregano, and ground red pepper; cook 1 minute. Add tomatoes with their juice and heat to boiling. Reduce heat and simmer, stirring occasionally, until slightly thickened, 15 to 20 minutes longer. Makes 6 main-dish servings.

Each serving: About 326 calories, 33g protein, 10g carbohydrate, 18g total fat (6g saturated), 94mg cholesterol, 758mg sodium.

4

MEAT

Meat is the major source of protein in the American diet, so it is important to know how to choose it and cook it properly.

BUYING MEAT

All meat in the United States is inspected by the United States Department of Agriculture (USDA) to ensure that it is safe to eat and free of disease, although some diseases, such as *E. coli* and salmonella, cannot be detected by the naked eye.

Grading is a voluntary procedure, and the grade given to any particular piece of meat reflects its tenderness: The higher the grade, the more tender the meat. There are different criteria for grading beef, lamb, and veal. In general, meat is graded according to age (the older the animal, the tougher the flesh) and the amount of marbling (streaks or flecks of fat within the flesh). This internal fat melts into the meat during the cooking process, moistening and flavoring the meat; the external fat that surrounds chops and steaks can be trimmed away.

The meat available to consumers is graded prime, choice, and select or good. Beef has the largest number of grading levels because the degree of tenderness varies much more from cut to cut. Lamb is also graded but veal only occasionally. Pork is rarely graded because only the highest grade is sold to consumers. One good bit of advice: Always buy the highest grade of meat you can afford.

STORING MEAT

Always store raw meat in the coldest part of the refrigerator (usually the bottom shelf), away from cooked and ready-to-eat foods. Place the meat on a plate or tray to catch any drips. Refrigerate uncooked meat for up to two days or freeze for up to six months. Ground meat can be refrigerated for one or two days or frozen for up to three months.

For short-term storage (up to two days in the refrigerator or up to two weeks in the freezer), leave raw meat in its original store wrapping. For longer freezing, or if the wrapping is torn, carefully rewrap the meat in freezer wrap or heavy-duty foil, pressing out all the air. Stack steaks, chops, and patties between sheets of freezer paper before wrapping. Label each package with the name of the cut, the number of servings, and the date.

Thaw frozen meat, on a plate to catch any drips, overnight in the refrigerator, not at room temperature. Do not refreeze uncooked meat or the texture will suffer. And for best results, do not freeze meat, raw or cooked, for longer than three months. Large roasts, however, can be frozen for up to one year.

COOKING TECHNIQUES

The USDA recommends that all meat be cooked until well-done (160°F) to kill any bacteria that could cause illness. We sometimes recommend cooking temperatures that are below this figure, because some meat tastes best cooked medium-rare or medium. Food-borne illnesses are relatively rare and usually affect only infants, the elderly, or people with weak immune systems. The degree to which you cook meat is a matter of personal taste, but also keep in mind for whom you are cooking.

Roasting

There is only one way to guarantee that meat is roasted to the desired doneness: Use a meat thermometer. Always insert a thermometer into the center or thickest part of the roast without touching any bone or fatty sections. Boneless roasts are tied to help them keep their shape during roasting. In our recipes, we sometimes place boneless roasts on a rack in the roasting pan so the heat can circulate under the meat, preventing the meat from cooking in its juices. Not all boneless roasts need to be cooked on racks, however. Tenderloin and some loin roasts cook so quickly that they don't have time to create juices. Rib roasts and other bone-in cuts come with their own natural built-in racks. Always remove a roast from the oven when it reaches 5° to 10°F less than the desired temperature, as the temperature will continue to rise as the meat stands. It is not necessary to cover the meat; the density of the hot roast will keep it from cooling too quickly. A foil tent would only trap the steam and soften the roast's delicious crusty exterior.

Panfrying and Sautéing

These fastest of cooking methods yield quick, tasty results. Before sautéing, pat the meat dry with paper towels so it can easily brown. Be sure to use a heavy-bottomed skillet so the heat is conducted evenly. We don't advise using a nonstick skillet; its slick surface inhibits the formation of a good crust. And don't crowd the meat in the pan or it will steam instead of brown. Cook over medium-high to high heat to sear the meat and give it rich flavor.

Braising and Stewing

Few dishes satisfy as much as a long-simmered stew or braised pot roast. The key is to be patient when slow simmering tough cuts of meat: It takes a long time for the collagen in the meat to melt and for the meat to become fork-tender. The key word here is "simmering." Tip: Do not let the liquid cook at more than a slow simmer or the meat will end up dry and tough.

Braising is usually done in a Dutch oven: a sturdy pot with a tight-fitting lid and a handle at each side that can go from the stovetop to the oven (and directly to the table if you like). Enameled cast-iron Dutch ovens are somewhat expensive but can last a lifetime. Old-fashioned, less expensive cast-iron Dutch ovens work equally well.

Broiling and Grilling

These dry-heat cooking methods are close "cousins." In broiling, the heat source is on top of the food, while in grilling, the heat source is below. Whether broiled or grilled, the food gets caramelized from the intense heat, which greatly contributes to its flavor. To make up for the lack of delicious smoky flavor when broiling, we like to use a flavorful marinade or dry rub. See Grilling page 300.

Always preheat a broiler on high for about ten minutes. Stoves with separate broiling units have adjustable broiler racks that enable them to be positioned as close to or as far away from the heating element as desired. Electric ovens that double as broilers are problematic. There is usually only one upper-rack position that is close to the heating element, but it is sometimes farther away than the ideal distance. This makes preheating especially important.

Carving Meat

Steaks and roasts benefit from a resting period before being served. This allows time for the internal juices to get redistributed throughout the meat, making the meat juicy and firming it for easier carving. Steaks should be transferred to a warm platter to keep them from cooling off, but they only need to stand for a

---

MEAT THERMOMETERS

Old-fashioned meat thermometer: Inserted into the meat before cooking and is left in the meat while it is being roasted.

Instant-read thermometer: Inserted into the meat for an almost immediate reading, then removed.

Probe thermometer: The desired temperature is set on a display and a probe is inserted into the meat. When the desired temperature is reached, an alert sounds. Allows you to roast meat to an exact temperature without having to open the oven to check.

minute or two before being served. Average-size roasts (about three pounds) should stand for ten minutes, and larger roasts for up to fifteen minutes.

For safety's sake, it's a good idea to place a towel under the carving board to prevent it from moving. Always carve with a sharp thin-bladed knife and use a two-tine meat fork to steady the roast. Carve across the grain, not parallel to the fibers of the meat; this produces shorter fibers, making the meat more tender.

MEAT SAFETY

When handling any raw meat, keep it separate from other ingredients until ready to combine. If the meat comes in contact with the work surface, the surface should be thoroughly washed, along with your hands, knives, and any other utensils in hot, soapy water.

Do not allow raw meat to stand at room temperature longer than one hour. Some cookbooks suggest letting meat stand out until it reaches room temperature so the meat will roast more evenly. We don't agree.

We use refrigerator-temperature meat for all of our recipes. If you are serving cooked meat as part of a buffet, do not let it stand at room temperature longer than two hours.

BEEF

Beef is still America's favorite meat. Whether you're enjoying a grilled steak, a juicy burger, or a savory stew, beef's deep, hearty flavor is sure to come through.

BUYING BEEF

Choose meat that is bright to deep red; any fat should be creamy white. As with all meat, color is a good indicator of quality. Cut edges should look freshly cut and moist—never wet. Vacuum-packed beef is darker and often looks more purple than red. Last, remember that the names of steaks and roasts often vary from state to state: A "strip steak" in California is known as a "shell steak" in New York.

ROASTING TIMES FOR BEEF

This roasting chart gives guidelines for cooking a variety of cuts from medium-rare to well-done when cooking without a recipe. Start with meat at refrigerator temperature. Remove a roast from the oven when it reaches 5° to 10°F below desired doneness; temperature will continue to rise as it stands.

| **APPROXIMATE COOKING TIME (MINUTES PER POUND)** | | | | | |
CUT	**OVEN TEMPERATURE**	**WEIGHT**	**MEDIUM-RARE (135°-140°F)**	**MEDIUM (145°-155°F)**	**WELL-DONE (OVER 160°F)**
Rib roast	325°F	4 to 6 pounds	24 to 30 minutes	30 to 36 minutes	34 to 38 minutes
(chine bone removed)		6 to 8 pounds	15 to 20 minutes	22 to 26 minutes	27 to 30 minutes
Rib-eye roast	350°F	4 to 6 pounds	15 to 20 minutes	18 to 22 minutes	20 to 24 minutes
Whole tenderloin	450°F	4 to 5 pounds	40 to 60 minutes *(total time)*		
Half tenderloin	450°F	2 to 3 pounds	40 to to 50 minutes *(total time)*		
Round tip roast	325°F	3 to 4 pounds	25 to 30 minutes	30 to 35 minutes	35 to 38 minutes
		6 to 8 pounds	22 to 25 minutes	26 to 32 minutes	30 to 35 minutes
Eye round roast	325°F	2 to 3 pounds	20 to 25 minutes	25 to 30 minutes	30 to 35 minutes

POPULAR BEEF CUTS

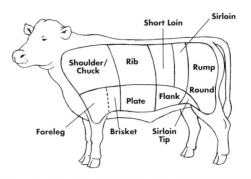

Short Loin · Sirloin · Shoulder/Chuck · Rib · Rump · Round · Plate · Flank · Sirloin Tip · Foreleg · Brisket

Beef rib roast, small end

Also called standing rib roast *(roast)*.

Beef rib-eye roast

Large center muscle of rib with bones and seam fat removed *(roast)*.

Beef bottom round roast

Also called beef bottom round pot roast; suitable for roasting if high quality *(braise, roast)*.

Beef chuck shoulder pot roast, boneless

Also called boneless cross-rib pot roast *(braise)*.

Beef chuck short ribs

Also called flanken short ribs *(braise)*.

Beef top loin steak

Also called shell, strip, New York, club, and Delmonico steak. Also available boneless *(broil, grill, panfry)*.

Beef loin porterhouse steak Includes tenderloin at least 1¼ inches in diameter *(broil, grill, panfry)*.

Beef rib-eye steak

Boneless steak also called fillet or Spencer steak; cut from beef rib-eye roast. Also available bone-in *(broil, panfry)*.

Beef round top round steak

Also known as London broil. Best when marinated *(broil, grill)*.

Beef loin tenderloin roast

Cut from tenderloin muscle; very tender, boneless, with very little (or no) fat covering. Also called beef tenderloin *(roast)*.

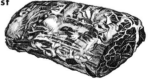

Beef Rib Roast with Creamy Horseradish Sauce

If you like, reserve the fat from the pan drippings to make Yorkshire Pudding (right), then prepare an au jus sauce. Add 2 cups of homemade Brown Beef Stock (page 61) to the pan drippings and bring to a boil, scraping up all the flavorful browned bits.

Prep: 25 minutes   Roast: 3 hours

- 1 (4-rib) beef rib roast from small end (7 pounds), trimmed and chine bone removed
- 3 tablespoons whole tricolor peppercorns (red, green, and black)
- 1 teaspoon salt
  Creamy Horseradish Sauce (below)

1. Preheat oven to 325°F. In medium roasting pan (14" by 10"), place rib roast, fat side up. In mortar, with pestle, crush peppercorns with salt. Use to rub on fat side of roast.

2. Roast beef until meat thermometer inserted in thickest part of meat (not touching bone) reaches 140°F, about 3 hours. Internal temperature of meat will rise to 145°F (medium) upon standing. Or roast until desired doneness.

3. When roast is done, transfer to warm large platter and let stand 15 minutes to set juices for easier carving. Meanwhile, prepare Creamy Horseradish Sauce. Makes 10 main-dish servings.

Each serving without sauce: About 317 calories, 39g protein, 1g carbohydrate, 16g total fat (7g saturated), 113mg cholesterol, 322mg sodium.

Creamy Horseradish Sauce

In small bowl, combine **1 jar (6 ounces) white horseradish,** drained, **½ cup mayonnaise, 1 teaspoon sugar,** and **½ teaspoon salt.** Whip **½ cup heavy or whipping cream;** fold into horseradish mixture. Makes about 1⅔ cups.

Each tablespoon: About 49 calories, 0g protein, 1g carbohydrate, 5g total fat (2 g saturated), 9mg cholesterol, 74mg sodium.

Yorkshire Pudding

Preheat oven to 450°F. In medium bowl, with wire whisk, combine **1½ cups all-purpose flour** and **¾ teaspoon salt.** Add **1½ cups milk** and **3 large eggs,** beaten. Beat until smooth. Pour **3 tablespoons drippings** from roast beef pan into small metal baking pan (13" by 9"); bake 2 minutes. Remove pan from oven and pour batter over drippings. Bake until puffed and lightly browned, about 25 minutes. Cut into squares. Makes 8 accompaniment servings.

Each serving: About 183 calories, 6g protein, 20g carbohydrate, 8g total fat (4g saturated), 90mg cholesterol, 246mg sodium.

CARVING A RIB ROAST

 Test Kitchen Tip The chine bone should be removed by your butcher so you can carve the roast between the rib bones. Carving will be easier and the meat will be juicier if the roast stands at least 15 minutes after you have removed it from the oven.

Place the roast, rib side down, on cutting board. With a carving knife, make a vertical cut toward the ribs, cutting a slice about ¼ inch thick.

Release the slice by cutting horizontally along the top of the rib bone. Transfer the slice to a warm platter.

Repeat to cut more slices. As each rib bone is exposed, cut it away from the roast and add to the platter. This will make it easier to carve the remaining meat.

Beef Eye Round au Jus

Roast some herbed new potatoes at the same time. And for the tenderest results, do not roast this cut to more than medium rare.

Prep: 30 minutes   Roast: 1 hour 10 minutes

- 1 beef eye round roast (4½ pounds), trimmed
- 1½ teaspoons salt
- ½ teaspoon dried thyme
- ¼ teaspoon ground black pepper
- 2 tablespoons olive oil
- 1 bag (16 ounces) carrots, peeled and cut into 2" by ¼" matchstick strips
- 1 pound leeks (3 medium), white and light green parts, cut into 2" by ¼" matchstick strips
- 4 garlic cloves, thinly sliced
- 1¼ cups dry red wine
- ½ cup water
- 1 bay leaf

1. Preheat oven to 450°F. In small bowl, combine salt, thyme, and pepper; use to rub on roast. In 10-inch skillet, heat oil over medium-high heat until very hot. Add beef and cook until browned on all sides, about 10 minutes. Transfer beef to nonreactive medium roasting pan (14" by 10").

2. Add carrots, leeks, and garlic to skillet and cook, stirring occasionally, until carrots are tender, about 7 minutes. Arrange vegetable mixture around beef.

3. Roast beef 25 minutes. Add wine, water, and bay leaf to roasting pan. Turn oven control to 325°F and roast until meat thermometer inserted in center of roast reaches 140°F, about 45 minutes longer. Internal temperature of meat will rise to 145°F (medium) upon standing. Or roast until desired doneness. Remove and discard bay leaf.

4. When roast is done, transfer to warm large platter and let stand 15 minutes to set juices for easier slicing. To serve, cut roast into thin slices and serve with vegetables. Makes 12 main-dish servings.

Each serving: About 232 calories, 33g protein, 6g carbohydrate, 8g total fat (2g saturated), 76mg cholesterol, 358mg sodium.

Stuffed Beef Tenderloin with Mushroom Gravy

This is a real showstopper that's great for entertaining. We gild the lily by dressing up this already exquisite roast with a melt-in-your-mouth stuffing.

Prep: 45 minutes   Roast/Cook: 1 hour

- Spinach-Mushroom Stuffing (opposite)
- 2 teaspoons chopped fresh thyme
- 1 teaspoon salt
- 1 teaspoon coarsely ground black pepper
- 1 whole beef tenderloin, trimmed (4 pounds)
- 2 tablespoons butter or margarine
- ¼ cup plain dried bread crumbs
- 1 can (14½ ounces) chicken broth or 1¾ cups Chicken Broth (page 62)
- 2 tablespoons dry vermouth
- 8 ounces mushrooms, trimmed and sliced
- 2 tablespoons all-purpose flour

1. Prepare Spinach-Mushroom Stuffing; set aside.

2. Preheat oven to 425°F. In small bowl, combine thyme, salt, and pepper; use to rub on tenderloin. Turn thinner end of meat under tenderloin to make meat an even thickness. With sharp knife, cut 1½-inch-deep slit in tenderloin, beginning 2 inches from thicker end of meat and ending 2 inches from opposite end.

3. Spoon Spinach-Mush-room Stuffing into slit in tenderloin. With string, tie tenderloin at 2-inch intervals to help hold its shape. Place stuffed tenderloin on rack in large roasting pan  (17" by 11½"); roast tenderloin 30 minutes.

4. Meanwhile, in 1-quart saucepan, melt 1 tablespoon butter over low heat. Remove saucepan from heat; stir in bread crumbs.

5. Remove tenderloin from oven; sprinkle bread-crumb topping on stuffing. Roast tenderloin until meat thermometer inserted in center of meat reaches 140°F, about 10 minutes longer. Internal temperature of meat will rise to 145°F (medium) upon standing. Or roast until desired doneness. Transfer tenderloin to warm platter and let stand 10 minutes to set juices for easier slicing.

6. Meanwhile, prepare mushroom gravy: Add ½ cup broth and vermouth to drippings in roasting pan; stir over low heat until browned bits are loosened from bottom of pan. Pour drippings mixture into 4-cup measuring cup; let stand until fat separates from meat juice. Skim and discard fat from meat-juice mixture. Add remaining broth and enough water to equal 2½ cups; set aside.

7. In 12-inch skillet, melt remaining 1 tablespoon butter over medium-high heat. Add mushrooms and cook until golden and liquid has evaporated, about 12 minutes. Stir in flour. Gradually stir meat-juice mixture into mushrooms and cook, stirring constantly, until gravy has thickened slightly and boils; boil 1 minute.

8. To serve, remove string and cut tenderloin into slices. Serve with mushroom gravy. Makes 10 main-dish servings.

Each serving with gravy: About 371 calories, 35g protein, 8g carbohydrate, 21g total fat (10g saturated), 114mg cholesterol, 679mg sodium.

Spinach-Mushroom Stuffing

In 12-inch skillet, melt **4 tablespoons butter or margarine** over medium-high heat; add 1 pound mushrooms, coarsely chopped, and cook until golden and liquid has evaporated, 12 to 15 minutes. Stir in **2 tablespoons dry vermouth;** cook 1 minute longer. Remove skillet from heat; stir in **1 package (10 ounces) frozen chopped spinach,** thawed and squeezed dry, **2 tablespoons freshly grated Parmesan cheese, 2 tablespoons plain dried bread crumbs, 1 teaspoon chopped fresh thyme, ¼ teaspoon salt,** and **½ teaspoon coarsely ground black pepper.** Cool.

SAUCES FOR BEEF TENDERLOIN

 Test Kitchen Tip
Béarnaise Sauce (page 433) is perfect with Roasted Beef Tenderloin. Cilantro Sauce (page 434) is a good choice for the Asian-Flavored Tenderloin. For the Southwestern-Flavored variation, try either Cilantro Sauce or Tomato Salsa (page 437) or Orange-Fennel Salsa (page 437).

Roasted Beef Tenderloin

Beef tenderloin can be brushed with a mixture of spices and fresh herbs of your choice. Served hot or at room temperature, it's perfect party fare.

Prep: 5 minutes   Roast: 50 minutes

- **2** tablespoons butter or margarine, melted
- **2** teaspoons Worcestershire sauce
- **1** teaspoon salt
- **1** teaspoon coarsely ground black pepper
- **1** whole beef tenderloin (5 pounds), trimmed and tied

1. Preheat oven to 450°F. In small bowl, combine butter, Worcestershire, salt, and pepper. Brush mixture on tenderloin.

2. Place tenderloin in 15½" by 10½" jelly-roll pan and roast until meat thermometer inserted in center of meat reaches 140°F, about 50 minutes. Internal temperature of meat will rise to 145°F (medium) upon standing. Or roast until desired doneness.

3. Transfer tenderloin to warm platter and let stand 15 minutes to set juices for easier slicing. Makes 12 main-dish servings.

Each serving: About 251 calories, 29g protein, 0g carbohydrate, 14g total fat (6g saturated), 92mg cholesterol, 276mg sodium.

Southwestern-Flavored Tenderloin

In small bowl, combine **1 tablespoon vegetable oil, 1 teaspoon honey, 1 tablespoon chili powder, 2 teaspoons ground cumin, 1 teaspoon salt,** and **¼ teaspoon dried oregano,** crumbled. Brush mixture on tenderloin instead of butter mixture; roast as directed.

Asian-Flavored Tenderloin

In small bowl, combine **2 teaspoons soy sauce, 2 teaspoons Asian sesame oil, 1 teaspoon honey, 1 teaspoon Chinese five-spice powder, ¼ teaspoon ground ginger,** and **⅛ teaspoon ground red pepper (cayenne).** Brush mixture on tenderloin instead of butter mixture; roast as directed.

Ropa Vieja

In Spanish, *ropa vieja* means "old clothes." The stew is simmered a long time so the meat can be shredded into thin strips resembling tattered fabric.

Prep: 45 minutes   Cook: 3 hours 30 minutes

- 1 beef flank steak (1¾ pounds)
- 1 medium onion, coarsely chopped
- 1 carrot, peeled and coarsely chopped
- 1 bay leaf
- 2 teaspoons salt
- 5 cups water
- 4 teaspoons olive oil
- 1 large onion (12 ounces), sliced
- 1 red pepper, cut into ½-inch-wide strips
- 1 yellow pepper, cut into ½-inch-wide strips
- 1 green pepper, cut into ½-inch-wide strips
- 3 garlic cloves, crushed with garlic press
- 3 serrano or jalapeño chiles, seeded and finely chopped
- ¼ teaspoon ground cinnamon
- 1 can (14 to 16 ounces) tomatoes
- capers

1. Cut flank steak crosswise into thirds. In nonreactive 5-quart Dutch oven, combine flank steak, chopped onion, carrot, bay leaf, 1 teaspoon salt, and water; heat to boiling over high heat. Reduce heat; cover and simmer until meat is very tender, 2 hours 30 minutes to 3 hours. Remove Dutch oven from heat. Remove cover and let flank steak stand 30 minutes.

2. In 12-inch skillet, heat oil over medium-high heat. Add sliced onion, red, yellow, and green peppers, and remaining 1 teaspoon salt; cook, stirring often, until vegetables are tender, about 15 minutes. Stir in garlic, serrano chiles, and cinnamon; cook 30 seconds. Stir in tomatoes with their juice, breaking them up with side of spoon, and cook 5 minutes.

3. With slotted spoon, transfer beef to large bowl; strain broth. Set aside 2 cups broth (reserve remaining broth for another use). Using two forks, shred beef into fine strips.

4. Stir 2 cups broth and shredded meat into pepper mixture and simmer, stirring occasionally, 10 minutes. Sprinkle with capers to serve. Makes 6 main-dish servings.

Each serving: About 246 calories, 25g protein, 10g carbohydrate, 12g total fat (4g saturated), 57mg cholesterol, 779mg sodium.

Brisket with Mushrooms

Humble beef brisket becomes a company dish when combined with a heady combination of fresh and dried mushrooms and served with a rich red wine sauce. To prepare at Passover, use matzoh meal instead of flour.

Prep: 1 hour 30 minutes   Bake: 2 hours 30 minutes

- ¾ cup boiling water
- ½ ounce dried porcini mushrooms (½ cup)
- 8 ounces small shiitake mushrooms, stems removed
- 8 ounces white mushrooms, trimmed
- ¼ cup vegetable oil
- 1 fresh beef brisket (4 pounds), well trimmed
- 4 medium red onions, sliced
- 2 garlic cloves, sliced
- 3 tablespoons all-purpose flour
- 1 can (14½ ounces) beef broth or 1¾ cups Brown Beef Stock (page 61)
- 1 cup dry red wine
- ¼ cup brandy
- 4 large fresh sage leaves
- 1 bay leaf
- 1½ teaspoons fresh thyme
- ½ teaspoon salt
- ¼ teaspoon coarsely ground black pepper
- ¼ cup chopped fresh parsley

1. In small bowl, pour boiling water over porcini mushrooms; let stand 30 minutes.

2. With slotted spoon, remove porcini, reserving mushroom liquid. Rinse mushrooms to remove any grit, then chop. Strain liquid through sieve lined with paper towels; set aside.

3. Preheat oven to 325°F. In 8-quart Dutch oven, heat oil over medium-high heat until very hot. Add brisket and cook until browned, about 10 minutes. Transfer brisket to platter; set aside. Add onions to Dutch oven and cook over medium heat, stirring occasionally, until lightly browned, about 15 minutes. Stir in garlic and cook 30 seconds. Stir in flour and cook, stirring until golden brown, about 2 minutes.

4. Return brisket to Dutch oven. Stir in porcini mushrooms, mushroom liquid, shiitake and white mushrooms, broth, wine, brandy, sage leaves, bay leaf, thyme, salt, pepper, and 2 tablespoons parsley. Heat to boiling over high heat. Cover and place in oven. Bake until brisket is tender, about 2 hours 30 minutes.

5. Transfer meat from Dutch oven to warm platter; let stand 15 minutes. Skim and discard fat from liquid in Dutch oven. Discard sage leaves and bay leaf. Heat liquid in pot to boiling over high heat. Reduce heat to medium; cook, uncovered, until thickened, about 15 minutes.

6. Slice brisket thinly across the grain. Stir remaining 2 tablespoons parsley into brisket liquid. Spoon some over meat; pass remaining liquid separately. Makes 10 main-dish servings.

Each serving: About 333 calories, 34g protein, 12g carbohydrate, 16g total fat (4g saturated), 90mg cholesterol, 447mg sodium.

COOKING BEEF

Test Kitchen Tip To cook up a tender piece of beef, it's best to match the cut of meat to the right cooking technique.

Broiling, Grilling, and Panfrying Choose porterhouse steak, T-bone steak, London broil (top round), top loin, rib-eye, sirloin steak, tenderloin, flank steak, skirt steak, cube steak, minute steak, and ground beef.

Braising and Stewing Choose chuck roast, brisket, short ribs, shin (shank cross cuts), and oxtails. Cubes for stew are usually cut from boneless chuck or bottom round, but chuck gives the moistest results. Bone-in cuts add flavor and body to stews.

Roasting Choose standing rib roast, tenderloin, rib-eye, eye round, and tri-tip.

Country Pot Roast

This is blue-ribbon country cooking. To give the home-style sauce a bit more body and flavor, we puree half of the vegetables.

Prep: 25 minutes   Bake: 3 hours

- 1 tablespoon vegetable oil
- 1 boneless beef chuck cross-rib pot roast or boneless chuck eye roast (4 pounds), trimmed
- 1 large onion (12 ounces), coarsely chopped
- 1 carrot, peeled and coarsely chopped
- 1 stalk celery, coarsely chopped
- 2 garlic cloves, finely chopped
- 1 can (15 ounces) crushed tomatoes
- ½ cup chicken broth
- 1 teaspoon salt
- ½ teaspoon dried thyme, crumbled
- ¼ teaspoon ground black pepper
- 1 bay leaf

1. Preheat oven to 350°F. In nonreactive 5-quart Dutch oven, heat oil over high heat until very hot. Add roast and cook until browned. Transfer roast to plate.

2. Add onion, carrot, and celery to Dutch oven and cook over medium-high heat until lightly browned. Add garlic; cook, stirring constantly, until fragrant, about 20 seconds.

3. Return roast to Dutch oven; add tomatoes, broth, salt, thyme, pepper, and bay leaf; heat to boiling. Cover and place in oven. Bake, turning roast once, until roast is tender, about 3 hours.

4. When roast is done, transfer to large platter and keep warm. Discard bay leaf. Skim and discard fat from liquid in Dutch oven. Transfer half of vegetables and liquid to blender; cover, with center part of cover removed to let steam escape, and puree until smooth. Pour pureed mixture into Dutch oven and stir until combined; heat to boiling. Cut meat into thin slices and serve with vegetables and sauce. Makes 8 main-dish servings.

Each serving: About 304 calories, 35g protein, 6g carbohydrate, 15g total fat (5g saturated), 114mg cholesterol, 573mg sodium.

Grillades

This New Orleans–style smothered steak is often served with grits for breakfast. We like it for lunch and dinner, too.

Prep: 15 minutes   Cook: 1 hour

- 4 beef minute steaks (6 ounces each)
- ½ teaspoon salt
- ¼ teaspoon ground black pepper
- 3 teaspoons vegetable oil
- 1 medium onion, chopped
- 1 green pepper, chopped
- 1 stalk celery, chopped
- 2 garlic cloves, finely chopped
- 1 can (14 to 16 ounces) tomatoes in puree
- 1 cup beef broth
- 1 teaspoon Worcestershire sauce
- 2 bay leaves
- 1 tablespoon red wine vinegar

1. Sprinkle beef with salt and black pepper. In non-stick 12-inch skillet, heat 1 teaspoon oil over medium-high heat until very hot. Add steaks and cook until browned, about 2 minutes per side, transferring steaks to plate as they are browned.

2. Add remaining 2 teaspoons oil to skillet; reduce heat to medium. Add onion and cook, stirring, 5 minutes. Add green pepper, celery, and garlic; cook, stirring, 3 minutes longer. Add tomatoes with their puree, breaking them up with side of spoon. Stir in broth, Worcestershire, and bay leaves. Increase heat to high; heat to boiling.

3. Return steaks to skillet and reduce heat. Cover and simmer 40 minutes. Transfer steaks to platter; keep warm. Increase heat to high; stir in vinegar and heat to boiling. Boil until sauce has thickened, about 5 minutes. Discard bay leaves. To serve, spoon sauce over steaks. Makes 4 main-dish servings.

Each serving: About 437 calories, 37g protein, 13g carbohydrate, 26g total fat (9g saturated), 107mg cholesterol, 772mg sodium.

New England Boiled Dinner

(Pictured on page 78)

Gently simmering the meat for hours creates its melt-in-your-mouth quality. If you like, substitute turnips or parsnips for the rutabaga, or add a few additional potatoes so you can make Corned Beef Hash (right) with the tasty leftovers.

Prep: 15 minutes   Cook: 3 hours 30 minutes

- 1 corned beef brisket (4 to 4½ pounds)
- 1 medium onion studded with 4 whole cloves
- 8 cups water
- 8 medium all-purpose potatoes (2½ pounds), peeled and each cut in half
- 8 carrots, peeled and each cut in half
- 1 small rutabaga (2 pounds), peeled and cut in half, each half cut into 8 wedges
- 1 small green cabbage (2 pounds), cut into 8 wedges
- 2 tablespoons chopped fresh parsley
  Dijon mustard
  bottled white horseradish

1. In 8-quart Dutch oven, place brisket, clove-studded onion, and water and heat to boiling over high heat. With slotted spoon, skim and discard foam from surface. Reduce heat; cover and simmer until brisket is tender, 2 hours 30 minutes to 3 hours.

2. Add potatoes, carrots, and rutabaga to Dutch oven; heat to boiling over high heat. Reduce heat; cover and simmer until vegetables are tender, about 30 minutes.

3. With slotted spoon, transfer brisket and vegetables to deep large platter; keep warm.

4. Heat liquid remaining in Dutch oven to boiling over high heat. Add cabbage; heat to boiling. Cover and boil until cabbage is tender, about 5 minutes.

5. Slice brisket very thinly across the grain. Transfer sliced meat to platter with vegetables. Place cabbage wedges on platter, sprinkle parsley on vegetables, and serve mustard and horseradish alongside. Makes 8 main-dish servings.

Each serving: About 587 calories, 35g protein, 43g carbohydrate, 31g total fat (10g saturated), 157mg cholesterol, 1,887mg sodium.

Corned Beef Hash

A breakfast tradition, especially with a freshly poached egg on top. By adding chopped cooked beets to the mixture, you get Red Flannel Hash, a Yankee classic. Purchase cooked corned beef or use leftovers from New England Boiled Dinner (left).

Prep: 15 minutes   Cook: 25 minutes

- 3 tablespoons butter or margarine
- 1 large onion (12 ounces), chopped
- 2 cups chopped lean cooked corned beef
- 2 cups chopped cooked all-purpose potatoes
- ¼ teaspoon coarsely ground pepper
- 1 tablespoon chopped fresh parsley

1. In 10-inch skillet, melt butter over medium heat. Add onion and cook, stirring often, until tender, about 5 minutes.

2. Stir in corned beef, potatoes, and pepper until well combined. Cook, pressing hash down firmly with spatula, until bottom of hash has browned, about 15 minutes.

3. With spatula, turn hash over one small section at a time. Press down with spatula and cook until second side has browned, 5 to 10 minutes longer. Sprinkle with parsley. Makes 4 main-dish servings.

Each serving: About 337 calories, 23g protein, 21g carbohydrate, 18g total fat (9g saturated), 89mg cholesterol, 947mg sodium.

Red Flannel Hash

Prepare as directed, adding **1 cup finely chopped cooked beets** with corned beef, potatoes, and pepper.

Filet Mignon with Mustard-Caper Sauce

A well-browned exterior is the key to maximum flavor with sautéed beef. Be sure to cook it over high heat.

Prep: 5 minutes   Cook: 20 minutes

- 4 beef tenderloin steaks (filet mignon), 1½ inches thick (6 ounces each)
- ½ teaspoon salt
- ¼ teaspoon coarsely ground black pepper
- 1 tablespoon olive oil
- 3 tablespoons finely chopped shallots
- ⅓ cup dry white wine
- ⅓ cup beef broth
- ⅓ cup heavy or whipping cream
- 3 tablespoons capers, drained
- 1 tablespoon Dijon mustard
- ¼ cup chopped watercress leaves plus additional leaves

1. Sprinkle steaks with salt and pepper. In nonstick 12-inch skillet, heat oil over high heat until very hot. Add steaks and cook, without turning, until browned, about 7 minutes. Turn steaks and cook 7 minutes longer for medium-rare or until desired doneness. Transfer to plates; keep warm.

2. Add shallots to drippings in skillet; cook 30 seconds. Stir in wine; cook, stirring, until browned bits are loosened from bottom of skillet. Stir in broth and boil 1 minute. Stir in cream; boil 1 minute longer. Stir in capers, mustard, and chopped watercress.

3. To serve, spoon sauce over meat and garnish with watercress. Makes 4 main-dish servings.

Each serving: About 334 calories, 27g protein, 3g carbohydrate, 22g total fat (9g saturated), 105mg cholesterol, 799mg sodium.

Steak au Poivre

Prepare as directed but in Step 1 use **2 tablespoons crushed black peppercorns.** In Step 2 omit shallots, broth, capers, and mustard; stir in wine and **2 tablespoons brandy,** stirring until browned bits are loosened. Stir in cream and boil until thickened. Replace watercress with **1 tablespoon chopped fresh parsley.**

Flank Steak with Red Onion Marmalade

This juicy panfried steak, topped with a sweet and tangy red onion mixture, is an easy weeknight dish to put-together.

Prep: 10 minutes   Cook: 35 minutes

- 3 tablespoons butter or margarine
- 2 medium red onions (1 pound), thinly sliced
- 3 tablespoons distilled white vinegar
- 3 tablespoons sugar
- 1 teaspoon salt
- 1 beef flank steak (1½ pounds)
- ¼ teaspoon coarsely ground pepper

1. In nonstick 12-inch skillet, melt 2 tablespoons butter over medium heat. Add onions and cook, stirring occasionally, until tender, about 15 minutes. Stir in vinegar, sugar, and ½ teaspoon salt. Reduce heat and simmer 5 minutes. Spoon red onion marmalade into small bowl; keep warm.

2. Wash skillet and wipe dry. Sprinkle steak with pepper and remaining ½ teaspoon salt. In skillet, melt remaining 1 tablespoon butter over medium-high heat. Add steak and cook 6 to 8 minutes per side for medium-rare or until desired doneness.

3. Slice steak and serve with red onion marmalade. Makes 6 main-dish servings.

Each serving: About 281 calories, 24g protein, 14g carbohydrate, 14g total fat (7g saturated), 72mg cholesterol, 150mg sodium.

Steak with Red Wine Sauce

Try this simple sauce with any panfried beef, from burgers to filet mignon. It is thickened with a little butter at the end, a French cooking technique that rounds out the wine and enriches the sauce. (Do not use margarine; it will not thicken the sauce.)

Prep: 5 minutes   Cook: 20 minutes

- 2 teaspoons vegetable oil
- 4 boneless beef strip (shell) steaks, 1 inch thick (8 ounces each)
- ½ teaspoon salt
- ¼ teaspoon ground black pepper
- ¼ cup finely chopped shallots
- 1 cup dry red wine
    pinch dried thyme, crumbled
- 2 tablespoons butter, cut into pieces
- 2 teaspoons chopped fresh tarragon or flat-leaf parsley

1. In nonstick 12-inch skillet, heat oil over medium-high heat until very hot. Sprinkle steaks with salt and pepper. Cook 5 to 6 minutes per side for medium-rare or until desired doneness. Transfer steaks to warm platter.

2. Discard drippings from skillet. Add shallots to pan and cook, stirring, until tender, about 1 minute. Add wine and thyme; heat to boiling over high heat. Boil until sauce has reduced to ⅓ cup, about 5 minutes. Remove pan from heat; stir in butter, stirring just until incorporated.

3. Cut steaks into thin slices. Transfer to warm platter; pour sauce on top and sprinkle with tarragon. Makes 4 main-dish servings.

Each serving: About 436 calories, 49g protein, 3g carbohydrate, 24g total fat (10g saturated), 145mg cholesterol, 179mg sodium.

STEAK SUCCESS

 Test Kitchen Tip The easiest way to check the doneness of steak is to cut into its center. You can also use the "touch test." The longer a steak cooks, the firmer the meat becomes as its juices evaporate. Press the steak in the center. If the steak is somewhat soft, it is medium-rare. If it bounces back slightly, the steak is medium. If firm, the steak is well-done.

Tuscan Pan-Seared Strip Steak

Tuscan cooks know that all it takes to bring out the flavor of a rich cut of beef is a squeeze of fresh lemon juice.

Prep: 5 minutes Cook: 12 minutes

- 4 boneless beef strip (shell) steaks, 1 inch thick (8 ounces each)
- 2 teaspoons olive oil
- 1 tablespoon chopped fresh rosemary or 1 teaspoon dried rosemary, crumbled
- 1 teaspoon salt
- 1 teaspoon coarsely ground black pepper
- 4 lemon wedges

1. Heat 12-inch skillet over high heat until very hot. Brush steaks with olive oil. In small bowl, combine rosemary, salt, and pepper. Use to rub on steaks.

2. Place steaks in skillet; reduce heat to medium-high. Cook steaks 7 minutes; turn and cook 5 minutes longer for medium-rare or 7 minutes longer for medium. Serve with lemon wedges. Makes 4 main-dish servings.

Each serving: About 375 calories, 49g protein, 1g carbohydrate, 18g total fat (6g saturated), 129mg cholesterol, 699mg sodium.

OTHER MEAT CHOICES

Beyond USDA inspections and voluntary grading, a consumer has other choices when buying meat.

Kosher meat is processed according to Jewish dietary laws. Only certain cuts of meat from certain animals can be consumed, and the meat must be eaten within 72 hours of slaughter. Because it is not aged, it is not very tender or very flavorful.

Halal butchers in Muslim communities butcher beef, goat, and lamb according to Islamic law. Halal meat is never more than two days old and is never frozen.

Natural and Organic Natural meat has been processed without artificial color, flavor, or preservatives. Some states, have laws that define organic meat as meat from animals raised without antibiotics, pesticides, or steroids and in a way that will minimally affect the environment.

Fajitas

Fajitas are ideal party fare. Serve with your favorite salsa, homemade if time permits (pages 436–437).

Prep: 15 minutes plus marinating
Cook/Broil: 20 minutes

- 3 tablespoons fresh lime juice
- 3 tablespoons fresh orange juice
- ¾ teaspoon salt
- ½ teaspoon dried oregano, crumbled
- 1 beef skirt steak (1¾ pounds)
- 1 tablespoon olive oil
- 2 medium onions, thinly sliced
- 2 garlic cloves, thinly sliced
- 3 large red peppers, cut into ½-inch-thick strips
- 1 large green pepper, cut into ½-inch-thick strips
- 2 teaspoons finely chopped pickled jalapeño chile
- 12 (6-inch) flour tortillas

1. In cup, combine lime and orange juices, ½ teaspoon salt, and oregano. Transfer to ziptight plastic bag; add meat, turning to coat. Seal bag, pressing out as much air as possible. Refrigerate beef 1 hour to marinate, turning bag once.

2. Preheat broiler. Meanwhile, in 12-inch skillet, heat oil over medium heat. Add onions and garlic and cook, stirring frequently, until onions are tender, about 5 minutes. Add red and green peppers, jalapeño, and remaining ¼ teaspoon salt; cook, stirring frequently, until red and green peppers are tender, about 7 minutes.

3. Remove meat from marinade and place on rack in broiling pan. Broil steak 6 inches from heat source 3 to 4 minutes per side for medium-rare or until desired doneness. Cut meat into thin slices across the grain and serve with tortillas and pepper mixture. Makes 6 main-dish servings.

Each serving: About 418 calories, 30g protein, 34g carbohydrate, 17g total fat (6g saturated), 66mg cholesterol, 531mg sodium.

GROUND BEEF

Some of America's favorite dishes start with ground beef: meat loaf, meatballs, burgers, chili, and casseroles, and that's just the beginning. Its popularity is well-deserved: It delivers big-time flavor at relatively low cost.

Buying and Storing

The label on ground beef often denotes the percentage of lean meat to fat, but sometimes the cut of meat is also listed. You can buy ground chuck, which is about 80 percent lean; ground sirloin, which is 90 to 95 percent extra-lean; and ground round, which at 85 percent lean is juicy, flavorful, and the most popular cut. If meat is labeled "ground beef," it comes from a combination of cuts and is only 70 percent lean. Keep in mind that the amount of fat in ground beef affects the moistness and texture of the cooked dish, so you will get different results when using ground chuck, ground round, or ground sirloin.

Ground beef should be cherry red. Don't worry if the meat in the center looks darker than the meat on the exterior. The darker color comes from a lack of oxygen. When exposed to the air, this darker meat will become redder.

E. coli, a strain of potentially deadly bacteria, has been found in mass-produced meat patties. To guard against this bacteria, always purchase ground beef from a reliable source and shape your own burgers.

Cooking Ground Beef Safely

Disease-causing bacteria like *E. coli* contaminate only the surface of food, so the inside of a roast or steak is not affected. The bacteria are killed when the outside of the food is exposed to high temperatures, when grilling and roasting, for example. When beef is ground, any outer surface contamination gets mixed throughout the meat. The bacteria on the surface of a grilled burger may be killed, but unless the interior of the meat is cooked to 160°F, dangerous bacteria can still be present. To eliminate this danger, always cook ground beef until well-done. When pressed in the center, a burger or patty should feel firm and spring back.

Danish Meatballs

These tender meatballs have a creamy sauce just made for spooning over noodles or rice. If you wish, serve the meatballs as they do in Denmark, with a dollop of lingonberry preserves.

Prep: 25 minutes   Cook: 15 minutes

1½	pounds ground beef chuck or ground meat for meat loaf (beef, pork, and veal)
½	cup plain dried bread crumbs
1	large egg
¼	cup chopped fresh flat-leaf parsley
2	tablespoons chopped fresh dill
1	tablespoon grated onion
1	teaspoon salt
¼	teaspoon ground black pepper
⅛	teaspoon ground nutmeg
2	tablespoons butter or margarine
2	tablespoons all-purpose flour
1½	cups milk
1	cup low-sodium chicken broth
	lingonberry preserves (optional)

1. In large bowl, combine ground beef, bread crumbs, egg, parsley, dill, onion, salt, pepper, and nutmeg just until well blended but not overmixed. Shape mixture into 24 meatballs, handling meat as little as possible.

2. In 12-inch skillet, melt butter over medium-high heat. Add meatballs and cook until browned, using slotted spoon to transfer meatballs to clean large bowl as they are browned. Discard all but 2 tablespoons drippings from skillet.

3. Stir flour into drippings in skillet; cook over medium heat, stirring, 1 minute. Gradually add milk and broth; cook, stirring constantly, until mixture has thickened and boils.

4. Add meatballs to skillet; heat to boiling. Reduce heat; cover and simmer 10 minutes. Serve with lingonberry preserves, if desired. Makes 6 main-dish servings.

Each serving: About 330 calories, 28g protein, 12g carbohydrate, 19g total fat (9g saturated), 125mg cholesterol, 991mg sodium.

Mexican Meatballs

If chipotle chiles are hard to find, substitute 1 seeded and minced jalapeño chile and ¼ teaspoon liquid smoke.

Prep: 30 minutes   Cook: 45 minutes

- 1½ pounds ground beef chuck
- ¾ cup plain dried bread crumbs
- 1 large egg
- 3 garlic cloves, finely chopped
- 1 teaspoon salt
- ½ teaspoon ground black pepper
- ¼ cup water
- 1 can (28 ounces) tomatoes
- 1 chipotle chile in adobo (page 25)
- 2 teaspoons vegetable oil
- 1 small onion, finely chopped
- 1 teaspoon ground cumin
- 1 cup chicken broth
- ¼ cup chopped fresh cilantro

1. In large bowl, combine ground beef, bread crumbs, egg, one-third of garlic, salt, pepper, and water just until well blended but not overmixed. Shape mixture into 1-inch meatballs, handling meat as little as possible.

2. In blender, puree tomatoes with their juice and chipotle chile until smooth.

3. In nonreactive 5-quart Dutch oven, heat oil over medium heat. Add onion and cook, stirring often, until tender, about 5 minutes. Stir in cumin and remaining garlic; cook 30 seconds. Stir in tomato mixture and broth; heat to boiling over high heat.

4. Add meatballs; heat to boiling. Reduce heat and simmer 30 minutes. To serve, sprinkle with cilantro. Makes 6 main-dish servings.

Each serving: About 318 calories, 28g protein, 18g carbohydrate, 15g total fat (5g saturated), 106mg cholesterol, 1,001mg sodium.

Greek Meatballs

These baked meatballs are prepared with a combination of beef and lamb, a touch of mint, and some feta cheese. Offer some Tzatziki (page 31) alongside, if you like.

Prep: 20 minutes   Bake: 20 minutes

- 1 pound ground beef chuck
- 1 pound lean ground lamb
- 1 cup fresh bread crumbs (about 2 slices bread)
- 2 large eggs
- 4 ounces feta cheese, finely crumbled (1 cup)
- 3 bunches green onions, finely chopped (1 cup)
- ¼ cup chopped fresh flat-leaf parsley
- 2 garlic cloves, finely chopped
- 1 tablespoon dried mint, crumbled
- 2 tablespoons olive oil
- 1 tablespoon red wine vinegar
- ½ teaspoon salt
- ¼ teaspoon ground black pepper

1. Preheat oven to 425°F. In large bowl, combine ground beef, ground lamb, bread crumbs, eggs, feta, green onions, parsley, garlic, mint, oil, vinegar, salt, and pepper just until well blended but not overmixed.

2. Shape mixture into scant ¼-cup meatballs, handling meat as little as possible. Place 1 inch apart in two jelly-roll pans. Bake until cooked through, 20 to 25 minutes. Makes 8 main-dish servings.

Each serving: About 365 calories, 26g protein, 5g carbohydrate, 27g total fat (11g saturated), 143mg cholesterol, 425mg sodium.

Tamale Pie

This tamale pie has a velvety soft cornmeal top and bottom crust. If you prefer firm slices, be sure to let it rest for at least 25 minutes before serving.

Prep: 25 minutes   Bake: 45 minutes

- 2 teaspoons vegetable oil
- 1 medium onion, chopped
- 1 pound ground beef chuck
- 1 tablespoon chili powder
- 1 teaspoon ground cumin
- 1 cup medium-hot salsa
- 1 can (15¼ to 16 ounces) whole-kernel corn, drained
- 4 cups water
- 1 cup cornmeal
- 1 teaspoon salt
- 2 ounces Cheddar cheese, shredded (½ cup)

1. Preheat oven to 350°F. In nonstick 12-inch skillet, heat oil over medium-high heat; add onion and cook until tender and golden, about 5 minutes. Stir in ground beef and cook, breaking up meat with side of spoon, until meat is browned, about 5 minutes. Skim and discard any fat. Stir in chili powder and cumin and cook 2 minutes longer. Remove from heat and stir in salsa and corn.

2. In 2-quart saucepan, heat water to boiling. With wire whisk, gradually whisk in cornmeal and salt. Cook over medium heat, whisking frequently, 5 minutes.

3. Pour half of cornmeal mixture into shallow 2-quart casserole. Spoon beef mixture over cornmeal; spoon remaining cornmeal over beef and sprinkle Cheddar on top. Bake 45 minutes. Remove casserole from oven and let stand 15 to 25 minutes before serving. Makes 6 main-dish servings.

Each serving: About 334 calories, 21g protein, 33g carbohydrate, 13g total fat (5g saturated), 57mg cholesterol, 1,026mg sodium.

"Susan's" Meat Loaf

This delicious basic meat loaf is from the "Susan, Our Teenage Cook" series, which ran in *Good Housekeeping* for decades. Ground chuck makes it tender and tasty.

Prep: 15 minutes   Bake: 1 hour

- 2 pounds ground beef chuck
- 2 large eggs
- 2 cups fresh bread crumbs (about 4 slices bread)
- 2 green onions, finely chopped
- 1 medium onion, finely chopped
- ¾ cup ketchup
- ¼ cup milk
- 2 tablespoons bottled white horseradish
- 1½ teaspoons salt
- 1 teaspoon dry mustard

1. Preheat oven to 400°F. In large bowl, combine ground beef, eggs, bread crumbs, green onions, onion, ¼ cup ketchup, milk, horseradish, salt, and dry mustard just until well blended but not overmixed.

2. Spoon mixture into 9" by 5" metal loaf pan, pressing firmly. Spread remaining ½ cup ketchup on top of loaf. Bake 1 hour. Let stand 10 minutes to set juices for easier slicing. Makes 8 main-dish servings.

Each serving: About 283 calories, 27g protein, 15g carbohydrate, 13g total fat (5g saturated), 125mg cholesterol, 845mg sodium.

MEAT LOAF DONE JUST RIGHT

Test Kitchen Tip

It's important to cook a meatloaf just until cooked through so that it remains moist and tasty. In our recipes we give the exact time needed to cook up a flavorful loaf. But you can also use an instant-read thermometer, which is the most fail-safe way to determine doneness for ground meat in loaves and in patties. Insert the thermometer into the thickest portion of the loaf or in the middle, inserting it halfway in. For patties, insert it horizontally until it reaches the center. The thermometer should read 160°F. Be sure to wash the thermometer before you reinsert it if needed.

Cajun Meat Loaf

Cajun Meat Loaf

This spicy meat loaf is for those who like a bit of kick in their comfort food.

Prep: 20 minutes   Bake: 1 hour 15 minutes

- 2 **tablespoons butter or margarine**
- 2 **carrots, peeled and finely chopped**
- 1 **large onion (12 ounces), chopped**
- 1 **large stalk celery, chopped**
- 1 **small green pepper, finely chopped**
- 2 **garlic cloves, crushed with garlic press**
- 2 **pounds ground meat for meat loaf (beef, pork, and veal)**
- 2 **large eggs**
- 1 **cup fresh bread crumbs (about 2 slices bread)**
- ½ **cup plus 2 tablespoons ketchup**
- ¼ **cup milk**
- 1 **tablespoon Worcestershire sauce**
- 2 **teaspoons salt**
- 1 **teaspoon ground cumin**
- ½ **teaspoon dried thyme**
- ½ **teaspoon ground nutmeg**
- ½ **teaspoon ground red pepper (cayenne)**
- ½ **teaspoon coarsely ground black pepper**

1. In nonstick 12-inch skillet, melt butter over medium heat. Add carrots, onion, celery, and green pepper and cook, stirring occasionally, until vegetables are tender, about 15 minutes. Add garlic and cook 1 minute longer. Set aside to cool slightly.

2. Preheat oven to 375°F. In large bowl, combine ground meat, eggs, bread crumbs, ½ cup ketchup, milk, Worcestershire, salt, cumin, thyme, nutmeg, ground red pepper, black pepper, and cooked vegetable mixture just until well blended but not overmixed.

3. In 13" by 9" baking pan, shape meat mixture into 10" by 5" loaf, pressing firmly. Brush remaining 2 tablespoons ketchup on top of loaf. Bake 1 hour 15 minutes. Let stand 10 minutes to set juices for easier slicing. Makes 8 main-dish servings.

Each serving: About 364 calories, 24g protein, 14g carbohydrate, 23g total fat (10g saturated), 149mg cholesterol, 961mg sodium.

VEAL

Veal has always been regarded as one of the finest meats, and it is associated with some very elegant dishes. This lean, delicate meat resembles poultry more than beef, and it has a versatility that lends itself to a variety of seasonings and cooking techniques. But remember, veal requires a bit of extra attention to keep it from becoming overcooked and dried out.

Buying Veal

Veal calves are raised for eight to sixteen weeks. In order to maintain the meat's delicate texture, the calves are never subjected to excessive movement. The finest and most expensive veal is *milk-fed*, either their mother's milk or a special milk formula. Milk-fed veal is rarely labeled as such but can be recognized by its pale pink, almost white color.

Grain-fed veal comes from older calves that were raised on grain or grass. It has a deep rosy pink color and a slightly stronger flavor than milk-fed veal. This veal is sometimes labeled "calf" but more often it is just labeled "veal."

When buying veal at the supermarket, let your eye be your guide. Look for meat that is fine-textured and pale. While marbling in beef is desirable, veal should have very little marbling, and what fat there is should be firm and very white. The bones of milk-fed veal have reddish marrow. Prime veal is usually milk-fed, whereas grain-fed veal is usually graded choice. Veal marketed under brand names is rarely graded.

Veal cutlets are readily available but vary in quality. The cutlets are ideally cut from a single muscle, usually the top or bottom round. If they are cut from two or three muscles, they will curl when cooked.

Storing Veal

Because veal is a moist meat, it is fairly perishable. Large cuts and stew meat will only keep for two days, tightly wrapped, in the refrigerator. Be sure to cook veal cutlets the day of purchase.

Cooking Veal

Broiling, Grilling and Panfrying For broiling or grilling, choose thick chops and steaks so they won't dry out. Veal cutlets, which are thin, are usually panfried.

ROASTING TIMES FOR VEAL
(OVEN TEMPERATURE OF 325°F)

Start with meat at refrigerator temperature. Remove roast from oven when it reaches 5°F below desired doneness; temperature will continue to rise as roast stands.

CUT	MEAT THERMOMETER READING	APPROXIMATE COOKING TIME (MINUTES PER POUND)
Boneless shoulder roast	160°F	35 to 40 minutes
Leg rump or round roast (boneless)	160°F	35 to 40 minutes
Boneless leg roast	160°F	25 to 30 minutes
Rib roast	160°F	30 to 35 minutes

Best Bets: Shoulder or blade steaks, loin or rib chops, ground veal, and cutlets.

Braising and Stewing Bone-in pieces are especially suited to braising and stewing. Veal stew meat, cut from the neck or shoulder, is readily available and delicious.

Best Bets: Shanks, shank cross cuts (osso buco), arm (shoulder) or blade steak, breast, and shoulder.

Roasting Veal roasts are generally very lean, so you'll get juicier results by cooking them to only 155°F, since the temperature will rise as it stands. Veal breast and shoulder roasts should be cooked until well done and tender.

Best Bets: Rib roast, loin roast, round, shoulder roast, and breast.

POPULAR VEAL CUTS

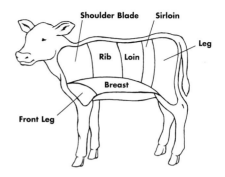

Shoulder Blade · Sirloin · Leg · Loin · Rib · Breast · Front Leg

Veal shoulder roast, boneless

Shoulder cut with bones removed; rolled and tied to keep its shape *(braise, roast)*.

Veal breast

Also called breast of veal. Contains lower ribs, lean meat, and layers of fat, making it juicy and flavorful *(braise, roast)*.

Veal breast riblets

Also called veal riblets; long, narrow cuts containing rib bones with thin fat covering *(braise)*.

Veal shoulder blade steak

Also called veal shoulder steak or veal shoulder chop *(braise, panfry)*.

Veal rib chops

Contain big rib-eye muscle. Expensive and tasty *(braise, panfry, grill, broil)*.

Veal loin chops

Muscles include top loin and tenderloin *(braise, panfry, grill, broil)*.

Veal top loin chops

Same as veal loin chops except do not contain tenderloin *(braise, panfry, grill, broil)*.

Veal cutlets

Very lean, thin, boneless slices from leg that are pounded thinly. Also called scallopini *(braise, panfry)*.

Veal shank cross cuts

Cut crosswise from hindshank, usually 1 to $2\frac{1}{2}$ inches thick. Also called osso buco *(braise)*.

Fruit-Stuffed Veal Roast

Fruit is frequently included in pork stuffings, but many fruits also complement the mild flavor of veal. If you like, use one type of dried fruit, such as apples, pears, or prunes.

Prep: 35 minutes   Roast: 1 hour 20 minutes

- 2 slices firm white bread, cut into ½-inch cubes
- 4 teaspoons olive oil
- 2 shallots, finely chopped
- 1 garlic clove, finely chopped
- ½ cup mixed dried fruit, coarsely chopped
- 2 teaspoons Dijon mustard
- ¾ teaspoon salt
- ½ teaspoon dried rosemary, crumbled
- 1 boneless veal shoulder roast (2½ pounds)
- ½ cup chicken broth
- 1 Golden Delicious apple, peeled, cored, and chopped
- ¼ cup applejack brandy or Calvados
- ½ cup heavy or whipping cream

1. Preheat oven to 375°F. Place bread cubes on cookie sheet and bake until lightly browned, about 5 minutes. Transfer to medium bowl. Turn oven control to 425°F.

2. In 1-quart saucepan, heat 2 teaspoons oil over medium heat. Add half of shallots and garlic and cook, stirring, until shallot is tender, about 4 minutes; add to bowl with croutons. Add dried fruit, mustard, ¼ teaspoon salt, and ¼ teaspoon rosemary; toss to combine.

3. Using sharp knife, cut roast lengthwise three-quarters of the way through, being careful not to cut all the way through. Open and spread flat like a book. Spoon fruit mixture on roast, leaving 1-inch border all around. Roll up roast from one long side to enclose filling; tie with string at 1-inch intervals to secure. Rub ¼ teaspoon of salt and remaining ¼ teaspoon rosemary on veal.

4. Place roast in small roasting pan (13" by 9") and roast until lightly browned, about 30 minutes. Turn oven control to 375°F and roast until meat thermometer inserted in center of roast reaches 155°F, about 50 minutes longer. Internal temperature of meat will rise to 160°F (medium) upon standing. Transfer roast to warm platter and let stand 10 minutes to set juices for easier slicing.

5. Meanwhile, skim and discard fat from roasting pan. Add broth and heat to boiling, stirring until browned bits are loosened from bottom of pan. Remove from heat and set aside.

6. Heat remaining 2 teaspoons oil in small skillet over medium heat. Add remaining shallots and cook, stirring frequently, until tender, about 4 minutes. Add apple and cook, stirring frequently, until tender-crisp, about 4 minutes. Remove from heat and add applejack. Return to heat and cook until liquid has evaporated. Add broth from roasting pan and heat to boiling; boil 3 minutes. Add cream and boil until sauce has slightly thickened, about 5 minutes. Stir in remaining ¼ teaspoon salt.

7. Slice veal and serve with applejack sauce. Makes 8 main-dish servings.

Each serving: About 323 calories, 30g protein, 13g carbohydrate, 15g total fat (7g saturated), 145mg cholesterol, 463mg sodium.

Stuffed Breast of Veal

This cut of meat can always be counted on for being moist, flavorful, and easy on the wallet. Here, it is filled with the classic Sicilian combination of spinach and golden raisins. Or use our Bacon and Collard Greens Stuffing (right) for a change of pace. Serve the veal hot or at room temperature; either way, it will be delicious.

Prep: 25 minutes plus cooling
Bake: 2 hours 15 minutes

- 1 tablespoon olive oil
- 1 small onion, chopped
- 3 garlic cloves, finely chopped
- 2 packages (10 ounces each) frozen chopped spinach, thawed and squeezed dry
- 1 lemon
- ⅓ cup golden raisins
- ¾ teaspoon salt
- 1 bone-in veal breast (4 pounds), with pocket for stuffing
- 1 cup chicken broth

1. Preheat oven to 425°F. In 12-inch skillet, heat oil over medium-low heat. Add onion and garlic and cook, stirring frequently, until onion is tender, about 5 minutes. Add spinach and cook, stirring frequently, until liquid has evaporated, about 2 minutes. Remove from heat.

2. From lemon, grate ¾ teaspoon peel and squeeze 2 tablespoons juice; set juice aside. Add raisins, ½ teaspoon salt, and lemon peel to spinach. Cool to room temperature. Spoon mixture into pocket of veal.

3. Place breast, meat side up, in medium roasting pan (14" by 10"). Sprinkle remaining ¼ teaspoon salt on meat side (not rib side) of veal and roast 1 hour. Turn veal, rib side up, and pour broth and lemon juice into bottom of roasting pan. Cover veal with loose tent of foil and bake until tender, about 1 hour 15 minutes longer.

4. Transfer veal, rib side down, to cutting board and let stand 10 minutes to set juices for easier carving. Skim and discard fat from drippings in pan. Carve veal by slicing down along one rib bone. Cut away rib bone and discard, then continue carving. Transfer slices to warm platter and serve with pan juices. Makes 6 main-dish servings.

Each serving: About 425 calories, 51g protein, 13g carbohydrate, 18g total fat (6g saturated), 183mg cholesterol, 637mg sodium.

Bacon and Collard Greens Stuffing

Substitute ¼ **cup minced shallots** for the onion and cook with the garlic as directed. Stir in **2 packages (10 ounces) each of thawed and squeezed dry frozen chopped collard greens** instead of the spinach. Omit the grated lemon and raisins and stir **4 slices of crisp-cooked and chopped bacon** into the greens mixture. Proceed as directed.

Braised Veal Chops with Tomatoes and Peas

The bones in the shoulder chops contribute extra flavor and body to the sauce. Two large chops will easily feed four people.

Prep: 10 minutes   Cook: 1 hour 15 minutes

- 2 veal shoulder blade chops, 1 inch thick (1 pound each)
- 1 slice bacon, chopped
- ¼ teaspoon salt
- ⅛ teaspoon ground black pepper
- 1 medium onion, chopped
- 2 garlic cloves, finely chopped
- 1 can (14½ ounces) tomatoes in puree
- 1 cup chicken broth
- ½ cup dry white wine
- ¼ teaspoon dried sage, crumbled
- 1 cup frozen peas

1. In nonstick 12-inch skillet, cook bacon over medium-high heat until browned. With slotted spoon, transfer bacon to paper towels to drain; reserve.

2. Pat veal dry with paper towels. Sprinkle chops with salt and pepper. Cook chops in drippings in skillet over medium-high heat until browned, about 5 minutes per side. Transfer veal to plate.

3. Reduce heat to medium. Add onion to skillet and cook, stirring occasionally, until lightly browned, about 5 minutes. Stir in garlic and cook 1 minute longer. Stir in tomatoes with their puree, broth, wine, and sage and heat to boiling, breaking up tomatoes with side of spoon.

4. Return chops to skillet; cover and simmer over medium-low heat until veal is tender, about 45 minutes. Transfer veal to platter; keep warm. Add peas to skillet and cook 5 minutes. To serve, cut veal into serving portions, spoon sauce over veal, and sprinkle bacon on top. Makes 4 main-dish servings.

Each serving: About 289 calories, 35g protein, 16g carbohydrate, 9g total fat (3g saturated), 139mg cholesterol, 782mg sodium.

Osso Buco with Gremolata

This aromatic recipe from northern Italy is especially wonderful when served with Creamy Polenta (page 258).

Prep: 40 minutes   Bake: 2 hours

- 4 meaty veal shank cross cuts (osso buco), each about 2 inches thick (1 pound each)
- ½ teaspoon salt
- ¼ teaspoon ground black pepper
- 1 tablespoon olive oil
- 2 medium onions, chopped
- 3 carrots, peeled and chopped
- 2 stalks celery, chopped
- 4 garlic cloves, finely chopped
- 1 can (14½ to 16 ounces) tomatoes in puree
- 1 cup dry white wine
- 1 cup chicken broth
- 1 bay leaf
- 2 tablespoons chopped fresh parsley
- ½ teaspoon freshly grated lemon peel

1. Preheat oven to 350°F. Sprinkle shanks with salt and pepper. In nonreactive 5-quart Dutch oven, heat oil over medium-high heat until very hot. Add shanks and cook until browned, about 10 minutes, transferring shanks to plate as they are browned.

2. Add onions to Dutch oven and cook over medium heat, stirring occasionally, until slightly browned, about 5 minutes. Add carrots, celery, and three-fourths of garlic; cook 2 minutes longer.

3. Return veal to Dutch oven. Stir in tomatoes with their puree, wine, broth, and bay leaf; heat to boiling over high heat. Cover and place in oven. Bake until veal is tender when pierced with fork, about 2 hours.

4. Meanwhile, prepare gremolata: In small bowl, mix parsley, lemon peel, and remaining garlic. Cover and refrigerate until ready to serve.

5. Transfer veal to platter. Heat sauce in Dutch oven to boiling over high heat; boil until it has reduced to 4 cups, about 10 minutes. Pour sauce over veal and sprinkle with gremolata. Makes 4 main-dish servings.

Each serving: About 374 calories, 53g protein, 20g carbohydrate, 8g total fat (2g saturated), 183mg cholesterol, 874mg sodium.

Veal Stew with Gremolata

Use **2½ pounds boneless veal shoulder,** cut into 1½-inch pieces. Proceed as in Step 1 but brown veal in batches, transferring meat to bowl as it is browned. Continue as directed but bake only 1 hour 30 minutes. Makes 6 main-dish servings.

Veal Scallopini Marsala

Simple, elegant, and scrumptious, this quintessential Italian dish takes only minutes to prepare.

Prep: 10 minutes   Cook: 15 minutes

- 1 pound veal cutlets
- ¼ cup all-purpose flour
- ¼ teaspoon salt
- ⅛ teaspoon coarsely ground pepper
- 3 tablespoons butter or margarine
- ½ cup dry Marsala wine
- ½ cup chicken broth
- 1 tablespoon chopped fresh parsley

1. Place cutlets between two sheets of plastic wrap or waxed paper. With meat mallet or rolling pin, pound cutlets to ⅛-inch thickness. Cut cutlets into 3" by 3" pieces. On waxed paper, combine flour, salt, and pepper; coat veal with seasoned flour, shaking off excess.

2. In nonstick 10-inch skillet, melt butter over medium-high heat. Cook veal, in batches, until lightly browned, 45 to 60 seconds per side, using tongs to transfer pieces to warm platter as they are browned; keep warm.

3. Add Marsala and broth to veal drippings in pan and cook, stirring until browned bits are loosened from bottom of skillet, until syrupy, 4 to 5 minutes. Pour sauce over veal and sprinkle with parsley. Makes 6 main-dish servings.

Each serving: About 179 calories, 17g protein, 5g carbohydrate, 7g total fat (4g saturated), 75mg cholesterol, 288mg sodium.

Vitello Tonnato

Serve this delicious cold buffet dish with bowls of roasted red peppers, potato salad, and a variety of olives.

**Prep: 20 minutes plus cooling and chilling
Cook: 1 hour 50 minutes**

- 1 rolled boneless veal shoulder roast (2¾ to 3 pounds), trimmed and tied
- 10 anchovy fillets
- 2 garlic cloves, thinly sliced
- 3 cups water
- 1 can (14½ ounces) chicken broth or 1¾ cups Chicken Broth (page 62)
- 1 cup dry white wine
- 1 medium onion, thinly sliced
- 2 carrots, peeled and thinly sliced
- 1 can (6 ounces) tuna packed in oil, undrained
- ½ cup mayonnaise
- ½ cup heavy or whipping cream
- 1 tablespoon fresh lemon juice
- ½ teaspoon salt
- ¼ teaspoon dried sage
- 2 tablespoons chopped fresh parsley

1. With sharp knife, make slits all over veal. Coarsely chop 2 anchovies; insert chopped anchovies and garlic into slits.

2. In nonreactive 5-quart Dutch oven, combine water, broth, wine, onion, and carrots and heat to boiling over medium heat. Add roast to Dutch oven. Reduce heat; cover and simmer until veal is tender, about 1 hour and 45 minutes.

3. Remove from heat; let veal cool in broth 1 hour, then transfer veal to plate and refrigerate to cool completely. Strain broth, reserving ¾ cup; discard remaining broth. Transfer reserved broth to food processor fitted with knife blade. Add tuna, mayonnaise, cream, lemon juice, salt, sage, and remaining 8 anchovies; puree until smooth.

4. Cut veal into thin slices; transfer to deep platter large enough to hold veal in one or two layers. Pour sauce over veal; cover and refrigerate at least 1 hour or up to 24 hours. Serve chilled or at room temperature, sprinkled with parsley. Makes 8 main-dish servings.

Each serving: About 401 calories, 37g protein, 3g carbohydrate, 26g total fat (7g saturated), 172mg cholesterol, 801mg sodium.

Wiener Schnitzel

Travelers to Vienna rarely leave without enjoying at least one meal of these thin, tender, breaded veal cutlets.

Prep: 15 minutes   Cook: 20 minutes

- 6 veal cutlets (1½ pounds)
- 2 large eggs
- 1⅓ cups all-purpose flour
- 1 teaspoon salt
- ½ teaspoon coarsely ground black pepper
- 1½ cups plain dried bread crumbs
- 4 tablespoons butter or margarine
- 6 anchovy fillets (optional)
- 2 tablespoons capers, drained
- 2 tablespoons chopped fresh parsley
- 2 lemons, each cut into 6 wedges

1. Place cutlets between two sheets of plastic wrap or waxed paper. With meat mallet or rolling pin, pound cutlets to ⅛-inch thickness.

2. In pie plate, beat eggs; on waxed paper, combine flour, salt, and pepper. Place bread crumbs on separate sheet of waxed paper. Coat cutlets in seasoned flour, dip in eggs, and then coat evenly with bread crumbs.

3. In nonstick 12-inch skillet, melt 2 tablespoons butter over medium-high heat. Add cutlets, a few at a time, and cook until browned, 3 to 4 minutes per side, adding remaining 2 tablespoons butter as needed. Using tongs, transfer cutlets to warm platter as they are browned.

4. To serve, top cutlets with anchovies, if using, and capers; sprinkle with parsley and garnish with lemon wedges. Makes 6 main-dish servings.

Each serving: About 348 calories, 30g protein, 25g carbohydrate, 13g total fat (6g saturated), 180mg cholesterol, 920mg sodium.

Schnitzel à la Holstein

Prepare Wiener Schnitzel as directed but serve each cutlet topped with **1 fried egg.**

Veal Parmigiana

Smothered in marinara sauce and topped with moz-zarella cheese, this Italian-restaurant favorite is easy to make at home.

Prep: 30 minutes   Cook: 25 minutes

- 2 cups Marinara Sauce (page 222) or bottled marinara sauce
- 1 cup plain dried bread crumbs
- ½ teaspoon salt
- ⅛ teaspoon ground black pepper
- 1 large egg
- 2 tablespoons water
- 6 veal cutlets (1½ pounds)
- 3 tablespoons butter or margarine
- ¼ cup freshly grated Parmesan cheese
- 4 ounces part-skim mozzarella cheese, shredded (1 cup)

1. Prepare Marinara Sauce, if using.

2. On waxed paper, combine bread crumbs, salt, and pepper. In pie plate, beat egg and water. Dip cut-lets in egg mixture, then in bread crumbs; repeat to coat each cutlet twice.

3. In 12-inch skillet, melt butter over medium heat. Add cutlets, a few at a time, and cook until browned, about 5 minutes per side, using tongs to transfer cut-lets to platter as they are browned.

4. Return cutlets to skillet. Spoon sauce evenly over cutlets. Sprinkle with Parmesan and top with moz-zarella. Reduce heat to low; cover and cook just until cheese has melted, about 5 minutes. Makes 6 main-dish servings.

Each serving: About 367 calories, 35g protein, 19g carbohydrate, 17g total fat (8g saturated), 154mg cholesterol, 913mg sodium.

Chicken Parmigiana

Substitute 1½ **pounds skinless, boneless chicken breast halves** for veal and prepare as directed above.

Veal Piccata

This piquant dish depends on real dairy butter for its success. Do not use margarine; the sauce will not thicken properly.

Prep: 10 minutes   Cook: 15 minutes

- ¼ cup all-purpose flour
- ½ teaspoon salt
- ¼ teaspoon ground black pepper
- 1 pound veal cutlets
- 4 teaspoons olive or vegetable oil
- ⅓ cup dry white wine
- 1 cup chicken broth
- 2 tablespoons fresh lemon juice
- 1 tablespoon butter
- 1 tablespoon chopped fresh flat-leaf parsley

1. Place cutlets between two sheets of plastic wrap or waxed paper. With meat mallet or rolling pin, pound cutlets to ¼-inch thickness. On waxed paper, combine flour, salt, and pepper. Coat cutlets with sea-soned flour, shaking off excess.

2. In nonstick 12-inch skillet, heat 2 teaspoons oil over medium-high heat until very hot. Add half of cut-lets and cook until browned, about 2 minutes. Turn cutlets and cook 1 minute longer. Using tongs, transfer cutlets to platter; keep warm. Repeat with remaining 2 teaspoons oil and remaining veal.

3. Increase heat to high and add wine to skillet, stir-ring until browned bits are loosened from bottom of skillet. Add broth and heat to boiling; boil until sauce has reduced to ½ cup, 4 to 6 minutes. Stir in lemon juice, butter, and parsley. When butter has melted, pour sauce over veal. Makes 4 main-dish servings.

Each serving: About 226 calories, 26g protein, 7g carbohydrate, 10g total fat (3g saturated), 96mg cholesterol, 643mg sodium.

Veal with Tomato and Arugula Salad

Crispy veal cutlets topped with a zesty salad offer a mouthwatering combination of contrasting colors, flavors, and textures—perfect for a late supper.

Prep: 20 minutes   Cook: 10 minutes

- 2 teaspoons fresh lemon juice
- 6 tablespoons olive oil
- 1 teaspoon salt
- ¾ teaspoon ground black pepper
- 1 large tomato (12 ounces), coarsely chopped
- 1 cup loosely packed basil leaves
- ¼ cup coarsely chopped red onion
- 1 pound veal cutlets
- 2 large eggs
- ½ cup all-purpose flour
- 1 cup plain dried bread crumbs
- 1 bunch arugula (10 ounces), trimmed

1. In medium bowl, combine lemon juice, 2 tablespoons oil, ½ teaspoon salt, and ¼ teaspoon pepper. Stir in tomato, basil, and onion; set aside.

2. Place cutlets between two sheets of plastic wrap or waxed paper. With meat mallet or rolling pin, pound cutlets to ⅛-inch thickness.

3. In pie plate, beat eggs with remaining ½ teaspoon each salt and pepper. Place flour on waxed paper; place bread crumbs on separate sheet of waxed paper. Coat cutlets in flour, dip in egg mixture, and then coat evenly in bread crumbs.

4. In nonstick 12-inch skillet, heat 2 tablespoons oil over medium-high heat until very hot. Add half of cutlets and cook about 3 minutes per side. Using tongs, transfer to platter large enough to hold cutlets in single layer; keep warm. Repeat with remaining 2 tablespoons oil and remaining veal.

5. To serve, add arugula to tomato mixture and toss to combine. Spoon on top of hot veal. Makes 4 main-dish servings.

Each serving: About 538 calories, 35g protein, 39g carbohydrate, 27g total fat (5g saturated), 195mg cholesterol, 939mg sodium.

PORK

From bacon to pork chops, from holiday ham to grilled sausage, there are many delicious ways to enjoy pork. Surprisingly, only one-third of American pork is served fresh: The rest is smoked, salted, cured, or made into tasty sausage.

Modern breeding methods have standardized pork to the degree that the various cuts are no longer graded. Simply check the label for the cut you need. And since pork is slaughtered at an early age, it is naturally tender.

Buying Pork

Look for fresh pork that's pinkish white to grayish pink (the leg and shoulder cuts tend to be darker than the loin cuts). The flesh should be firm to the touch. The amount of marbled fat should be minimal, and any external fat should be firm and white. Cured and smoked pork products, however, are darker in color due to the curing process.

Storing Pork

Fresh pork can be refrigerated, tightly wrapped, for up to two days. Cured and smoked products, if unsliced and sealed in their original packaging, will last for two weeks or longer, but only one week after being opened. Do not store according to the "purchase by" date on the package, as supermarket refrigerators are colder than those at home.

Cooking Pork Safely

Like other meats, today's pork is much leaner than in the past. Recipes used to require pork to be cooked to 170°F to prevent any possible infection from trichinosis, a disease that could be passed to humans through undercooked pork. Not only has trichinosis been eradicated from pork products, but the parasite that carries the disease is killed at 137°F. So for tender, juicy pork it should not be cooked above 160°F. The exception is large cuts like fresh ham, which should be cooked to 170°F. When carved, they will have just a hint of pink at the center (with a deeper pink color near the bone), but the juices will run clear. Cook ground pork just until no trace of pink remains in the center. And to keep pork chops juicy, cook just until the meat is opaque at the bone.

POPULAR PORK CUTS

Shoulder (Boston Butt)
Ribs
Loin
Picnic Shoulder
Spareribs
Leg
Bacon
Jowl

Pork shoulder arm picnic

Also called picnic or whole fresh picnic *(roast)*.

Pork shoulder arm roast

Also called pork arm roast *(roast)*.

Pork leg roast, boneless

Also called rolled fresh ham. Also available bone-in *(roast)*.

Pork loin center rib roast

Contains loin eye muscle and rib bones; also called pork loin roast and center cut pork roast. Also available boneless *(roast)*.

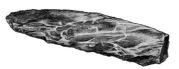

Pork loin tenderloin

Very tender and lean; cut into slices for panfrying or stir-frying. Also called pork tenderloin *(roast, broil, panfry, grill)*.

Pork spareribs

Contain long rib bones with thin covering of meat on outside of and between ribs *(roast, bake, braise, broil, grill)*.

Pork loin country-style ribs

Actually blade end loin chops that have been split. Also called country-style spareribs *(roast, bake, braise, broil, grill)*.

Pork loin rib chops

Contain loin eye muscle and backbone. Also called center cut chops *(braise, panfry, broil, grill)*.

Pork loin chops

Contain eye muscle and tenderloin separated by T-shaped bone. Also called loin end chops *(braise, panfry, broil, grill)*.

Pork loin sirloin chops

From sirloin end of loin. Also called sirloin pork chops or sirloin pork steaks *(braise, panfry, broil, grill)*.

Pork loin sirloin cutlets

Boneless, tender slices cut from sirloin end of loin *(braise, panfry, broil, grill)*.

Pork loin blade chops

From blade end of loin. Also called pork loin blade steaks *(braise, panfry, broil, grill)*.

TYPES OF HAM

Smoked ham comes from the hind leg of pork, whereas picnic ham comes from the shoulder. These hams are labeled either "partially cooked" or "fully cooked." In either case, be sure to follow the label's instructions.

Partially cooked ham must be cooked to 155°F before eating.

Fully cooked ham is ready to serve, but its flavor is much improved by heating it to an internal temperature of 130° to 140°F. It is available:

- bone-in-whole, shank, or butt portions
- semiboneless- the aitch and shank bones have been removed; only the leg bone remains
- boneless- rolled and shaped or formed

Spiral-sliced ham is ham that has been cut in one long continuous slice, and is ideal buffet food.

Canned ham is cured but not always smoked.

Boneless smoked pork shoulder (also called boneless pork butt), rolled and wrapped in a mesh stockinette that is removed before serving, is much smaller than ham. It's a great way to serve smoked pork to a small number of people.

Country hams, such as Smithfield and Virginia, are heavily salted and smoked. They should be soaked in cold water for 24 to 36 hours to remove the excess salt, then thoroughly cooked.

Prosciutto and prosciutto de Parma are cured, air-dried ham that have not been smoked. Imported and domestic prosciutto can be purchased in specialty food stores and in many supermarkets.

ROASTING TIMES FOR PORK
(OVEN TEMPERATURE OF 350°F)

Start with meat at refrigerator temperature. Remove roast from oven when it reaches 5°F below desired doneness; temperature will continue to rise as roast stands.

CUT	WEIGHT	MEAT THERMOMETER READING	APPROXIMATE COOKING TIME (MINUTES PER POUND)
FRESH PORK (WITH BONE)			
Crown roast	6 to 10 pounds	160°F	25 to 30 minutes
Center loin roast	3 to 5 pounds	160°F	25 to 30 minutes
Boneless top loin roast	2 to 4 pounds	160°F	25 to 30 minutes
Whole leg (fresh ham)	10 to 14 pounds	160° to 170°F	25 to 30 minutes
Leg half, shank or butt portion	3 to 5 pounds	160° to 170°F	40 minutes
Boston butt	3 to 6 pounds	160° to 170°F	45 minutes
Tenderloin (roast at 425° to 450°F)	½ to 1½ pounds	160°F	25 to 35 minutes total
SMOKED, COOK BEFORE EATING (HEAT AT 325°F)			
Whole ham	14 to 16 pounds	160°F	15 to 18 minutes
SMOKED FULLY COOKED PORK			
Whole ham	14 to 16 pounds	130° to 140°F	1 to 1¾ hours total
Half ham	6 to 8 pounds	130° to 140°F	1 hour total

Fresh Ham with Spiced Apple Glaze

A whole ham will provide enough meat for your grandest dinner party. A fragrant blend of cinnamon, cloves, and nutmeg—ideal with pork—is rubbed on before roasting. Serve with everal kinds of mustard.

Prep: 15 minutes   Bake: 5 hours

- 1 whole pork leg (fresh ham, 15 pounds), trimmed
- 2 teaspoons dried thyme
- 2 teaspoons ground cinnamon
- 2 teaspoons salt
- 1 teaspoon coarsely ground black pepper
- ½ teaspoon ground nutmeg
- ½ teaspoon ground cloves
- 1 jar (10 ounces) apple jelly
- ¼ cup balsamic vinegar

1. Preheat oven to 350°F. With knife, remove skin and trim excess fat from pork leg, leaving only a thin layer of fat.

2. In cup, combine thyme, cinnamon, salt, pepper, nutmeg, and cloves. Use to rub on pork. Place pork, fat side up, on rack in large roasting pan (17" by 11½"). Roast pork 3 hours. Cover pork loosely with tent of foil. Continue roasting until meat thermometer inserted into thickest part of pork (not touching bone) registers 150°F, about 1 hour.

3. Meanwhile, in 1-quart saucepan, heat apple jelly and vinegar to boiling over high heat; boil 2 minutes. Set aside.

4. When pork has reached 150°F, remove foil and brush pork with glaze. Continue roasting pork, brushing occasionally with remaining glaze, until meat thermometer registers 165°. (Meat near bone will be slightly pink.) Internal temperature of pork will rise to 170° upon standing.

5. When roast is done, transfer to warm large platter; let stand 20 minutes to set juices for easier carving. Makes 24 main-dish servings.

Each serving: About 298 calories, 38g protein, 6g carbohydrate, 12g total fat (4g saturated), 123mg cholesterol, 232mg sodium.

CARVING A WHOLE HAM

Place cooked ham on a cutting board. Using a carving fork to steady the ham, cut a few slices from the thin side of ham. Turn the ham over. Cut a few slices from the meaty end.

Cut out a small wedge of meat at the shank end of the ham.

Cut even slices along the ham, cutting through to the bone. Release the meat by cutting horizontally along the top of the bone. Transfer the slices to a warm platter.

PORK SAUSAGE

Test Kitchen Tip

Fresh sausage is simply seasoned ground pork that has been stuffed into casings or formed into patties; it must be cooked. *Cured and smoked sausages* sometimes require further cooking. *Andouille*, a spicy smoked sausage, is an important ingredient in Cajun cooking. *Kielbasa* (Polish sausage) is a good substitute for andouille and is delicious grilled. *Chorizo* is available fresh or smoked. It is seasoned with paprika and chiles and is used in Spanish and Mexican cooking. Many *German-style sausages*, such as bratwurst (a combination of pork and veal), are fresh sausages and must be cooked. *Dried and cured sausages*, such as salami and pepperoni, are usually presliced and don't require cooking.

Pineapple-Glazed Ham

Here's our recipe for this time-honored classic, along with two delicious glaze variations. A spiral-cut ham is an easy alternative.

Prep: 15 minutes   Bake: 2 hours 10 minutes

- 1 fully cooked smoked bone-in ham (14 pounds)
- 1 can (20 ounces) crushed pineapple, drained
- 1 cup packed dark brown sugar
- 1 tablespoon Dijon mustard

1. Preheat oven to 325°F. With sharp knife, remove skin and trim fat from ham, leaving about ¼-inch-thick layer of fat. Place ham on rack in large roasting pan (17" by 11½"). Bake ham 1 hour 45 minutes.

2. Meanwhile, prepare pineapple glaze: In medium bowl, combine pineapple, brown sugar, and mustard until blended. Remove ham from oven. Brush pineapple mixture on ham. Bake until meat thermometer inserted in thickest part of ham (not touching bone) reaches 135°F, 25 to 30 minutes longer. Internal temperature of ham will rise to 140°F upon standing. Transfer ham to warm platter and let stand 15 minutes to set juices for easier slicing. Makes 20 main-dish servings.

Each serving: About 193 calories, 21g protein, 15g carbohydrate, 5g total fat (2g saturated), 47mg cholesterol, 1,151mg sodium.

Melba-Glazed Ham

Prepare ham as directed but in Step 2 in small saucepan, heat ⅔ **cup peach preserves** and ½ **cup red raspberry jelly or jam** until melted and smooth. During the last thirty minutes of roasting time, brush the glaze over the ham two or three times. Makes about 1 cup.

Tomato and Onion Glazed Ham

Prepare ham as directed but in Step 2 in small saucepan, melt **1 tablespoon butter or margarine** over medium heat. Add **2 tablespoons finely chopped onion** and cook until tender. Stir in **1 can (8 ounces) tomato sauce, 2 tablespoons brown sugar,** and **1 teaspoon Worcestershire sauce;** heat to boiling. Reduce heat; simmer until glaze thickens, about 5 minutes. During the last thirty minutes of roasting time, brush the glaze over the ham two or three times. Makes about 1 cup.

MORE WAYS TO ENJOY HAM

Here are just a few ways to use leftovers and to add the rich smoky flavor of ham to your meals.

ZESTY SANDWICH SPREAD

In food processor, grind enough ham to equal 2 cups. Transfer to medium bowl and stir in ½ cup sweet pickle relish, ½ cup finely chopped celery, and 1 package (3 ounces) cream cheese. Serve as sandwich spread or with unsalted crackers.

EGGS BENEDICT

For Sunday brunch, serve thinly sliced ham on a toasted English muffin, topped with poached egg and Hollandaise Sauce (page 432).

HEARTY SOUPS

Use ham bone in split-pea soup, bean soup, or German Lentil Soup (page 53).

OPEN-FACED GRILLED SANDWICHES

Brown slices of ham and pineapple in butter or margarine. Place on toasted kaiser roll halves, top with Cheddar cheese, and broil until cheese melts.

FLAVORFUL SAUCE

Add some minced ham to Béchamel (White Sauce, page 432), and serve over chicken or vegetables.

MAIN-DISH SALADS

Toss some chopped ham into macaroni, potato, or rice salad for a tasty main dish. Or add ¼ cup chopped ham to Creamy Potato Salad (page 418).

HAM AND MELON

Arrange thinly sliced ham on thinly sliced melon wedges or other fruit to serve for breakfast, lunch, or as a first course.

HAM BISCUITS

Make biscuits (page 447). Split, spread with butter and top with thinly sliced ham.

Pork Roast with Fennel and Garlic

Our flavorful secret is a spice paste. For greater flavor absorption, rub the meat ahead of time and refrigerate for up to twenty-four hours. Bone-in cuts, such as this loin roast, take a little longer to cook than boneless cuts but are the most flavorful.

Prep: 10 minutes   Roast: 1 hour 30 minutes

- 4 garlic cloves, finely chopped
- 2½ teaspoons fennel seeds, crushed
- 1 teaspoon salt
- ½ teaspoon ground black pepper
- 2 teaspoons olive oil
- 1 bone-in pork loin roast (4 pounds), trimmed
- ⅓ cup dry white wine
- ⅔ cup chicken broth

1. Preheat oven to 450°F. In cup, combine garlic, fennel seeds, salt, pepper, and oil to make paste.

2. Place roast in small roasting pan (13" by 9") and rub fennel paste on outside of pork and between bones. Roast pork 45 minutes. Turn oven control to 350°F, cover meat loosely with tent of foil, and roast until meat thermometer inserted in thickest part of roast (not touching bone) reaches 155°F, about 45 minutes longer. Internal temperature of meat will rise to 160°F upon standing. When roast is done, transfer to warm platter and let stand 15 minutes to set juices for easier carving.

3. Meanwhile, add wine to roasting pan and heat to boiling over high heat, stirring until browned bits are loosened from bottom of pan. Add broth and heat to boiling. Remove from heat; skim and discard fat. Serve sauce with roast. Makes 8 main-dish servings.

Each serving: About 270 calories, 35g protein, 1g carbohydrate, 13g total fat (4g saturated), 99mg cholesterol, 440mg sodium.

Pork Roast with Fresh Sage

Prepare as above but substitute ¼ **cup fresh parsley, 2 tablespoons chopped fresh sage**, and ½ **teaspoon dried thyme** for fennel seeds.

French Roast Pork

The spice mixture rubbed onto the pork is a classic French combination known as *quatre épices*, which means "four spices." We've taken the liberty of adding one more for good measure. Once the pork begins roasting, the aroma of warm spices will fill your kitchen.

Prep: 5 minutes   Roast: 1 hour

- 1 boneless pork loin roast (2 pounds), trimmed
- 1 teaspoon salt
- ¾ teaspoon dried thyme
- ½ teaspoon ground cinnamon
- ½ teaspoon ground black pepper
- ⅛ teaspoon ground nutmeg
- ⅛ teaspoon ground cloves
- ⅓ cup dry white wine
- ⅔ cup chicken broth
  applesauce

1. Preheat oven to 350°F. Pat pork dry with paper towels.

2. In cup, combine salt, thyme, cinnamon, pepper, nutmeg, and cloves. Use to rub on pork.

3. Place roast on rack in small roasting pan (13" by 9"). Roast pork until meat thermometer inserted in center of roast reaches 155°F, about 1 hour. Internal temperature of meat will rise to 160°F upon standing.

4. When roast is done, transfer to warm platter and let stand 15 minutes to set juices for easier slicing.

5. Meanwhile, add wine to roasting pan and heat to boiling over high heat, stirring until browned bits are loosened from bottom of pan. Add broth and heat to boiling; boil 2 minutes. Remove from heat; skim and discard fat. Serve pan juices and applesauce with pork. Makes 6 main-dish servings.

Each serving: About 254 calories, 33g protein, 1g carbohydrate, 11g total fat (4g saturated), 93mg cholesterol, 561mg sodium.

Spice-Brined Pork Loin

Brining in a blend of kosher salt, sugar, and spices infuses this pork with wonderful flavor and keeps it tender and juicy. Allow the pork to soak in the brine for 18 to 24 hours before roasting.

Prep: 20 minutes plus marinating 18 to 24 hours
Roast: 1 hour

- 2 cups cold water
- ¼ cup sugar
- ¼ cup kosher salt
- 2 tablespoons coriander seeds
- 2 tablespoons cracked black pepper
- 2 tablespoons fennel seeds
- 2 tablespoons cumin seeds
  peel from 1 navel orange, white pith removed
- 3 cups ice
- 1 boneless pork loin roast (about 3 pounds), trimmed
- 4 garlic cloves, crushed with side of chef's knife

1. In 2-quart saucepan, heat 1 cup water, sugar, salt, coriander, pepper, fennel, cumin, and orange peel to boiling over high heat. Reduce heat to low; simmer 2 minutes. Remove saucepan from heat; stir in ice until almost melted. Stir in remaining cup water.

2. Place pork in large zip-tight plastic bag. Add garlic and brine; seal bag, pressing out excess air. Place bag in large bowl or small roasting pan and refrigerate 18 to 24 hours.

3. When ready to cook pork, preheat oven to 400°F. Remove pork from bag; discard brine (it's alright if some spices stick to pork). Place roast on rack in medium roasting pan (14" by 10"). Roast pork 1 hour to 1 hour 15 minutes or until meat thermometer inserted into center of roast reaches 150°F. Internal temperature of meat will rise to 160°F upon standing. Transfer pork to cutting board and let stand 10 minutes to allow juices to set for easier slicing.

Each serving: About 175 calories, 24g protein, 1g carbohydrate, 8g total fat (3g saturated), 67mg cholesterol, 445mg sodium.

Spice-Brined Pork Loin

COOKING PORK

Test Kitchen Tip

Since pork is usually tender, many cuts are perfectly suitable for these cooking methods.

Broiling, Grilling, Panfrying & Stir-frying
Many lean cuts lend themselves to these methods.
Best Bets: Tenderloin, loin, rib and loin chops, sirloin chops and cutlets, blade chops, and sausages. Spareribs are good broiled or grilled if first precooked.

Braising & Stewing Many cuts of pork stand up well to long, slow cooking in liquid.
Best Bets: Sirloin chops, blade chops, shoulder, spareribs and pork cubes for stew.

Roasting Use tender cuts from the loin.
Best Bets: Rib crown roast, shoulder arm roast, arm picnic roast, fresh ham, whole boneless tenderloin, bone-in and boneless loin, spareribs, and country-style ribs.

Caribbean Pork Roast

The seasonings that give this dish its Caribbean flavor are similar to those used in jerk cooking. The piquant sauce would also go well with grilled chicken or fish.

Prep: 10 minutes   Roast: 1 hour 20 minutes

- 1 boneless pork shoulder blade roast (fresh pork butt, 2½ pounds), trimmed
- 1½ teaspoons salt
- 1¼ teaspoons sugar
- ¾ teaspoon ground ginger
- ½ teaspoon ground allspice
- ½ teaspoon ground black pepper
- 3 teaspoons Dijon mustard
- ⅔ cup mango chutney, chopped
- 6 tablespoons fresh lime juice
- 2 tablespoons water

1. Preheat oven to 425°F. Using sharp knife, cut roast lengthwise almost in half, being careful not to cut all the way through. Open and spread flat like a book. In cup, combine salt, sugar, ginger, allspice, and pepper. Brush cut side of pork with 2 teaspoons mustard and sprinkle with half of seasoning mixture. Close pork "book" and rub remaining seasoning mixture on outside of pork. Tie roast with string at 1-inch intervals.

2. Place roast on rack in small roasting pan (13" by 9"). Roast pork 1 hour. Turn oven control to 350°F and roast until meat thermometer inserted in center of roast reaches 155°F, about 20 minutes longer. Internal temperature of meat will rise to 160°F upon standing. Let stand 10 minutes to set juices for easier slicing.

3. Meanwhile, in small bowl, combine chutney, lime juice, water, and remaining 1 teaspoon mustard. Serve sauce with sliced pork. Makes 6 main-dish servings.

Each serving: About 417 calories, 35g protein, 28g carbohydrate, 17g total fat (6g saturated), 124mg cholesterol, 1,050mg sodium.

Oven-Barbecued Spareribs

These sweet and sticky ribs are worth getting your fingers dirty for! Nevertheless, keep the napkins handy.

Prep: 10 minutes   Roast: 1 hour 30 minutes

- 6 pounds pork spareribs, cut into 1-rib portions
- 1 can (6 ounces) tomato paste
- ¼ cup packed brown sugar
- ½ cup water
- ¼ cup honey
- ¼ cup cider vinegar
- 2 tablespoons vegetable oil
- 1 tablespoon grated onion
- 2 teaspoons chili powder
- 2 teaspoons salt

1. Preheat oven to 325°F. Arrange spareribs in single layer in large roasting pan (17" by 11½"). Roast spareribs 1 hour.

2. Meanwhile, prepare glaze: In medium bowl, combine tomato paste with brown sugar, water, honey, vinegar, oil, onion, chili powder, and salt until well blended.

3. Brush ribs with glaze. Continue roasting ribs, brushing frequently with glaze, until ribs are tender, about 30 minutes longer. Makes 6 main-dish servings.

Each serving: About 849 calories, 53g protein, 27g carbohydrate, 59g total fat (20g saturated), 214mg cholesterol, 1,178mg sodium.

Caribbean Pork Roast

Mexican-Style Spareribs

A heady blend of tequila, orange juice, lime juice, and jalapeño pepper gives these pork ribs their personality. If you wish, the ribs can be marinated overnight.

Prep: 15 minutes   Roast: 1 hour 50 minutes

- 1 cup firmly packed fresh cilantro leaves and stems
- ½ small onion, thinly sliced
- 4 garlic cloves, crushed with garlic press
- 1 pickled jalapeño chile
- ½ cup fresh lime juice
- ¼ cup fresh orange juice
- ¼ cup tequila
- 1 tablespoon olive oil
- 2 tablespoons sugar
- ½ teaspoon dried oregano
- 3 pounds pork spareribs

1. Preheat oven to 350°F.

2. In blender, combine cilantro, onion, garlic, pickled jalapeño, lime and orange juices, tequila, oil, sugar, and oregano and puree until smooth.

3. Place spareribs in nonreactive roasting pan just large enough to hold them in single layer. Pour cilantro mixture over ribs, turning to coat well. Roast, turning ribs twice, 1 hour 30 minutes. Turn oven control to 450°F and roast ribs until very tender and richly colored, about 20 minutes longer.

4. Transfer ribs to warm platter. Skim and discard fat from sauce remaining in pan and spoon sauce over ribs. Makes 4 main-dish servings.

Each serving: About 610 calories, 40g protein, 13g carbohydrate, 44g total fat (15g saturated), 161mg cholesterol, 183mg sodium.

Pulled Pork Barbecue

This easy indoor pork barbecue is so tender it can be pulled apart. For authentic smoky flavor, brown the pork on the grill.

Prep: 10 minutes plus cooling
Cook: 2 hours 45 minutes

- 3 pounds boneless pork shoulder blade roast, trimmed and tied
- ½ teaspoon salt
- ¼ teaspoon ground black pepper
- 1 tablespoon vegetable oil
- 2 cups water
- 1 cup ketchup
- ¼ cup distilled white vinegar
- ¼ cup Worcestershire sauce
- ⅓ cup packed brown sugar
- 1 tablespoon dry mustard
- ¼ to ½ teaspoon crushed red pepper
- 10 hamburger buns, split

1. Pat pork dry with paper towels. Sprinkle roast with salt and pepper. In nonreactive 5-quart Dutch oven, heat oil over medium-high heat until very hot. Add roast and cook until browned, about 5 minutes. Transfer pork to plate; discard drippings from pan.

2. Combine water, ketchup, vinegar, Worcestershire, brown sugar, dry mustard, and crushed red pepper in Dutch oven. Add pork and heat to boiling over high heat. Reduce heat; cover and simmer, turning roast every 30 minutes, 2 hours 30 minutes.

3. Transfer roast to plate and cool. Boil pot liquid until it has reduced and thickened, about 5 minutes.

4. When roast is cool enough to handle, discard strings. Separate meat into chunks, removing as much fat as possible. With hands or fork, shred meat into bite-size pieces. Return pork to Dutch oven, stirring; heat through. Serve pulled pork on hamburger buns. Makes 10 main-dish servings.

Each serving: About 408 calories, 31g protein, 37g carbohydrate, 15g total fat (4g saturated), 93mg cholesterol, 806mg sodium.

Orange-Glazed Pork Rolls

When you want smoky pork flavor but don't want to serve ham, roast a smoked pork shoulder roll. Its neat shape makes for easy serving, so it's no trouble to prepare several.

Prep: 5 minutes   Cook/Bake: 1 hour 50 minutes

- 2 smoked pork shoulder rolls (3 pounds each)
- ¼ teaspoon whole black peppercorns
- 1 bay leaf
- 1 jar (10 to 12 ounces) orange marmalade
- 2 tablespoons bottled white horseradish

1. Remove stockinette casing (if any) from pork rolls, if directed on label. In 8-quart saucepot, place shoulder rolls, peppercorns, bay leaf, and enough *water* to cover meat; heat to boiling over high heat. Reduce heat; cover and simmer until pork rolls are tender, about 1 hour 30 minutes.

2. Preheat oven to 350°F. In small bowl, combine orange marmalade and horseradish.

3. When shoulder rolls are done, arrange in 13" by 9" baking pan; bake, brushing occasionally with marmalade mixture, 20 minutes.

4. To serve, cut rolls into slices and arrange on warm platter. Makes 12 main-dish servings.

Each serving: About 605 calories, 33g protein, 18g carbohydrate, 44g total fat (16g saturated), 126mg cholesterol, 1,847mg sodium.

Breaded Pork Tenderloin

This recipe shows just how quickly pork tenderloin can be transformed into a delicious meal. Serve with your favorite salsa or with lemon wedges.

Prep: 20 minutes   Cook: 10 minutes

- 1 pork tenderloin (12 ounces), trimmed
- 1 large egg
- 2 tablespoons water
- ½ teaspoon salt
- ¼ teaspoon dried rosemary, crumbled
- ¾ cup plain dried bread crumbs
- 3 tablespoons vegetable oil

1. Using sharp knife, cut tenderloin lengthwise almost in half, being careful not to cut all the way through. Open and spread flat like a book. Place pork between two sheets of plastic wrap or waxed paper. With meat mallet or rolling pin, pound pork to ¼-inch thickness; cut crosswise into 4 equal pieces.

2. In pie plate, with fork, lightly beat egg, water, salt, and rosemary. Place bread crumbs on waxed paper. Using tongs, dip pork in egg mixture, then in bread crumbs. Repeat to coat each piece of pork twice.

3. In 12-inch skillet, heat oil over medium-high heat until very hot. Add pork and cook until browned and cooked through, about 5 minutes per side. Makes 4 main-dish servings.

Each serving: About 291 calories, 22g protein, 15g carbohydrate, 15g total fat (3g saturated), 108mg cholesterol, 522mg sodium.

MEAT BARGAINS

Test Kitchen Tip

You don't have to deplete your savings to incorporate quality meat into a meal. While less-expensive cuts often require more time to cook or marinate to keep them tender, the end result will be rich and flavorful. Here are some tips to help stretch your dinner dollar:

- Buy larger cuts of meat; they're often sold at a lower price per pound than smaller ones. Ask the butcher to cut the pork shoulder arm picnic, beef chuck shoulder, beef rump, or bottom round roast into smaller pieces, or purchase family packs of meat in bulk from a club store.

Label and freeze any portions you're not going to use right away.

- Look for the bone-in choices from less tender meats. They tend to cost less, and the bone adds a depth of flavor to stews and soups. Look for chuck blade steaks, shoulder lamb chops, veal breast, and lamb shanks.
- Don't shy away from fat. The leaner the cut, the more expensive it'll be. Fresh ham, beef chuck, and cross-rib pot roast are tender and juicy after a long braise, and the fat can easily be skimmed off after cooking.

Choucroute Garni

For sauerkraut lovers! Serve this filling, homey dish, best made during the cold winter months, with boiled potatoes, a pot of good-quality mustard, and a loaf of crusty bread.

Prep: 20 minutes   Cook: 50 minutes

- 4 slices bacon, cut into 1-inch pieces
- ¼ cup water
- 1 large onion (12 ounces), thinly sliced
- 2 McIntosh apples, each peeled, cut into quarters, and thinly sliced
- 2 bags (16 ounces each) sauerkraut, rinsed and drained
- 1½ cups fruity white wine, such as riesling
- 6 juniper berries, crushed
- 1 bay leaf
- 6 smoked pork chops, ½ inch thick (4 ounces each)
- 1 pound kielbasa (smoked Polish sausage), cut into 1½-inch pieces

1. In nonreactive 5-quart Dutch oven, combine bacon and water; cook over medium-low heat until bacon is lightly crisped, about 4 minutes. Add onion and cook, stirring frequently, until onion is tender and golden, about 7 minutes.

2. Add apples and cook until tender, about 3 minutes. Stir in sauerkraut, wine, juniper berries, and bay leaf and heat to boiling. Reduce heat; cover and simmer 15 minutes.

3. Nestle pork chops and kielbasa into cabbage mixture; cover and cook until pork is heated through and sauerkraut is tender, about 20 minutes. Discard bay leaf and serve. Makes 6 main-dish servings.

Each serving: About 524 calories, 27g protein, 19g carbohydrate, 37g total fat (13g saturated), 106mg cholesterol, 3,151mg sodium.

Oven-Baked Pepper Bacon

The perfect way to make bacon for a crowd: in the oven! This method works best when using lean bacon, but if the bacon renders an excessive amount of fat, pour it off before switching racks.

Prep: 10 minutes   Bake: 25 minutes

- 1½ pounds sliced lean bacon
- 2½ teaspoons coarsely ground black pepper

1. Preheat oven to 400°F. Arrange bacon slices in two jelly-roll or roasting pans, overlapping the lean edge of each bacon slice with fat edge of the next. Sprinkle pepper evenly over bacon. Bake until bacon is golden brown and crisp, about 25 minutes, rotating baking pans between upper and lower oven racks halfway through baking.

2. Transfer bacon to paper towels. Keep warm until ready to serve. Makes 12 accompaniment servings.

Each serving: About 93 calories, 5g protein, 0g carbohydrate, 8g total fat (3g saturated), 13mg cholesterol, 254mg sodium.

Choucroute Garni

Stuffed Pork Chops

The aroma of this dish will remind you of childhood trips to your grandparents for Sunday supper. If you don't have rye bread for the stuffing, use whole wheat.

Prep: 20 minutes   Cook: 30 minutes

- 4 teaspoons vegetable oil
- 1 small onion, chopped
- 1 Golden Delicious apple, peeled, cored, and chopped
- ½ teaspoon caraway seeds
  pinch dried thyme
- 2 slices rye bread, toasted and cut into ¼-inch pieces
- 2 tablespoons plus ½ cup chicken broth
- 1 tablespoon spicy brown mustard
- 4 pork loin chops, 1 inch thick (8 ounces each)
- ¼ teaspoon salt

1. In 10-inch skillet, heat 2 teaspoons oil over medium heat. Add onion and cook until tender, about 5 minutes. Add apple, caraway seeds, and thyme and cook 3 minutes longer. Transfer apple mixture to medium bowl. Wipe skillet clean.

2. Stir bread pieces, 2 tablespoons broth, and mustard into apple mixture. Pat pork dry with paper towels. Holding knife parallel to surface, cut a horizontal pocket in each chop. Stuff apple mixture into pocket of each chop and secure with toothpicks. Sprinkle with salt.

3. In 12-inch skillet, heat remaining 2 teaspoons oil over medium heat until hot. Cook chops until they just lose their pink color throughout, about 7 minutes per side. Transfer chops to warm platter.

4. Increase heat to high. Add remaining ½ cup broth to skillet and heat to boiling, stirring to loosen brown bits from bottom of pan. Boil broth until reduced to ¼ cup, 3 to 5 minutes. Pour sauce over chops. Makes 4 main-dish servings.

Each serving: About 367 calories, 39g protein, 15g carbohydrate, 15g total fat (4g saturated), 102mg cholesterol, 540mg sodium.

Italian Sausage and Broccoli Rabe

In this rustic classic, sweet sausage balances the pleasant bite of broccoli rabe. Fans of this bitter green may want to double the amount used.

Prep: 5 minutes   Cook: 30 minutes

- 1 bunch broccoli rabe (1 pound), tough ends trimmed
- 2 teaspoons salt
- 1 pound sweet Italian-sausage links, pricked with fork
- ¼ cup water
- 1 tablespoon olive oil
- 1 large garlic clove, finely chopped
- ⅛ teaspoon crushed red pepper

1. In 5-quart saucepot, heat *4 quarts water* to boiling. Add broccoli rabe and salt. Cook just until stems are tender, about 5 minutes; drain. When cool enough to handle, coarsely chop broccoli rabe.

2. Meanwhile, in 10-inch skillet, heat sausage links and water to boiling over medium heat. Cover and cook 5 minutes. Remove cover and cook, turning sausages frequently, until water has evaporated and sausages are well browned, about 20 minutes longer. Using tongs, transfer sausages to paper towels to drain; cut each sausage on diagonal in half.

3. Discard fat from skillet but do not wipe clean. To drippings in skillet, add oil, garlic, and crushed red pepper. Cook, stirring, until very fragrant, about 15 seconds. Add broccoli rabe and cook, stirring, until well coated and heated through, about 2 minutes. Stir in sausages and remove from heat. Makes 4 main-dish servings.

Each serving: About 325 calories, 19g protein, 6g carbohydrate, 25g total fat (8g saturated), 65mg cholesterol, 1,079mg sodium.

Polenta and Sausage Casserole

Layers of creamy polenta, cheese, and a tomato-sausage sauce make this a terrific casserole for a potluck party, buffet, or brunch.

Prep: 1 hour   Bake: 35 minutes

- 8 ounces sweet Italian-sausage links, casings removed
- 8 ounces hot Italian-sausage links, casings removed
- 1 tablespoon olive oil
- 1 large onion (12 ounces), chopped
- 1 large stalk celery, chopped
- 1 carrot, peeled and chopped
- 1 can (28 ounces) plum tomatoes in puree
- 2 cups yellow cornmeal
- 1 can (14½ ounces) chicken broth or 1¾ cups Chicken Broth (page 62)
- ¾ teaspoon salt
- 4½ cups boiling water
- ½ cup freshly grated Parmesan cheese
- 8 ounces Fontina or mozzarella cheese, shredded (2 cups)

1. Prepare tomato-sausage sauce: In nonreactive 5-quart Dutch oven, cook sweet and hot sausage meat over medium-high heat, breaking up meat with side of spoon, until browned. With slotted spoon, transfer meat to bowl. Discard fat from Dutch oven.

2. Add oil to Dutch oven. Add onion, celery, and carrot and cook over medium-high heat until browned. Stir in sausage and tomatoes with their puree, breaking up tomatoes with side of spoon. Heat to boiling over high heat. Reduce heat; cover and simmer 10 minutes. Remove cover and simmer 10 minutes longer.

3. Preheat oven to 350°F. Prepare polenta: In 4-quart saucepan with wire whisk, mix cornmeal, broth, and salt. Over medium-high heat, add boiling water and cook, whisking constantly, until mixture has thickened, about 5 minutes. Whisk in Parmesan.

4. Grease 13" by 9" baking dish. Evenly spread half of polenta mixture in prepared dish; top with half of tomato-sausage sauce, then half of Fontina. Repeat with remaining polenta mixture and sauce.

5. Bake casserole 15 minutes. Sprinkle with remaining Fontina; bake until mixture is bubbling and cheese is golden, about 20 minutes longer. Let stand 15 minutes for easier serving. Makes 8 main-dish servings.

Each serving: About 466 calories, 23g protein, 38g carbohydrate, 25g total fat (11g saturated), 70mg cholesterol, 1,323mg sodium.

Balsamic-Glazed Pork Chops

Balsamic vinegar is very versatile; it's not just for salad dressing. Here it's turned into a sweet-tart sauce just made for tender pork.

Prep: 5 minutes   Cook: 10 minutes

- 8 boneless pork loin chops, ½ inch thick (3 ounces each), trimmed
- ½ teaspoon salt
- ¼ teaspoon ground black pepper
- 1 tablespoon olive oil
- 3 tablespoons finely chopped shallot or onion
- ⅓ cup balsamic vinegar
- ¼ cup packed brown sugar

1. Pat pork dry with paper towels. Sprinkle chops with salt and pepper. In nonstick 12-inch skillet, heat oil over medium-high heat until hot. Cook pork 4 minutes on one side; turn and cook 3 minutes on second side. Transfer pork to platter; keep warm.

2. Increase heat to high. Stir shallot into pan juices; cook 1 minute. Stir in vinegar and sugar and cook 1 minute longer. Pour sauce over pork. Makes 4 main-dish servings.

Each serving: About 275 calories, 28g protein, 15g carbohydrate, 11g total fat (3g saturated), 76mg cholesterol, 364mg sodium.

LAMB

The unique, relatively mild flavor of lamb calls for bold seasonings like garlic, rosemary, and wine or intriguing combinations of assertive, exotic spices and sweet fruits.

Buying Lamb

Americans generally prefer the milder taste of young lamb, and the good news is that most supermarket lamb is from animals six to twelve months old. Baby lamb (milk-fed lamb) is less than two months old and has a delicate flavor and pale pink color. Even though it is raised year-round, so-called spring lamb (Easter lamb) comes from slightly older sheep up to five months old. Both of these younger lambs are specialty items that are most easily found during the holiday season at ethnic butchers. Look for lamb from Australia and New Zealand in supermarkets and in butcher shops. The cuts are smaller than those of American lamb, since they come from smaller—not younger—animals, but you can count on the meat to be tender and flavorful.

When shopping for lamb, look for meat that is pinkish red. Darker meat indicates an older animal, and it will have a stronger flavor. The fat should look white, firm, and waxy. The bones should be porous and un-splintered, with a reddish tinge at the cut end. If you buy a large cut of lamb, such as a whole leg, be sure the fell (the thin membrane covering the fat) has been removed. If necessary, peel it off with the help of a sharp knife. In any case, the fat should be trimmed away so only a thin covering remains.

Storing Lamb

Lamb chops, stew meat, and roasts can be stored for up to two days in the refrigerator. Ground lamb is quite perishable, so it should be used within one day of purchase.

ROASTING TIMES FOR LAMB
(OVEN TEMPERATURE OF 350°F)

Start with meat at refrigerator temperature. Remove roast from oven when it reaches 5°F below desired doneness; temperature will continue to rise as it stands.

CUT	WEIGHT	APPROXIMATE COOKING TIME (MINUTES PER POUND)		
		MEDIUM-RARE (135°-140°F)	MEDIUM (145°-155°F)	WELL-DONE (OVER 160°F)
Whole leg	5 to 7 pounds	15 minutes	15 to 18 minutes	20 minutes
	7 to 9 pounds	20 minutes	20 to 23 minutes	25 minutes
Leg shank half	3 to 4 pounds	20 to 25 minutes	30 minutes	35 to 40 minutes
Leg sirloin half	3 to 4 pounds	20 to 23 minutes	25 to 30 minutes	35 minutes
Leg roast (boneless)	4 to 7 pounds	15 to 18 minutes	20 to 23 minutes	25 minutes
Rib roast or rack (roast at 375°F)	1½ to 2½ pounds	20 to 25 minutes	30 minutes	35 minutes
Crown roast, unstuffed (roast at 375°F)	2 to 3 pounds	20 minutes	25 minutes	30 minutes
Shoulder roast	4 to 6 pounds	20 minutes	25 minutes	30 minutes
Shoulder roast (Boneless)	3½ to 6 pounds	35 minutes	40 minutes	45 minutes

POPULAR LAMB CUTS

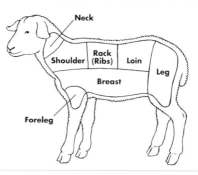

Neck

Shoulder | Rack (Ribs) | Loin

Leg

Breast

Foreleg

Lamb rib roast

Elegant and expensive. Also called rack of lamb *(roast)*.

Lamb shoulder neck slices

Cross cuts of neck. Also called neck of lamb and bone-in lamb for stew *(braise)*.

Lamb rib chops

Also called rack lamb chops *(broil, grill, panfry, roast, bake)*.

Lamb loin chops

Meaty area has both rib-eye muscle and tenderloin *(broil, grill, panfry)*.

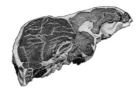

Lamb leg sirloin chop

Includes three different muscles. Also called lamb sirloin steak *(broil, grill, panfry)*.

Lamb shoulder arm chops

Cut from arm portion of shoulder. Also called arm cut chops, round bone chops, or shoulder chops *(braise, broil, grill)*.

Lamb shoulder blade chops

From blade portion of the shoulder. Also called lamb shoulder chops or blade cut chops *(braise, broil, grill, panfry)*.

Lamb shanks

Cut from arm of shoulder *(braise)*.

Lamb leg whole

Also called leg of lamb; available bone-in and boneless *(roast)*.

Lamb leg shank half

Sirloin half removed. Lower half of leg and round leg bone included *(roast)*.

Lamb breast riblets

Cut from breast, contain long and narrow ribs with layers of meat and fat *(braise)*.

Lamb breast

Also called breast of lamb. Part of forequarter, containing row of ribs *(braise, roast)*.

Roasted Leg of Lamb with Pistachio-Mint Crust

To prevent the nut crust from burning, don't spread it over the roast until after it has cooked for one hour. Some Indian markets and specialty stores sell shelled pistachios, or simply shell your own.

Prep: 30 minutes   Roast: 2 hours 15 minutes

- 1 whole bone-in lamb leg (7 pounds), trimmed
- 2 large garlic cloves, sliced
- 1½ teaspoons salt
- 2 tablespoons butter or margarine
- 1 small onion, chopped
- 1½ slices firm white bread, torn into ¼-inch pieces
- ½ cup pistachios, finely chopped
- 2 tablespoons coarsely chopped fresh mint
- ¼ teaspoon coarsely ground black pepper
- ½ cup port wine
- 3 tablespoons all-purpose flour
- 1 can (14½ ounces) chicken broth or 1¾ cups Chicken Broth (page 62)

1. Preheat oven to 325°F. Cut about a dozen ½-inch-long slits in lamb and insert slice of garlic in each. Sprinkle lamb with 1 teaspoon salt. Place lamb, fat side up, on rack in large roasting pan (17" by 11½"). Roast lamb 1 hour.

2. Meanwhile, in 10-inch skillet, melt butter over medium heat. Add onion and cook until lightly browned and tender, about 10 minutes; remove from heat. Stir in bread, pistachios, mint, remaining ½ teaspoon salt, and pepper. After lamb has roasted 1 hour, carefully pat mixture onto lamb.

3. Roast lamb 1 hour 15 to 30 minutes longer, until meat thermometer inserted in thickest part of lamb (not touching bone) reaches 140°F. Internal temperature of meat will rise to 145°F (medium) upon standing. Or roast until desired doneness. When lamb is done, transfer to warm platter and let stand 15 minutes to set juices for easier carving.

4. Meanwhile, prepare gravy: Remove rack from roasting pan; pour pan drippings into 2-cup measuring cup. Add port to pan, stirring until browned bits are loosened from bottom of pan. Pour into drippings in cup; let stand until fat separates out. Skim 2 tablespoons fat from drippings; return to roasting pan. Discard any remaining fat.

5. With wire whisk, whisk flour into fat in roasting pan over medium-high heat until well blended. Gradually whisk in meat juice and broth and heat to boiling, stirring constantly; boil 1 minute. Pour gravy into gravy boat and serve with lamb. Makes 10 main-dish servings.

Each serving: About 404 calories, 46g protein, 8g carbohydrate, 18g total fat (7g saturated), 144mg cholesterol, 680mg sodium.

Rosemary Leg of Lamb

The French often roast lamb that has first been rubbed with a mix of fragrant dried herbs. We like to do it, too.

Prep: 5 minutes   Roast: 1 hour 45 minutes

- 1 whole bone-in lamb leg (7½ pounds), trimmed
- ½ teaspoon dried rosemary, crumbled
- ½ teaspoon dried thyme, crumbled
- ½ teaspoon salt
- ¼ teaspoon ground black pepper

1. Preheat oven to 450°F. Place lamb in large roasting pan (17" by 11½"). In cup, combine rosemary, thyme, salt, and pepper. Use to rub on lamb.

2. Roast lamb 15 minutes. Turn oven control to 350°F and roast, basting every 15 minutes with pan juices, until meat thermometer inserted in thickest part of lamb (not touching bone)  reaches 140°F, 1 hour 30 to 45 minutes longer. Internal temperature of meat will rise to 145°F (medium) upon standing. Or roast until desired doneness.

3. When lamb is done, transfer to cutting board and let stand 15 minutes to set juices for easier carving.

4. Carve lamb into slices and arrange on warm platter. Makes 10 main-dish servings.

Each serving: About 312 calories, 46g protein, 0g carbohydrate, 13g total fat (5g saturated), 145mg cholesterol, 227mg sodium.

Roast Rack of Lamb

When you feel like showing off, few dishes do it more elegantly than a classic rack of lamb. For easy carving, ask the butcher to loosen the backbone from the ribs.

Prep: 10 minutes   Roast: 20 to 25 minutes

- 2 **teaspoons dried rosemary, crumbled**
- 2 **teaspoons olive oil**
- ½ **teaspoon dried thyme**
- 1 **large garlic clove, minced**
- ½ **teaspoon salt**
- ¼ **teaspoon freshly ground black pepper**
- 2 **lamb rib roasts (racks of lamb), 8 ribs each, (1¼ pounds each), trimmed**

1. Preheat oven to 450°F. In a small cup, combine rosemary, oil, thyme, garlic, salt, and pepper to form a paste. Rub paste on tops (fat side) of racks. Place racks, rub side up, in a large shallow roasting pan.

2. Roast lamb until meat thermometer inserted in center of lamb (not touching bone) reaches 135° to 140°F for medium-rare, 20 to 25 minutes. Transfer to a cutting board and let stand 10 minutes to set juices. Cut between ribs to serve. Makes 4 main-dish servings.

Each serving: About 675 calories, 31g protein, 1g carbohydrate, 60g total fat (25g saturated), 145mg cholesterol, 379mg sodium.

Crumb-Topped Roast Rack of Lamb

In small bowl, combine **1 cup fresh bread crumbs (2 slices firm white bread), 1 teaspoon olive oil, ⅛ teaspoon salt** and **⅛ teaspoon black pepper**. Follow directions for roast rack of lamb, rubbing racks with paste. After roasting lamb for 10 minutes, remove from oven. Spread **2 tablespoons Dijon mustard** over tops of racks. Press bread crumb mixture over mustard and pat to stick. Roast lamb to 135° to 140°F for medium-rare, 10 to 15 minutes longer.

CARVING A LEG OF LAMB

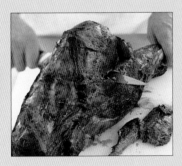

Cut a slice from the thin side of the leg so it can lie flat for easier carving; turn the leg cut side down. Holding the meat steady with a carving fork, make a vertical cut to the bone 1 inch from the shank. Holding the knife horizontally, cut along the top of the bone about halfway down its length.

Holding the leg steady by grasping the bone or by inserting a carving fork into the lamb, slice the meat that has been released from the bone. Make a second horizontal cut almost to the end of the leg, then slice the remaining lamb.

Turn the leg over. With the knife blade almost flat and working away from you, cut long slices following the line of the bone.

Lamb Shanks with White Beans and Roasted Endive

Lamb shanks, a Mediterranean favorite, are paired with endive that is roasted in the oven at the same time as the lamb for a rich, mellow flavor.

Prep: 1 hour 30 minutes   Bake: 2 hours

White Beans and Lamb Shanks

- 1 package (16 ounces) dry Great Northern beans
- 8 small lamb shanks (about 1 pound each)
- 2½ teaspoons salt
- 1 teaspoon coarsely ground pepper
- 2 tablespoons vegetable oil
- 6 medium garlic cloves, crushed with side of chef's knife
- 4 carrots, peeled and cut into 1-inch pieces
- 1 large onion (12 ounces), coarsely chopped
- ¼ cup all-purpose flour
- 2 tablespoons tomato paste
- 2 cups dry white wine
- 1 can (14 to 14½ ounces) chicken broth or 1¾ cups Chicken Broth (page 62)
- 2 sprigs fresh rosemary, plus 8 sprigs for garnish

Roasted Endive

- 1 tablespoon olive oil
- ½ teaspoon salt
- ¼ teaspoon coarsely ground pepper
- 8 medium heads Belgian endive (about 1½ pounds)

1. Prepare white beans: In 4-quart saucepan, combine beans and enough *water* to cover by 2 inches; heat to boiling over high heat. Cook 3 minutes; remove from heat. Cover and set aside until beans are softened, about 1 hour. Drain and rinse beans. (Or, if you prefer, soak beans overnight in cold water. Drain and rinse.)

2. Meanwhile, prepare lamb shanks: Pat shanks dry with paper towels; sprinkle with 1 teaspoon salt and ½ teaspoon pepper. In 8-quart Dutch oven, heat oil over medium-high heat until very hot but not smoking. Add shanks, in batches, and cook, until browned, 12 to 15 minutes, using tongs to transfer shanks to large bowl as they are browned. If necessary, reduce heat to medium before adding second batch of shanks to prevent overbrowning.

3. Preheat oven to 375°F. Add garlic, carrots, and onion to Dutch oven; cook, stirring frequently, until browned and tender, about 10 minutes. Add flour, tomato paste, and remaining 1½ teaspoons salt and ½ teaspoon pepper; cook, stirring constantly, 2 minutes. Add wine and heat to boiling, stirring until browned bits are loosened from bottom of Dutch oven; boil 5 minutes. Add broth and 1 cup water; heat to boiling. Stir in beans and 2 sprigs rosemary. Return shanks to Dutch oven; heat to boiling. Cover Dutch oven and bake 1 hour.

4. Meanwhile, prepare roasted endive: In large bowl, with fork, mix oil, salt, and pepper. Trim root ends of endive and cut each lengthwise in half. Add endive to oil mixture and toss until evenly coated. Arrange endive, cut sides down, in 15½" by 10½" jelly-roll pan.

5. After 1 hour, turn shanks and replace cover. Place endive in same oven. Bake shanks and endive until meat is fork-tender and easily separates from bone and endive is very tender and bottoms begin to brown, about 1 hour.

6. When shanks are done, transfer to large bowl. Skim and discard fat from liquid in Dutch oven. Remove and discard rosemary. To serve, spoon some beans and cooking liquid onto each of 8 large dinner plates. Top each with 1 lamb shank and 2 endive halves. Garnish with a rosemary sprig. Makes 8 main-dish servings.

Each serving lamb and beans: About 725 calories, 67g protein, 46g carbohydrate, 28g total fat (11g saturated), 198mg cholesterol, 1,110mg sodium.

Each serving endive: About 30 calories, 1g protein, 3g carbohydrate, 2g total fat (0g saturated), 0mg cholesterol, 145mg sodium.

Lamb Steak with Red Pepper Relish

Lamb steak, an often overlooked cut, is simply a thick crosswise slice of lamb leg that is every bit as delicious as you'd expect.

Prep: 30 minutes   Broil: 10 minutes

- ⅓ cup cider vinegar
- ¼ cup sugar
- 1¼ teaspoons salt
-     pinch dried thyme, crumbled
-     pinch fennel seeds, crushed
- 2 small red peppers, chopped
- 1 medium Golden Delicious apple, peeled, cored, and chopped
- 2 jalapeño chiles, seeded and finely chopped
- 1 center-cut lamb steak, 1 inch thick (1½ pounds), or 8 lamb loin chops, 1 inch thick (4 ounces each)

1. In 2-quart saucepan, combine vinegar, sugar, 1 teaspoon salt, thyme, and fennel seeds; heat to boiling over high heat. Add red peppers, apple, and jalapeños; heat to boiling. Reduce heat and simmer, stirring occasionally, until liquid has evaporated, 15 to 20 minutes. Keep warm.

2. Meanwhile, preheat broiler. Sprinkle lamb with remaining ¼ teaspoon salt. Place lamb on rack in broiling pan. Place pan in broiler at closest position to heat source and broil lamb 5 minutes. Turn lamb and broil 5 minutes longer for medium-rare or until desired doneness. Serve lamb with warm red pepper relish. Makes 4 main-dish servings.

Each serving: About 267 calories, 26g protein, 21g carbohydrate, 9g total fat (3g saturated), 82mg cholesterol, 799mg sodium.

Glazed Rosemary Lamb Chops

These rosemary-scented lamb chops are broiled with an apple-jelly and balsamic-vinegar glaze. Keep this glaze in mind for pork, too.

Prep: 10 minutes   Broil: 10 minutes

- 8 lamb loin chops, 1 inch thick (4 ounces each)
- 1 large garlic clove, cut in half
- 2 teaspoons chopped fresh rosemary or ½ teaspoon dried rosemary, crumbled
- ¼ teaspoon salt
- ¼ teaspoon coarsely ground black pepper
- ¼ cup apple jelly
- 1 tablespoon balsamic vinegar

1. Preheat broiler. Rub both sides of chops with cut side of garlic; sprinkle with rosemary, salt, and pepper. In cup, combine apple jelly and vinegar.

2. Place chops on rack in broiling pan. Place pan in broiler at closest position to heat source; broil chops 4 minutes. Brush chops with half of apple-jelly mixture; broil 1 minute. Turn chops and broil 4 minutes longer. Brush chops with remaining jelly mixture and broil 1 minute longer for medium-rare or until desired doneness.

3. Transfer lamb to warm platter. Skim and discard fat from drippings in pan. Serve chops with pan juices, or drizzle with additional balsamic vinegar. Makes 4 main-dish servings.

Each serving: About 240 calories, 26g protein, 14g carbohydrate, 8g total fat (3g saturated), 82mg cholesterol, 223mg sodium.

Shepherd's Pie

Traditional shepherd's pie is made with lamb. If you use beef instead, it's called Cottage Pie. Either way, it's real comfort food.

Prep: 40 minutes   Bake: 20 minutes

- 2 pounds all-purpose potatoes, peeled and cut into quarters
- ½ cup milk
- 3 tablespoons butter or margarine
- ¼ cup plus 1 tablespoon freshly grated Parmesan cheese
- 1 teaspoon salt
- ¼ plus ⅛ teaspoon ground black pepper
- 1 medium onion, chopped
- 2 carrots, peeled and chopped
- 1 pound ground lamb
- 2 tablespoons tomato paste
- 2 tablespoons all-purpose flour
- ¼ cup dry red wine
- 1 cup chicken broth
- ¼ teaspoon dried thyme
- 1 cup frozen peas

1. Preheat oven to 425°F. In 4-quart saucepan, combine potatoes and enough *water* to cover; heat to boiling. Boil until potatoes are tender, about 20 minutes; drain and return to saucepan. With potato masher, mash potatoes with milk and 2 tablespoons butter. Stir in ¼ cup Parmesan, ½ teaspoon salt, and ¼ teaspoon pepper; set aside.

2. Meanwhile, in nonstick 10-inch skillet, melt remaining 1 tablespoon butter over medium heat. Add onion and carrots; cook until vegetables are tender, about 5 minutes. Add ground lamb and cook over medium-high heat, stirring and breaking up meat with spoon, until lamb is no longer pink, about 5 minutes. Skim and discard fat. Add tomato paste and cook, stirring, 1 minute. Add flour and cook, stirring, 1 minute longer. Stir in wine and cook until wine has evaporated. Add broth, thyme, remaining ½ teaspoon salt, and remaining ⅛ teaspoon pepper, stirring until browned bits are loosened from bottom of skillet. Heat to boiling; stir in peas.

3. Transfer lamb mixture to 9-inch deep-dish pie plate. Spoon mashed potatoes evenly on top and sprinkle with remaining 1 tablespoon Parmesan. Place on foil-lined cookie sheet and bake until slightly browned, about 20 minutes. Makes 4 main-dish servings.

Each serving: About 599 calories, 31g protein, 50g carbohydrate, 31g total fat (15g saturated), 113mg cholesterol, 1,272mg sodium.

Panfried Calf's Liver and Bacon

A classic combination of crispy bacon and panfried liver.

Prep: 10 minutes   Cook: 8 minutes

- 4 slices bacon
- 3 tablespoons all-purpose flour
- 4 slices calf's liver, ½ inch thick (1 pound)
- ¼ teaspoon salt
  chopped fresh parsley
- 1 small lemon, cut into 4 wedges

1. In 12-inch skillet, cook bacon over medium-high heat until browned. With slotted spoon, transfer bacon to paper towels to drain; keep warm.

2. Place flour on waxed paper. Coat liver with flour, shaking off excess.

3. Discard all but 1 tablespoon bacon drippings from skillet. Add liver slices to hot drippings in skillet and cook over medium-high heat until crisp and browned but slightly pink inside, 1½ to 2 minutes per side. (Don't overcook, or liver will be tough.) Sprinkle with salt.

4. Place liver and bacon on warm platter; sprinkle with parsley and serve with lemon wedges. Makes 4 main-dish servings.

Each serving: About 233 calories, 23g protein, 10g carbohydrate, 11g total fat (4g saturated), 358mg cholesterol, 331mg sodium.

5

POULTRY

All around the globe, poultry has found its way into just about every kitchen. It is prized for its versatility and for the ease with which it can be combined with a vast range of ingredients. Whether you are preparing chicken gumbo to be served over steamed rice, a succulent and juicy golden brown turkey to grace the holiday table, or an Italian classic like chicken cacciatore, these dishes are guaranteed to satisfy family and friends alike.

The United States Department of Agriculture inspection sticker on poultry guarantees that it was raised and processed according to strict government guidelines. Grade A birds, the most common variety in supermarkets, are the highest quality. And more than 90 percent of all broiler-fryers (chickens that range from about 2 ½ to 4 pounds) are marketed under a brand name, a further assurance of quality.

KNOW YOUR CHICKEN

Broiler-fryers Tender young birds that weigh 3 to 5 pounds. They can be roasted, fried, sautéed, grilled, or broiled.

Roasters Meaty birds that usually weigh 6 to 8 pounds and are best when roasted.

Cornish hens Small birds that weigh up to 2 pounds each. They are tasty grilled, broiled, and roasted.

Fowl Also called stewing hens, these tough older birds are available especially around the holidays. They are always braised or stewed and make the tastiest chicken broth.

Capons Neutered male chickens that weigh 8 to 10 pounds on average. They are very meaty and tender and are usually roasted.

POULTRY SHOPPING CHOICES

Organic The term *organic* is not recognized by the USDA, so it cannot appear on labels. The term can be used in advertisements to promote a brand, however. Generally, organic poultry has been raised on organically grown, antibiotic-free feed.

Free-range These birds have been raised in an environment that provides access to open spaces but not necessarily an open farmyard. This free movement allows them to develop more muscle, which contributes to fuller-flavored meat.

All-natural This simply means that the poultry has been minimally processed. Its feed was not necessarily organic and might have contained antibiotics.

Kosher Kosher birds have been processed according to Kosher dietary laws under the strict supervision of a rabbi. The procedure includes salting to draw out the blood and season the meat.

Halal If you live in an area that has a Muslim community, there is probably a Halal butcher. These birds are not fed hormones and are slaughtered manually while a special prayer is recited.

POULTRY SENSE

POULTRY	READY-TO-COOK WEIGHT	SERVINGS	STUFFING
Broiler-fryer	2½ to 4½ pounds	2 to 4	1 to 3 cups
Roasting chicken	5 to 7 pounds	5 to 7	3 to 6 cups
Capon	6 to 8 pounds	6 to 8	3 to 6 cups
Cornish hen	1 to 2 pounds	1 to 2	¾ to 1½ cups
Turkey	8 to 12 pounds	6 to 8	6 to 9 cups
	12 to 16 pounds	12 to 16	9 to 12 cups
	16 to 20 pounds	16 to 20	12 to 15 cups
	20 to 24 pounds	20 to 24	15 to 18 cups
Turkey breast	4 to 6 pounds	5 to 8	—
Turkey breast (boneless)	4 to 6 pounds	5 to 8	—
Duck	4 to 5 pounds	4	3 to 4 cups
Goose	10 to 12 pounds	6 to 8	6 to 9 cups

BUYING FRESH AND FROZEN POULTRY

Look for fresh whole birds that appear plump and have meaty breasts. Chicken sold as parts should also look plump. Poultry skin should be smooth and moist and free of bruises and pinfeathers. The color of the skin can range from creamy white to yellow, depending on the bird's feed and breed, and is not an indication of flavor or quality. In general, tenderness depends on the age of the bird.

Buy fresh poultry according to the "sell-by" date on the package. When you open the package, the chicken may have a slight odor. This is caused by oxidation and should disappear once the bird is rinsed with cold running water. If the poultry still smells, return it to the market. Be sure to avoid packages with leaks or tears.

If you buy frozen poultry, be sure the meat is rock-hard and without any signs of freezer burn, and make sure there are no ice crystals. The packaging should be tightly sealed and intact. Frozen liquid in the bottom can indicate that the bird was thawed and refrozen.

HANDLING AND STORING POULTRY

Store raw poultry in its original store wrapping on a plate to catch any leaks. If wrapped in butcher paper, remove the paper and place the bird in a large plastic bag. Keep poultry in the coldest part of the refrigerator (usually the bottom shelf), away from cooked or ready-to-eat foods and use within two days. Store uncooked giblets separately in the refrigerator and use within a day, or wrap and freeze for up to one month.

Be sure to wash your hands, the cutting board, and any utensils that have come in contact with raw poultry with hot, soapy water. To destroy germs, bleach your cutting board once a week or so with a solution of 1 tablespoon chlorine bleach to 1 gallon warm water.

Freeze raw poultry for up to six months. Ground poultry will keep in the refrigerator for one day or in the freezer for up to three months. Cool cooked poultry as quickly as possible, then cover and refrigerate up to three days, or tightly wrap and freeze for up to three months.

THAWING POULTRY SAFELY

For safety's sake, thaw poultry either in the refrigerator or by immersion in cold water—not on the kitchen counter at room temperature.

Thawing in the refrigerator This is the preferred method. Leave the bird in its original wrapper, and place it on a tray to catch any drips. As a general rule, allow about six hours per pound. For example, a 24-pound turkey will take approximately four days to thaw completely.

Thawing in cold water If there's no time to thaw the bird in the refrigerator, use this method, which takes less time but requires more attention. Place the bird (in its original wrapper or in a watertight plastic bag) in a large pan or in the sink with enough cold water to cover. (Warm water thaws poultry too quickly and can encourage bacterial growth.) Change the water every 30 minutes to maintain the temperature. Allow about 30 minutes of thawing time per pound, then add 1 hour to that total.

5 THAWING TIPS

- Frozen poultry should be thawed completely before being cooked.
- Remove giblets as soon as possible during thawing, then wrap and refrigerate.
- A bird is thawed if the ice crystals have disappeared from the body cavity and the meat is soft and the joints are flexible.
- Once thawed, cook the bird within 12 hours.
- For reasons of texture—not safety—do not refreeze thawed poultry.

ROASTING TIMES

POULTRY	READY-TO-COOK WEIGHT	COOKING TIME (UNSTUFFED)	COOKING TIME (STUFFED)
Chicken (at 350°F)	2½ to 3 pounds	1¼ to 1½ hours	1¼ to 1½ hours
	3 to 4½ pounds	1½ to 1¾ hours	1½ to 1¾ hours
	5 to 7 pounds	2 to 2¼ hours	2 to 2¼ hours
Capon (at 325°F)	5 to 6 pounds	2 to 2½ hours	2½ to 3 hours
	6 to 8 pounds	2½ to 3½ hours	3 to 4 hours
Cornish hen (at 350°F)	1 to 2 pounds	1 to 1¼ hours	1 to 1¼ hours
Turkey (at 325°F)	Variations in roasting conditions could increase indicated roasting times up to 30 minutes.		
	8 to 12 pounds	2¾ to 3 hours	3 to 3½ hours
	12 to 14 pounds	3 to 3¾ hours	3½ to 4 hours
	14 to 18 pounds	3¾ to 4¼ hours	4 to 4¼ hours
	18 to 20 pounds	4¼ to 4½ hours	4¼ to 4¾ hours
	20 to 24 pounds	4½ to 5 hours	4¾ to 5½ hours
Duck (at 350°F)	4 to 5 pounds	2½ to 2¾ hours	2½ to 2¾ hours
Goose (at 350°F)	10 to 12 pounds	2¾ to 3¼ hours	3 to 3½ hours

Apple and Thyme Roast Chicken

The tempting aroma of fresh apples, thyme sprigs, and allspice will fill your kitchen.

Prep: 20 minutes	Roast: 1 hour

- 1 chicken (3½ pounds)
- 2 sprigs plus 1 tablespooon chopped fresh thyme
- ¾ teaspoon salt
- ¼ teaspoon coarsely ground black pepper
- ⅛ teaspoon ground allspice
- 1 jumbo onion (1 pound), cut into 12 wedges
- ¼ cup water
- 2 teaspoons olive oil
- 2 large Granny Smith apples, each cored and cut into quarters
- 2 tablespoons applejack brandy or Calvados
- ½ cup chicken broth

1. Preheat oven to 450°F. Remove giblets and neck from chicken; reserve for another use. Pat chicken dry with paper towels.

2. With fingertips, gently separate skin from meat on chicken breast. Place 1 thyme sprig under skin of each breast half. In cup, combine chopped thyme, salt, pepper, and allspice.

3. With chicken breast side up, lift wings up toward neck, then fold wing tips under back of chicken so wings stay in place. Tie legs together with string.

4. In medium roasting pan (14" by 10"), toss onion, chopped-thyme mixture, water, and oil. Push onion mixture to sides of pan. Place chicken, breast side up, on small rack in center of roasting pan.

5. Roast chicken and onion mixture 40 minutes. Add apples to pan; roast about 20 minutes longer. Chicken is done when temperature on meat thermometer inserted in thickest part of thigh, next to body, reaches 175° to 180°F and juices run clear when thigh is pierced with tip of knife.

6. Transfer chicken to warm platter; let stand 10 minutes to set juices for easier carving.

7. Meanwhile, remove rack from roasting pan. With slotted spoon, transfer onion mixture to platter with chicken. Skim and discard fat from drippings in pan. Add applejack to pan  drippings; cook 1 minute over medium heat, stirring constantly. Add broth; heat to boiling. Serve pan-juice mixture with chicken. Remove skin from chicken before eating, if desired. Makes 4 main-dish servings.

Each serving with skin: About 589 calories, 49g protein, 22g carbohydrate, 33g total fat (9g saturated), 159mg cholesterol, 708mg sodium.

Each serving without skin: About 441 calories, 43g protein, 22g carbohydrate, 20g total fat (5g saturated), 132mg cholesterol, 686mg sodium.

CARVING TIPS

Test Kitchen Tip Letting the bird rest after roasting results in firmer, juicier meat that is easier to carve. Poultry should stand at least ten minutes before carving so the simmering juices can relax back into the meat. When carving, use a sharp thin-bladed knife that is long enough to slice off the breast of large birds like turkey or long-bodied birds such as duck or goose.

Roast Chicken with Forty Cloves of Garlic

Slow roasting mellows garlic to a sweet nuttiness. Serve with lots of crusty bread for spreading the extra garlic.

Prep: 15 minutes   Roast: 1 hour

- 1 chicken (3½ pounds)
- 6 thyme sprigs
- ½ teaspoon salt
- ¼ teaspoon coarsely ground black pepper
- 40 garlic cloves (2 heads), loose papery skin discarded but not peeled
- 1 cup chicken broth

1. Preheat oven to 450°F. Remove giblets and neck from chicken; reserve for another use. Pat chicken dry with paper towels.

2. With fingertips, gently separate skin from meat on chicken breast. Place 2 thyme sprigs under skin of each breast half. Place remaining 2 sprigs inside cavity of chicken. Sprinkle salt and pepper on outside of chicken.

3. With chicken breast side up, lift wings up toward neck, then fold wing tips under back of chicken so wings stay in place. Tie legs together with string. Place chicken, breast side up, on rack in small roasting pan (13" by 9").

4. Roast chicken 30 minutes. Add garlic cloves to pan; roast about 30 minutes longer. Chicken is done when temperature on meat thermometer inserted in thickest part of thigh, next to body, reaches 175° to 180°F and juices run clear when thigh is pierced with tip of knife.

5. Transfer chicken to warm platter; let stand 10 minutes to set juices for easier carving.

6. Meanwhile, remove rack from roasting pan. With slotted spoon, transfer garlic cloves to small bowl. Skim and discard fat from drippings in pan. Remove and discard skin from 6 garlic cloves; return peeled garlic to roasting pan and add broth. Heat broth mixture to boiling over medium heat, stirring to loosen browned bits from bottom of pan and mashing garlic with back of spoon until well blended. Serve chicken with pan juices and remaining garlic cloves. Remove skin from chicken before eating, if desired. Makes 4 main-dish servings.

CARVING A ROAST CHICKEN

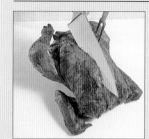

To remove the breast meat, using a thin sharp knife, start along one side of the breastbone, cutting down along the rib cage (scraping against the bones as you go), cutting off the breast meat in one piece. Repeat on the other side.

To carve the breast meat, holding the knife at a slight angle, cut the meat crosswise into even slices.

To remove a chicken leg, force it away from the body with a carving fork until it pops out of its socket. Separate the thigh from the body by cutting through the joint. If you like, separate the drumstick from the thigh by cutting through the center joint. Repeat on the other side. To remove the wings, cut through the joints where the wings meet the body.

Each serving with skin: About 501 calories, 50g protein, 11g carbohydrate, 28g total fat (8g saturated), 157mg cholesterol, 688mg sodium.

Each serving without skin: About 352 calories, 44g protein, 10g carbohydrate, 14g total fat (4g saturated), 129mg cholesterol, 667mg sodium.

Mahogany Roast Chicken

Give your roast chicken a deep amber glaze by brushing it with a simple mix of balsamic vinegar, brown sugar, and dry vermouth.

Prep: 10 minutes   Roast: 1 hour 15 minutes

- 1 chicken (3½ pounds)
- ¾ teaspoon salt
- ½ teaspoon coarsely ground black pepper
- 2 tablespoons dark brown sugar
- 2 tablespoons balsamic vinegar
- 2 tablespoons dry vermouth
- ¼ cup water

1. Preheat oven to 375°F. Remove giblets and neck from chicken; reserve for another use. Rinse chicken inside and out with cold running water; drain. Pat dry with paper towels. Sprinkle salt and pepper on outside of chicken.

2. With chicken breast side up, lift wings up toward neck, then fold wing tips under back of chicken so wings stay in place. Tie legs together with string. Place chicken, breast side up, on rack in small roasting pan (13" by 9"). Roast chicken 45 minutes.

3. Meanwhile, prepare glaze: In small bowl, stir brown sugar, vinegar, and vermouth until sugar has dissolved.

4. After chicken has roasted 45 minutes, brush with some glaze. Turn oven control to 400°F and roast chicken, brushing with glaze twice more during roasting, until chicken is deep brown, about 30 minutes longer. Chicken is done when temperature on meat thermometer inserted in thickest part of thigh, next to body, reaches 175° to 180°F and juices run clear when thigh is pierced with tip of knife.

5. Transfer chicken to warm platter; let stand 10 minutes to set juices for easier carving.

6. Meanwhile, remove rack from roasting pan. Skim and discard fat from drippings in pan. Add water to pan; heat to boiling over medium heat, stirring until browned bits are loosened from bottom of pan. Serve chicken with pan juices. Makes 4 main-dish servings.

Each serving with skin: About 446 calories, 48g protein, 7g carbohydrate, 24g total fat (7g saturated), 154mg cholesterol, 583mg sodium.

Roast Lemon Chicken

For an easy dinner when company calls, roast a succulent extra-large chicken.

Prep: 10 minutes   Roast: 1 hour 30 minutes to 2 hours

- 1 roasting chicken or capon (7 pounds)
- 2 lemons
- 1 bunch thyme
- 2 garlic cloves
- ¾ teaspoon salt
- ½ teaspoon ground black pepper
- 1¼ cups chicken broth
- 2 teaspoons cornstarch
- 1 tablespoon cold water

1. Preheat oven to 375°F. Remove giblets and neck from chicken; reserve for another use. Pat chicken dry with paper towels.

2. From 1 lemon, cut 4 thin round slices. Cut remainder of lemon and second lemon into quarters. With fingertips, separate skin from meat on chicken breast. Place 2 lemon slices under skin of each breast half. Set aside several thyme sprigs for garnish. Place garlic cloves, lemon quarters, and remaining thyme sprigs inside cavity of chicken. Sprinkle chicken with ½ teaspoon salt and ¼ teaspoon pepper.

3. With chicken breast side up, lift wings up toward neck, then fold wing tips under back of chicken so wings stay in place. Tie legs together with string. Place chicken, breast side up, on rack in medium roasting pan (14" by 10").

4. Roast chicken, basting occasionally with pan drippings, 1 hour 30 minutes to 2 hours. When chicken turns golden brown, cover loosely with tent of foil to prevent overbrowning. Chicken is done when temperature on meat thermometer inserted in thickest part of thigh, next to body, reaches 175°F and juices run clear when thigh is pierced with tip of knife.

5. Transfer chicken to warm platter; let stand 15 minutes to set juices for easier carving.

6. Meanwhile, prepare gravy: Remove rack from roasting pan. Skim and discard fat from drippings. Add broth to pan, stirring until browned bits are loosened from pan. In cup, blend cornstarch and water. Stir cornstarch mixture into broth. Add remaining ¼ teaspoon each salt and pepper. Heat to boiling over high heat, stirring; boil 1 minute.

7. Garnish chicken with reserved thyme sprigs. Serve with gravy. Remove skin from chicken before eating, if desired. Makes 8 main-dish servings.

Each serving with skin: About 469 calories, 50g protein, 3g carbohydrate, 28g total fat (8g saturated), 156mg cholesterol, 525mg sodium.

Each serving without skin: About 291 calories, 42g protein, 3g carbohydrate, 11g total fat (3g saturated), 125mg cholesterol, 500mg sodium.

Lemon-Roasted Chicken for a Crowd

When you need a special dish for a big party but you don't have time to fuss, turn to this tasty crowd-pleasing recipe.

Prep: 20 minutes   Roast: 1 hour 30 minutes

- 1½ cups fresh lemon juice (7 large lemons)
- ¼ cup vegetable oil
- 1 large onion (12 ounces), finely chopped
- 2 large garlic cloves, crushed with garlic press
- 1 tablespoon plus 2 teaspoons salt
- 1 tablespoon dried thyme
- 2 teaspoons ground black pepper
- 5 chickens (3 pounds each),
     each cut into quarters

1. Preheat oven to 375°F. In medium bowl, combine lemon juice, oil, onion, garlic, salt, thyme, and pepper. In two large roasting pans (17" by 11½"), arrange chicken, skin side up. Pour lemon-juice mixture over chicken.

2. Roast chicken, basting occasionally with pan juices, until juices run clear when thickest part of chicken is pierced with tip of knife, about 1 hour 30 minutes.

3. Transfer chicken to warm platters. Skim and discard fat from drippings in pan; pour pan drippings into medium bowl. Spoon some pan juices over chicken and serve chicken with remaining juices. Makes 20 main-dish servings.

Each serving: About 381 calories, 41g protein, 3g carbohydrate, 22g total fat (6g saturated), 132mg cholesterol, 706mg sodium.

CUTTING UP A RAW CHICKEN

To remove a leg, cut down between the thigh and the body. Bend the leg portion back; twist to crack the hip joint. Cut through the joint. Repeat for the other leg.

To separate the leg from the thigh, place the leg skin side down and cut through the center joint. Repeat with the other leg.

To remove a wing, pull the wing away from the body, then cut between the wing joint and the breast. Repeat with the other wing.

Using kitchen shears, cut through the rib cage along one side of the backbone from the tail to the neck. Repeat on the other side to remove the backbone in one piece.

Place the breast skin side down and cut in half by placing a heavy knife lengthwise along the center of the breastbone. Press the knife to cut through the bone and meat.

Baked "Fried" Chicken

For this healthier version of fried chicken, skinless chicken pieces are dipped in a spicy bread-crumb coating and baked until crispy and golden brown. We guarantee that you won't miss the calories.

Prep: 15 minutes   Bake: 35 minutes

- olive oil nonstick cooking spray
- ½ cup plain dried bread crumbs
- ¼ cup freshly grated Parmesan cheese
- 2 tablespoons cornmeal
- ½ teaspoon ground red pepper (cayenne)
- 1 large egg white
- ½ teaspoon salt
- 1 chicken (3½ pounds), cut into 8 pieces and skin removed from all but wings

1. Preheat oven to 425°F. Grease 15½" by 10½" jelly-roll pan with cooking spray.

2. On waxed paper, combine bread crumbs, Parmesan, cornmeal, and ground red pepper. In pie plate, beat egg white and salt.

3. Dip each piece of chicken in egg-white mixture, then coat with crumb mixture, pressing firmly so mixture adheres. Arrange chicken in prepared pan; lightly coat chicken with cooking spray.

4. Bake chicken until coating is crisp and golden brown and juices run clear when thickest part of chicken is pierced with tip of knife, about 35 minutes. Makes 4 main-dish servings.

Each serving: About 329 calories, 46g protein, 14g carbohydrate, 9g fat (3g saturated), 137mg cholesterol, 660mg sodium.

Thyme-Roasted Chicken and Vegetables

In just over an hour, you can have a one-dish meal of roasted chicken with fennel, potatoes, and onion ready to bring to the table.

Prep: 20 minutes   Roast: 50 minutes

- 1 chicken (3½ pounds), cut into 8 pieces and skin removed from all but wings
- 1 pound all-purpose potatoes (3 medium), not peeled, cut into 2-inch pieces
- 1 large fennel bulb (1½ pounds), trimmed and cut into 8 wedges
- 1 large red onion, cut into 8 wedges
- 1 tablespoon chopped fresh thyme or 1 teaspoon dried thyme
- 1 teaspoon salt
- ½ teaspoon ground black pepper
- 2 tablespoons olive oil
- ⅓ cup water

1. Preheat oven to 450°F. In large roasting pan (17" by 11½"), arrange chicken, and place potatoes, fennel, and onion around it. Sprinkle chicken with thyme, salt, and pepper. Drizzle oil over chicken and vegetables.

2. Roast chicken and vegetables 20 minutes; baste with drippings in pan. Roast, basting once more, until juices run clear when chicken breasts are pierced with tip of knife, about 20 minutes longer. Transfer chicken breasts to platter; keep warm.

3. Continue roasting remaining chicken pieces until juices run clear when thickest part of chicken is pierced with tip of knife and vegetables are fork-tender, about 10 minutes longer. Transfer chicken and vegetables to platter with breasts; keep warm.

4. Skim and discard fat from drippings in pan. To drippings, add water; heat to boiling over medium heat, stirring until brown bits are loosened from bottom. Spoon pan juices over chicken and vegetables. Makes 4 main-dish servings.

Each serving: About 401 calories, 43g protein, 28g carbohydrate, 13g total fat (2g saturated), 124mg cholesterol, 870mg sodium.

Picnic Chicken with Three Sauces

This walnut-crusted baked chicken is delicious hot or cold, especially when dipped into one of our easy sauces.

Prep: 30 minutes   Bake: 30 minutes

olive oil nonstick cooking spray
1¾ cups walnuts (about 8 ounces)
1 cup plain dried bread crumbs
1½ teaspoons salt
¼ to ½ teaspoon ground red pepper (cayenne)
2 large eggs
8 medium bone-in chicken breast halves (4 pounds), skin removed
8 medium chicken drumsticks (1¾ pounds), skin removed
choice of sauce (right)

1. Preheat oven to 425°F. Grease two 15½" by 10½" jelly-roll pans with cooking spray.

2. In food processor with knife blade attached, process walnuts with ¼ cup bread crumbs until walnuts are finely ground. In medium bowl, combine nut mixture, salt, ground red pepper, and remaining ¾ cup bread crumbs; stir until well mixed. In pie plate, beat eggs.

3. Cut each chicken breast half crosswise into two pieces. One at a time, dip breast pieces and drumsticks in beaten egg, then into walnut mixture to coat evenly, pressing firmly so mixture adheres. Arrange chicken in jelly-roll pans; lightly coat chicken with cooking spray.

4. Bake chicken until golden brown and juices run clear when thickest part of chicken is pierced with tip of knife, 30 to 35 minutes, rotating pans between upper and lower oven racks halfway through baking.

5. Meanwhile, prepare sauce. Cover and refrigerate sauce if not serving right away.

6. Serve chicken hot with dipping sauce, or cool chicken slightly, cover, and refrigerate to serve cold later with sauce. Makes 12 main-dish servings.

Each serving without sauce: About 311 calories, 32g protein, 10g carbohydrate, 16g total fat (2g saturated), 113mg cholesterol, 468mg sodium.

REMOVING SKIN FROM RAW CHICKEN

To remove the skin from a chicken thigh, grasp the skin tightly and pull it off in one piece. If you like, grasp the skin with a piece of paper towel or dip your fingers into a little coarse salt to get a better grip.

To remove the skin from a drumstick, grasp the skin at the meaty end of the drumstick; pull the skin down and off the end of the drumstick. (If necessary, use a sharp knife to cut the skin off.)

To remove the skin from a chicken breast, grasp the skin at the thin end of breast and pull it off. (It is difficult to remove the skin from chicken wings—don't bother.)

Blue-Cheese Sauce

In medium bowl, combine **4 ounces blue cheese, crumbled (1 cup), ½ cup mayonnaise, ½ cup plain lowfat yogurt, ½ teaspoon hot pepper sauce,** and **¼ teaspoon coarsely ground black pepper** until blended. Makes about 1½ cups sauce.

Each tablespoon: About 53 calories, 1g protein, 1g carbohydrate, 5g total fat (1g saturated), 7mg cholesterol, 98mg sodium.

Creamy Honey-Mustard Sauce

In medium bowl, combine **⅔ cup Dijon mustard, ¼ cup sour cream, ¼ cup honey,** and **¾ teaspoon Worcestershire sauce** until well blended. Makes about 1¼ cups sauce.

Each tablespoon: About 27 calories, 0g protein, 4g carbohydrate, 1g total fat (0g saturated), 1mg cholesterol, 197mg sodium.

Apricot-Balsamic Sauce

In medium bowl, combine **1 jar (12 ounces) apricot preserves, 2 tablespoons balsamic vinegar, 1 tablespoon soy sauce,** and **¼ teaspoon freshly grated orange peel** until well blended. Makes about 1¼ cups sauce.

Each tablespoon: About 42 calories, 0g protein, 11g carbohydrate, 0g total fat (0g saturated), 0mg cholesterol, 58mg sodium.

Asparagus-Chicken Roulades

When food is butterflied, it is cut horizontally almost in half, then opened flat, resembling a butterfly.

Prep: 18 minutes   Cook 10 minutes

- 4 medium skinless, boneless chicken breast halves (1¼ pounds)
- 1 lemon
- 3 ounces goat cheese, softened
- ½ cup loosely packed fresh mint leaves, chopped
- ¾ pound thin asparagus, trimmed
- ¼ teaspoon ground black pepper
- ¼ teaspoon salt
- 1 tablespoon olive oil
- ½ cup chicken broth

1. Holding knife parallel to work surface and against a long side of chicken-breast half, cut chicken almost in half, making sure not to cut all the way through. Open breast half and spread flat like a book. Repeat with remaining chicken.

2. From lemon, grate ½ teaspoon peel and squeeze 1 tablespoon juice; set aside juice. In small bowl, stir goat cheese, mint, and lemon peel until mixed.

3. Spread goat-cheese mixture evenly on cut sides of breast halves. Place one-fourth of uncooked asparagus on a long side of each breast half. Roll up each breast half to enclose asparagus, allowing ends of stalks to stick out if necessary; secure with toothpicks. Sprinkle chicken roulades with pepper and salt.

4. In nonstick 12-inch skillet, heat oil over medium-high heat until hot. Add roulades and cook, covered, 9 to 11 minutes or until chicken loses its pink color throughout, turning roulades to brown all sides.

5. Transfer roulades to cutting board; keep warm. To same skillet, add broth and reserved lemon juice; heat to boiling, scraping up any browned bits. Remove skillet from heat.

6. To serve, discard toothpicks from roulades. Cut roulades crosswise into 1-inch-thick slices. Place each sliced roulade on a dinner plate; drizzle with pan sauce. Makes 4 main-dish servings.

Each serving: About 265 calories, 39g protein, 2g carbohydrate, 10g total fat (4g saturated), 92mg cholesterol, 450mg sodium.

Coq au Vin

This well-known dish, which is basically chicken stewed in a red-wine sauce, is a specialty of the Burgundy region of France. Use a moderately priced California or Oregon Pinot Noir, which is made from the same grape as more expensive French Burgundy.

Prep: 45 minutes   Bake: 45 minutes

4	slices bacon, cut into ¾-inch pieces
4	tablespoons butter or margarine
¼	teaspoon salt
⅛	teaspoon ground black pepper
1	chicken (3½ pounds), cut into 8 pieces and skin removed from all but wings
1	small onion, finely chopped
1	carrot, peeled and finely chopped
18	pearl onions (generous 1 cup), peeled
10	ounces mushrooms, trimmed
⅓	cup all-purpose flour
2	cups dry red wine
1⅓	cups chicken broth
2	tablespoons tomato paste
1	stalk celery
12	sprigs plus 3 tablespoons chopped parsley
2	bay leaves

1. Preheat oven to 325°F. In 5-quart Dutch oven, cook bacon over medium-high heat until crisp. With slotted spoon, transfer to paper towels to drain. Reduce heat to medium and add butter to drippings in pot. Sprinkle chicken with salt and pepper. Add chicken to Dutch oven, in batches if necessary, and cook until golden brown, about 5 minutes per side, using tongs to transfer chicken pieces to bowl as they are browned.

2. Add chopped onion and carrot to Dutch oven and cook until lightly browned, about 5 minutes. With slotted spoon, transfer to bowl with chicken. Add pearl onions to Dutch oven and cook, stirring, until browned, about 6 minutes; transfer to bowl. Add mushrooms to pot and cook, stirring, until browned, about 6 minutes; transfer to bowl.

3. Add flour to Dutch oven and cook, stirring, 2 minutes. With wire whisk, whisk in ½ cup wine until smooth. Add remaining 1½ cups wine, broth, and tomato paste. Heat to boiling, whisking constantly; boil 2 minutes. Return chicken, vegetables, and three-fourths of bacon to Dutch oven.

4. With string, tie together celery, parsley sprigs, and bay leaves; add to Dutch oven. Cover and place in oven. Bake, stirring occasionally, 45 minutes.

5. When chicken is tender and sauce is slightly thickened, skim fat and discard celery bundle. Sprinkle coq au vin with remaining bacon and chopped parsley. Makes 6 main-dish servings.

Each serving: About 414 calories, 32g protein, 17g carbohydrate, 24g total fat (10g saturated), 115mg cholesterol, 645mg sodium.

Chicken Curry

Serve curry over rice with an array of condiments. Chopped cilantro, chopped peanuts, shredded coconut, golden raisins, cucumber sticks, mango chutney, toasted slivered almonds, and sliced bananas are popular items but by no means the only possibilities.

Prep: 15 minutes plus cooling
Cook: 1 hour 15 minutes

1	chicken (3½ pounds), cut into 8 pieces
4	medium onions, finely chopped
2	carrots, peeled and finely chopped
2	stalks celery with leaves, finely chopped
8	parsley sprigs
1	lime
4	tablespoons butter or margarine
2	Granny Smith apples, peeled, cored, and chopped
3	garlic cloves, finely chopped
1	tablespoon curry powder
3	tablespoons all-purpose flour
½	cup half-and-half or light cream
⅓	cup golden raisins
2	tablespoons mango chutney, chopped
2	teaspoons minced, peeled fresh ginger
½	teaspoon salt
	pinch ground red pepper (cayenne)

1. In 5-quart Dutch oven, combine chicken, one-fourth onions, carrots, celery, and parsley sprigs. Add just enough *water* to cover. Heat to boiling over high heat. Reduce heat; partially cover and simmer, turning once, until chicken loses its pink color throughout, 25 to 30 minutes. Using tongs, transfer chicken to bowl. When cool enough to handle, remove and discard skin and bones; with hands, shred chicken.

2. Meanwhile, strain broth through sieve, discarding vegetables. Return broth to Dutch oven; heat to boiling and boil until reduced to 2 cups. Skim and discard fat from broth; reserve broth.

3. From lime, grate ½ teaspoon peel and squeeze 5 teaspoons juice; set aside.

4. In 12-inch skillet, melt butter over medium heat. Add remaining three-fourths onions, apples, garlic, and curry powder and cook, stirring, until apples are tender, about 10 minutes. Sprinkle with flour, stirring to blend. Gradually add 2 cups reserved broth, stirring constantly until broth has thickened and boils. Stir in lime peel and juice, half-and-half, raisins, chutney, ginger, salt, and ground red pepper. Reduce heat and simmer, stirring occasionally, 5 minutes. Add chicken and heat through. Makes 6 main-dish servings.

Each serving: About 379 calories, 30g protein, 33g carbohydrate, 14g total fat (7g saturated), 117mg cholesterol, 449mg sodium.

Chicken Mole

Mole (MO-lay) is a thick, rich, dark brown Mexican sauce traditionally made with dried chiles, spices, seeds such as pumpkin, nuts, and a touch of unsweetened chocolate. Serve with rice and crisp tortillas.

Prep: 10 minutes   Cook: 45 minutes

1	can (14½ ounces) diced tomatoes
1	can (4 to 4½ ounces) chopped mild green chiles
½	cup whole blanched almonds
½	small onion, coarsely chopped
1	small garlic clove, peeled
1	tablespoon chili powder
1	teaspoon ground cumin
1	teaspoon ground coriander
¾	teaspoon ground cinnamon
¾	teaspoon salt
½	teaspoon sugar
1	tablespoon olive oil
3	pounds bone-in chicken parts, skin removed from all but wings
½	square (½ ounce) unsweetened chocolate, chopped
¼	cup water
2	tablespoons chopped fresh cilantro

1. Prepare mole sauce: In blender or in food processor with knife blade attached, puree tomatoes, chiles, almonds, onion, garlic, chili powder, cumin, coriander, cinnamon, salt, and sugar until smooth.

2. In nonstick 12-inch skillet, heat oil over medium-high heat until very hot. Add chicken and cook until golden brown, about 5 minutes per side, using tongs to transfer chicken pieces to large bowl as they are browned.

3. Add mole sauce, chocolate, and water to skillet; cook, stirring, until chocolate melts. Return chicken to skillet; heat to boiling. Reduce heat; cover and simmer until chicken juices run clear when chicken thigh is pierced with tip of knife, 30 to 35 minutes. Sprinkle with cilantro to serve. Makes 6 main-dish servings.

Each serving: About 263 calories, 27g protein, 9g carbohydrate, 14g total fat (3g saturated), 76mg cholesterol, 617mg sodium.

CUCUMBER RAITA

This classic accompaniment to Indian dishes can tame the heat of even the fiercest curry. Peel, seed, and coarsely shred 1 medium cucumber. Squeeze out as much liquid as possible. In a small bowl, combine the cucumber with 1 cup (8 ounces) plain yogurt. Season with salt and pepper. Add a tablespoon of chopped fresh mint, if you like.

Country Captain Casserole

Though the exact origin of this well-known dish is often debated, its great flavor is never in dispute.

Prep: 30 minutes   Bake: 1 hour

- 2 tablespoons plus 1 teaspoon vegetable oil
- 2 chickens (3½ pounds each), each cut into 8 pieces and skin removed from all but wings
- 2 medium onions, chopped
- 1 large Granny Smith apple, peeled, cored, and chopped
- 1 large green pepper, chopped
- 3 large garlic cloves, finely chopped
- 1 tablespoon grated, peeled fresh ginger
- 3 tablespoons curry powder
- ½ teaspoon coarsely ground black pepper
- ¼ teaspoon ground cumin
- 1 can (28 ounces) plum tomatoes in puree
- 1 can (14½ ounces) chicken broth or 1¾ cups Chicken Broth (page 62)
- ½ cup dark seedless raisins
- 1 teaspoon salt
- ¼ cup chopped fresh parsley

1. In nonreactive 8-quart Dutch oven, heat 2 tablespoons oil over medium-high heat until very hot. Add chicken, in batches, and cook until golden brown, about 5 minutes per side. Using tongs, transfer chicken pieces to bowl as they are browned.

2. Preheat oven to 350°F. In same Dutch oven, heat remaining 1 teaspoon oil over medium-high heat. Add onions, apple, green pepper, garlic, and ginger; cook, stirring frequently, 2 minutes. Reduce heat to medium; cover and cook 5 minutes longer.

3. Stir in curry powder, black pepper, and cumin; cook 1 minute. Add tomatoes with their puree, broth, raisins, salt, and chicken pieces, breaking up tomatoes with side of spoon. Heat to boiling over high heat; boil 1 minute. Cover and place in oven. Bake 1 hour. Sprinkle with parsley. Makes 8 main-dish servings.

Each serving: About 347 calories, 43g protein, 19g carbohydrate, 11g total fat (2g saturated), 133mg cholesterol, 825mg sodium.

Country Captain Casserole

Arroz con Pollo

From Madrid to Miami, different versions of this comforting dish are served almost anywhere Spanish is spoken.

Prep: 15 minutes   Cook: 40 minutes

1 tablespoon vegetable oil
6 medium bone-in chicken thighs (1½ pounds), skin and fat removed
1 medium onion, finely chopped
1 red pepper, chopped
1 garlic clove, finely chopped
⅛ teaspoon ground red pepper (cayenne)
1 cup regular long-grain rice
1 can (14½ ounces) chicken broth or 1¾ cups Chicken Broth (page 62)
¼ cup water
1 strip (3" by ½") lemon peel
¼ teaspoon dried oregano
¼ teaspoon salt
1 cup frozen peas
¼ cup chopped pimiento-stuffed olives (salad olives)
¼ cup chopped fresh cilantro
    lemon wedges

1. In 5-quart Dutch oven, heat oil over medium-high heat until very hot. Add chicken and cook until golden brown, about 5 minutes per side. With tongs, transfer chicken pieces to bowl as they are browned.

2. Reduce heat to medium. Add onion and red pepper to Dutch oven and cook until tender, about 5 minutes. Stir in garlic and ground red pepper and cook 30 seconds. Add rice and cook, stirring, 1 minute. Stir in broth, water, lemon peel, oregano, salt, and chicken; heat to boiling. Reduce heat; cover and simmer until juices run clear when thickest part of chicken is pierced with tip of knife, about 20 minutes.

3. Stir in peas; cover and heat through. Remove from heat and let stand 5 minutes.

4. Transfer chicken to serving bowl. Sprinkle with olives and cilantro; serve with lemon wedges. Makes 4 main-dish servings.

Each serving: About 387 calories, 26g protein, 48g carbohydrate, 9g total fat (2g saturated), 81mg cholesterol, 927mg sodium.

Chicken Cacciatore

Food prepared *alla cacciatore,* "hunter-style," includes mushrooms in the sauce. This dish is representative of the kind of home cooking that found its way first into Italian restaurants and then into American kitchens. Serve over wide, flat noodles.

Prep: 15 minutes   Cook: 40 minutes

2 tablespoons olive oil
1 chicken (3½ pounds), cut into 8 pieces and skin removed from all but wings
3 tablespoons all-purpose flour
1 medium onion, finely chopped
4 garlic cloves, crushed with garlic press
8 ounces mushrooms, trimmed and thickly sliced
1 can (14 to 16 ounces) tomatoes
½ teaspoon salt
½ teaspoon dried oregano, crumbled
¼ teaspoon dried sage
⅛ teaspoon ground red pepper (cayenne)

1. In nonstick 12-inch skillet, heat oil over medium-high heat until very hot. On waxed paper, coat chicken with flour, shaking off excess. Add chicken to skillet and cook until golden brown, about 3 minutes per side. With tongs, transfer chicken pieces to bowl as they are browned.

2. Add onion and garlic to skillet. Reduce heat to medium-low and cook, stirring occasionally, until onion is tender, about 5 minutes. Add mushrooms and cook, stirring frequently, until just tender, about 3 minutes.

3. Add tomatoes with their juice, breaking them up with side of spoon. Add salt, oregano, sage, ground red pepper, and chicken and heat to boiling over high heat. Reduce heat; cover and simmer until juices run clear when thickest part of chicken is pierced with tip of knife, about 25 minutes.

4. Transfer chicken to serving bowl. Spoon sauce over chicken. Makes 4 main-dish servings.

Each serving: About 371 calories, 44g protein, 18g carbohydrate, 13g total fat (3g saturated), 133mg cholesterol, 608mg sodium.

Chicken with Rosemary Dumplings

It doesn't take hours to make a stew when you're using chicken breasts. The tender, melt-in-your-mouth dumplings make this stew a complete meal.

Prep: 15 minutes   Cook: 1 hour

- 2 tablespoons vegetable oil
- 6 large bone-in chicken breast halves (3¼ pounds), skin removed
- 4 large carrots, peeled and cut into 1-inch pieces
- 2 large stalks celery, cut into ¼-inch-thick slices
- 1 medium onion, finely chopped
- 1 cup plus 2 tablespoons all-purpose flour
- 2 teaspoons baking powder
- 1½ teaspoons chopped fresh rosemary or ½ teaspoon dried rosemary, crumbled
- 1 teaspoon salt
- 1 large egg
- 1½ cups milk
- 2 cups water
- 1 can (14½ ounces) low-sodium chicken broth or 1¾ cups Chicken Broth (page 62)
- ¼ teaspoon ground black pepper
- 1 package (10 ounces) frozen peas

1. In 8-quart Dutch oven, heat 1 tablespoon oil over medium-high heat until very hot. Add 3 chicken breast halves; cook until golden brown, about 5 minutes per side. With tongs, transfer chicken pieces to bowl as they are browned. Repeat with remaining chicken.

2. Add remaining 1 tablespoon oil to drippings in Dutch oven. Add carrots, celery, and onion and cook, stirring frequently, until vegetables are golden brown and tender, about 10 minutes.

3. Prepare dumplings: In small bowl, combine 1 cup flour, baking powder, rosemary, and ½ teaspoon salt. In cup, with fork, beat egg with ½ cup milk. Stir egg mixture into flour mixture until just blended.

4. Return chicken to Dutch oven; add water, broth, pepper, and remaining ½ teaspoon salt. Heat to boiling over high heat. Drop dumpling mixture by rounded tablespoons on top of chicken and vegetables to make 12 dumplings. Reduce heat; cover and simmer 15 minutes.

5. With slotted spoon, transfer dumplings, chicken, and vegetables to serving bowl; keep warm. Reserve broth in Dutch oven.

6. In cup, blend remaining 2 tablespoons flour with remaining 1 cup milk until smooth; stir into broth mixture. Heat to boiling over high heat; boil 1 minute to thicken slightly. Add peas and heat through. Pour sauce over chicken and dumplings. Makes 6 main-dish servings.

Each serving: About 437 calories, 46g protein, 38g carbohydrate, 10g total fat (3g saturated), 137mg cholesterol, 951mg sodium

Mediterranean Chicken with Soft Polenta

You can buy packages of cornmeal labeled polenta in specialty food stores, but we find that regular yellow cornmeal works—and tastes—equally good.

Prep: 15 minutes   Cook: 40 minutes

- 2 tablespoons all-purpose flour
- ¾ teaspoon salt
- ¼ teaspoon ground black pepper
- 4 medium chicken leg quarters (2¼ pounds), skin and fat removed
- 1 tablespoon olive oil
- 1 small onion, cut in half and thinly sliced
- ½ cup dry white wine
- 1 can (14½ ounces) diced tomatoes
- ½ cup Kalamata olives, pitted and coarsely chopped
- 4 strips (3" by 1" each) fresh lemon peel
- 6 sprigs fresh thyme plus additional for garnish
- 2¼ cups whole milk
- 1 can (14 to 14½ ounces) chicken Broth or 1¾ cups Chicken Broth (page 62)
- 1 cup yellow cornmeal
- 2 tablespoons butter or margarine, cut into pieces
- ⅛ teaspoon ground black pepper

1. Prepare chicken: On waxed paper, combine flour, ½ teaspoon salt, and pepper. Use to coat chicken legs shaking off excess.

2. In nonstick 12-inch skillet, heat oil over medium heat until hot. Add legs and cook, turning over once, until browned, 10 to 12 minutes. With slotted spoon, transfer legs to plate.

3. To drippings in skillet, add onion and cook, stirring frequently, until golden brown, about 5 minutes. Add wine; boil until reduced by half, about 2 minutes. Add tomatoes with their juice, olives, lemon peel, 6 thyme sprigs, and remaining ¼ teaspoon salt. Return legs with any accumulated juices to skillet, stirring to coat; heat to boiling over high heat. Reduce heat to low; cover and simmer just until juices run clear when thickest part of leg is pierced with tip of knife, about 20 minutes.

4. Meanwhile, prepare soft polenta: In 3-quart nonreactive saucepan, heat milk and broth to boiling over high heat. Reduce heat to low; gradually whisk in cornmeal. Cook, stirring occasionally, until mixture is very thick, about 10 minutes. Remove saucepan from heat; stir in butter and pepper.

5. Remove lemon peel and thyme sprigs from chicken mixture. Divide polenta among 4 dinner plates; top each with 1 chicken leg and some sauce. Garnish with remaining thyme sprigs. Makes 4 main-dish servings.

Each serving: About 550 calories, 41g protein, 43g carbohydrate, 23g total fat (6g saturated), 139mg cholesterol, 1,685mg sodium.

Spicy Peanut Chicken

This recipe is based on the cuisines of Africa. A crisp cucumber salad and jasmine or basmati rice, available in most supermarkets, are the usual accompaniments.

Prep: 15 minutes   Cook: 1 hour 10 minutes

1	teaspoon ground cumin
¼	teaspoon ground cinnamon
4	medium chicken leg quarters (2¼ pounds), skin and fat removed
1	tablespoon vegetable oil
1	medium onion, thinly sliced
1	can (28 ounces) plum tomatoes, drained, juice reserved, and coarsely chopped
¼	cup creamy peanut butter
¼	cup packed fresh cilantro leaves plus additional sprigs
2	garlic cloves, peeled
½	teaspoon salt
¼	teaspoon crushed red pepper

1. In cup, combine cumin and cinnamon. Use to rub on chicken.

2. In nonstick 12-inch skillet, heat oil over medium-high heat until very hot. Add chicken and cook until golden brown, about 5 minutes per side. Add onion and cook until golden, about 5 minutes.

3. Meanwhile, in blender or in food processor with knife blade attached, puree reserved tomato juice, peanut butter, cilantro, garlic, salt, and crushed red pepper until smooth.

4. Pour peanut-butter mixture and chopped tomatoes over chicken; heat to boiling. Reduce heat; cover and simmer until juices run clear when thickest part of chicken is pierced with tip of knife, about 40 minutes. Garnish with cilantro sprigs. Makes 4 main-dish servings.

Each serving: About 361 calories, 36g protein, 16g carbohydrate, 18g fat (3g saturated), 116mg cholesterol, 817mg sodium.

Chicken Thighs Provençal

The quintessentially Provençal combination of thyme, basil, fennel, and orange makes sensational chicken.

Prep: 30 minutes   Cook: 1 hour 15 minutes

- 2 pounds skinless, boneless chicken thighs, fat removed and each cut into quarters
- ¾ teaspoon salt
- 3 teaspoons olive oil
- 2 red peppers, cut into ¼-inch-wide strips
- 1 yellow pepper, cut into ¼-inch-wide strips
- 1 jumbo onion (1 pound), thinly sliced
- 3 garlic cloves, crushed with garlic press
- 1 can (28 ounces) plum tomatoes
- ¼ teaspoon dried thyme
- ¼ teaspoon fennel seeds, crushed
- 3 strips (3" by 1" each) orange peel
- ½ cup loosely packed fresh basil leaves, chopped

1. Sprinkle chicken with ½ teaspoon salt. In nonreactive 5-quart Dutch oven, heat 1 teaspoon oil over medium-high heat until very hot. Add half of chicken and cook until golden brown, about 5 minutes per side. With tongs, transfer chicken pieces to bowl as they are browned. Repeat with 1 teaspoon oil and remaining chicken.

2. Reduce heat to medium. To drippings in Dutch oven, add remaining 1 teaspoon oil, red and yellow peppers, onion, and remaining ¼ teaspoon salt. Cook, stirring frequently, until vegetables are tender and lightly browned, about 20 minutes. Add garlic; cook 1 minute longer.

3. Return chicken to Dutch oven. Add tomatoes with their juice, thyme, fennel seeds, and orange peel; heat to boiling, breaking up tomatoes with side of spoon. Reduce heat; cover and simmer until chicken loses its pink color throughout, about 15 minutes.

4. Transfer to serving bowl and sprinkle with basil to serve. Makes 8 main-dish servings.

Each serving: About 204 calories, 24g protein, 12g carbohydrate, 7g total fat (1g saturated), 94mg cholesterol, 480mg sodium.

Poule au Pot with Tarragon

Stewed chicken and vegetables is a favorite Sunday supper in France. Use the leftover broth as the base for a soup later in the week.

Prep: 15 minutes   Cook: 1 hour

- 3 medium leeks (about 1 pound)
- 1 chicken (3½ pounds), cut into 8 pieces
- 1 pound small red potatoes
- 1 bag (16 ounces) carrots, peeled and cut into 3-inch pieces
- 4 cups water
- 1 can (14½ ounces) chicken broth or 1¾ cups Chicken Broth (page 62)
- ½ teaspoon salt
- ¼ teaspoon dried thyme
- ¼ teaspoon ground black pepper
- 1 large sprig plus 1 tablespoon chopped fresh tarragon

1. Cut off roots and trim dark green tops from leeks; cut each leek lengthwise in half, then crosswise into 3-inch pieces. Rinse in large bowl of cold water, swishing to remove sand; transfer to colander to drain, leaving sand in bottom of bowl.

2. In 6- to 8-quart Dutch oven, combine leeks, chicken, potatoes, carrots, water, broth, salt, thyme, pepper, and tarragon sprig. Heat to boiling over high heat. Reduce heat; cover and simmer until chicken loses its pink color throughout, about 45 minutes.

3. With slotted spoon, transfer chicken and vegetables to serving bowl. Remove and discard skin from chicken. Skim and discard fat from broth. Pour 1 cup broth over chicken (refrigerate remaining broth for another use). To serve, sprinkle chopped tarragon on top. Makes 4 main-dish servings.

Each serving: About 472 calories, 47g protein, 44g carbohydrate, 11g total fat (3g saturated), 127mg cholesterol, 859mg sodium.

Southern Fried Chicken

Here it is: our favorite recipe for this all-time classic. Mashed potatoes or biscuits are a must.

Prep: 35 minutes plus chilling and standing
Cook: 40 minutes

- 2 cups buttermilk
- 2 tablespoons hot pepper sauce
- 1 tablespoon salt
- 2 chickens (3½ pounds each), each cut into 8 pieces
- 2 cups all-purpose flour
- 1½ teaspoons baking powder
- 1 teaspoon ground black pepper
- 1 teaspoon paprika
- 5 cups vegetable oil or shortening for frying

1. In extra-large (2- to 2½-gallon) zip-tight plastic bag, combine buttermilk, hot pepper sauce, and 1 teaspoon salt. Add chicken pieces, turning to coat. Seal bag, pressing out excess air. Place bag in bowl; refrigerate 2 to 24 hours to marinate, turning bag over once.

2. In pie plate, stir flour, baking powder, pepper, paprika, and remaining 2 teaspoons salt until well mixed. Remove chicken, a few pieces at a time, from buttermilk, shaking off excess. Add chicken to flour mixture, turning to coat well. Place chicken pieces so that they do not touch one another on wire rack, set over waxed paper. Repeat with remaining chicken. Let stand until coating has set, about 15 minutes. Discard buttermilk mixture.

3. Meanwhile, preheat oven to 250°F. Line two 15½" by 10½" jelly-roll pans or large cookie sheets with paper towels. Divide oil between two 12-inch skillets, preferably electric (there should be about ½ inch oil in each skillet), and heat over medium heat until temperature reaches 360°F on deep-fry thermometer.

4. To each skillet, add 4 chicken pieces, skin side down, being careful to avoid crowding. Cover skillets and cook until chicken is light golden brown on bottom, 4 to 5 minutes. Turn pieces and cook, covered (reducing heat to medium-low if necessary to maintain a temperature of 300°F), 8 to 10 minutes longer for white meat, 13 to 15 minutes longer for dark meat, turning pieces every 4 or 5 minutes, until well browned on all sides and juices run clear when thickest part is pierced with tip of knife. Using tongs, transfer chicken pieces to lined jelly-roll pans to drain; keep warm in oven. Repeat with remaining chicken. Makes 8 main-dish servings.

Each serving: About 545 calories, 39g protein, 25g carbohydrate, 31g total fat (6g saturated), 140mg cholesterol, 845mg sodium.

POACHED CHICKEN BREASTS WITH TWO SAUCES

Poached chicken breasts are versatile—and healthful.

Poached Chicken Breasts
In 12-inch skillet, combine 6 small skinless, boneless chicken breast halves (1¾ pounds), 1 medium onion, thinly sliced, 3 cups water, and 1 bay leaf. Heat to boiling over high heat. Reduce heat; cover and simmer 1 minute, turning chicken over halfway through cooking. Remove skillet from heat; cover and let stand 10 minutes. Transfer chicken to plate; cover loosely and refrigerate until chilled. Makes 6 servings.

Turkish Chicken in Walnut Sauce
In food processor with knife blade attached, process 1¼ cups toasted walnuts and 3 slices firm white bread, torn until walnuts are finely ground. Add 1 cup chicken broth, 1 small garlic clove, minced, ¾ teaspoon salt, ½ teaspoon paprika, and ⅓ teaspoon ground red pepper (cayenne); process until well combined. Stir half of walnut sauce into chicken until combined. Spoon onto serving platter. Pour remaining sauce on top. Cover with plastic wrap and let stand 30 minutes, or refrigerate up to 8 hours. Makes 6 main-dish servings.

Chicken Breasts Tonnato
In blender or in food processor with knife blade attached, blend 1 can (6½ ounces white tuna in oil, 4 anchovy fillets, 2 tablespoons capers, drained, ¼ cup olive oil, ¼ cup fresh lemon juice, ¼ teaspoon salt, and ¾ cup reserved poaching liquid until smooth. Line platter with 1 bunch arugula or lettuce leaves. Dip each cold chicken breast half into tuna sauce to coat; arrange on arugula. Pour any remaining sauce over chicken. Garnish with lemon slices and 2 teaspoons capers. Makes 6 main-dish servings.

Chicken Breasts with Lemon-Caper Sauce

Preparing chicken *alla Francese* reverses the order in which chicken is ordinarily coated. Here, the chicken is dipped first in flour and then in beaten egg. The result is deep golden chicken with a delicate, puffy coating.

Prep: 15 minutes   Cook: 20 minutes

- 4 medium skinless, boneless chicken breast halves (1¼ pounds)
- 2 tablespoons plus 1½ teaspoons all-purpose flour
- ½ teaspoon salt
- 1 large egg
- 2 teaspoons olive oil
- 2 tablespoons butter or margarine
- 2 lemons, each cut in half
- 3 garlic cloves, crushed with side of chef's knife
- ½ cup chicken broth
- ¼ cup dry white wine
- 2 tablespoons capers, drained
- 1 tablespoon chopped fresh parsley

1. Place chicken breast halves between two sheets of plastic wrap or waxed paper. With meat mallet or rolling pin, pound to ½-inch thickness. On waxed paper, combine 2 tablespoons flour and salt. In pie plate, beat egg.

2. In nonstick 12-inch skillet, heat oil over medium-high heat until very hot. Stir in 1 tablespoon butter until melted. One by one, coat each chicken breast with flour mixture, dip in egg, and add to skillet; cook 5 minutes. Reduce heat to medium, turn chicken, and cook until chicken loses its pink color throughout, 8 to 10 minutes longer. Using tongs, transfer chicken breasts to platter; keep warm.

3. From ½ lemon, cut thin slices; from remaining 1½ lemons, squeeze 2 tablespoons juice. To drippings in skillet, add lemon slices and garlic; cook, stirring, until garlic is golden. In small bowl, blend broth, wine, lemon juice, and remaining 1½ teaspoons flour until smooth; stir into mixture in skillet. Heat sauce to boiling; boil 1 minute. Stir in capers and remaining 1 tablespoon butter until butter melts. Discard garlic. Arrange lemon slices over and between chicken breasts. Pour sauce over chicken; sprinkle with chopped parsley. Makes 4 main-dish servings.

Each serving: About 287 calories, 35g protein, 7g carbohydrate, 11g total fat (5g saturated), 151mg cholesterol, 773mg sodium.

Thai Chicken with Basil

This easy stir-fry is a good example of Thai cooking, which is defined by the blending of cool and hot flavors, such as cilantro, basil, ginger, garlic, and chiles.

Prep: 20 minutes plus marinating   Cook: 10 minutes

- 1 pound skinless, boneless chicken breast halves
- 3 tablespoons Asian fish sauce (nuoc nam, page 26)
- 1 tablespoon soy sauce
- 1 tablespoon brown sugar
- 2 teaspoons vegetable oil
- 1 large onion (12 ounces), cut into ¼-inch-thick slices
- 2 red or green chiles (serrano or jalapeño), seeded and cut into matchstick strips
- 2 teaspoons minced, peeled fresh ginger
- 2 garlic cloves, crushed with garlic press
- 1½ cups loosely packed fresh basil leaves

1. With knife held in slanting position, almost parallel to cutting surface, cut each chicken breast half crosswise into ¼-inch-thick slices. In medium bowl, combine fish sauce, soy sauce, and brown sugar; add chicken slices, tossing to coat. Let marinate 5 minutes.

2. In nonstick 12-inch skillet, heat oil over medium-high heat until very hot. Add chicken with marinade and cook, stirring frequently (stir-frying), until chicken loses its pink color throughout, 3 to 4 minutes. With slotted spoon, transfer chicken to bowl.

3. Add onion to marinade remaining in skillet and cook, stir-frying, until tender-crisp, about 4 minutes. Stir in chiles, ginger, and garlic; cook 1 minute longer.

4. Return chicken to skillet; heat through. Stir in basil leaves just before serving. Makes 4 main-dish servings.

Each serving: About 238 calories, 31g protein, 16g carbohydrate, 5g total fat (1g saturated), 66mg cholesterol, 784mg sodium.

Thai Chicken with Basil

GROUND CHICKEN AND GROUND TURKEY

To answer the public's demand for reduced-fat ground meats, poultry producers now offer both ground turkey and ground chicken. Each type of ground poultry has a different fat content, and since fat provides moisture and flavor, expect different results when cooking with different varieties. For example, lean ground turkey breast works well when cooked in a liquid (think along the lines of turkey meatballs in tomato sauce), but it is less successful when made into turkey burgers, where its lack of fat may make the burgers dry.

Ground chicken Made from white and dark chicken meat with skin, its fat content is about ten percent. It is an excellent all-purpose ground poultry, but any recipe prepared with this product will have a slightly softer texture than the same dish prepared with ground turkey.

Ground turkey breast Ninety-nine percent lean, this is simply white turkey breast meat, ground without any skin or fat.

Ground turkey This is a mixture of white and dark turkey meat; ground with the skin, which adds moisture. It has about seven percent fat, which is similar to the fat content of ground beef sirloin.

Ground turkey (dark meat) Usually found in the frozen section of the supermarket, packed in plastic tubes, it contains about 15 percent fat. Ground dark turkey meat may be less expensive, but it has the same fat content as ground beef round, so it doesn't offer much in the way of fat reduction.

Leaner Meatballs

Enjoy some of these tasty Italian-style meatballs with your favorite pasta and sauce, and freeze the rest. Let them cool in the pan on a wire rack, then transfer the meatballs to a jelly-roll pan and place in the freezer until frozen. Transfer them to large zip-tight plastic bags and freeze for up to one month.

Prep: 25 minutes   Bake: 15 minutes

- ⅓ cup water
- 1½ cups fresh bread crumbs (about 3 slices firm white bread)
- 1 pound lean ground beef
- 1 pound lean ground turkey meat
- 2 large egg whites
- ⅓ cup freshly grated Romano or Parmesan cheese
- 3 tablespoons grated onion
- 2 tablespoons chopped fresh parsley
- 1 garlic clove, minced
- 1 teaspoon salt
- ¼ teaspoon coarsely ground black pepper

1. Preheat oven to 425°F. Line 15½" by 10½" jelly-roll pan with foil and lightly grease.

2. In large bowl, pour water over bread crumbs. With hands, toss until bread is evenly moistened. Add ground beef, ground turkey, egg whites, Romano, onion, parsley, garlic, salt, and pepper; with hands, combine just until well blended but not overmixed.

3. Shape mixture into twenty-four 2-inch meatballs (for easier shaping, use slightly wet hands), handling meat as little as possible. Arrange meatballs in prepared pan and bake until lightly browned and cooked through, 15 to 20 minutes. Makes 24 meatballs.

Each meatball: About 80 calories, 8g protein, 2g carbohydrate, 4g total fat (1g saturated), 44mg cholesterol, 166mg sodium.

Turkey Meat Loaf

Thickly slice any leftover meat loaf and place between slices of hearty bread that have been spread with mango chutney for the best ever brown-bag lunch.

Prep: 15 minutes   Bake: 1 hour

- 1 tablespoon olive oil
- 1 medium onion, finely chopped
- 2 garlic cloves, finely chopped
- 2 pounds ground turkey meat
- 2 large eggs
- 1 cup fresh bread crumbs (about 2 slices firm white bread)
- ¼ cup milk
- ¼ cup mango chutney, chopped
- 2 tablespoons ketchup
- 1¼ teaspoons salt
- ½ teaspoon dried sage

1. Preheat oven to 350°F. In 6-inch skillet, heat oil over medium heat. Add onion and garlic and cook, stirring frequently, until tender, about 5 minutes. Transfer to medium bowl; cool to room temperature.

2. Add ground turkey, eggs, bread crumbs, milk, chutney, ketchup, salt, and sage to bowl; combine just until well blended but not overmixed. Spoon mixture into 9" by 5" metal loaf pan; press down gently. Cover with foil and bake until meat thermometer inserted in center of meat loaf registers 170°F, about 1 hour. Cool in pan 10 minutes; turn out onto warm platter and slice. Makes 8 main-dish servings.

Each serving: About 261 calories, 23g protein, 14g carbohydrate, 12g total fat (3g saturated), 137mg cholesterol, 657mg sodium.

CORNISH HENS

These small birds, a crossbreed of the White Plymouth and Cornish chicken strains, weigh between 1½ and 1¾ pounds and yield two servings. For a bird small enough for a single serving, look for *poussin* at specialty butcher shops. Pronounced "poose-AHN," these small chickens weigh about 1 pound each. You can substitute poussin for Cornish hens in most recipes, but reduce the cooking time by about one-third.

Cornish Hens Milanese

(Pictured on page 126)

Gremolata, a tasty blend of chopped fresh parsley, freshly grated lemon peel, and pungent garlic, is a popular way to finish a food dish in Italy. We also love gremolata scattered over steamed green beans or new potatoes.

Prep: 5 minutes   Roast: 50 minutes

- 2 Cornish hens (1½ pounds each)
- 3 tablespoons chopped fresh parsley
- 1 teaspoon extra-virgin olive oil
- ¼ teaspoon salt
- ⅛ teaspoon ground black pepper
- 1 small garlic clove, minced
- ½ teaspoon freshly grated lemon peel

1. Preheat oven to 375°F. Remove giblets and necks from hens; reserve for another use. With poultry shears, cut each hen lengthwise in half. Rinse hen halves with cold running water; pat dry with paper towels.

2. In small bowl, combine 2 tablespoons parsley, oil, salt, and pepper. With fingertips, carefully separate skin from meat on each hen half; spread parsley mixture under skin. Place hens, skin side up, in large roasting pan (17" by 11½").

3. Roast hens, basting with drippings 3 times, until juices run clear when thickest part of thigh is pierced with tip of knife, about 50 minutes.

4. Arrange hens warm on platter. In cup, combine remaining 1 tablespoon parsley, garlic, and lemon peel; sprinkle over hens. Makes 4 main-dish servings.

Each serving: About 384 calories, 32g protein, 0g carbohydrate, 27g total fat (7g saturated), 187mg cholesterol, 236mg sodium.

Chicken Livers Marsala

In this classic preparation, Marsala wine mellows and sweetens the assertive flavor of the chicken livers. Serve with rice or noodles to soak up the juices.

Prep: 15 minutes   Cook: 15 minutes

- 1 pound chicken livers, trimmed and cut in half
- 3 tablespoons butter or margarine
- ¾ teaspoon salt
- 1 medium onion, chopped
- 8 ounces mushrooms, trimmed and cut in half
- ¼ teaspoon ground black pepper
- ¼ cup dry Marsala wine
- 1 tablespoon chopped fresh parsley

1. Pat livers dry with paper towels. In 10-inch skillet, melt 1 tablespoon butter over medium-high heat. Add livers, sprinkle with ½ teaspoon salt, and cook, stirring often, until livers are browned but still pink in center, 3 to 4 minutes. Transfer livers to bowl.

2. Add remaining 2 tablespoons butter to skillet. Add onion and cook until tender, about 5 minutes. Add mushrooms, pepper, and remaining ¼ teaspoon salt and cook until mushrooms are tender. Stir in Marsala and heat to boiling. Add livers and heat through. Sprinkle with parsley. Makes 4 main-dish servings.

Each serving: About 272 calories, 22g protein, 12g carbohydrate, 13g total fat (7g saturated), 522mg cholesterol, 619mg sodium.

MARSALA WINE

Test Kitchen Tip

Marsala, Italy's most famous fortified wine, is produced by a process similar to the one used in Spain to make sherry. Marsala is made in several different styles: *secco* (dry), *semisecco* (semisweet), and *dolce* (sweet). It is also classified based on its flavor characteristics and aging:

Fine is usually aged less than one year

Superiore is aged at least two years

Superiore Riserva is aged at least four years

Vergine e/o Soleras is aged at least five years

Vergine e/o Soleras Stravecchio or **Vergine e/o Solveras Riserva** is aged at least ten years

TURKEY

Choose your turkey by size—there is no difference in flavor or texture between a tom (male) and a hen (female). Fresh birds are especially delicious, but if you choose to buy a frozen bird, be sure to allow enough time for thorough thawing. Farm-raised wild turkeys, found in specialty butcher shops, have a mildly gamy flavor and are never as big or as meaty as the supermarket variety.

TURKEY PARTS

Turkey parts are readily available and can be prepared in as many ways as chicken. Whole turkey breast is a good way to feed a crowd and makes tasty leftovers for sandwiches. Turkey drumsticks, both economical and tasty, are an excellent choice for a weeknight meal. Lean turkey cutlets (boneless sliced turkey breast) cook quickly and look elegant, but take care not to overcook them or they will toughen and dry out.

Traditional Roast Turkey with Giblet Gravy

Here it is—the traditional Thanksgiving centerpiece. The chart on page 129 will tell you, in a flash, how much time you'll need to roast the perfect bird, no matter how small or how large.

Prep: 1 hour (not including stuffing)
Roast: 3 hours 45 minutes

choice of stuffing (pages 159–161)
1 turkey (14 pounds)
1½ teaspoons salt
½ teaspoon coarsely ground black pepper
Giblet Gravy (page 152)

1. Prepare desired stuffing; set aside.

2. Preheat oven to 325°F.  Remove giblets and neck from turkey; reserve for making Giblet Gravy. Rinse turkey inside and out with cold running water and drain well; pat dry with paper towels.

3. Loosely spoon some stuffing into neck cavity. Fold neck skin over stuffing; fasten neck skin to turkey back with one or two skewers.

4. Loosely spoon remaining stuffing into body cavity (bake any leftover stuffing in small covered casserole during last 30 minutes of roasting time). Fold skin over cavity opening; skewer closed, if necessary.  Tie legs and tail together with string, push drumsticks under band of skin, or use stuffing clamp. Secure wings to body with string, if desired.

5. Place turkey, breast side up, on rack in large roasting pan (17" by 11½"). Sprinkle salt and pepper on outside of turkey. Cover with loose tent of foil. Roast about 3 hours 45 minutes. Start  checking for doneness during last hour of roasting.

6. To brown turkey, remove foil during last hour of roasting and baste occasionally with pan drippings. Turkey is done when temperature on meat thermometer inserted in thickest part of thigh, next to body, reaches 180° to 185°F and juices run clear when thickest part of thigh is pierced with tip of knife. (Breast temperature should be 170° to 175°F, stuffing temperature 160° to 165°F.)

7. While turkey is roasting, prepare giblets and neck to use in Giblet Gravy.

8. Transfer turkey to large platter; keep warm. Let stand at least 15 minutes to set juices for easier carving.

9. Meanwhile, prepare Giblet Gravy.

10. Serve turkey with stuffing and gravy. Makes 14 main-dish servings.

Each serving without skin, stuffing, or gravy: About 143 calories, 25g protein, 0g carbohydrate, 4g total fat (1g saturated), 65mg cholesterol, 146mg sodium.

Giblet Gravy

Prepare giblets and neck: In 3-quart saucepan, combine **gizzard, heart, neck,** and enough **water** to cover; heat to boiling over high heat. Reduce heat; cover and simmer 45 minutes. Add **liver** and cook 15 minutes longer. Strain giblet broth through sieve into large bowl. Pull meat from neck; discard bones. Coarsely chop neck meat and giblets. Cover and refrigerate meat and broth separately.

To make gravy, remove rack from roasting pan. Strain **pan drippings** through sieve into 4-cup measuring cup or medium bowl. Add **1 cup giblet broth** to hot roasting pan and heat to boiling, stirring until browned bits are loosened from bottom of pan; add to drippings in measuring cup. Let stand 1 minute, or until fat separates from meat juice. Spoon **2 tablespoons fat** from drippings into 2-quart saucepan; skim and discard any remaining fat. Add **remaining giblet broth** and enough *water* to meat juice in cup to equal 3½ cups.

Heat fat in saucepan over medium heat. Stir in **2 tablespoons all-purpose flour** and ½ **teaspoon salt** and cook, stirring, until flour turns golden brown. With wire whisk, gradually whisk in **meat-juice mixture** and cook, whisking, until gravy has thickened slightly and boils; boil 1 minute. Stir in reserved giblets and neck meat; heat through. Pour gravy into gravy boat. Makes about 3½ cups gravy.

Each ¼ cup gravy: About 128 calories, 17g protein, 1g carbohydrate, 5g total fat (2g saturated), 153mg cholesterol, 152mg sodium.

CARVING A ROAST TURKEY

Cut through the skin where the leg is attached. To remove the leg, force it away from the body with a carving fork until it pops out of the socket. Separate the thigh from the body by cutting through the joint. If you like, separate the drumstick from the thigh by cutting through the center joint. To carve the leg, slice the thigh and drumstick meat, cutting parallel to the bones. Repeat on the other side.

To carve the breast, make a horizontal cut above the wing joint along the length of the bird, making sure to cut down to the bone.

With the knife parallel to the rib cage, cut the breast meat into thin slices. Cut off the wing. Repeat on the other side.

GIBLETS

Giblets, poultry organs that can be cooked and eaten, include the liver, heart, and gizzard; some of them may be used to enrich gravy or to make a quick, flavorful broth. (Don't add livers to broth, they will make it bitter.) Giblets are usually wrapped in a separate package along with the neck and placed in the cavity of a bird, but the content varies from producer to producer. For your holiday giblet gravy, we recommend buying giblets separately to be sure of what you are buying.

Rosemary Roast Turkey Breast

When a whole turkey is too much, use just the breast. It will make white-meat fans very happy.

Prep: 20 minutes   Roast: 2 hours 15 to 30 minutes

- 1   bone-in turkey breast (6 to 7 pounds)
- 1½ teaspoons dried rosemary, crumbled
- 1   teaspoon salt
- ¾   teaspoon coarsely ground black pepper
- 1   cup chicken broth

1. Preheat oven to 350°F. Rinse turkey breast with cold running water and drain well; pat dry with paper towels. In cup, combine rosemary, salt, and pepper. Rub rosemary mixture on both inside and outside of turkey breast.

2. Place turkey, skin side up, on rack in small roasting pan (13" by 9"). Cover turkey with loose tent of foil. Roast turkey 1 hour 30 minutes. Remove foil; roast, occasionally basting with pan drippings, 45 to 60 minutes longer. Start checking for doneness during last 30 minutes of cooking. Turkey breast is done when temperature on meat thermometer inserted into thickest part of breast (not touching bone) reaches 170°F and juices run clear when thickest part of breast is pierced with tip of knife.

3. Transfer turkey to warm platter. Let stand 15 minutes to set juices for easier carving.

4. Meanwhile, pour broth into drippings in hot roasting pan; heat to boiling, stirring until browned bits are loosened from bottom of pan. Strain pan-juice mixture through sieve into 1-quart saucepan; let stand 1 minute. Skim and discard fat. Heat pan-juice mixture over medium heat until hot; serve with turkey. Remove skin before eating. Makes 10 main-dish servings.

Each serving without skin and with pan juices: About 251 calories, 55g protein, 0g carbohydrate, 2g total fat (0g saturated), 152mg cholesterol, 428mg sodium.

Turkey Marsala with Mushrooms

Turkey cutlets are an excellent and economical substitute for veal scallopini, and this recipe proves it.

Prep: 15 minutes   Cook: 15 minutes

- 2   tablespoons butter or margarine
- 10 ounces mushrooms, trimmed and sliced
- ¾   teaspoon salt
- 1   pound turkey cutlets, large pieces cut in half
- 3   tablespoons all-purpose flour
- ¼   teaspoon ground black pepper
- 1   tablespoon olive oil
- ½   cup dry Marsala wine
- ¼   cup water

1. In nonstick 12-inch skillet, melt 1 tablespoon butter over medium-high heat. Add mushrooms and ¼ teaspoon salt; cook until mushrooms are golden brown and liquid has evaporated, about 7 minutes. With slotted spoon, transfer mushrooms to medium bowl.

2. Meanwhile, with meat mallet or between two sheets of plastic wrap or waxed paper with rolling pin, pound turkey cutlets to ¼-inch thickness. On waxed paper, combine flour, pepper, and remaining ½ teaspoon salt; use to coat cutlets, shaking off excess.

3. In same skillet, melt remaining 1 tablespoon butter with oil over medium-high heat. Add half of cutlets and cook until cutlets are golden brown and lose their pink color throughout, 1 to 2 minutes per side. Transfer cutlets to bowl with mushrooms; keep warm. Repeat with remaining cutlets.

4. To skillet, add Marsala and water; cook 1 minute. Stir in turkey cutlets and mushrooms, turning to coat with sauce. Makes 4 main-dish servings.

Each serving: About 284 calories, 30g protein, 9g carbohydrate, 10g total fat (4g saturated), 86mg cholesterol, 556mg sodium.

Turkey Thighs Osso Buco–Style

Cooked in a manner usually reserved for veal shanks, turkey thighs make an excellent stew. Serve with soft polenta or rice pilaf.

Prep: 20 minutes   Bake: 1 hour 30 minutes

- ¼ teaspoon salt
- ¼ teaspoon ground black pepper
- 2 turkey thighs (1¼ pounds each), skin removed
- 2 teaspoons vegetable oil
- 2 medium onions, finely chopped
- 4 carrots, peeled and cut into ¾-inch pieces
- 2 stalks celery, cut into ½-inch pieces
- 4 garlic cloves, finely chopped
- 1 can (14½ ounces) tomatoes in puree
- ½ cup dry red wine
- 1 bay leaf
- ¼ teaspoon dried thyme

1. Preheat oven to 350°F. Sprinkle salt and pepper on turkey. In nonreactive 5-quart Dutch oven, heat oil over medium-high heat until very hot. Add 1 turkey thigh and cook, turning occasionally, until golden brown, about 5 minutes. With tongs, transfer thigh to plate; repeat with second thigh. Discard all but 1 tablespoon fat from Dutch oven.

2. Reduce heat to medium. Add onions to Dutch oven and cook, stirring occasionally, 5 minutes. Add carrots, celery, and garlic; cook, stirring frequently, 2 minutes longer.

3. Stir in tomatoes with puree, wine, bay leaf, and thyme, breaking up tomatoes with side of spoon; heat to boiling. Add browned turkey; cover and place in oven. Bake until turkey is tender, about 1 hour 30 minutes. Discard bay leaf. Remove turkey meat from bones and cut into bite-size pieces; return meat to Dutch oven and stir well. Makes 4 main-dish servings.

Each serving: About 323 calories, 36g protein, 24g carbohydrate, 9g total fat (3g saturated), 122mg cholesterol, 483mg sodium.

Turkey Tetrazzini

The original Chicken Tetrazzini was named in honor of the Italian opera star Luisa Tetrazzini. This recipe is just about the best way to use up Thanksgiving turkey leftovers.

Prep: 30 minutes   Bake: 30 minutes

- 4 tablespoons butter or margarine
- ¼ cup all-purpose flour
- 2¼ cups chicken broth
- ¼ cup dry white wine
- ¼ teaspoon dried thyme
- pinch ground nutmeg
- ½ cup heavy or whipping cream
- 1 small onion, chopped
- 10 ounces mushrooms, trimmed and cut into quarters
- 8 ounces linguine, cooked as label directs
- 12 ounces cooked turkey, coarsely chopped (3 cups)
- 3 tablespoons freshly grated Parmesan cheese

1. Preheat oven to 400°F. In 2-quart saucepan, melt 3 tablespoons butter over medium heat. Stir in flour and cook 3 minutes. With wire whisk, whisk in broth, wine, thyme, and nutmeg until smooth. Heat to boiling, whisking constantly. Reduce heat and simmer, whisking frequently, 5 minutes. Stir in cream; set sauce aside.

2. In 10-inch skillet, melt remaining 1 tablespoon butter over medium heat. Add onion and cook until tender, about 5 minutes. Add mushrooms and cook, stirring occasionally, 10 minutes longer.

3. In 2- to 2½-quart shallow casserole, combine cooked linguine, mushroom mixture, and turkey. Stir in sauce and sprinkle with Parmesan. Bake until bubbly, about 30 minutes. Makes 6 main-dish servings.

Each serving: About 458 calories, 30g protein, 37g carbohydrate, 21g total fat (11g saturated), 104mg cholesterol, 648mg sodium.

Turkey Potpie with Cornmeal Crust

Chock full of turkey and vegetables, this potpie is the last word in comfort food.

Prep: 30 minutes   Bake: 35 minutes

- 1 tablespoon vegetable oil
- 1 medium rutabaga (1 pound), peeled and cut into ½-inch pieces
- 3 carrots, peeled and cut into ½-inch pieces
- 1 large onion (12 ounces), chopped
- 1 pound all-purpose potatoes (3 medium), peeled and cut into ½-inch pieces
- 2 large stalks celery, chopped
- ¾ teaspoon salt
- 1 pound cooked turkey or chicken, cut into ½-inch pieces (4 cups)
- 1 package (10 ounces) frozen peas
- 1 can (14½ ounces) chicken broth or 1¾ cups Chicken Broth (page 62)
- 1 cup milk
- ¼ cup all-purpose flour
- ¼ teaspoon ground black pepper
- ⅛ teaspoon dried thyme
  Cornmeal Crust (right)
- 1 large egg, beaten

1. Prepare potpie filling: In nonstick 12-inch skillet, heat oil over medium-high heat; add rutabaga, carrots, and onion and cook 10 minutes. Stir in potatoes, celery, and ½ teaspoon salt; cook, stirring frequently, until rutabaga is tender-crisp, about 10 minutes longer. Spoon into 13" by 9" baking dish; add turkey and peas.

2. In 2-quart saucepan, heat broth to boiling. Meanwhile, in small bowl, blend milk and flour until smooth. Stir milk mixture into broth. Add pepper, thyme, and remaining ¼ teaspoon salt; heat to boiling over high heat, stirring. Stir sauce into chicken-vegetable mixture in baking dish.

3. Prepare Cornmeal Crust. Preheat oven to 425°F.

4. On lightly floured surface, with floured rolling pin, roll dough into rectangle 4 inches larger than top of baking dish. Arrange dough rectangle over filling; trim edge, leaving 1-inch overhang. Fold overhang under; flute. Brush crust with some egg. If desired, reroll trimmings; cut into decorative shapes to garnish top of pie. Brush dough cutouts with egg. Cut several slits in crust to allow steam to escape during baking.

5. Place potpie on foil-lined cookie sheet to catch any overflow during baking. Bake potpie until crust is golden brown and filling is hot and bubbling, 35 to 40 minutes. During last 10 minutes of baking, cover edges of crust with foil to prevent overbrowning. Makes 10 main-dish servings.

Each serving: About 416 calories, 21g protein, 42g carbohydrate, 18g total fat (5g saturated), 60mg cholesterol, 644mg sodium.

Cornmeal Crust

In large bowl, combine **1½ cups all purpose-flour, ¼ cup cornmeal,** and **¾ teaspoon salt.** With pastry blender or two knives used scissor-fashion, cut in **⅔ cup vegetable shortening** until mixture resembles coarse crumbs. Sprinkle **6 to 7 tablespoons cold water,** 1 tablespoon at a time, over flour mixture, mixing with fork after each addition until dough is just moist enough to hold together.

Turkey Potpie with Cornmeal Crust

Old-Fashioned Creamed Turkey

This old-time favorite, sometimes called turkey hash, deserves a place in the Comfort Food Hall of Fame. You can stir in leftover cooked vegetables—carrots, peas, and potatoes are all good—along with the turkey. Spoon it over noodles, mashed potatoes, or rice.

Prep: 10 minutes   Cook: 20 minutes

- 2 tablespoons butter or margarine
- 1 small onion, finely chopped
- 3 tablespoons all-purpose flour
- 2 cups milk
- ½ teaspoon salt
- ⅛ teaspoon ground black pepper
  pinch ground nutmeg
- 8 ounces cooked turkey or chicken, cut into ½-inch pieces (2 cups)
- 2 tablespoons chopped fresh parsley

1. In 3-quart saucepan, melt butter over medium heat. Add onion and cook, stirring, until tender, about 5 minutes. Stir in flour and cook, stirring constantly, 1 minute. With wire whisk, gradually whisk in milk, salt, pepper, and nutmeg. Heat to boiling over medium-high heat, whisking. Reduce heat and simmer, whisking occasionally, 5 minutes.

2. Stir turkey into sauce and heat through. Stir in parsley and serve. Makes 4 main-dish servings.

Each serving: About 277 calories, 26g protein, 13g carbohydrate, 13g total fat (7g saturated), 87mg cholesterol, 462mg sodium.

GOOSE

Goose is the holiday bird of choice for many families. It has dark, deep-flavored, firm-textured flesh and, when roasted properly, sports an irresistibly crisp, golden skin. A goose is a large bird that isn't very meaty, but the meat is fairly rich. Serve it in small portions, accompanied by generous helpings of stuffing.

Crispy Roasted Goose with Orange Sauce

Piercing the skin of goose helps drain off the large amount of fat and also crisps the skin. Serve with one of our homemade cranberry sauces (pages 438–439) or chutneys (pages 439–440). Pour all the flavorful fat through a fine sieve and freeze for up to four months. Use for browning potatoes.

Prep: 30 minutes   Roast: 4 hours 25 minutes

- 1 goose (12 pounds)
- 5 navel oranges, each cut in half
- 1 bunch thyme
- 4 bay leaves
- ½ teaspoon dried thyme
- 1¼ teaspoons salt
- ½ teaspoon coarsely ground black pepper
- 3 tablespoons orange-flavored liqueur
- 2 tablespoons cornstarch
- ½ cup orange marmalade

1. Preheat oven to 400°F. Remove giblets and neck from goose; reserve for another use. Trim and discard fat from body cavity and any excess skin. Rinse goose inside and out with cold running water and drain well; pat dry with paper towels. With goose breast side up, lift wings up toward neck, then fold wing tips under back of goose so wings stay in place. Place 6 orange halves, thyme sprigs, and bay leaves in body cavity. Tie legs and tail together with string. Fold neck skin over back. With two-tine fork, prick skin in several places to drain fat during roasting.

2. Place goose, breast side up, on rack in large roasting pan (17" by 11½"). In cup, combine dried thyme, 1 teaspoon salt, and pepper; rub mixture over goose. Cover goose and roasting pan with foil. Roast 1 hour 30 minutes; turn oven control to 325°F and roast 2 hours longer.

3. Meanwhile, in small bowl, from remaining 4 orange halves, squeeze ¾ cup juice. Stir in 1 tablespoon liqueur, cornstarch, and remaining ¼ teaspoon salt; set aside. In cup, mix orange marmalade with remaining 2 tablespoons liqueur.

4. With spoon or bulb baster, remove as much fat from roasting pan as possible. Remove foil and roast goose 45 minutes longer. Remove goose from oven and turn oven control to 450°F. Brush marmalade mixture over goose. Roast goose until skin is golden brown and crisp, about 10 minutes longer. Transfer goose to warm platter; let stand at least 15 minutes for juices to set for easier carving.

5. Prepare sauce: Remove rack from roasting pan. Strain pan drippings through sieve into 8-cup measuring cup or large bowl. Let stand until fat separates from meat juice; skim and reserve fat for another use (there should be about 5 cups fat). Measure meat juice; if necessary, add enough water to meat juice to equal 1 cup. Return meat juice to pan and add reserved orange-juice mixture. Heat sauce to boiling over medium heat, stirring; boil 1 minute. (Makes about 1¾ cups.) Serve sauce with goose. Remove skin before eating, if desired. Makes 10 main-dish servings.

Each serving with skin: About 810 calories, 66g protein, 5g carbohydrate, 57g total fat (18g saturated), 235mg cholesterol, 472mg sodium.

Each serving without skin: About 488 calories, 57g protein, 5g carbohydrate, 25g total fat (9g saturated), 188mg cholesterol, 440mg sodium.

DUCK

Most supermarket ducks are of the Pekin (Long Island) breed. While the meat is flavorful, it can also be fatty. Cutting a duck into quarters helps render the excess fat. Specialty butchers often carry Moulard or Muscovy ducks, which are leaner and meatier than the Pekin variety but also much more expensive.

Ginger-Glazed Duck

To ensure crisp, flavorful skin, this glazed duck is roasted at high heat during the last 10 minutes.

Prep: 10 minutes	Roast: 2 hours 10 minutes

- 1 duck (4½ pounds), cut into quarters, fat removed
- 3 teaspoons grated, peeled fresh ginger
- ½ teaspoon salt
- ¼ teaspoon ground black pepper
- 2 tablespoons honey
- 1 tablespoon soy sauce

1. Preheat oven to 350°F. Pat duck dry with paper towels. With two-tine fork, prick skin in several places.

2. In cup, combine 1 teaspoon ginger, salt, and pepper. Use to rub on meat side of duck quarters. Place duck, skin side up, on rack in large (17" by 11½") foil-lined roasting pan. Roast 2 hours, using spoon or bulb baster to remove fat from pan occasionally.

3. Meanwhile, in cup, combine honey, soy sauce, and remaining 2 teaspoons ginger.

4. Turn oven control to 450°F. Remove duck from oven and brush all over with ginger glaze. Return to oven and roast 10 minutes longer. Makes 4 main-dish servings.

Each serving: About 690 calories, 37g protein, 9g carbohydrate, 55g total fat (19g saturated), 163mg cholesterol, 662mg sodium.

Chipotle-Glazed Duck

Prepare as directed but omit ginger, honey, and soy sauce. While duck roasts, press **2 tablespoons chopped canned chipotle chiles in adobo** (page 25) through sieve into small bowl; discard skin and seeds. Stir **2 tablespoons light (mild) molasses** into chipotle chiles. Proceed as in Step 4.

Red-Cooked Duck

Chinese "red-cooked" food is simmered in a soy-sauce mixture that turns the food a dark reddish brown.

Prep: 25 minutes   Bake: 2 hours

- 4 green onions
- 1 duck (4½ pounds), cut into 8 pieces, fat removed
- 1 tablespoon olive oil
- ¼ cup soy sauce
- 2 tablespoons dry sherry
- 1 tablespoon minced, peeled fresh ginger
- 3 garlic cloves, each cut in half
- 1 tablespoon brown sugar
- 2 whole star anise or ½ teaspoon anise seeds
- ¼ teaspoon ground red pepper (cayenne)
- ¾ cup water

1. Preheat oven to 350°F. Cut green onions on diagonal into 1½-inch pieces.

2. Pat duck dry with paper towels.

3. In 8-quart Dutch oven, heat oil over high heat until very hot. Cook duck, in batches, until golden brown, about 8 minutes, using tongs to transfer duck pieces to large bowl as they are browned. Discard all but 1 tablespoon fat from Dutch oven. Add green onions and cook, stirring, until lightly browned, about 5 minutes.

4. Stir in soy sauce, sherry, ginger, garlic, brown sugar, star anise, ground red pepper, and water. Heat to boiling over high heat, stirring until browned bits are loosened from bottom of Dutch oven.

5. Return duck to Dutch oven. Cover and place in oven. Bake 2 hours, basting duck several times with pan liquid.

6. With tongs, transfer duck to warm deep platter. Strain sauce through sieve; skim and discard fat. Serve duck topped with sauce. Makes 4 main-dish servings.

Each serving: About 721 calories, 38g protein, 8g carbohydrate, 59g total fat (19g saturated), 163mg cholesterol, 1,293mg sodium.

STUFFING POULTRY

Tradition often dictates a stuffed bird (especially the holiday turkey), so the juices of the bird can moisten the stuffing. But some cooks prefer to roast their birds unstuffed and heat the stuffing in a separate baking dish. If you prefer your poultry stuffed, here are some pointers on how to do it safely.

- One important rule of thumb: Remember that the stuffing is only being heated through while inside the bird and does not actually cook. Therefore, it is important that the ingredients be thoroughly cooked before being combined.

- To save time, cut up the raw stuffing ingredients the night before, then cover and refrigerate. If you wish, you can cook the vegetables and meat, then cool, cover, and refrigerate. When you're ready to put the stuffing together, reheat the cooked ingredients in a large skillet before proceeding with the recipe.

- Stuff the bird just before roasting—never in advance—and roast immediately. Use warm cooked ingredients and hot broth or stock for your stuffing. A warm stuffing will reach the safe temperature of 160°F more quickly. At this safe temperature, bacteria, including salmonella, are killed.

- Lightly stuff the body and neck cavities; do not pack. Stuffing needs room to expand during cooking. You will rarely be able to fit all of the stuffing inside the bird, so bake the extra stuffing in a covered buttered baking dish for about 30 minutes or until heated through.

- After cooking, the stuffing temperature should have reached 160°F to be safe. Check the temperature with a meat thermometer inserted deep into the stuffing. If the poultry has reached the proper temperature but the stuffing hasn't, transfer the stuffing to a buttered baking dish, cover, and continue baking until it reaches 160°F.

- Any leftover stuffing should be promptly removed from the bird (to avoid potential bacterial growth). Transfer the stuffing to a covered container and use within three days, or freeze up to one month.

Southwest Corn Bread Stuffing

This old-style stuffing starts with moist homemade Monterey Jack corn bread. Crumble the corn bread, drizzle with chicken broth, and you've got stuffing!

**Prep: 20 minutes plus cooling
Bake: 1 hour 45 minutes**

- 2 cups yellow cornmeal
- 2 teaspoons baking powder
- 1 teaspoon baking soda
- 1 teaspoon salt
- 2 cups buttermilk
- ½ cup butter or margarine (1 stick), melted and cooled
- 1 can (14¾ ounces) cream-style corn
- 2 cans (4 to 4½ ounces each) chopped mild green chiles
- 8 ounces Monterey Jack cheese, shredded (2 cups)
- 4 large eggs, lightly beaten
- ½ cup chicken broth

1. Preheat oven to 350°F. Grease 13" by 9" baking pan or deep oven-safe 12-inch skillet (if skillet is not oven-safe, wrap handle with double layer of foil).

2. In large bowl, combine cornmeal, baking powder, baking soda, and salt. Stir in buttermilk, melted butter, corn, chiles, cheese, and eggs and stir until thoroughly blended. Pour batter into baking pan.

3. Bake corn bread until top is browned and toothpick inserted in center comes out clean, 60 to 65 minutes. Cool in pan on wire rack. (The cornbread can be used after cooling to make stuffing, but it will make a firmer stuffing if allowed to stale slightly. If desired, cover and reserve corn bread up to 2 days.)

4. Prepare stuffing: Crumble corn bread into large bowl. Drizzle with broth; toss to mix well. Use to stuff 12- to 16-pound turkey, or heat in baking dish and serve alongside poultry or ham: Spoon stuffing into greased 13" by 9" baking dish; cover with foil and bake in preheated 325°F oven until heated through, about 45 minutes. Makes about 11 cups stuffing.

Each ½ cup stuffing: About 161 calories, 6g protein, 15g carbohydrate, 9g total fat (5g saturated), 62mg cholesterol, 481mg sodium.

Country Sausage and Corn Bread Stuffing

It's hard to resist this all-time favorite stuffing of pecans, sausage, and store-bought stuffing mix.

Prep: 45 minutes   Bake: 45 minutes

- 1 pound pork sausage meat
- 4 tablespoons butter or margarine
- 3 stalks celery, coarsely chopped
- 1 large onion (12 ounces), coarsely chopped
- 1 red pepper, coarsely chopped
- 1 can (14½ ounces) chicken broth or 1¾ cups Chicken Broth (page 62)
- ½ teaspoon coarsely ground black pepper
- ¾ cup water
- 1 package (14 to 16 ounces) corn bread stuffing mix
- 1½ cups pecans (6 ounces), toasted and coarsely chopped
- ¼ cup chopped fresh parsley

1. Heat 12-inch skillet over medium-high heat until very hot. Add sausage meat and cook, breaking up sausage with side of spoon, until browned, about 10 minutes. With tongs, transfer sausage to large bowl.

2. Discard all but 2 tablespoons sausage drippings. Add butter, celery, onion, and red pepper to skillet; cook, stirring occasionally, until vegetables are golden brown and tender. Stir in broth, black pepper, and water; heat to boiling, stirring until browned bits are loosened from bottom of skillet.

3. Add vegetable mixture, stuffing mix, pecans, and parsley to sausage; stir to combine well. Use to stuff 12- to 16-pound turkey, or heat in baking dish and serve alongside poultry or ham: Spoon stuffing into greased 13" by 9" baking dish; cover with foil and bake in preheated 325°F oven until heated through, about 45 minutes. Makes about 12 cups stuffing.

Each ½ cup stuffing: About 174 calories, 4g protein, 15g carbohydrate, 11g total fat (3g saturated), 13mg cholesterol, 407mg sodium.

Chestnut and Apple Stuffing

It's easiest to peel chestnuts while they're warm. Peel only a few at a time while you keep the rest hot.

Prep: 1 hour   Bake: 45 minutes

2 pounds fresh chestnuts
10 cups ½-inch cubes day-old French bread (one 16-ounce loaf)
6 tablespoons butter or margarine
2 stalks celery, sliced
1 medium onion, coarsely chopped
1¾ pounds Rome Beauty or Crispin apples (3 large), peeled, cored, and coarsely chopped
2 teaspoons poultry seasoning
1 can (14½ ounces) chicken broth or 1¾ cups Chicken Broth (page 62)
1 cup water
1 teaspoon salt

1. Preheat oven to 400°F. With sharp knife, slash shell of each chestnut. Place in jelly-roll pan and roast until shells burst open, about 20 minutes. When cool enough to handle, with paring knife, peel chestnuts. Chop chestnut meat; place in large bowl. Add bread cubes to bowl with chestnuts and toss to combine.

2. In 3-quart saucepan, melt butter over medium-high heat. Add celery and onion and cook until golden brown and tender, about 10 minutes. Add apples and poultry seasoning; cook, stirring occasionally, 2 minutes longer. Stir in broth, water, and salt; heat to boiling over high heat.

3. Pour hot vegetable mixture over chestnut mixture; stir to combine well. Use to stuff 12- to 16-pound turkey, or heat in baking dish and serve alongside poultry or ham: Spoon stuffing into greased 13" by 9" baking dish; cover with foil and bake in preheated 325°F oven until heated through, about 45 minutes. Makes about 12 cups stuffing.

Each ½ cup stuffing: About 158 calories, 3g protein, 28g carbohydrate, 4g total fat (2g saturated), 8mg cholesterol, 321mg sodium.

Northwest Fruit Stuffing

The sour-cherry orchards of the Northwest are celebrated in this fruit-studded stuffing.

Prep: 40 minutes   Bake: 45 minutes

½ cup butter or margarine (1 stick)
1 large red onion, coarsely chopped
1 medium fennel bulb (1¼ pounds), trimmed and coarsely chopped
2 large pears, peeled, cored, and coarsely chopped
1 large Granny Smith apple, peeled, cored, and coarsely chopped
1½ loaves (16 ounces each) sliced firm white bread, cut into ¾-inch cubes and lightly toasted
1 cup chicken broth
⅔ cup dried tart cherries
½ cup golden raisins
⅓ cup chopped fresh parsley
2 teaspoons chopped fresh thyme
1 teaspoon chopped fresh sage
1 teaspoon salt
½ teaspoon coarsely ground black pepper

1. In 12-inch skillet, melt butter over medium-high heat. Add onion and fennel and cook, stirring occasionally, until vegetables are golden brown and tender, 10 to 12 minutes. Add pears and apple and cook 5 minutes longer. Transfer to large bowl.

2. Add bread cubes, broth, cherries, raisins, parsley, thyme, sage, salt, and pepper to bowl with pears and apple; toss to combine well. Use to stuff 12- to 16-pound turkey, or heat in baking dish and serve alongside poultry or ham: Spoon stuffing into greased 13" by 9" baking dish; cover with foil and bake in preheated 325°F oven until heated through, about 45 minutes. Makes about 12 cups stuffing.

Each ½ cup stuffing: About 151 calories, 3g protein, 24g carbohydrate, 5g total fat (3g saturated), 11mg cholesterol, 351mg sodium.

Moist Bread Stuffing

This is the traditional stuffing most of us grew up with. For the best results, use firm white bread. If you wish, set the bread cubes out overnight so they become stale.

Prep: 25 minutes   Bake: 45 minutes

- ½ cup butter or margarine (1 stick)
- 5 stalks celery, finely chopped
- 1 medium onion, finely chopped
- 2 loaves (16 ounces each) sliced firm white bread, cut into ¾-inch cubes
- 1 can (14½ ounces) chicken broth or 1¾ cups Chicken Broth (page 62)
- ¼ cup chopped fresh parsley
- 1 teaspoon dried thyme
- ¾ teaspoon salt
- ½ teaspoon ground black pepper
- ½ teaspoon dried sage

1. In 5-quart Dutch oven, melt butter over medium heat. Add celery and onion and cook, stirring occasionally, until tender, about 15 minutes.

2. Remove Dutch oven from heat. Add bread cubes, broth, parsley, thyme, salt, pepper, and sage; toss to combine well. Use to stuff 12- to 16-pound turkey, or heat in baking dish and serve alongside poultry or ham: Spoon stuffing into greased 13" by 9" baking dish; cover with foil and bake in preheated 325°F oven until heated through, about 45 minutes. Makes about 10 cups stuffing.

Each ½ cup stuffing: About 170 calories, 4g protein, 24g carbohydrate, 6g total fat (3g saturated), 13mg cholesterol, 473mg sodium.

Parsnips, Swiss Chard, and Bacon Stuffing

The unusual pairing of parsnips and Swiss chard with bacon will surprise and delight your family and guests.

Prep: 45 minutes   Bake: 45 minutes

- 8 ounces sliced bacon, cut into ½-inch pieces
- 1 pound parsnips, peeled and coarsely chopped
- 3 stalks celery, coarsely chopped
- 1 large onion (12 ounces), coarsely chopped
- 1½ pounds Swiss chard, tough stems trimmed and leaves cut into 2-inch pieces
- 1 can (14½ ounces) chicken broth or 1¾ cups Chicken Broth (page 62)
- ½ teaspoon coarsely ground black pepper
- 2 packages (8 ounces each) herb-seasoned stuffing mix

1. In 12-inch skillet, cook bacon over medium-low heat until browned. With slotted spoon, transfer to large bowl.

2. Discard all but ¼ cup bacon drippings from skillet. Increase heat to medium-high; add parsnips, celery, and onion and cook, stirring occasionally, until vegetables are golden and tender, about 15 minutes. Add Swiss chard; cook, stirring frequently, until chard wilts, about 2 minutes. Stir in broth and pepper.

3. Add vegetable mixture and stuffing mix to bacon in bowl; toss to combine well. Use to stuff 12- to 16-pound turkey, or heat in baking dish and swerve alongside poultry or ham: Spoon stuffing into greased 13" by 9" baking dish; cover with foil and bake in preheated 325°F oven until heated through, about 45 minutes. Makes about 14 cups stuffing.

Each ½ cup stuffing: About 112 calories, 3g protein, 17g carbohydrate, 3g total fat (1g saturated), 3mg cholesterol, 390mg sodium.

6

FISH & SHELLFISH

The growing popularity of fish and shellfish is hardly a surprise. Seafood is a rich source of protein, vitamins, and minerals and is low in fat. And oily fish, such as salmon and tuna, are high in omega-3 fatty acids, which can lower blood cholesterol levels.

BUYING FISH AND SHELLFISH

The surface of a whole fish should glisten but not look slimy. Ask the fishmonger to show you the gills; they should be bright red with no tinge of brown. The eyes should not be sunken, but don't worry if they are clouded over, because the eyes of some fish lose their shine soon after they are caught.

Fish fillets and steaks are often sold in plastic-wrapped trays. Look for fish that appears moist and has no gaps in the flesh, which should feel firm through the plastic. The meat of dark fish, such as tuna, should not contain any rainbow streaks.

Mollusks (including clams, mussels, and oysters), must be purchased alive because their viscera deteriorate quickly once dead. Tightly closed shells indicate the mollusks are alive, but if you tap a gaping shell and it closes, it's also fine. Don't buy mollusks with broken shells. And if a clam or mussel feels especially heavy, it could be filled with mud, so discard it. Mollusks sold out of their shells, like scallops and squid, should be as sweet smelling as an ocean breeze. And the siphons of soft-shell clams should retract slightly when touched.

Crustaceans, including crabs and lobsters, should be purchased alive from a store with a large turnover and appear lively. Fresh shrimp should also be subjected to the sniff test; black spots on the shell mean the shrimp are over the hill.

STORING FISH AND SHELLFISH

- Keep fish and shellfish as cold as possible. Have the seafood you purchase packed in ice, or place it in the same bag as your frozen food.
- Store fish in the coldest part of the refrigerator, where the temperature is between 35° and 40°F. Or store on ice: Fill a baking dish with ice, and place the wrapped seafood on top, replenishing the ice as needed. You can also cover frozen artificial ice packets with a kitchen towel and place the wrapped fish on top.
- It is especially important to keep oily fish, such as mackerel and bluefish, as cold as possible. Their high fat content means they can go rancid quickly at less-than-ideal temperatures.
- If you must freeze seafood, be sure it is very fresh, and wrap it tightly in plastic wrap and heavy-duty foil. Freeze for up to three months.
- Shellfish should also be placed in the coldest part of the refrigerator. Store live clams, mussels, and oysters in a large bowl covered with a wet towel; use within one day. Refrigerate crabs in a tightly closed heavy-duty paper bag poked with a few airholes; cook within one day of purchase. Lobsters should be cooked on the day of purchase because they don't last long once out of water. Keep them well wrapped in a wet cloth or in several layers of newspaper in the refrigerator.

Mussels with Tomato and White Wine

- Cooked crab and lobster should be eaten within one day of purchase. Shucked oysters and crabmeat are often pasteurized, which extends their shelf life but decreases their flavor.

COOKING SUCCESS

Here's the simple secret to cooking fish successfully: Don't overcook it. Cook it until the flesh is just opaque throughout; it will continue to cook after it has been removed from the heat.

Before cooking fillets, especially thick ones, run your fingers over the flesh to feel for any stray bones. Remove them with tweezers set aside for that purpose.

To check fish fillets or steaks for doneness, use the tip of a small knife to separate the flesh in the thickest part; it should be uniformly opaque. To check whole fish, make an incision at the backbone to see if the flesh is opaque or insert an instant-read thermometer in the thickest part near the backbone; it should read 135° to 140°F.

When cooking clams, mussels, or oysters, scrub the shells well under cold running water to remove any surface sand and grit.

KNOW YOUR FISH

Fish is categorized two ways: by shape (round or flat) and by fat content (lean to oily). It is helpful to know the fat content, flavor, and texture of various fish so you can easily substitute one for another.

Round fish have a plump, cylindrical shape and an eye on each side of the head. The backbone runs down the center of the fish, separating the two thick fillets. Round fish are generally filleted or cut into steaks but can also be cooked whole. Common round fish include salmon, red snapper, sea bass, monkfish, and catfish.

Flatfish have wide, thin bodies with both eyes on the same side of the head. The backbone runs down the center of the fish, with two lines of bones fanning out on either side, separating the top and bottom fillets. Flatfish are usually filleted. The most common are sole, flounder, and halibut.

The fat content of a fish is a good indicator of the flavor you can expect. *Lean fish* make up the majority of fish. They have the blandest flavor and most delicate

THE FISH EXCHANGE

Lean	Moderate	Oily
Cod, Scrod	Bluefish	Bluefin tuna
Flounder	Catfish	Butterfish
Grouper	Mahi-mahi	Herring
Haddock	Rainbow trout	Lake trout
Halibut	Striped bass	Mackerel
Monkfish	Swordfish	Pompano
Ocean perch	Yellowfin tuna	Salmon
Orange roughy		Shad
Pike		Whitefish
Pollock		
Red snapper		
Rockfish		
Sea bass		
Sole		
Tilapia		
Tilefish		
Turbot		
Whiting		

texture. *Moderately oily fish* have a slightly higher fat content, a pleasant texture, and a mild flavor. Some fish, such as tuna, can be categorized as either moderately oily or oily, depending on the species. *Oily fish* have flesh that is strong-tasting, firm, and meaty. They are high in omega-3 fatty acids.

FISH GLOSSARY

Here is a glossary of some of the fish you are likely to find in your market.

Arctic char Very similar to salmon; usually farm-raised. Also known as salmon trout.

Bluefish A dark-fleshed, strong-flavored, oily fish. The fresher it is, the milder the flavor.

Catfish A beloved freshwater fish of the American South. Farm-raised catfish are readily available.

Cod This saltwater fish, found in both Atlantic and Pacific waters, is known for its mild flavor and white, flaky flesh. Small cod are called scrod.

Flounder A popular flatfish with white flesh, a delicate texture, and mild flavor.

Grouper Has firm, meaty, white flesh and is sold whole or filleted.

Halibut A large flatfish with firm, flavorful flesh. Often sold as fillets, but one of the few flatfish thick enough to be cut into steaks.

Mackerel An oily fish with a pronounced fish flavor. When large, it is called *Spanish mackerel.*

Monkfish A favored fish in Provence, monkfish has firm flesh and a lobsterlike flavor.

Pompano On the West Coast, pompano is called *yellowtail.* It has somewhat oily flesh and a firm texture.

Red snapper An excellent all-purpose fish and one of the few fillets firm enough to be grilled.

Salmon Much of the salmon in our markets is farm-raised, even when labeled "Atlantic" or "Norwegian." Wild salmon, such as *coho, king*, and *sockeye*, has superior flavor but is available in limited quantities.

Sole A flatfish with firm white flesh and a distinctively delicate flavor.

Striped bass Most striped bass in today's markets is a farm-raised hybrid of striped bass and white bass.

Swordfish A fish with a firm and meaty texture that is a good choice for broiling and grilling.

Trout Rainbow trout and brook trout are about 12 ounces each and serve one person.

Tuna A huge fish with plenty of muscle and flavor. The most common varieties are *bluefin, yellowfin, albacore*, and *skipjack.* Tuna is also known as *ahi* and *bonito.*

KNOW YOUR SHELLFISH

Mollusks have soft bodies that are protected by shells consisting of one or more parts. This glossary lists the most popular shellfish.

Clams. Hard-shell clams, the most common Atlantic Coast variety, are categorized by size. *Littlenecks* are the smallest, *cherrystones* are medium, and *chowder clams* are the largest.

Soft-shell clams have delicate shells that don't completely close because of the long necklike siphon that protrudes between the two halves of the shell. On the East Coast, they are usually called *steamers*, because they are so delicious when steamed. They are also know as *Ipswich* clams, so named for the location of one of the largest clam beds. West Coast soft-shell clams include the huge *geoduck* (GOO-ee-duck) and the long *razor clam.*

Mussels Most markets carry *blue mussels,* which have bluish black shells and are harvested wild or cultivated. *New Zealand green mussels* are slightly larger and have a bright green shell.

Oysters Oysters are usually named for the location of their beds: *Wellfleet, Chincoteague,* and *Apalachicola* on the East Coast and *Westcott Bay, Tomales Bay,* and the tiny *Olympia* on the West Coast are examples.

Scallops *Sea scallops* are gathered year round and are relatively large. Small *bay scallops* are only available in the fall and winter. *Calico scallops* are very small, but they have the least flavor and the toughest texture.

Squid Also called calamari, many fish markets sell it already cleaned.

CRUSTACEANS

Crustaceans have elongated bodies that are covered by jointed shells.

Crab On the West Coast, there is *Dungeness crab,* whose season runs from October to April. *King crab,* usually from Alaska, provides the large legs that are sold fresh or frozen. Small *blue crabs* are found along the East and Gulf Coasts. The large pieces of meat from the body are sold as lump, jumbo, or backfin crabmeat.

Soft-shell crabs Blue crabs caught during the short period after they have shed their hard shells and before their new, soft shells have hardened. They are available fresh from May to September.

Stone crabs Popular in Florida, the claws are harvested, and the rest of the crab is tossed back into the water so new claws can regenerate.

Lobster There are two types: *American (Maine) lobster,* from the North Atlantic coast, and *rock (spiny) lobster,* which is harvested off Florida, California, Australia, and New Zealand. It is usually sold as frozen lobster tail.

Shrimp More than 95 percent of the shrimp sold has been previously frozen. *Warm-water shrimp* live in tropical waters and are usually categorized by the color of their shell: pink, white, blue, or black tiger.

Tarragon-Roasted Salmon

No fish poacher? Roast a whole salmon in the oven instead. This herb-stuffed fish is a delicious dish that serves up to ten people. Any leftovers can be turned into tasty salmon cakes or salmon salad.

Prep: 10 minutes   Roast: 40 minutes

- 2 **large lemons, thinly sliced**
- 1 **whole salmon (5½ pounds), cleaned and scaled**
- 2 **tablespoons olive oil**
- ½ **teaspoon salt**
- ½ **teaspoon coarsely ground black pepper**
- 1 **large bunch tarragon**
- 1 **small bunch parsley**
  Caper Sauce (right)
  lemon wedges

1. Preheat oven to 450°F. Line jelly-roll pan with foil. Arrange one-third of lemon slices in row down center of pan.

2. Rinse salmon inside and out with cold running water; pat dry with paper towels. Rub outside of salmon with oil. Place salmon on top of lemon slices. Sprinkle cavity with salt and pepper. Place tarragon and parsley sprigs and half of remaining lemon slices in cavity. Arrange remaining lemon slices on top of fish. Roast salmon until just opaque throughout when knife is inserted at backbone, about 40 minutes.

3. Meanwhile, prepare Caper Sauce.

4. Carefully remove lemon slices and peel off skin from top of salmon; discard. Using two wide spatulas, transfer salmon to cutting board.

5. To serve, slide cake server under front section of top fillet and lift off fillet; transfer to warm large platter. Slide server under backbone and lift it away from bottom fillet; discard. Slide cake server between bottom fillet and skin and transfer fillet to platter. Serve with lemon wedges and caper sauce. Makes 10 main-dish servings.

Each serving without sauce: About 325 calories, 33g protein, 1g carbohydrate, 20g total fat (4g saturated), 96mg cholesterol, 213mg sodium.

SMOKED AND PROCESSED FISH

 Test Kitchen Tip

Anchovies These tiny salted fish are an important seasoning in Mediterranean cooking. They are usually found filleted, salt-cured, and canned in oil. Because most recipes call only for a few fillets, you will often have leftover anchovies; cover the can tightly with plastic wrap and use within one week. Anchovy paste is a convenient product because there is no waste. About ½ teaspoon of anchovy paste equals one fillet.

Caviar Real caviar is the salted roe of sturgeon. You may see lumpfish and salmon "caviar," but they are not really caviar—they're just fish eggs. Caviar is rare, costly, and uniquely delicious. There are three categories: *beluga* (large dark gray eggs), *osetra* (medium eggs that range in color from yellow to brown), and *sevruga* (smaller eggs that are light gray).

Salt Cod Cod that has been salted and dried. Buy thick white pieces; salt cod turns gray as it ages. Salt cod is always soaked thoroughly and rinsed before cooking to remove the salt.

Smoked Salmon *Nova* is named after the true Nova Scotia salmon, which is rarely seen in our markets. It has been cured in brine and then smoked. *Lox* is salmon that has been pickled in a spiced brine but is not always smoked.

Caper Sauce

In medium bowl, mix ¾ **cup sour cream,** ½ **cup mayonnaise,** ¼ **cup milk, 3 tablespoons capers,** drained and chopped, **2 tablespoons chopped fresh tarragon,** ½ **teaspoon freshly grated lemon peel,** and ⅛ **teaspoon coarsely ground black pepper** until blended. Cover and refrigerate until ready to serve, up to two days. Makes about 1⅔ cups.

Each tablespoon: About 58 calories, 0g protein, 1g carbohydrate, 6g total fat (2g saturated), 7mg cholesterol, 90mg sodium.

Cold Poached Salmon Steaks with Watercress Sauce

One of the best warm-weather entrées around. Fast and easy, and you don't even have to turn on the oven.

Prep: 15 minutes plus cooling   Cook: 10 minutes

- 1 medium lemon
- 4 salmon steaks, 1 inch thick (6 ounces each)
- ¾ teaspoon salt
- ½ teaspoon coarsely ground black pepper
- 1 medium onion, thinly sliced
  Watercress Sauce (below)

1. From lemon, squeeze juice; reserve for Watercress Sauce. Set lemon shells aside. Rub salmon steaks evenly with salt and pepper.

2. In 12-inch skillet, heat ½ *inch water* to boiling over high heat. Add salmon, onion, and lemon shells; heat to boiling. Reduce heat; cover and simmer until fish is just opaque throughout, 5 to 8 minutes. With slotted spatula, transfer fish to platter. Let cool 30 minutes, or cover and refrigerate to serve later.

3. Meanwhile, prepare Watercress Sauce.

4. Remove skin and bones from salmon, if you like. Serve with sauce. Makes 4 main-dish servings.

Each serving without sauce: About 274 calories, 30g protein, 0g carbohydrate, 16g total fat (3g saturated), 88mg cholesterol, 231mg sodium.

Watercress Sauce

In blender or in food processor with knife blade attached, puree ½ **bunch watercress,** tough stems trimmed (1 cup), ½ **cup sour cream, 1 tablespoon fresh lemon juice, 1 teaspoon chopped fresh tarragon or ⅛ teaspoon dried tarragon, 1½ teaspoons sugar,** and **1 teaspoon salt** until smooth. Cover and refrigerate. Makes about ½ cup sauce.

Each tablespoon: About 35 calories, 1g protein, 2g carbohydrate, 3g total fat (2g saturated), 6mg cholesterol, 301mg sodium.

Salt-Baked Fish

Baking a whole fish in a crust of kosher salt seals in the juices and guarantees exquisitely moist—and surprisingly unsalty—fish.

Prep: 5 minutes   Bake: 30 minutes

- 4 cups kosher salt
- 1 whole red snapper, striped bass, or porgy (1½ to 2 pounds), cleaned and scaled
- 1 lemon
- 3 rosemary or thyme sprigs

1. Preheat oven to 450°F. Line 13" by 9" baking pan with foil; spread 2 cups salt in bottom of pan.

2. Rinse snapper inside and out with cold running water; pat dry with paper towels. From lemon, cut 3 slices. Cut remaining lemon into wedges. Place lemon slices and rosemary in cavity of fish. Place fish on bed of salt; cover with remaining 2 cups salt. Bake until fish is just opaque throughout when knife is inserted at backbone, about 30 minutes.

3. To serve, tap salt crust to release from top of fish; discard. Slide cake server under front section of top fillet and lift off fillet; transfer to platter. Slide server under backbone and lift it away from bottom fillet; discard. Slide cake server between bottom fillet and skin and transfer fillet to platter. Serve with reserved lemon wedges. Makes 2 main-dish servings.

Each serving: About 188 calories, 37g protein, 6g carbohydrate, 3g total fat (1g saturated), 66mg cholesterol, 800mg sodium.

Roast Striped Bass

Prepare as directed above substituting **1 whole striped bass (2¼ pounds),** cleaned and scaled, for snapper and omitting salt. Make diagonal slashes on each side of fish at 1-inch intervals, about ¼ inch deep. Place bass in medium roasting pan (14" by 10"). Proceed as above. Makes 4 main-dish servings.

Trout Meunière

Here's the classic way to prepare trout, along with four tasty seasoning variations. One trout per person makes a generous serving.

Prep: 10 minutes plus standing Cook: 20 minutes

- 4 brook or rainbow trout (10 to 12 ounces each), cleaned and scaled
- 1 cup milk
- ¼ cup all-purpose flour
- ½ teaspoon salt
- 4 tablespoons vegetable oil
- ¼ cup fresh lemon juice
- 4 tablespoons butter or margarine
- ¼ cup chopped fresh parsley

1. Rinse trout inside and out with cold running water; pat dry with paper towels. Soak trout in milk 10 minutes. On waxed paper, combine flour and salt. Remove trout from milk and coat evenly with flour mixture, shaking off excess.

2. In 12-inch skillet, heat 2 tablespoons oil over medium heat until very hot. Add 2 trout and cook until just opaque throughout when knife is inserted at backbone, 4 to 5 minutes per side. Transfer to platter and keep warm. Repeat with remaining 2 tablespoons oil and remaining fish.

3. Pour off any fat remaining in skillet and wipe skillet clean with paper towels. Return skillet to heat; add lemon juice and cook 15 seconds. Add butter; cook until foamy, about 2 minutes. Stir in parsley and pour butter sauce over fish. Makes 4 main-dish servings.

Each serving: About 493 calories, 41g protein, 8g carbohydrate, 32g total fat (10g saturated), 143mg cholesterol, 468mg sodium.

Trout with Brown Butter and Sage

Prepare as directed through Step 2. In Step 3, substitute **2 tablespoons chopped fresh sage** for parsley and cook until butter is lightly browned, about 3 minutes. Add **1 teaspoon fresh lemon juice.** Pour sauce over fish.

Trout Amandine

Prepare as directed through Step 2. In Step 3, omit parsley. Add ¼ **cup sliced almonds** to skillet with butter and cook until almonds are golden, 2 to 3 minutes. Add **1 teaspoon fresh lemon juice.** Pour sauce over fish.

Trout Grenobloise

Prepare as directed through Step 2. In Step 3, omit lemon juice. From **1 lemon,** remove peel and white pith. Cut lemon into ¼-inch-thick slices; discard seeds. Cut slices into ½-inch pieces. After cooking butter until foamy, add lemon, **4 teaspoons capers,** and **1 tablespoon chopped fresh parsley.** Spoon sauce over fish.

Trout with Cornmeal and Bacon

Prepare as directed through Step 2, substituting ⅓ **cup cornmeal** for flour in Step 1 and bacon drippings from **4 strips bacon** for oil in Step 2. Omit Step 3. Garnish fish with **crumbled cooked bacon.**

TROUT

Rainbow trout and brook trout are marketed at just the right size for single servings: between 8 and 12 ounces. They belong to the *Salmonidae* (salmon) family. Rainbow trout has a green or blue back, silvery sides covered with tiny dark spots, and a thin red strip running along each side. Brook trout, on the other hand, has a green-brown back and green sides, and its skin is mottled with yellow and red spots. Although trout is still caught in the wild, most of the trout in stores have been farmed in springwater–fed ponds. Trout is mild flavored and delicate and is best enjoyed when prepared simply as in our tasty recipes.

Broiled Salmon Steaks

Broiling is a quick—and easy—way to get healthful, flavorful salmon steaks onto the dinner table in less than 15 minutes.

Prep: 3 minutes   Broil: 10 minutes

- 4 salmon steaks, 1 inch thick (6 ounces each)
- 1 teaspoon vegetable oil
  pinch salt
  pinch ground black pepper

1. Preheat broiler. Rub both sides of salmon steaks with oil and sprinkle with salt and pepper.

2. Place salmon on rack in broiling pan. Place pan in broiler, 4 inches from heat source. Broil salmon 5 minutes, then turn and broil until fish is just opaque throughout, about 5 minutes longer. Makes 4 main-dish servings.

Each serving: About 284 calories, 30g protein, 0g carbohydrate, 17g total fat (3g saturated), 88mg cholesterol, 123mg sodium.

Salmon Steaks Teriyaki

Prepare as above, omitting salt and pepper in Step 1. In small saucepan, combine **6 tablespoons soy sauce, ½ teaspoon Asian sesame oil, 3 tablespoons brown sugar, 1 garlic clove,** crushed, and **1 teaspoon minced, peeled fresh ginger;** heat to boiling over medium-high heat. Boil until mixture has thickened slightly, about 3 minutes. Strain through fine-mesh sieve; discard solids. In Step 2, broil salmon 3 minutes, then brush with glaze and broil 2 minutes more. Turn steaks and broil 3 minutes; brush with glaze and broil 2 minutes more. To serve, sprinkle with **2 green onions,** cut on diagonal into thin slices. Makes 4 main-dish servings.

Each serving: About 313 calories, 36g protein, 13g carbohydrate, 12g total fat (2g saturated), 93mg cholesterol, 1,550mg sodium.

Pan-Seared Tuna

This is a great way to cook tuna steaks: Get the oil in the pan very hot and sear the fish very quickly. The oil in the marinade moistens the fish but adds hardly any fat at all.

Prep: 10 minutes plus marinating   Cook: 6 minutes

- 4 large lemons
- 6 tablespoons olive oil
- 6 tablespoons chopped fresh parsley
- ½ teaspoon salt
- ¼ teaspoon ground black pepper
- 4 tuna steaks, ¾ inch thick (5 ounces each)

1. From lemons, grate 1 teaspoon peel and squeeze ⅔ cup juice. In 9-inch square baking dish, with wire whisk, whisk lemon peel and juice, 3 tablespoons oil, 5 tablespoons parsley, salt, and pepper until mixed. Add tuna, turning to coat. Cover and refrigerate 45 minutes to marinate, turning occasionally.

2. In 10-inch cast-iron skillet or other heavy skillet, heat remaining 3 tablespoons oil over medium-high heat until hot. Add tuna and cook until pale pink in center (medium), about 3 minutes per side, or until desired doneness. Transfer to plates and sprinkle with remaining 1 tablespoon parsley. Makes 4 main-dish servings.

Each serving: About 246 calories, 30g protein, 1g carbohydrate, 13g total fat (2g saturated), 48mg cholesterol, 341mg sodium.

Halibut Braised in Red Wine

Red wine *does* go with fish! Here the slight acidity of the wine accents the mild flavor of the halibut. Other tasty fish options include salmon and monkfish.

Prep: 10 minutes   Cook: 30 minutes

- 2 tablespoons butter or margarine
- ½ cup finely chopped shallots (3 large)
- 1 garlic clove, finely chopped
- 1 carrot, peeled and thinly sliced
- 2 cups dry red wine
- ¾ cup chicken broth
- ½ teaspoon salt
- ¼ teaspoon dried thyme
- 4 skinless, boneless halibut steaks, 1 inch thick (6 ounces each)
- 2 tablespoons chopped fresh parsley

1. In nonstick 12-inch skillet, melt 1 tablespoon butter over low heat. Add shallots and garlic and cook, stirring occasionally, until shallots are tender, about 4 minutes. Add carrot and cook 4 minutes longer. Add wine and heat to boiling over high heat; boil 2 minutes. Add broth, salt, and thyme. Slip in halibut and reduce heat to low. Cover and cook until fish is just opaque throughout, about 8 minutes. With slotted spatula, transfer fish to platter and keep warm.

2. Increase heat to high and boil wine mixture until it has reduced by half, 7 to 10 minutes. Remove from heat and swirl in remaining 1 tablespoon butter until melted. Strain sauce through fine-mesh sieve. To serve, spoon sauce over fish and sprinkle with parsley. Makes 4 main-dish servings.

Each serving: About 277 calories, 37g protein, 8g carbohydrate, 10g total fat (4g saturated), 70mg cholesterol, 643mg sodium.

Swordfish Steaks Broiled with Maître d'Hôtel Butter

Swordfish is terrific with the classic lemon-and-herb butter, but any of the other flavored butters (page 434) would be just as inviting. If you like, top each steak with a tablespoon of the herbed butter before serving.

Prep: 15 minutes   Broil: 8 minutes

- 4 teaspoons Maître d'Hôtel Butter (page 434)
- 4 swordfish steaks, 1 inch thick (6 ounces each)

1. Prepare Maître d'Hôtel Butter.

2. Preheat broiler. Place swordfish on rack in broiling pan. Spread ½ teaspoon Maître d'Hôtel Butter on each side of each fish steak. Place pan in broiler, 4 inches from heat source. Broil swordfish, without turning, until just opaque throughout, 8 to 10 minutes. Spoon pan juices over fish to serve. Makes 4 main-dish servings.

Each serving: About 217 calories, 30g protein, 0g carbohydrate, 10g total fat (4g saturated), 69mg cholesterol, 175mg sodium.

Swordfish Steaks Broiled with Maître d'Hôtel Butter

Broiled Cod Steaks Montauk

A flavored mayonnaise topping is a quick way to add punch to broiled fish.

Prep: 5 minutes   Broil: 6 minutes

¼ cup mayonnaise
½ teaspoon Dijon mustard
⅛ teaspoon salt
⅛ teaspoon ground black pepper
4 cod steaks, ½ inch thick (6 ounces each)

1. Preheat broiler.
2. In small bowl, mix mayonnaise, mustard, salt, and pepper until blended.
3. Lightly oil rack in broiling pan. Place cod on rack in broiling pan. Place pan in broiler, 4 inches from heat source. Broil cod until just opaque throughout, 5 to 7 minutes. Remove broiling pan from broiler. Brush mayonnaise mixture on fish. Return pan to broiler; broil until mayonnaise mixture is lightly browned and bubbling, 1 to 2 minutes longer. Makes 4 main-dish servings.

Each serving: About 222 calories, 27g protein, 0g carbohydrate, 12g total fat (2g saturated), 72mg cholesterol, 247mg sodium.

Lemon Topping
Prepare as directed but substitute ½ **teaspoon freshly grated lemon peel** for Dijon mustard.

Horseradish Topping
Prepare as directed but substitute **1 teaspoon bottled white horseradish** for Dijon mustard.

Dill-Pepper Topping
Prepare as directed but substitute **2 tablespoons chopped fresh dill** for Dijon mustard and **¼ teaspoon coarsely ground black pepper** for ground black pepper.

Lime-Jalapeño Topping
Prepare as directed but substitute **½ teaspoon freshly grated lime peel** for Dijon mustard and add **1 small jalapeño,** seeded and minced, to mayonnaise mixture.

Parmesan Topping
Prepare as directed but substitute **2 tablespoons freshly grated Parmesan cheese** for Dijon mustard.

Dried Tomato Topping
Prepare as directed (left) but substitute **1 dried tomato,** finely chopped, for Dijon mustard.

Cod Veracruz

This is fish, Mexican-style. Chile aficionados may want to add a little more cayenne pepper or hot chili powder.

Prep: 15 minutes   Cook: 35 minutes

4 tablespoons vegetable oil
1 yellow pepper, cut into thin strips
1 medium onion, thinly sliced
1 jalapeño chile, seeded and finely chopped
1 garlic clove, thinly sliced
¾ teaspoon chili powder
½ teaspoon salt
1 can (14½ to 16 ounces) tomatoes in puree
½ teaspoon ground coriander
¼ teaspoon ground cumin
⅛ teaspoon ground red pepper (cayenne)
4 cod steaks, ¾ inch thick (4 ounces each)

1. In nonstick 12-inch skillet, heat 2 tablespoons oil over medium heat. Add yellow pepper and onion and cook, stirring, until tender and golden, 15 minutes. Add jalapeño, garlic, ½ teaspoon chili powder, and ¼ teaspoon salt and cook, stirring, 3 minutes.
2. Add tomatoes with their puree and cook, breaking up tomatoes with side of spoon, until mixture has slightly reduced, about 10 minutes.
3. Meanwhile, in cup, combine coriander, cumin, remaining ¼ teaspoon each chili powder and salt, and ground red pepper. Sprinkle both sides of cod steaks with spice mixture.
4. In 10-inch skillet, heat remaining 2 tablespoons oil over medium-high heat until hot. Add cod and cook until steaks are just opaque throughout and nicely browned, 3 to 4 minutes per side. To serve, arrange fish on platter and top with warm tomato sauce. Makes 4 main-dish servings.

Each serving: About 254 calories, 19g protein, 12g carbohydrate, 14g total fat (2g saturated), 43mg cholesterol, 508mg sodium.

Roasted Salmon in Tarragon and Capers

A whole salmon fillet with a crusty crumb-and-herb topping looks festive, tastes fabulous, and is surprisingly quick and easy to prepare.

Prep: 10 minutes   Roast: 30 minutes

- 3 tablespoons butter or margarine
- 1/3 cup plain dried bread crumbs
- 1/4 cup loosely packed fresh parsley leaves, minced
- 3 tablespoons drained capers, minced
- 1 teaspoon dried tarragon
- 2 teaspoons freshly grated lemon peel
- 1/4 teaspoon salt
- 1/4 teaspoon coarsely ground black pepper
- 1 whole salmon fillet (2 to 2 1/2 pounds)
  lemon wedges

1. Preheat oven to 450°F. Line jelly-roll pan with foil; grease foil.

2. In 1-quart saucepan, melt butter over low heat. Remove saucepan from heat; stir in bread crumbs, parsley, capers, tarragon, lemon peel, salt, and pepper.

3. Place salmon, skin side down, in prepared pan. Pat crumb mixture on top. Roast until salmon turns opaque throughout and topping is lightly browned, about 30 minutes.

4. With two large spatulas, carefully transfer salmon to platter (it's okay if salmon skin sticks to foil). Serve with lemon wedges. Makes 6 main-dish servings.

Each serving: About 325 calories, 28g protein, 5g carbohydrate, 21g total fat (4g saturated), 76mg cholesterol, 425mg sodium.

Fennel-Crusted Bluefish

If you prefer to grill, rub the bluefish with olive oil, then with the fennel mixture. Serve with lemon wedges.

Prep: 5 minutes   Cook: 8 minutes

- 2 teaspoons fennel seeds, crushed
- 1/2 teaspoon whole black peppercorns, crushed
- 1/2 teaspoon salt
- 4 pieces bluefish fillet (6 ounces each)
- 1 tablespoon butter or margarine
- 1 teaspoon olive oil

1. In cup, combine fennel seeds, peppercorns, and salt. Use to rub on both sides of bluefish fillets.

2. In nonstick 12-inch skillet, melt butter with oil over medium-high heat. Add bluefish and cook until fish is just opaque throughout, 4 to 6 minutes per side. Makes 4 main-dish servings.

Each serving: About 247 calories, 34g protein, 0g carbohydrate, 11g total fat (3g saturated), 108mg cholesterol, 422mg sodium.

TURNING FILLETS IN FRYING SKILLET

To turn fish fillets so they don't fall apart, use a wide slotted spatula, supporting the fillet with your fingers as you turn it.

Fried Catfish

Before frying, let the coated fish fillets stand for a few minutes to set the crust; it will adhere better and fry to crispy perfection.

Prep: 15 minutes plus standing   Cook: 20 minutes

- ¾ cup cornmeal
- 2 tablespoons all-purpose flour
- ½ teaspoon salt
- ¼ teaspoon ground black pepper
- ¼ cup milk
- 6 catfish fillets (6 ounces each)
- 4 tablespoons vegetable oil
- lemon wedges

1. In zip-tight plastic bag, combine cornmeal, flour, salt, and pepper. Pour milk into pie plate. Dip catfish fillets, one at a time, into milk to coat well, then into cornmeal mixture, shaking bag to coat fish. Place coated catfish on wire rack set over waxed paper; set aside to dry 20 minutes.

2. In 10-inch skillet, heat 2 tablespoons oil over medium-high heat until hot. Add 3 catfish fillets to skillet and fry until just opaque throughout and golden, 4 to 5 minutes per side. Transfer to paper towels to drain. Repeat with remaining 2 tablespoons oil and remaining catfish. Serve with lemon wedges. Makes 6 main-dish servings.

Each serving: About 377 calories, 28g protein, 16g carbohydrate, 22g total fat (4g saturated), 58mg cholesterol, 255mg sodium.

Codfish Cakes

Crisp but tender fish cakes are a great weekend supper; serve with homemade Tartar Sauce (page 434).

Prep: 30 minutes plus chilling   Cook: 10 minutes

- 3 tablespoons vegetable oil
- 2 large stalks celery, chopped
- 1 small onion, chopped
- 1½ cups fresh bread crumbs (about 3 slices bread)
- 1 pound cod fillet
- 1 large egg, lightly beaten
- 2 tablespoons light mayonnaise
- 1 tablespoon chopped fresh parsley
- 1 teaspoon fresh lemon juice
- ¼ teaspoon hot pepper sauce
- ½ teaspoon salt
- lemon wedges

1. In 12-inch skillet, heat 1 tablespoon oil over medium heat. Add celery and onion and cook, stirring occasionally, until onion is tender and lightly browned, about 10 minutes. Remove skillet from heat.

2. Place two-thirds of bread crumbs on waxed paper. Place remaining crumbs in medium bowl. With tweezers, remove any bones from cod. With large chef's knife, finely chop fish; add to bowl with bread crumbs. Stir in celery-onion mixture, egg, mayonnaise, parsley, lemon juice, pepper sauce, and salt until well combined.

3. Shape fish mixture into four 3-inch patties (mixture will be very soft and moist). Refrigerate patties until firm, at least 30 minutes. Wipe skillet clean.

4. Use bread crumbs on waxed paper to coat patties, patting crumbs to adhere. In same skillet, heat remaining 2 tablespoons oil over medium-low heat until hot. Add patties to skillet and cook until browned and cooked through, 5 to 6 minutes per side. Serve with lemon wedges. Makes 4 main-dish servings.

Each serving: About 298 calories, 24g protein, 15g carbohydrate, 16g total fat (2g saturated), 105mg cholesterol, 565mg sodium.

Cod, Cabbage, and Bacon in Parchment

Curly savoy cabbage is more delicate than plain green cabbage and goes especially well with the subtle flavor of cod.

Prep: 20 minutes   Bake: 20 minutes

- 2   slices bacon, chopped
- 2   teaspoons vegetable oil
- ½   head (¾ pound) savoy cabbage, thinly sliced (6 cups)
- ½   plus ⅛ teaspoon salt
- ¼   plus ⅛ teaspoon ground black pepper pinch dried thyme
- 4   thick pieces cod fillet (6 ounces each)
- 4   squares (12 inches each) cooking parchment or foil
- 1   tablespoon butter or margarine, cut into very small pieces

1. Preheat oven to 400°F.

2. In 12-inch skillet, cook bacon over medium-low heat until browned. With slotted spoon, transfer to paper towels to drain. Discard drippings from skillet; wipe skillet clean.

3. In same skillet, heat oil over high heat. Add cabbage, ½ teaspoon salt, ¼ teaspoon pepper, and thyme; cook, stirring, until cabbage is tender. Stir in bacon.

4. With tweezers, remove any bones from cod. Place one-fourth cabbage mixture on one half of each parchment square. Place fillets on top of cabbage. Sprinkle fillets with remaining ⅛ teaspoon each salt and pepper and evenly dot with butter.

5. Fold unfilled half of parchment over cod. To seal packets, beginning at a corner where parchment is folded, make ½-inch-wide folds, with each new fold overlapping the previous one, until packet is  completely sealed. Packet will resemble half-circle. Place packets in jelly-roll pan. Bake 20 minutes (packets will puff up and brown). Cut packets open to serve. Makes 4 main-dish servings.

Each serving: About 232 calories, 33g protein, 7g carbohydrate, 8g total fat (3g saturated), 84mg cholesterol, 567mg sodium.

Baked Scrod with Fennel and Potatoes

Here's a simple dish that needs only a crisp green salad to become a complete meal.

Prep: 15 minutes   Bake: 55 minutes

- 1½   pounds red potatoes (4 large), not peeled, thinly sliced
- 1   medium fennel bulb (1 pound), trimmed and thinly sliced, feathery tops reserved
- 1   garlic clove, finely chopped
- 2   tablespoons olive oil
- ¾   plus ⅛ teaspoon salt
- ½   teaspoon coarsely ground black pepper
- 4   pieces scrod fillet (5 ounces each)
- 1   large ripe tomato (8 ounces), seeded and chopped

1. Preheat oven to 425°F.

2. In shallow 2½-quart baking dish, toss potatoes, fennel, garlic, oil, ¾ teaspoon salt, and ¼ teaspoon pepper until well combined; spread evenly in baking dish. Bake, stirring once, until vegetables are tender and lightly browned, about 45 minutes.

3. With tweezers, remove any bones from scrod. Sprinkle scrod with remaining ⅛ teaspoon salt and remaining ¼ teaspoon pepper. Arrange on top of potato mixture. Bake until fish is just opaque throughout, 10 to 15 minutes.

4. Sprinkle with tomato and garnish with reserved fennel tops. Makes 4 main-dish servings.

Each serving: About 335 calories, 30g protein, 35g carbohydrate, 8g total fat (1g saturated), 61mg cholesterol, 679mg sodium.

Scrod with Lemon-Garlic Bread Crumbs

Want an easy way to bake up flaky scrod fillets? Top them with lots of garlicky bread crumbs.

Prep: 20 minutes   Bake: 10 minutes

- 2 tablespoons butter or margarine
- 1 garlic clove, finely chopped
- 1 cup fresh bread crumbs (about 2 slices bread)
- 4 pieces scrod or cod fillet (6 ounces each)
- 2 tablespoons fresh lemon juice
- ½ teaspoon salt
- 1 tablespoon chopped fresh parsley
  lemon wedges

1. Preheat oven to 450°F. In 10-inch skillet, melt butter over medium heat. Add garlic; cook until golden. Add bread crumbs and cook, stirring frequently, until lightly toasted. Remove skillet from heat.

2. With tweezers, remove any bones from scrod. In 13" by 9" baking dish, arrange fillets in single layer; sprinkle with lemon juice and salt. Press bread-crumb mixture onto fillets. Bake until fish is just opaque throughout, 10 to 15 minutes.

3. Sprinkle scrod with parsley and serve with lemon wedges. Makes 4 main-dish servings.

Each serving: About 231 calories, 32g protein, 8g carbohydrate, 7g total fat (4g saturated), 89mg cholesterol, 517mg sodium.

Oven-Fried Fish

Here's a reduced-fat method for getting crispy fish without lots of oil. To keep the fat profile low, serve with Tartar Sauce (page 434), made with lowfat mayonnaise or simply sprinkle the fish with malt vinegar. For fish and chips, serve with crisp Oven Fries (page 365) and malt vinegar.

Prep: 10 minutes   Bake: 12 minutes

- 2 teaspoons vegetable oil
- ¼ cup all-purpose flour
- ½ teaspoon salt
- ¼ teaspoon ground red pepper (cayenne)
- 2 large egg whites
- 1 cup plain dried bread crumbs
- 1 pound flounder or sole fillets, cut on diagonal into 1-inch-wide strips

1. Preheat oven to 450°F. Grease cookie sheet with oil; set aside.

2. On waxed paper, combine flour, salt, and ground red pepper. In shallow bowl, beat egg whites just until foamy. On separate sheet of waxed paper, place bread crumbs. Coat flounder strips with seasoned flour, shaking off excess. Dip strips into egg white, then coat in bread crumbs, patting crumbs to adhere. Arrange fish strips on prepared cookie sheet.

3. Place cookie sheet on lowest oven rack and bake fish 5 minutes. With wide spatula, turn fish. Bake until just opaque throughout and golden, 4 to 5 minutes longer. Makes 4 main-dish servings.

Each serving: About 267 calories, 27g protein, 26g carbohydrate, 5g total fat (1g saturated), 54mg cholesterol, 642mg sodium.

Asian-Style Flounder Baked in Parchment

Baking in parchment packets is a simple way to seal in the juices and the flavor of delicate fish. Substitute foil for the parchment paper, if necessary.

Prep: 15 minutes **Bake:** 8 minutes

- 2 large green onions
- 2 tablespoons soy sauce
- 2 tablespoons seasoned rice vinegar
- 4 flounder fillets (6 ounces each)
- 4 sheets (12" by 15") cooking parchment or foil
- 2 teaspoons grated, peeled fresh ginger

1. Cut green onion tops into 2" by ¼" matchstick strips; reserve for garnish. Thinly slice white part of green onions.

2. In small bowl, combine soy sauce and vinegar.

3. Preheat oven to 425°F. Place 1 flounder fillet on one half of each parchment sheet. Sprinkle with ginger and sliced green onions; drizzle with soy-sauce mixture. Fold unfilled half of parchment over fish. To seal packets, beginning at a corner where parchment is folded, make ½-inch-wide folds, with each new fold overlapping previous one, until packet is completely sealed. Packet will resemble half-circle. Place packets in jelly-roll pan. Bake 8 minutes (packets will puff up and brown).

4. Cut packets open and garnish fish with reserved green-onion strips. Makes 4 main-dish servings.

Each serving: About 170 calories, 33g protein, 3g carbohydrate, 2g total fat (0g saturated), 82mg cholesterol, 802mg sodium.

Whole Flounder in Parchment

Prepare as above, but use a **3-pound whole flounder,** cleaned and scaled, and 2 sheets 24" by 12" of parchment or foil. Preheat oven to 400°F. Line rimmed baking pan with parchment paper. Follow Steps 1 and 2. Place fish on parchment in pan. Sprinkle with ginger and sliced green onions; drizzle with soy-sauce mixture. Top with second sheet of parchment. To seal fish, beginning at one corner, make ½-inch-wide folds, with each new fold overlapping previous one, until packet is sealed. Roast fish about 30 minutes, or until fish is just opaque when knife is inserted at backbone. Cut parchment open and using two wide slotted spatulas, transfer fish to large platter. Pour pan juices over fish and garnish with reserved green-onion strips. Makes 4 main-dish servings.

Baked Flounder with Savory Crumb Topping

Need a fast and flavorful midweek supper recipe? Our tasty flounder is the answer. If you don't have an open bottle of dry white wine, substitute dry vermouth or reduced-sodium chicken broth.

Prep: 15 minutes **Bake:** 10 minutes

- 1½ cups fresh bread crumbs (about 3 slices bread)
- 2 tablespoons chopped fresh parsley
- ¼ cup dry white wine
- 4 flounder fillets (5 ounces each)
- ¼ teaspoon salt
- ¼ cup mayonnaise

1. Preheat oven to 400°F. In 10-inch skillet, toast bread crumbs over medium heat, stirring frequently, until golden, about 10 minutes. Remove from heat and stir in parsley.

2. Pour wine into 13" by 9" baking dish; add flounder fillets, turning to coat. Arrange fillets, skinned side up, in dish, tucking thin ends under. Sprinkle with salt and spread mayonnaise on top. Gently pat bread-crumb mixture over mayonnaise. Bake until fish is just opaque throughout and topping has crisped, about 10 minutes. Makes 4 main-dish servings.

Each serving: About 295 calories, 29g protein, 11g carbohydrate, 13g total fat (2g saturated), 76mg cholesterol, 452mg sodium.

Parmesan Cheese Fillets

Prepare as directed above but use only **⅔ cup plain dried bread crumbs** and add **⅓ cup freshly grated Parmesan cheese** to bread-crumb mixture.

Sesame Seed Fillets

Prepare as directed above but use only **¾ cup plain dried bread crumbs** and add **¼ cup sesame seeds** to bread-crumb mixture.

Rolled Sole Stuffed with Crab

For a stress-free dinner party, stuff and roll up the sole fillets and refrigerate for up to four hours before baking them. The sauce can also be prepared several hours ahead, then reheated gently just before serving.

Prep: 20 minutes   Bake: 25 minutes

- 2 tablespoons butter or margarine
- 4 tablespoons finely chopped shallots
- 8 ounces lump crabmeat, picked over
- ½ cup fresh bread crumbs (about 1 slice bread)
- 1 tablespoon chopped fresh parsley
- 2 teaspoons fresh lemon juice
- ½ plus ⅛ teaspoon salt
- ⅛ teaspoon plus pinch ground black pepper
- 6 sole or flounder fillets (6 ounces each)
- 1 can (14 to 16 ounces) tomatoes, drained
- ¼ cup heavy or whipping cream
- 1 teaspoon chopped fresh tarragon or parsley

1. Preheat oven to 400°F. Grease 13" by 9" baking dish; set aside.

2. In nonstick 10-inch skillet, melt 1 tablespoon butter over medium heat. Add 2 tablespoons shallots and cook until tender, about 2 minutes. Transfer to medium bowl. Add crabmeat, bread crumbs, parsley, lemon juice, ¼ teaspoon salt, and ⅛ teaspoon pepper to shallots; toss with fork until evenly combined.

3. Sprinkle skinned side of sole fillets with ¼ teaspoon salt. Spoon crabmeat mixture evenly over fillets. Roll up fillets and place, seam side down, in prepared baking dish. Bake until fish is just opaque throughout, about 25 minutes.

4. Meanwhile, in blender, puree tomatoes until smooth. In same 10-inch skillet, melt remaining 1 tablespoon butter over medium heat. Add remaining 2 tablespoons shallots and cook until tender, about 2 minutes. Add pureed tomatoes, remaining ⅛ teaspoon salt, and remaining pinch pepper; increase heat to high and cook, stirring frequently, until liquid has almost evaporated, about 5 minutes. Stir in cream and heat to boiling. Remove from heat and stir in tarragon.

5. With wide slotted spatula, transfer fish to warm platter. Stir any juices in baking dish into sauce; spoon sauce over fish. Makes 6 main-dish servings.

Each serving: About 298 calories, 41g protein, 7g carbohydrate, 11g total fat (5g saturated), 144mg cholesterol, 665mg sodium.

Rolled Sole Stuffed with Crab

CRABMEAT: DELICIOUS DELICACY

Test Kitchen Tip

Although live crabs are often available at the fish counter, buying cooked crabmeat is easiest way when you need to use the meat as a recipe ingredient.

Lump or **backfin** consists of large whole lumps from the body and backfin. It is very expensive and tasty.

Special crabmeat is made up of lump crabmeat and flaked meat from the rest of the body.

Flaked crabmeat contains all of the meat from the body but no lump meat.

Claw crabmeat is meat from the claws.

Crabmeat is sold fresh by the half pound and pound. It should have a sweet aroma and look moist and snowy white. Canned crabmeat is good in a pinch, but it lacks the special flavor of the fresh.

Portuguese-Style Monkfish

Here, chunks of firm monkfish are cooked in a spicy sausage-tomato sauce until tender. Serve over rice or pasta.

Prep: 25 minutes   Cook: 40 minutes

- 1 tablespoon olive oil
- 1 medium onion, chopped
- 3 garlic cloves, finely chopped
- 1 fully cooked chorizo sausage (3 ounces), cut lengthwise into quarters, then crosswise into thin slices
- 1 red pepper, chopped
- 2/3 cup chicken broth
- 1 can (14 to 16 ounces) tomatoes, chopped
- 1/4 teaspoon salt
- 1/4 teaspoon crushed red pepper
- 1½ pounds monkfish, dark membrane removed, cut into 1-inch pieces
- 1/4 cup chopped fresh parsley

1. In nonstick 10-inch skillet, heat oil over medium-low heat. Add onion and garlic and cook, stirring frequently, until onion is tender, about 5 minutes.

2. Add chorizo and chopped red pepper and cook, stirring frequently, until pepper is tender, about 5 minutes. Add broth and heat to boiling. Stir in tomatoes with their juice, salt, and crushed red pepper; heat to boiling.

3. Add monkfish to skillet. Reduce heat; cover and simmer until monkfish is tender, about 10 minutes. With slotted spoon, transfer monkfish to bowl. Increase heat to high and boil liquid until sauce has reduced and thickened, about 5 minutes. Return fish to skillet and stir in parsley. Makes 4 main-dish servings.

Each serving: About 308 calories, 32g protein, 11g carbohydrate, 15g total fat (4g saturated), 61mg cholesterol, 781mg sodium.

Red Snapper in Parchment with Tomatoes and Basil

Here, the snapper juices mingle with the tomatoes and basil in a parchment packet to create a fabulous sauce.

Prep: 25 minutes   Bake: 15 minutes

- 1 tablespoon butter or margarine
- 1 large garlic clove, finely chopped
- 1 pound ripe plum tomatoes, seeded and chopped (2 cups)
- 1/4 plus 1/8 teaspoon salt
- 1/4 teaspoon ground black pepper
- 1/3 cup chopped fresh basil
- 4 red snapper fillets (6 ounces each), skin removed
- 4 squares (12 inches each) cooking parchment or foil

1. Preheat oven to 400°F.

2. In 12-inch skillet, melt butter over medium-high heat. Add garlic and cook 30 seconds. Add tomatoes, 1/4 teaspoon salt, and 1/8 teaspoon pepper. Cook, stirring frequently, until liquid has almost evaporated, about 5 minutes. Remove from heat and stir in basil.

3. With tweezers, remove any bones from snapper fillets. Place 1 fillet, skinned side down, on one half of each parchment square. Sprinkle with remaining 1/8 teaspoon each salt and pepper; top with tomato mixture.

4. Fold unfilled half of parchment over fish. To seal packets, beginning at a corner where parchment is folded, make 1/2-inch-wide folds, with each new fold overlapping previous one, until packet is completely sealed. Packet will resemble half-circle. Place packets in jelly-roll pan. Bake 15 minutes (packets will puff up and brown). Cut packets open to serve. Makes 4 main-dish servings.

Each serving: About 207 calories, 33g protein, 6g carbohydrate, 5g total fat (2g saturated), 65mg cholesterol, 359mg sodium.

Baked Salmon Fillets

Thick center-cut pieces of salmon bake in about 20 minutes. If using thinner pieces cut nearer the tail, check after 15 minutes. There are many sauces that go well with baked salmon; try Salmoriglio Sauce (page 435) or a fruit salsa (pages 437–438).

Prep: 5 minutes   Bake: 15 minutes

- 4 pieces salmon fillet with skin (6 ounces each)
- 1 teaspoon olive oil
- ⅛ teaspoon salt
- ⅛ teaspoon ground black pepper

1. Preheat oven to 400°F and grease 13" by 9" baking dish.

2. With tweezers, remove any bones from salmon fillets. Arrange fillets in prepared baking dish; rub with oil and sprinkle with salt and pepper. Bake until salmon is just opaque throughout, 15 to 20 minutes. Makes 4 main-dish servings.

Each serving: About 331 calories, 34g protein, 0g carbohydrate, 21g total fat (4g saturated), 100mg cholesterol, 174mg sodium.

Salmon and Lentils

This nicely herbed dish features a sprightly lemon dressing that is spooned over flavorful salmon and lentils. Serve a green vegetable or salad on the side.

Prep: 10 minutes   Cook/Bake: 50 minutes

- 1 cup lentils, rinsed and picked through
- 2¼ cups water
- ¾ plus ⅛ teaspoon salt
- 4 pieces salmon fillet with skin (6 ounces each)
- 1 teaspoon plus 2 tablespoons olive oil
- ⅛ plus ¼ teaspoon coarsely ground black pepper
- 1 lemon
- 1 teaspoon Dijon mustard
- 4 teaspoons chopped fresh tarragon
- 1 tablespoon butter or margarine
- ¼ cup finely chopped shallots
- ¼ cup chopped fresh parsley

1. Preheat oven to 400°F. In 2-quart saucepan, combine lentils, water, and ½ teaspoon salt; heat to boiling over high heat. Reduce heat; cover and simmer until lentils are tender, 20 to 30 minutes. Drain.

2. Meanwhile, grease 13" by 9" baking dish. With tweezers, remove any bones from salmon. Arrange fillets in single layer in prepared baking dish. Rub with 1 teaspoon oil and sprinkle with ⅛ teaspoon each salt and pepper. Bake until fish is just opaque throughout, 15 to 20 minutes.

3. While salmon is baking, prepare dressing: From lemon, grate ½ teaspoon peel and squeeze 2 tablespoons juice. In small bowl, with wire whisk, whisk together lemon juice, mustard, and remaining ¼ teaspoon salt. Gradually whisk in remaining 2 tablespoons oil, then stir in 2 teaspoons tarragon.

4. In 10-inch skillet, melt butter over medium heat. Add shallots and cook, stirring, 2 minutes. Stir in lentils, lemon peel, and remaining ¼ teaspoon pepper. Remove from heat and stir in parsley and remaining 2 teaspoons tarragon. Spread lentil mixture on platter. Arrange salmon on top of lentils and spoon dressing over salmon. Makes 4 main-dish servings.

Each serving: About 582 calories, 48g protein, 30g carbohydrate, 30g total fat (7g saturated), 108mg cholesterol, 604mg sodium.

SAUCES FOR FISH

Test Kitchen Tip

Unlike meat and poultry dishes, where pan sauces are often created from the cooking juices, many fish sauces are separate recipes. For a Mediterranean touch, try Salmoriglio Sauce (page 435) or Salsa Verde (page 435). Some favorite mayonnaise-based sauces include Tartar Sauce (page 434), and Easy Aïoli (page 33). Salsas, such as Olive and Lemon or Orange-Fennel (pages 436–437), are excellent condiments for grilled fish, or top fish with a pat of Olive Butter or Ginger-Cilantro Butter (page 434).

Fresh Salmon Burgers with Capers and Dill

Our lemon-caper sauce is easy as well as delicious. It also makes a tasty sandwich spread and is a great dipper for shrimp and scallops.

Prep: 25 minutes   Grill: 6 minutes

- 1 large lemon
- ¼ cup light mayonnaise
- 1 tablespoon capers, drained and coarsely chopped
- 1 pound salmon fillet, skin removed
- ¼ cup loosely packed fresh dill, chopped
- 2 green onions, thinly sliced
- ½ cup plain dried bread crumbs
- ¾ teaspoon salt
  nonstick cooking spray
- 4 whole-wheat hamburger buns, split and toasted
  green-leaf lettuce leaves

1. Prepare outdoor grill for direct grilling.

2. Meanwhile, from lemon, grate 1 teaspoon peel and squeeze 1 tablespoon juice.

3. In small bowl, stir lemon juice, ½ teaspoon lemon peel, mayonnaise, and capers until blended. Set lemon-caper sauce aside. Makes about ⅓ cup.

4. With tweezers, remove any bones from salmon. With large chef's knife, finely chop salmon; place in medium bowl. Add dill, green onions, ¼ cup bread crumbs, salt, and remaining ½ teaspoon lemon peel; gently mix with fork until combined. Shape salmon mixture into four 3-inch round burgers.

5. Sprinkle both sides of burgers with remaining bread crumbs; pat gently to adhere. Spray both sides of burgers with nonstick spray.

6. Place burgers on grill over medium heat. Cook burgers 6 to 8 minutes for medium or until desired doneness, turning once.

7. Serve burgers on buns with lettuce and lemon-caper mayonnaise. Makes 4 main-dish servings.

Each serving: About 380 calories, 27g protein, 34g carbohydrate, 15g total fat (3g saturated), 65mg cholesterol, 990mg sodium.

Salmon Teriyaki Burgers

Prepare as above, but omit lemon-caper sauce. In Step 3, substitute ½ **cup diced water chestnuts,** ¼ **cup teriyaki sauce,** and ¼ **teaspoon crushed red pepper** for dill, green onions, bread crumbs, salt, and lemon peel. Do not sprinkle burgers with bread crumbs. Proceed as directed. To serve, place burgers on buns with lettuce and spoon **1 tablespoon hoisin sauce** over each.

Five-Spice Salmon Fillets

Chinese five-spice powder adds an intriguing hint of licorice to rich salmon.

Prep: 5 minutes   Cook: 8 minutes

- 4 pieces salmon fillet (4 ounces each), skin removed
- 2 teaspoons Chinese five-spice powder
- 1 teaspoon all-purpose flour
- ½ teaspoon salt
- ¼ teaspoon cracked black pepper
- 2 teaspoons vegetable oil

1. With tweezers, remove any bones from salmon fillets. On waxed paper, combine five-spice powder, flour, salt, and pepper. Use to rub on both sides of fillets.

2. In nonstick 10-inch skillet, heat oil over medium heat until hot. Add salmon; cook until just opaque throughout, 4 to 5 minutes per side. Makes 4 main-dish servings.

Each serving: About 222 calories, 21g protein, 2g carbohydrate, 14g total fat (3g saturated), 63mg cholesterol, 353mg sodium.

Snapper Livornese

Vibrant with olives, capers, and basil, this preparation works beautifully with any lean white fish.

Prep: 10 minutes   Cook: 25 minutes

- 1 tablespoon olive oil
- 1 garlic clove, finely chopped
- 1 can (14 to 16 ounces) tomatoes
- ⅛ teaspoon salt
- ⅛ teaspoon ground black pepper
- 4 red snapper fillets (6 ounces each)
- ¼ cup chopped fresh basil
- ¼ cup Kalamata or Gaeta olives, pitted and chopped
- 2 teaspoons capers, drained

1. In nonstick 10-inch skillet, heat oil over medium heat. Add garlic and cook just until very fragrant, about 30 seconds. Stir in tomatoes with their juice, salt, and pepper, breaking up tomatoes with spoon. Heat to boiling; reduce heat and simmer 10 minutes.

2. With tweezers, remove any bones from snapper fillets. Place fillets, skin side down, in skillet. Cover and simmer until fish is just opaque throughout, about 10 minutes. With wide slotted spatula, transfer fish to warm platter. Stir basil, olives, and capers into tomato sauce and spoon over snapper. Makes 4 main-dish servings.

Each serving: About 250 calories, 36g protein, 6g carbohydrate, 8g total fat (1g saturated), 63mg cholesterol, 571mg sodium.

REMOVING PIN BONES

Test Kitchen Tip

Run your fingers along each fillet to check for pin bones. Use tweezers or pin-nose pliers (set aside for that purpose) to pull them out. Or use a sharp knife to cut along each side of the strip of bones and remove it.

Snapper Livornese

Kedgeree

A traditional British breakfast dish, kedgeree is also delicious for brunch or supper.

Prep: 35 minutes   Bake: 30 minutes

- 1 tablespoon butter or margarine
- 1 small onion, chopped
- ¾ teaspoon curry powder
- 1½ cups regular long-grain rice
- 3 cups water
- 1 teaspoon salt
- ¼ teaspoon coarsely ground black pepper
- 1 pound smoked haddock fillet (finnan haddie)
- 1 lemon
- 4 large hard-cooked eggs, coarsely chopped
- ¼ cup chopped fresh parsley
- ½ cup heavy or whipping cream

1. In 2-quart saucepan, melt butter over medium heat. Add onion and cook until tender, about 5 minutes. Stir in curry powder and rice. Add water, salt, and pepper; heat to boiling. Reduce heat; cover and simmer, without stirring or lifting lid, until rice is tender and all liquid has been absorbed, about 20 minutes. Transfer to large bowl.

2. Meanwhile, in 10-inch skillet, combine smoked haddock fillet with enough *water* to cover; heat to boiling. Reduce heat and simmer just until haddock begins to flake, 5 to 10 minutes. Drain and cool slightly.

3. Preheat oven to 350°F. From lemon, grate ½ teaspoon peel and squeeze 1 tablespoon juice; add lemon peel and juice to rice, fluffing with fork. Flake haddock, discarding any skin or bones. Add fish, eggs, and parsley to rice, tossing gently. Transfer to 13" by 9" baking dish, spreading evenly; drizzle cream over top. Cover with foil and bake 30 minutes. Makes 6 main-dish servings.

Each serving: About 406 calories, 27g protein, 42g carbohydrate, 14g total fat (7g saturated), 232mg cholesterol, sodium n/a.

Brandade

A little of this flavorful, velvety Provençal hors d'oeuvre goes a long way. Spread on thin slices of toasted bread.

Prep: 20 minutes plus 24 to 36 hours to soak cod
Cook: 20 minutes

- 1 pound salt cod fillets
- 1 large baking potato (12 ounces), peeled and thinly sliced
- 3 garlic cloves, peeled
- 1 cup heavy or whipping cream
  pinch ground nutmeg
- 2 tablespoons extra-virgin olive oil
  thinly sliced French bread, toasted

1. In medium bowl, combine salt cod fillets and enough *cold water* to cover generously. Cover and refrigerate, changing water several times, 24 to 36 hours. Drain and rinse well.

2. In 3-quart saucepan, combine potato, garlic, and *3 cups water;* heat to boiling over high heat. Reduce heat and simmer until potato is tender, 12 to 15 minutes. Drain, reserving 1 cup water. Mash potato and garlic until almost smooth. Transfer mixture to medium bowl.

3. Meanwhile, in clean 3-quart saucepan, combine cod and enough *water* to cover; heat to boiling. Reduce heat and simmer until fish can be flaked with fork, 5 to 10 minutes; drain. When cool enough to handle, discard any skin or bones. Transfer cod to food processor with knife blade attached and pulse until flaked.

4. In clean 3-quart saucepan, heat cream over low heat. With wooden spoon, stir in cod, potato mixture, reserved potato water, and nutmeg; stir until well combined. With wire whisk, gradually whisk in oil. Serve with toast. Makes 4 cups or 12 first-course servings.

Each ¼ cup without toast: About 216 calories, 25g protein, 5g carbohydrate, 11g total fat (5g saturated), 85mg cholesterol, sodium n/a.

Portuguese-Style Salt Cod

They say that the Portuguese have 365 ways to cook salt cod. This is certainly one of the best.

Prep: 35 minutes plus 24 to 36 hours to soak cod
Cook/Bake: 1 hour 20 minutes

- 1 pound salt cod fillets
- ¼ cup olive oil, preferably extra-virgin
- 3 small onions, thinly sliced
- 2 garlic cloves, thinly sliced
- 1 pound (5 small) all-purpose potatoes
- 1 can (28 ounces) tomatoes, drained and chopped
- ¼ cup plus 1 tablespoon chopped fresh parsley
- ¼ teaspoon salt
- ¼ teaspoon ground black pepper
- 2 large hard-cooked eggs, each cut lengthwise into quarters
- 16 oil-cured black olives, pitted
- 2 teaspoons capers, drained

1. In medium bowl, combine salt cod fillets and enough *cold water* to cover generously. Cover and refrigerate, changing water several times, 24 to 36 hours. Drain and rinse well.

2. In 3-quart saucepan, combine cod and enough *water* to cover; heat to boiling. Reduce heat and simmer until fish can be flaked with fork, 5 to 10 minutes; drain. When cool enough to handle, discard any skin or bones and coarsely flake cod.

3. Meanwhile, in 10-inch skillet, heat oil over medium heat. Add onions and garlic and cook, stirring, until very tender and golden, about 10 minutes. With slotted spoon, transfer onions to bowl. Pour oil in skillet into cup; reserve.

4. In 5-quart Dutch oven, combine potatoes and enough salted *cold water* to cover; heat to boiling. Cook just until potatoes are tender when pierced with fork, about 20 minutes. When cool enough to handle, peel potatoes and cut into thin slices.

5. Preheat oven to 350°F. Lightly oil 8-inch square baking dish. In dish, layer potatoes, tomatoes, ¼ cup parsley, half of onions, cod, and remaining onions, lightly sprinkling each layer with salt and pepper. Bake until golden and heated through, about 35 minutes.

6. To serve, drizzle with reserved oil. Arrange eggs on top and sprinkle with olives, capers, and remaining 1 tablespoon parsley. Makes 4 main-dish servings.

Each serving: About 697 calories, 80g protein, 39g carbohydrate, 25g total fat (4g saturated), 279mg cholesterol, sodium n/a.

Chinese Steamed Clams

Serve this Asian-inspired dish with steamed white rice so all of the flavorful broth can be enjoyed.

Prep: 10 minutes   Cook: 10 minutes

- 1 tablespoon vegetable oil
- 2 green onions, finely chopped
- 1 tablespoon minced, peeled fresh ginger
- 1 garlic clove, finely chopped
- 2 dozen cherrystone or littleneck clams, scrubbed (page 186), or mussels, scrubbed and debearded (page 187)
- ½ cup water
- 3 tablespoons dry sherry
- 2 tablespoons soy sauce
- 2 tablespoons chopped fresh cilantro

In 8-quart saucepot, heat oil over high heat. Add green onions, ginger, and garlic; cook until green onions are tender, about 1 minute. Add clams, water, sherry, and soy sauce; heat to boiling. Reduce heat; cover and simmer 5 to 10 minutes, transferring clams to large platter as they open. Discard any clams that have not opened. Pour broth over clams on platter and sprinkle with cilantro. Makes 4 first-course servings.

Each serving: About 131 calories, 14g protein, 5g carbohydrate, 4g total fat (1g saturated), 36mg cholesterol, 576mg sodium.

Scrub the clams well under cold running water to remove all the grit.

Protecting your hand with a folded towel, hold the clam with the "hinge" facing you; wedge the thin edge of a clam knife between the shells.

Slide the knife around to separate the shells.

Open the shell. Cut the clam meat away from the top shell; discard the top shell.

Slide the knife underneath the meat in the bottom shell to release it.

Steamed Soft-Shell Clams

A great appetizer or main dish to have with an ice-cold beer on a hot summer day!

Prep: 5 minutes   Cook: 10 minutes

6 dozen steamer (soft-shell) clams
melted butter or margarine (optional)

1. In very large bowl or in kitchen sink, place clams and enough *cold water* to cover; drain. Repeat rinsing and draining until sand no longer falls to bottom of bowl.

2. In steamer or 8-quart saucepot fitted with rack, heat enough *water* to cover pan bottom to boiling over high heat. Place clams on rack in steamer. Reduce heat; cover and steam until clams open, 5 to 10 minutes, transferring clams to bowl as they open. Discard any clams that have not opened.

3. Strain clam broth through sieve lined with paper towels and pour into 6 soup cups or mugs.

4. To eat, with fingers, pull clams from shells by neck; peel off and discard black sheath that covers neck. Dip clams first in broth to remove any sand, then into melted butter, if you like. When sand has settled to bottom, broth can be sipped, if desired. Makes 6 first-course servings.

Each serving without butter: About 76 calories, 13g protein, 3g carbohydrate, 1g total fat (0g saturated), 35mg cholesterol, 57mg sodium.

Mussels with Tomatoes and White Wine

(Pictured on page 162)

This saucy dish should be served with plenty of good crusty bread for dipping.

Prep: 20 minutes   Cook: 25 minutes

1	tablespoon olive or vegetable oil
1	small onion, chopped
2	garlic cloves, finely chopped
¼	teaspoon crushed red pepper
1	can (14 to 16 ounces) tomatoes
¾	cup dry white wine
4	pounds large mussels, scrubbed and debearded (right)
2	tablespoons chopped fresh parsley

1. In nonreactive 5-quart Dutch oven, heat oil over medium heat. Add onion and cook until tender and golden, 6 to 8 minutes. Add garlic and crushed red pepper and cook 30 seconds longer. Stir in tomatoes with their juice and wine, breaking up tomatoes with side of spoon. Heat to boiling; boil 3 minutes.

2. Add mussels; heat to boiling. Reduce heat; cover and simmer until mussels open, about 5 minutes, transferring mussels to large bowl as they open. Discard any mussels that have not opened. Pour mussel broth over mussels and sprinkle with parsley. Makes 8 first-course or 4 main-dish servings.

Each first-course serving: About 104 calories, 9g protein, 6g carbohydrate, 3g total fat (1g saturated), 18mg cholesterol, 277mg sodium.

Moules à la Marinière

Prepare as above, substituting **butter** for olive oil, if you like, and ⅓ **cup chopped shallots** for onion. Omit crushed red pepper and tomatoes; use **1½ cups wine.** Proceed as directed.

SCRUBBING AND DEBEARDING MUSSELS

Scrub mussels well under cold running water. To debeard, grasp the hair-like beard firmly with your thumb and forefinger and pull it away, or scrape it off with a knife. (Cultivated mussels usually do not have beards.)

Panfried Oysters

Large plump oysters work best in this seaside favorite.

Prep: 15 minutes   Cook: 10 minutes

1	pint shucked oysters, drained
⅔	cup finely crushed saltine crackers
2	tablespoons butter or margarine
2	tablespoons vegetable oil
	lemon wedges

1. Gently pat oysters dry with paper towels. Place cracker crumbs on waxed paper and coat oysters with crumbs.

2. In 10-inch skillet, heat 1 tablespoon butter and 1 tablespoon oil over medium-high heat until hot. Add half of oysters to skillet and cook until golden brown, 2 to 3 minutes per side. Repeat with remaining butter, oil, and oysters. Serve with lemon wedges. Makes 4 first-course servings.

Each serving: About 249 calories, 10g protein, 13g carbohydrate, 17g total fat (5g saturated), 85mg cholesterol, 353mg sodium.

Scalloped Oysters

Bake these crumb-topped oysters in individual ramekins, if you have them, or in a shallow 2½ quart baking dish. The baking time will depend on the depth of the dish.

Prep: 40 minutes   Bake: 15 minutes

- 10 slices firm white bread, torn into 1-inch pieces
- 4 tablespoons butter or margarine, melted
- 1½ pints shucked oysters with their liquid
- ¾ cup heavy or whipping cream
- ¼ teaspoon salt
- ⅛ teaspoon coarsely ground black pepper
- 2 tablespoons chopped fresh parsley

1. Preheat oven to 400°F. Place bread pieces in jelly-roll pan and drizzle with melted butter, tossing to coat evenly. Toast bread in oven, stirring occasionally, until crisp and golden, about 25 minutes.

2. Meanwhile, drain oysters, reserving liquid, and refrigerate. In 1-quart saucepan, heat oyster liquid to boiling over high heat. Reduce heat to medium and cook until oyster liquid has reduced to 3 tablespoons, about 5 minutes. Add cream, salt, and pepper; heat to boiling. Remove saucepan from heat.

3. In large bowl, gently combine toasted bread pieces, oysters, and parsley. Spoon mixture into eight 12-ounce ramekins, dividing it evenly. Pour about 2 tablespoons cream mixture over each. Bake just until edges of oysters begin to curl, about 15 minutes. Makes 8 first-course servings.

Each serving: About 288 calories, 10g protein, 22g carbohydrate, 18g total fat (10g saturated), 99mg cholesterol, 436mg sodium.

Scallops Provençal

A hint of orange peel gives this tomato sauce a flavor reminiscent of southern France. If you wish, make the sauce in advance and reheat at serving time. You can substitute bay scallops for the sea scallops.

Prep: 20 minutes   Cook: 20 minutes

- 1 large leek (8 ounces)
- 2 tablespoons olive oil
- 2 garlic cloves, finely chopped
- 1 can (14 to 16 ounces) tomatoes, chopped
- 1 teaspoon salt
- ½ teaspoon freshly grated orange peel
  pinch ground red pepper (cayenne)
- 1 pound sea scallops
- ¼ cup all-purpose flour

1. Cut off roots and trim dark green tops from leek; cut lengthwise in half, then crosswise into thin slices. Rinse in large bowl of cold water, swishing to remove sand; transfer to colander to drain, leaving sand in bottom of bowl.

2. In nonstick 10-inch skillet, heat 1 tablespoon oil over medium heat. Add leek and garlic and cook, stirring frequently, until leek is tender, about 7 minutes. Add tomatoes with their juice, ½ teaspoon salt, orange peel, and ground red pepper; heat to boiling. Reduce heat and simmer until sauce has thickened slightly, about 5 minutes.

3. Meanwhile, pull off and discard tough crescent-shaped muscle from each scallop. Pat scallops dry with paper towels. Cut each scallop horizontally in half if large.

4. In 12-inch skillet, heat remaining 1 tablespoon oil over medium-high heat until hot. Place flour on waxed paper and coat scallops with flour, shaking off excess. Sprinkle remaining ½ teaspoon salt on scallops. Add scallops to skillet and cook, stirring, until just opaque throughout and lightly golden, about 4 minutes. Stir in sauce and heat through. Makes 4 main-dish servings.

Each serving: About 227 calories, 21g protein, 17g carbohydrate, 8g total fat (1g saturated), 37mg cholesterol, 944mg sodium.

Scallop and Asparagus Stir-Fry

Tossing this dish with chopped basil just before serving adds a pleasing touch of fresh flavor. With steamed rice, you have a complete meal.

Prep: 20 minutes   Cook: 15 minutes

- 1 **pound sea scallops**
- 2 **tablespoons reduced-sodium soy sauce**
- 1 **tablespoon minced, peeled fresh ginger**
- 2 **tablespoons vegetable oil**
- 2 **garlic cloves, thinly sliced**
- 1½ **pounds asparagus, trimmed and cut into 2-inch pieces**
- ¼ **teaspoon crushed red pepper**
- ½ **cup loosely packed fresh basil leaves, chopped, plus additional leaves**

1. Pull off and discard tough crescent-shaped muscle from each scallop. In bowl, toss scallops with 1 tablespoon soy sauce and ginger.

2. In nonstick 12-inch skillet, heat 1 tablespoon oil over medium-high heat. Add garlic and cook, stirring often, until golden. With slotted spoon, transfer garlic to medium bowl.

3. Add asparagus and crushed red pepper to skillet and cook, stirring frequently (stir-frying), until asparagus is tender-crisp, about 7 minutes. Transfer asparagus to bowl with garlic.

4. Add remaining 1 tablespoon oil to skillet; add scallop mixture and stir-fry until scallops are just opaque throughout, 3 to 5 minutes.

5. Return asparagus and garlic to skillet, along with remaining 1 tablespoon soy sauce; heat through. Add chopped basil, tossing to combine. Spoon mixture onto warm platter and top with basil leaves. Makes 4 main-dish servings.

Each serving: About 204 calories, 24g protein, 10g carbohydrate, 8g total fat (1g saturated), 37mg cholesterol, 487mg sodium.

Scallop and Asparagus Stir-Fry

Panfried Scallops

Try these during the fall and winter months, when small bay scallops are in season. Otherwise, substitute sea scallops and increase the cooking time accordingly.

Prep: 5 minutes   Cook: 5 minutes

- 1 **pound bay scallops**
- 2 **tablespoons olive oil**
- ½ **teaspoon salt**
- 2 **tablespoons chopped fresh parsley**
- 4 **lemon wedges**

Pat scallops dry with paper towels. In 12-inch skillet, heat oil over medium-high heat until hot. Add scallops to skillet and sprinkle with salt. Cook, stirring, until just opaque throughout, about 4 minutes. Add parsley and toss. Serve with lemon wedges. Makes 4 main-dish servings.

Each serving: About 160 calories, 19g protein, 3g carbohydrate, 8g total fat (1g saturated), 37mg cholesterol, 473mg sodium.

Panfried Soft-Shell Crabs

Here's the classic way to prepare soft-shell crabs so they're crispy outside and moist inside.

Prep: 30 minutes   Cook: 12 minutes

- ½ cup all-purpose flour
- ¾ teaspoon salt
- ½ teaspoon ground black pepper
- 8 live soft-shell crabs (6 ounces each), cleaned
- 4 tablespoons butter or margarine
  lemon wedges

1. On waxed paper, combine flour, salt, and pepper. Coat crabs with seasoned flour, shaking off excess.

2. In 12-inch skillet, melt 2 tablespoons butter over medium heat until hot; add 4 crabs and cook until golden, 3 to 4 minutes per side. Transfer crabs to platter and keep warm. Repeat with remaining butter and remaining crabs. Serve with lemon wedges. Makes 4 main-dish servings.

Each serving: About 256 calories, 19g protein, 12g carbohydrate, 15g total fat (8g saturated), 188mg cholesterol, 1,207mg sodium.

Panfried Soft-Shell Crabs

CLEANING SOFT-SHELL CRABS

Test Kitchen Tip — Soft-shell crabs are sometimes available already cleaned, but it is better to do it yourself at home, because crabs begin to spoil once their viscera are removed. To clean, with kitchen shears, cut across each crab ¼ inch behind the eyes; discard front portion. Cut off the flat pointed "apron" on the underside. Bend back the top shell on each side and snip off the spongy gills. Rinse with cold running water; pat dry with paper towels.

Crab Boil

A big pot of spiced boiled crabs, a Chesapeake Bay tradition, is a delicious but messy affair. Cover the table with newspaper and have lots of big napkins on hand. Serve with coleslaw and rolls. (If you want to cook crab so you can pick the meat for another recipe, omit the crab boil seasoning and red pepper.)

Prep: 8 minutes   Cook: 40 minutes

- 2 medium onions, coarsely chopped
- 1 carrot, peeled and coarsely chopped
- 1 stalk celery, coarsely chopped
- 1 lemon, sliced
- ½ cup crab boil seasoning
- 1 tablespoon crushed red pepper
- 1 tablespoon salt
- 1 gallon (16 cups) water
- 1 can or bottle (12 ounces) beer
- 2 dozen live hard-shell blue crabs, rinsed

1. In 12-quart stockpot, combine onions, carrot, celery, lemon, crab boil seasoning, crushed red pepper, salt, water, and beer. Heat to boiling over high heat; cook 15 minutes.

2. Using tongs, transfer crabs to stockpot. Cover and heat to boiling; boil 5 minutes (crabs will turn red). With tongs, transfer crabs to colander to drain, then place on warm platter.

3. To eat crab, twist off claws and legs, then crack shell to remove meat. Break off flat pointed apron from underside of crab; remove top shell. Discard feathery gills. With kitchen shears or hands, break body in half down center. With fingers or lobster pick, remove meat. Makes 4 main-dish servings.

Each serving: About 123 calories, 24g protein, 0g carbohydrate, 2g total fat (0g saturated), 119mg cholesterol, 1,410mg sodium.

HOW TO STORE
HARD-SHELLED CRABS

 It's best to cook crabs the day they are purchased, but they can be stored up to two days. Place the crabs in a large shallow bowl, then nestle the bowl in a larger bowl of ice. Cover the crabs with a damp kitchen towel. Refrigerate, replacing the ice as needed.

Steamed Lobster

Quite simply, a seafood lover's dream.

Prep: 5 minutes   Cook: 20 minutes

- **2 live lobsters (1¼ to 1½ pounds each)**
- **4 tablespoons butter or margarine, melted**
- **2 teaspoons fresh lemon juice**

1. In 12-quart stockpot, heat *1½ inches water* to boiling over high heat. Plunge lobsters, headfirst, into boiling water. Cover and heat to boiling; steam 12 minutes. With tongs, transfer lobsters to colander to drain, then place on platter.

2. Combine melted butter and lemon juice; transfer to small cups for dipping lobster.

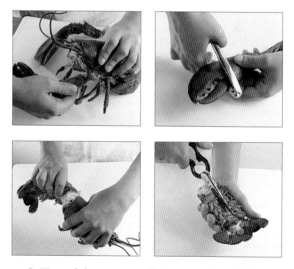

3. To eat lobster, twist off claws and legs. With lobster cracker, nut cracker, or hammer, crack large claws; remove meat. Separate legs at joints; push out meat. Twist to separate tail from body. Reserve any red roe (coral) and greenish liver (tomalley) separately, if desired. With kitchen shears, cut down along center of underside of tail; gently remove meat. Lift bony portion behind small legs from shell; with lobster pick or fork, remove small nuggets of meat. Dip lobster into lemon butter. Makes 2 main-dish servings.

Each serving with butter: About 340 calories, 29g protein, 2g carbohydrate, 24g total fat (15g saturated), 162mg cholesterol, 760mg sodium.

Shrimp Curry

This is a mildly seasoned curry prepared in the French style with cream. Serve over rice, if you like.

Prep: 20 minutes   Cook: 12 minutes

- 2 tablespoons butter or margarine
- 2 garlic cloves, finely chopped
- 2 teaspoons minced, peeled fresh ginger
- 2 teaspoons curry powder
- ½ teaspoon ground coriander
- ½ teaspoon ground cumin
- ¾ cup heavy or whipping cream
- 1 teaspoon salt
- 1 medium zucchini (8 ounces), cut lengthwise in half, then crosswise into thin slices
- 1 pound medium shrimp, shelled and deveined (opposite)
- ½ teaspoon ground black pepper
- 2 tablespoons chopped fresh cilantro

1. In 2-quart saucepan, melt 1 tablespoon butter over medium heat. Add garlic, ginger, curry powder, coriander, and cumin; cook, stirring, 1 minute. Stir in cream and ½ teaspoon salt; increase heat to high and boil until curry sauce has thickened, about 5 minutes.

2. In 10-inch skillet, melt remaining 1 tablespoon butter over medium-high heat. Add zucchini and cook, stirring, until zucchini begins to brown, 2 to 3 minutes. Stir in shrimp, pepper, and remaining ½ teaspoon salt; cook, stirring, until shrimp are just opaque throughout, about 2 minutes. Stir shrimp and zucchini into curry sauce; sprinkle with cilantro. Makes 4 main-dish servings.

Each serving: About 318 calories, 21g protein, 5g carbohydrate, 24g total fat (14g saturated), 216mg cholesterol, 797mg sodium.

Thai Shrimp

To serve, spoon this chunky shrimp-and-vegetable mixture over fragrant jasmine rice.

Prep: 30 minutes   Cook: 15 minutes

- 2 medium limes
- 3 teaspoons vegetable oil
- 1 small onion, finely chopped
- 1 small red pepper, thinly sliced
- 2 teaspoons grated, peeled fresh ginger
- ⅛ to ¼ teaspoon ground red pepper (cayenne)
- 4 ounces medium mushrooms, cut into quarters
- ½ teaspoon salt
- 1 can (13¾ to 15 ounces) light coconut milk (not cream of coconut)
- 1 pound large shrimp, shelled and deveined (opposite)
- 2 ounces snow peas, strings removed and cut into 2" by ¼" matchstick strips
- ⅓ cup loosely packed fresh cilantro leaves

1. From limes, with vegetable peeler, peel six 1" by ¾" strips of peel; squeeze 2 tablespoons juice. Set aside.

2. In nonstick 12-inch skillet, heat 2 teaspoons oil over medium heat. Add onion and cook until tender, about 5 minutes. Add sliced red pepper and cook 1 minute. Stir in ginger and ground red pepper; cook 1 minute. Transfer onion mixture to small bowl.

3. In same skillet, heat remaining 1 teaspoon oil over medium-high heat. Add mushrooms and salt and cook until tender and lightly browned, about 3 minutes. Stir in coconut milk, lime peel and juice, and onion mixture and heat to boiling. Add shrimp and cook until shrimp are opaque throughout, about 2 minutes. Stir in snow peas and cilantro. Makes 4 main-dish servings.

Each serving: About 222 calories, 20g protein, 11g carbohydrate, 11g total fat (4g saturated), 140mg cholesterol, 456mg sodium.

Shrimp Étouffée

Étouffée means "smothered" in Cajun French, and that's just what these shrimp are—smothered in a scrumptious sauce loaded with vegetables and plenty of flavor.

Prep: 30 minutes   Cook: 1 hour

- 4 tablespoons butter or margarine
- ¼ cup all-purpose flour
- 1 yellow pepper, chopped
- 2 medium onions, chopped
- 2 stalks celery with some leaves, chopped
- 2 garlic cloves, finely chopped
- 3 cups water
- 3 tablespoons tomato paste
- 2 bay leaves
- 1½ teaspoons salt
- ¾ teaspoon chili powder
- ¼ teaspoon dried thyme
- ¼ teaspoon ground black pepper
- 1½ pounds medium shrimp, shelled and deveined (below)
- 1 cup chopped green onions (5 medium)
- ¼ cup plus 2 tablespoons chopped fresh parsley
- 1 cup regular long-grain rice, cooked as label directs

1. In 4-quart Dutch oven, melt butter over medium heat. With wooden spoon, gradually stir in flour until blended and cook, stirring constantly, until flour mixture is color of peanut butter; do not let burn. Add yellow pepper, onions, celery, and garlic. Cook, stirring frequently, until onions are tender, about 5 minutes. Stir in water and tomato paste and heat to boiling. Add bay leaves, salt, chili powder, thyme, and black pepper; reduce heat and simmer 30 minutes.

2. Stir in shrimp, green onions, and ¼ cup parsley. Return to simmer and cook 3 minutes. Remove from heat, cover, and let stand 10 minutes. Discard bay leaves and sprinkle étouffée with remaining 2 tablespoons parsley. Serve with hot rice. Makes 6 main-dish servings.

Each serving without rice: About 229 calories, 21g protein, 15g carbohydrate, 10g total fat (5g saturated), 161mg cholesterol, 882mg sodium.

Crawfish Étouffée

Prepare as directed but substitute **1 pound fresh or frozen cooked crawfish tail meat** for shrimp.

Each serving without rice: About 217 calories, 20g protein, 14g carbohydrate, 9g total fat (5g saturated), 155mg cholesterol, 797mg sodium.

SHELLING AND DEVEINING SHRIMP

With kitchen shears or a small knife, cut the shrimp shell along the outer curve, just deep enough into the flesh to expose the dark vein.

Peel back the shell from the cut and gently separate the shell from the shrimp. Discard the shell (or use to make fish stock).

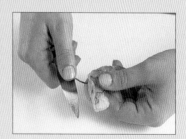

Remove the vein with the tip of a small knife; discard. Rinse the shrimp with cold running water. Pat dry with paper towel.

Shrimp Tempura

Shrimp tempura waits for no one—it gets soggy quickly. Serve as soon as the shrimp are lifted out of the pot and drained.

Prep: 25 minutes   Cook: 15 minutes

vegetable oil for frying

Dipping Sauce

- ⅓ cup chicken broth
- 3 tablespoons soy sauce
- 2 tablespoons water
- 1 tablespoon plus 1 teaspoon seasoned rice vinegar
- 2 teaspoons sugar
- 1 teaspoon minced, peeled fresh ginger

Batter

- ¾ cup ice-cold water
- 1 cup cake flour (not self-rising)
- 1 teaspoon baking powder
- ¼ teaspoon salt

- 1 pound large shrimp, shelled, deveined, and butterflied (right)

1. In 5-quart Dutch oven, heat 2½ inches vegetable oil until temperature reaches 400°F on deep-fat thermometer.

2. Meanwhile, in small saucepan, combine broth, soy sauce, 2 tablespoons water, vinegar, sugar, and ginger; heat to boiling over high heat. Boil 2 minutes. Strain through sieve into small bowl and keep dipping sauce warm.

3. Pour ice-cold water into medium bowl; sift flour, baking powder, and salt into water. With fork, stir just until barely incorporated; a few lumps may remain.

4. Dip 4 shrimp at a time into batter to coat lightly. Allowing excess batter to drip off, add shrimp to hot oil and fry, turning once or twice, until coating is very pale golden, 1 to 2 minutes. With slotted spoon, transfer shrimp to paper towels to drain. Serve immediately with warm dipping sauce. Makes 4 main-dish servings.

Each serving: About 309 calories, 22g protein, 27g carbohydrate, 12g total fat (2g saturated), 140mg cholesterol, 1,355mg sodium.

Beer-Batter Fried Shrimp

Prepare as above, omitting Step 2. In Step 3, omit baking powder and substitute **1 cup beer** for water and proceed as directed. Serve shrimp with Tartar Sauce (page 434). Makes 6 first-course servings.

BUTTERFLYING SHRIMP

Remove the shell, leaving the tail segment in place. With kitchen shears or a small knife, cut the shrimp along the outer curve, about three-fourths of the way through the flesh.

Spread the flesh open and remove the dark vein with the tip of the knife. Rinse the butterflied shrimp with cold running water.

Shrimp and Potatoes in Feta-Tomato Sauce

Feta cheese gives this Greek-style dish a tangy finish.

Prep: 20 minutes   Cook: 50 minutes

- 1 tablespoon olive oil
- 2 medium onions, chopped
- 1½ pounds all-purpose potatoes, peeled and cut into 1-inch pieces
- 1 large garlic clove, finely chopped
  pinch ground red pepper (cayenne)
- ¾ cup water
- ½ teaspoon salt
- 1 can (14 to 16 ounces) tomatoes
- 1 pound medium shrimp, shelled and deveined (page 193)
- 4 ounces feta cheese, crumbled (1 cup)
- ¼ cup chopped fresh dill

1. In nonstick 10-inch skillet, heat oil over medium heat. Add onions and cook, stirring frequently, until tender and golden, about 10 minutes.

2. Add potatoes and cook, stirring, until potatoes begin to brown, about 10 minutes. Stir in garlic and ground red pepper and cook 30 seconds. Stir in water and salt; cover and cook until potatoes are almost tender, about 10 minutes.

3. Add tomatoes with their juice, breaking up tomatoes with side of spoon. Cook, uncovered, until liquid has thickened slightly, about 10 minutes.

4. Stir in shrimp and feta. Cover and cook until shrimp are opaque throughout, 3 to 5 minutes. Remove from heat and stir in dill. Makes 4 main-dish servings.

Each serving: About 359 calories, 27g protein, 37g carbohydrate, 11g total fat (5g saturated), 165mg cholesterol, 926mg sodium.

Fried Calamari Fra Diavolo

Crispy golden-fried squid is served with a tomato dipping sauce that is often as spicy as the devil (*fra diavolo* means "brother devil"). Or simply serve with lemon wedges, if you prefer.

Prep: 10 minutes   Cook: 25 minutes

- 1 tablespoon olive oil
- 2 garlic cloves, crushed with side of chef's knife
- ⅛ to ¼ teaspoon crushed red pepper
- 1 can (14 to 16 ounces) tomatoes
- ¾ teaspoon salt
- 1 pound cleaned squid
- ⅔ cup all-purpose flour
- 1 cup water
  vegetable oil for frying

1. In nonreactive 1-quart saucepan, heat olive oil over medium heat. Add garlic and crushed red pepper; cook until garlic is golden, about 30 seconds. Add tomatoes with their juice and ½ teaspoon salt, breaking up tomatoes with side of spoon; heat to boiling. Reduce heat; cover and simmer 10 minutes. Keep warm.

2. Rinse squid with cold running water and gently pat dry with paper towels. Slice squid bodies crosswise into ¾-inch rings. Cut tentacles into pieces if large.

3. To make batter, in small bowl, with fork, mix flour and water until smooth. In 10-inch skillet, heat ½ inch vegetable oil over medium heat until very hot. (A small piece of bread dropped into oil should sink, then rise to top and begin bubbling.) In small batches, drop squid into batter. Allowing excess batter to drip off, add squid to hot oil. Fry, turning to brown on all sides, until golden, about 2 minutes. With slotted spoon, transfer squid to paper towels to drain; sprinkle with remaining ¼ teaspoon salt. Serve with tomato sauce for dipping. Makes 4 first-course servings.

Each serving: About 325 calories, 21g protein, 25g carbohydrate, 16g total fat (2g saturated), 264mg cholesterol, 660mg sodium.

7

EGGS & CHEESE

EGGS

There is an old saying that "The egg is to cuisine what the article is to speech." Like the little words that help to provide a sentence with structure, the humble egg is taken for granted. Without eggs, cakes would be tough and flat, custards wouldn't set, a meringue would be just a pile of sugar, soufflés wouldn't puff, mayonnaise wouldn't thicken, meat loaves would crumble, and breakfast just wouldn't be the same. The egg is an indispensable, invaluable ingredient that no kitchen can do entirely without. It is a good source of protein, iron, and vitamins. And while whole eggs and egg yolks are relatively high in fat and cholesterol, egg whites are completely fat and cholesterol free.

SALMONELLA AND EGGS

Raw eggs pose a health concern because they can be contaminated with salmonella, a bacterium that can cause food poisoning. Salmonella is killed at 160°F, so be sure to cook eggs to at least that temperature (this is easily reached with scrambled eggs, "over-hard" fried eggs, custards, and other favorite egg dishes). Certain people, such as the elderly, infants, pregnant women, and those with compromised immune systems, are especially susceptible to infection and should not eat undercooked eggs. After handling raw eggs, thoroughly wash your hands and any utensils that have come in contact with the eggs with hot, soapy water.

Pasteurized eggs Available in the dairy case, these eggs are free from salmonella, *E. coli*, and listeria. Cook them the way you would any other eggs.

Egg substitutes These products, which are pasteurized and salmonella free, are used by people with special dietary needs. Liquid egg substitute (colored egg whites) can be substituted for whole eggs, but don't expect the rich flavor real eggs deliver.

Dehydrated egg whites and meringue powder No need to overcrowd the refrigerator with cartons or to separate fresh eggs for meringue recipes. Just follow the reconstituting directions on the package.

CHOOSING EGGS

As defined by the United States Department of Agriculture, eggs that are sold are sized and graded. An egg's grade is based on many factors, including the appearance of the shell, the quality of the interior of the egg, and the size of the air pocket at the top of the egg (usually determined by candling, a process in which the egg is held against a strong light to illuminate its interior). The grades are as follows:

Grade AA eggs With firm, high yolks and thick whites, they are the best choice for frying, poaching, and cooking in the shell.

Grade A eggs Fine all-purpose eggs with whites that are thinner than those of Grade AAs. They are good for baking.

Grade B eggs These have the thinnest white. They are rarely available to the consumer.

The *chalaza*, the thin white cord that attaches the yolk to the shell, is especially prominent in a very fresh egg and disappears as an egg ages. (When making a custard, you may want to strain the custard to remove the chalazae, which become hard when cooked.)

The size of an egg is determined by its weight. Eggs are graded jumbo, extra large, large, medium, and small. All of the recipes in this book use large eggs unless otherwise noted. Using the right size egg is important, especially in recipes that call for a large number.

An eggshell's color is determined solely by the breed of hen. Cooks in the Northeast often prefer brown eggs, but they are no different from the white variety. It is important, however, that the eggshells be clean and uncracked; never buy cracked eggs. Before purchasing eggs, move them in the carton to make sure they haven't cracked and stuck.

STORING EGGS

Eggs should be stored in their carton in a cool part of the refrigerator. The open egg compartment on the refrigerator door is not the ideal place, because it is exposed to warm air every time the door is opened. Also, keep eggs away from strong-smelling foods, such as cheese or onions. Aromas and flavors can easily pass through an egg's thin shell, which is another good reason to keep eggs in their protective carton. To keep the yolks centered, store eggs pointed end down. If stored at around 40°F, eggs will keep for about one month.

The Sell-By Date Keep eggs refrigerated until ready to use, because they deteriorate quickly at room temperature. As fresh eggs age, their thick translucent whites thin out and their round firm yolks flatten. For poaching and frying, use very fresh eggs, because they hold their shape the best. The carton "sell-by" date is the easiest way to tell how old eggs are: It can never be more than thirty days past the packing date. Some states show the packing date in Julian numbers, which run from 001 (January 1) to 365 (December 31).

The Buoyancy Test If you don't have the egg carton and want to check for freshness, all you need is a glass of water. As an egg ages, its liquid begins to evaporate, making the air space at the top of the egg bigger and the egg increasingly buoyant. When placed in a glass of water, a fresh egg will sink to the bottom, a slightly older egg will stand upright, and an old egg will float. As a last resort, there's always the smell test. Break the egg into a saucer and give it a sniff. An egg should have no odor at all or smell absolutely clean and slightly sweet. There's no mistaking the aroma of a bad egg.

Egg Yolk Color The color of an egg yolk can range from yellow to orange. It is determined solely by the hen's diet and is not an indication of taste or freshness. You will sometimes see a small blood spot on an egg yolk. This is caused by a ruptured blood vessel and does not denote freshness. If desired, it can easily be removed with the tip of a knife.

SEPARATING EGGS

To separate an egg, sharply tap the eggshell along its middle to make a crosswise crack. With your thumbs, gently pull open the shell along the crack, letting some of the white run into a bowl. Slowly transfer the yolk back and forth from one half-shell to the other, being careful not to break the yolk on any sharp shell edges, until all the white has run into the bowl. If any yolk does get into the whites, it can sometimes be removed with a small spoon or the edge of an eggshell.

BEATING EGG WHITES

When beating egg whites, keep in mind that their volume will increase six to nine times, so use a large enough bowl. The bowl and the beaters must be absolutely clean; even the tiniest bit of fat will prevent peaks from forming. Stainless-steel or glass bowls do the best job. A little cream of tartar will stabilize egg whites, but salt discourages foaming.

Room-temperature egg whites beat to the fullest volume. Let chilled whites stand for 30 minutes to warm up. Or, place the bowl of egg whites into a separate bowl of hot water; stir for one or two minutes.

If a recipe says to beat egg whites until "foamy" or "frothy," beat them until they form a mass of tiny clear bubbles. For "soft peaks," beat until the whites form soft rounded peaks that droop when the beaters are lifted.

For "stiff glossy peaks," beat until the whites form peaks that hold their shape when the beaters are lifted but are still moist. Overbeaten whites look lumpy and watery—there is no way to salvage them.

How sugar is added to egg whites is crucial. Sugar should be added gradually so it has time to dissolve. Beat the egg whites to the soft peak stage, then begin adding the sugar, about 2 tablespoons at a time, beating until the whites are stiff and glossy.

Basic Omelets

A well-made omelet can be a quick supper or a satisfying breakfast. Mix up a batch of eggs, prepare your fillings, and you're ready for quick assembly-line production. For lower-fat omelets, use 4 large eggs and 8 egg whites.

Prep: 5 minutes plus preparing filling
Cook: 2 minutes per omelet

choice of filling (right and page 200)
8 large eggs
½ cup water
½ teaspoon salt
4 teaspoons butter or margarine

1. Prepare filling; keep warm. In medium bowl, with wire whisk, beat eggs, water, and salt.

2. In nonstick 10-inch skillet, melt 1 teaspoon butter over medium-high heat. Pour ½ cup egg mixture into skillet. Cook, gently lifting edge of eggs with

heat-safe rubber spatula and tilting pan to allow uncooked eggs to run underneath, until eggs are set, about 1 minute. Spoon one-fourth of filling over half of omelet. Fold unfilled half of omelet over filling and slide onto warm plate. Repeat with remaining butter, egg mixture, and filling. If desired, keep omelets warm in 200°F oven until all omelets are cooked. Makes 4 main-dish servings.

Each omelet without filling: About 183 calories, 13g protein, 1g carbohydrate, 14g total fat (5g saturated), 435mg cholesterol, 455mg sodium.

Creamy Mushroom Filling

In nonstick 10-inch skillet, melt **1 tablespoon butter or margarine** over medium-high heat. Add **1 medium onion,** finely chopped; cook until tender, about 5 minutes. Stir in **8 ounces mushrooms,** trimmed and thinly sliced, ¼ **teaspoon salt,** and ⅛ **teaspoon ground black pepper;** cook until liquid has evaporated. Stir in ¼ **cup heavy cream;** boil until thickened, about 3 minutes. Stir in **2 tablespoons chopped fresh parsley.** Use one-fourth mushroom mixture for each omelet.

Each filled omelet: About 291 calories, 15g protein, 8g carbohydrate, 23g total fat (11g saturated), 463mg cholesterol, 637mg sodium.

Black Bean and Salsa Filling

In nonstick 10-inch skillet, cook **1 cup canned black beans,** rinsed and drained, and **1 cup medium-hot salsa** over medium-high heat, stirring frequently, until liquid has evaporated. Divide black-bean mixture, **1 ripe medium avocado,** peeled and chopped, and ¼ **cup sour cream** among omelets.

Each filled omelet: About 365 calories, 17g protein, 18g carbohydrate, 25g total fat (9g saturated), 442mg cholesterol, 1,307mg sodium.

Red Pepper and Goat Cheese Filling

In nonstick 10-inch skillet, melt **2 teaspoons butter or margarine** over medium-high heat. Add **2 red peppers,** thinly sliced, and ¼ **teaspoon salt;** cook until tender and lightly browned. Add **1 garlic clove,** finely chopped; cook 1 minute. Divide red pepper, **2 ounces goat cheese,** and ½ **cup loosely packed, trimmed and torn arugula** among omelets.

Each filled omelet: About 257 calories, 16g protein, 3g carbohydrate, 20g total fat (10g saturated), 452mg cholesterol, 692mg sodium.

Basic Omelet with Garden-Vegetable Filling

Garden-Vegetable Filling

In nonstick 10-inch skillet, heat **1 tablespoon olive oil** over medium heat. Add **1 small onion,** chopped, **1 small zucchini (6 ounces),** chopped, **1 small yellow pepper,** chopped, **½ teaspoon salt,** and **⅛ teaspoon ground black pepper;** cook until vegetables are tender, about 10 minutes. Stir in **2 ripe plum tomatoes,** chopped, and **¼ cup chopped fresh basil;** heat through. Use one-fourth mixture for each omelet.

Each filled omelet: About 239 calories, 14g protein, 7g carbohydrate, 17g total fat (6g saturated), 435mg cholesterol, 749mg sodium.

Western Filling

In nonstick 10-inch skillet, heat **1 tablespoon olive oil** over medium heat. Add **1 small onion,** chopped, **1 green pepper,** chopped, **8 ounces mushrooms,** trimmed and thinly sliced, and **¼ teaspoon salt;** cook until vegetables are tender and liquid has evaporated, about 10 minutes. Add **4 ounces sliced ham,** finely chopped (1 cup), and heat through. Use one-fourth filling for each omelet.

Each filled omelet: About 294 calories, 19g protein, 8g carbohydrate, 21g total fat (7g saturated), 452mg cholesterol, 974mg sodium.

Egg White Omelet

Prepare filling. Blend **2 tablespoons skim milk** and **1 tablespoon all-purpose flour** until smooth. Whisk in **4 large egg whites, ½ teaspoon salt,** and **¼ teaspoon ground tumeric** if using. In nonstick 8-inch skillet, heat **2 teaspoons olive oil** over medium heat. Add egg white mixture and cook until just set, about 2 minutes. Spoon filling, if using, over half of omelet. Continue as for Basic Omelet (page 199). Makes 1 main-dish serving.

Each omelet without filling: About 186 calories, 16g protein, 9g carbohydrate, 9g total fat (1g saturated), 1mg cholesterol, 1,393mg sodium.

Scrambled Eggs with Cream Cheese

These rich and creamy scrambled eggs are not everyday fare. This is a great large-batch recipe for brunch, but it is easily halved.

Prep: 10 minutes   Cook: 10 minutes

14	large eggs
¼	teaspoon ground black pepper
3	tablespoons butter or margarine
2	packages (3 ounces each) cream cheese, cut into 1-inch cubes

1. In large bowl, with wire whisk, beat eggs and pepper until well blended.

2. In nonstick 12-inch skillet, melt butter over medium heat; add eggs. With heat-safe spatula, gently push egg mixture as it begins to set to form soft curds.

3. When eggs are partially cooked, top with cream cheese. Continue cooking, stirring occasionally, until eggs have thickened and no visible liquid egg remains. Serve on warm platter. Makes 8 main-dish servings.

Each serving: About 243 calories, 13g protein, 2g carbohydrate, 20g total fat (10g saturated), 407mg cholesterol, 217mg sodium.

Scrambled Eggs with Cream Cheese and Salmon

Prepare as directed above but sprinkle **4 ounces smoked salmon,** chopped, over eggs with cream cheese. To serve, top with **¼ cup chopped green onions.**

Each serving: About 260 calories, 15g protein, 2g carbohydrate, 21g total fat (10g saturated), 410mg cholesterol, 501mg sodium.

Basic Fluffy Omelet

Beaten egg whites give this oven-baked omelet extra lift. For a cheese omelet, sprinkle top with your favorite shredded cheese during the last minute of baking.

Prep: 10 minutes Cook/Bake: 15 minutes

- 4 large eggs, separated
- 2 tablespoons water
- ⅛ teaspoon salt
- 1 tablespoon butter or margarine

1. Preheat oven to 350°F. In medium bowl, with mixer at high speed, beat egg whites until stiff peaks form when beaters are lifted. In large bowl, with mixer at high speed, beat egg yolks, water, and salt until egg-yolk mixture has thickened. With rubber spatula, gently fold one-third of beaten egg whites into egg-yolk mixture. Fold in remaining egg whites until just blended.

2. In oven-safe nonstick 10-inch skillet (if skillet is not oven-safe, wrap handle with double layer of foil), melt butter over medium-low heat. Add egg mixture and cook until top has puffed and underside is golden, about 3 minutes.

3. Place skillet in oven. Bake until top of omelet is golden and center springs back when lightly touched with finger, about 10 minutes.

4. To serve, loosen omelet from skillet and slide onto warm platter. Makes 2 main-dish servings.

Each serving: About 200 calories, 13g protein, 1g carbohydrate, 16g total fat (7g saturated), 441mg cholesterol, 331mg sodium.

Spaghetti Frittata

This is a great way to use up leftover pasta, even if it is coated with tomato sauce. (You'll need about 3 cups of cooked pasta.)

Prep: 20 minutes Cook/Broil: 10 minutes

- 6 large eggs
- ¼ cup milk
- ⅓ cup freshly grated Parmesan cheese
- ¼ cup chopped fresh basil
- ½ teaspoon salt
- ¼ teaspoon ground black pepper
- 6 ounces thin spaghetti, broken in half and cooked as label directs
- 1 tablespoon olive oil

1. Preheat broiler. In large bowl, with wire whisk, beat eggs, milk, Parmesan, basil, salt, and pepper until well blended. Add pasta and toss to combine.

2. In oven-safe nonstick 10-inch skillet (if skillet is not oven-safe, wrap handle with double layer of foil), heat oil over medium-low heat. Add pasta-egg mixture, pressing lightly with spatula to flatten. Cook until mixture is almost set in center, about 10 minutes. Place skillet in broiler 6 inches from heat source. Broil until frittata is set, about 1 minute.

3. To serve, loosen frittata from skillet and slide onto warm platter; cut into 4 wedges. Makes 4 main-dish servings.

Each serving: About 347 calories, 19g protein, 34g carbohydrate, 14g total fat (5g saturated), 327mg cholesterol, 545mg sodium.

QUICK NO-COOK FILLINGS FOR OMELETS

mango chutney and sour cream • diced avocado, salsa, and sour cream • chopped tomato and pesto • chopped smoked salmon, cubed cream cheese, and capers • chopped smoked turkey, thinly sliced red onion, and cubed Brie cheese • chopped tomato, crumbled feta cheese, and dill • diced ham, chopped green onions, and shredded Pepper Jack cheese • ricotta cheese, berries, and confectioners' sugar • chopped fresh herbs, green onions, and sour cream

Chive and Goat Cheese Frittata

A frittata is an Italian omelet in which the ingredients are mixed with the eggs rather than folded inside. The frittata is often slipped under the broiler to brown the top. Ours is packed with the delicious flavors of tangy goat cheese, ripe tomato, and fresh chives.

Prep: 15 minutes   Cook/Bake: 20 minutes

- 8 large eggs
- 1/3 cup milk
- 1/2 teaspoon salt
- 1/8 teaspoon freshly ground pepper
- 1 ripe medium tomato, chopped
- 2 tablespoons snipped fresh chives
- 1 tablespoon butter or olive oil
- 1 package (3 1/2 ounces) goat cheese

1. Preheat oven to 375°F. In medium bowl, with wire whisk, beat eggs, milk, salt, and pepper until well blended. Stir in tomato and chives.

2. In oven-safe nonstick 10-inch skillet (if skillet is not oven-safe, wrap handle with a double layer of foil), melt butter over medium heat. Pour in egg mixture. Drop tablespoons of goat cheese on top of egg mixture, cook, without stirring, until egg mixture begins to set around edge, 3 to 4 minutes.

3. Place skillet in oven; bake until frittata is set, 8 to 10 minutes. To serve, loosen frittata from skillet and slide onto warm platter; cut into 4 wedges. Makes 4 main-dish servings.

Each serving: About 262 calories, 18g protein, 4g carbohydrate, 19g total fat (9g saturated), 447mg cholesterol, 552mg sodium.

Potato and Ham Frittata

Prepare egg mixture as directed above but omit tomato, chives, and goat cheese. Cut **2 large red potatoes** into 1/2-inch pieces. Coarsely chop **1 medium onion.** Heat oil in skillet over medium heat. Add potatoes and onion; cover and cook, stirring occasionally, until potatoes are tender, about 12 minutes. Stir in **4 ounces cooked ham,** finely chopped (1 cup). Cook 2 minutes. Spread potato mixture evenly in skillet. Pour egg mixture into skillet and follow remaining cooking directions.

Asparagus and Romano Frittata

Omit tomato, chives, and goat cheese. Prepare egg mixture as directed. Cut **1 pound asparagus** into 1-inch pieces. Thinly slice **4 green onions.** Melt butter in skillet over medium-high heat. Stir in asparagus; cook 4 minutes. Reduce heat to medium, add onions, cook 2 minutes, stirring. Spread vegetable mixture in skillet. Stir 1/2 **cup freshly grated Romano cheese** into eggs and pour into skillet. Cook as directed.

Quiche Lorraine

This is the classic version that put quiche on the culinary map in the 1970s.

Prep: 35 minutes   Bake: 55 minutes

Pastry Dough for 1-Crust Pie (page 534)
- 4 large eggs
- 2 cups milk
- 1/2 teaspoon salt
- 1/8 teaspoon ground black pepper
  pinch ground nutmeg
- 4 slices bacon, cooked and crumbled
- 4 ounces Gruyère or Swiss cheese, shredded (1 cup)

1. Prepare Pastry Dough for 1-Crust Pie. Preheat oven to 425°F. Use dough to line 9-inch pie plate. Line pie shell with foil and fill with pie weights or dry beans. Bake 10 minutes. Remove foil with weights; bake until golden, 5 to 10 minutes longer. Cool on wire rack. Turn oven control to 350°F.

2. In medium bowl, with wire whisk, beat eggs, milk, salt, pepper, and nutmeg until well blended. Sprinkle bacon and Gruyère over bottom of crust; pour egg mixture over bacon and cheese.

3. Place pie plate on foil-lined cookie sheet to catch any overflow. Bake until knife inserted in center comes out clean, 55 to 60 minutes. Cool on wire rack 15 minutes. Serve hot or at room temperature. Makes 8 main-dish servings.

Each serving: About 304 calories, 12g protein, 18g carbohydrate, 20g total fat (10g saturated), 149mg cholesterol, 439mg sodium.

Mushroom Quiche

Prepare and bake pastry dough. Prepare egg mixture as directed but omit bacon and Gruyère. In 10-inch skillet, melt **2 tablespoons butter or margarine** over medium-high heat. Add **8 ounces mushrooms,** trimmed and very thinly sliced, **2 tablespoons finely chopped onion,** ¼ **teaspoon salt,** ⅛ **teaspoon coarsely ground black pepper,** and **pinch dried thyme;** cook, stirring frequently, until mushrooms are tender and liquid has evaporated, about 10 minutes. Add to egg mixture, stirring to mix. Pour into piecrust. Proceed with Step 4, but reduce baking time to 45 to 50 minutes.

Asparagus Quiche

Prepare and bake pastry dough. Prepare egg mixture as directed but omit bacon. Trim **1 pound asparagus** and cut into ¾-inch pieces (2½ cups). In 2-quart saucepan, heat *4 cups water* to boiling over high heat. Add asparagus and cook until tender, 6 to 8 minutes; drain. Rinse asparagus with cold running water; drain. Spread asparagus over bottom of crust and sprinkle with Gruyère; pour egg mixture over. Proceed with Step 4, but reduce baking time to 40 to 45 minutes.

Bite-Size Bacon Quiches

Prepare Pastry Dough for 2-Crust Pie (page 533). On lightly floured surface, with floured rolling pin, roll dough ⅛ inch thick. Using 3-inch round cookie cutter, cut dough into 36 circles, rerolling trimmings. Line thirty-six 1¾-inch mini muffin-pan cups with dough circles. Cover and refrigerate. Prepare egg mixture as directed, using **2 eggs, 1 cup milk,** and ¼ **teaspoon salt.** Divide bacon and cheese evenly among pastry cups. Spoon a scant tablespoon egg mixture into each cup. Bake until egg mixture is set, about 25 minutes. Remove quiches from pans and serve hot. Makes 36 bite-size quiches.

Each serving: About 90 calories, 3g protein, 6g carbohydrate, 6g total fat (3g saturated), 24mg cholesterol, 105mg sodium.

Huevos Rancheros

Hungry ranchers know that this Mexican country-style egg dish is an excellent source of energy before a long, hard workday.

Prep: 10 minutes   Cook/Bake: 20 minutes

1	tablespoon vegetable oil
1	medium onion, coarsely chopped
1	garlic clove, finely chopped
1	jalapeño chile, seeded and finely chopped
1	can (14 to 16 ounces) tomatoes
¼	teaspoon salt
4	(6-inch) corn or flour tortillas
3	tablespoons butter or margarine
4	large eggs
2	tablespoons sour cream
1	tablespoon chopped fresh cilantro
1	ripe medium avocado, pitted, peeled, and cut crosswise into thin slices

1. Preheat oven to 350°F. In nonreactive 2-quart saucepan, heat 1 tablespoon oil over medium-high heat. Add onion, garlic, and jalapeño and cook, stirring occasionally, until onion is tender, about 5 minutes. Stir in tomatoes with their juice and salt; heat to boiling over high heat, breaking up tomatoes with side of spoon. Reduce heat; cover and simmer, stirring occasionally, 5 minutes.

2. Wrap tortillas in foil; place in oven until heated through, about 10 minutes.

3. Meanwhile, in 10-inch skillet, melt butter over medium heat. Break 1 egg into small cup and, holding cup close to skillet, slip egg into skillet; repeat with remaining eggs. Reduce heat to low; cook slowly, spooning butter over eggs to baste them and turning eggs to cook on both sides, until egg whites are completely set and egg yolks begin to thicken but are not hard.

4. Place tortillas on warm plates; place 1 fried egg on each tortilla and spoon 2 tablespoons tomato sauce over each. Top with some sour cream and sprinkle with cilantro; garnish with avocado slices. Serve with remaining tomato sauce. Makes 4 main-dish servings.

Each serving: About 403 calories, 11g protein, 25g carbohydrate, 31g total fat (10g saturated), 239mg cholesterol, 521mg sodium.

Classic Cheese Soufflé

An all-American soufflé made with sharp Cheddar cheese. For the most height, don't overfold the cheese mixture before pouring it into the soufflé dish.

Prep: 20 minutes   Bake: 55 minutes

2	tablespoons plain dried bread crumbs or freshly grated Parmesan cheese
4	tablespoons butter or margarine
¼	cup all-purpose flour
1½	cups milk, warmed
8	ounces sharp Cheddar cheese, shredded (2 cups)
¼	teaspoon salt
⅛	teaspoon ground red pepper (cayenne)
5	large eggs, separated
1	large egg white

1. Preheat oven to 325°F. Grease 2-quart soufflé dish; sprinkle evenly with bread crumbs.

2. Prepare cheese sauce: In heavy 2-quart saucepan, melt butter over low heat. Add flour and cook, stirring, 1 minute. With wire whisk, gradually whisk in warm milk. Cook over medium heat, stirring constantly with wooden spoon, until sauce has thickened and boils. Reduce heat and simmer, stirring frequently, 3 minutes. Stir in Cheddar, salt, and ground red pepper; cook, stirring, just until cheese has melted and sauce is smooth. Remove saucepan from heat.

3. In bowl, with wire whisk, lightly beat egg yolks; gradually whisk in ½ cup hot cheese sauce. Gradually whisk egg-yolk mixture into cheese sauce in saucepan, stirring rapidly to prevent curdling. Pour cheese mixture back into bowl.

4. In large bowl, with mixer at high speed, beat 6 egg whites until stiff peaks form when beaters are lifted. With rubber spatula, gently fold one-third of beaten egg whites into cheese mixture. Fold in remaining whites just until blended.

5. Pour mixture into prepared soufflé dish. If desired, to create top-hat effect (center will rise higher than edge), with back of spoon, make 1-inch-deep indentation all around top of soufflé about 1 inch from edge of dish. Bake until soufflé has puffed and is golden brown and knife inserted 1 inch from edge comes out clean, 55 to 60 minutes. Serve hot. Makes 6 main-dish servings.

Each serving: About 356 calories, 18g protein, 9g carbohydrate, 27g total fat (15g saturated), 246mg cholesterol, 519mg sodium.

Gruyère-Spinach Soufflé

Prepare as directed (left) but substitute **8 ounces Gruyère cheese** for Cheddar and stir **1 package (10 ounces) frozen chopped spinach,** thawed and squeezed dry, into cheese mixture before folding in beaten egg whites. Substitute **pinch ground nutmeg** for ground red pepper.

Each serving: About 372 calories, 21g protein, 11g carbohydrate, 27g total fat (15g saturated), 248mg cholesterol, 446mg sodium.

Southwestern Soufflé

Prepare as directed (left) but substitute **8 ounces Monterey Jack cheese** for Cheddar and stir **½ cup chopped cooked ham** into cheese mixture before folding in beaten egg whites.

Each serving: About 366 calories, 21g protein, 9g carbohydrate, 27g total fat (15g saturated), 253mg cholesterol, 662mg sodium.

HOW MANY? HOW MUCH?

Test Kitchen Tip

If you are measuring eggs by volume, use these amounts:

1 large egg white = about 2 tablespoons
1 large egg yolk = about 1 tablespoon
5 large eggs = about 1 cup
8 large egg whites = about 1 cup

Southwestern Soufflé

Eggs Benedict

This brunch classic serves eight, allowing one egg and one muffin half per diner (if you're serving friends or family with large appetites, however, it will serve four).

Prep: 25 minutes   Cook: 10 minutes

Hollandaise Sauce (page 432)
8 slices Canadian bacon
4 English muffins, split and toasted
8 large eggs

1. Prepare Hollandaise Sauce; keep warm.

2. In jelly-roll pan, arrange toasted English muffins in single layer and top each with slice of Canadian bacon; keep warm.

3. Poach eggs: In 12-inch skillet, heat *1½ inches water* to boiling. Reduce heat to medium-low. Break 1 egg into small cup; holding cup close to surface of water, slip into simmering water. Repeat with remaining eggs.  Cook until egg whites have set and egg yolks begin to thicken but are not hard, 3 to 5 minutes.

4. Place jelly-roll pan with bacon-topped English muffins next to poaching eggs. With slotted spoon, carefully remove eggs, one at a time, from water and very briefly drain (still held in spoon) on paper towels; set 1 egg on top of each slice of Canadian bacon. Spoon hollandaise sauce over. Serve hot. Makes 8 main-dish servings.

Each serving: About 311 calories, 15g protein, 15g carbohydrate, 21g total fat (10g saturated), 337mg cholesterol, 786mg sodium.

Basic Crepes

These delicate pancakes can be stuffed with one of our fillings or rolled up with some jam. The crepes can be prepared up to one day ahead; wrap a stack tightly in plastic wrap and refrigerate.

Prep: 5 minutes plus chilling   Cook: 25 minutes

3 large eggs
1½ cups milk
4 tablespoons butter or margarine, melted
⅔ cup all-purpose flour
½ teaspoon salt

1. In blender, blend eggs, milk, 2 tablespoons butter, flour, and salt until smooth, scraping down sides of blender. Transfer batter to medium bowl; cover and refrigerate at least 1 hour or up to overnight to allow flour to absorb liquid.

2. Heat nonstick 10-inch skillet over medium-high heat. Brush bottom of skillet lightly with some remaining butter. With wire whisk, throughly mix batter to blend well. Pour scant ¼ cup batter into skillet; tilt  pan to coat bottom completely with batter. Cook crepe until top is set and underside is lightly browned, about 1½ minutes.

3. With heat-safe rubber spatula, loosen edge of crepe; turn. Cook until second side has browned, about 30 seconds. Slip crepe onto waxed paper. Repeat with remaining batter, brushing pan lightly with butter before cooking each crepe and stacking crepes between sheets of waxed paper. Makes about 12 crepes.

Each crepe: About 97 calories, 3g protein, 7g carbohydrate, 6g total fat (3g saturated), 68mg cholesterol, 166mg sodium.

Crepes with Pipérade Filling

In the Basque region, which straddles the mountainous Spanish-French border, *pipérade* is a favorite component of egg dishes.

Prep: 45 minutes   Cook/Bake: 45 minutes

Basic Crepes (left)
- 1 tablespoon olive oil
- 1 medium onion, thinly sliced
- 1 red pepper, thinly sliced
- 1 yellow or green pepper, thinly sliced
- ¾ teaspoon salt
- 1 garlic clove, finely chopped
- ⅛ teaspoon ground red pepper (cayenne)
- 1 can (14 to 16 ounces) tomatoes
- 3 ounces Gruyère cheese, shredded (¾ cup)
- 1 tablespoon chopped fresh parsley

1. Prepare Basic Crepes. Set aside 8 crepes. (Reserve remaining crepes for another use.) Preheat oven to 400°F.

2. In 10-inch skillet, heat oil over medium heat. Add onion, red and yellow peppers, and salt; cover and cook until vegetables are tender, about 15 minutes. Stir in garlic and ground red pepper; cook 30 seconds. Add tomatoes with their juice, breaking them up with side of spoon. Cook, uncovered, until juices have thickened, about 15 minutes.

3. Place crepes on surface; sprinkle one-fourth of Gruyère over each crepe, leaving 1-inch border. Spread generous ¼ cup filling down center of each crepe. Roll up crepes and place, seam side down, in shallow 2-quart baking dish. Bake until heated through, about 15 minutes. Sprinkle with parsley. Makes 4 main-dish servings.

Each serving: About 360 calories, 15g protein, 25g carbohydrate, 23g total fat (11g saturated), 159mg cholesterol, 1,019mg sodium.

Crepes Filled with Apples and Gruyère

Apples and Gruyère, a match made in heaven, make an easy but delicious crepe filling.

Prep: 45 minutes   Cook/Bake: 10 minutes

Basic Crepes (opposite)
- 1 tablespoon butter or margarine
- 2 Golden Delicious apples, each peeled, cored, and cut into 16 wedges
- 4 ounces Gruyère cheese, shredded (1 cup)

1. Prepare Basic Crepes. Set aside 8 crepes. (Reserve remaining crepes for another use.) Preheat oven to 400°F. Grease large cookie sheet.

2. In nonstick 10-inch skillet, melt butter over medium-high heat. Add apples and cook, stirring frequently, until tender and beginning to brown, about 5 minutes.

3. Place crepes on surface; sprinkle one-fourth of Gruyère over half of each crepe. Place one-fourth of apples over Gruyère. Fold crepes over to enclose filling; place on prepared cookie sheet. Bake until cheese melts, about 5 minutes. Makes 4 main-dish servings.

Each serving: About 372 calories, 15g protein, 23g carbohydrate, 25g total fat (14g saturated), 174mg cholesterol, 457mg sodium.

CREPE FILLINGS

Here are some other tasty fruit and cheese combinations for filling crepes.

Strawberries and Goat Cheese Use 2 cups hulled and sliced strawberries and 8 ounces of fresh (mild) goat cheese. Prepare as directed above but cook the strawberries only until slightly softened, about 2 minutes.

Red Plums and Swiss Cheese Use 4 large plums and 4 ounces Swiss cheese. Prepare as directed above.

Blueberries and Ricotta Cheese Use 2 cups blueberries and 8 ounces ricotta cheese. Prepare as directed above, but cook the blueberries just until slightly softened, about 3 minutes.

Puffy Apple Pancake

Caramelized apples are an easy and delicious enhancement for our basic puffy pancake.

Prep: 15 minutes   Cook/Bake: 30 minutes

2   tablespoons butter or margarine
½   cup plus 2 tablespoons sugar
¼   cup water
6   medium Granny Smith or Newtown Pippin apples (2 pounds), each peeled, cored, and cut into 8 wedges
3   large eggs
¾   cup milk
¾   cup all-purpose flour
¼   teaspoon salt

1. Preheat oven to 425°F. In oven-safe 12-inch skillet (if skillet is not oven-safe, wrap handle with double layer of foil), combine butter, ½ cup sugar, and water; heat to boiling over medium-high heat. Add apples; cook, stirring occasionally, until apples are golden and sugar mixture begins to caramelize, about 15 minutes.

2. Meanwhile, in blender or in food processor with knife blade attached, blend eggs, milk, flour, remaining 2 tablespoons sugar, and salt until smooth.

3. Pour batter over apples. Place skillet in oven and bake until pancake has puffed and is golden, about 15 minutes. Serve hot. Makes 6 main-dish servings.

Each serving: About 301 calories, 6g protein, 54g carbohydrate, 8g total fat (4g saturated), 121mg cholesterol, 181mg sodium.

Simple Puffy Pancake

Prepare as directed above but omit apple mixture in Step 1. In Step 3, add **2 tablespoons butter or margarine** to skillet and heat in oven until melted. Pour batter into skillet and bake as directed. Serve filled with a mixture of fresh berries and bananas, or a simple drizzle of maple syrup. Makes 6 main-dish servings.

French Toast

If you like, try adding a pinch of cinnamon, nutmeg, orange peel, and/or vanilla extract to the egg mixture.

Prep: 5 minutes   Cook: 15 minutes

3   large eggs
¾   cup milk
⅛   teaspoon salt
4   tablespoons butter or margarine
8   slices (½ inch thick) sourdough or other firm white bread
      softened butter or margarine, maple syrup, or honey

1. Preheat oven to 250°F. In pie plate, with wire whisk, beat eggs, milk, and salt until well blended. In nonstick 12-inch skillet, melt 2 tablespoons butter over medium-high heat.

2. Dip 4 bread slices, one at a time, in beaten egg mixture to coat both sides well. Place in skillet and cook until browned, about 4 minutes per side. Transfer to cookie sheet; keep warm in oven. Repeat with remaining 2 tablespoons butter and remaining 4 bread slices. Serve hot with butter, maple syrup, or honey. Makes 4 main-dish servings.

Each serving without butter, syrup, or honey: About 341 calories, 11g protein, 32g carbohydrate, 18g total fat (10g saturated), 197mg cholesterol, 605mg sodium.

EGG SIZE EQUIVALENTS

Almost any size egg can be used for frying, scrambling, hard-cooking, and poaching. For baking and custards, however, large-size eggs are usually used. To substitute one size egg for another, follow our guidelines.

EGG SIZE EQUIVALENTS

LGE	JUMBO	X-LGE	MED	SMALL
1	1	1	1	1
2	2	2	2	3
3	3	2	3	4
4	3	4	5	5
5	4	4	6	7
6	5	5	7	8

Overnight Baked French Toast

(Pictured on page 196)

With its glorious brown-sugar crust, this rich, eggy French toast is a beautiful choice for company—and it's made with very little effort. Garnish with a sprinkling of confectioners' sugar and fresh berries.

Prep: 10 minutes plus overnight to chill   Bake: 1 hour

- 12 slices firm white bread
- 6 large eggs
- 2 cups milk
- 1 teaspoon vanilla extract
- ¼ teaspoon ground cinnamon
- ¼ teaspoon ground nutmeg
      pinch salt
- ½ cup packed brown sugar
- 4 tablespoons butter or margarine, softened
- 1 tablespoon maple syrup

1. Arrange bread slices in four stacks in 8-inch square baking dish.

2. In blender, combine eggs, milk, vanilla, cinnamon, nutmeg, and salt and blend until mixture is smooth. Slowly pour egg mixture over bread slices; press bread down to absorb egg mixture, spooning egg mixture over any uncoated bread. Cover and refrigerate overnight.

3. Preheat oven to 350°F. In small bowl, stir brown sugar, butter, and maple syrup until combined. Spread evenly over each stack of bread. Bake until knife inserted 1 inch from center comes out clean, about 1 hour. Let stand 15 minutes before serving. To serve, cut each stack diagonally in half. Makes 8 servings.

Each serving: About 308 calories, 10g protein, 37g carbohydrate, 13g total fat (6g saturated), 184mg cholesterol, 364mg sodium.

Spinach Strata

This strata is best when assembled the night before, then baked the next day. For a real treat, use fresh mozzarella.

Prep: 15 minutes plus chilling   Bake: 1 hour

- 8 slices firm white bread
- 4 ounces mozzarella cheese, shredded (1 cup)
- 1 package (10 ounces) frozen chopped spinach, thawed and squeezed dry
- 1 tablespoon butter or margarine
- 6 large eggs
- 2 cups milk
- ½ teaspoon salt
- ¼ teaspoon ground black pepper

1. Lightly grease 8-inch square baking dish. Arrange 4 bread slices in bottom of dish. Sprinkle with ½ cup mozzarella and top with spinach; sprinkle with remaining ½ cup mozzarella. Spread butter on one side of remaining 4 bread slices and arrange, butter side up, over mozzarella.

2. In large bowl, with wire whisk, beat eggs, milk, salt, and pepper until well blended. Slowly pour egg mixture over bread slices; press bread down to absorb egg mixture, spooning egg mixture over any uncoated bread. Cover and refrigerate at least 4 hours or up to overnight.

3. Preheat oven to 350°F. Remove cover and bake strata until golden and knife inserted in center comes out clean, about 1 hour. Let stand 15 minutes before serving. Makes 6 main-dish servings.

Each serving: About 313 calories, 17g protein, 25g carbohydrate, 16g total fat (7g saturated), 244mg cholesterol, 624mg sodium.

Stuffed Eggs

Stuffed eggs are make-ahead appetizers that work as well with large as with small groups.

Prep: 30 minutes   Cook: 10 minutes plus standing

6 large eggs
¼ cup mayonnaise
1 tablespoon milk
⅛ teaspoon salt

1. In 3-quart saucepan, place eggs and enough *cold water* to cover by at least 1 inch; heat to boiling over high heat. Immediately remove saucepan from heat and cover tightly; let stand 15 minutes. Pour off hot water and run cold water over eggs to cool. Peel eggs.

2. Slice eggs lengthwise in half. Gently remove yolks and place in medium bowl; with fork, finely mash yolks. Stir in mayonnaise, milk, and salt until evenly blended. Egg-yolk mixture and egg whites can be covered separately and refrigerated up to 24 hours.

3. Place egg whites in jelly-roll pan lined with paper towels (to prevent eggs from rolling). Spoon egg-yolk mixture into pastry bag fitted with star tip or zip-tight plastic bag with one corner cut off. Pipe about 1 tablespoon yolk mixture into each egg-white half, or simply spoon mixture. Cover eggs and refrigerate up to 4 hours. Makes 12 appetizers.

Each appetizer: About 72 calories, 3g protein, 0g carbohydrate, 6g total fat (1g saturated), 109mg cholesterol, 82mg sodium.

Bacon-Horseradish Stuffed Eggs

Prepare as directed above but add **2 tablespoons crumbled crisp-cooked bacon** and **1 tablespoon bottled white horseradish** to yolk mixture. If not serving right away, sprinkle crumbled bacon on top of stuffed eggs instead of adding to yolk mixture.

Each appetizer: About 80 calories, 4g protein, 1g carbohydrate, 7g total fat (2g saturated), 110mg cholesterol, 102mg sodium.

Dried Tomato–Caper Stuffed Eggs

Prepare as directed (left) but add **1 tablespoon plus 2 teaspoons chopped dried tomatoes packed in oil and herbs, 1 tablespoon plus 2 teaspoons chopped drained capers,** and **⅛ teaspoon coarsely ground black pepper** to yolk mixture.

Each appetizer: About 78 calories, 3g protein, 1g carbohydrate, 7g total fat (1g saturated), 109mg cholesterol, 143mg sodium.

Lemon-Basil Stuffed Eggs

Prepare as directed (left) but add **1 tablespoon chopped fresh basil, ¼ teaspoon freshly grated lemon peel,** and **¼ teaspoon coarsely ground black pepper** to yolk mixture.

Each appetizer: About 73 calories, 3g protein, 0g carbohydrate, 6g total fat (1g saturated), 109mg cholesterol, 82mg sodium.

Pimiento-Studded Stuffed Eggs

Prepare as directed (left) but add **2 tablespoons chopped pimientos, 2 teaspoons Dijon mustard,** and **⅛ teaspoon ground red pepper (cayenne)** to yolk mixture.

Each appetizer: About 74 calories, 3g protein, 1g carbohydrate, 6g total fat (1g saturated), 109mg cholesterol, 102mg sodium.

Lemon-Basil Stuffed Eggs

CHEESE

No matter how you slice it, cheese is simply coagulated milk curd. The final product depends on many variables. What kind of milk was used? Cow's is the most common, but many cheeses are made from sheep's or goat's milk. How long was the cheese aged? In general, the older the cheese, the harder the texture. Was any special bacteria, yeast, or mold added to the cheese to give it distinction? Penicillin molds give blue cheeses their unique taste and veined appearance. Brie is treated with a mold that forms an edible rind that cures the cheese from the outside in. Whether you appreciate cheese by itself as an appetizer or dessert course or use it in casseroles, pizzas, salads, paninis, or other dishes, this delicious food delivers a lot of flavor, even in small amounts.

HOW CHEESE IS MADE

Cheese is made by combining milk with a starter: a bacterial culture that curdles the milk to form curds (solids) and whey (liquid). The whey is then drained off. For some fresh cheeses, the curds are served in their soft state (cottage cheese, for example), but for most cheeses, the curds are further coagulated. This is usually accomplished by adding an animal product called rennet. The cheese is then cured by pressing (which removes more whey and makes the cheese harder), cooking, or adding bacterial agents.

HOW CHEESE IS CATEGORIZED

Cheese is often categorized by its texture. *Hard cheeses*, such as Parmigiano-Reggiano and Romano, can be grated. Sliceable cheeses, such as Monterey Jack and Gouda, are considered *semihard*. *Semisoft cheeses*, such as Camembert and triple-crèmes, are spreadable. *Fresh cheeses*, such as cottage cheese and mascarpone, are soft and usually quite perishable. Blue cheeses and goat cheeses have distinctive flavors that put them in their own separate categories. They can be creamy or crumbly, very sharp or quite mild. *Processed cheese* is made from pasteurized cheese that has been combined with emulsifiers and other ingredients to create a moister, more uniform product. Since processed cheese only has to contain 51 percent actual cheese, its flavor is much milder than that of natural cheese.

BUYING CHEESE

Cheese is a living organism and needs to be treated with respect and a certain amount of care. To buy the best cheese, find a cheese or specialty food store that prides itself on the quality of its merchandise. A cheese seller will be able to recommend cheeses that are ripe and ready to eat, as well as those that should be served at a later date. Avoid cheese that has an ammonia odor. Also, do not buy any hard or semihard cheese with beads of moisture on the surface or with dry, cracked rinds. Semisoft cheese should yield to gentle pressure. Any powdery "bloom" on the rind should be evenly colored and slightly moist.

STORING CHEESE

Store cheese in the refrigerator, tightly wrapped to prevent it from drying out. Leave the original wrapping intact, or rewrap in waxed paper and then in foil. To prolong the life of a cheese, change the wrapping every few days. Strong-smelling cheese should be stored in an airtight container so its aroma doesn't affect other foods in close proximity.

In general, the harder a cheese, the longer it will keep. Soft cheese, especially goat cheese, should be eaten as soon as possible. Semihard cheeses will keep for a few weeks if wrapped tightly. If a cheese (like Cheddar) dries out, grate it and use in cooked dishes. Hard grating cheeses, such as Romano and Parmesan, can be stored for up to several months.

If a hard cheese develops a moldy spot, cut it away; the remaining cheese is fine to eat. Discard any soft cheese that has developed mold, because it could have permeated the cheese.

If absolutely necessary, you can freeze hard or semihard cheese, but when thawed, the cheese will lose moisture and become crumbly. Use it for cooking, not eating. To freeze, wrap the cheese airtight in moisture-proof wrapping and freeze for up to three months.

A CHEESE GLOSSARY

Asiago A sharp cow's milk cheese made in northern Italy since the 16th century. The most readily available version is a domestic hard grating cheese.

Blue cheese An entire category of cheese with blue-green veins that give the cheese a tart, sharp flavor and aroma. American, Canadian, and Danish varieties are simply called "blue cheese." *Danish blue cheese* is especially good in salad dressings. *French Roquefort*, considered the king of blue cheeses, is made with sheep's milk and is crumbly and sharp, with distinct blue veining. *Italian Gorgonzola*, made from cow's milk, has a creamy texture and milder flavor. Young *dolce Gorgonzola* has the softest texture and mildest flavor (although it is still quite tangy), while aged *naturale Gorgonzola* is firmer and more assertive. *British Stilton*, with its inedible thick rind, is another highly regarded cow's milk blue cheese.

Brie Brie is a semisoft cheese with an edible white rind. When purchased, it should have a soft, not runny, consistency.

Camembert A perfectly ripe Camembert has a creamy, runny center and rich buttery flavor. This semisoft cheese has a "bloomed" (velvety looking) edible rind.

Cheddar A semihard cheese that ranges in flavor from mild to extrasharp and in color from ivory to orange. It is named after the British village that specializes in its production, but it has become an American classic.

Edam A mild-flavored Dutch cheese made from partially skimmed cow's milk and shaped into a flattened ball. Edam from Holland is coated with red paraffin and wrapped in red cellophane. Domestic Edam is coated in red paraffin.

Farmer cheese True farmer cheese is a soft fresh curd cheese that is firm enough to slice. It has a mild, tangy flavor.

Feta Depending on its country of origin and the type of milk used, the flavor of feta varies. It is always stored in brine, which imparts an inherent saltiness. European feta cheese is usually made from sheep's milk. *Greek feta* is crumbly, salty, and sharp; *Bulgarian feta* has a more delicate taste and a creamier texture; and *French feta* is milder still. *American feta* is made in the Greek style but is usually made from cow's or goat's milk.

Fontina The classic Fontina d'Aosta, smooth-textured and mildly pungent, is one of the great cheeses of Italy. There are also tasty American, Danish, and Swedish versions.

Goat cheese Sharp, tangy, and brilliant white, this cheese is sometimes referred to by its French name, *chèvre*. It can be young and soft or aged and hard. Some are coated in herbs, spices, or wood ash, wrapped in leaves, or soaked in olive oil. They can be round, button-shaped, or resemble a pyramid; many have rinds. French chèvres are highly revered, but there are excellent American versions.

Gouda Similar in flavor and appearance to Edam but made from cow's milk. Aged Gouda is sharp-tasting and butterscotch in color.

Gruyère See Swiss cheese.

Havarti Danish Havarti is a brick-shaped cheese dotted with tiny holes. It has a mild flavor and soft texture.

Manchego In America, this golden yellow Spanish sheep's milk cheese is available in two stages of ripeness: one-year-old *curado* and two-year-old *añejo*. Some liken its sharp flavor and dry, crumbly texture to fine Cheddar cheese.

Mascarpone This mild clotted cream has a thick, creamy texture. It is best known as a key ingredient in the delectable Italian dessert called tiramisú.

Blue cheeses: Maytag Blue, Roquefort, Stilton, Danish Blue, Gorgonzola

Goat's and sheep's milk cheeses: Classic ash-coated log, buttons, pyramid, ricotta salata, Bûcheron, feta

Monterey Jack An American original developed by Scotsman David Jacks near Monterey, California, in the 1890s. Soft-textured with a mild acidic bite, true Monterey Jack has tiny holes running through it. Jack cheese is sometimes flavored with jalapeño peppers. *Dry Jack* is a very hard, aged cheese that is used primarily for grating.

Mozzarella Mozzarella is one of the best melting cheeses. In southern Italy, it is often made from *bufala* (water buffalo) milk and hand-formed into balls. Domestically, the version found most often is factory-produced from whole or partially skimmed cow's milk. Specialty food stores carry fresh mozzarella that is hand-formed, smoked mozzarella, and imported buffalo milk mozzarella.

Muenster American Muenster is a brick-shaped, paprika-sprinkled cheese with a mild flavor and smooth texture. It is a good melting cheese. There are French, Danish, and German Munsters (note the different spelling), but they are much stronger.

Parmesan There is only one authentic Parmigiano-Reggiano. Protected by Italian law, Parmigiano-Reggiano can be made only in a geographically defined area around Parma, Italy. It is aged for at least fourteen months, and its name is repeatedly stamped on the rind. Whenever possible, buy Parmigiano by the wedge and grate it just before serving.

Port-Salut Formerly made by French Trappist monks, this cheese is now factory-produced. It has a mild flavor, a semisoft texture, and an edible orange-colored rind.

Provolone The somewhat soft, mild provolone found in most supermarkets is the American version. It comes in a variety of shapes, from balls to cylinders, but it is always bound with rope to maintain its form. Italian provolone is often aged until sharp and firm.

Queso blanco A popular cheese in Latino cooking, it is pressed into firm blocks; when sliced and heated, it melts. It is often confused with *queso fresco*, which has a dry texture and does not melt.

Raclette A semisoft cheese from Switzerland with excellent melting qualities.

Ricotta Its name literally means "recooked." The traditional version of this soft, fresh Italian cheese is prepared from the whey collected after making other cheeses. The whey is cooked a second time with coagulants to produce a mild, granular cheese. The ricotta cheese sold in American supermarkets is usually a blend of whey and cow's milk, either partially skimmed or whole.

Ricotta Salata No relation to soft ricotta, this is a pressed, lightly salted Sicilian sheep's milk cheese with a slightly crumbly, firm texture.

Soft-ripened cheeses: Brie, Camembert, Explorateur

Hard (grating) cheeses: Pecorino Romano, Parmigiano-Reggiano

Romano A hard grating cheese that is often used as a substitute for Parmesan. Romano has a slightly salty, more piquant taste that goes beautifully with the robust tomato sauces and vegetable dishes of southern Italy. Italian *Pecorino Romano* is made from sheep's milk.

Swiss cheese Americans refer to any cheese with holes as Swiss cheese, but there are distinct types. Generic Swiss cheese is American-made, usually in California or Wisconsin. There are two classic Swiss-made cheeses that are indispensable in fondue: *Gruyère* and *Emmental*. As they age, their characteristic holes are formed by carbon dioxide trapped in the cheese. Gruyère has pea-size holes and a full, rich flavor. The French version is called Comté. Emmental has holes of various shapes and a nutty flavor. *Jarlsberg*, one of the most popular of all imported cheeses, is a Norwegian version of Emmental, but with larger holes and a softer texture.

Taleggio This cow's milk cheese has a soft interior with flavor that can range from tart and salty to rich and buttery. Its reddish brown crust should be dry and uncracked. It is made in the Lombardy region of northern Italy.

Triple-crème cheese A category of cheeses made with cow's milk and enriched with cream, resulting in buttery rich texture and flavor. *Brillat-Savarin*, *St.-André*, and *Explorateur* are three of the best-known triple-crème cheeses.

Broccoli-Cheddar Puff

Serve this golden puff as a side dish or as the star of a holiday brunch.

Prep: 35 minutes   Bake: 40 minutes

5	tablespoons butter or margarine
6	tablespoons all-purpose flour
½	teaspoon salt
⅛	teaspoon ground red pepper (cayenne)
2¼	cups milk
8	ounces sharp Cheddar cheese, shredded (2 cups)
2	boxes (10 ounces each) frozen chopped broccoli, thawed and squeezed dry
7	large eggs, separated
1½	cups coarse soft fresh bread crumbs (about 3 slices firm white bread)

1. In 4-quart sauce pan, melt 4 tablespoons butter over medium-low heat. Stir in flour, salt, and ground red pepper until blended; cook 1 minute, stirring. Gradually stir in milk; cook until mixture boils and thickens, stirring frequently. Stir in Cheddar; cook just until melted. Remove from heat. Stir in broccoli.

2. In small bowl, with fork, lightly beat egg yolks. Stir in about ½ cup cheese sauce. Gradually pour egg-yolk mixture into cheese sauce, stirring rapidly to prevent curdling. Cool slightly.

3. Meanwhile, preheat oven to 325°F. Grease shallow 3½-quart ceramic casserole or 13" by 9" glass baking dish. In microwave-safe small bowl, heat remaining 1 tablespoon butter in microwave oven on High 15 to 20 seconds or until melted, swirling bowl once. Add bread crumbs; stir until well combined.

4. In large bowl, with mixer at high speed, beat egg whites until stiff peaks form when beaters are lifted. With rubber spatula, gently fold one third of whites into cheese mixture. Fold cheese mixture gently back into remaining whites.

5. Pour mixture into prepared casserole. Sprinkle crumb mixture on top. Bake 40 minutes or until top is browned and knife inserted in center comes out clean. Serve immediately. Makes 15 accompaniment servings.

Each serving: About 190 calories, 9g protein, 9g carbohydrate, 13g total fat (7g saturated), 131mg cholesterol, 280mg sodium.

Mozzarella in Carrozza

Mozzarella in carrozza, "mozzarella in a carriage," is usually deep-fried, but we panfry ours. It is served with a buttery anchovy sauce that can be drizzled over each serving, if you like.

Prep: 20 minutes   Cook: 5 minutes

- 8 ounces part-skim mozzarella cheese
- 8 slices firm white bread, crusts removed
- 2 large eggs, well beaten
- ¼ cup milk
- ¼ cup all-purpose flour
- ½ teaspoon salt
- ¼ teaspoon ground black pepper
- ½ cup plain dried bread crumbs
- 3 tablespoons vegetable oil
- 4 tablespoons butter or margarine
- 8 anchovy fillets, drained
- 1 tablespoon chopped fresh parsley
- 1 teaspoon capers, drained
- 1 teaspoon fresh lemon juice

1. Stand mozzarella on its side and cut lengthwise into 4 equal slices. Place 1 slice cheese between 2 slices bread to form sandwich. Repeat with remaining cheese and bread.

2. Preheat oven to 200°F.

3. In pie plate, with wire whisk, beat eggs and milk. On waxed paper, combine flour, salt, and pepper; spread bread crumbs on separate sheet of waxed paper. Dip sandwiches, one at a time, in flour mixture, shaking off excess, then in egg mixture, and finally in bread crumbs, shaking off excess.

4. In nonstick 12-inch skillet, heat oil over medium heat until hot. Add sandwiches; cook until golden brown, about 1½ minutes per side. Cut each sandwich on diagonal in half. Arrange on platter in single layer. Keep warm in oven.

5. In same skillet, melt butter; add anchovies and cook, stirring constantly, 1 minute. Add parsley, capers, and lemon juice; cook 30 seconds longer. Transfer sauce to small bowl. Serve sauce with sandwiches. Makes 8 appetizer servings.

Each serving: About 309 calories, 13g protein, 22g carbohydrate, 19g total fat (8g saturated), 89mg cholesterol, 713mg sodium.

Mozzarella in Carrozza

Classic Swiss Fondue

Eating fondue, Switzerland's most famous cheese dish, is a social occasion, best saved for small groups. It is important to use a dry, slightly acidic wine, such as sauvignon blanc, or the cheese won't melt smoothly.

Prep: 15 minutes   Cook: 15 minutes

- 1 garlic clove, cut in half
- 1½ cups dry white wine
- 1 tablespoon kirsch or brandy
- 8 ounces Swiss or Emmental cheese, shredded (2 cups)
- 8 ounces Gruyère cheese, shredded (2 cups)
- 3 tablespoons all-purpose flour
- ⅛ teaspoon ground black pepper
  pinch ground nutmeg
- 1 loaf (16 ounces) French bread, cut into 1-inch cubes

1. Rub inside of fondue pot or heavy nonreactive 2-quart saucepan with garlic; discard garlic. Pour wine into fondue pot. Heat over medium-low heat until very hot but not boiling; stir in kirsch.

2. Meanwhile, in medium bowl, toss Swiss cheese, Gruyère, and flour until mixed. Add cheese mixture, one handful at a time, to wine, stirring constantly and vigorously until cheese has melted and mixture is thick and smooth. If mixture separates, increase heat to medium, stirring just until smooth. Stir in pepper and nutmeg.

3. Transfer fondue to table; place over tabletop heater to keep hot, if you like. To eat, spear cubes of French bread onto long-handled fondue forks and dip into cheese mixture. Makes 6 first-course servings.

Each serving: About 567 calories, 29g protein, 45g carbohydrate, 25g total fat (14g saturated), 76mg cholesterol, 689mg sodium.

Savory Ricotta Cheesecake

This basil-scented cheesecake can be served warm or cool with a salad of baby greens or tomatoes and crusty bread.

Prep: 15 minutes   Bake: 1 hour 10 minutes

- 2 garlic cloves, peeled
- 1 cup loosely packed fresh basil leaves
- 1 container (32 ounces) part-skim ricotta cheese
- 1 package (8 ounces) cream cheese
- ⅓ cup freshly grated Parmesan cheese
- 4 large eggs
- 3 tablespoons all-purpose flour
- ¾ teaspoon freshly grated orange peel
- ½ teaspoon salt
- ¼ teaspoon ground black pepper

1. Preheat oven to 350°F. Lightly grease 9-inch springform pan. Place on cookie sheet.

2. In 1-quart saucepan, heat *2 cups water* to boiling over high heat. Add garlic and cook 3 minutes to blanch; drain.

3. In food processor with knife blade attached, process garlic and basil until chopped. Add ricotta, cream cheese, Parmesan, eggs, flour, orange peel, salt, and pepper; puree until smooth and well combined. Pour into prepared pan.

4. Bake until cake is just set and toothpick inserted in center comes out clean, about 1 hour 10 minutes. Cool in pan on wire rack 10 minutes. With small knife, carefully loosen cheesecake from side of pan; remove side of pan. To serve, cut into wedges. Makes 12 first-course servings.

Each serving: About 222 calories, 14g protein, 7g carbohydrate, 15g total fat (9g saturated), 117mg cholesterol, 319mg sodium.

Welsh Rabbit

Whether you call it rarebit or rabbit (perhaps named by an unsuccessful hunter), this is classic comfort food. If you top it with bacon, it becomes Yorkshire rabbit.

Prep: 10 minutes   Cook: 10 minutes

2	tablespoons butter or margarine
¼	cup all-purpose flour
1	cup milk, warmed
⅔	cup beer
8	ounces sharp Cheddar cheese, shredded (2 cups)
1	teaspoon Dijon mustard
½	teaspoon Worcestershire sauce
⅛	teaspoon ground red pepper (cayenne)
9	slices white bread, toasted

1. In 2-quart saucepan, melt butter over medium heat. With wooden spoon, stir in flour. With wire whisk, gradually whisk in warm milk until smooth. Whisk in beer and heat to boiling, whisking constantly. Reduce heat and simmer 1 minute. Stir in Cheddar, mustard, Worcestershire, and ground red pepper; remove from heat. Stir until smooth.

2. Cut toast slices on diagonal in half. Arrange 3 toast halves on each plate and spoon cheese mixture over. Makes 6 main-dish servings.

Each serving: About 342 calories, 14g protein, 26g carbohydrate, 19g total fat (11g saturated), 56mg cholesterol, 521mg sodium.

Lacy Parmesan Crisps

Called *frico* in Italy, these delicious wafers are simply spoonfuls of grated cheese that are baked and cooled. Reusable nonstick bakeware liners, available at most kitchenware stores and bakery suppliers, yield the best results and are easy to use, but you can use a nonstick cookie sheet instead.

Prep: 20 minutes   Bake: 6 minutes per batch

6	ounces Parmesan cheese, coarsely grated (1½ cups)

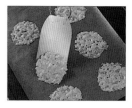

1. Preheat oven to 375°F. Line large cookie sheet with reusable nonstick bakeware liner. Drop level tablespoons Parmesan 3 inches apart onto cookie sheet; spread to form 2-inch rounds.

2. Bake Parmesan rounds until edges just begin to color, 6 to 7 minutes. Transfer crisps, still on bakeware liner, to wire rack; cool 2 minutes. Transfer to paper towels to drain. Repeat with remaining Parmesan. Makes about 24 crisps.

Each crisp: About 28 calories, 3g protein, 0g carbohydrate, 2g total fat (1g saturated), 5mg cholesterol, 114mg sodium.

Cheddar Crisps

Prepare as directed above but substitute **6 ounces sharp Cheddar cheese,** coarsely shredded (1½ cups) for Parmesan. Bake until bubbling but not browned, 6 to 7 minutes per batch.

Lacy Parmesan Crisps

8

PASTA & PASTA SAUCES

Pasta has become a weeknight favorite for many cooks; it's nutritious, easy to prepare, and delicious. Best of all, pasta is extremely versatile. It can be rich and satisfying when combined with meat, light and luscious when tossed with vegetables or seafood, or positively mouthwatering when layered and baked until golden and bubbling.

We use dried Italian-style pasta for most of our recipes, as it is readily available. For special occasions, homemade or store-bought fresh pasta is an excellent choice. Made with eggs, fresh pasta has a delicate texture that works well with creamy sauces. Dried pasta, made from flour and water, is more economical, lower in fat, and a good match for a wide variety of sauces.

BUYING AND STORING PASTA

For the best taste and texture, buy dried pasta made from durum wheat flour or from semolina flour. Store dried pasta in a cool, dry, dark place for up to one year, but if it is made of whole wheat, store up to six months. Even though clear plastic pasta storage containers are attractive, do not use them. Light destroys riboflavin, a key nutrient in pasta. We recommend buying pasta that comes in cardboard boxes for the same reason.

Store commercially made fresh pasta in the refrigerator for up to one week, or freeze for up to one month. Homemade pasta can be refrigerated for up to three days or frozen for up to one month. For the best results, don't thaw frozen pasta before cooking.

A PASTA GLOSSARY

Long Strands
Bucatini Long, thick tubes resembling hollow spaghetti.
Capellini Also called *capelli d' angelo* or angel hair. Very thin, delicate strands.
Fusilli Long strands resembling a telephone cord but also the name for short spirals.
Spaghetti Italian for "lengths of cord."
Vermicelli Very thin spaghetti.

Flat Ribbons
Egg noodles American-style noodles enriched with egg yolks.
Fettuccine Flat noodles about ¼ inch wide.
Lasagna Very wide flat pasta noodles, also available in a no-boil version.
Linguine Ribbons of pasta that are ⅛ inch wide.
Mafalde Wide ribbons with one long ruffled edge.
Pappardelle Ribbons about 1 inch wide.
Tagliatelle Slightly wider than fettuccine.

Tubular Pastas
Elbow macaroni Small curved tubular pasta.
Mostaccioli Tubes about 2 inches long, available smooth and ribbed.
Penne Tubes with diagonally cut ends.
Rigatoni Large ribbed tubes.
Ziti Medium tubes about 1 inch long.

Small Pastas
Acini di pepe Tiny pasta stubs.
Alphabets Tiny letter-shaped pasta.

Penne with Vodka Sauce

Ditalini Very short macaroni; also called *tubettini*.

Orzo Although rice-shaped, *orzo* means "barley" in Italian.

Pastina Very, very small pasta flakes.

Miscellaneous Shapes

Cavatelli Small elongated ridged pasta.

Conchiglie Medium shells good for sauce.

Creste di gallo Curly medium-ribbed pasta that resembles a rooster's crest.

Farfalle Italian for "butterflies," also called bow ties.

Gemelli Two short spaghettilike strands that are twisted together.

Manicotti Large tubes of pasta meant for stuffing.

Orecchiette Disks that resemble small ears.

Radiatori Small deeply ribbed pasta resembling little radiators.

Rotini Corkscrew pasta, also called *fusilli* and *rotelle*.

Ruote Wagon wheel–shaped pasta.

Asian Noodles

Cellophane noodles Called bean threads or *mai fun*.

Chinese-style egg noodles Tender whole-wheat strands, similar to egg linguine.

Rice sticks Very thin rice stick noodles, also called *mai fun* or rice vermicelli.

Soba Thin brownish gray noodles made from buckwheat flour.

Udon noodles Long, thick, Japanese wheat noodles.

PERFECT PASTA

Cook the Right Amount of Pasta

Most packages list a 2-ounce serving size, but a more generous main-dish measure is 4 ounces dried pasta or 3 ounces fresh pasta per person. The cooked yield of pasta depends on its shape: Four ounces of tube-shaped pasta, like penne, equals 2½ cups cooked; 4 ounces of long-strand pasta, like spaghetti, equals 2 cups cooked; 4 ounces of egg noodles equals 3 cups cooked.

Cook Pasta in Enough Water

Use at least four quarts of water for each pound of pasta. Cover the pot and bring the water to a rapid boil over high heat. Salt the water, then stir in the pasta.

Be Sure to Salt the Water

Pasta doesn't contain salt, so it needs to be cooked in salted water to be seasoned properly. If you are concerned about the amount of sodium in your diet, rest assured that only 10 percent of the salt in the cooking water is absorbed by the pasta. The basic proportion is 2 teaspoons of salt per pound of pasta.

Stir Frequently

Stirring ensures even cooking and keeps pasta from clumping together and sticking to the bottom of the pot. Do not add oil to the cooking water; it prevents sauce from clinging to the pasta.

Don't Overcook Pasta

The cooking time on pasta packages is only a guide, so start checking for doneness before the suggested time and check often. To test pasta for doneness, remove a piece from the boiling water, rinse it briefly under warm water, and bite into it. When pasta is perfectly cooked, it should be *al dente* ("to the tooth") with no raw flour taste and a tiny chalk white center. After it's drained, pasta will continue to cook from the residual heat and from the hot sauce with which it's tossed. If the pasta is to be baked, undercook it slightly, since it will continue to cook in the oven.

Drain Well and Don't Rinse

Drain the pasta in a colander, shaking to remove excess water. Don't rinse pasta; rinsing cools down pasta and removes both the surface starch that keeps it firm and its essential nutrients. Only lasagna noodles and pasta for salad should be rinsed.

Serve It Hot

When pasta stands, it gets cold and unappetizingly gummy. So call everyone to the table while you're tossing the pasta. To keep it as hot as possible, return the drained pasta to the cooking pot, which will still be warm, and combine it with the sauce there. Or warm the serving bowl and the individual bowls.

Cavatelli

Manicotti

Rotini

Gemelli

Conchiglie

Stelline

Orecchiette

Creste di gallo

Linguine

Ruote

Radiatori

Farfalle

Orzo

Marinara Sauce

This sauce is very versatile—we use it in recipes throughout the book. For a toothsome alternative, stir 8 ounces of sweet or hot Italian-sausage links, cooked and crumbled, into the sauce. Or top each serving with a spoonful of ricotta cheese for a creamy treat.

Prep: 5 minutes   Cook: 30 minutes

- 2 tablespoons olive oil
- 1 small onion, chopped
- 1 garlic clove, finely chopped
- 1 can (28 ounces) plum tomatoes
- 2 tablespoons tomato paste
- 2 tablespoons chopped fresh basil or parsley (optional)
- ½ teaspoon salt

1. In nonreactive 3-quart saucepan, heat oil over medium heat; add onion and garlic and cook, stirring, until onion is tender, about 5 minutes.

2. Stir in tomatoes with their juice, tomato paste, basil if using, and salt. Heat to boiling, breaking up tomatoes with side of spoon. Reduce heat; partially cover and simmer, stirring occasionally, until sauce has thickened slightly, about 20 minutes. Use to coat 1 pound pasta for 4 main-dish servings. Makes 3½ cups.

Each ½ cup: About 67 calories, 1g protein, 7g carbohydrate, 4g total fat (1g saturated), 0mg cholesterol, 388mg sodium.

Arrabbiata Sauce

Prepare as directed above, but add ¼ to ½ **teaspoon crushed red pepper** with onion and garlic in Step 1. Omit fresh herbs and proceed as directed.

Spaghetti all'Amatriciana

Prepare as directed above, but use **1 tablespoon oil** in Step 1. Add **4 ounces sliced pancetta,** chopped, and cook until crisp before adding ¼ **teaspoon crushed red pepper** with onion and garlic. In Step 3, omit tomato paste and basil and proceed as directed. Toss pasta with sauce and ¼ **cup chopped fresh parsley.**

Pesto

Pesto is the perfect use for all that fresh summer basil. To serve the pesto with pasta, add ¼ cup pasta cooking water. To store pesto, spoon into half-pint containers and top with a few tablespoons of olive oil. Cover and refrigerate up to one week.

Prep: 10 minutes

- 2 cups firmly packed fresh basil leaves
- 1 garlic clove, crushed with garlic press
- 2 tablespoons pine nuts (pignoli) or walnuts
- ¼ cup olive oil
- 1 teaspoon salt
- ¼ teaspoon coarsely ground black pepper
- ½ cup freshly grated Parmesan cheese

In blender or in food processor with knife blade attached, puree basil, garlic, pine nuts, oil, salt, and pepper until smooth. Add Parmesan and blend until combined. Makes about ¾ cup sauce (enough to coat 1 pound pasta).

Each tablespoon: About 66 calories, 2g protein, 1g carbohydrate, 6g total fat (1g saturated), 3mg cholesterol, 256mg sodium.

Penne with Vodka Sauce

(Pictured on page 218)

This restaurant favorite is a cinch to prepare at home. Don't hesitate to add the vodka. You won't taste it; it just melds the flavors.

Prep: 15 minutes   Cook: 30 minutes

- 1 tablespoon olive oil
- 1 small onion, chopped
- 1 garlic clove, finely chopped
- 1/8 to 1/4 teaspoon crushed red pepper
- 1 can (28 ounces) tomatoes in puree, coarsely chopped
- 3 tablespoons vodka (optional)
- 1/2 teaspoon salt
- 1/2 cup heavy or whipping cream
- 1 cup frozen peas, thawed
- 1 package (16 ounces) penne or rotini
- 1/2 cup loosely packed fresh basil leaves, thinly sliced

1. In nonstick 12-inch skillet, heat oil over medium heat. Add onion and cook until tender, about 5 minutes. Add garlic and crushed red pepper; cook until garlic is golden, about 30 seconds longer. Stir in tomatoes with their puree, vodka if using, and salt; heat to boiling over high heat. Reduce heat and simmer until sauce has thickened, 15 to 20 minutes. Stir in cream and peas; heat to boiling.

2. Meanwhile, in large saucepot, cook pasta as label directs. Drain. In warm serving bowl, toss pasta with sauce and sprinkle with basil. Makes 4 main-dish servings.

Each serving: About 652 calories, 20g protein, 107g carbohydrate, 17g total fat (8g saturated), 41mg cholesterol, 763mg sodium.

Linguine with Red Clam Sauce

If you wish, substitute two cans (10 ounces each) of whole baby clams plus one-fourth of the clam liquid for the littleneck clams.

Prep: 20 minutes   Cook: 1 hour

- Marinara Sauce (opposite)
- 1/2 cup dry white wine
- 2 dozen littleneck clams, scrubbed (page 186)
- 1 package (16 ounces) linguine
- 1 tablespoon butter or margarine, cut into pieces (optional)
- 1/4 cup chopped fresh parsley

1. Prepare Marinara Sauce.

2. In nonreactive 12-inch skillet, heat wine to boiling over high heat. Add clams; cover and cook until clams open, 5 to 10 minutes, transferring clams to bowl as they open. Discard any clams that have not opened. Strain clam broth through sieve lined with paper towels; reserve 1/4 cup. When cool enough to handle, remove clams from shells and coarsely chop. Discard shells.

3. Meanwhile, in large saucepot, cook pasta as label directs. Drain.

4. In same clean 12-inch skillet, combine marinara sauce, reserved clam broth, and clams; cook over low heat until heated through. In warm serving bowl, toss pasta with sauce and butter, if using. Sprinkle with parsley and serve. Makes 6 main-dish servings.

Each serving: About 429 calories, 20g protein, 67g carbohydrate, 9g total fat (2g saturated), 29mg cholesterol, 582mg sodium.

Linguine with Fresh Tomato Sauce

If the ripe summer tomatoes you use taste a bit acidic, simply add 1 teaspoon sugar to the sauce. If using juicy beefsteak tomatoes instead of meaty plum tomatoes, simmer the sauce uncovered for about 20 minutes to allow the excess juices to evaporate.

Prep: 15 minutes   Cook: 30 minutes

- 1 tablespoon olive oil
- 1 small onion, chopped
- 2 pounds ripe plum tomatoes or beefsteak tomatoes, peeled and coarsely chopped
- ½ teaspoon salt
- 3 tablespoons butter, cut into pieces, or olive oil
- 2 tablespoons chopped fresh sage or ½ cup chopped fresh basil
- 1 package (16 ounces) linguine or penne

1. In nonstick 10-inch skillet, heat oil over medium heat. Add onion and cook until tender and golden, about 10 minutes. Add tomatoes with their juice and salt; heat to boiling over high heat. Reduce heat; cover and simmer, stirring and breaking up tomatoes with side of spoon, until sauce has thickened, 15 to 20 minutes. Stir in butter and sage.

2. Meanwhile, in large saucepot, cook pasta as label directs. Drain. In warm serving bowl, toss pasta with sauce. Makes 6 main-dish servings.

Each serving: About 388 calories, 11g protein, 65g carbohydrate, 10g total fat (4g saturated), 16mg cholesterol, 334mg sodium.

Spaghetti with Roasted Tomatoes

Oven-roasted tomatoes have a sweet, intense flavor that is hard to resist. They make a terrific pasta sauce. If you like, you can use 3 pints of whole grape tomatoes to replace the plum tomatoes; reduce the roasting time to 20 to 30 minutes. No need to peel!

Prep: 10 minutes plus cooling   Roast/Cook: 1 hour

- 2 tablespoons olive oil
- 3 pounds ripe plum tomatoes (16 medium), cut lengthwise in half
- 6 garlic cloves, not peeled
- 1 package (16 ounces) spaghetti or linguine
- ¾ teaspoon salt
- ¼ teaspoon coarsely ground black pepper freshly grated Pecorino Romano cheese (optional)

1. Preheat oven to 450°F. Brush jelly-roll pan with 1 tablespoon oil. Arrange tomatoes, cut side down, in pan; add garlic. Roast tomatoes and garlic until tomatoes are well browned and garlic has softened, 50 to 60 minutes.

2. When cool enough to handle, peel tomatoes over medium bowl to catch any juices. Place tomatoes in bowl; discard skins. Squeeze garlic to separate pulp from skins. Add garlic to tomatoes.

3. Meanwhile, in large saucepot, cook pasta as label directs. Drain.

4. With back of spoon, crush tomatoes and garlic. Stir in salt, pepper, and remaining 1 tablespoon oil. Serve sauce at room temperature or transfer to saucepan and heat through over low heat. In warm serving bowl, toss pasta with sauce. Serve with Pecorino, if you like. Makes 4 main-dish servings.

Each serving: About 552 calories, 17g protein, 101g carbohydrate, 10g total fat (1g saturated), 0mg cholesterol, 570mg sodium.

Radiatori with Arugula, Cherry Tomatoes, and Pancetta

No need to cook the arugula in this easy dish; it quickly wilts when tossed with the hot pasta and sauce.

Prep: 15 minutes   Cook: 25 minutes

- 4 ounces sliced pancetta or bacon, chopped
- 1 garlic clove, crushed with garlic press
- 1 pound cherry tomatoes, cut into quarters
- ½ teaspoon salt
- ¼ teaspoon coarsely ground black pepper
- 1 package (16 ounces) radiatori or rotini
- 2 bunches arugula (10 ounces each), trimmed
- ¼ cup freshly grated Parmesan cheese

1. In nonstick 10-inch skillet, cook pancetta over medium heat until lightly browned. (If cooking bacon, discard all but 1 tablespoon bacon drippings.) Add garlic and cook, stirring, 30 seconds. Add tomatoes, salt, and pepper and cook until tomatoes are warmed through, 1 to 2 minutes longer.

2. Meanwhile, in large saucepot, cook pasta as label directs. Drain. In warm serving bowl, toss pasta with pancetta mixture, arugula, and Parmesan. Makes 4 main-dish servings.

Each serving: About 557 calories, 22g protein, 93g carbohydrate, 11g total fat (4g saturated), 14mg cholesterol, 676mg sodium.

KNOW YOUR PASTA

Choose the right sauce for your pasta. Here are some tried-and-true guidelines:

- Thin pastas, such as capellini and vermicelli, should be dressed with delicate, light sauces that will cling to the skinny strands.
- Fettuccine and linguine are excellent with light meat, vegetable, seafood, cheese, and cream sauces.
- Tubular pastas are great with meat sauces: The nuggets of meat nestle right inside the tubes. Chunky vegetable or olive sauces are also a good match for macaroni-type pastas as well as for baked dishes.
- Tiny pastas are best saved for soups or combined with other ingredients.

Penne with No-Cook Tomato Sauce

This sauce is spectacular in summer, when tomatoes are at their peak. Use equal amounts of red and yellow tomatoes for a jewel-like effect.

Prep: 20 minutes plus standing   Cook: 25 minutes

- 2 pounds ripe tomatoes (6 medium), chopped
- 1 cup loosely packed fresh basil leaves, thinly sliced
- 8 ounces fresh mozzarella cheese, cut into ½-inch cubes
- 2 tablespoons olive oil
- 1 tablespoon red wine vinegar
- 1 teaspoon salt
- ¼ teaspoon coarsely ground black pepper
- 1 package (16 ounces) penne or rotini

1. In medium bowl, combine tomatoes, basil, mozzarella, oil, vinegar, salt, and pepper, tossing gently to mix. Let sauce stand at least 15 minutes or up to 1 hour at room temperature to blend flavors.

2. Meanwhile, in large saucepot, cook pasta as label directs. Drain. In warm serving bowl, toss pasta with sauce. Makes 4 main-dish servings.

Each serving: About 698 calories, 27g protein, 99g carbohydrate, 21g total fat (1g saturated), 40mg cholesterol, 749mg sodium.

Bow Ties with Tomatoes and Lemon

Prepare as directed, but omit mozzarella and substitute **¼ cup loosely packed fresh mint leaves,** chopped, for basil in Step 1. Add **1 teaspoon grated lemon peel** and **1 garlic clove,** crushed with garlic press, to tomato mixture. In Step 2, substitute **1 package (16 ounces) bow ties or ziti** for penne.

Fettuccine with Mushroom Sauce

The combination of dried porcini and fresh shiitake mushrooms gives this sauce a rich, earthy flavor.

Prep: 20 minutes plus standing Cook: 25 minutes

- ½ cup boiling water
- 1 package (.35 ounce) dried porcini mushrooms
- 2 tablespoons olive oil
- 1 medium onion, chopped
- 2 garlic cloves, finely chopped
- 8 ounces shiitake mushrooms, stems removed and caps thinly sliced
- 12 ounces white mushrooms, trimmed and thinly sliced
- ½ teaspoon salt
- ¼ teaspoon freshly ground black pepper
- 1¼ cups chicken broth
- 1 pound fresh fettuccine
- 2 tablespoons butter, cut into pieces (optional)
- ¼ cup chopped fresh parsley

1. In small bowl, pour boiling water over porcini mushrooms; let stand about 15 minutes. With slotted spoon, remove porcini, reserving liquid. Rinse mushrooms to remove any grit, then chop. Strain mushroom liquid through sieve lined with paper towels; set aside.

2. In 12-inch skillet, heat 1 tablespoon oil over low heat. Add onion and garlic and cook, stirring frequently, until onion is tender. Add shiitake mushrooms; increase heat to medium and cook, stirring, 5 minutes. Add remaining 1 tablespoon oil, white and porcini mushrooms, salt, and pepper; cook until mushrooms are tender, about 7 minutes. Add reserved mushroom liquid and cook, stirring frequently, until liquid has evaporated, about 2 minutes. Add broth and heat to boiling; cook until broth has reduced by one-third.

3. Meanwhile, in large saucepot, cook pasta as label directs. Drain. In warm serving bowl, toss pasta with mushroom sauce, butter if using, and parsley. Makes 6 main-dish servings.

Each serving without butter: About 366 calories, 13g protein, 64g carbohydrate, 6g total fat (1g saturated), 0mg cholesterol, 475mg sodium.

Pasta Primavera

With its lively medley of vegetables this pasta dish is a perfect way to celebrate the arrival of spring and the first asparagus of the season.

Prep: 15 minutes Cook: 25 minutes

- ½ cup heavy or whipping cream
- 3 tablespoons butter or margarine
- 4 ounces shiitake mushrooms, stems removed and caps thinly sliced
- 2 very small yellow squash or zucchini (4 ounces each), cut into 2" by ¼" matchstick strips
- 4 green onions, thinly sliced
- 1 tablespoon chopped fresh parsley
- 1 package (16 ounces) fettuccine
- 1 pound asparagus, trimmed and cut on diagonal into 1½-inch pieces
- 4 ounces sugar snap peas, strings removed
- ¾ cup freshly grated Parmesan cheese
- ¼ teaspoon salt

1. In 1-quart saucepan, heat cream to boiling and boil 1 minute. Remove from heat and set aside.

2. In nonstick 10-inch skillet, melt butter over medium heat. Add mushrooms and cook, stirring, 1 minute. Add squash and cook, stirring, until vegetables are tender, about 3 minutes. Remove from heat; stir in green onions and parsley. Keep warm.

3. Meanwhile, in large saucepot, cook pasta as label directs. After pasta has cooked 7 minutes, add asparagus and sugar snap peas to pasta water. Cook until pasta and vegetables are tender, 3 to 5 minutes longer. Drain, reserving ½ cup pasta water.

4. In warm bowl, toss pasta and vegetables with reserved pasta water, Parmesan, and salt. Stir in cream and mushroom mixture. Makes 6 main-dish servings.

Each serving: About 491 calories, 18g protein, 64g carbohydrate, 18g total fat (11g saturated), 52mg cholesterol, 462mg sodium.

Spaghetti with Garlic and Oil

The classic combination of garlic and oil gives this simple pasta its heady flavor. Serve with lots of freshly grated Parmesan or Pecorino-Romano cheese.

Prep: 5 minutes   Cook: 25 minutes

- 1 package (16 ounces) spaghetti or linguine
- ¼ cup olive oil
- 1 large garlic clove, finely chopped
- ⅛ teaspoon crushed red pepper (optional)
- ¾ teaspoon salt
- ¼ teaspoon coarsely ground black pepper
- 2 tablespoons chopped fresh parsley

1. In large saucepot, cook pasta as label directs. Drain, reserving ½ cup cooking water.

2. Meanwhile, in 1-quart saucepan, heat oil over medium heat. Add garlic and cook just until golden, about 1 minute; add crushed red pepper if using, and cook 30 seconds longer. Remove saucepan from heat; stir in salt and black pepper. In warm serving bowl, toss pasta with sauce and parsley, using cooking water to moisten pasta as necessary. Makes 6 main-dish servings.

Each serving: About 362 calories, 10g protein, 57g carbohydrate, 10g total fat (1g saturated), 0mg cholesterol, 361mg sodium.

Garlicky Broccoli Pasta

Pasta with garlic and broccoli is a time-honored tradition and with good reason: It is absolutely delicious.

Prep: 15 minutes   Cook: 30 minutes

- 1 package (16 ounces) orecchiette or fusilli
- 1 bunch broccoli (about 1 pound)
- 2 tablespoons extra-virgin olive oil
- 3 garlic cloves, thinly sliced
- ¼ cup water
- ½ teaspoon salt
- ½ cup freshly grated Romano cheese

1. In large saucepot, cook pasta as label directs.

2. Meanwhile, trim broccoli. Coarsely chop stems and florets. You should have about 5 cups broccoli.

3. In nonstick 12-inch skillet, heat oil over medium heat until hot. Add garlic and cook, stirring, until golden, 2 to 3 minutes. Stir in broccoli, water, and salt. Cover and cook, stirring occasionally, until broccoli is tender, 8 to 10 minutes.

4. Drain pasta, reserving ½ cup pasta cooking water. Return pasta to saucepot. Add Romano, broccoli mixture, and reserved cooking water to pasta; toss until well combined. Makes 6 main-dish servings.

Each serving: About 370 calories, 14g protein, 61g carbohydrate, 8g total fat (2g saturated), 7mg cholesterol, 395mg sodium.

EASY ADD-INS FOR GARLIC AND OIL SAUCE

Test Kitchen Tip Spaghetti with Garlic and Oil (left) is just the starting point for many delicious possibilities.

- Add 4 to 6 coarsely chopped anchovy fillets in oil, drained (or 1 to 1½ teaspoons anchovy paste), and 2 tablespoons capers, drained, to cooked garlic-oil mixture; reduce heat and stir until anchovies break up, about 30 seconds.

- Add ½ cup Gaeta, Kalamata, or green Sicilian olives, pitted and chopped, to cooked garlic-oil mixture; reduce heat and stir until olives are heated through, about 1 minute.

- Add 2 to 3 ounces crumbled firm goat cheese to tossed pasta; toss again.

- Add ⅓ cup chopped dried tomatoes to pasta with garlic-oil mixture and parsley; toss.

- Substitute 2 to 4 tablespoons chopped fresh basil, oregano, chives, or tarragon for parsley.

- Add 1 bag (10 ounces) cleaned spinach, 1 can garbanzo beans, drained and rinsed, and ½ cup golden raisins.

Fettuccine Alfredo

Roman restaurateur Alfred di Lello created this luscious, creamy dish in the early 1900s, and its popularity has never waned. Be sure to use only freshly grated Parmesan cheese (preferably Italian Parmigiano-Reggiano) when making this indulgent pasta.

Prep: 10 minutes Cook: 25 minutes

- 1 package (16 ounces) fettuccine
- 1½ cups heavy or whipping cream
- 1 tablespoon butter or margarine
- ½ teaspoon salt
- ¼ teaspoon coarsely ground black pepper
- ¾ cup freshly grated Parmesan cheese
   chopped fresh parsley

1. In large saucepot, cook pasta as label directs. Drain.

2. Meanwhile, in 2-quart saucepan, heat cream, butter, salt, and pepper to boiling over medium-high heat. Boil until sauce has thickened slightly, 2 to 3 minutes. In warm serving bowl, toss pasta with sauce and Parmesan. Sprinkle with parsley. Makes 6 main-dish servings.

Each serving: About 558 calories, 16g protein, 59g carbohydrate, 29g total fat (17g saturated), 96mg cholesterol, 532mg sodium.

Farfalle with Gorgonzola Sauce

Farfalle, which means "butterflies" in Italian, are commonly called bow ties. Here, we've combined them with a creamy blue-cheese sauce and a sprinkling of toasted walnuts for fabulous flavor.

Prep: 10 minutes Cook: 25 minutes

- 1 package (16 ounces) bow ties or penne
- 1 cup half-and-half or light cream
- ¾ cup chicken broth
- 4 ounces Gorgonzola or blue cheese, crumbled
- ¼ teaspoon coarsely ground black pepper
- 1 cup frozen peas, thawed
- ½ cup chopped walnuts, toasted

1. In large saucepot, cook pasta as label directs. Drain.

2. Meanwhile, in 2-quart saucepan, heat half-and-half and broth just to boiling over medium-high heat. Reduce heat to medium; cook 5 minutes. Add Gorgonzola and pepper, stirring constantly until cheese has melted and sauce is smooth. Stir in peas. In warm serving bowl, toss pasta with sauce; sprinkle with walnuts. Makes 6 main-dish servings.

Each serving: About 486 calories, 18g protein, 63g carbohydrate, 18g total fat (8g saturated), 31mg cholesterol, 499mg sodium.

Pasta with Bacon and Peas

You probably already have most of the ingredients for this dish on hand. The sauce is quickly prepared while the pasta is cooking.

Prep: 10 minutes Cook: 20 minutes

- 1 package (16 ounces) thin spaghetti or vermicelli
- 1 package (10 ounces) frozen peas
- 4 slices bacon
- 1 medium onion, chopped
- 1 container (15 ounces) part-skim ricotta cheese
- ½ cup freshly grated Pecorino Romano cheese
- ½ teaspoon salt
- ¼ teaspoon coarsely ground black pepper

1. In large saucepot, cook pasta as label directs. After pasta has cooked 6 minutes, add frozen peas to pasta water. Cook until pasta is tender, about 2 minutes longer. Drain, reserving 1 cup pasta water. Return pasta and peas to saucepot.

2. Meanwhile, in 12-inch skillet, cook bacon over medium heat until browned. With tongs, transfer bacon to paper towels to drain. Discard all but 1 tablespoon bacon drippings from skillet. Add onion and cook until tender and golden, about 10 minutes.

3. Add reserved pasta water, onion, ricotta, Pecorino, salt, and pepper to pasta and peas in saucepot; toss to combine. Crumble in bacon; toss again. Makes 4 main-dish servings.

Each serving: About 738 calories, 37mg protein, 104mg carbohydrate, 19g fat (9g saturated), 51mg cholesterol, 845mg sodium.

Linguine with White Clam Sauce

Start with fresh clams and add a few ingredients to cook up one of the best of all pasta dishes. Don't overcook the clams or they will become tough.

Prep: 15 minutes   Cook: 30 minutes

- ½ cup dry white wine
- 2 dozen littleneck clams, scrubbed (page 186)
- 1 package (16 ounces) linguine or spaghetti
- ¼ cup olive oil
- 1 large garlic clove, finely chopped
- ¼ teaspoon crushed red pepper
- ¼ cup chopped fresh parsley

1. In nonreactive 5-quart Dutch oven, heat wine to boiling over high heat. Add clams; cover and cook until clams open, 5 to 10 minutes, transferring clams to bowl as they open. Discard any clams that have not opened.

2. Strain clam broth through sieve lined with paper towels; set aside. When cool enough to handle, remove clams from shells and coarsely chop. Discard shells.

3. Meanwhile, in large saucepot, cook pasta as label directs. Drain.

4. Add oil, garlic, and crushed red pepper to same clean Dutch oven. Cook over medium heat, stirring occasionally, just until garlic turns golden. Stir in parsley, clams, and clam broth; heat just to simmering. Add pasta to Dutch oven and toss until combined. Makes 6 main-dish servings.

Each serving: About 427 calories, 19g protein, 59g carbohydrate, 11g total fat (1g saturated), 24mg cholesterol, 111mg sodium.

Pasta with Tuna Puttanesca

This tomatoless, no-cook version of puttanesca sauce is simply mouthwatering. The unusual mix of greens, shallots, capers, and lemon hits the spot. For the most authentic Italian flavor, use tuna packed in olive oil.

Prep: 15 minutes   Cook: 25 minutes

- 1 package (16 ounces) rotini or medium shells
- 3 tablespoons capers, drained and chopped
- 3 tablespoons finely chopped shallots
- ½ teaspoon freshly grated lemon peel
- 2 tablespoons red wine vinegar
- 1 tablespoon olive oil
- ½ teaspoon salt
- ¼ teaspoon coarsely ground black pepper
- 1 can (6 ounces) light tuna in olive oil
- 2 bunches watercress (4 to 6 ounces each), tough stems removed
- ½ cup loosely packed fresh basil leaves, chopped

1. In large saucepot, cook pasta as label directs. Drain, reserving ½ cup pasta water.

2. Meanwhile, in large bowl, with fork, mix capers, shallots, lemon peel, vinegar, oil, salt, and pepper until well combined. Add undrained tuna and watercress; toss.

3. In pasta saucepot, toss pasta, basil, tuna mixture, and reserved pasta water. Makes 6 main-dish servings.

Each serving: About 374 calories, 18g protein, 59g carbohydrate, 7g total fat (1g saturated), 11mg cholesterol, 630mg sodium.

Pad Thai

Authentic Pad Thai is made with rice noodles (use the ⅛-inch-wide ones) that are available at Asian markets. If you can't find them, use angel hair pasta or linguine (cooked according to the package directions).

Prep: 25 minutes plus soaking noodles   Cook: 5 minutes

- 1 package (7 to 8 ounces) rice stick noodles (rice vermicelli) or 8 ounces angel hair pasta
- ¼ cup fresh lime juice
- ¼ cup Asian fish sauce (nam pla, page 26)
- 2 tablespoons sugar
- 1 tablespoon vegetable oil
- 8 ounces medium shrimp, shelled and deveined (page 193), then cut lengthwise in half
- 2 garlic cloves, finely chopped
- ¼ teaspoon crushed red pepper
- 3 large eggs, lightly beaten
- 6 ounces bean sprouts (2 cups), rinsed and drained
- ⅓ cup unsalted roasted peanuts, coarsely chopped
- 3 green onions, thinly sliced
- ½ cup loosely packed fresh cilantro leaves
  lime wedges

1. In large bowl, soak rice stick noodles, if using, in enough *hot water* to cover for 20 minutes. Drain. With kitchen shears, cut noodles into 4-inch lengths. If using angel hair pasta, break in half, cook in large saucepot as label directs, drain, and rinse with cold running water.

2. Meanwhile, in small bowl, combine lime juice, fish sauce, and sugar. Assemble all remaining ingredients and place next to stove.

3. In 12-inch skillet, heat oil over high heat until hot. Add shrimp, garlic, and crushed red pepper; cook, stirring, 1 minute. Add eggs and cook, stirring, until just set, about 20 seconds. Add drained noodles and cook, stirring, 2 minutes. Add fish-sauce mixture, half of bean sprouts, half of peanuts, and half of green onions; cook, stirring, 1 minute.

4. Transfer Pad Thai to warm platter or serving bowl. Top with remaining bean sprouts and sprinkle with remaining peanuts, remaining green onions, and cilantro. Serve with lime wedges. Makes 4 main-dish servings.

Each serving: About 495 calories, 25g protein, 65g carbohydrate, 17g total fat (3g saturated), 235mg cholesterol, 827mg sodium.

Pad Thai

ASIAN NOODLES

Test Kitchen Tip Noodles are a worldwide favorite. In Asia, the purported area of their origin, they are consumed for breakfast, lunch, and dinner, and they are simmered in broth, stir-fried with meat and/or vegetables, and deep-fried. They are categorized not by country but by the type of flour—bean, rice, or wheat—from which they are made. Asian noodles are not interchangeable because some require different amounts of presoaking or precooking, and others do not. For the best results, use what your recipe calls for. Asian noodles are available fresh, dried, and frozen at Asian markets, specialty stores, and some well-stocked supermarkets.

Seafood Fra Diavolo

Packed with shrimp, mussels, and rings of tender squid, this pasta is a seafood lover's dream.

Prep: 25 minutes Cook: 1 hour

- 8 ounces cleaned squid
- 1 tablespoon olive oil
- 1 large garlic clove, finely chopped
- ¼ teaspoon crushed red pepper
- 1 can (28 ounces) plum tomatoes
- ½ teaspoon salt
- 1 dozen mussels, scrubbed and debearded (page 187)
- 8 ounces medium shrimp, shelled and deveined (page 193)
- 1 package (16 ounces) linguine or spaghetti
- ¼ cup chopped fresh parsley

1. Rinse squid and pat dry with paper towels. Slice squid bodies crosswise into ¼-inch rings. Cut tentacles into several pieces if they are large.

2. In nonreactive 4-quart saucepan, heat oil over medium heat. Add garlic and crushed red pepper; cook just until fragrant, about 30 seconds. Stir in tomatoes with their juice and salt, breaking up tomatoes with side of spoon. Heat to boiling over high heat. Add squid and heat to boiling. Reduce heat; cover and simmer 30 minutes. Remove cover and simmer 15 minutes longer. Increase heat to high. Add mussels; cover and cook 3 minutes. Stir in shrimp; cover and cook until mussels open and shrimp are opaque throughout, about 2 minutes longer. Discard any mussels that have not opened.

3. Meanwhile, in large saucepot, cook pasta as label directs. Drain. In warm serving bowl, toss pasta with seafood mixture and parsley. Makes 6 main-dish servings.

Each serving: About 410 calories, 25g protein, 65g carbohydrate, 5g total fat (1g saturated), 140mg cholesterol, 588mg sodium.

Neapolitan Pasta Sauce

This is the kind of old-time pasta sauce that simmers for hours, filling the kitchen with enticing aromas. It makes a big batch, enough to coat about 5 pounds of pasta, so plan to freeze the leftovers. Serve this richly flavored sauce with a sturdy pasta such as rigatoni.

Prep: 15 minutes Cook: 4 hours 15 minutes

- 2 pounds boneless pork shoulder blade roast (fresh pork butt), trimmed
- 1 garlic clove, thinly sliced
- 1 tablespoon olive oil
- 1 pound sweet Italian-sausage links
- 8 ounces hot Italian-sausage links
- 2 large onions (12 ounces each), finely chopped
- 4 garlic cloves, finely chopped
- 4 cans (28 ounces each) plum tomatoes
- 1 can (28 ounces) tomato puree
- 1 tablespoon sugar
- ½ teaspoon salt

1. With small knife, make several slits in pork shoulder and insert garlic slices. In nonreactive 12-quart saucepot, heat oil over medium heat until very hot. Cook pork and sweet and hot sausages in batches until lightly browned, using slotted spoon to transfer meat to bowl as it is browned.

2. Add onions and chopped garlic to saucepot; cook until onion is tender, about 5 minutes. Add tomatoes with their juice, tomato puree, sugar, and salt; heat to boiling, breaking up tomatoes with side of spoon.

3. Return pork to saucepot. Reduce heat; partially cover and simmer 3 hours. Add sausage and cook until pork is very tender, about 45 minutes longer. Remove pork and cut into bite-size pieces; return to saucepot (keep sausages whole). Use 3 cups sauce to coat 1 pound pasta for 6 main-dish servings. Makes 16 cups.

Each ½ cup: About 139 calories, 9g protein, 5g carbohydrate, 9g total fat (3g saturated), 35mg cholesterol, 318mg sodium.

Spaghetti and Meatballs

These large meatballs are all cooked at the same time in one skillet. If you prefer smaller meatballs, you'll need to cook them in two skillets or in batches, or simply bake them in a jelly-roll pan at 450°F for 20 minutes. If you like, substitute Leaner Meatballs (page 148).

Prep: 20 minutes   Cook: 1 hour

Marinara Sauce (page 222)
1½ pounds ground meat for meat loaf
     (beef, pork, and/or veal) or ground beef chuck
1 cup fresh bread crumbs (about 2 slices bread)
1 large egg
¼ cup freshly grated Pecorino Romano or
     Parmesan cheese
¼ cup chopped fresh parsley
1 garlic clove, crushed with garlic press
1 teaspoon salt
¼ teaspoon ground black pepper
2 teaspoons olive oil
1 package (16 ounces) spaghetti

1. Prepare Marinara Sauce.

2. Meanwhile, prepare meatballs: In large bowl, combine ground meat, bread crumbs, egg, Pecorino, parsley, garlic, salt, and pepper just until blended but not overmixed. Shape into twelve 2-inch meatballs, handling meat as little as possible.

3. In nonstick 10-inch skillet, heat oil over medium heat until hot. Add meatballs and cook, gently turning, until browned and just cooked through, about 20 minutes. Add sauce to meatballs and heat to boiling, stirring to loosen browned bits from bottom of skillet. Reduce heat and simmer while you cook the pasta.

4. In large saucepot, cook pasta as label directs. Drain. In warm serving bowl, gently toss pasta with meatballs and sauce. Makes 6 main-dish servings.

Each serving: About 692 calories, 34g protein, 69g carbohydrate, 30g total fat (10g saturated), 129mg cholesterol, 1,077mg sodium.

Classic Bolognese Sauce

A staple in Bologna, Italy, this tomato-based meat sauce, enriched with cream and mellowed by long simmering, is well worth the time. Freeze leftovers in small batches.

Prep: 10 minutes   Cook: 1 hour 25 minutes

2 tablespoons olive oil
1 medium onion, chopped
1 carrot, peeled and finely chopped
1 stalk celery, finely chopped
1½ pounds ground meat for meat loaf
     (beef, pork, and/or veal) or ground beef chuck
½ cup dry red wine
1 can (28 ounces) plum tomatoes, chopped
2 teaspoons salt
¼ teaspoon ground black pepper
⅛ teaspoon ground nutmeg
¼ cup heavy or whipping cream

1. In nonreactive 5-quart Dutch oven, heat oil over medium heat. Add onion, carrot, and celery and cook, stirring occasionally, until tender, about 10 minutes.

2. Add ground meat and cook, breaking up meat with side of spoon, until no longer pink. Stir in wine and heat to boiling. Stir in tomatoes with their juice, salt, pepper, and nutmeg. Heat to boiling over high heat. Reduce heat and simmer, stirring occasionally, 1 hour.

3. Stir in cream and heat through, stirring constantly. Use 2½ cups sauce to coat 1 pound pasta for 6 main-dish servings. Makes 5 cups.

Each serving pasta with sauce: About 678 calories, 32g protein, 68g carbohydrate, 30g total fat (11g saturated), 104mg cholesterol, 1,210mg sodium.

Penne with Sausage

This simple dish proves that a pasta sauce doesn't have to cook forever to be flavorful.

Prep: 15 minutes   Cook: 30 minutes

- 8 ounces sweet Italian-sausage links, casings removed
- 2 garlic cloves, finely chopped
- 1 pound mushrooms, trimmed and sliced
- 1 can (28 ounces) plum tomatoes
- 1 teaspoon sugar
- ¾ teaspoon salt
- 1 package (16 ounces) penne or rotini

1. In nonstick 12-inch skillet, cook sausage and garlic over medium-high heat, breaking up sausage with side of spoon, until sausage is browned, about 5 minutes. Add mushrooms and cook over high heat, stirring, until all liquid has evaporated and mushrooms are browned. Stir in tomatoes with their juice, sugar, and salt, breaking up tomatoes with side of spoon; heat to boiling. Reduce heat and simmer until thickened, 5 to 8 minutes.

2. Meanwhile, in large saucepot, cook pasta as label directs. Drain. In warm serving bowl, toss pasta with sauce. Makes 4 main-dish servings.

Each serving: About 690 calories, 27g protein, 100g carbohydrate, 20g total fat (7g saturated), 43mg cholesterol, 1,283mg sodium.

A SIDE OF PASTA — FOUR WAYS

Cook 1 cup orzo or 1¾ cups mini bow-tie pasta as label directs. Then make one of these delicious side dishes.

Prep: 10 minutes   Cook: 25 minutes

Confetti Pasta

In 10-inch skillet, heat 2 teaspoons olive oil over medium heat. Add 2 carrots, shredded, 1 medium zucchini (8 ounces), shredded, 1 garlic clove, crushed with garlic press, ¾ teaspoon salt, and ¼ teaspoon coarsely ground black pepper and cook 5 minutes. Stir in cooked pasta; heat through. Makes 4 accompaniment servings.

Each serving: About 203 calories, 7g protein, 37g carbohydrate, 3g total fat (0g saturated), 0mg cholesterol, 490mg sodium.

Pasta with Peas and Onion

In 10-inch skillet, heat 2 teaspoons olive oil over medium heat. Add 1 small onion, chopped, and 2 tablespoons water and cook until onion is golden, about 10 minutes. Stir in cooked pasta and 1 cup frozen peas, thawed, and heat through. Makes 4 accompaniment servings.

Each serving: About 216 calories, 8g protein, 39g carbohydrate, 3g total fat (0g saturated), 0mg cholesterol, 81mg sodium.

Orange-Fennel Pasta

In 10-inch skillet, heat 2 teaspoons olive oil over medium heat. Add 1 garlic clove, crushed with garlic press, ¾ teaspoon salt, and ¼ teaspoon coarsely ground black pepper and cook 30 seconds. Stir in 1 teaspoon freshly grated orange peel and ½ teaspoon fennel seeds, crushed. Stir in cooked pasta and 2 tablespoons chopped fresh parsley; heat through. Makes 4 accompaniment servings.

Each serving: About 181 calories, 6g protein, 32g carbohydrate, 3g total fat (0g saturated), 0mg cholesterol, 477mg sodium.

Tubetti with Lemon and Cream

In 2-quart saucepan, combine ¼ cup plus 2 tablespoons heavy cream, ½ teaspoon lemon peel, ¼ teaspoon salt, and a pinch of pepper; heat to boiling over medium-high heat. Boil 1 minute. Stir in 1½ cups tubetti (7 ounces), cooked as label directs, and 1 tablespoon chopped fresh parsley and cook over medium heat, stirring constantly, 1 minute. Transfer to warm serving bowl and sprinkle with 1 tablespoon chopped fresh parsley. Makes 6 accompaniment servings.

Each serving: About 175 calories, 5g protein, 25g carbohydrate, 6g total fat (3g saturated), 20mg cholesterol, 132mg sodium.

Beef and Sausage Lasagna

Always let lasagna stand for a good 15 minutes after baking so the ingredients have time to settle—it makes for easier cutting.

Prep: 1 hour   Bake: 45 minutes

8 ounces hot Italian-sausage links, casings removed
8 ounces ground beef chuck
1 medium onion, chopped
1 can (28 ounces) plum tomatoes
2 tablespoons tomato paste
1¼ teaspoons salt
12 lasagna noodles (10 ounces)
1 container (15 ounces) part-skim ricotta cheese
1 large egg
¼ cup chopped fresh parsley
⅛ teaspoon coarsely ground black pepper
8 ounces part-skim mozzarella cheese, shredded (2 cups)

1. Prepare meat sauce: In nonreactive 4-quart saucepan, cook sausage, ground beef, and onion over high heat, breaking up sausage and meat with side of spoon, until meat is well browned. Discard fat. Add tomatoes with their juice, tomato paste, and 1 teaspoon salt; heat to boiling, breaking up tomatoes with side of spoon. Reduce heat; cover and simmer, stirring occasionally, 30 minutes.

2. Meanwhile, in large saucepot, cook lasagna noodles as label directs but do not add salt to water. Drain and rinse with cold running water. Return to saucepot with enough *cold water* to cover.

3. Preheat oven to 375°F. In medium bowl, stir ricotta, egg, parsley, remaining ¼ teaspoon salt, and pepper until well combined.

4. Drain noodles on clean kitchen towels. In 13" by 9" baking dish, arrange 6 lasagna noodles, overlapping to fit. Spread with all of ricotta mixture and sprinkle with half of mozzarella; top with half of meat sauce. Cover with remaining 6 noodles and spread with remaining meat sauce. Sprinkle with remaining mozzarella.

5. Cover lasagna with foil and bake 30 minutes. Remove foil and bake until sauce is bubbling and top has lightly browned, about 15 minutes longer. Let stand 15 minutes for easier serving. Makes 10 main-dish servings.

Each serving: About 363 calories, 23g protein, 31g carbohydrate, 16g total fat (7g saturated), 74mg cholesterol, 780mg sodium.

Beef and Sausage Lasagna

PASTA FOR LASAGNA

Test Kitchen Tip

When you're shopping for lasagna noodles, you are faced with several options. Domestic pasta is on the thick side, whereas imported pasta is thinner and more delicate. Choosing one over the other is just a matter of personal preference.

No-boil pasta eliminates the need for boiling the pasta before assembling the lasagna. It has been pre-cooked, then dried: During baking it soaks up liquid from the other ingredients and softens. Follow the instructions on the package for cooking no-boil noodles properly. If you use your own recipe, stir about 1 cup of additional water or tomato juice into your finished sauce so it contains more liquid. Or use your recipe without any changes, but reconstitute the sheets of pasta before using: Let them soak in enough warm water to cover until supple, 5 to 10 minutes, then drain the noodles and assemble the lasagna.

Curly Mac 'n' Cheese

Kids will absolutely love the curly corkscrew pasta in this ever-popular supper dish.

Prep: 30 minutes   Bake: 25 minutes

- 1 package (16 ounces) rotini
- 6 cups milk
- 3 tablespoons cornstarch
- ¾ teaspoon salt
- ⅛ teaspoon ground nutmeg
- ½ cup freshly grated Parmesan cheese
- 8 ounces sharp Cheddar cheese, shredded (2 cups)

1. Preheat oven to 375°F. In large saucepot, cook pasta as label directs. Drain.

2. Meanwhile, in 4-quart saucepan, with wire whisk, mix milk, cornstarch, salt, and nutmeg until smooth. Cook over medium heat, whisking frequently, until mixture has thickened slightly and boils. Boil, whisking constantly, 1 minute. Remove pan from heat. Gradually whisk in Parmesan until cheese has melted and sauce is smooth.

3. Spoon pasta into shallow 3½-quart or 13" by 9" baking dish. Pour sauce over pasta and stir to thoroughly mix. Sprinkle Cheddar over top. Bake until Cheddar has melted and mixture is hot and bubbling, about 25 minutes. Makes 8 main-dish servings.

Each serving: About 476 calories, 23g protein, 54g carbohydrate, 18g total fat (11g saturated), 60mg cholesterol, 650mg sodium.

DRESS UP YOUR MAC 'N' CHEESE

Here are some delicious cheese and macaroni variations your family is sure to enjoy. Prepare as directed, replacing the Cheddar with:

- 4 ounces fontina and 4 ounces gorgonzola
- 4 ounces goat cheese and 4 ounces Monterey Jack
- 3 ounces sharp Cheddar, 3 ounces Asiago, 3 ounces dry Jack cheese
- 4 ounces sharp white Cheddar, 4 ounces Asiago

Northern-Style Lasagna

This is the classic lasagna of northern Italy: lasagna noodles separated by layers of full-flavored meat sauce, rich béchamel sauce, and a blend of cheeses. Here dried porcini mushrooms give additional flavor to the meat sauce without much effort.

**Prep: 1 hour 15 minutes plus standing
Bake: 50 minutes**

Meat Sauce

- ½ cup boiling water
- ½ ounce dried porcini mushrooms (about ½ cup)
- 2 tablespoons extra-virgin olive oil
- 3 large garlic cloves, finely chopped
- 2 large carrots, peeled and finely chopped
- 1 large onion (12 ounces), chopped
- 8 ounces lean (90%) ground beef
- 8 ounces ground pork
- 8 ounces ground veal
- ½ cup dry red wine
- 1 can (28 ounces) diced tomatoes
- ½ teaspoon salt

Béchamel Sauce

- 4 tablespoons butter or margarine
- ⅓ cup all-purpose flour
- ½ teaspoon freshly ground black pepper
- ½ teaspoon salt
- ¼ teaspoon ground nutmeg
- 2½ cups milk

Cheese Filling

- 8 ounces Fontina cheese, shredded (2 cups)
- ½ cup freshly grated Parmesan cheese

- 1 package (8 to 9 ounces) no-boil lasagna noodles (6½" by 3½" each)

1. Prepare meat sauce: In small bowl, pour boiling water over porcini mushrooms; let stand 15 minutes.

2. Meanwhile, in 12-inch skillet, heat oil over medium heat until hot. Add garlic, carrots, and onion and cook, stirring occasionally, until vegetables are tender, about 15 minutes. Increase heat to high. Add beef,

Northern-Style Lasagna

pork, and veal and cook, breaking up meat with side of spoon, until meat is browned, about 10 minutes.

3. Meanwhile, with slotted spoon, remove porcini, reserving liquid. Rinse mushrooms to remove any grit, then coarsely chop. Strain mushroom liquid through sieve lined with paper towels; set aside.

4. Add wine to meat in skillet and heat to boiling; boil until most of liquid has evaporated, 2 to 3 minutes. Stir in tomatoes with their juice, salt, mushrooms, and reserved soaking liquid; heat to boiling. Reduce heat to medium-low; simmer, uncovered, until sauce thickens slightly, about 20 minutes, stirring occasionally.

5. Preheat oven to 375°F. Meanwhile, prepare béchamel sauce: In nonreactive 2-quart saucepan, melt butter over medium heat. With wire whisk, stir in flour, pepper, salt, and nutmeg and cook 1 minute. Whisking continuously, gradually add milk and heat to boiling. Remove saucepan from heat; set aside.

6. Prepare filling: In small bowl, toss Fontina and Parmesan until well combined.

7. Assemble lasagna: In bottom of 13" by 9" baking dish, evenly spread 1 cup meat sauce. Arrange 4 noodles over sauce, overlapping slightly to fit and making sure they do not touch sides of dish. (If your package of lasagna noodles has only 12 noodles, use 3 noodles per layer and do not overlap them.) Spoon about 1½ cups meat sauce over noodles. Spread about ⅔ cup béchamel sauce over meat sauce and sprinkle with about ½ cup cheese filling. Repeat layering 3 more times with remaining noodles, meat sauce, béchamel sauce, and cheese.

8. Cover lasagna with foil and bake 30 minutes. Remove foil and bake until heated through and cheese is lightly browned, about 20 minutes longer. Let stand 15 minutes for easier serving. Makes 10 main-dish servings.

Each serving: About 460 calories, 29g protein, 34g carbohydrate, 23g total fat (11g saturated), 98mg cholesterol, 933mg sodium.

Sausage-and-Pepper Baked Ziti

This new twist on baked ziti will please kids as well as adults. If you like, assemble it up to a day ahead, refrigerate, and bake just before serving.

Prep: 40 minutes plus standing
Bake: 20 minutes

- 1½ pounds sweet and/or hot Italian-sausage links, cut crosswise into 1-inch-thick pieces
- 4 garlic cloves, thinly sliced
- 2 large green, yellow, and/or red peppers, cut into ¼-inch-thick slices
- 1 jumbo onion (about 1 pound), cut in half, then cut crosswise into ¼-inch-thick slices
- 1 can (28 ounces) whole tomatoes in puree
- 1 can (15 ounces) tomato puree
- 1 teaspoon salt
- 1 pound ziti or penne pasta
- 1 package (8 ounces) part-skim mozzarella cheese, cut into ½-inch cubes
- ½ cup freshly grated Pecorino Romano cheese

1. Prepare sauce: In deep nonstick 12-inch skillet, cook sausage over medium-high heat, stirring occasionally, until browned on all sides, about 5 minutes.

2. Reduce heat to medium. Discard all but 2 tablespoons sausage drippings from skillet. Add garlic, peppers, and onion to sausage and cook, covered, until vegetables are tender, about 10 minutes, stirring occasionally. Stir in tomatoes with their puree, tomato puree, and salt; heat to boiling over medium heat, breaking up tomatoes with side of spoon. Reduce heat to low; cover and simmer 10 minutes.

3. Meanwhile, preheat oven to 400°F. In large saucepot, cook pasta 2 minutes less than directed on label. Drain pasta; return to saucepot. Add sauce and stir until pasta is evenly coated. Add mozzarella; toss to combine.

4. Transfer pasta mixture to 13" by 9" baking dish and spread evenly; sprinkle with Romano. Bake, uncovered, until hot and bubbling and top is brown, 20 to 25 minutes. Let stand 10 minutes for easier serving. Makes 10 main-dish servings.

Each serving: About 520 calories, 25g protein, 49g carbohydrate, 23g total fat (10g saturated), 65mg cholesterol, 1,190mg sodium.

Baked Rigatoni and Peas

This is a terrific dish for a big party. Place one dish on the buffet table, and keep the other warm in the oven. To make a day ahead, prepare through the making of the topping in Step 4. Cover and refrigerate the rigatoni and topping separately. To serve, sprinkle the topping over the rigatoni and bake, allowing for some extra baking time since the rigatoni will be cold.

Prep: 45 minutes   Bake: 30 minutes

- 14 tablespoons butter or margarine (1¾ sticks)
- ½ cup all-purpose flour
- 7 cups milk, warmed
- 2 cups freshly grated Parmesan cheese
- 2 teaspoons plus 1 tablespoon salt
- 2 packages (16 ounces each) rigatoni or ziti
- 1 bag (20 ounces) frozen peas, thawed
- 2 cans (14½ ounces each) diced tomatoes
- 1 cup loosely packed fresh basil leaves, thinly sliced
- ½ cup plain dried bread crumbs

1. Prepare cheese sauce: In heavy 4-quart saucepan, melt 10 tablespoons butter over low heat. Add flour and cook, stirring, 2 minutes. With wire whisk, gradually whisk in warm milk. Cook over medium heat, stirring constantly with wooden spoon, until sauce has thickened and boils. Reduce heat and simmer, stirring frequently, about 5 minutes. Stir in 1½ cups Parmesan and 2 teaspoons salt. Remove from heat.

2. Meanwhile, in 12-quart saucepot, cook pasta as label directs, adding remaining 1 tablespoon salt to water; drain. Return rigatoni to saucepot.

3. Preheat oven to 350°F. Pour cheese sauce over rigatoni in saucepot, stirring to combine. Stir in peas, tomatoes with their juice, and basil. Spoon pasta mixture into two shallow 3½- to 4-quart casseroles or two 13" by 9" baking dishes.

4. In small saucepan, melt remaining 4 tablespoons butter over low heat. Remove from heat and stir in bread crumbs and remaining ½ cup Parmesan. Sprinkle topping over pasta. Bake until hot and bubbling and topping is golden, 30 to 35 minutes. Makes 20 main-dish servings.

Each serving: About 390 calories, 15g protein, 48g carbohydrate, 15g total fat (9g saturated), 41mg cholesterol, 703mg sodium.

Spicy Szechuan Noodles

Once you cook up these flavorful noodles, you may never order them again from take-out.

Prep: 10 minutes   Cook: 25 minutes

- 1½ pounds ground pork
- 3 garlic cloves, crushed with garlic press
- 3 tablespoons dry sherry
- 3 tablespoons grated, peeled fresh ginger
- 3 tablespoons soy sauce
- ¾ teaspoon crushed red pepper
- 1 can (14 to 14½ ounces) chicken broth, or 1¾ cups Chicken Broth (page 62)
- ¼ cup peanut butter
- 1 tablespoon vegetable oil
- 2 bunches green onions, cut into 2-inch pieces
- 1 package (16 ounces) linguine or thin spaghetti
- 1 tablespoon Asian sesame oil or hot chili oil (optional)

1. In medium bowl, mix pork, garlic, sherry, ginger, soy sauce, and crushed red pepper until blended but not overmixed. In 4-cup measuring cup, with fork, stir broth and peanut butter until well blended.

2. In 12-inch skillet, heat oil over high heat. Add green onions and cook until wilted, 2 to 3 minutes. Transfer onions to another medium bowl. In same skillet, in batches, cook pork, breaking up meat with side of spoon, just until it is no longer pink, 1 to 2 minutes.

3. Return onions to pork mixture in skillet and stir in broth mixture; heat to boiling over high heat. Reduce heat to medium; cook, uncovered, until mixture thickens slightly, 12 to 14 minutes.

4. Meanwhile, in large saucepot, cook pasta as label directs. Drain pasta; return to saucepot. Add sesame oil, if using; toss to coat. Transfer linguine to large serving bowl; top with pork mixture. Makes 6 main-dish servings.

Each serving: About 560 calories, 38g protein, 63g carbohydrate, 16g total fat (4g saturated), 69mg cholesterol, 905mg sodium.

Szechuan Peanut Noodles

Loaded with taste and texture, this quick-and-easy dish is sure to please the peanut butter lovers in your family—adults as well as children. Turn this tasty noodle dish into a hearty main dish by tossing in cooked shrimp or shredded deli roast chicken.

Prep: 15 minutes   Cook: 10 minutes

- 1 package (16 ounces) linguine or spaghetti
- 4 ounces snow peas, strings removed
- 1 small cucumber (6 ounces), peeled, seeded, and cut into 2″ by ¼″ matchstick strips Asian Peanut Sauce (page 436)
- ¼ cup unsalted dry roasted peanuts, coarsely chopped
- 2 green onions, chopped

1. In large saucepot, cook linguine as label directs. Add snow peas during last 1 minute of cooking time. Drain linguini and snow peas and rinse with cold water until cool. Drain well.

2. Remove snow peas and cut into ¼-inch-wide matchstick strips.

3. In large bowl, combine peanut sauce and linguine. Add snow peas and cucumber; toss until linguine is coated with sauce. Sprinkle peanuts and green onions on top. Makes 5 main-dish or 8 accompaniment servings.

Each main-dish serving: About 618 calories, 22g protein, 81g carbohydrate, 24g total fat (4g saturated), 0mg cholesterol, 916mg sodium.

Ricotta Gnocchi with Browned Butter and Sage

They are also delicious with Marinara Sauce (page 222) and a sprinkling of Parmesan.

Prep: 1 hour   Cook: 17 minutes

- 3 **tablespoons butter**
- 1 **teaspoon chopped fresh sage**
- ¾ **teaspoon salt**
- ¼ **teaspoon ground black pepper**
- 1 **container (15 ounces) ricotta cheese**
- 6 **tablespoons freshly grated Parmesan cheese**
- ¾ **cup chopped fresh parsley**
- ¾ **cup all-purpose flour or as needed**

1. Prepare sage butter: In 2-quart saucepan, melt butter over medium heat. Continue to cook, stirring, until butter turns golden brown. (If butter gets too dark, it will be bitter). Remove from heat and stir in sage, ¼ teaspoon salt, and pepper; set aside.

2. In medium bowl, combine ricotta, Parmesan, parsley, and remaining ½ teaspoon salt. Sprinkle flour over ricotta mixture and, with your hands, work mixture into soft, smooth dough. If dough is sticky, add some flour. Work dough just until flour is incorporated into cheese mixture; do not overwork.

3. Break off piece of dough; on lightly floured surface, roll into ¾-inch-thick rope. (If rope doesn't hold together, return to bowl with remaining dough and work in more flour.) Cut dough rope into ¾-inch lengths. Place one piece of dough on inside curve of fork tines, gently pressing on dough with thumb as you roll dough along tines. Allow dough to drop off fork, slightly curling in on itself, forming an oval. One side of gnocchi will have ridges and opposite side will have an indentation. Repeat rolling, cutting, and shaping with remaining dough. (Gnocchi can be made up to 4 hours ahead to this point. Arrange in single layer in floured jelly-roll pan; cover and refrigerate.)

4. In 5-quart saucepot, heat *4 quarts water* to boiling over high heat. Add half of gnocchi and cook until gnocchi float to surface, 2 to 3 minutes. With slotted spoon, transfer gnocchi to warm shallow serving bowl. Repeat with remaining gnocchi. To serve, toss gnocchi with sage butter. Makes 8 first-course servings.

Each serving: About 196 calories, 9g protein, 11g carbohydrate, 13g total fat (8g saturated), 42mg cholesterol, 394mg sodium.

Ricotta Gnocchi with Browned Butter and Sage

Gnocchi

Usually served as a first course, these Italian potato dumplings are perfect with Marinara Sauce (page 222) or Neapolitan Sauce, (page 232). Or drizzle with butter, top with Parmesan cheese, and broil just until the cheese has melted.

Prep: 1 hour   Cook: 30 minutes

- 5 all-purpose potatoes (1½ pounds)
- 1 teaspoon salt
- 1½ cups all-purpose flour

1. In 4-quart saucepan, heat potatoes and enough *water* to cover to boiling over high heat. Reduce heat; cover and simmer until potatoes are tender, 20 to 25 minutes. Drain. Cool slightly; peel potatoes.

2. Press warm potatoes through food mill or ricer. With wooden spoon, stir in salt and flour until dough begins to come together. Gently press dough into a ball; divide in half.

3. On floured surface, with floured hands, knead each dough half until smooth. Divide each half into 6 equal pieces. On lightly floured surface, roll one piece of dough at a time into about ¾-inch-thick rope. Cut rope into ¾-inch lengths.

4. Place one piece of dough on inside curve of fork tines, gently pressing on dough with thumb as you roll dough along tines. Allow dough to drop off fork, slightly curling in on itself, forming an oval. One side of gnocchi will have ridges and opposite side will have an indentation. Repeat rolling, cutting, and shaping with remaining dough.

(Gnocchi can be made up to 4 hours ahead to this point. Arrange in single layer in floured jelly-roll pan; cover and refrigerate.)

5. In 5-quart saucepot, heat *4 quarts water* to boiling over high heat. Add one-third of gnocchi to boiling water. When gnocchi float to surface, cook 30 seconds. With slotted spoon, transfer gnocchi to warm shallow serving bowl. Repeat with remaining gnocchi. Makes 8 first-course servings.

Each serving without sauce: About 160 calories, 4g protein, 35g carbohydrate, 0g total fat, 0mg cholesterol, 295mg sodium.

Dried Fruit Kugel

This heavenly lowfat version of sweet noodle pudding is studded with dried plums. If you prefer an even sweeter dessert, use dates.

Prep: 20 minutes   Bake: 35 minutes

- 8 ounces wide egg noodles
- 1 container (8 ounces) lowfat (1%) cottage cheese
- 1 container (8 ounces) reduced-fat sour cream
- ¼ cup packed brown sugar
- 1 large egg
- ⅓ cup water
- 1 teaspoon vanilla extract
- 1 cup chopped dried plums (prunes) or dates

1. Preheat oven to 350°F. In medium saucepot, cook noodles as label directs. Drain.

2. In large bowl, with wire whisk, mix cottage cheese, sour cream, brown sugar, egg, water, and vanilla. Add prunes and noodles and toss well. Spoon mixture into 9-inch square baking dish. Bake until golden brown, about 35 minutes. Serve warm or at room temperature. Makes 6 dessert servings.

Each serving: About 347 calories, 14g protein, 56g carbohydrate, 8g total fat (3g saturated), 85mg cholesterol, 229mg sodium.

9

BEANS, RICE & OTHER GRAINS

BEANS

For many cultures, beans and grains are the major source of protein. Although this lowfat, high-fiber dynamic duo also provides a healthful amount of minerals and vitamins, the protein in beans or grains alone is incomplete. Luckily, the amino acids missing from beans can be found in grains, and vice versa, so when served together, they create a complete protein. Beans or grains can also be served along with small amounts of meat or dairy to complete the protein.

Dry beans encompass a variety of legumes, including split peas and lentils. Since tofu is made from soybeans (actually soy milk), it is included here as well.

Dry beans keep for about one year, but they become less flavorful and drier as time passes, and older beans take longer to cook. Buy them in small quantities and use within six months. Store in an airtight container in a cool, dry place.

Canned beans are a great time-saver because they don't require soaking or cooking. However, they do need to be rinsed under cold water and drained before being used. This quick rinse freshens their flavor and removes some of their sodium. One can of beans (15 to 19 ounces) yields about 2 cups beans once drained.

SOAKING DRY BEANS

Before soaking, always sort through beans to remove tiny stones or debris. Place the beans in a colander and rinse well with cold water. Transfer the beans to a bowl. (Dry beans rehydrate to at least double their size, so use

a large bowl.) Add enough cold water to cover by 2 inches. The standard overnight soaking time is really for the cook's convenience. The job is done when the beans have swelled to about double their size, which takes about four hours, but beans can be soaked for up to 24 hours. In hot weather, to prevent the beans from fermenting, refrigerate them while they soak.

When time is of the essence, use this quick-soak technique: Combine the beans and water in a pot and heat to boiling; cook for three minutes. Remove from the heat, cover tightly, and set aside for one hour. Drain and rinse the beans.

COOKING DRY BEANS

There are two reasons to soak dried beans before they're cooked. Soaking returns moisture to the beans and softens them. In so doing, it reduces the cooking time and also allows some of the hard-to-digest complex sugars to dissolve in the water.

There is an enormous range of cooking times for dry beans. Use the directions on the package as a guide, then taste often to check for doneness.

Dry beans should always be cooked in soft water or they will be tough. If you live in an area with hard water, be sure to add a pinch of baking soda to the cooking water. Because water boils at a lower temperature at high altitudes, beans will take longer to cook, so be sure they are well soaked and softened before cooking. Adding salt to beans at the beginning of cooking toughens the skins and increases the cooking time. But beans usually taste better when seasoned early, so we often use a minimal amount of salt when the cooking begins, then add the remainder at the end.

BEAN YIELDS

Although the volume changes with each bean variety, in general, 1 cup dried beans yields about 2 cups cooked beans. Large beans, like limas, yield about 2½ cups, whereas small beans, such as black beans, yield just under 2 cups. Cover leftover cooked beans with some of their cooking liquid in airtight containers; refrigerate for up to five days or freeze for up to six months.

BEANS AND BEAN PRODUCTS GLOSSARY

Black Also called turtle beans. They're the major component of black bean soup and burrito fillings; often mixed with rice for greater nutrition.

Black-eyed peas Beige beans with a black circular "eye," they are also called cowpeas.

Black-eyed peas, garbanzo beans, red beans

Fava Also known as broad beans, these flat light-brown beans resemble large limas.

Garbanzo Also called chickpeas, they're best known as the base for hummus.

Great Northern These white beans have a delicate flavor. They can be used in place of other white beans in most recipes.

Lima Also called butter beans, these large oval beans hold their shape well when cooked.

Miso Used in Japanese cooking, this is a salty paste made from fermented soybeans. Several varieties are available: the lighter the color, the milder the flavor.

Navy (pea) Small white beans, also called Yankee beans. They're most often used in baked bean dishes.

Pinto Spanish for "speckled," these pale pink beans have reddish brown streaks. They are used in refried beans, soups, and stews.

Red Small red beans that are the main ingredient in red beans and rice. They are also called chili or Mexican red beans.

Red kidney Good all-purpose beans that have a firm, burgundy-colored skin, sweet and pale flesh, and a slightly mealy texture.

Split peas (yellow or green) Dried peas that have been peeled and split in half.

Tofu Made from soy milk that has been coagulated and pressed into cubes. Tofu can be extra-firm, firm, or soft. Silken tofu, sold in aseptic boxes, has not been pressed. Available soft or firm, this tofu is more delicate than the pressed variety.

White kidney (cannellini) These beans are creamier and milder than the red variety.

Great Northern beans, white kidney beans, pink beans

KNOW YOUR LENTILS

Protein-packed lentils don't need to be presoaked, and they cook faster than other dried beans.

Black beluga lentils These tiny lentils are named for their caviarlike appearance.

Brown lentils This common variety of lentils has a firm texture and a mild, nutty flavor.

Green lentils Popular in European cooking, they have a firm texture and a nutty, earthy taste.

Red lentils A smaller round variety, they become yellow and soft when cooked; often used in Indian dals.

Small green French lentils (Puy) These tiny plump lentils are considered to have superior flavor. They cook quickly, hold their shape well, and nutty taste.

Hoppin' John

This moist and delicious rice-and-black-eyed-pea mixture is served in the South on New Year's Day for luck: The peas represent coins, ensuring a prosperous year.

Prep: 15 minutes   Cook: 1 hour

- 1 tablespoon vegetable oil
- 2 stalks celery, chopped
- 1 large onion (12 ounces), chopped
- 1 red pepper, chopped
- 2 garlic cloves, finely chopped
- 1 package (16 ounces) dry black-eyed peas, rinsed and picked through
- 1 large smoked ham hock (12 ounces)
- 4 cups water
- 2 cans (14½ ounces each) chicken broth or 3½ cups Chicken Broth (page 62)
- 2 teaspoons salt
- ¼ teaspoon crushed red pepper
- 1 bay leaf
- 2 cups regular long-grain rice

1. In 4-quart saucepan, heat oil over medium heat; add celery, onion, and chopped red pepper. Cook, stirring frequently, until onion is golden, about 10 minutes. Add garlic; cook 2 minutes longer.

2. Add black-eyed peas, ham hock, water, broth, 1 teaspoon salt, crushed red pepper, and bay leaf to celery mixture; heat to boiling over high heat. Reduce heat; cover and simmer, stirring occasionally, until black-eyed peas are tender, about 40 minutes. Discard bay leaf.

3. Prepare rice as label directs, adding remaining 1 teaspoon salt. (Do not add butter or margarine.)

4. In large bowl, combine pea mixture and rice. Makes 14 cups or 18 accompaniment servings.

Each serving: About 188 calories, 9g protein, 33g carbohydrate, 2g total fat (0g saturated), 3mg cholesterol, 549mg sodium.

Old-Fashioned Baked Beans

An heirloom recipe for not-too-sweet baked beans. This makes a batch big enough for a Fourth-of-July barbecue or a winter potluck party.

Prep: 15 minutes plus soaking beans
Bake: 3 hours 30 minutes

- 2 packages (16 ounces each) dry navy (pea) beans, soaked and drained (page 243)
- 7½ cups water
- 4 slices bacon, cut into 1-inch pieces, or 4 ounces salt pork, finely chopped
- 2 medium onions, chopped
- ½ cup dark molasses
- ⅓ cup packed brown sugar, preferably dark
- 5 teaspoons salt
- 4 teaspoons dry mustard

Preheat oven to 350°F. In 8-quart Dutch oven, combine beans and water; heat to boiling over high heat. Cover and place in oven. Bake 1 hour. Stir in bacon, onions, molasses, brown sugar, salt, and dry mustard. Cover and bake, stirring occasionally, 1 hour. Remove cover and bake until sauce is thickened and coats beans, 1 hour 30 minutes to 2 hours longer. Makes about 11 cups or 14 accompaniment servings.

Each serving: About 312 calories, 15g protein, 54g carbohydrate, 5g total fat (2g saturated), 4mg cholesterol, 895mg sodium.

HAM HOCKS

Ham hocks, a traditional ingredient in Southern cooking, are used to flavor greens and other vegetables. Their delicious smoky flavor makes them a "must" for split pea soup, especially when a ham bone is not available.

The hock, which is the ankle part of a smoked ham, doesn't contain enough meat to be eaten on its own. Smoked ham hocks are found in supermarkets in the refrigerated meat case alongside other pork products, and are usually sold in packages of two or three. Wrap unused hocks in heavy-duty foil and freeze for up to six months.

Tuscan White Beans with Sage

Leave it to the Italians to give us flawlessly flavored beans. These are perfect with Pork Roast with Fennel and Garlic (page 109).

Prep: 15 minutes plus soaking beans
Bake: 45 minutes

- 1 package (16 ounces) white kidney beans (cannellini), soaked and drained (page 243)
- 3 slices bacon
- 2 small onions, very thinly sliced
- 4 garlic cloves, crushed with side of chef's knife
- 2 sprigs plus 2 teaspoons thinly sliced fresh sage leaves
- 1 bay leaf
- 3 tablespoons olive oil
- 2 teaspoons salt
- 1/2 teaspoon ground black pepper

1. Preheat oven to 325°F. In 5-quart Dutch oven, combine beans, bacon, onions, garlic, sage sprigs, bay leaf, oil, and enough *water* to cover by 2 inches; heat to boiling over high heat. Cover and place in oven. Bake until beans are tender but still retain their shape, 45 to 60 minutes.

2. Drain beans, reserving cooking liquid. Discard bacon, sage sprigs, and bay leaf. Return beans to pot and stir in sliced sage, salt, pepper, and 1/2 to 1 cup bean cooking liquid until desired consistency. Spoon into serving bowl and serve hot, warm, or at room temperature. Makes about 6 cups or 8 accompaniment servings.

Each serving: About 263 calories, 14g protein, 37g carbohydrate, 7g total fat (1g saturated), 2mg cholesterol, 617mg sodium.

Indian-Style Lentils

Fresh ginger and cumin give lentils an Indian-flavor twist, while diced sweet potatoes add flavor and color.

Prep: 20 minutes   Cook: 45 minutes

- 1 tablespoon vegetable oil
- 1 medium onion, chopped
- 1 tablespoon minced, peeled fresh ginger
- 1 large garlic clove, finely chopped
- 1 1/2 teaspoons cumin seeds
- 1/8 teaspoon ground red pepper (cayenne)
- 1 pound sweet potatoes, peeled and cut into 3/4-inch pieces (3 cups)
- 1 cup brown lentils, rinsed and picked through
- 1 can (14 1/2 ounces) chicken or vegetable broth or 1 3/4 cups Chicken Broth (page 62) or Vegetable Broth (page 61)
- 1 cup water
- 1/4 teaspoon salt
- 1 container (8 ounces) plain lowfat yogurt
- 1/4 cup chopped fresh mint or cilantro

1. In 3-quart saucepan, heat oil over medium heat. Add onion and cook, stirring, until tender, about 5 minutes. Stir in ginger, garlic, cumin seeds, and ground red pepper; cook 30 seconds. Stir in sweet potatoes, lentils, broth, water, and salt; heat to boiling over high heat. Reduce heat; cover and simmer, stirring occasionally, until lentils are just tender, about 30 minutes. Transfer to serving bowl.

2. In small bowl, combine yogurt and mint. Serve with lentils. Makes 6 accompaniment servings.

Each serving: About 234 calories, 13g protein, 38g carbohydrate, 4g total fat (1g saturated), 2mg cholesterol, 421mg sodium.

SLICING FRESH HERBS WITH EASE

Here's the easiest way to slice fresh herbs such as sage and basil. Stack the leaves, then tightly roll them up lengthwise, cigar style. Place on a cutting board and cut crosswise with a large sharp knife into thin or thick slices. This is sometimes referred to as *chiffonade*.

Quick "Baked" Beans

With convenience ingredients and a few pantry staples, you can have authentic-tasting baked beans on the table in only 25 minutes.

Prep: 10 minutes   Cook: 15 minutes

- 2 teaspoons olive oil
- 1 small onion, chopped
- 1 cup ketchup
- ½ cup water
- 3 tablespoons light (mild) molasses
- 1 tablespoon Dijon mustard
- ½ teaspoon Worcestershire sauce
- ¼ teaspoon salt
  pinch ground cloves
- 1 can (15 to 19 ounces) black beans, rinsed and drained
- 1 can (15 to 19 ounces) red kidney beans, rinsed and drained
- 1 can (15 to 19 ounces) pink beans, rinsed and drained
- 1 can (15 to 19 ounces) white beans, such as Great Northern, rinsed and drained

1. In 4-quart saucepan, heat oil over medium-low heat. Add onion and cook until tender and golden, 5 to 8 minutes.

2. Stir in ketchup, water, molasses, mustard, Worcestershire, salt, and cloves until blended. Add black, red kidney, pink, and white beans; heat to boiling over high heat. Reduce heat; cover and simmer 5 minutes. Makes about 6 cups or 8 accompaniment servings.

Each serving: About 233 calories, 12g protein, 43g carbohydrate, 2g total fat (0g saturated), 0mg cholesterol, 709mg sodium.

Refried Beans

As a Mexican-style side dish, refried beans are hard to beat. Lard is the traditional cooking medium, but we prefer the smoky flavor of bacon.

Prep: 10 minutes   Cook: 22 minutes

- 3 slices bacon, coarsely chopped
- 2 tablespoons water
- 1 medium onion, chopped
- 3 garlic cloves, finely chopped
- 2 cans (15 to 19 ounces each) pinto beans, rinsed and drained
- ¾ cup chicken broth

1. In 12-inch skillet, cook bacon with water over medium heat until browned. With slotted spoon, transfer bacon to paper towels to drain.

2. Add onion and garlic to drippings in skillet; cook, stirring frequently, until onion is tender, about 7 minutes. Add beans and ¼ cup broth. With potato masher or wooden spoon, mash beans. Continue cooking beans until liquid has been absorbed, about 3 minutes. Add ¼ cup broth and stir until beans are piping hot and almost all liquid has been absorbed, about 3 minutes. Add remaining ¼ cup broth and heat to boiling. Spoon onto platter and sprinkle with bacon. Makes 4 cups or 4 accompaniment servings.

Each serving: About 241 calories, 11g protein, 25g carbohydrate, 11g total fat (4g saturated), 11mg cholesterol, 661mg sodium.

BAKED BEAN ADD-INS

Here are some easy ways to vary the flavor of baked beans:

- Stir in a few slices of crisp-cooked bacon.
- Add some diced ham or smoked boneless pork chop.
- Add a few drops of hickory liquid smoke.
- Substitute a favorite barbecue sauce for the ketchup.
- Use yellow mustard instead of Dijon.
- Add about 1 tablespoon minced chipotles in adobo.
- Stir in a little chili powder.
- Add some maple syrup or honey.
- Transfer the simmered beans to a shallow baking dish; top with buttered crumbs, and run under the broiler.

RICE

The USDA divides rice into three categories: long-, medium-, and short-grain. In general, shorter grains contain the most starch. Most Americans are familiar with long-grain white rice, which has had the hull and bran removed. Brown rice retains its bran layer, as do other whole-grain rice varieties that are covered with a black or red bran layer.

Store rice in a cool, dry, insect-free area in its own package. White rice will keep for up to two years; brown rice for up to one year.

COOKING RICE

There's no need to rinse most domestic rice before cooking, as the rice was cleaned before being milled. You should, however, rinse wild rice and imported varieties such as basmati or jasmine, which may be dirty or dusty. Brown rice and sticky (glutinous) rice will cook more quickly if presoaked overnight, but do not soak any other kinds of rice.

There are two methods for cooking rice: immersion and absorption:

Immersion In this method, the rice is boiled like pasta in a large unmeasured amount of salted water until tender, then drained. Unfortunately, the nutrients are also drained away.

Absorption Here the rice is cooked in a measured quantity of liquid, all of which is absorbed, thus conserving the nutrients. The cooking time and amount of liquid depend on the variety of rice.

KNOW YOUR RICE

Long-Grain Rice

Aromatic Some rice varieties become fragrant when cooked. The best-known is basmati, a rice valued for its perfumed scent, delicate taste, and fluffy texture. When cooked, the slender grains swell lengthwise, resulting in thin dry grains perfect for pilafs. Similar fragrant rice varieties include *jasmine* and *popcorn.*

Instant Rice that has been partially or fully cooked, then dehydrated. It cooks quickly.

Parboiled (converted) Rice that has been steamed, pressure treated, and dehydrated; the grains remain firm and separate after cooking.

Regular Slender, polished, elongated white grains that cook into dry grains that separate easily.

Medium-Grain Rice

Arborio The traditional rice for Italian risotto; this plump, roundish medium-grain rice has a high starch content and yields a moist, creamy texture. *Vialone Nano* and *Carnaroli* rice varieties can also be used to make risotto.

Japanese (sushi) Starchy medium-grain rice that clings together after cooking, making it the perfect rice for sushi.

Paella (Valencia) The preferred rice in Spanish and Latino dishes, it cooks up creamy and slightly sticky.

Short-Grain Rice

Sticky Also called glutinous or sweet rice. An opaque white short-grain rice with a slightly sweet taste and a soft, sticky texture.

Brown and Black Rice

Brown The outer hull has been removed, but the nutritious, high-fiber bran layer remains. Brown rice can be long-, medium, or short-grain. Other varieties include *Wehani,* a new brown rice, and *red rice,* which has a red bran layer.

Black There are many varieties of this hulled rice with its black bran, including *Thai black sticky rice* and *Chinese black rice.*

Wild Rice

Wild rice Not truly a rice but the seed of a water grass. The hand-harvested variety of wild rice, *manohmin,* is gathered the traditional way: in canoes. The rice grains vary in both length and color and have a slightly smoky, earthy flavor and a chewy texture. Commercially cultivated wild rice is uniform in size and color, less expensive than the true wild variety, and available in supermarkets.

OTHER GRAINS

When we cook grains, we are actually using the fruits of grasses, which are called kernels. Whole kernels are also known as berries or groats, while finely cracked groats are called grits. The kernels can be coarsely ground into meal or finely ground into flour.

Each kernel has three components: the bran, the endosperm, and the germ. The bulk of the kernel is the endosperm. The bran is the fiber-rich outer coating of the kernel, and the germ is the seed. Some grains also have an inedible husk, which is always removed. A grain that has the bran, endosperm, and germ intact is called a whole grain. Grains often have their bran and germ removed. These processed grains are often enriched with vitamins to replace some that were lost.

To prevent their oils from turning rancid quickly, store uncooked grains in an airtight container at cool room temperature or in the refrigerator for up to one month, or freeze for up to three months.

COOKING GRAINS

Rinsing Before cooking, whole grains should be washed in cold water to remove any dust, chaff, or natural coatings that could impart a bitter taste. Place the grains in a sieve, then place in a bowl of cold water and swish the sieve back and forth. Lift out the sieve, pour off the water, and repeat until the water looks clear. Give the grains a final rinse, then drain.

Soaking Whole berries and brown rice cook more quickly if presoaked. At least eight or up to 24 hours before cooking, place the rinsed grain berries in a large bowl of cold water and let stand at room temperature. (In hot weather, let stand in the refrigerator.) Drain well before cooking.

Toasting Grains are sometimes toasted (lightly precooked) before using to enhance their aroma and flavor. Millet is toasted to bring out its flavor and texture, and kasha is coated with beaten egg and then toasted to keep the grains separated. In rice pilaf the rice is toasted in the saucepan to firm up the outside layer, making the cooked rice firmer, while in risottos the rice is toasted to seal in the starch. To toast whole grains, place them in a heavy skillet over medium heat. (Add 1 or 2 tablespoons of oil or butter to the pan first, if you wish.) Cook, stirring almost constantly, until the grains are fragrant but not colored, 3 to 5 minutes.

Cooking The rule of thumb when cooking grains is 2 cups of liquid to 1 cup of grain. If the cooking liquid is absorbed before the grain is tender, simply add more hot liquid. Or, if the grain is tender and some liquid remains, simply drain it off. Follow the instructions on the package for exact liquid measurements and estimated cooking times.

As with beans, the outer coating of some whole grains, like whole-wheat berries and amaranth, toughens and prohibits the proper absorption of liquid if salt is present. When in doubt, cook the grains in unsalted water and season when they are almost tender.

COOKING RICE	RICE VARIETY (1 CUP)	AMOUNT OF LIQUID	COOKING TIME	YIELD
In all cases, for 1 cup rice, combine the rice, cooking liquid (you can use water, but broth adds flavor), optional salt, and butter or margarine in a 2- to 3-quart saucepan. Heat to boiling. Reduce heat; cover and simmer until done. Do not uncover the saucepan to check on the	Regular long-grain	1¾ to 2 cups	18 to 20 minutes	3 cups
	Medium- or short-grain	1½ to 1¾ cups	18 to 20 minutes	3 cups
	Brown	2 to 2½ cups	45 to 50 minutes	3 to 4 cups
	Wild	2 to 2½ cups	45 to 60 minutes	2⅔ cups

rice's progress until the last 5 minutes of cooking. When the rice is tender, remove suacepan from heat and let stand, covered, for 5 minutes. This short waiting period ensures a better texture. Fluff the rice with a fork before serving.

GRAINS GLOSSARY

Barley Pearl barley has been polished (milled) to remove the outer hull. Quick-cooking pearl barley has been presteamed.

Buckwheat A grain with an earthy flavor. Kasha is roasted buckwheat kernels.

Bulgur Wheat kernels that have been steamed, dried, and crushed. Bulgur is available fine, medium, and coarse.

Cornmeal Dried corn kernels that have been ground to a fine, medium, or coarse texture. Stone-ground cornmeal has not been degerminated (had its germ removed).

Couscous Not a grain but actually tiny pellets of semolina pasta. Most couscous is precooked and needs only a soaking in hot liquid to soften.

Hominy Corn kernels first soaked in a lime or lye solution to remove the hulls and germ, then dried.

Quinoa (KEEN-wah) Quinoa is rich in protein and nutrients. The tiny quick-cooking seeds have a slightly earthy taste, resilient texture, and are translucent.

Rye Cooked rye berries are softer than wheat berries and have a slightly tangy flavor.

Triticale A laboratory-engineered hybrid that is a cross between wheat and rye.

Wheat Cooked wheat berries are often served in pilafs and salads. The most common type of wheat berry is red winter wheat.

Hot Fluffy Rice

For drier rice, use only 1¾ cups water; for extra-tender rice, use 2⅓ cups water and cook a bit longer.

Prep: 5 minutes   Cook: 25 minutes

- 2 cups water
- 1 cup regular long-grain rice
- 1 tablespoon butter or margarine (optional)
- 1 teaspoon salt

In 3-quart saucepan, heat water to boiling over high heat. Stir in rice, butter if using, and salt; heat to boiling. Reduce heat; cover and simmer, without stirring or lifting lid, until rice is tender and all liquid has been absorbed, 18 to 20 minutes. Remove from heat and let stand 5 minutes. Fluff rice with fork. Makes about 3 cups or 4 accompaniment servings.

Each serving: About 169 calories, 3g protein, 37g carbohydrate, 0g total fat (0g saturated), 0mg cholesterol, 585mg sodium.

Brown Rice

Prepare as directed for Hot Fluffy Rice but use **2½ cups water, 1 cup long-grain brown rice,** and **1 teaspoon salt.** Simmer 45 to 50 minutes. Or prepare as label directs. Makes 4 cups or 6 accompaniment servings.

Each serving: About 114 calories, 2g protein, 24g carbohydrate, 1g total fat (0g saturated), 0mg cholesterol, 391mg sodium.

Aromatic Rice

Follow these basic directions to cook up fluffy rice, then add the desired flavoring for one of the options opposite.

Prep: 5 minutes   Cook: 25 minutes

- 1 cup chicken broth
- ¾ cup water
- 1 cup regular long-grain rice
- ¼ teaspoon salt
  seasonings (right)

In 3-quart saucepan, heat broth and water to boiling over high heat. Stir in rice and salt; heat to boiling. Reduce heat; cover and simmer, without stirring or lifting lid, until rice is tender and all liquid has been absorbed, 18 to 20 minutes. Remove from heat and let stand 5 minutes. Fluff rice with fork and add seasoning. Makes about 3 cups or 4 accompaniment servings.

Each serving: About 176 calories, 4g protein, 37g carbohydrate, 1g total fat (0g saturated), 0mg cholesterol, 395mg sodium.

Lemon-Parsley Rice

Cook as directed. Stir in **2 tablespoons chopped fresh parsley** and **1 teaspoon freshly grated lemon peel.**

Asian Rice

Cook as directed but omit salt. Stir in **2 green onions,** chopped, **2 teaspoons soy sauce,** and **¼ teaspoon Asian sesame oil.**

Lemon-Parmesan Rice

Cook as directed. Stir in **¼ cup freshly grated Parmesan cheese, 1 teaspoon freshly grated lemon peel,** and **¼ teaspoon ground black pepper.**

Pepper Jack Rice

Cook as directed. Stir in **2 ounces Monterey Pepper-Jack cheese with jalapeño chiles,** shredded (½ cup), and **3 green onions,** thinly sliced.

Coconut Rice

Cook as directed. Stir in **½ cup unsweetened coconut milk** (not cream of coconut), **½ teaspoon freshly grated lime peel,** and **pinch ground red pepper (cayenne).**

Green Rice

Cook as directed but after the rice has cooked 15 minutes, stir in **1 package (10 ounces) frozen chopped spinach,** thawed; cover and cook 5 minutes longer. Stir in **2 ounces feta cheese,** finely crumbled (½ cup).

Baked Rice

Here's an alternative to rice cooked on the stove. Substitute chicken or beef broth for the water, if you wish, in which case, delete the salt.

Prep: 5 minutes   Bake: 30 minutes

- 2 cups boiling water
- 1 cup regular long-grain rice
- 1 tablespoon butter or margarine, cut into pieces
- ½ teaspoon salt

Preheat oven to 350°F. Grease shallow 1½-quart casserole or 8-inch square baking dish. In casserole, combine boiling water, rice, butter, and salt. Cover and bake until rice is tender and all liquid has been absorbed, 30 to 35 minutes. Fluff with fork. Makes about 3 cups or 4 accompaniment servings.

Each serving: About 194 calories, 3g protein, 37g carbohydrate, 3g total fat (2g saturated), 8mg cholesterol, 321mg sodium.

Persian Rice Pilaf

Sweet currants and a touch of spice create heavenly fragrant rice. Try this with grilled chicken or butterflied leg of lamb.

Prep: 10 minutes   Cook: 30 minutes

- 1 tablespoon butter or margarine
- 1 small onion, finely chopped
- 1 cup regular long-grain rice
- 1 can (14½ ounces) chicken or vegetable broth or 1¾ cups Chicken Broth (page 62) or Vegetable Broth (page 61)
- ¼ cup water
- ¼ cup dried currants
- ⅛ teaspoon ground black pepper
      pinch ground cinnamon
- ½ teaspoon freshly grated orange peel
- ¼ cup pine nuts (pignoli), toasted
- ¼ cup chopped fresh parsley

1. In 2-quart saucepan, melt butter over medium heat. Add onion and cook, stirring, until tender, about 4 minutes. Add rice; cook, stirring, 1 minute. Stir in broth, water, currants, pepper, and cinnamon; heat to boiling. Reduce heat; cover and simmer, without stirring or lifting lid, until rice is tender and all liquid has been absorbed, 18 to 20 minutes.

2. Remove rice from heat; let stand 5 minutes. Add orange peel, fluffing rice with fork until combined. Stir in pine nuts and parsley. Makes 4 cups or 4 accompaniment servings.

Each serving: About 291 calories, 7g protein, 48g carbohydrate, 9g total fat (3g saturated), 8mg cholesterol, 463mg sodium.

Paella

Every Spanish cook has his or her own version of paella, which may include a wide range of ingredients. The crucial ingredient in every paella is the rice. Opt for a medium-grain rice, such as Spanish Valencia, or a short-grain rice, such as Italian Arborio, for their distinctive texture and the way the grains cling together when cooked. (Long-grain rice, which cooks up fluffy, can be substituted in a pinch.)

Prep: 30 minutes   Cook: 1 hour

- 1 tablespoon olive oil
- 1½ pounds skinless, boneless chicken thighs, cut into 2-inch pieces
- 2 fully cooked chorizo sausages (3 ounces each)
- 1 medium onion, finely chopped
- 1 red pepper, finely chopped
- 2 garlic cloves, finely chopped
- ¼ teaspoon ground red pepper (cayenne)
- ½ cup canned tomatoes in puree
- ½ cup dry white wine
- 2 cups medium- or short-grain rice
- 4 ounces green beans, cut into 1-inch pieces
- 2½ cups water
- 1 can (14½ ounces) chicken broth or 1¾ cups Chicken Broth (page 62)
- 1½ teaspoons salt
- ¼ teaspoon loosely packed saffron threads, crumbled
- ⅛ teaspoon dried thyme
- ½ bay leaf
- 1 pound mussels, scrubbed and debearded (page 187)
- 12 ounces medium shrimp, shelled and deveined (page 193)
- ¼ cup chopped fresh parsley
  lemon wedges

1. In deep nonreactive 12-inch skillet, heat oil over medium-high heat until very hot. Add chicken and chorizo; cook until browned, about 10 minutes. With slotted spoon, transfer chicken and chorizo to bowl.

2. Reduce heat to medium. Add onion and chopped red pepper to skillet; cook, stirring frequently, until onion is tender, about 5 minutes. Stir in garlic and ground red pepper; cook, stirring, 30 seconds. Add tomatoes with their puree and wine; cook, breaking up tomatoes with side of spoon, until liquid has evaporated.

3. Stir rice, green beans, water, broth, salt, saffron, thyme, and bay leaf into skillet. Thinly slice chorizo; return chorizo and chicken to skillet. Heat to boiling over high heat. Reduce heat; cover and simmer 20 minutes.

4. Tuck mussels into paella; cover and cook 3 minutes. Tuck shrimp into paella; cover and cook just until mussels have opened and shrimp are opaque throughout, about 3 minutes longer. Remove from heat and let stand 5 minutes. Discard bay leaf and any mussels that have not opened. Sprinkle paella with parsley and serve with lemon wedges. Makes 8 main-dish servings.

Each serving: About 467 calories, 35g protein, 45g carbohydrate, 15g total fat (4g saturated), 146mg cholesterol, 1,110mg sodium.

A PAELLA PRIMER

Test Kitchen Tip

Paella is known worldwide as a Spanish rice dish that may contain chicken, rabbit, sausage, lobster, shrimp, mussels, or any combination thereof. Originally, however, the word *paella* referred only to the pan in which this dish was cooked, a *paellera*, from the Latin word for frying pan, *patella*. The dish became so popular in Spain that eventually the word came to mean the food itself.

There are likely as many variations of paella as there are cooks who prepare it, though some of the renditions depend upon the region in which the paella is cooked. Among Spanish cooks, however, the one constant in this dish is the rice that is used: Valencia, a short-grain rice that has been harvested in Spain for more than one thousand years.

A paella pan, an inexpensive shallow metal two-handled affair, which ranges in size from about 10 inches to well over several feet across, is the pan of choice, but a skillet will do in a pinch.

Cumin Rice with Black Beans

The time-honored combination of rice and beans is found throughout Latin America and the Caribbean. Serve as a side dish for a juicy grilled steak.

Prep: 10 minutes   Cook: 30 minutes

- 1 tablespoon vegetable oil
- 1 medium onion, finely chopped
- 1 garlic clove, finely chopped
- 2 teaspoons cumin seeds
- 1½ cups regular long-grain rice
- 1 can (14½ ounces) chicken or vegetable broth or 1¾ cups Chicken Broth (page 62) or Vegetable Broth (page 61)
- 1¼ cups water
- ¼ teaspoon salt
- 1 can (15 to 19 ounces) black beans, rinsed and drained
- 2 tablespoons chopped fresh cilantro lime wedges

1. In 3-quart saucepan, heat oil over medium heat. Add onion and cook, stirring, until tender, about 5 minutes. Stir in garlic and cumin seeds; cook, stirring, until fragrant. Add rice and cook, stirring, 1 minute. Add broth, water, and salt; heat to boiling over high heat. Reduce heat; cover and simmer, without stirring or lifting lid, until rice is tender and most of liquid has been absorbed, about 15 minutes.

2. Stir beans into rice. Cover and cook 5 minutes longer. Remove from heat and let stand 5 minutes. Spoon into serving bowl and sprinkle with cilantro. Serve with lime wedges. Makes about 6 cups or 6 accompaniment servings.

Each serving: About 256 calories, 7g protein, 48g carbohydrate, 4g total fat (1g saturated), 0mg cholesterol, 515mg sodium.

Brown Rice and Vegetable Pilaf

Fragrant herbs and a variety of fresh vegetables complement the nutty flavor of brown rice in this tasty and nutritious vegetarian dish. Serve as a hearty accompaniment or main course.

Prep: 15 minutes   Cook: 1 hour 10 minutes

- 1 tablespoon olive or vegetable oil
- 1 medium onion, finely chopped
- 1 stalk celery, finely chopped
- 8 ounces mushrooms, trimmed and sliced
- 1 garlic clove, finely chopped
- 1 cup regular long-grain brown rice
- 2¼ cups water
- 2 carrots, peeled and chopped
- 1¼ teaspoons salt
- ⅛ teaspoon dried thyme
- ⅛ teaspoon ground black pepper pinch dried sage

In 10-inch skillet, heat oil over medium heat. Add onion and celery; cook, stirring frequently, until onion is tender, about 5 minutes. Stir in mushrooms; increase heat to medium-high and cook until mushrooms begin to brown and liquid has evaporated. Stir in garlic. Add rice; cook, stirring, 30 seconds. Stir in water, carrots, salt, thyme, pepper, and sage; heat to boiling. Reduce heat; cover and simmer until rice is tender and all liquid has been absorbed, about 45 minutes. Fluff with fork. Makes about 4½ cups or 6 accompaniment servings.

Each serving: About 167 calories, 4g protein, 31g carbohydrate, 3g total fat (0g saturated), 0mg cholesterol, 503mg sodium.

Jambalaya

A Cajun favorite, jambalaya is a rice dish that has countless variations. Though it can be made with almost any favorite meat, poultry, or shellfish, we are partial to the combination of sausage and shrimp.

Prep: 20 minutes plus cooling   Cook: 55 minutes

- 8 ounces hot Italian-sausage links, pricked with fork
- 1 medium onion, finely chopped
- 1 green pepper, chopped
- 1 stalk celery, chopped
- 1 garlic clove, finely chopped
- 1/8 teaspoon ground red pepper (cayenne)
- 1 1/2 cups regular long-grain rice
- 1 can (14 1/2 ounces) chicken broth or 1 3/4 cups Chicken Broth (page 62)
- 1 1/4 cups water
- 1/4 teaspoon salt
- 1/8 teaspoon dried thyme
- 1 can (14 to 16 ounces) tomatoes, drained and chopped
- 1 pound medium shrimp, shelled and deveined (page 193)
- 2 green onions, thinly sliced hot pepper sauce (optional)

1. In nonreactive 5-quart Dutch oven, cook sausages over medium heat until browned, about 10 minutes. With slotted spoon, transfer sausages to paper towels to drain. When cool enough to handle, cut sausages into 1/2-inch pieces.

2. To drippings in Dutch oven, add onion, green pepper, and celery; cook, stirring frequently, until tender, about 10 minutes. Stir in garlic and ground red pepper and cook, stirring, 30 seconds. Add rice and cook, stirring, 1 minute. Stir in sausages, broth, water, salt, and thyme; heat to boiling over high heat. Reduce heat; cover and simmer 15 minutes.

3. Stir in tomatoes; cover and cook 5 minutes. Stir in shrimp; cover and cook until shrimp are opaque throughout, about 5 minutes longer. Transfer to serving bowl and sprinkle with green onions. Serve with hot pepper sauce, if you like. Makes 6 main-dish servings.

Each serving: About 405 calories, 23g protein, 45g carbohydrate, 14g total fat (5g saturated), 122mg cholesterol, 873mg sodium.

Lemony Shrimp Risotto

(Pictured on page 242)

We tested this recipe in an 1,100-watt microwave oven. If your microwave has less or more power, you may have to make adjustments in cooking times in order to reach the desired doneness.

Prep: 5 minutes   Cook: 25 minutes

- 2 lemons
- 2 cans (14 1/2 ounces each) chicken broth or 3 1/2 cups Chicken Broth (page 62)
- 1 cup water
- 1/2 cup dry white wine
- 2 teaspoons butter or margarine
- 2 teaspoons olive oil
- 1 medium shallot, minced (2 tablespoons)
- 2 cups Arborio rice (Italian short-grain rice) or medium-grain rice
- 1 pound medium shrimp, shelled and deveined (page 193), leaving tail part of shell on, if you like
- 1 cup frozen peas
- 3/4 teaspoon salt
- 1/4 teaspoon coarsely ground black pepper

1. From lemons, grate 2 teaspoons peel and squeeze 1/4 cup juice. In covered 2-quart saucepan, heat lemon juice, broth, water, and wine to boiling over high heat.

2. Meanwhile, in 3- to 3 1/2-quart microwave-safe casserole, combine butter, oil, and shallot. Cook, uncovered, in microwave oven on High until shallot softens, about 2 minutes. Add rice and stir to coat. Cook on High (100% power) 1 minute.

3. Stir hot broth mixture and lemon peel into rice mixture. Cover casserole with lid or vented plastic wrap and cook on Medium (50% power), stirring once, until most of liquid is absorbed, about 15 minutes.

4. Stir in shrimp, frozen peas, salt, and pepper. Cover and cook on Medium (50% power), stirring once, just until shrimp turn opaque throughout and rice is tender but still firm, 3 to 4 minutes longer. Makes 4 main-dish servings.

Each serving: About 620 calories, 31g protein, 99g carbohydrate, 8g total fat (1g saturated), 4g fiber, 140mg cholesterol, 1,515mg sodium.

Risotto Milanese

Saffron-infused Risotto Milanese is the traditional accompaniment to Osso Buco (page 101). It is also delicious as a first course or as a meatless main course when followed by a generous mixed salad.

Prep: 10 minutes Cook: 35 minutes

- 3½ cups water
- 1 can (14½ ounces) chicken broth or 1¾ cups Chicken Broth (page 62)
- 2 tablespoons butter or olive oil
- 1 small onion, finely chopped
- 2 cups Arborio rice (Italian short-grain rice) or medium-grain rice
- 1 teaspoon salt
- ½ cup dry white wine
- ¼ teaspoon loosely packed saffron threads
- ½ cup freshly grated Parmesan cheese

1. In 2-quart saucepan, heat water and broth to boiling over high heat. Reduce heat to low; cover.

2. Meanwhile, in 4-quart saucepan, melt butter over medium heat. Add onion and cook, stirring occasionally, until tender, about 5 minutes. Add rice and salt and cook, stirring frequently, until rice grains are opaque. Add wine; cook until wine has been absorbed.

3. Add about ½ cup hot broth to rice, stirring until liquid has been absorbed. Continue cooking, adding broth about ½ cup at a time and stirring until most of liquid has been absorbed. After cooking 10 minutes, crumble saffron into rice. Continue cooking, adding remaining broth ½ cup at a time and stirring, until all broth has been absorbed and rice is tender but still firm, about 15 minutes longer (risotto should have a creamy consistency). Remove pot from heat; stir in Parmesan cheese. Makes about 5½ cups.

Each serving: About 216 calories, 6g protein, 35g carbohydrate, 6g total fat (3g saturated), 13mg cholesterol, 649mg sodium.

GREAT RISOTTOS

Risotto Primavera

Follow Steps 1 through 3; (left) but omit saffron. After cooking 10 minutes, stir 2 cups vegetables (use a combination of shredded carrots, finely diced zucchini, sliced asparagus, and frozen peas) into rice. Follow remaining directions. Stir ½ teaspoon grated lemon peel in with Parmesan cheese. Makes about 6½ cups.

Mushroom Risotto

Prepare risotto (left) but omit saffron. In a small bowl, pour ½ cup boiling water over ½ ounce dried porcini mushrooms (about ½ cup). Let stand 15 minutes. With slotted spoon remove porcini and rinse to remove any grit. Chop porcini. Strain mushroom soaking liquid through sieve lined with paper towels set over a separate small bowl. In Step 1 reduce water to 3¼ cups, and add mushroom liquid. Melt 1 tablespoon butter in 4-quart saucepan and stir in 1 pound trimmed and sliced white mushrooms and ¼ teaspoon salt; cook until mushrooms are tender and liquid has evaporated, about 10 minutes. Stir in chopped porcini and transfer to a bowl. Follow Step 2, using 1 tablespoon butter. Follow Step 3 but after cooking 10 minutes, stir in mushroom mixture. Makes about 7 cups.

Shrimp Risotto

Prepare risotto (left) but omit saffron and Parmesan cheese. Shell and devein 1 pound medium shrimp, reserving shells. In Step 1 increase water to 4 cups and add shrimp shells. Heat to boiling; reduce heat and simmer 15 minutes. Strain broth through sieve set over a bowl and measure. If necessary, add enough water to equal 5 cups. Return broth to same clean saucepan; heat to boiling. Reduce heat; cover and simmer. In 4-quart saucepan melt 1 tablespoon butter over medium-high heat. Add shrimp and ½ teaspoon salt; cook, stirring, until shrimp are just opaque but not fully cooked, 1½ to 2 minutes. Transfer shrimp to a bowl. Follow Step 2, using 1 tablespoon butter. Follow Step 3. Stir in 1 cup frozen baby peas and shrimp and cook until heated through, 1 to 2 minutes. Stir in ¼ cup chopped parsley. Makes about 8 cups.

Wild Rice Pilaf with Dried Cranberries

Sautéed vegetables and dried cranberries add flavor and color to this savory wild- and white-rice mixture.

Prep: 20 minutes   Cook: 45 to 60 minutes

- 1   cup wild rice
- 4   cups water
- ¾   cup dried cranberries
- 4   tablespoons butter or margarine
- 3   carrots, peeled and chopped
- 1   stalk celery, chopped
- ½   small fennel bulb (8 ounces), trimmed and chopped
- 1   medium onion, chopped
- 1½ teaspoons chopped fresh thyme or ¼ teaspoon dried thyme
- 2   cups regular long-grain rice
- 1   can (14½ ounces) chicken broth or 1¾ cups Chicken Broth (page 62)
- ¾   teaspoon salt
- ¼   teaspoon coarsely ground black pepper

1. Rinse wild rice; drain. In 3-quart saucepan, combine wild rice and 2 cups water; heat to boiling over high heat. Reduce heat; cover and simmer until wild rice is tender and some grains have popped, 45 to 60 minutes. Stir in dried cranberries; heat 1 minute. Drain, if necessary.

2. Meanwhile, in 5-quart Dutch oven, melt butter over medium-high heat. Add carrots, celery, fennel, and onion; cook, stirring occasionally, until vegetables are tender and lightly browned, about 20 minutes. Stir in thyme; cook 1 minute. Transfer vegetables to medium bowl.

3. In same 5-quart Dutch oven, combine white rice, broth, and remaining 2 cups water; heat to boiling over high heat. Reduce heat; cover and simmer, without stirring or lifting lid, until rice is tender and all liquid has been absorbed, 18 to 20 minutes. Stir in salt, pepper, wild-rice mixture, and vegetable mixture; heat through. Makes about 12 cups or 12 accompaniment servings.

Each serving: About 240 calories, 5g protein, 44g carbohydrate, 5g total fat (3g saturated), 10mg cholesterol, 354mg sodium.

Couscous

Couscous is not a grain but a tiny Moroccan pasta made from semolina flour. Here's a basic recipe and some mouthwatering variations.

Prep: 5 minutes   Cook: 5 minutes

- 1¼ cups water
- ¼   cup dark seedless raisins, dried currants, dried cranberries, or dried cherries (optional)
- 1   tablespoon butter or margarine
- ¾   teaspoon salt
- 1   cup couscous (Moroccan pasta)

In 3-quart saucepan, combine water, raisins if using, butter, and salt; heat to boiling over high heat. Stir in couscous. Remove from heat; cover and let stand 5 minutes. Fluff couscous with fork. Makes about 3 cups or 4 accompaniment servings.

Each serving: About 226 calories, 6g protein, 43g carbohydrate, 3g total fat (2g saturated), 8mg cholesterol, 471mg sodium.

Lime Couscous
Prepare couscous as directed but omit raisins and add **1 tablespoon fresh lime juice** and **½ teaspoon freshly grated lime peel** to water.

Moroccan Couscous
Prepare couscous as directed but add **¼ teaspoon ground cinnamon, ¼ teaspoon ground turmeric (optional),** and **¼ teaspoon ground cumin** to water.

Dried Tomato and Green Onion Couscous
Prepare couscous as directed but omit raisins and add **1 green onion,** sliced, and **5 dried tomato halves,** chopped, to water.

Creamy Polenta

Long a popular staple in northern Italy, polenta has acquired a devoted American following. Our method ensures lump-free results.

Prep: 5 minutes   Cook: 30 minutes

- 2 cups cold water
- 1 teaspoon salt
- 1½ cups yellow cornmeal
- 4½ cups boiling water
- ½ cup freshly grated Parmesan cheese
- 4 tablespoons butter or margarine, cut into pieces

1. In 5-quart Dutch oven, combine cold water and salt. With wire whisk, gradually beat in cornmeal until smooth. Whisk in boiling water. Heat to boiling over high heat. Reduce heat to medium-low and cook, stirring frequently with wooden spoon, until mixture is very thick, 20 to 25 minutes.

2. Stir Parmesan and butter into polenta until butter has melted. Serve immediately. Makes 8 accompaniment servings.

Each serving: About 173 calories, 5g protein, 20g carbohydrate, 8g total fat (5g saturated), 20mg cholesterol, 464mg sodium.

Microwave Polenta

In deep 4-quart microwave-safe bowl or casserole, combine **2 cups lowfat milk, 1½ cups cornmeal,** and **1 teaspoon salt** until blended. Stir in **4½ cups boiling water.** Cook in microwave oven on High about 12 to 15 minutes. After first 5 minutes of cooking, with wire whisk, stir vigorously until smooth (mixture will be lumpy at first). Stir two more times during cooking. When polenta is thick and creamy, stir in **4 tablespoons butter,** cut into pieces, and **½ cup freshly grated Parmesan cheese.**

Broiled Polenta Wedges

Line 13" by 9" baking pan with foil, extending foil over rim. Prepare Creamy Polenta as directed but use only 3½ cups boiling water and cook until mixture is very thick and indentation remains when a spoon is dragged through polenta, 30 to 35 minutes. Stir in Parmesan and butter as directed. Spoon mixture into prepared pan, smoothing top. Refrigerate until very firm, at least 1 hour. Preheat broiler. Lift foil with polenta from baking pan; place on cookie sheet. Cut polenta into 16 triangles; separate triangles. Brush **1 tablespoon melted butter or margarine** on polenta wedges. Broil 5 to 7 inches from heat source until lightly browned and heated through, about 10 minutes.

Rosemary Polenta Wedges

Prepare Broiled Polenta Wedges as directed (left) but add **½ teaspoon chopped fresh rosemary** or **¼ teaspoon dried rosemary,** crumbled, to melted butter.

Puffy Cheddar Grits

Serve this cheese-filled casserole for brunch along with bacon and sausages or as a side dish for dinner. If you wish, refrigerate the cooked grits overnight and bake them the next morning; just add 20 minutes to the baking time.

Prep: 20 minutes   Bake: 45 minutes

- 3½ cups milk
- 2 cups water
- 2 tablespoons butter or margarine
- 1 teaspoon salt
- 1¼ cups quick hominy grits
- 8 ounces Cheddar cheese, shredded (2 cups)
- 5 large eggs
- 1 teaspoon hot pepper sauce
- ¼ teaspoon ground black pepper

1. Preheat oven to 325°F. Grease shallow 2½-quart casserole. In 4-quart saucepan, combine 1½ cups milk, water, butter, and salt; heat to boiling over medium-high heat. With wire whisk, gradually whisk in grits, beating constantly to prevent lumps. Reduce heat; cover and cook, stirring occasionally with wooden spoon, 5 minutes (grits will be very stiff). Remove from heat; stir in Cheddar.

2. In medium bowl, with wire whisk, beat eggs, remaining 2 cups milk, hot pepper sauce, and black pepper until blended. Gradually stir egg mixture into grits.

3. Pour grits mixture into prepared casserole. Bake until knife inserted in center comes out clean, about 45 minutes. Makes 8 main-dish servings.

Each serving: About 338 calories, 16g protein, 24g carbohydrate, 20g total fat (11g saturated), 185mg cholesterol, 604mg sodium.

Spoonbread

Soft enough to eat with a spoon, this Southern classic is a cross between a bread and a soufflé.

Prep: 15 minutes plus standing   Bake: 40 minutes

- 3 cups milk
- ½ teaspoon salt
- ¼ teaspoon ground black pepper
- 1 cup cornmeal
- 4 tablespoons butter or margarine, cut into pieces
- 3 large eggs, separated

1. Preheat oven to 400°F. Generously grease shallow 1½-quart baking dish.

2. In 4-quart saucepan, combine milk, salt, and pepper; heat to boiling over medium-high heat. Remove from heat; with wire whisk, whisk in cornmeal. Add butter, whisking until melted. Let stand 5 minutes.

Spoonbread

3. Whisk egg yolks, one at a time, into cornmeal mixture until blended. In medium bowl with mixer at high speed, beat egg whites just until soft peaks form when beaters are lifted. Gently fold beaten egg whites, one-half at a time, into cornmeal mixture just until blended. Pour evenly into prepared baking dish. Bake until spoonbread is set, about 40 minutes. Serve immediately. Makes 8 accompaniment servings.

Each serving: About 203 calories, 7g protein, 18g carbohydrate, 11g total fat (6g saturated), 108mg cholesterol, 272mg sodium.

Mushroom-Barley Pilaf

Serve barley instead of rice for a flavorful change.

Prep: 15 minutes   Cook: 55 minutes

- 1 cup pearl barley
- 2 tablespoons butter or margarine
- 1 medium onion, chopped
- 2 stalks celery, cut into ¼-inch-thick slices
- 12 ounces mushrooms, trimmed and sliced
- 1 can (14½ ounces) chicken or vegetable broth or 1¾ cups Chicken Broth (page 62) or Vegetable Broth (page 61)
- ¾ cup water
- ½ teaspoon salt
- ⅛ teaspoon dried thyme
- ⅛ teaspoon ground black pepper
- ¼ cup chopped fresh parsley

1. In 3-quart saucepan, toast barley over medium heat, shaking pan occasionally, until barley begins to brown, about 4 minutes. Transfer to bowl.

2. In same saucepan, melt butter over medium heat. Add onion and celery; cook until onion is tender, about 5 minutes. Stir in mushrooms; cook until mushrooms are tender and liquid has evaporated. Stir in toasted barley, broth, water, salt, thyme, and pepper. Heat to boiling over high heat. Reduce heat; cover and simmer until barley is tender, about 30 minutes. Stir in parsley. Makes 4 cups or 6 accompaniment servings.

Each serving: About 187 calories, 6g protein, 32g carbohydrate, 5g total fat (3g saturated), 10mg cholesterol, 536mg sodium.

Basic Bulgur

Bulgur has a pleasant nutty flavor and takes only minutes to prepare.

Prep: 2 minutes   Cook: 20 minutes

1	can (14½ ounces) chicken broth or 1¾ cups Chicken Broth (page 62)
¼	cup water
¼	teaspoon dried thyme
	pinch ground nutmeg
1	cup medium-grind bulgur

In 2-quart saucepan, combine broth, water, thyme, and nutmeg; heat to boiling over high heat. Stir in bulgur. Reduce heat; cover and simmer until all liquid has been absorbed, 10 to 15 minutes. Fluff with fork. Makes 3 cups or 4 accompaniment servings.

Each serving: About 133 calories, 5g protein, 27g carbohydrate, 1g total fat (0g saturated), 0mg cholesterol, 434mg sodium.

Quinoa

Although unfamiliar to many, quinoa (KEEN-wah) has been a staple grain since the time of the Incas, who called it the "mother grain." It is considered a super grain because it contains more protein—including all eight essential amino acids—than any other grain.

Prep: 10 minutes   Cook: 25 minutes

1	cup quinoa
1¾	cups water
¾	teaspoon salt
3	medium ears corn, husks and silk removed
1	tablespoon butter or margarine
4	green onions, sliced
¼	teaspoon ground black pepper
½	teaspoon freshly grated lemon peel

1. In sieve, rinse quinoa with cold running water. In 2-quart saucepan, combine water, quinoa, and ½ teaspoon salt; heat to boiling over high heat. Reduce heat; cover and simmer until water has been absorbed, about 15 minutes.

2. Meanwhile, cut corn kernels from cobs. In 10-inch skillet, melt butter over medium-high heat. Add corn, green onions, remaining ¼ teaspoon salt, and pepper. Cook, stirring frequently, until corn is tender-crisp, about 3 minutes. Stir in lemon peel. Add quinoa and cook, stirring, until evenly combined. Makes about 5 cups or 6 accompaniment servings.

Each serving: About 188 calories, 6g protein, 34g carbohydrate, 4g total fat (1g saturated), 5mg cholesterol, 340mg sodium.

A TASTE OF THE MIDDLE EAST: BULGUR PILAF WITH APRICOTS

This bulgur-based side dish is especially delicious with grilled lamb or chicken.

In 3-quart saucepan, melt 2 tablespoons butter or margarine over medium heat. Add 1 medium onion, chopped, and cook, stirring, until tender, about 5 minutes. Add 1 cup medium-grind bulgur wheat and cook, stirring, 2 minutes.

Stir in 1 can (15 to 19 ounces) garbanzo beans, rinsed and drained, ⅓ cup dried chopped apricots, 1 can (14½ ounces) chicken broth, 1 cinnamon stick (3inches), ¼ teaspoon salt, and ⅛ teaspoon ground black pepper; heat to boiling over high heat. Reduce heat; cover and simmer 15 minutes.

Remove from heat and let stand 15 minutes. With fork, fluff pilaf. Discard cinnamon stick. Makes 3 cups or 6 accompaniment servings.

Wheat Berries with Brown Butter and Pecans

Wheat berries have an appealing chewy texture. Combining them with pecans and brown butter brings out the grain's nutty flavor.

Prep: 10 minutes plus overnight to soak
Cook: 1 hour 20 minutes

- 1 cup wheat berries (whole-grain wheat)
- 2 tablespoons butter or margarine
- 1 medium onion, chopped
- ½ cup pecans, coarsely chopped
- ½ teaspoon salt
- ⅛ teaspoon ground black pepper
- 1 tablespoon water
- 2 tablespoons chopped fresh parsley

1. In bowl, place wheat berries with enough *water* to cover by 2 inches. Soak overnight. Drain.

2. In 3-quart saucepan, combine wheat berries and *3 cups water*; heat to boiling over high heat. Reduce heat; cover and simmer until wheat berries are tender but still firm to the bite, about 1 hour. Drain.

3. In same clean saucepan, melt butter over medium heat. Add onion and cook, stirring frequently, until tender, about 5 minutes. Stir in pecans, salt, and pepper. Cook, stirring, until pecans are lightly toasted and butter begins to brown, about 3 minutes. Stir in wheat berries and water; heat through. Stir in parsley. Makes 3½ cups or 6 accompaniment servings.

Each serving: About 212 calories, 5g protein, 27g carbohydrate, 11g total fat (3g saturated), 10mg cholesterol, 233mg sodium.

Hazelnut-Honey Granola

Eat this granola as a snack, or serve as a breakfast cereal.

Prep: 20 minutes Bake: 30 minutes

- 3 cups old-fashioned oats, uncooked
- ¾ cup honey
- 4 tablespoons butter or margarine, melted
- 1½ teaspoons vanilla extract
- 1 cup hazelnuts (filberts) and/or whole natural almonds, coarsely chopped
- ½ cup toasted wheat germ
- ½ cup sesame seeds
- 1 cup dried tart cherries (4 ounces) or dark seedless raisins
- ½ cup dried apricots (3 ounces), thinly sliced
- ½ cup golden raisins

1. Preheat oven to 350°F. Divide oats between two jelly-roll pans; bake, stirring twice, until lightly toasted, about 15 minutes.

2. In large bowl, combine honey, melted butter, and vanilla. Add toasted oats, hazelnuts, wheat germ, and sesame seeds, stirring to coat. Spread mixture evenly in same jelly-roll pans.

3. Bake, stirring every 5 minutes, until mixture is dark golden brown, 15 to 20 minutes. Cool granola in pans on wire racks. Transfer granola to bowl and stir in cherries, apricots, and golden raisins. Store in airtight container. Makes 9 cups.

Each ¼ cup: About 118 calories, 2g protein, 18g carbohydrate, 5g total fat (1g saturated), 3mg cholesterol, 15mg sodium.

10

QUICK & EASY WEEKNIGHT MEALS

A balanced, delicious meal does not mean slaving away for hours, which is a good thing in today's busy world. You can have a meal on the table in 30 minutes or less, using some simple steps:

- Have all the tools and cookware that you need out and ready when starting the meal.
- The foods you use can affect how long dinner will take to cook. Choose ingredients that can be purchased partially prepared such as bagged precut vegetables. Take advantage of supermarket convenience foods. Store-bought glazes, rubs, and marinades can add a whole lot of flavor in very little time.
- When a recipe calls for moist heat, turn to your microwave. Salmon steaks, for example, cook more rapidly and are easier to handle than when they're poached on the stovetop. The higher the wattage, the faster food cooks; our recipes were tested in 1,000-watt ovens.
- Have a slow cooker? Before leaving the house for work or errands, load an electric slow cooker with the ingredients for stew or chili. For best results, choose a cooker that has a heating element in the sidewall for even heating, both high and low settings, and a liner or crock that can be removed for cleaning.

UTENSILS

The utensils you use can make all the difference. Here is our list of must-haves:
- heavy 12-inch nonstick skillet with a lid
- paring knife for trimming vegetables and fruits
- chef's knife for fast chopping and slicing
- serrated knife for cutting delicate foods
- kitchen scissors for snipping herbs
- heatproof silicone spatula
- Microplane® grater for grating citrus peel and ginger

GROCERY SHOPPING

When grocery shopping, go to the store with menu concepts for at least several meals. Check your pantry for needed staples before you head out, and stock up on foods that are running low. In the produce aisle, let freshness be your guide.

Good Housekeeping's *Favorite Fast Foods:*
fresh pasta • couscous • quick-cooking brown rice • marinated or precooked meats and poultry • presliced meats and poultries • spiced blends • salad dressing • packaged salad greens and vegetables • frozen vegetables • flavored cheeses

Faster Food: Favorite Shortcuts
- Take a few minutes to assemble all the ingredients; it saves time in the long run.
- If you're going to need noodles for your dinner, put the water on to boil as soon as you get home.
- Do two tasks at once, but make sure only one requires close attention.
- Use your microwave to precook ingredients that take a long time such as potatoes and squash.
- Cut meat into cubes to speed up cooking time.
- Thinly slice long-cooking vegetables like carrots and parsnips.

Turkey Cutlets with Chopped Salad

Steak Pizzaiola

Made with ingredients typically found at neighborhood pizzerias, this dish is perfect for a midweek supper. If you like, serve the steak on grilled Italian bread.

Prep: 15 minutes   Cook: 15 minutes

- 2 tablespoons olive oil
- 1 large onion (12 ounces), thinly sliced
- 2 garlic cloves, finely chopped
- 1 large red pepper, thinly sliced
- 1 large yellow pepper, thinly sliced
- 4 ounces mushrooms, trimmed and thickly sliced
- 1 can (15 ounces) crushed tomatoes
- ¾ teaspoon salt
- 8 beef minute steaks (2 ounces each)

1. In nonreactive 12-inch skillet, heat 1 tablespoon oil over medium heat. Add onion and garlic and cook, stirring frequently, until onion is tender-crisp, about 2 minutes.

2. Add red and yellow peppers and mushrooms and cook, stirring frequently, until peppers are tender-crisp, about 2 minutes longer.

3. Add tomatoes and ¼ teaspoon salt; cook just until sauce has slightly thickened, about 2 minutes longer. Transfer to medium bowl; keep warm.

4. Wipe skillet with paper towels, then heat remaining 1 tablespoon oil over medium-high heat until very hot. Sprinkle beef with remaining ½ teaspoon salt; cook steaks, in batches, until just cooked through, about 2 minutes per side, transferring steaks to warm platter as they are cooked. Spoon sauce over steaks. Makes 4 main-dish servings.

Each serving: About 355 calories, 26g protein, 14g carbohydrate, 22g total fat (7g saturated), 72mg cholesterol, 668mg sodium.

Steak Pizzaiola

Tuscan Steak and Beans

For the most flavor, be sure to purchase steaks with marbling (streaks of internal fat), which will ensure moistness and great taste.

Prep: 5 minutes   Cook: 20 minutes

- 1 teaspoon olive oil
- 2 boneless beef strip (shell) or rib-eye steaks, ¾ inch thick (about 10 ounces each)
- ½ teaspoon salt
- ½ teaspoon coarsely ground black pepper
- 1 medium onion, sliced
- ⅓ cup balsamic vinegar
- 2 teaspoons chopped fresh rosemary
- 2 tablespoons water
- 1 pint grape or cherry tomatoes
- 1 can (15 to 19 ounces) white kidney beans (cannellini), rinsed and drained
  fresh rosemary leaves for garnish

1. In 10-inch skillet, heat oil over medium-high heat until very hot. Sprinkle steaks with salt and pepper. Add steaks to skillet and cook, turning once, 8 to 10 minutes for medium-rare or until desired doneness. Transfer steaks to cutting board; keep warm.

2. Reduce heat to medium. Add onion to drippings in skillet and cook, stirring, until browned and tender, about 5 minutes. Add vinegar, chopped rosemary, and water, stirring until browned bits are loosened from bottom of skillet. Stir in tomatoes and beans; cook, stirring occasionally, until heated through, about 2 minutes.

3. Cut steaks into thin slices and serve with tomato-and-bean mixture. Garnish with rosemary leaves. Makes 4 main-dish servings.

Each serving: About 495 calories, 35g protein, 29g carbohydrate, 25g total fat (10g saturated), 76mg cholesterol, 540mg sodium.

2. In 12-inch skillet, heat 1 tablespoon oil over high heat until very hot. Add beef mixture and cook, stirring frequently (stir-frying), just until beef is no longer pink, about 1 minute. Transfer beef to clean bowl.

3. Add remaining 1 teaspoon oil to skillet. Add onion and stir-fry until tender-crisp, about 3 minutes. Stir in chiles, garlic, and ginger; cook, stir-frying, 30 seconds.

4. Return beef and any juices to skillet and add basil; heat through. Makes 4 main-dish servings.

Each serving: About 291 calories, 31g protein, 20g carbohydrate, 10g total fat (2g saturated), 65mg cholesterol, 779mg sodium.

Thai Beef with Basil

Simple and fresh-tasting, this easy but exotic stir-fry is seasoned with fish sauce, one of the basic ingredients of of Thai cooking.

Prep: 15 minutes plus marinating   Cook: 6 minutes

- 3 tablespoons Asian fish sauce (nam pla, page 26)
- 1 tablespoon soy sauce
- 1 tablespoon brown sugar
- 1 beef top round steak (1 pound)
- 1 tablespoon plus 1 teaspoon vegetable oil
- 1 jumbo sweet onion (1 pound), cut into ¼-inch-thick slices
- 3 long red chiles or serrano chiles, seeded and thinly sliced
- 3 garlic cloves, cut into long, thin slices
- 2 teaspoons minced, peeled fresh ginger
- 1 cup loosely packed basil leaves

1. In medium bowl, combine fish sauce, soy sauce, and brown sugar. Cut round steak lengthwise in half, then cut into ⅛-inch-thick slices across the grain. Add beef to fish-sauce mixture, tossing to coat well; cover and refrigerate beef 30 minutes to marinate.

Thai Beef with Basil

Chipotle Skirt Steak with Avocado Salsa

Serve this Southwestern winner at your next barbecue.

Prep: 10 minutes plus standing   Grill: 6 minutes

- 1 tablespoon chipotle chile powder
- ¾ teaspoon salt
- 1¼ pounds beef skirt steak
- 2 plum tomatoes, coarsely chopped
- 1 ripe medium avocado, pitted and peeled, cut into ½-inch pieces
- ½ cup salsa verde or mild salsa

1. Prepare outdoor grill for direct grilling over medium heat. In cup, with fork, stir chipotle chile powder and salt. Use to rub on steak.

2. Prepare salsa: In medium bowl, stir tomatoes, avocado, and salsa. (Makes 2 cups.)

3. Place steak on grill over medium heat. Cook steak, turning once, 6 to 8 minutes for medium-rare or until desired doneness. Transfer steak to cutting board and let stand 5 minutes to set juices for easier slicing. Cut against the grain into thin slices. Serve with avocado salsa. Makes 4 main-dish servings.

Each serving: About 420 calories, 29g protein, 9g carbohydrate, 30g total fat (10g saturated), 92mg cholesterol, 640mg sodium.

No-Bake Tamale Pie

No-Bake Tamale Pie

Making tamale pie is usually a time-consuming job, but our speedy filling is cooked in a skillet and the typical saucepan topping is replaced by sliced precooked polenta.

Prep: 10 minutes   Cook: 20 minutes

- 4 teaspoons vegetable oil
- 1 small onion, chopped
- 2 garlic cloves, crushed with garlic press
- 1 pound lean (90%) ground beef
- 2 teaspoons chili powder
- 1 teaspoon ground cumin
- ½ teaspoon salt
- 1 log (16 ounces) precooked polenta, cut crosswise into 8 slices
- 1 jar (16 ounces) medium-hot salsa (about 1¾ cups)
- 1 cup frozen whole-kernel corn
- ½ cup loosely packed fresh cilantro leaves, chopped

1. In nonstick 12-inch skillet, heat 2 teaspoons oil over medium-high heat. Add onion and cook, stirring frequently, until golden, about 3 minutes. Stir in garlic; cook 30 seconds.

2. Stir in ground beef and cook, breaking up meat with side of spoon, until meat is no longer pink, about 5 minutes. Stir in chili powder, cumin, and salt; cook 1 minute, stirring.

3. In nonstick 10-inch skillet, heat remaining 2 teaspoons oil over medium-high heat. Add polenta and cook until golden on both sides and heated through, about 10 minutes.

4. Meanwhile, stir salsa and frozen corn into meat mixture; simmer 3 to 5 minutes to blend flavors. Stir in cilantro.

5. Spoon meat mixture into 9-inch deep-dish pie plate or shallow 1½-quart casserole. Arrange polenta on top. Spoon 2 polenta slices and some chile onto each of 4 dinner plates. Makes 4 main-dish servings.

Each serving: About 425 calories, 32g protein, 38g carbohydrate, 17g total fat (5g saturated), 69mg cholesterol, 1,325mg sodium.

Picadillo

The unusual seasoning of this crowd-pleasing ground-beef stew, a Latino classic, calls for a simple accompaniment of steamed rice and a crisp green salad. To use the mixture as a filling for empanadas or turnovers, cook it until almost all of the liquid has evaporated.

Prep: 10 minutes   Cook: 25 minutes

- 4 teaspoons olive oil
- 1 medium onion, finely chopped
- 4 garlic cloves, finely chopped
- 2 pounds ground beef chuck
- 1 can (15 ounces) crushed tomatoes
- ½ cup pimiento-stuffed olives (salad olives), coarsely chopped
- ⅓ cup dark seedless raisins
- 3 tablespoons tomato paste
- 1 tablespoon red wine vinegar
- 1 teaspoon unsweetened cocoa
- 1 teaspoon ground cumin
- ½ teaspoon salt
- ¼ cup slivered almonds, toasted

1. In 12-inch skillet, heat oil over medium heat. Add onion and garlic and cook, stirring frequently, until onion is tender, about 5 minutes. Stir in ground beef and cook, breaking up meat with side of spoon, until meat is no longer pink, about 5 minutes.

2. Add tomatoes, olives, raisins, tomato paste, vinegar, cocoa, cumin, and salt; stir to combine and heat to boiling. Reduce heat and simmer until slightly thickened, about 5 minutes. Stir in almonds and serve. Makes 6 main-dish servings.

Each serving: About 397 calories, 34g protein, 17g carbohydrate, 23g total fat (7g saturated), 94mg cholesterol, 743mg sodium.

Stuffed Tomatoes

Be sure to use the ripest and most flavorful tomatoes you can find for this dish.

Prep: 10 minutes   Cook: 20 minutes

- 1 medium onion, finely chopped
- 1 pound lean (90%) ground beef
- 4 ripe jumbo tomatoes (about 14 ounces each)
- ½ cup uncooked instant white rice or ¾ cup cooked rice
- 1¼ teaspoons salt
- 1¼ teaspoons ground black pepper
- 1 cup loosely packed fresh mint leaves

1. In nonstick 12-inch skillet, cook onion and ground beef over medium-high heat, breaking up meat with spoon, until meat is browned, about 10 minutes.

2. Meanwhile, cut thin slice from stem end of each tomato; reserve. With spoon, scoop out seeds and pulp from each; reserve. Transfer tomato shells to microwave-safe plate and cook in microwave oven on High just until heated through, about 2 minutes.

3. Chop reserved tomato slices and pulp. Stir tomatoes, rice, salt, and pepper into meat mixture. Cover and cook over medium heat 10 minutes.

4. Meanwhile, chop mint. Stir into meat mixture.

5. Fill tomato shells with hot meat mixture. Makes 4 main-dish servings.

Each serving: About 365 calories, 29g protein, 33g carbohydrate, 15g total fat (5g saturated), 71mg cholesterol, 835mg sodium.

VARIATIONS ON A STUFFED TOMATO

Use our tasty beef-rice mixture to stuff other vegetables. Use one type or a combination, if you like. Substitute the chopped flesh from the vegetables for the tomato pulp.

Zucchini Halve, seed, and microwave, covered, just until tender, 3 to 5 minutes. Remove all but a ¼-inch wall of flesh.

Baby eggplant Halve lengthwise and steam or microwave just until tender. Remove all but a ¼-inch wall of flesh.

Meatball Stroganoff

As an accompaniment to this dish, toss 1 pound green beans, Brussels sprouts, or broccoli florets with 1 tablespoon olive oil and ¼ teaspoon salt. Spread in jelly-roll pan and roast at 450°F until tender, 15 to 20 minutes.

Prep: 10 minutes   Cook: 20 minutes

8	ounces wide egg noodles
1	pound lean (90%) ground beef
12	saltine crackers, crushed
1	small onion, finely chopped
1	large egg
¼	teaspoon salt
3	tablespoons water
1	tablespoon all-purpose flour
1	teaspoon paprika
1	can (14½ ounces) chicken broth or 1¾ cups Chicken Broth (page 62)
½	cup reduced-fat sour cream

1. In covered 4-quart saucepan, heat *3 quarts salted water* to boiling over high heat. Add noodles and cook as label directs.

2. Meanwhile, in medium bowl, combine beef, saltines, onion, egg, salt, and water just until well blended but not overmixed. Shape mixture into 16 meatballs, handling meat as little as possible.

3. Spray nonstick 12-inch skillet with vegetable cooking spray; heat over medium-high heat until hot. Add meatballs and cook, turning frequently, until meat is browned and no longer pink in center, about 12 minutes. Transfer meatballs to plate.

4. Stir flour and paprika into drippings in pan; cook, stirring, 30 seconds. Stir in broth and heat to boiling; boil until thickened, about 2 minutes. Reduce heat to low. Stir in sour cream. Return meatballs to pan; heat through.

5. Drain noodles. To serve, spoon meatball mixture over noodles. Makes 4 main-dish servings.

Each serving: About 560 calories, 36g protein, 52g carbohydrate, 22g total fat (9g saturated), 190mg cholesterol, 865mg sodium.

Meatball Stroganoff

Easy Stuffed Cabbage

This simple version of the classic dish steams up to look like open flower leaves. Serve it with a cucumber salad.

Prep: 15 minutes   Cook: 20 minutes

- 1 can (28 ounces) diced tomatoes
- 1¼ pounds lean (90%) ground beef
- 1 bag (8.8 ounces) heat-and-serve precooked rice pilaf (do not heat)
- 1 cup loosely packed fresh mint leaves, coarsely chopped
- ¾ teaspoon salt
- ½ teaspoon ground black pepper
- 1 small head green cabbage (about 2 pounds), cored

1. Transfer 1 cup canned tomatoes with some juice to medium bowl. Pour remaining tomatoes with juice into nonstick 12-inch skillet.

2. To tomatoes in bowl, add beef, rice, mint, salt, and pepper; stir until blended.

3. Remove 8 large cabbage leaves from head. Spoon ½ cup meat mixture into center of each leaf; arrange, open side up, in skillet over tomatoes. Cover skillet and cook mixture over medium-high heat until beef loses its pink color throughout, about 20 minutes.

4. To serve, place 2 meat-filled cabbage leaves on each of 4 dinner plates. Spoon tomato sauce over cabbage. Makes 4 main-dish servings.

Each serving: About 405 calories, 34g protein, 28g carbohydrate, 17g total fat (6g saturated), 88mg cholesterol, 1,550mg sodium.

STROGANOFF HISTORY

Test Kitchen Tip As one story goes, when a senior member of the affluent Stroganov family could no longer chew chunks of beef, his clever chef thinly shaved the meat, browned, it, then cooked it in sauce. Others believe the dish made its debut at one of the high-class open dinners given by Count Alexander Stroganov of Russia.

Veal Cutlets with Arugula and Tomato Salad

This dish is usually prepared with breaded cutlets fried in a large amount of oil. To lighten it up, we sautéed the veal with no coating in just a film of oil. Even without the richness of extra calories, however, this dish is delicious! Try it with turkey or chicken cutlets, too.

Prep: 20 minutes   Cook: 8 minutes

- 1 tablespoon minced shallot
- 1 tablespoon balsamic vinegar
- 1 tablespoon olive oil
- ¾ teaspoon salt
- ½ teaspoon ground black pepper
- 1 pound veal cutlets
- 1 bag (5 ounces) baby arugula or 2 small bunches (3 to 4 ounces each) arugula, tough stems trimmed and leaves coarsely chopped
- 1 cup grape tomatoes, each cut in half
- ½ ounce Parmesan-cheese shavings

1. In large bowl, whisk shallot, vinegar, 2 teaspoons oil, ¼ teaspoon salt, and ¼ teaspoon pepper until blended; set aside.

2. If veal cutlets are large, cut each crosswise in half. If necessary, with meat mallet or with rolling pin, between two sheets of plastic wrap or waxed paper, pound cutlets to even ⅛-inch thickness.

3. In nonstick 12-inch skillet, heat ½ teaspoon oil over medium-high heat until very hot. Add half of cutlets; sprinkle with ¼ teaspoon salt and ⅛ teaspoon pepper and cook, turning once, until cutlets just lose their pink color throughout, about 2 minutes. Transfer cutlets to warm platter. Repeat with remaining cutlets, remaining ½ teaspoon oil, remaining ¼ teaspoon salt, and remaining ⅛ teaspoon pepper.

4. Add arugula and tomatoes to dressing in bowl and toss until evenly coated. To serve, spoon salad over cutlets on platter and top with Parmesan shavings. Makes 4 main-dish servings.

Each serving: About 225 calories, 31g protein, 5g carbohydrate, 9g total fat (2g saturated), 94mg cholesterol, 585mg sodium.

Pork Tenderloin with Roasted Grapes

If you have never had roasted grapes, try this! They are absolutely delicious and a perfect match for the pork.

Prep: 5 minutes Cook: 25 minutes

- 1 teaspoon fennel seeds, crushed
- ½ teaspoon salt
- ½ teaspoon coarsely ground black pepper
- 1 pork tenderloin (1 pound)
- 2 teaspoons extravirgin olive oil
- 3 cups seedless red and green grapes (about 1 pound)
- ½ cup chicken broth

1. Preheat oven to 475°F. In cup, with fork, stir fennel seeds, salt, and pepper. Use to rub all over pork.

2. In 12-inch skillet with oven-safe handle (if skillet is not oven-safe, wrap handle of skillet with double layer of foil), heat oil over medium-high heat until very hot. Add pork and cook 5 minutes, turning to brown all sides.

3. Add grapes and broth to skillet; heat to boiling. Cover and place in oven. Roast until meat thermometer inserted in center of roast reaches 150°F, 15 to 18 minutes. Internal temperature of meat will rise to 155°F upon standing. Transfer pork to warm platter.

4. Meanwhile, heat grape mixture to boiling over high heat; boil until liquid has thickened slightly, about 1 minute. Slice pork; serve with grapes and pan juices. Makes 4 main-dish servings.

Each serving: About 245 calories, 25g protein, 22g carbohydrate, 7g total fat (2g saturated), 74mg cholesterol, 475mg sodium.

Pork Tenderloin with Roasted Grapes

Gingered Pork and Vegetable Stir-fry

2. In nonstick 12-inch skillet, heat 1 teaspoon oil over medium-high heat until hot. Add snow peas, zucchini, and green onions and cook, stirring frequently (stir-frying), until lightly browned and tender-crisp, about 5 minutes. Transfer vegetables to large bowl.

3. In same skillet, heat remaining 1 teaspoon oil; add pork and stir-fry until pork just loses its pink color, about 3 minutes. Transfer to bowl with vegetables.

4. Stir cornstarch mixture; add to skillet and heat to boiling. Boil, stirring constantly, until sauce thickens slightly, about 1 minute. Return pork and vegetables to skillet and stir until coated with sauce; heat through. Makes 4 main-dish servings.

Each serving: About 186 calories, 21g protein, 8g carbohydrate, 8g total fat (1g saturated), 55mg cholesterol, 430mg sodium.

Curried Pork with Olives and Dried Plums

This Indian-inspired dish calls for a good-quality curry powder for authentic flavor.

Prep: 5 minutes Cook: about 20 minutes

- 2 pork tenderloins (about 12 ounces each), trimmed
- 1 tablespoon curry powder
- 1 can (14½ ounces) low-sodium chicken broth or 1¾ cups Chicken Broth (page 62)
- ½ cup pitted dried plums (prunes)
- ¼ cup chopped pimiento-stuffed olives (salad olives)

1. Spray nonstick 10-inch skillet with vegetable cooking spray; heat over medium-high heat until hot. Meanwhile, rub pork with curry powder.

2. Add pork to skillet and cook 5 to 7 minutes, turning to brown all sides. Add broth, dried plums, and olives; heat to boiling. Partially cover skillet and cook, turning meat occasionally, 10 to 15 minutes longer or until meat thermometer inserted in center of pork reaches 155°F.

3. Transfer pork to cutting board. Slice pork and serve with dried plums, olives, and pan juices. Makes 6 main-dish servings.

Each serving: About 195 calories, 29g protein, 10g carbohydrate, 4g total fat (1g saturated), 68mg cholesterol, 225mg sodium.

Gingered Pork and Vegetable Stir-fry

Serve each person ¾ cup cooked rice, preferably brown, on the side. To make 4 servings, use 1 cup uncooked rice.

Prep: 15 minutes Cook: 15 minutes

- 1 pork tenderloin (12 ounces), trimmed and thinly sliced
- 2 tablespoons grated peeled fresh ginger
- 1 cup low-sodium chicken broth
- 2 tablespoons teriyaki sauce
- 2 teaspoons cornstarch
- 2 teaspoons canola oil
- 8 ounces snow peas, strings removed
- 1 medium zucchini (8 ounces), cut lengthwise in half and thinly sliced crosswise
- 3 green onions, cut into 3-inch pieces

1. In medium bowl, toss pork and ginger. In cup, whisk broth, teriyaki sauce, and cornstarch until smooth; set aside.

Orange Pork and Asparagus Stir-fry

Citrus fruit and grated peel are often used to flavor lean and/or mild-tasting food. Here, pieces of juicy orange, freshly squeezed juice, and grated peel perk up thin slices of lean pork tenderloin that are quickly cooked with fresh asparagus.

Prep: 20 minutes   Cook: 10 minutes

- 2 navel oranges
- 1 teaspoon olive oil
- 1 pork tenderloin (about 12 ounces), trimmed and thinly sliced on diagonal
- ¾ teaspoon salt
- ¼ teaspoon ground black pepper
- 1½ pounds thin asparagus, trimmed and each stalk cut in half
- 1 garlic clove, crushed with garlic press
- ¼ cup water

1. From 1 orange, grate 1 teaspoon peel and squeeze ¼ cup juice. Cut peel and white pith from remaining orange. Cut orange crosswise into ¼-inch-thick slices; cut each slice into quarters.

2. In nonstick 12-inch skillet, heat ½ teaspoon oil over medium-high heat until very hot. Add half of pork slices and sprinkle with ¼ teaspoon salt and ⅛ teaspoon pepper; cook, stirring frequently (stir-frying), until pork just loses its pink color, about 2 minutes. Transfer pork to plate. Repeat with remaining ½ teaspoon oil, pork, ¼ teaspoon salt, and remaining ⅛ teaspoon pepper. Transfer pork to same plate.

3. To same skillet, add asparagus, garlic, orange peel, remaining ¼ teaspoon salt, and water; cover and cook, stirring occasionally, until asparagus is tender-crisp, about 2 minutes.

4. Return pork and any juices to skillet. Add orange juice and orange pieces; cook, stirring often, until heated through. Makes 4 main-dish servings.

Each serving: About 165 calories, 24g protein, 8g carbohydrate, 4g total fat (1g saturated), 50mg cholesterol, 495mg sodium.

Latin Pork Chops with Black Beans

Serve with a mixed green salad and steamed white rice.

Prep: 15 minutes   Cook: 15 minutes

- 4 boneless pork loin chops, ¾ inch thick (5 ounces each), well trimmed
- ½ teaspoon ground cumin
- ½ teaspoon ground coriander
- ¼ teaspoon dried thyme
- ⅛ teaspoon ground allspice
- ½ teaspoon salt
- 1 teaspoon olive oil
- 1 medium onion, chopped
- 3 garlic cloves, crushed with garlic press
- 1 can (15 to 19 ounces) black beans, rinsed and drained
- ½ cup chicken broth
- 1 tablespoon fresh lime juice
- ¼ teaspoon coarsely ground black pepper
- ¼ cup packed fresh cilantro leaves, chopped fresh orange wedges (optional)

1. Pat pork chops dry with paper towels. In cup, with fork, stir cumin, coriander, thyme, allspice, and ¼ teaspoon salt. Use to rub on pork chops.

Latin Pork Chops with Black Beans

2. Spray nonstick 12-inch skillet with vegetable cooking spray; heat over medium-high heat until hot. Add pork chops and cook 4 minutes; turn pork and cook until lightly browned on the outside and still slightly pink on the inside, 3 to 4 minutes longer. Transfer to platter; cover loosely with foil to keep warm.

3. In same skillet, heat oil over medium heat. Add onion and cook, stirring frequently, until golden, about 5 minutes. Add garlic and cook, stirring, 1 minute longer. Add beans, broth, lime juice, pepper, and remaining ¼ teaspoon salt; heat through.

4. To serve, spoon bean mixture over pork; sprinkle with cilantro. Serve with orange wedges, if you like. Makes 4 main-dish servings.

Each serving: About 340 calories, 42g protein, 25g carbohydrate, 11g total fat (3g saturated), 76mg cholesterol, 760mg sodium.

Ham Steak with Apple Chutney

This freshly made, sweet-and-tangy chutney is perfect with ham steak, but you can also serve it with grilled pork or chicken.

Prep: 10 minutes   Cook: 35 minutes

- 2 teaspoons vegetable oil
- 1 medium onion, chopped
- 2 Golden Delicious apples, peeled, cored, and chopped
- 1 teaspoon minced, peeled fresh ginger
- ¾ cup apple juice
- 1 tablespoon cider vinegar
- ¼ cup golden raisins
- ½ teaspoon freshly grated orange peel
- ¼ teaspoon salt
- 1 fully cooked smoked-ham center slice, 1 inch thick (2 pounds)

1. In nonreactive 2-quart saucepan, heat oil over medium heat. Add onion and cook, stirring occasionally, 5 minutes. Stir in apples and ginger and cook 3 minutes longer. Stir in apple juice, vinegar, raisins, orange peel, and salt; heat to boiling. Reduce heat and simmer 10 minutes. (Makes 2⅔ cups chutney.)

2. Meanwhile, heat 10-inch skillet over medium heat until very hot. Add ham steak and cook until heated through and lightly browned, 8 to 10 minutes per side. Serve with chutney. Makes 6 main-dish servings.

Each serving: About 257 calories, 29g protein, 17g carbohydrate, 8g total fat (2g saturated), 65mg cholesterol, 1,922mg sodium.

Ham Steak with Creamy Cheese Grits

For an appetizer, place a bowl of orange and grapefruit sections on the table for everyone to enjoy while the ham and grits cook. Serve this classic combination with toasted pumpernickel-raisin bread from the bakery.

Prep: 5 minutes   Cook: 15 minutes

- 1¼ cups milk
- 1 can (14½ ounces) low-sodium chicken broth or vegetable broth or 1¾ cups Chicken Broth (page 62)
- ¼ teaspoon ground red pepper (cayenne)
- ¼ teaspoon dried thyme
- ¾ cup quick-cooking grits
- 4 ounces Cheddar cheese, shredded (1 cup)
- 1 fully cooked smoked-ham center slice, ½ inch thick (about 1¼ pounds)
- 2 tablespoons light brown sugar
  green onions for garnish

1. In nonreactive 2-quart saucepan, whisk milk, broth, ground red pepper, and thyme; heat to boiling over high heat. Slowly whisk grits into liquid. Reduce heat to low; cover and simmer, stirring occasionally, until mixture has thickened, 5 to 7 minutes. Remove saucepan from heat and stir in Cheddar.

2. While grits are cooking, prepare ham: Spray nonstick 12-inch skillet with vegetable cooking spray; heat over medium-high heat until very hot. Pat ham dry with paper towels. Coat both sides of ham with brown sugar. Cook ham, turning once, until glazed and heated through, about 5 minutes. To serve, arrange ham on platter with pan juices and grits. Garnish with green onions. Makes 4 main-dish servings.

Each serving: About 537 calories, 45g protein, 33g carbohydrate, 24g total fat (12g saturated), 122mg cholesterol, 2,499mg sodium.

Italian Sausage and Potatoes

Turn this delicious dish into Italian street-festival fare by omitting the potatoes and dividing the sausage-and-pepper mixture among four split hero rolls.

Prep: 10 minutes   Roast: 30 minutes

- 1 pound sweet and/or hot Italian sausages links, cut crosswise into thirds
- 1 pound small red potatoes, each cut in half
- 1 jumbo onion (about 1 pound), cut into 12 wedges
- 2 red and/or yellow peppers, each cut lengthwise into 8 pieces
- 1 tablespoon olive oil
- ½ teaspoon salt
- ¼ teaspoon ground black pepper

1. Preheat oven to 450°F.

2. In 15½" by 10½" jelly-roll pan, combine sausages, potatoes, onion, peppers, oil, salt, and pepper; toss to coat.

3. Roast sausage mixture, stirring once halfway through roasting, until potatoes are fork-tender and sausages are lightly browned, 30 to 35 minutes. Makes 4 main-dish servings.

Each serving: About 545 calories, 20g protein, 37g carbohydrate, 32g total fat (12g saturated), 80mg cholesterol, 925mg sodium.

SAUSAGES

 Sausage is nothing more than ground meat mixed with fat, flavorings, salt, filler, and sometimes preservatives stuffed into an edible casing. Here are a few of the most common:

Andouille Cajun andouille is a heavily smoked and spiced sausage made from pork butt or shank meat.

Chorizo Coarsely ground pork that is generously seasoned with chili powder, garlic, and other seasonings. Spanish chorizo is made with smoked pork, and Mexican chorizo is made with fresh pork.

Italian Sausage (sweet or hot) Coarsely ground pork flavored with black pepper and often with fennel seed.

Kielbasa A staple of Polish cuisine, it comes in many varieties, but the most common is thick and fully cooked.

Chorizo and Bean Burritos

For the best results, choose Spanish chorizo, a fully cooked smoked pork sausage seasoned with chiles and garlic. Some brands come with a casing that should be removed before cooking. Check before slicing.

Prep: 20 minutes   Cook: 10 minutes

- ⅔ cup regular long-grain rice
- 2 cans (15 to 16 ounces each) low-sodium pinto beans, not drained
- 1 teaspoon vegetable oil
- 1 small onion, chopped
- 2 teaspoons chili powder
- ¼ teaspoon ground cumin
- 8 ounces fully cooked chorizo sausage, sliced
- 6 burrito-size (10-inch) flour tortillas, warmed
- 4 ounces Cheddar cheese, shredded (1 cup)
- ½ cup packed fresh cilantro
- 1 large ripe tomato, chopped

1. Prepare rice as label directs.

2. In food processor with knife blade attached, process beans with their liquid until coarsely chopped.

3. In nonstick 10-inch skillet, heat oil over medium heat until hot. Add onion and cook, stirring occasionally, until lightly browned, 3 to 4 minutes. Stir in chili powder, cumin, and chorizo; cook 2 minutes. Add beans and cook, stirring frequently, until heated through, about 2 minutes.

4. Place tortillas on work surface. Spoon equal amounts of rice, bean mixture, Cheddar, cilantro, and tomato across center of each tortilla. Fold sides of tortilla over filling. Makes 6 main-dish servings.

Each serving: About 730 calories, 32g protein, 89g carbohydrate, 28g total fat (11g saturated), 53mg cholesterol, 940mg sodium.

Red Beans and Rice

Creole cooks traditionally made this dish on wash day (Monday) because it could simmer unattended all day long. Here's our quick, lowfat version, which can be served whenever the mood strikes.

Prep: 10 minutes Cook: 20 minutes

- 1 tablespoon vegetable oil
- 2 stalks celery with leaves, sliced
- 1 medium red onion, coarsely chopped
- 2 garlic cloves, finely chopped
- ½ teaspoon dried thyme
- 1 bay leaf
- 2 cans (15 to 19 ounces each) red kidney beans, rinsed and drained
- 1 package (6 ounces) sliced Canadian bacon, cut into thin strips
- 1 cup low-sodium chicken broth
- 5 tablespoons chopped fresh parsley
- 1 teaspoon Worcestershire sauce
- ⅛ to ¼ teaspoon hot pepper sauce
- 1 cup regular long-grain rice, cooked as label directs

1. Prepare rice as label directs.

2. Meanwhile, in 4-quart saucepan, heat oil over medium heat. Add celery, onion, garlic, thyme, and bay leaf; cook, stirring occasionally, until vegetables are tender and lightly browned, about 10 minutes.

3. Stir in beans, Canadian bacon, broth, 4 tablespoons parsley, Worcestershire, and hot pepper sauce. Cook, stirring occasionally, until heated through. Discard bay leaf.

4. To serve, spoon hot rice into 4 large soup bowls. Top each with bean mixture, and sprinkle with remaining 1 tablespoon parsley. Serve with additional hot pepper sauce, if you like. Makes 4 main-dish servings.

Each serving: About 468 calories, 26g protein, 71g carbohydrate, 8g total fat (2g saturated), 21mg cholesterol, 1,085mg sodium.

Chicken Caesar Salad

Have a little extra time? Add cherry tomatoes that have been cut in half and sliced cucumbers to greens when tossing. Use your vegetable peeler to make thin shavings of fresh Parmesan cheese to garnish the top of the salad.

Prep: 10 minutes Cook: 5 minutes

- 12 ounces chicken-breast tenders
- 1 tablespoon vegetable oil
- ¼ teaspoon salt
- 1 bag (7½ to 10 ounces) regular or reduced-fat Caesar salad kit
- 1 bag (5 to 6 ounces) baby romaine or baby spinach leaves
- 2½ ounces carrots, cut into 2" by ¼" matchstick strips (about ¾ cup)
- ⅛ teaspoon coarsely ground black pepper

1. Heat ridged grill pan or heavy 10-inch skillet over medium-high heat until very hot.

2. Meanwhile, in medium bowl, toss chicken with oil and salt until evenly coated.

3. Add chicken to grill pan and cook, turning once, just until chicken loses its pink color throughout, 4 to 5 minutes.

4. Meanwhile, in large bowl, toss lettuce, dressing, croutons, and Parmesan from Caesar salad kit with romaine and carrots.

5. Add cooked chicken to salad and toss again. Sprinkle with pepper. Makes 4 main-dish servings.

Each serving: About 250 calories, 22g protein, 3g carbohydrate, 14g total fat (2g saturated), 60mg cholesterol, 435mg sodium.

THE ORIGIN OF CAESAR SALAD

Test Kitchen Tip

During Prohibition, a popular spot for a night out was Caesar's Palace in Tijuana, Mexico. On the evening of July 24, 1924, Caesar Cardini had just about run out of food. He improvised by putting together a salad with what was on hand: romaine lettuce, olive oil, some cheese, and eggs. He then prepared the salad tableside, creating an immediate sensation.

Chicken Breasts with Six Quick Sauces

A choice of easy sauces makes this recipe one for the file.

Prep: 2 minutes plus making sauce   Cook: 10 minutes

- 1 teaspoon vegetable oil
- 4 small skinless, boneless chicken breast halves (1 pound)
   choice of sauce (below)

1. In nonstick 12-inch skillet, heat oil over medium-high heat until very hot. Add chicken and cook until chicken is golden brown and loses its pink color throughout, 4 to 5 minutes per side. Transfer chicken to platter; keep warm.

2. Prepare sauce and spoon over chicken. Makes 4 main-dish servings.

Apple-Curry Sauce

After removing chicken from skillet, reduce heat to medium. Add **2 teaspoons vegetable oil** to skillet. Add **1 Golden Delicious apple,** peeled, cored, and chopped, and **1 small onion,** chopped. Cook, stirring, until tender. Stir in **1½ teaspoons curry powder** and **¼ teaspoon salt;** cook, stirring, 1 minute. Stir in **½ cup mango chutney, ½ cup frozen peas,** and **½ cup water.** Heat to boiling; boil 1 minute. Spoon over chicken.

Each serving with chicken: About 352 calories, 34g protein, 38g carbohydrate, 5g total fat (1g saturated), 82mg cholesterol, 596mg sodium.

Black Bean Salsa

After removing chicken from skillet, reduce heat to medium. Add **1 can (15 to 19 ounces) black beans,** rinsed and drained, **1 jar (10 ounces) thick-and-chunky salsa, 1 can (8¾ ounces) whole-kernel corn,** drained, **2 tablespoons chopped fresh cilantro,** and **¼ cup water** to skillet. Cook, stirring, until heated through, about 1 minute. Spoon over chicken.

Each serving with chicken: About 282 calories, 38g protein, 22g carbohydrate, 4g total fat (1g saturated), 82mg cholesterol, 1,086mg sodium.

Chinese Ginger Sauce

After removing chicken from skillet, reduce heat to medium. Add **1 teaspoon vegetable oil** to skillet. Add **1 red pepper,** thinly sliced, and cook until tender-crisp. Add **½ cup water, 2 tablespoons soy sauce, 2 tablespoons seasoned rice vinegar,** and **1 tablespoon grated, peeled fresh ginger.** Heat to boiling; boil 1 minute. Sprinkle with **2 green onions,** chopped. Spoon over chicken.

Each serving with chicken: About 195 calories, 34g protein, 4g carbohydrate, 4g total fat (1g saturated), 82mg cholesterol, 757mg sodium.

Provençal Sauce

After removing chicken from skillet, reduce heat to medium. Add **1 teaspoon olive or vegetable oil** to skillet. Add **1 medium onion,** chopped, and cook, stirring, until tender. Stir in **1 can (14½ ounces) Italian-style stewed tomatoes, ½ cup pitted ripe olives,** each cut in half, **1 tablespoon drained capers,** and **¼ cup water.** Cook, stirring, until heated through, about 1 minute. Spoon over chicken.

Each serving with chicken: About 253 calories, 35g protein, 11g carbohydrate, 7g total fat (1g saturated), 82mg cholesterol, 785mg sodium.

Creamy Mushroom Sauce

After removing chicken from skillet, add **1 teaspoon vegetable oil** to skillet. Add **10 ounces mushrooms,** trimmed and sliced, **1 medium onion,** thinly sliced, and **¾ teaspoon salt.** Cook, stirring, until vegetables are golden brown and tender. Reduce heat to low; stir in **½ cup light sour cream** and **¼ cup water;** heat through (do not boil). Spoon over chicken.

Each serving with chicken: About 260 calories, 37g protein, 9g carbohydrate, 8g total fat (3g saturated), 92mg cholesterol, 548mg sodium.

Dijon Sauce

After removing chicken from skillet, reduce heat to low. Add ½ **cup half-and-half or light cream, 2 tablespoons Dijon mustard with seeds,** and ¾ **cup seedless red or green grapes,** each cut in half, to skillet. Cook, stirring to blend flavors, until sauce has thickened, about 1 minute. Spoon over chicken.

Each serving with chicken: About 234 calories, 34g protein, 7g carbohydrate, 7g total fat (3g saturated), 93mg cholesterol, 285mg sodium.

Chicken with Smashed Potatoes, Potpie Style

To save time, use half of a 10-ounce bag of shredded carrots. You can also create a leaner version of this recipe that cuts the fat by 6 grams by increasing the broth to 1¼ cups and omitting the cream.

Prep: 10 minutes   Cook: 20 minutes

1½	pounds baby red potatoes, each cut in half
1	tablespoon vegetable oil
4	medium skinless, boneless chicken breast halves (about 1¼ pounds)
½	teaspoon salt
¼	teaspoon ground black pepper
2	medium carrots, cut into 2" by ¼" matchstick strips (about 1½ cups)
1	cup chicken broth
¼	cup heavy or whipping cream
½	teaspoon dried tarragon, crumbled
1	cup tiny frozen peas, thawed
1	tablespoon butter or margarine

1. In 5-quart Dutch oven, combine potatoes and enough *water* to cover; heat to boiling over high heat. Reduce heat to medium. Cover and simmer until tender, about 12 minutes.

2. Meanwhile, in nonstick 12-inch skillet, heat oil over medium-high heat until very hot. Add chicken and sprinkle with ¼ teaspoon salt and ⅛ teaspoon pepper; cook 6 minutes. Turn chicken and reduce heat to medium; cover and cook until chicken loses its pink color throughout, about 8 minutes longer. Transfer chicken to plate; keep warm.

3. To same skillet, add carrots, broth, cream, and dried tarragon; cover and cook over medium-high heat until carrots are tender, about 5 minutes. Remove skillet from heat and stir in peas.

4. Drain potatoes and return to pot. Coarsely mash potatoes with butter and remaining ¼ teaspoon salt and ⅛ teaspoon pepper.

5. To serve, spoon potatoes onto large platter; top with chicken and spoon vegetable mixture over all. Makes 4 main-dish servings.

Each serving: About 456 calories, 40g protein, 41g carbohydrate, 14g total fat (6g saturated), 110mg cholesterol, 637mg sodium.

Chicken with Smashed Potatoes, Potpie Style

Chicken with Pears and Marsala

To complete the meal, serve with steamed broccoli and rice. Or combine green and starch: Cook 1 cup white rice as label directs; stir in 1 cup cooked frozen peas at end.

Prep: 10 minutes   Cook: 20 minutes

- 1 teaspoon vegetable oil
- 4 small skinless, boneless chicken breast halves (about 1 pound)
- ¼ teaspoon salt
- ⅛ teaspoon ground black pepper
- 2 ripe Bosc or Anjou pears, peeled, cored, and each cut in quarters
- ¾ cup chicken broth
- ½ cup dry Marsala wine
- 1 tablespoon cornstarch
- 2 teaspoons chopped fresh sage leaves

1. In nonstick 10-inch skillet, heat oil over medium-high heat until very hot. Add chicken; sprinkle with salt and pepper. Cook, turning once, until chicken loses its pink color throughout, 10 to 12 minutes. Transfer to plate; keep warm.

2. To skillet, add pears and cook until browned on all sides, 3 to 5 minutes.

3. Meanwhile, in small bowl, whisk broth, wine, cornstarch, and sage until smooth.

4. Carefully add broth mixture to skillet. Heat to boiling, stirring, until sauce has thickened slightly, 1 minute. Return chicken with any juices to skillet; heat through. Makes 4 main-dish servings.

Each serving: About 195 calories, 27g protein, 12g carbohydrate, 3g total fat (1g saturated), 66mg cholesterol, 410mg sodium.

Thai Chicken

Rich coconut-milk sauce infused with seasonings typical of Asian cuisine turns an ordinary chicken dinner into an exotic feast.

Prep: 10 minutes   Cook: 20 minutes

- 2 teaspoons vegetable oil
- 4 small skinless, boneless chicken breast halves (about 1 pound)
- ¼ teaspoon salt
- 1 medium lime
- 1 small onion, minced
- 1 tablespoon minced, peeled fresh ginger
- 2 garlic cloves, minced
- ¼ teaspoon crushed red pepper
- ⅓ cup well-stirred unsweetened coconut milk (not cream of coconut)
- 1 tablespoon Asian fish sauce (nam pla, page 26)
- ⅓ cup water
- ¼ cup packed fresh cilantro leaves, chopped

1. In nonstick 12-inch skillet, heat 1 teaspoon oil over medium-high heat until very hot. Add chicken; sprinkle with salt and cook 6 minutes. Reduce heat to medium; turn chicken and cook until it loses its pink color throughout, 6 to 8 minutes longer. Transfer chicken to platter; keep warm.

2. Meanwhile, from lime, with vegetable peeler, remove 3 strips peel (2" by 1" each) and squeeze 2 teaspoons juice.

3. In same skillet, heat remaining 1 teaspoon oil over medium heat. Add onion and ginger and cook, stirring occasionally, until onion is tender and golden, about 5 minutes. Add garlic, crushed red pepper, and lime peel; cook, stirring, 30 seconds.

4. Add coconut milk, fish sauce, lime juice, and water to skillet; heat to boiling over medium-high heat.

5. To serve pour sauce over chicken; sprinkle with cilantro. Makes 4 main-dish servings.

Each serving: About 210 calories, 28g protein, 5g carbohydrate, 12g total fat (5g saturated), 66mg cholesterol, 400mg sodium.

Spicy Ginger Chicken in Lettuce Cups

You can use ground turkey or pork in this dish if you prefer, or use a mix of ground meats.

Prep: 15 minutes   Cook: 10 minutes

- 3 tablespoons soy sauce
- 1 tablespoon grated, peeled fresh ginger
- 1 teaspoon sugar
- ⅛ teaspoon crushed red pepper
- 1 garlic clove, crushed with press
- 1 pound ground chicken
- 2 medium stalks celery, chopped
- ½ cup sliced water chestnuts, chopped
- ¼ cup dry-roasted peanuts, coarsely chopped
- 8 to 12 large Boston lettuce leaves

1. In cup, with fork, stir soy sauce, ginger, sugar, crushed red pepper, and garlic; set aside.

2. Spray nonstick 10-inch skillet with vegetable cooking spray; heat over medium-high heat until hot. Add chicken and cook, breaking up meat with side of spoon, until no longer pink, 4 to 5 minutes.

3. Add celery to chicken in skillet, and cook 2 minutes, stirring occasionally. Add water chestnuts and soy-sauce mixture, cook, stirring constantly, 1 minute to blend flavors. Stir in peanuts.

4. Divide chicken mixture among lettuce leaves. Fold leaves over chicken mixture and eat out of hand. Makes 4 main-dish servings.

Each serving: About 305 calories, 24g protein, 8g carbohydrate, 20g total fat (1g saturated), 66mg cholesterol, 825mg sodium.

Maple-Roasted Chicken Thighs with Sweet Potatoes

A mixed-greens salad or green beans with almonds would go nicely with this hearty autumn dish.

Prep: 15 minutes   Roast: 40 minutes

- 4 large bone-in chicken thighs (about 1½ pounds), skin and fat removed
- 2 small sweet potatoes (about 1 pound total), peeled and cut into 1-inch pieces
- 1 small onion, cut into 1-inch pieces
- ½ (16-ounce) bag baby carrots or 8 ounces parsnips, cut into 1-inch pieces
- ¼ cup maple syrup
- 1 teaspoon salt
- ½ teaspoon ground black pepper

1. Preheat oven to 450°F.

2. In jelly-roll pan or large shallow roasting pan, combine chicken, sweet potato, onion, carrots, maple syrup, salt, and pepper; toss to coat.

3. Roast chicken mixture, stirring vegetables once and turning chicken halfway through roasting, until juices run clear when thickest part of thigh is pierced with tip of knife and liquid in pan thickens slightly, 40 to 45 minutes. Makes 4 main-dish servings.

Each serving: About 290 calories, 21g protein, 41g carbohydrate, 4g total fat (1g saturated), 80mg cholesterol, 695mg sodium.

Spicy Ginger Chicken in Lettuce Cups

Easy Cobb Salad

This California classic has been enjoyed since 1937, when it was created in the Brown Derby restaurant.

Prep: 25 minutes

- 6 slices fully cooked, ready-to-serve bacon
- 2 bags (5 ounces each) mixed baby greens (about 16 cups loosely packed)
- 1 pint red or yellow cherry or grape tomatoes, each cut in half
- 2 cups corn kernels cut from cobs (about 4 ears)
- 2 cups (½-inch cubes) skinless cooked chicken meat (about 10 ounces)
- ½ English (seedless) cucumber, unpeeled, cut into ¼-inch pieces
- 3 ounces blue cheese, crumbled (¾ cup)
- ⅓ cup Tomato Vinaigrette (page 428) or bottled vinaigrette salad dressing

1. Heat bacon in microwave oven as label directs; cool slightly, then coarsely chop.

2. Line deep large platter with baby greens. Arrange cherry tomatoes, corn, chicken, cucumber, blue cheese, and bacon in striped pattern over greens. Serve with Tomato Vinaigrette or favorite dressing. Makes 6 main-dish servings.

Each serving without dressing: About 215 calories, 21g protein, 16g carbohydrate, 10g total fat (4g saturated), 49mg cholesterol, 655mg sodium.

South of the Border Cobb

Prepare as directed above replacing blue cheese with **queso fresco or mild goat cheese**. Add **2 tablespoons chopped cilantro** to vinaigrette.

Mediterranean Cobb

Prepare as directed above replacing corn with **sliced roasted red peppers**. Substitute **feta** for blue cheese and ½ **cup pitted kalamata olives** for bacon. Add **2 tablespoons chopped fresh mint** to vinaigrette.

Turkey Cutlets with Chopped Salad

(Pictured on page 262)

Turkey cutlets sautéed until golden, then served over arugula and tomato salad, warm the vegetables just enough to bring out all their flavor.

Prep: 15 minutes   Cook: 12 minutes

- 1 green onion, thinly sliced
- 2 tablespoons freshly grated Parmesan cheese
- 4 tablespoons olive oil
- 1 tablespoon red wine vinegar
- ½ teaspoon Dijon mustard
- ¼ teaspoon salt
- ¼ teaspoon coarsely ground black pepper
- 1 pound turkey cutlets
- ⅓ cup seasoned dried bread crumbs
- 1 pound plum tomatoes (4 large), cut into ¾-inch pieces
- 2 small bunches arugula (6 to 8 ounces), coarsely chopped

1. Prepare dressing: In medium bowl, with fork, mix green onion, Parmesan, 2 tablespoons oil, vinegar, mustard, salt, and pepper; set aside.

2. Place turkey cutlets between two sheets of plastic wrap or waxed paper. With meat mallet or rolling pin, pound cutlets to ¼-inch thickness. Coat cutlets with bread crumbs.

3. In nonstick 12-inch skillet, heat remaining 2 tablespoons oil over medium-high heat until very hot. Add turkey cutlets, a few at a time, and cook until cutlets are golden brown and lose their pink color throughout, about 2½ minutes per side. Transfer cutlets to warm plate as they are done.

4. Add tomatoes and arugula to reserved dressing; gently toss to mix well. Pile salad on platter and top with turkey cutlets. Makes 4 main-dish servings.

Each serving: About 336 calories, 33g protein, 15g carbohydrate, 16g total fat (3g saturated), 73mg cholesterol, 559mg sodium.

Sautéed Turkey Cutlets

This tender cut is a midweek time-saver: It cooks in just five minutes. Take your pick of the three easy, delicious sauces to spoon over the top.

Prep: 15 minutes plus making sauce   Cook: 15 minutes

- 1 pound turkey cutlets
- ¼ teaspoon salt
- ¼ teaspoon coarsely ground black pepper
- 2 teaspoons olive oil
  choice of sauce (below)

1. With meat mallet or with rolling pin, between two sheets of plastic wrap or waxed paper, pound turkey cutlets to ¼-inch thickness. Sprinkle cutlets with salt and pepper.

2. In nonstick 12-inch skillet, heat oil over medium-high heat until very hot. Add turkey cutlets, a few at a time, and cook until cutlets are golden brown and lose their pink color throughout, about 2 minutes per side, transferring cutlets to platter as they are done. Keep warm while sauce is prepared.

3. In same skillet, prepare one of the sauces. Spoon sauce over turkey cutlets. Makes 4 main-dish servings.

Tomato-Olive Sauce

To drippings in skillet, add **2 teaspoons olive oil** and **1 small onion,** finely chopped. Cook over medium heat, stirring frequently, until tender, about 5 minutes. Add **1 garlic clove,** finely chopped; cook, stirring, 1 minute. Stir in **1 can (14½ ounces) diced tomatoes with their juice.** Sprinkle with **2 tablespoons coarsely chopped pitted Kalamata olives.** Spoon over turkey cutlets.

Each serving with turkey: About 211 calories, 29g protein, 8g carbohydrate, 7g total fat (1g saturated), 70mg cholesterol, 443mg sodium.

Mushroom Sauce

To drippings in skillet, add **2 teaspoons olive oil** and **1 garlic clove,** crushed with garlic press; cook over medium heat 10 seconds. Add **1 pound mushrooms,** trimmed and sliced, and ¼ **teaspoon dried thyme;** cook, stirring frequently, until mushrooms are golden brown and liquid has evaporated, about 10 minutes. In cup, blend **1 cup chicken broth and 1 teaspoon cornstarch** until smooth. Stir broth mixture into skillet; heat to boiling, stirring. Boil 1 minute.

Each serving with turkey: About 206 calories, 31g protein, 6g carbohydrate, 6g total fat (1g saturated), 70mg cholesterol, 453mg sodium.

Curry-Apricot Sauce

To drippings in skillet, add **2 teaspoons olive oil** and **1 small onion,** chopped; cook over medium heat, stirring occasionally, until onion is tender and golden, 6 to 8 minutes. Increase heat to medium-high. Add **1 teaspoon curry powder** and ½ **teaspoon ground coriander;** cook, stirring, 1 minute. In cup, blend **1 cup chicken broth and 1 teaspoon cornstarch** until smooth. Stir broth mixture and ½ **cup dried apricots,** coarsely chopped, into skillet; heat to boiling, stirring. Boil 1 minute. Spoon over turkey cutlets.

Each serving with turkey: About 259 calories, 36g protein, 13g carbohydrate, 6g total fat (0g saturated), 88mg cholesterol, 465mg sodium.

TYPES OF OLIVE OIL

Test Kitchen Tip

Supermarkets and specialty food stores carry an array of olive oils from Italy, Spain, Greece, France, and the U.S. The best are cold-pressed, meaning that the oil is extracted through pressure. *Extravirgin olive oil* is produced by the first pressing of the olives and is considered the finest. *Virgin olive oil* is also a first-press oil but with a higher amount of acidity. *Olive oil* contains a mix of olive oil and virgin or extravirgin olive oil. And *light olive oil* has had some of the flavor removed so it is light (meaning "delicate") in taste.

Red-Cooked Turkey Thighs with Leeks

A slow cooker is perfect for this Chinese method of long cooking, which makes the turkey very tender. "Red-cooked" refers to the dark burnished color of the meat after it has been braised in the aromatic cooking liquid.

Prep: 20 minutes
Slow Cook: 8 hours on low or 4 hours on high

- 4 large leeks (about 2 pounds)
- ½ cup dry sherry
- ⅓ cup soy sauce
- ¼ cup packed brown sugar
- 2 tablespoons minced, peeled fresh ginger
- 1 teaspoon Chinese five-spice powder
- 3 small bone-in turkey thighs (about 1 pound each), skin removed
- 3 garlic cloves, crushed with garlic press
- 2 cups (about half 16-ounce bag) peeled baby carrots

1. Cut off roots and dark green tops from leeks. Discard tough outer leaves. Cut each leek lengthwise in half, then crosswise in half. Rinse leeks in large bowl of cold water, swishing to remove sand. Transfer to colander to drain, leaving sand in bottom of bowl. Repeat several times, until no sand remains. Drain well.

2. In 4½- to 6-quart slow-cooker bowl, combine sherry, soy sauce, sugar, ginger, and five-spice powder. Add leeks, turkey, garlic, and carrots; toss to coat with soy mixture. Cover and cook as manufacturer directs on low setting 8 to 10 hours or on high 4 to 5 hours.

3. Transfer turkey and vegetables to deep platter. Skim and discard fat from cooking liquid. Spoon cooking liquid over turkey and vegetables. Makes 6 main-dish servings.

Each serving: About 355 calories, 41g protein, 24g carbohydrate, 10g total fat (3g saturated), 112mg cholesterol, 1,005mg sodium.

Turkey and White Bean Chili

We love chili made with ground turkey (or even chicken); it is much lighter—and more healthful—than beef versions but just as flavorful.

Prep: 5 minutes   Cook: 15 minutes

- 1 tablespoon olive oil
- 1 medium onion, chopped
- 1 pound ground turkey
- 2 teaspoons ground coriander
- 2 teaspoons ground cumin
- 2 teaspoons fresh thyme leaves
- 2 cans (15 to 19 ounces each) Great Northern beans, rinsed and drained
- 1 can (4 to 4½ ounces) chopped mild green chiles, not drained
- 1 can (14½ ounces) chicken broth or 1¾ cups Chicken Broth (page 62)
- 2 small ripe tomatoes (about 4 ounces each), coarsely chopped
- 1 lime, cut into wedges

1. In nonstick 12-inch skillet, heat oil over medium-high heat. Add onion and cook, stirring frequently, until tender and golden, about 5 minutes. Add turkey and cook, breaking up turkey with side of spoon, until it loses its pink color throughout, about 5 minutes. Stir in coriander, cumin, and thyme; cook, stirring frequently, 1 minute.

2. Meanwhile, in small bowl, mash half of beans.

3. Stir mashed beans, remaining whole beans, chiles with their liquid, and broth into turkey mixture; heat to boiling over medium-high heat. Boil until chili has thickened slightly, about 1 minute. Stir in tomatoes. Serve with lime wedges. Makes 4 main-dish servings.

Each serving: About 495 calories, 35g protein, 49g carbohydrate, 18g total fat (4g saturated), 90mg cholesterol, 1,040 sodium.

Cod Livornese

Fish fillets, especially thick ones like cod, may have a few bones. Before cooking, run your fingers over the flesh, and if you find any strays, use tweezers to remove them.

Prep: 10 minutes   Cook: 20 minutes

- 2 teaspoons olive oil
- 1 medium onion, cut lengthwise in half and thinly sliced
- 2 garlic cloves, crushed with garlic press
- ⅓ cup dry white wine
- 1 can (14½ ounces) diced tomatoes
- ¼ cup pitted Kalamata olives
- ¼ cup loosely packed fresh parsley leaves, chopped
- 2 tablespoons drained capers
- ¼ teaspoon crushed red pepper
- 4 pieces cod or scrod fillet (about 6 ounces each)
- ¼ teaspoon salt
- 1 lemon, cut into wedges

1. In nonstick 12-inch skillet, heat oil over medium-high heat. Add onion and cook, stirring occasionally, until lightly browned and tender, about 8 minutes. Stir in garlic; cook, stirring, 30 seconds. Add wine; cook 1 minute. Stir in tomatoes with their juice, olives, parsley, capers, and crushed red pepper; heat to boiling.

2. Arrange cod fillets in single layer over tomato mixture, overlapping as necessary; sprinkle with salt. Cover and cook just until cod turns opaque throughout, 8 to 9 minutes. To serve, squeeze lemon over cod. Makes 4 main-dish servings.

Each serving: About 210 calories, 32g protein, 9g carbohydrate, 5g total fat (1g saturated), 73mg cholesterol, 845mg sodium.

Cod Livornese

Roast Cod with Bacon, Potatoes, and Kale

Using frozen chopped kale and frozen mashed potatoes really cuts down on the prep time while still providing the nutrients for a healthy meal.

Prep: 15 minutes   Cook/Roast: 20 minutes

- 1 package (10 ounces) frozen chopped kale
- 1 package (16 ounces) frozen mashed potatoes
- 2 slices bacon, cut crosswise into ½-inch-long pieces
- 1 pound cod or scrod fillet, 1 inch thick, cut into 4 pieces
- ¼ teaspoon salt
- 2 tablespoons cornmeal
- 1 large onion (12 ounces), thinly sliced
- ½ cup chicken broth
- 2 teaspoons cider vinegar

Roast Cod with Bacon, Potatoes, and Kale

1. In microwave oven, cook kale as label directs; drain. Transfer kale to medium bowl.

2. In microwave oven, heat potatoes as label directs. Add potatoes to bowl with kale and stir until blended. Cover and keep warm.

3. Preheat oven to 450°F. In nonstick 12-inch skillet, cook bacon over medium heat until browned. With slotted spoon, transfer bacon to paper towels to drain. Pour off and discard drippings from skillet.

4. Place cod on waxed paper; sprinkle with salt, then cornmeal, turning to coat.

5. In same skillet, over medium-high heat, cook cod until lightly browned, about 2 minutes per side. Transfer cod to pie plate; place in oven and roast cod until opaque throughout, 8 to 10 minutes.

6. While cod is roasting, to same skillet, add onion. Reduce heat to medium; cover and cook, stirring once, until onion is browned, about 5 minutes. Add broth; cover and cook until onion has wilted, about 4 minutes. Remove from heat; stir in vinegar and bacon.

7. To serve, reheat potato mixture in microwave oven. Divide potato mixture among plates; top with cod, then onion mixture. Makes 4 main-dish servings.

Each serving: About 315 calories, 28g protein, 31g carbohydrate, 9g total fat (4g saturated), 67mg cholesterol, 845mg sodium.

Asian Flounder Bake

To toast sesame seeds: Place seeds in a small, dry skillet and cook, stirring, over medium-high heat until fragrant and golden, about one minute.

Prep: 10 minutes   Bake: 12 minutes

- ¼ cup reduced-sodium soy sauce
- 2 tablespoons dry sherry
- 1 teaspoon sugar
- 1 teaspoon grated, peeled fresh ginger
- 1 teaspoon Asian sesame oil
- 1 bag (10 ounces) shredded carrots (about 3 cups)
- 1 bag (5 to 6 ounces) baby spinach
- 4 flounder or sole fillets (about 5 ounces each)
- 1 green onion, thinly sliced
- 1 tablespoon sesame seeds, toasted (optional)

1. Preheat oven to 450°F. In small bowl, with fork, stir soy sauce, sherry, sugar, ginger, and sesame oil until blended.

2. In 13" by 9" baking dish, spread carrots evenly. Cover carrots with spinach, then top with flounder. Pour soy-sauce mixture evenly over flounder. Bake until fish turns opaque throughout, 12 to 14 minutes.

3. To serve, sprinkle with green onion and top with sesame seeds, if using. Makes 4 main-dish servings.

Each serving: About 200 calories, 30g protein, 11g carbohydrate, 3g total fat (1g saturated), 68mg cholesterol, 735mg sodium.

Halibut with Braised Fennel

You can substitute other mild white fish for halibut, if you like. Flounder, orange roughy, scrod, and whiting are excellent choices.

Prep: 10 minutes   Cook: 20 minutes

- 2 teaspoons olive oil or vegetable oil
- 1 teaspoon fennel seeds
- 2 medium fennel bulbs (about 1 pound each), trimmed and cut lengthwise into very thin slices
- ¾ teaspoon salt
- ¼ teaspoon coarsely ground black pepper
- ¼ cup balsamic vinegar
- 2 tablespoons water
- 4 halibut steaks, 1 inch thick (about 6 ounces each)

1. In nonstick 12-inch skillet, heat oil over medium-high heat. Add fennel seeds; toast, stirring, 1 minute. Add sliced fennel, ½ teaspoon salt, and ⅛ teaspoon pepper; cover and cook, stirring occasionally, 5 minutes. Stir in vinegar and water; cover and cook, stirring occasionally, until sauce has thickened and glazes fennel, about 3 minutes.

2. Reduce heat to medium. Arrange halibut in single layer on top of fennel; sprinkle with remaining ¼ teaspoon salt and remaining ⅛ teaspoon pepper. Cover and cook until halibut turns opaque throughout and flakes easily when tested with a fork, about 10 minutes. Makes 4 main-dish servings.

Each serving: About 270 calories, 38g protein, 14g carbohydrate, 7g total fat (1g saturated), 54mg cholesterol, 615mg sodium.

BALSAMIC VINEGAR

Authentic balsamic vinegar can only be produced in two areas in Italy: Modena and Reggio Emilia. The bottles labels must say that the vinegar is *Aceto Balsamico Tradizionale* as an assurance of quality. This very expensive vinegar is most often used for drizzling—not cooking. Commercial balsamic vinegar from these regions is readily available in the U.S. A well-made commercial balsamic has a delicious rich sweetness with a hint of sourness and a deep brown color; it is ideal for everyday cooking.

Roasted Scrod with Tomato Relish

A sweet-and-sour relish is just the thing to perk up the simply prepared scrod fillets in this dish.

Prep: 15 minutes   Cook/Roast: 40 minutes

- 3 teaspoons vegetable oil
- 1 small onion, chopped
- 2 tablespoons water
- 1 can (28 ounces) plum tomatoes, drained and each tomato cut into quarters
- ¼ cup red wine vinegar
- 2 tablespoons brown sugar
- ½ teaspoon salt
- 4 pieces scrod fillet (6 ounces each)
- ¼ teaspoon coarsely ground black pepper

1. Preheat oven to 450°F.

2. In 2-quart saucepan, heat 2 teaspoons oil over medium heat. Add onion and water and cook until onion is tender and golden, about 10 minutes. Stir in tomatoes, vinegar, brown sugar, and ¼ teaspoon salt; heat to boiling over high heat. Continue cooking over high heat, stirring frequently, until relish has thickened, about 15 minutes.

3. Meanwhile, with tweezers, remove any bones from scrod. Arrange fillets in 9-inch square baking dish; sprinkle with remaining 1 teaspoon oil, pepper, and remaining ¼ teaspoon salt. Roast scrod until just opaque throughout, 12 to 15 minutes. To serve, transfer fish to platter and spoon tomato relish on top. Makes 4 main-dish servings.

Each serving: About 248 calories, 32g protein, 18g carbohydrate, 5g total fat (1g saturated), 73mg cholesterol, 708mg sodium.

Salmon Fillets with Tomato Jam

The tartness of orange peel, vinegar, and marinara sauce complement the richness of the salmon. Serve with brown rice, which adds a nutty flavor element to this meal.

Prep: 10 minutes   Bake/Cook: 15 minutes

- 4 pieces salmon fillets (about 6 ounces each), skin removed
- 3 teaspoons olive oil
- ⅛ teaspoon salt
- ⅛ teaspoon ground black pepper
- 1 medium onion, chopped
- 2 large garlic cloves, crushed with garlic press
- ½ teaspoon dried basil
- ¼ teaspoon dried oregano
- 1 tablespoon sugar
- ¼ cup red wine vinegar
- 1 cup marinara sauce
- ½ teaspoon freshly grated orange peel orange slices

1. Preheat oven to 400°F. Grease 13" by 9" baking dish; set aside.

2. With tweezers, remove any bones from salmon. Arrange salmon in single layer in prepared dish; rub with 1 teaspoon oil and sprinkle with salt and pepper. Bake salmon until it turns opaque throughout and flakes easily when tested with a fork, about 15 minutes.

3. Meanwhile, in nonstick 10-inch skillet, heat remaining 2 teaspoons oil over medium heat. Add onion; cook, stirring occasionally, until lightly browned, about 3 minutes. Stir in garlic, basil, and oregano; cook 20 seconds. Add sugar; cook until sugar begins to caramelize, about 1 minute. Add vinegar and heat to boiling; boil until almost evaporated, about 1 minute. Stir in marinara sauce and orange peel; cook until sauce has a jamlike consistency, about 5 minutes.

4. Serve salmon with tomato jam. Garnish with orange slices. Makes 4 main-dish servings.

Each serving: About 360 calories, 30g protein, 12g carbohydrate, 21g total fat (4g saturated), 80mg cholesterol, 410mg sodium.

Seafood with Zesty Tomatoes and Wine

You would never guess that the base for this authentic-tasting fish stew is marinara sauce from a jar.

Prep: 20 minutes   Cook: 15 minutes

- 1 tablespoon olive oil
- 1 small onion, chopped
- 2 large garlic cloves, crushed with garlic press
- ¼ teaspoon crushed red pepper
- 1 jar (14 to 16 ounces) marinara sauce
- ¾ cup dry white wine
- ¾ pound monkfish, dark membrane removed, cut into 2-inch pieces
- 2 pounds medium mussels, scrubbed and debearded
- ½ pound large shrimp, shelled and deveined
- 1 tablespoon chopped fresh parsley leaves

1. In 5-quart Dutch oven, heat oil over medium heat. Add onion; cover and cook, stirring occasionally, until golden brown and tender, about 5 minutes. Add garlic and crushed red pepper and cook, uncovered, 30 seconds. Stir in marinara sauce and wine; cook 3 minutes longer.

2. Increase heat to medium-high. Stir in monkfish; cover and cook 2 minutes. Stir in mussels; cover and cook 2 minutes. Stir in shrimp; cover and cook until mussels open and fish and shrimp turn opaque, about 2 minutes. Discard any mussels that have not opened.

3. To serve, sprinkle with parsley. Makes 4 main-dish servings.

Each serving: About 430 calories, 36g protein, 43g carbohydrate, 11g total fat (2g saturated), 122mg cholesterol, 1,040mg sodium.

Jeweled Cinnamon Couscous

You can whip up this hearty nonmeat main dish in just ten minutes. If you crave something green, toss in a cup of frozen peas or serve with a crisp salad.

Prep: 10 minutes   Cook: 10 minutes

- 1 tablespoon butter or margarine
- ½ medium red onion, chopped
- 1 package (8 ounces) sliced mushrooms
- 1 can (14½ ounces) low-sodium vegetable broth or 1¾ cups Vegetable Broth (page 61)
- ¼ cup water
- 1 can (15 to 19 ounces) low-sodium garbanzo beans, rinsed and drained
- ½ cup dried cranberries
- ½ cup golden raisins
- ¼ cup dry sherry
- 1 teaspoon salt
- ½ teaspoon ground cinnamon
- ¼ teaspoon ground black pepper
- 1 package (10½ ounces) plain couscous (Moroccan pasta)

1. In deep 12-inch skillet, melt butter over medium-high heat. Add onion and mushrooms; cook, stirring occasionally, 3 minutes.

2. While vegetables are cooking, in 1-quart saucepan, heat broth and water to boiling over high heat.

3. Stir garbanzo beans, cranberries, raisins, sherry, salt, cinnamon, and pepper into mushroom mixture. Remove skillet from heat.

4. Add couscous to skillet; stir in hot broth. Cover and let mixture stand until liquid has been absorbed, about 5 minutes. Fluff with fork before serving. Makes about 8 cups or 4 main-dish servings.

Each serving: About 601 calories, 21g protein, 116g carbohydrate, 6g total fat (2g saturated), 8mg cholesterol, 653mg sodium.

Black-Bean and Sweet-Potato Chili

This hearty chili is great for cool nights in early fall. Try it with pinto, cannellini, kidney, or pink beans, or use a combination thereof for a colorful entrée.

Prep: 10 minutes   Cook: about 25 minutes

- 1 tablespoon olive oil
- 1 medium onion, chopped
- 2 garlic cloves, chopped
- 2 medium sweet potatoes (about 12 ounces each), peeled and cut into ½-inch pieces
- 1 tablespoon chili powder
- 1 jar (16 ounces) mild salsa (about 1¾ cups)
- 1 cup water
- 2 cans (15 to 19 ounces each) low-sodium black beans, not drained
- ½ cup reduced-fat sour cream
- ¼ cup loosely packed fresh cilantro leaves, chopped

1. In 4-quart saucepan, heat oil over medium-high heat. Add onion and garlic; cook, stirring occasionally, until soft, about 4 minutes. Stir in sweet potatoes, chili powder, salsa, and water; heat to boiling. Reduce heat to medium-low and cook, stirring occasionally, until potatoes are tender, 12 to 15 minutes. Add beans with their liquid and cook 3 minutes to blend flavors.

2. In small bowl, combine sour cream and cilantro. Serve chili with cilantro cream. Makes about 10 cups or 4 main-dish servings.

Each serving: About 520 calories, 23g protein, 91g carbohydrate, 9g total fat (3g saturated), 12mg cholesterol, 950mg sodium.

Black Bean Cakes

Serve these "burgers" on toasted sesame buns with a side of sweet potato fries for a tasty vegetarian entrée. They also make delicious appetizers served on a bed of shredded lettuce.

Prep: 10 minutes   Cook: 7 minutes

- 1 can (15 to 19 ounces) black beans, rinsed and drained
- 2 tablespoons reduced-fat mayonnaise
- ¼ cup chopped fresh cilantro
- 1 tablespoon plain dried bread crumbs
- ½ teaspoon ground cumin
  pinch dried oregano, crumbled
- ¼ teaspoon hot pepper sauce
- 2 tablespoons olive oil
- 2 tablespoons all-purpose flour
- ¼ cup mild or medium salsa
- 8 teaspoons sour cream

1. In large bowl, with potato masher, mash beans and mayonnaise until almost smooth, leaving some lumps. Stir in cilantro, bread crumbs, cumin, oregano, and hot pepper sauce. With lightly floured hands, shape into four 3-inch patties.

2. In 10-inch skillet, heat oil over medium heat. Dust patties with flour, shaking off excess. Cook patties until crusty and lightly browned, about 3 minutes per side, transferring them to plates as they are done.

3. To serve, top each cake with 1 tablespoon salsa and 2 teaspoons sour cream. Makes 4 servings.

Each serving: About 204 calories, 6g protein, 24g carbohydrate, 11g total fat (2g saturated), 6mg cholesterol, 410mg sodium.

Potato Pancake with Broccoli and Cheddar

Meatless doesn't have to be bland, as evidenced by this "cheesy" main dish. It's perfect for those times when a satisfying meatless meal is what you want.

Prep: 5 minutes   Cook: 20 minutes

- 1 tablespoon butter or margarine
- 1 medium onion, chopped
- 1 bag (12 ounces) broccoli flowerets, each cut in half if large
- 1 teaspoon salt
- 2 tablespoons water
- 4 cups refrigerated shredded hash brown potatoes (20 ounces)
- ⅛ teaspoon ground black pepper
- 1 tablespoon vegetable oil
- 4 ounces sharp Cheddar cheese, shredded (1 cup)

1. In nonstick 12-inch skillet, melt butter over medium heat. Add onion and cook, stirring frequently, until golden and tender, about 5 minutes. Stir in broccoli, ¼ teaspoon salt, and water; cover and cook, stirring once, until broccoli is tender, about 3 minutes. Transfer broccoli mixture to medium bowl.

2. In large bowl, combine potatoes, pepper, and remaining ¾ teaspoon salt. In same skillet, heat oil over medium-high heat. Add half the potato mixture, gently patting with rubber spatula to cover bottom of skillet. Leaving 1-inch border, top potatoes with broccoli mixture. Sprinkle Cheddar over broccoli. Cover cheese with remaining potato mixture, patting so that mixture extends to edge of skillet. Cook until golden brown on bottom, about 5 minutes.

3. Place large round platter or cookie sheet upside down over skillet. Grasping platter and skillet firmly together, very carefully and quickly flip skillet over to invert pancake onto platter. Slide pancake back into skillet. Cook until browned, about 5 minutes longer. Cut in quarters. Makes 4 main-dish servings.

Each serving: About 321 calories, 13g protein, 32g carbohydrate, 17g total fat (8g saturated), 37mg cholesterol, 837mg sodium.

Spinach and Jack Cheese Bread Pudding

Spinach and Jack Cheese Bread Pudding

Rich in eggs and cheese, this easy-to-fix casserole can make a satisfying light dinner or a hearty brunch.

Prep: 10 minutes   Cook: 20 minutes

- 6 large eggs
- 2 cups lowfat milk (1%)
- ¼ teaspoon dried thyme
- ¼ teaspoon salt
- ¼ teaspoon coarsely ground black pepper pinch ground nutmeg
- 1 package (10 ounces) frozen chopped spinach, thawed and squeezed dry
- 4 ounces Monterey Jack cheese, shredded (1 cup)
- 8 slices firm white bread, torn into ¾-inch pieces

1. Preheat oven to 375°F.

2. In large bowl, with wire whisk, beat eggs, milk, thyme, salt, pepper, and nutmeg until well blended. With rubber spatula, stir in spinach, Monterey Jack, and bread pieces.

3. Pour mixture into 13" by 9" baking dish. Bake bread pudding until browned and puffed and knife inserted in center comes out clean, 20 to 25 minutes.

4. Remove bread pudding from oven; let stand 5 minutes before serving. Makes 6 main-dish servings.

Each serving: About 280 calories, 17g protein, 22g carbohydrate, 13g total fat (6g saturated), 233mg cholesterol, 545mg sodium.

Mexican-Style Bread Pudding

Prepare as directed but substitute **4 ounces Pepper Jack cheese,** shredded, for Monterey Jack cheese and add **4 ounces sliced pepperoni** in Step 2. Serve with your favorite salsa.

11

GRILLING

Whether you cook over a shoebox-size hibachi or in a state-of-the-art gas-powered "kettle," grilling imparts a unique flavor. The intense heat, the smoke, and the pleasure of cooking—and eating—outdoors, all enhance the natural flavor of food.

TYPES OF GRILLS

Charcoal These grills are fueled by charcoal briquettes or natural hardwood charcoal. The simplest is the Japanese-style hibachi, a small cast-iron grill just right for a small patio. For more ambitious grilling, choose a large covered "kettle" grill. Or choose the middle-size uncovered grill, called a brazier.

Gas Gas grills are available with a variety of options, including electric ignition, fuel gauge, extra burners, warming racks, and storage cabinets.

Electric Like gas grills, most electric units have artificial briquettes for authentic smoky flavor. There are large electric grills for the backyard as well as tabletop models.

GRILLING EQUIPMENT

Grill topper If you like seafood and vegetables, you'll want a grill topper: a perforated metal sheet or mesh screen that provides a flat surface.

Grilling basket A good option for delicate or small foods. There are fish-shaped baskets for whole fish as well as square and oblong baskets with handles.

Tongs Better than a fork for turning foods, because they don't pierce the surface and release juices.

Spatula Use a long-handled spatula with a heatproof handle for flipping burgers and moving food on a grill topper.

Skewers Long metal skewers are a must for kabobs. Choose skewers with flat shafts, which prevent the food from slipping around.

Basting brush A heatproof handle and a long shaft are musts. Silicone or natural bristles stand up to the heat better than synthetic ones.

Instant-read thermometer Insert it into the food, and the dial gives you a reading in seconds.

Grilling mitts These are long to protect more of your forearm and well insulated to protect you from the heat.

Water spray bottle The kind used to mist plants; adjust it so it shoots a narrow stream to quash flare-ups.

Brass-bristled scrub brush Use this brush to clean the grill rack.

LIGHTING

Gas and electric grills are easy to light; just follow the manufacturer's directions. A charcoal fire requires a little more work: Spread an even layer of briquettes over the bottom of the firebox, then stack them into a pyramid. Allow 30 to 40 minutes for the coals to burn down to gray ash before cooking. The following will help you get the fire going:

Chimney starter An open-ended metal cylinder with a handle. Place crumpled newspaper in the bottom, top with briquettes, and light the paper through an opening in the bottom.

Electric starter A loop-shaped heating element with a handle, this device is placed in a bed of briquettes; plug it in and the briquettes ignite.

Self-starting briquettes These are impregnated with starter fluid. A match will ignite them immediately. Don't add them to a fire that's already hot.

Solid fire starter Place these waxy-looking cubes in the firebox, pile briquettes on top, and light.

FINE-TUNING THE FIRE

Coals are ready when they are about 80 percent ash gray. To test the heat, hold your palm above the coals at cooking height (about 6 inches): If the fire is low (above 200°F), you'll be able to keep your hand there for 5 to 6 seconds. If you can bear the heat for 4 to 5 seconds, the fire is moderate (above 300°F). If you can hold your palm over the fire for just 2 to 3 seconds, the fire is hot (above 375°F).

Tapping the coals will remove their ash cover and make the fire hotter. Pushing the coals together intensifies the heat, whereas spreading them apart decreases it. Opening the vents on a covered grill increases the temperature; partially closing them lowers it.

SAFETY TIPS

- Except for grills intended to be used indoors, always cook in the open air. You're safe under a carport or in the doorway of a garage, but never use a charcoal or gas grill inside.
- Have a bucket of sand or water near the grill in case the fire gets out of hand.
- Never add liquid fire starter to an existing fire, as the stream of fluid could ignite.
- Keep an eye on the grill at all times, especially when children and/or pets are around.
- Don't wear scarves or clothing with loose, billowy sleeves or fringes.
- If the fire flares up or food catches fire, raise the rack and spread the coals apart. If necessary, spray the fire with water.
- If you want to coat the grill rack with nonstick cooking spray, do so while the rack is cold.

MARINADES, RUBS, AND SAUCES

When food is cooked by dry heat, marinating and basting help keep it moist. Although the smoky taste of grilled food is naturally delicious, marinades and dry seasoning rubs can add extra flavor.

Marinades are a classic way to flavor food. Delicate foods, such as seafood and boneless chicken breasts, benefit from 15 minutes of marinating and should not be marinated for more than 30 minutes unless directed in the recipe. Large cuts of beef and pork and bone-in chicken parts should be marinated for at least 1 hour but no more than 24 hours. A marinade can be brushed onto food as it grills, but stop basting 10 minutes before the food is done, or the marinade will not have sufficient time to cook. Discard any leftover marinade.

Seasoning rubs are combinations of spices, dried herbs, salt, and, sometimes, moist ingredients such as mustard, oil, or pureed fresh herbs. The mixture is rubbed onto the food before grilling. Apply the rub 1 or 2 hours ahead for maximum flavor.

Basting sauces, including barbecue sauce, should be thick enough to adhere to food. Sauces containing honey, molasses, or sugar, are likely to burn, so wait until the last 15 minutes of cooking time before brushing them on.

FLAVORING THE FIRE

In addition to seasoning the food you'll be grilling, you can also flavor the fire. This works best in a covered grill.

Grilling woods are sold in chunks or chips to be tossed onto a charcoal fire or gas grill. Chips require about 30 minutes of soaking; larger chunks should be soaked for up to 2 hours. Use oak and mesquite for beef and pork, and hickory for turkey, chicken, and pork. Fruitwoods, such as apple and cherry, are mild enough to use with chicken and seafood. If using chunks of wood, add them to the fire at the beginning; place chips on the coals later on. Whole spices and fresh or dried herbs can be placed directly on a fire if first soaked for 30 minutes.

Red Wine and Rosemary Porterhouse

This robust marinade can season a thick, juicy steak in 15 minutes. Marinate for up to one hour for more intense flavor. It's also good on lamb, pork, or poultry. Serve with Lemon-Garlic Potato Packet (page 326) and Crumb-Topped Tomatoes (page 327). For a dry red wine that would work well in this recipe, try a shiraz, merlot, chianti, or cabernet.

Prep: 10 minutes plus marinating   Grill: 15 minutes

½ cup dry red wine
1 tablespoon Worcestershire sauce
1 tablespoon tomato paste
1 tablespoon Dijon mustard
1 tablespoon balsamic vinegar
1 tablespoon chopped fresh rosemary
1 large garlic clove, crushed with garlic press
1 beef porterhouse or T-bone steak,
   1½ inches thick (about 1½ pounds)
1 lemon, cut into wedges

1. In 13" by 9" baking dish, combine red wine, Worcestershire, tomato paste, mustard, vinegar, rosemary, and garlic.

2. Place steak in marinade, turning to coat both sides. Cover and let stand 15 minutes at room temperature or refrigerate up to 1 hour, turning once.

3. Prepare outdoor grill for direct grilling over medium heat.

4. Remove steak from baking dish; discard marinade. Place steak on grill over medium heat and cook, turning once, 15 to 20 minutes for medium-rare or until desired doneness.

5. Transfer steak to cutting board and let stand 10 minutes to set juices for easier slicing. Cut into thin slices and serve with lemon wedges. Makes 4 main-dish servings.

Each serving: About 395 calories, 32g protein, 1g carbohydrate, 28g total fat (11g saturated), 104mg cholesterol, 125mg sodium.

GRILLING BEEF

To test the internal temperature, insert an instant-read thermometer into the center or thickest part of the meat. If it is ½ inch thick or less, insert the thermometer horizontally into the meat, halfway in. Always let steak rest approximately 10 minutes before serving or slicing, so the juices have time to redistribute throughout the meat. During the resting time, the internal temperature of the meat will rise about 5 degrees.

CUT	MEDIUM-RARE COOK TO TEMPERATURE	APPROXIMATE COOKING TIME
Steaks (porterhouse, T-bone, sirloin, rib-eye, top round):		
¾" thick	145°F	6–8 minutes
1" thick	145°F	11–14 minutes
Steaks (flank or skirt)	145°F	15–20 minutes
Tenderloin, whole	135°F	30–40 minutes
Burgers, 1" thick	160°F	10–12 minutes

Pepper-Crusted Filet Mignon

These very tender steaks make great company fare, plus they're a snap to cook and can be prepared ahead. Simply coat them with crushed spices as directed, then cover and refrigerate for up to one day until ready to cook.

Prep: 15 minutes plus standing   Grill: 16 minutes

- 1 tablespoon whole black peppercorns
- 1 teaspoon whole fennel seeds
- 4 beef tenderloin steaks (filet mignon), each 1 inch thick (about 4 ounces each)
- 3 medium peppers (red, yellow, and/or orange)
- 1 tablespoon minced fresh parsley
- 1 teaspoon olive oil
- ¾ teaspoon salt

1. Prepare outdoor grill for covered direct grilling over medium-high heat.

2. In mortar with pestle or in zip-tight plastic bag with rolling pin, crush peppercorns and fennel seeds. Use to rub on steaks. Place steaks in 13" by 9" baking dish; cover and refrigerate until ready to cook.

3. Cut each pepper lengthwise in half; remove and discard stems and seeds. With hand, flatten each pepper half. Place peppers, skin side down, on grill. Cover grill and cook, without turning, until skins are charred and blistered, 8 to 10 minutes. Transfer peppers to bowl; cover with plate and let steam at room temperature until cool enough to handle, about 15 minutes. If using gas grill, reset temperature to medium.

4. Remove peppers from bowl. Peel skins and discard. Cut peppers lengthwise into ¼-inch-wide strips and return to same bowl. Add parsley, oil, and ¼ teaspoon salt; toss until peppers are evenly coated.

5. Sprinkle steaks with remaining ½ teaspoon salt. Place steaks on grill over medium heat. Cover grill and cook, turning once, 8 to 10 minutes for medium-rare or until desired doneness. Serve steaks topped with peppers. Makes 4 main-dish servings.

Each serving: About 230 calories, 26g protein, 9g carbohydrate, 10g total fat (3g saturated), 71mg cholesterol, 495mg sodium.

Flank Steak with Chimichurri Sauce

Chimichurri is a thick green herb sauce that is served with grilled meats in Argentina. It can be prepared ahead and refrigerated for up to two days. Bring it to room temperature before serving.

Prep: 15 minutes   Grill: 12 minutes

- 1½ cups loosely packed fresh parsley leaves, chopped
- 1½ cups loosely packed fresh cilantro leaves, chopped
- ¼ cup olive oil
- 3 tablespoons red wine vinegar
- 1 garlic clove, crushed with garlic press
- ¾ teaspoon salt
- ¼ teaspoon ground black pepper
  pinch crushed red pepper
- ½ teaspoon chili powder
- ½ teaspoon sugar
- ¼ teaspoon ground coriander
- ¼ teaspoon ground cumin
- 1 beef flank steak (1½ pounds)

1. Prepare outdoor grill for direct grilling over medium heat.

2. Meanwhile prepare chimichurri sauce: In small bowl, combine parsley, cilantro, oil, vinegar, garlic, ¼ teaspoon salt, black pepper, and crushed red pepper; set aside.

3. In cup, combine chili powder, sugar, coriander, cumin, and remaining ½ teaspoon salt. Use to rub on flank steak.

4. Place steak on grill and cook about 6 minutes per side for medium-rare or until desired doneness.

5. Transfer steak to cutting board. Holding knife in slanting position, almost parallel to cutting board, slice steak thinly across the grain. Serve with sauce. Makes 4 main-dish servings.

Each serving with 1 tablespoon sauce: About 239 calories, 25g protein, 2g carbohydrate, 14g total fat (5g saturated), 62mg cholesterol, 497mg sodium.

Pastrami-Spiced Flank Steak

Pastrami, a popular New York City deli item, probably came to us via the Romanians, who prepared many of their meats by smoking. Although our pastrami isn't smoked, it is similarly coated with coarse pepper and other aromatic spices. Serve it on sliced rye with a side of coleslaw, deli style!

Prep: 15 minutes plus marinating   Grill: 13 minutes

- 1 tablespoon coriander seeds
- 1 tablespoon paprika
- 1 tablespoon cracked black pepper
- 2 teaspoons ground ginger
- 1½ teaspoons salt
- 1 teaspoon sugar
- ½ teaspoon crushed red pepper
- 3 garlic cloves, crushed with garlic press
- 1 beef flank steak (about 1½ pounds)
- 12 slices rye bread
     deli-style mustard

1. In mortar with pestle or in zip-tight plastic bag with rolling pin, crush coriander seeds. In cup, combine coriander, paprika, black pepper, ginger, salt, sugar, and crushed red pepper.

2. Rub garlic on both sides of steak, then rub with spice mixture. Place steak in large zip-tight plastic bag; seal bag, pressing out as much excess air as possible. Place bag on plate; refrigerate at least 2 hours, or up to 24 hours.

3. Prepare outdoor grill for direct grilling over medium heat.

4. Remove steak from bag. Place steak on grill over medium heat and cook, turning once, 13 to 15 minutes for medium-rare or until desired doneness.

5. Place bread slices on grill over medium heat and toast, without turning, just until grill marks appear on underside of bread.

6. Transfer steak to cutting board. Let stand 10 minutes to set juices for easier slicing. Cut steak across the grain into thin slices and serve with grilled rye bread and mustard. Makes 6 main-dish servings.

Each serving: About 380 calories, 33g protein, 35g carbohydrate, 12g total fat (4g saturated), 47mg cholesterol, 1,015mg sodium.

Pastrami-Spiced Flank Steak

Brisket with Chunky BBQ Sauce

A great do-ahead main dish for a summer picnic. You can slow-cook the brisket on the stovetop up to several days ahead. Then, 20 minutes before serving, brush it with sauce and grill until heated through.

Prep: 15 minutes   Cook/Grill: 3 hours 35 minutes

Brisket

- 1 fresh beef brisket (4½ pounds), well trimmed
- 1 medium onion, cut into quarters
- 1 large carrot, peeled and cut into 1½-inch pieces
- 1 bay leaf
- 1 teaspoon whole black peppercorns
- ¼ teaspoon whole allspice

Chunky BBQ Sauce

- 1 tablespoon vegetable oil
- 1 large onion (12 ounces), finely chopped
- 3 garlic cloves, finely chopped
- 2 tablespoons minced, peeled fresh ginger
- 1 teaspoon ground cumin
- 1 can (14½ ounces) tomatoes in puree, chopped
- 1 bottle (12 ounces) chili sauce
- ⅓ cup cider vinegar
- 2 tablespoons light (mild) molasses
- 2 tablespoons brown sugar
- 2 teaspoons dry mustard
- 1 tablespoon cornstarch
- 2 tablespoons water

1. Prepare brisket: In 8-quart Dutch oven, place brisket, onion, carrot, bay leaf, peppercorns, and allspice. Add enough *water* to cover and heat to boiling over high heat. Reduce heat; cover and simmer until meat is tender, about 3 hours.

2. Meanwhile, prepare Chunky BBQ Sauce: In nonstick 12-inch skillet, heat oil over medium heat. Add onion and cook, stirring occasionally, until tender, about 10 minutes. Add garlic and ginger and cook, stirring, 1 minute. Stir in cumin and cook 1 minute longer.

3. Stir in chopped tomatoes with their puree, chili sauce, vinegar, molasses, brown sugar, and dry mustard; heat to boiling over high heat. Reduce heat and simmer, stirring occasionally, 5 minutes.

4. In cup, blend cornstarch and water until smooth. After sauce has simmered 5 minutes, stir in cornstarch mixture. Heat to boiling, stirring; boil 1 minute. Cover and refrigerate sauce if not using right away. Makes about 4 cups.

5. When brisket is done, transfer to large platter. If not serving right away, cover and refrigerate until ready to serve.

6. Prepare outdoor grill for covered direct grilling over medium heat. Place brisket on grill, cover and cook 10 minutes. Turn brisket and cook 5 minutes longer. Spoon 1 cup barbecue sauce on top of brisket and cook until brisket is heated through, about 5 minutes longer. (Do not turn brisket after topping with sauce.)

7. Transfer brisket to cutting board. To serve, reheat remaining sauce in small saucepan on grill. Slice brisket thinly across the grain and serve with sauce. Makes 12 main-dish servings.

Each serving: About 241 calories, 26g protein, 6g carbohydrate, 11g total fat (4g saturated), 81mg cholesterol, 174mg sodium.

Each ¼ cup sauce: About 61 calories, 1g protein, 13g carbohydrate, 1g total fat (0g saturated), 0mg cholesterol, 328mg sodium.

Spice-Rubbed Beef Tenderloin

You can grill the meat right after seasoning it, or refrigerate it for up to 24 hours for even more flavor.

Prep: 5 minutes   Grill: 30 minutes

- 1 tablespoon fennel seeds, crushed
- 2 teaspoons salt
- ½ teaspoon ground ginger
- ½ teaspoon crushed red pepper
- 1 center-cut beef tenderloin roast (2½ pounds), trimmed and tied

1. Prepare outdoor grill for direct grilling over medium heat.

2. In cup, combine fennel seeds, salt, ginger, and crushed red pepper. Use to rub on beef tenderloin.

3. Place tenderloin on grill and cook, turning occasionally, until meat thermometer inserted in center of meat reaches 140°F, 30 to 40 minutes. Internal temperature of meat will rise to 145°F (medium) upon standing. Or cook until desired doneness. Transfer roast to cutting board and let stand 10 minutes to set juices for easier slicing. Cut into thin slices and serve. Makes 8 main-dish servings.

Each serving: About 177 calories, 22g protein, 1g carbohydrates, 9g total fat (3g saturated), 65mg cholesterol, 631mg sodium.

Korean Steak

Set out bowls of crisp romaine lettuce, rice, green onions, and sesame seeds and let each person assemble his or her own package.

Prep: 40 minutes plus marinating   Grill: 14 minutes

- ½ cup reduced-sodium soy sauce
- 2 tablespoons sugar
- 2 tablespoons minced, peeled fresh ginger
- 2 tablespoons seasoned rice vinegar
- 1 tablespoon Asian sesame oil
- ¼ teaspoons ground red pepper (cayenne)
- 3 garlic cloves, pressed
- 1½ pounds beef top round or sirloin steak, 1 inch thick
- 1 cup regular long-grain rice
- 3 green onions, thinly sliced
- 1 tablespoon sesame seeds, toasted
- 1 head romaine lettuce, separated into leaves

Korean Steak

1. In large zip-tight plastic bag, combine soy sauce, sugar, ginger, vinegar, sesame oil, ground red pepper, and garlic; add steak, turning to coat. Seal bag, pressing out excess air. Place on plate; refrigerate steak 1 to 4 hours to marinate, turning once.

2. Prepare outdoor grill for direct grilling over medium heat.

3. Just before grilling steak, prepare rice as label directs; keep warm.

4. Remove steak from bag; reserve marinade. Place steak on hot grill rack over medium heat and grill, turning once, 14 to 15 minutes for medium-rare or until desired doneness. Transfer steak to cutting board; let stand 10 minutes to allow juices to set for easier slicing.

5. In 1-quart saucepan, heat reserved marinade and ¼ cup water to boiling over high heat; boil 2 minutes.

6. To serve, thinly slice steak. Let each person place some steak slices, rice, green onions, and sesame seeds on a lettuce leaf, then drizzle with some cooked marinade. Fold side of lettuce leaf over filling to form a packet to eat like a sandwich. Makes 6 servings.

Each serving: About 370 calories, 30g protein, 35g carbohydrate, 11g total fat (3g saturated), 69mg cholesterol, 960mg sodium.

A SOY SAUCE PRIMER

Test Kitchen Tip

One of the oldest condiments known, naturally brewed soy sauce originated in China over 2,500 years ago. It wasn't until the sixth century, however, when Buddhism and its meatless principals were embraced, that it began to be used in Japan. The strict vegetarian diet meant giving up traditional meat- and fish-based seasonings. Luckily, a Japanese priest who had studied in China began making a seasoning from fermented soybeans— soy sauce in Japan. After some time, wheat was added to give the sauce a more balanced flavor.

Supermarkets carry two types of soy sauce:

Regular soy sauce, which is brewed from wheat, soybeans, water, and salt, is aged for several months to develop its flavor.

Reduced-sodium soy sauce is brewed the same way as is regular but it contains about 40 percent less sodium.

Stuffed Veal Chops

Thick, juicy veal chops, stuffed with a mixture of creamy cheese, roasted peppers, and basil, sit atop a bed of spicy greens. The combination of warm chops and cool greens is a real winner. Use a small paring knife to cut the pocket so that it is deep but not wide.

Prep: 15 minutes Grill: 10 to 12 minutes

- ¼ cup roasted red peppers (one-third 7-ounce jar), drained and chopped
- 3 tablespoons chopped fresh basil
- 4 veal rib chops, each 1 inch thick (about 10 ounces each)
- 2 ounces Fontina cheese, sliced
- ½ plus ⅛ teaspoon salt
- ½ plus ⅛ teaspoon coarsely ground black pepper
- 1 tablespoon olive oil
- 1 tablespoon balsamic vinegar
- ½ teaspoon Dijon mustard
- 4 ounces arugula, watercress, or baby spinach, tough stems removed

1. Prepare outdoor grill for direct grilling over medium-high heat.

2. In small bowl, mix roasted red peppers and 2 tablespoons chopped basil.

3. Pat veal dry with paper towels. Holding knife parallel to surface, cut a horizontal pocket in each chop. Tuck cheese slices into pocket of each chop, then stuff each with one-fourth of red-pepper mixture. Sprinkle chops with ½ teaspoon salt and ½ teaspoon pepper.

4. Place chops on grill and cook, turning once, until chops are lightly browned on both sides and just lose their pink color throughout, 10 to 12 minutes.

5. Meanwhile, in medium bowl, with wire whisk, mix oil, vinegar, remaining 1 tablespoon basil, mustard, remaining ⅛ teaspoon salt, and remaining ⅛ teaspoon pepper until blended. Add arugula to dressing bowl; toss until evenly coated.

6. To serve, spoon arugula mixture onto platter; arrange chops on top. Makes 4 servings.

Each serving: About 440 calories, 40g protein, 2g carbohydrate, 29g total fat (11g saturated), 181mg cholesterol, 655mg sodium.

THE PERFECT BURGER

- For juiciness and flavor, use relatively lean meat but not the very leanest. You need to have a little fat for great burgers.
- Don't overmix when combining meat and other ingredients, and don't squeeze or compress the mixture when shaping patties or you'll end up with dry, tough burgers.
- To prevent sticking, get the grill good and hot before putting on the burgers.
- Salt after cooking, not before; salt draws out juices.
- Never flatten or score burgers with a spatula as they cook or you'll lose precious juices.
- For safety's sake, cook thoroughly, until just a trace of pink remains in the center (160°F). Burgers don't have to be well done, but they should not be rare.
- Keep ground beef refrigerated up to two days in its supermarket wrap. For longer storage, rewrap in freezer wrap and freeze; use within three months.

Tex-Mex Burger

Classic Hamburgers

What could be more satisfying than a classic burger? Here's the way to do it right.

Prep: 5 minutes   Grill: 8 minutes

1¼ **pounds ground beef chuck**
½   **teaspoon salt**
¼   **teaspoon ground black pepper**

1. Prepare outdoor grill for direct grilling over medium-high heat.

2. Shape ground beef into 4 patties, each ¾ inch thick, handling meat as little as possible. Sprinkle patties with salt and pepper.

3. Place patties on grill rack and cook about 4 minutes per side for medium or until desired doneness. Makes 4 burgers.

Each burger: About 243 calories, 29g protein, 0g carbohydrate, 14g total fat (6g saturated), 88mg cholesterol, 391mg sodium.

Classic Cheeseburgers

Prepare as directed but during last 2 minutes of grilling top each burger with **1 ounce of sliced Cheddar or Swiss cheese.** Cover grill to melt cheese.

Grilled Hamburgers

Tex-Mex Burgers

Before shaping into patties, combine 2 tablespoons finely chopped onion, 2 tablespoons bottled salsa, 1 teaspoon salt, and 1 teaspoon chili powder with ground beef just until well blended but not overmixed. Grill or panfry as directed.

Each burger: About 249 calories, 29g protein, 1g carbohydrate, 14g total fat (6g saturated), 88mg cholesterol, 771mg sodium.

Teriyaki Burgers

Before shaping into patties, combine ¼ cup chopped green onions, 2 tablespoons soy sauce, 1 tablespoon brown sugar, and ¼ teaspoon ground red pepper (cayenne) with ground beef just until well blended but not overmixed. Grill or panfry as directed, but during last 2 minutes of cooking, brush burgers on each side with a mixture of 2 tablespoons apple jelly, 2 teaspoons minced, peeled fresh ginger, and 1 teaspoon soy sauce.

Each burger: About 290 calories, 29g protein, 12g carbohydrate, 14g total fat (6g saturated), 88mg cholesterol, 708mg sodium.

Greek Burgers

Before shaping into patties, combine ¼ cup chopped fresh parsley, 1 teaspoon dried mint, crumbled, 1 teaspoon salt, and ¼ teaspoon ground black pepper with ground beef just until well blended but not overmixed. Grill or panfry as directed.

Each burger: About 245 calories, 29g protein, 0g carbohydrate, 14g total fat (6g saturated), 88mg cholesterol, 686mg sodium.

Roquefort Burgers

Before shaping into patties, combine 1 tablespoon Worcestershire sauce and ½ teaspoon coarsely ground black pepper with ground beef just until well blended but not overmixed. Shape mixture into 4 balls. Make indentation in center of each ball; place ½ ounce crumbled Roquefort or blue cheese into each indentation. Shape ground-beef mixture around cheese; flatten each into ¾-inch-thick patty. Grill or panfry as directed.

Each burger: About 299 calories, 32g protein, 1g carbohydrate, 19g total fat (8g saturated), 101mg cholesterol, 399mg sodium.

Basic Grilled Pork Tenderloins

Lean, tasty pork tenderloins are perfect for grilling.

Prep: 15 minutes plus marinating   Grill: 18 minutes

- 1 pork tenderloin (about 1 pound)
  choice of dry spice rub (below)

1. Prepare outdoor grill for covered direct grilling over medium heat.

2. In cup, combine rub ingredients; use to rub on tenderloins.

3. Place tenderloins on grill, cover and cook, turning tenderloins once, until browned on the outside and still slightly pink in the center, 16 to 20 minutes. Meat thermometer inserted in thickest part of tenderloin should register 150°F.

4. Transfer tenderloin to cutting board; cover and let rest 5 minutes. Thinly slice. Makes 8 servings.

Each serving: About 177 calories, 26g protein, 0g carbohydrate, 7g total fat (2g saturated), 77mg cholesterol, 48mg sodium.

DRY SPICE RUBS

Curry Rub
Combine 2 tablespoons brown sugar, 1 tablespoon curry powder, 1/2 teaspoon salt, and 1/4 teaspoon ground black pepper.

Southwestern Rub
Combine 2 teaspoons chili powder, 1/2 teaspoon salt, 1/4 teaspoon ground cumin, 1/4 teaspoon ground coriander, 1/4 teaspoon ground red pepper (cayenne), and 1/4 teaspoon ground black pepper.

Middle Eastern Rub
Combine 1 tablespoon dried mint, crumbled, 1 teaspoon ground cumin, 1/2 teaspoon salt, and 1/4 teaspoon ground black pepper.

Herbes de Provence Rub
Combine 1 1/2 teaspoons dried thyme, crumbled, 1 teaspoon dried rosemary, crumbled, 1/2 teaspoon dried marjoram, crumbled, 1/2 teaspoon salt, and 1/4 teaspoon ground black pepper.

Jerk Pork Tenderloins

From Jamaica, jerk seasoning uses lots of allspice, which is native to the island. Combined with thyme, bay leaves, and hot chiles, it makes a unique and delicious rub for pork, chicken, and fish.

Prep: 15 minutes plus marinating   Grill: 18 minutes

- 1 bunch green onions, cut into 1-inch pieces
- 3 bay leaves, broken into pieces
- 3 garlic cloves, peeled
- 2 jalapeño chiles, seeded and coarsely chopped
- 2 tablespoons distilled white vinegar
- 1 tablespoon dried thyme
- 2 teaspoons ground allspice
- 1 teaspoon salt
- 1/2 teaspoon coarsely ground black pepper
- 2 whole pork tenderloins (1 pound each)
- 2 small or 1 large ripe pineapple

1. In food processor with knife blade attached, puree green onions, bay leaves, garlic, jalapeños, vinegar, thyme, allspice, salt, and pepper until thick paste is formed. Use to rub on tenderloins. Place pork on large plate; cover and refrigerate 1 hour or overnight.

2. Prepare outdoor grill for covered direct grilling over medium heat.

3. Meanwhile, with sharp knife, cut pineapples lengthwise through crown to stem end for total of 8 wedges, leaving on leafy crown.

4. Place tenderloins on grill, cover and cook, turning tenderloins once, until browned on outside and still slightly pink in center, 18 to 22 minutes. Meat thermometer inserted in thickest part of tenderloin should register 150°F. Transfer tenderloin to cutting board; cover and let stand 5 minutes.

5. Meanwhile, add pineapple wedges, cut sides down, to same grill rack; cook, turning once, until golden brown and heated through, 5 to 8 minutes.

6. Transfer pineapple to platter. Cut tenderloin into thin slices. Serve with pineapple wedges. Makes 8 main-dish servings.

Each serving: About 205 calories, 27g protein, 10g carbohydrate, 6g total fat (2g saturated), 78mg cholesterol, 340mg sodium.

Cut	Cook to Temperature	Approximate Cooking Time
Chops (rib or loin), 1" thick	150°F	10–12 minutes
Tenderloin, whole	150°F	13–23 minutes
Tenderloin steaks, ¼" thick	150°F	5–6 minutes

Pork Tenderloin Cutlets with Plum Glaze

The cutlets and glaze can be prepped in advance—up to several hours ahead—and the grilling takes only minutes. Serve with ginger iced tea and scallion pancakes.

Prep: 10 minutes   Grill: 6 minutes

- 1 pork tenderloin (1 pound), trimmed
- ¾ teaspoon salt
- ¼ teaspoon coarsely ground black pepper
- ½ cup plum jam or preserves
- 1 tablespoon brown sugar
- 1 tablespoon grated, peeled fresh ginger
- 2 garlic cloves, crushed with garlic press
- 1 tablespoon fresh lemon juice
- ½ teaspoon ground cinnamon
- 4 large plums (1 pound), each pitted and cut in half

1. Prepare outdoor grill for direct grilling over medium heat.

2. Using sharp knife, cut tenderloin lengthwise almost in half, being careful not to cut all the way through. Open and spread flat like a book. Place tenderloin between two sheets of plastic wrap or waxed paper. With meat mallet or rolling pin, pound meat to ¼-inch thickness. Cut crosswise into 4 equal pieces; sprinkle cutlets with salt and pepper.

3. In small bowl, combine plum jam, brown sugar, ginger, garlic, lemon juice, and cinnamon. Brush one side of each cutlet and cut side of each plum half with plum glaze. Place cutlets and plums on grill, glaze side down, and cook 3 minutes. Brush cutlets and plums with remaining plum glaze; turn pork and plums over and cook until cutlets are lightly browned on both sides and just lose their pink color throughout and plums are hot, about 3 minutes longer. Makes 4 main-dish servings.

Each serving: About 333 calories, 27g protein, 44g carbohydrate, 6g total fat (2g saturated), 80mg cholesterol, 509mg sodium.

Maple-Glazed Pork Tenderloins

Use leftovers for a sandwich treat of thinly sliced pork topped with sharp Cheddar cheese and apple slices.

Prep: 10 minutes plus refrigerating   Grill: 20 minutes

- 2 pork tenderloins (12 ounces each), trimmed
- ½ teaspoon salt
- ¼ teaspoon ground black pepper
- 8 wooden toothpicks
- 6 slices bacon
- ½ cup maple or maple-flavored syrup

1. Prepare outdoor grill for direct grilling over medium heat. Soak toothpicks in water for 30 minutes.

2. Sprinkle tenderloins with salt and pepper. Place pork in bowl; cover and refrigerate 30 minutes.

3. Wrap 3 bacon slices around each tenderloin and secure with toothpicks. Place tenderloins on grill and cook, brushing frequently with syrup and turning occasionally, until meat thermometer inserted in center of pork reaches 150°F, 20 to 25 minutes. Internal temperature will rise to 155°F upon standing. Let pork stand 5 minutes to set juices for easier slicing. Makes 6 main-dish servings.

Each serving: About 265 calories, 28g protein, 18g carbohydrate, 9g total fat (3g saturated), 86mg cholesterol, 352mg sodium.

Teriyaki Pork Chops with Grilled Pineapple Slices

Many fruits go well with pork, but pineapple certainly tops the list. Before grilling, the pork chops are marinated in a Polynesian-style mixture that deliciously complements the pineapple.

Prep: 15 minutes plus marinating   Grill: 20 minutes

- ⅓ cup soy sauce
- 2 tablespoons plus ¼ cup packed brown sugar
- 2 green onions, chopped
- 2 tablespoons grated, peeled fresh ginger
- 4 pork loin chops, ¾ inch thick (6 to 8 ounces each)
- 1 small pineapple

1. Prepare outdoor grill for direct grilling over medium heat.

2. In 13" by 9" baking dish, combine soy sauce, 2 tablespoons brown sugar, green onions, and ginger. Add chops, turning to coat. Let stand 20 minutes at room temperature to marinate.

3. Meanwhile, cut off crown and stem end from pineapple. Stand pineapple upright and cut off rind and eyes. Then place pineapple on its side and cut crosswise into ½-inch-thick slices. Sprinkle pineapple slices with remaining ¼ cup brown sugar.

4. Place pineapple on grill and cook, turning slices occasionally, until browned on both sides, 15 to 20 minutes. After pineapple has cooked 10 minutes, place chops on grill and cook, turning occasionally and brushing with remaining teriyaki mixture halfway through cooking, until chops are browned on both sides and juices run clear when center is pierced with tip of knife, about 10 minutes. Serve chops with grilled pineapple slices. Makes 4 main-dish servings.

Each serving: About 399 calories, 30g protein, 48g carbohydrate, 11g total fat (4g saturated), 78mg cholesterol, 1,433mg sodium.

Herbed Pork Chops

For a delicious and interesting change of pace, fennel seeds, with their subtle licoricelike flavor, perk up the pork chops. Crushing the seeds just before using them helps retain their flavor and fragrance.

Prep: 15 minutes   Grill: 11 minutes

- 1 tablespoon chopped fresh rosemary leaves
- 2 teaspoons fennel seeds, crushed
- ¾ teaspoon salt
- ⅛ teaspoon ground black pepper
- 4 bone-in pork loin or rib chops, ¾ inch thick (about 6 ounces each)
- 1 pound plum tomatoes, each cut lengthwise in half
- 1 tablespoon extravirgin olive oil
- 2 tablespoons chopped fresh parsley leaves
- 1 teaspoon grated fresh lemon peel
- 1 garlic clove, crushed with press

1. Prepare outdoor grill for covered direct grilling over medium heat.

2. Meanwhile, in cup, combine rosemary, fennel seeds, ½ teaspoon salt, and pepper. Use to rub on pork chops.

3. In medium bowl, combine tomatoes, oil, and remaining salt; set aside.

4. Place pork chops on grill, cover and cook chops 5 minutes. Turn chops and arrange on one side of grill. Place tomatoes, cut sides down, on other side of grill; set bowl aside. Cover grill and cook pork chops until browned on outside and still slightly pink on inside, 4 to 5 minutes; cook tomatoes until evenly charred on both sides, 6 to 7 minutes.

5. Transfer chops to platter and tomatoes to cutting board. Cool tomatoes slightly, then cut into large pieces. Return tomatoes and their juices to bowl; stir in parsley, lemon peel, and garlic. Serve chops with tomato salad. Makes 4 main-dish servings.

Each serving: About 315 calories, 28g protein, 6g carbohydrate, 19g total fat (6g saturated), 88mg cholesterol, 520mg sodium.

Barbecued Pork Spareribs

Plain spareribs? Of course not! It's the sauces that make these special. Here are three of our favorites.

Prep: 1 hour 20 minutes   Grill: 20 minutes

4 pounds pork spareribs, cut into 1- or 2-rib portions
choice of sauce (below)

1. Early in day or one day ahead, precook spareribs: In 8-quart Dutch oven, place ribs. Add enough *water* to cover and heat to boiling over high heat. Reduce heat; cover and simmer until spareribs are tender, about 1 hour. Transfer spareribs to platter; cover and refrigerate.

2. Prepare outdoor grill for direct grilling over medium heat.

3. Meanwhile, prepare desired barbecue sauce.

4. To grill: Place cooked spareribs on grill and cook, turning ribs frequently and brushing with barbecue sauce often, until heated through, about 20 minutes. Makes 8 main-dish servings.

Balsamic-Rosemary Sauce

In 1-quart saucepan, combine ⅔ **cup balsamic vinegar, 2 tablespoons brown sugar, 1 teaspoon salt,** and ½ **teaspoon ground black pepper** and heat to boiling over medium heat. Cook until sauce has reduced to ⅓ cup, about 15 minutes. Stir in **1 teaspoon dried rosemary,** crumbled.

Each serving with Balsamic-Rosemary Sauce: About 368 calories, 26g protein, 4g carbohydrate, 27g total fat (10g saturated), 107mg cholesterol, 376mg sodium.

Orange-Dijon Sauce

In cup, combine **1 cup sweet orange marmalade,** ¼ **cup Dijon mustard,** ¼ **cup packed brown sugar, 1 teaspoon freshly grated orange peel,** and 1½ **teaspoons salt.**

Each serving with Orange-Dijon Sauce: About 483 calories, 26g protein, 33g carbohydrate, 27g total fat (10g saturated), 107mg cholesterol, 723mg sodium.

Asian Barbecue Sauce

In 1-quart saucepan, heat **1 tablespoon vegetable oil** over medium heat; add **2 green onions,** finely chopped, and cook until tender, about 5 minutes. Add **2 teaspoons grated, peeled fresh ginger** and **1 garlic clove,** crushed with garlic press; cook, stirring frequently, 1 minute longer. Stir in ⅔ **cup packed brown sugar,** ¼ **cup soy sauce,** ¼ **cup dry sherry, 1 tablespoon cornstarch,** and ½ **teaspoon salt.** Heat to boiling over medium-high heat, stirring, until mixture has thickened and boils. Remove from heat; stir in **1 teaspoon Asian sesame oil.**

Each serving with Asian Barbecue Sauce: About 453 calories, 26g protein, 20g carbohydrate, 29g total fat (10g saturated), 107mg cholesterol, 750mg sodium.

PORK RIBS GLOSSARY

Test Kitchen Tip

Nothing says summer more than pork ribs on the grill. There are several types of ribs you are likely to find at your local supermarket.

Spareribs A rack, made up of the 13 ribs from the belly of a pig, weigh around 2 to 3 pounds, with lots of meat at the wider end. It will feed from two to three people.

Baby Back Ribs These are pork chop bones from the upper portion of the rib section of the loin with the boneless meat removed. Baby back ribs are not, as one might think, from baby pigs. These ribs have much less meat on them than spareribs, as the meat is cut very close to the bone. One rack will feed one or two people. With their smaill size, they make great cocktail food.

Country-Style Ribs These ribs are actually loin pork chops that have been split. These meaty, slightly fatty ribs are delicious grilled or braised. They are sold bone-in and boneless.

Plum-Good Baby Back Ribs

Licorice-flavored star anise—one of the spices in Chinese five-spice powder—gives these ribs their distinctive appeal. The ribs can be cooked in the seasoned liquid up to two days ahead, then cooled, covered, and refrigerated. Remove the ribs from the refrigerator while the grill heats, then proceed with the recipe.

Prep: 1 hour   Grill: 15 minutes

4	racks pork baby back ribs (about 1 pound each)
12	whole black peppercorns
2	bay leaves
10	whole star anise
2	cinnamon sticks (each 3 inches long)
¼	cup soy sauce
1	jar (12 ounces) plum jam (1 cup)
1	tablespoon grated, peeled fresh ginger
1	garlic clove, crushed with garlic press

1. In 8-quart saucepot, combine ribs, peppercorns, bay leaves, 4 star anise, and 1 cinnamon stick. Add enough *water* to cover and heat to boiling over high heat. Reduce heat to low; cover and simmer until ribs are fork-tender, 50 minutes to 1 hour. Transfer ribs to platter. If not serving right away, cover and refrigerate until ready to serve.

2. Prepare glaze: In 1-quart saucepan, heat soy sauce, remaining 6 star anise, and remaining cinnamon stick to boiling over high heat. Reduce heat to low; cover and simmer 5 minutes. Remove from heat; let stand, covered, 5 minutes. Strain mixture into bowl; discard star anise and cinnamon. Stir in plum jam, ginger, and garlic.

3. Prepare outdoor grill for direct grilling over medium heat.

4. Place ribs on grill and cook, turning once, until browned, about 10 minutes. Brush ribs with some glaze and grill, brushing with remaining glaze and turning frequently, 5 to 10 minutes longer. Makes 6 main-dish servings.

Each serving: About 690 calories, 37g protein, 38g carbohydrate, 43g total fat (16g saturated), 172mg cholesterol, 860mg sodium.

Sausage-and-Pepper Grill

For hearty sandwiches reminiscent of those found at Italian street fairs, grill Italian hero rolls, split them open, and top with this sausage, pepper, and onion mixture. If you prefer, toss the grilled sausages and vegetables with cooked ziti, add grated Parmesan cheese, and serve.

Prep: 15 minutes   Grill: 15 minutes

⅓	cup balsamic vinegar
1	teaspoon brown sugar
½	teaspoon salt
¼	teaspoon coarsely ground black pepper
2	medium red peppers, cut into 1½-inch-wide strips
2	medium green peppers, cut into 1½-inch-wide strips
2	large red onions (about 8 ounces each), each cut into 6 wedges
1	tablespoon olive oil
¾	pound sweet Italian sausage links
¾	pound hot Italian sausage links

1. Prepare outdoor grill for direct grilling over medium heat.

2. In cup, with fork, mix vinegar, brown sugar, salt, and black pepper. In large bowl, toss red and green peppers and onions with oil until evenly coated.

3. Place sausages and vegetables on grill. Cook sausages, turning occasionally, until golden brown and cooked through, 15 to 20 minutes. Cook vegetables, turning occasionally and brushing with some balsamic mixture during last 3 minutes of cooking, until tender, about 15 minutes. Transfer vegetables and sausages to platter as they finish cooking.

4. To serve, cut sausages diagonally into 2-inch-thick slices. Drizzle remaining balsamic mixture over vegetables. Makes 4 main-dish servings.

Each serving: About 500 calories, 27g protein, 19g carbohydrate, 36g total fat (12g saturated), 97mg cholesterol, 1,450mg sodium.

Southwestern Ham Steak

Serve with one of our fresh salsas (pages 436–438).

Prep: 5 minutes   Grill: 8 minutes

- 2 teaspoons chili powder
- ½ teaspoon ground cumin
- ¼ teaspoon ground coriander
- ¼ teaspoon ground red pepper (cayenne)
- ¼ teaspoon sugar
- 1 fully cooked smoked ham center slice, ½ inch thick (1¼ pounds)

1. Prepare outdoor grill for direct grilling over medium heat.

2. In small bowl, combine chili powder, cumin, coriander, ground red pepper, and sugar. Use to rub on ham steak.

3. Place ham steak on grill and cook until heated through and lightly browned, about 4 minutes per side. Makes 4 main-dish servings.

Each serving: About 171 calories, 27g protein, 1g carbohydrate, 6g total fat (2g saturated), 61mg cholesterol, 1,727mg sodium.

Grilled Lamb Chops with Spice Rub

Grilling chops that have been seasoned with a rub is the easiest way to guarantee lots of flavor.

Prep: 5 minutes   Grill: 10 minutes

- 4 lamb shoulder chops, ¾ inch thick (8 ounces each)
- choice of dry spice rub (page 300)

1. Prepare outdoor grill for direct grilling over medium heat.

2. In small bowl, combine rub ingredients; use to rub on lamb chops.

3. Place chops on grill and cook about 5 minutes per side for medium-rare or until desired doneness. Makes 4 main-dish servings.

Each serving: About 454 calories, 57g protein, 2g carbohydrate, 22g total fat (8g saturated), 196mg cholesterol, 470mg sodium.

Aromatic Leg of Lamb

Once your butcher has boned out a leg of lamb for you, ask for the lamb bone. Use it to cook up some flavorful lamb broth for an especially tasty stew or hearty soup.

Prep: 20 minutes   Grill: 15 minutes

- 3 pounds boneless lamb leg, butterflied and trimmed
- 3 garlic cloves, each cut in half and crushed with side of chef's knife
- 1 tablespoon olive oil
- 2 teaspoons fennel seeds, crushed
- 2 teaspoons cumin seeds, crushed
- 2 teaspoons coriander seeds, crushed
- 1½ teaspoons salt
- lemon wedges

1. Prepare outdoor grill for covered direct grilling over medium heat. Rub both sides of lamb with cut sides of garlic cloves; discard garlic.

2. In small bowl, combine oil, fennel seeds, cumin seeds, coriander seeds, and salt. Use to rub on lamb.

3. Place lamb on grill, cover and cook, turning lamb occasionally, 15 to 25 minutes for medium-rare or until desired doneness. Thickness of butterflied lamb will vary throughout; cut off sections of lamb as they are done and place on cutting board. Let stand 10 minutes to set juices for easier slicing. Cut into thin slices and serve lamb with lemon wedges. Makes 8 main-dish servings.

Each serving: About 265 calories, 36g protein, 1g carbohydrate, 12g total fat (4g saturated), 114mg cholesterol, 525mg sodium.

SPICES

Spices come from the bark, buds, fruit, roots, seeds, or stems of plants and trees, unlike herbs, which come from the leafy parts of plants. Spices have always been used for flavoring food and drinks as well as for medicinal and ceremonial purposes. The most common spices are allspice, anise, caraway, celery seed, chile powder, coriander, cumin, fennel, juniper, mustard, and pepper.

Grilled Leg of Lamb with Mint and Oregano

Flavored with lemon, garlic, and fresh herbs, this grilled lamb will please anyone craving a taste of the sun-drenched Aegean countryside. For a simple feast, serve with rice and sliced summer tomatoes.

Prep: 25 minutes plus overnight to marinate
Grill: 15 minutes

1	large bunch fresh mint
1	large bunch fresh oregano
3	tablespoons plus ¼ cup olive oil
3	tablespoons plus ¼ cup fresh lemon juice
1	garlic clove, finely chopped
1½	teaspoons salt
¾	teaspoon ground black pepper
3	pounds boneless lamb leg, butterflied and trimmed

1. Measure ¼ cup each mint and oregano leaves and chop, reserving remainder for sauce. In 13" by 9" baking dish, combine chopped mint and oregano, 3 tablespoons each oil and lemon juice, garlic, 1 teaspoon salt, and ½ teaspoon pepper. Add lamb, turning to coat. Cover with plastic wrap and refrigerate lamb overnight to marinate.

2. Prepare outdoor grill for direct grilling over medium heat.

3. Meanwhile, for sauce, chop 2 tablespoons each mint and oregano leaves. In small bowl, combine mint and oregano with remaining ¼ cup each oil and lemon juice, remaining ½ teaspoon salt, and remaining ¼ teaspoon pepper.

4. Remove lamb from marinade; discard marinade. Place lamb on grill and cook, turning occasionally, 15 to 25 minutes for medium-rare or until desired doneness. Thickness of butterflied lamb will vary throughout; cut off sections of lamb as they are done and place on cutting board. Let stand 10 minutes to set juices for easier slicing. Cut into thin slices and serve with herb sauce. Makes 8 main-dish servings.

Each serving: About 266 calories, 22g protein, 2g carbohydrate, 19g total fat (4g saturated), 69mg cholesterol, 491mg sodium.

Rosemary Lamb Kabobs

The fresh, clean flavors of orange and rosemary are wonderful with lamb. Serve alongside skewers of grilled cherry tomatoes and a bowl of yellow rice.

Prep: 30 minutes plus marinating   Grill: 10 minutes

3	oranges
1	tablespoon olive oil
1	tablespoon chopped fresh rosemary or 1½ teaspoons dried rosemary, crumbled
2	garlic cloves, each cut in half
¼	teaspoon salt
¼	teaspoon ground red pepper (cayenne)
1	pound boneless lamb leg, cut into 1½-inch pieces
8	metal skewers
1	red pepper, cut into 1½-inch squares
1	yellow pepper, cut into 1½-inch squares
1	orange pepper, cut into 1½-inch squares
1	pint cherry tomatoes
6	green onions, cut into 2-inch pieces
10	ounces small mushrooms, trimmed

1. Prepare outdoor grill for direct grilling over medium heat.

2. Meanwhile, from oranges, grate 1 teaspoon peel and squeeze 1 cup juice. In large bowl, combine orange peel and juice, oil, rosemary, garlic, salt, and ground red pepper. Add lamb, turning to coat, and let stand, stirring occasionally, 10 minutes at room temperature.

3. Thread lamb onto 4 metal skewers and thread vegetables onto remaining 4 skewers, alternating vegetables. Place skewers on grill. Cook lamb and vegetables, turning once, 10 to 12 minutes for medium-rare or until desired doneness. Transfer to platter. Makes 4 main-dish servings.

Each serving: About 245 calories, 28g protein, 12g carbohydrate, 10g total fat (3g saturated), 81mg cholesterol, 118mg sodium.

Different chicken parts require different amounts of time on the grill, but it is nice to be able to remove all of the chicken from the grill at the same time so it is equally hot. Here's an easy way to accomplish this: When grilling a cut-up chicken, put the legs on the grill first. After 5 minutes, place the breasts on the grill. After another 10 minutes, put the thighs on to cook.

Cut	Cook to Temperature	Approximate Cooking Time
Legs, bone-in	170°F	35–40 minutes
Thighs, bone-in	170°F	12–15 minutes
Thighs, boneless	170°F	10–12 minutes
Breasts, bone-in	165°F	30–35 minutes
Breasts, boneless	160°F	10–12 minutes
Cornish game hens, halved	170°F	35–45 minutes

Beer-Can Chicken

Your favorite brew keeps this chicken moist and juicy. If you're using a charcoal grill, add ten charcoal briquettes per side if cooking time is more than 1 hour.

Prep: 15 minutes plus standing   Grill: 1 hour

- 3 tablespoons paprika
- 1 tablespoon sugar
- 1 tablespoon salt
- 2 teaspoons coarsely ground black pepper
- 1 teaspoon onion powder
- 1 teaspoon garlic powder
- 1 teaspoon ground red pepper (cayenne)
- 2 whole chickens (about 3½ pounds each)
- 2 cans (12 ounces each) beer

1. Prepare charcoal fire for covered indirect-heat grilling with drip pan as manufacturer directs or preheat gas grill for covered indirect grilling over medium heat.

2. In cup, combine paprika, sugar, salt, black pepper, onion powder, garlic powder, and ground red pepper.

3. Remove giblets and necks from chickens. Rinse chickens inside and out with cold running water and drain well; pat dry with paper towels. Sprinkle 1 tablespoon spice mixture inside cavity of each chicken. Rub remaining spice mixture all over chickens.

4. Wipe beer cans clean. Open cans; pour ½ cup beer from each can and reserve for another use. With church key, make four more holes in top of each can. With partially filled can on flat surface, hold 1 chicken upright, with opening of body cavity down, and slide chicken over top of beer can so can fits inside cavity. Repeat with remaining chicken and can.

5. With large spatula, transfer chickens to center of grill rack, keeping cans upright. (If using charcoal, place chickens over drip pan.) Spread chicken legs to balance chickens on rack. Cover grill and cook chickens until juices run clear when thickest part of thigh is pierced with tip of knife, 1 hour to 1 hour 15 minutes.

6. With tongs and barbecue mitts, remove chickens and cans from grill, being careful not to spill beer. Let chickens stand 10 minutes before lifting from cans. Transfer chickens to large platter or cutting board; discard beer. Makes 8 main-dish servings.

Each serving: About 350 calories, 39g protein, 4g carbohydrate, 19g total fat (5g saturated), 152mg cholesterol, 985mg sodium.

All-American Barbecued Chicken

Our traditional-style barbecue sauce is perfect with grilled chicken, beef, or spareribs. We like to remove the skin from the chicken; it reduces the chance of flare-ups.

Prep: 1 hour   Grill: 40 minutes

- 2 tablespoons olive oil
- 1 large onion (12 ounces), chopped
- 2 cans (15 ounces each) tomato sauce
- 1 cup red wine vinegar
- ½ cup light (mild) molasses
- ¼ cup Worcestershire sauce
- ⅓ cup packed brown sugar
- ¾ teaspoon ground red pepper (cayenne)
- 2 chickens (3½ pounds each), each cut into quarters and skin removed from all but wings, if desired

1. In nonstick 10-inch skillet, heat oil over medium heat. Add onion and cook until tender, about 5 minutes. Stir in tomato sauce, vinegar, molasses, Worcestershire, brown sugar, and ground red pepper; heat to boiling over high heat. Reduce heat to medium-low and cook, stirring occasionally, until sauce has thickened slightly, about 45 minutes. (Makes about 3½ cups sauce.) If not using sauce right away, cover and refrigerate to use within 2 weeks.

2. Prepare outdoor grill for covered direct grilling over medium heat.

3. Reserve 1½ cups sauce to serve with chicken. Place chicken on grill, cover and cook turning once, 20 to 25 minutes. Generously brush chicken with some of remaining barbecue sauce and cook, brushing frequently with sauce and turning chicken often, until juices run clear when thickest part of chicken is pierced with tip of knife, about 20 minutes longer. Serve with reserved sauce. Makes 8 main-dish servings.

Each serving without additional sauce, without skin: About 370 calories, 42g protein, 21g carbohydrate, 13g total fat (3g saturated), 127mg cholesterol, 543mg sodium.

Each ¼ cup sauce: About 99 calories, 1g protein, 20g carbohydrate, 2g total fat (0g saturated), 0mg cholesterol, 422mg sodium.

Ginger-Grilled Chicken for a Crowd

When you have a crowd to feed at a backyard bash, try this honey-and-ginger party pleaser.

Prep: 10 minutes plus overnight to marinate
Grill/Broil: 35 minutes

- 1¼ cups soy sauce
- ¾ cup honey
- ¼ cup fresh lemon juice
- 2 tablespoons vegetable oil
- 2 tablespoons minced, peeled fresh ginger
- 2 garlic cloves, crushed with garlic press
- 3 chickens (3 pounds each), each cut into quarters

1. In small bowl, combine soy sauce, honey, lemon juice, oil, ginger, and garlic until well blended. Divide chicken and marinade among three zip-tight plastic bags, turning chicken to coat; place in 15" by 9" baking dish. Seal bags, pressing out as much air as possible. Refrigerate chicken overnight to marinate.

2. Prepare outdoor grill for covered direct grilling over medium heat.

3. Remove chicken from marinade; discard marinade. Place chicken on grill, cover and cook until golden brown, about 5 minutes per side. Move chicken to perimeter of grill (where it is cooler); cover and cook until juices run clear when thickest part of chicken is pierced with tip of knife, about 25 minutes longer.

To broil in oven: Marinate chicken as in Step 1. Preheat broiler. Place chicken, skin side down, on rack in large broiling pan. (Chicken may have to be broiled in batches.) Place pan in broiler 8 to 10 inches from heat source. Broil chicken until golden brown, about 20 minutes. Turn chicken skin side up; broil, brushing occasionally with marinade, until juices run clear when thickest part of chicken is pierced with tip of knife, about 20 minutes longer. Makes 12 main-dish servings.

Each serving: About 410 calories, 42g protein, 10g carbohydrate, 22g total fat (6g saturated), 132mg cholesterol, 988mg sodium.

Chicken with Gremolata Salsa

Instead of the usual salsa, we use gremolata, a piquant combination of parsley, lemon peel, and garlic, along with sun-ripened tomatoes to flavor the chicken. For something a little different, try grated orange peel instead of the lemon, and basil instead of the parsley. If you like, remove the skin from the chicken and brush the quarters with one tablespoon of oil before cooking to lighten the dish.

Prep: 15 minutes Grill: 40 minutes

- 4 ripe medium tomatoes, cut into ¼-inch pieces
- 2 tablespoons finely chopped fresh parsley
- 1 teaspoon freshly grated lemon peel
- 1 small garlic clove, minced
- 1 teaspoon olive oil
- 1 teaspoon salt
- ½ teaspoon coarsely ground black pepper
- 1 whole chicken (about 3½ pounds), cut into quarters

1. Prepare outdoor grill for covered direct grilling over medium heat.

2. Meanwhile, prepare salsa: In small bowl, combine tomatoes, parsley, lemon peel, garlic, oil, ½ teaspoon salt, and ¼ teaspoon pepper; set aside. Makes about 3 cups.

3. Sprinkle chicken with remaining ½ teaspoon salt and ¼ teaspoon pepper. Place chicken on grill rack, cover and cook 20 minutes. Turn chicken and cook until juices run clear when thickest part of chicken is pierced with tip of knife, 20 to 25 minutes longer. Serve chicken with salsa. Makes 4 main-dish servings.

Each serving: About 460 calories, 49g protein, 6g carbohydrate, 25g total fat (7g saturated), 154mg cholesterol, 740mg sodium.

Citrus-Sage Chicken

Sage makes an excellent addition to a garden or window box. It doesn't require much attention, and it grows more lush and beautiful each year. At summer's end, hang it upside down in bunches in a cool, dark place to dry.

Prep: 25 minutes plus marinating Grill: 30 minutes

- 2 large oranges
- 2 large lemons
- ¼ cup chopped fresh sage plus additional whole leaves
- 2 tablespoons olive oil
- 2 teaspoons salt
- ¾ teaspoon coarsely ground black pepper
- 2 chickens (3½ pounds each), each cut into 8 pieces and skin removed from all but wings

1. From oranges, grate 1 tablespoon peel and squeeze 3 tablespoons juice. From lemons, grate 1 tablespoon peel and squeeze 3 tablespoons juice.

2. In large bowl, with wire whisk, combine orange and lemon peels and juices, chopped sage, oil, salt, and pepper. Add chicken, turning to coat. Cover and refrigerate chicken 2 hours to marinate, turning three or four times.

3. Prepare outdoor grill for covered direct grilling over medium heat.

4. Place chicken, meat side down, on grill, cover and cook 20 minutes. Turn chicken and cook until juices run clear when thickest part of chicken is pierced with tip of knife, 10 to 15 minutes longer.

5. To serve, arrange chicken on warm platter; garnish with sage leaves. Makes 8 main-dish servings.

Each serving: About 307 calories, 41g protein, 2g carbohydrate, 14g total fat (3g saturated), 127mg cholesterol, 705mg sodium.

Tandoori-Style Grilled Chicken

A yogurt marinade seasoned with aromatic Indian spices keeps skinless chicken moist and succulent and provides lots of flavor without extra fat.

Prep: 10 minutes plus marinating   Grill: 20 minutes

- 1 tablespoon paprika, preferably sweet Hungarian
- ½ teaspoon ground cinnamon
- ½ teaspoon ground coriander
- ½ teaspoon ground cumin
- ¼ teaspoon ground cardamom
- 1 cup (8 ounces) plain lowfat yogurt
- 2 tablespoons fresh lemon juice
- 1 tablespoon olive oil
- ½ small onion, cut into quarters
- 2 garlic cloves
- 1 tablespoon sliced pickled jalapeño chile or diced fresh jalapeño chile with seeds
- 1 tablespoon sliced, peeled fresh ginger
- ½ teaspoon salt
- 1 chicken (3½ pounds), cut into 8 pieces and skin removed from all but wings
  lemon wedges (optional)

1. In 6-inch skillet, heat paprika, cinnamon, coriander, cumin, and cardamom over low heat until very fragrant, about 3 minutes. Transfer spices to blender. Add yogurt, lemon juice, oil, onion, garlic, jalapeño, ginger, and salt; puree until smooth.

2. Make several ¼-inch-deep slashes in each chicken piece. Place chicken in ziptight plastic bag, pour in yogurt mixture, and turn chicken to coat. Seal bag, pressing out as much air as possible. Refrigerate chicken 1 to 3 hours to marinate, turning once or twice.

3. Lightly grease grill rack. Prepare outdoor grill for covered direct grilling over medium heat.

4. Place chicken on grill over medium heat, cover and cook, turning chicken every 5 minutes, until juices run clear when thickest part of chicken is pierced with tip of knife, 20 to 25 minutes. Transfer to warm platter and serve with lemon wedges, if desired. Makes 4 main-dish servings.

Each serving: About 301 calories, 44g protein, 7g carbohydrate, 10g total fat (2g saturated), 136mg cholesterol, 466mg sodium.

GRILLED CHICKEN BREASTS

Prepare outdoor grill for direct grilling over medium heat. Place 4 medium skinless, boneless chicken breast halves (1¼ pounds) between sheets of plastic wrap and pound thick portion so the breasts are an even thickness. In medium bowl, toss chicken with 1 tablespoon olive oil, ¼ teaspoon salt, and ¼ teaspoon freshly ground pepper.

Oil grill rack and place chicken on grill; cook 5 minutes, turning once and cooking 4 to 5 minutes longer, or until juices run clear when chicken is pierced with tip of knife. Makes 4 main-dish servings.

Grilled Chicken Breasts with Lemon and Rosemary
Prepare grill and pound chicken breasts. From 2 lemons, grate 2 teaspoons peel, and squeeze 3 tablespoons juice. In bowl, combine lemon peel, lemon juice, 1 tablespoon chopped fresh rosemary, 1 finely chopped garlic clove, ½ teaspoon salt, and ¼ teaspoon freshly ground pepper. Add chicken breasts to bowl, turning to coat. Grill as directed above, brushing with remaining mixture.

Grilled Chicken Breasts with Cumin, Coriander, and Lime
Prepare grill and pound chicken breasts. In bowl, whisk 3 tablespoons fresh lime juice, 2 tablespoons olive oil, 1 teaspoon ground cumin, 1 teaspoon ground coriander, 1 teaspoon sugar, 1 teaspoon salt, and ⅛ teaspoon ground red pepper (cayenne). Add chicken, turning to coat. Grill as directed above, brushing with remaining lime mixture halfway through cooking.

Grilled Chicken Breasts with Tomato-Olive Relish
In small bowl, combine 2 medium tomatoes, chopped, ¼ cup coarsely chopped pitted Kalamata olives, 2 tablespoons finely chopped red onion, 2 tablespoons drained capers, 1 teaspoon olive oil, and 1 teaspoon red wine vinegar. Prepare chicken as directed above. Serve chicken topped with tomato mixture.

Jamaican Jerk Chicken Kabobs

Originally, jerk seasoning was only used to season pork shoulder, which was "jerked" apart into shreds before serving. Nowadays, this very popular power-packed seasoning rub is enjoyed on fish and chicken as well.

Prep: 15 minutes plus marinating Grill: 10 minutes

- 2 green onions, chopped
- 1 jalapeño chile, seeded and minced
- 1 tablespoon minced, peeled fresh ginger
- 2 tablespoons white wine vinegar
- 2 tablespoons Worcestershire sauce
- 3 teaspoons vegetable oil
- 1 teaspoon ground allspice
- 1 teaspoon dried thyme
- ½ teaspoon plus ⅛ teaspoon salt
- 1 pound skinless, boneless chicken breast halves, cut into 12 pieces
- 1 red pepper, cut into 1-inch pieces
- 1 green pepper, cut into 1-inch pieces
- 4 metal skewers

1. In blender or in food processor with knife blade attached, process green onions, jalapeño, ginger, vinegar, Worcestershire, 2 teaspoons oil, allspice, thyme, and ½ teaspoon salt until paste forms.

2. Place chicken in small bowl or in zip tight plastic bag and add green-onion mixture, turning to coat chicken. Cover bowl or seal bag and refrigerate chicken 1 hour to marinate.

3. Meanwhile, in small bowl, toss red and green peppers with remaining 1 teaspoon oil and remaining ⅛ teaspoon salt.

4. Prepare outdoor grill for direct grilling over medium heat. Alternately thread chicken and pepper pieces on each skewer.

5. Place kabobs on grill over medium heat. Brush kabobs with any remaining marinade. Cook kabobs 5 minutes; turn and cook until chicken loses its pink color throughout, about 5 minutes longer. Makes 4 main-dish servings.

Each serving: About 181 calories, 27g protein, 6g carbohydrate, 5g total fat (1g saturated), 66mg cholesterol, 525mg sodium.

Grilled Chicken Breasts Saltimbocca

In Italian, *saltimbocca* means "jump in your mouth" and these irresistible prosciutto-and-sage–topped chicken breasts will do just that. One note of caution: Don't slice the prosciutto paper-thin or it could burn.

Prep: 10 minutes Grill: 10 minutes

- 4 medium skinless, boneless chicken breast halves (1¼ pounds)
- ⅛ teaspoon salt
- ⅛ teaspoon ground black pepper
- 12 fresh sage leaves
- 4 large slices prosciutto (4 ounces)

1. Prepare outdoor grill for covered direct grilling over medium heat.

2. Sprinkle chicken with salt and pepper. Place 3 sage leaves on each breast half. Place 1 prosciutto slice on top of each breast half, tucking in edges if necessary; secure with toothpicks.

3. Place chicken, prosciutto side down, on grill, cover and cook 5 to 6 minutes. Turn and grill until chicken loses its pink color throughout, 5 to 6 minutes longer. Makes 4 main-dish servings.

Each serving: About 223 calories, 41g protein, 0g carbohydrate, 6g total fat (1g saturated), 105mg cholesterol, 690mg sodium.

Grilled Chicken Breasts Saltimbocca

Curried Chicken with Mango and Cantaloupe Slaw

Curried Chicken with Mango and Cantaloupe Slaw

Here, curry, crystallized ginger, and crushed red pepper bring out the full sweet flavor of fresh fruit.

Prep: 25 minutes plus marinating   Grill: 10 minutes

- 1 to 2 limes
- 1 container (6 ounces) plain lowfat yogurt
- ¾ teaspoon curry powder
- ¼ cup chopped crystallized ginger
- 1 teaspoon salt
- ¼ teaspoon crushed red pepper
- 4 medium skinless, boneless chicken breast halves (about 1¼ pounds)
- ½ small cantaloupe, rind removed, cut into julienne strips (2 cups)
- 1 large mango, peeled and cut into julienne strips (2 cups)
- ½ cup loosely packed fresh cilantro leaves, chopped
- 1 head Boston lettuce
  lime wedges (optional)

1. Prepare outdoor grill for covered direct grilling over medium heat.

2. From limes, grate ½ teaspoon peel and squeeze 2 tablespoons juice. In large bowl, combine 1 tablespoon lime juice and ¼ teaspoon lime peel with yogurt, curry powder, 2 tablespoons ginger, ¾ teaspoon salt, and ⅛ teaspoon crushed red pepper and whisk until blended. Add chicken, turning to coat with marinade. Cover and let stand 15 minutes at room temperature or 30 minutes in refrigerator, turning occasionally.

3. Prepare slaw: In medium bowl, with rubber spatula, gently stir cantaloupe and mango with cilantro, remaining 2 tablespoons ginger, 1 tablespoon lime juice, ¼ teaspoon lime peel, ¼ teaspoon salt, and ⅛ teaspoon crushed red pepper; set aside. Makes about 4 cups.

4. Grease grill rack. Remove chicken from marinade; discard marinade. Place chicken on grill. Cover and cook chicken, turning once, until juices run clear when thickest part of breast is pierced with tip of knife, 10 to 12 minutes. Transfer chicken to cutting board; cool slightly to set juices for easier slicing, then cut into long, thin slices.

5. To serve, divide lettuce leaves among 4 dinner plates; top with chicken and slaw. Serve with lime wedges, if you like. Makes 4 main-dish servings.

Each serving with lettuce: About 205 calories, 34g protein, 5g carbohydrate, 4g total fat (1g saturated), 92mg cholesterol, 330mg sodium.

Each ½ cup slaw: About 50 calories, 1g protein, 13g carbohydrate, 0g total fat, 0mg cholesterol, 150mg sodium.

Thai Chicken Saté

Chicken marinated in curried coconut milk is teamed with pickled cucumbers and creamy peanut sauce.

Prep: 45 minutes   Grill: 5 minutes

- 1 English (seedless) cucumber, cut crosswise into thin slices
- 1½ teaspoons salt
- 1 tablespoon Thai green curry paste
- ¼ cup plus ⅓ cup well-stirred unsweetened coconut milk (not cream of coconut)
- 4 medium skinless, boneless chicken breast halves (about 1¼ pounds), each cut diagonally into 6 strips
- ¼ cup creamy peanut butter
- 2 teaspoons soy sauce
- 1 teaspoon packed dark brown sugar
- ⅛ teaspoon ground red pepper (cayenne)
- 1 tablespoon hot water
- 1¼ cups rice vinegar
- 3 tablespoons granulated sugar
- 2 medium shallots, thinly sliced
- 1 jalapeño chile, seeded and minced
- 12 (12-inch) metal skewers

1. In medium bowl, toss cucumber with salt; let stand 30 minutes at room temperature.

2. In another bowl, stir curry paste and ¼ cup coconut milk until blended. Add chicken and turn to coat. Let stand 15 minutes at room temperature, stirring occasionally.

3. Prepare outdoor grill for covered direct grilling over medium heat.

4. Meanwhile, prepare peanut sauce: In small bowl, with wire whisk, mix peanut butter, soy sauce, brown sugar, ground red pepper, remaining ⅓ cup coconut milk, and hot water until blended and smooth. Transfer sauce to serving bowl. Makes about ⅔ cup.

5. Drain cucumber, discarding liquid in bowl. Pat cucumber dry with paper towels. Return cucumber to bowl. Add vinegar, granulated sugar, shallots, and jalapeño; toss to combine. Cover and refrigerate until ready to serve.

6. Thread 2 chicken strips, accordion-style, on each of 12 metal skewers; discard marinade. Place skewers on grill, cover grill and cook, turning skewers once, just until chicken loses its pink color throughout, 5 to 8 minutes. Makes 4 main-dish servings.

7. Arrange skewers on platter. Serve with peanut sauce and cucumbers.

Each serving without peanut sauce: About 260 calories, 34g protein, 15g carbohydrate, 6g total fat (3g saturated), 90mg cholesterol, 525mg sodium.

CHICKEN AND BEEF SATÉ

Here's another tasty recipe for this great party dish: Cut 1 pound skinless, boneless chicken breast halves lengthwise into ¾-inch-wide strips; place in bowl. Holding knife almost parallel to work surface, slice 1 boneless beef top sirloin steak, 1 (1-inch-thick) boneless beef top sirloin steak (about 1¼ pounds) crosswise into thin strips; place in separate bowl.

From 2 large limes, grate 2 teaspoons peel and squeeze 2 tablespoons juice. In small bowl, mix lime peel and juice, ¼ cup soy sauce, 1 tablespoon grated, peeled fresh ginger, 2 teaspoons sugar, and 2 garlic cloves, crushed with garlic press. Pour half of sauce over chicken and half over beef; stir to coat. Refrigerate 30 minutes.

Prepare outdoor grill for direct grilling over medium heat. Separately thread chicken strips and beef strips, accordion-style, onto metal skewers. Place skewers on hot grill rack and grill, turning once, until just cooked through, 3 to 7 minutes. Serve with peanut sauce, if desired (see Thai Chicken Saté.).

Portuguese Mixed Grill

This dish, with its vinegar marinade and use of chorizo sausage, is a good example of typical Portuguese cooking. The Portuguese use vinegar marinades to tenderize tough cuts of meat and poultry. Our chicken rarely needs tenderizing, but we like the zesty flavor.

Prep: 30 minutes plus marinating Grill: 25 minutes

- ¼ cup red wine vinegar
- 2 tablespoons olive oil
- 2 tablespoons chopped fresh oregano or 1 teaspoon dried oregano
- 1 teaspoon salt
- ½ teaspoon coarsely ground black pepper
- 8 medium bone-in skinless chicken thighs (1¾ pounds), fat removed
- 3 medium red onions, each cut into 6 wedges
- 3 long metal skewers
- 12 ounces fully cooked chorizo sausage links, each cut crosswise in half
- ⅔ cup assorted olives such as Kalamata, cracked green, and picholine

1. Prepare outdoor grill for direct grilling over medium heat.

2. In bowl, combine vinegar, 1 tablespoon oil, 1 tablespoon oregano, salt, and pepper. Add chicken, turning to coat. Cover and refrigerate 30 minutes to marinate, no longer.

3. Thread onion wedges onto each metal skewer. Place onion skewers on grill; brush with remaining 1 tablespoon oil and grill 5 minutes.

4. Place chicken on grill and cook, turning onions and chicken once, until onions are tender and juices run clear when thickest part of chicken is pierced with tip of knife, about 20 minutes longer.

5. About 10 minutes before onions and chicken are done, place chorizo pieces on grill and cook, turning occasionally, until lightly browned and heated through.

6. To serve, remove onion wedges from skewers and arrange on warm platter with chicken and chorizo. Scatter olives on top and sprinkle with remaining 1 tablespoon oregano. Makes 6 main-dish servings.

Each serving: About 482 calories, 34g protein, 11g carbohydrate, 33g total fat (10g saturated), 130mg cholesterol, 1,495mg sodium.

Portuguese Mixed Grill

PEPPERCORNS

Test Kitchen Tip

Pepper has been used to flavor foods for hundreds of years. Peppercorn berries grow in clusters on a plant that is native to India and Indonesia. Whether peppercorns end up being black, white, or green depends upon how they are processed. Black peppercorns are picked when the berries are not quite ripe, then dried until shriveled and brownish black. White peppercorns are picked ripe, then skinned and dried. They are smaller and milder than black peppercorns. Green peppercorns are soft, underripe berries and are usually processed in brine. They have a fresh, mild flavor. Whole black and white peppercorns can be stored in a cool, dark place for up to a year.

Port and Black Currant–Glazed Chicken Thighs

A robust combination of Port, Dijon mustard, and fresh tarragon makes a quick tasty marinade for these chicken thighs. A last-minute brush with a black currant–jelly glaze adds a sweet note that complements the flavors of the marinade.

Prep: 15 minutes plus marinating   Grill: 25 minutes

- ⅓ cup ruby Port
- ¼ cup Dijon mustard
- ½ teaspoon salt
- ¼ teaspoon coarsely ground black pepper
- 2 tablespoons chopped fresh tarragon
- 8 medium bone-in chicken thighs (about 2½ pounds), skin removed
- ¼ cup black currant jelly

1. Prepare outdoor grill for covered direct grilling over medium heat.

2. In large bowl, with wire whisk, mix Port, mustard, salt, pepper, and 1 tablespoon tarragon until well blended. Transfer 3 tablespoons marinade to small bowl; set aside.

3. Add chicken to marinade in large bowl; turn until evenly coated. Cover bowl and let stand 15 minutes at room temperature or 30 minutes in refrigerator.

4. Meanwhile, add black currant jelly to marinade in small bowl and whisk until blended; set aside.

5. Place chicken on grill, cover and cook, turning once, until juices run clear when thickest part of thigh is pierced with tip of knife, about 25 minutes. Brush jelly mixture all over chicken; grill, turning once, until glazed, 1 to 2 minutes longer. Transfer chicken to platter; sprinkle with remaining 1 tablespoon tarragon. Makes 4 main-dish servings.

Each serving: About 280 calories, 28g protein, 15g carbohydrate, 12g total fat (3g saturated), 99mg cholesterol, 290mg sodium.

Peking Chicken Roll-Ups

The traditional Chinese recipe for duck is quite labor-intensive and takes several days to make. Our version, prepared in minutes, is made with grilled boneless chicken thighs and served in flour tortillas with hoisin sauce.

Prep: 25 minutes   Grill: 10 minutes

- 8 (8-inch) flour tortillas
- 2 tablespoons honey
- 2 tablespoons soy sauce
- 1 tablespoon grated, peeled fresh ginger
- ⅛ teaspoon ground red pepper (cayenne)
- 2 garlic cloves, crushed with garlic press
- 6 skinless, boneless chicken thighs (about 1¼ pounds)
- 1 teaspoon vegetable oil
- ¼ cup hoisin sauce
- ½ English (seedless) cucumber, cut into 2" by ¼" matchstick strips
- 2 green onions, thinly sliced

1. Prepare outdoor grill for direct grilling over medium-high heat.

2. Stack tortillas and wrap in foil. In small bowl, mix honey, soy sauce, ginger, ground red pepper, and garlic until blended. Set aside tortillas and honey mixture.

3. Coat chicken with oil and place on grill and cook, turning once, 5 minutes. Brush chicken all over with honey mixture and cook, turning once, until juices run clear when thickest part of thigh is pierced with tip of knife, 5 to 7 minutes longer.

4. While chicken is cooking, place foil-wrapped tortillas on same grill rack and heat until warm, 3 to 5 minutes.

5. Transfer chicken to cutting board and cut into thin slices. Spread hoisin sauce on one side of each tortilla. Top each with chicken, cucumber, and green onions; roll up to serve. Makes 4 main-dish servings.

Each serving: About 400 calories, 27g protein, 50g carbohydrate, 10g total fat (3g saturated), 75mg cholesterol, 1,255mg sodium.

Summer Squash and Chicken

For this easy summer supper, simply toss the sliced squash on the grill along with the marinated chicken. You can use either zucchini or yellow squash alone, or a combination of the two.

Prep: 15 minutes plus marinating   Grill: 10 minutes

- 1 lemon
- 1 tablespoon olive oil
- ½ teaspoon salt
- ¼ teaspoon coarsely ground black pepper
- 4 medium skinless, boneless chicken thighs (about 1¼ pounds)
- 4 medium yellow summer squash and/or zucchini (about 6 ounces each), each cut lengthwise into 4 wedges
- ¼ cup snipped fresh chives

1. Prepare outdoor grill for covered direct grilling over medium heat.

2. From lemon, grate 1 tablespoon peel and squeeze 3 tablespoons juice. In medium bowl, combine lemon peel and juice, oil, salt, and pepper and whisk until blended. Transfer 2 tablespoons marinade to cup and set aside.

3. Add chicken thighs to bowl with marinade; turn to evenly coat. Cover and let stand 15 minutes at room temperature or 30 minutes in the refrigerator.

4. Remove chicken from marinade; discard marinade. Place chicken and squash on grill, cover and cook, turning chicken and squash once, until juices run clear when thickest part of thigh is pierced with tip of knife and squash is tender and browned, 10 to 12 minutes, transferring pieces to platter as they are done.

5. Transfer chicken and squash to cutting board. Cut chicken into 1-inch-wide strips; cut each squash wedge crosswise in half.

6. To serve, on large platter, toss squash with reserved marinade, then toss with chicken and sprinkle with chives. Makes 4 main-dish servings.

Each serving: About 255 calories, 29g protein, 8g carbohydrate, 8g total fat (3g saturated), 101mg cholesterol, 240mg sodium.

Summer Squash and Chicken

Charcoal-Grilled Whole Turkey

Grilled turkey has become so popular that some cooks serve it for Thanksgiving, but keep in mind that a 12-pound bird is the largest that comfortably fits on a grill. Don't be concerned about the pink color of the meat under the skin—it's caused by the smoke.

Prep: 15 minutes   Grill: 2 hours 15 minutes to 3 hours

- 1 turkey (12 pounds)
- 2 tablespoons vegetable oil
- 2 teaspoons dried sage
- 2 teaspoons dried thyme
- 2 teaspoons salt
- ½ teaspoon ground black pepper

1. Prepare grill: In bottom of covered charcoal grill, with vents open and grill uncovered, ignite 60 charcoal briquettes (not self-starting). Allow to burn until all coals are covered with thin coat of gray ash, about 30 minutes. With tongs, move hot briquettes to two opposite sides of grill and arrange in two piles. Place sturdy disposable foil pan (13" by 9" by 2") in center of grill between piles of coals to catch drips.

2. Remove giblets and neck from turkey; reserve for another use. Rinse turkey inside and out with cold running water and drain well; pat dry with paper towels.

3. Fasten neck skin to turkey back with skewers. Tie legs and tail together with string. Secure wings to body with string, if desired. In cup, combine oil, sage, thyme, salt, and pepper; use to rub on outside of turkey.

4. Place turkey, breast side up, on rack over foil pan. Cover grill and cook 2 hours 15 minutes to 3 hours, adding 8 or 9 briquettes to each side of grill every hour to maintain grill temperature of 325°F on oven or grill thermometer. Turkey is done when temperature on meat thermometer inserted in thickest part of thigh, reaches 175° to 180°F and juices run clear when thickest part of thigh is pierced with tip of knife.

5. When turkey is done, transfer to warm platter; let stand 15 minutes to set juices for easier carving. Skim and discard fat from drippings in bottom of pan; serve drippings with turkey. Makes 12 main-dish servings.

Each serving: About 524 calories, 73g protein, 0g carbohydrate, 23g total fat (7g saturated), 212mg cholesterol, 575mg sodium.

Spiced Grilled Turkey Breast

Soaking a whole turkey breast overnight in a spiced salt solution (brine) produces exceptionally tender and flavorful meat. You can also brine a whole chicken before roasting. Serve with Peach Salsa (page 438).

Prep: 35 minutes plus brining and standing
Grill: 25 minutes

Spiced Turkey

- ¼ **cup sugar**
- ¼ **cup kosher salt**
- 2 **tablespoons cracked black pepper**
- 2 **tablespoons ground ginger**
- 1 **tablespoon ground cinnamon**
- 1 **whole boneless turkey breast (about 4 pounds), skin removed and breast cut in half**
- 4 **garlic cloves, crushed with side of chef's knife**
  Peach Salsa (page 438)

Honey Glaze

- 2 **tablespoons honey**
- 2 **tablespoons Dijon mustard**
- 1 **chipotle chile in adobo, minced**
- 1 **teaspoon balsamic vinegar**

1. Prepare turkey: In 2-quart saucepan, heat sugar, salt, pepper, ginger, cinnamon, and *1 cup water* to boiling over high heat. Reduce heat to low; simmer 2 minutes. Remove from heat; stir in *3 cups ice water*.

2. Place turkey breast in large zip-tight plastic bag; add brine and garlic. Seal bag, pressing out excess air. Place bag in bowl and refrigerate breast, turning occasionally, 24 hours.

3. Prepare outdoor grill for covered direct grilling over medium heat.

4. Meanwhile, prepare glaze: In small bowl, stir honey, mustard, chipotle, and vinegar until blended; set aside.

5. Remove turkey from bag; discard brine and garlic. With paper towels, pat turkey dry and brush off most of pepper. With long-handled basting brush, oil grill rack. Place turkey on grill, cover and cook turkey, turning once, 20 minutes. Brush turkey with glaze and cook, basting and turning frequently, until temperature on meat thermometer inserted into thickest part of breast reaches 165°F, 5 to 10 minutes longer (depending on thickness of breast). Internal temperature will rise 5°F upon standing. Transfer turkey to cutting board and let rest 10 minutes to set juices for easier slicing.

6. While turkey rests, prepare Peach Salsa.

7. Serve turkey hot, or cover and refrigerate to serve cold. Accompany with salsa. Makes 12 main-dish servings.

Each serving turkey: About 170 calories, 34g protein, 4g carbohydrate, 1g total fat (0g saturated), 94mg cholesterol, 555mg sodium.

Grilled Whole Sea Bass with Lemon and Herbs

The firm white flesh of sea bass holds up well on the grill. If you can't get whole sea bass, substitute red snapper or striped bass.

Prep: 5 minutes   Grill: 16 minutes

- 2 whole sea bass (1½ pounds each), cleaned and scaled
- 1½ teaspoons salt
- 4 thin lemon slices, each cut in half
- 8 oregano or rosemary sprigs
- 1 tablespoon olive oil

1. Prepare outdoor grill for covered direct grilling over medium heat.

2. Rinse bass inside and out with cold running water; pat dry with paper towels. Make three diagonal slashes on each side of fish, cutting almost to bone. Sprinkle fish inside and out with salt. Place lemon slices and oregano sprigs in fish cavities. Rub oil all over bass.

3. Place bass on grill, cover and cook until just opaque when knife is inserted at backbone, about 8 minutes per side.

4. To serve, slide cake server under front section of top fillet of each fish and lift off fillet; transfer to platter. Slide server under backbone and lift it away from bottom fillet; discard. Slide cake server between bottom fillet and skin and transfer fillet to platter. Makes 4 main-dish servings.

Each serving: About 162 calories, 25g protein, 1g carbohydrate, 6g total fat (1g saturated), 54mg cholesterol, 673mg sodium.

Salmon with Mustard-Dill Sauce

We brought the flavors of Swedish gravlax to the grill. Traditional gravlax is made by marinating raw salmon in a savory mixture of fresh dill, sugar, and salt, then serving it with a sweet mustard sauce.

Prep: 15 minutes   Grill: 8 minutes

Grilled Salmon

- 2 tablespoons sugar
- 1 tablespoon chopped fresh dill
- 2 tablespoons white wine vinegar
- ¾ teaspoon salt
- ¼ teaspoon coarsely ground black pepper
- 4 salmon steaks, each ¾ inch thick (about 6 ounces each)

Mustard-Dill Sauce

- 3 tablespoons chopped fresh dill
- 3 tablespoons Dijon mustard
- 3 tablespoons light mayonnaise
- 2 teaspoons sugar
- 4 teaspoons white wine vinegar
- ¼ teaspoon coarsely ground black pepper

1. Prepare outdoor grill for direct grilling over medium heat.

2. Prepare salmon: In medium bowl, mix sugar, dill, vinegar, salt, and pepper.

3. With tweezers, remove small bones from salmon; add salmon steaks to bowl with sugar mixture, turning each to coat. Let stand at room temperature 10 minutes.

4. Meanwhile, prepare sauce: In small bowl, mix dill, mustard, mayonnaise, sugar, vinegar, and pepper.

5. Place salmon on grill and cook, turning once, until just opaque throughout, 8 to 9 minutes. Serve with mustard sauce. Makes 4 main-dish servings.

Each serving: About 270 calories, 30g protein, 13g carbohydrate, 11g total fat (1g saturated), 80mg cholesterol, 850mg sodium.

Glazed Salmon with Watermelon Salsa

We love blending sweet and spicy flavors, so we added a jalapeño chile to the fruit salsa—with delicious results.

Prep: 20 minutes   Grill: 9 minutes

Watermelon Salsa

- 1 lime
- 4 cups (½-inch cubes) seedless watermelon (from about 2½-pound piece)
- ¼ cup loosely packed fresh mint leaves, chopped
- 2 tablespoons chopped green onions
- 1 small jalapeño chile, seeded and finely chopped (1 tablespoon)

Glazed Salmon

- ¼ cup hoisin sauce
- ½ teaspoon Chinese five-spice powder
- 4 salmon steaks, 1 inch thick (about 6 ounces each)

1. Prepare outdoor grill for covered direct grilling over medium heat.

2. Meanwhile, prepare salsa: From lime, grate 1 teaspoon peel and squeeze 1 tablespoon juice. In serving bowl, toss lime peel and juice with watermelon, mint, green onions, and jalapeño. Makes about 3⅔ cups.

3. In cup, stir hoisin sauce and five-spice powder.

4. Place salmon on grill over medium heat. Brush salmon with half of hoisin mixture. Cover grill and cook salmon 3 minutes. Turn salmon over and brush with remaining hoisin mixture. Cover grill and cook 3 minutes. Turn salmon over again and cook until just opaque throughout, about 3 minutes longer. Serve salmon with salsa. Makes 4 main-dish servings.

Each serving: About 345 calories, 30g protein, 18g carbohydrate, 17g total fat (3g saturated), 81mg cholesterol, 260mg sodium.

Glazed Salmon with Watermelon Salsa

Grilled Spiced Salmon Steaks

Spice rubs are excellent with fresh fish that is not delicately flavored, like salmon.

Prep: 5 minutes   Grill: 8 minutes

- 1 tablespoon chili powder
- 2 teaspoons brown sugar
- 1 teaspoon ground cumin
- 1 teaspoon dried thyme
- 1 teaspoon salt
- 2 teaspoons olive oil
- 4 salmon steaks, ¾ inch thick (8 ounces each) lemon wedges

1. Prepare outdoor grill for covered direct grilling over medium heat. In cup, combine chili powder, brown sugar, cumin, thyme, salt, and oil. Use to rub on both sides of salmon steaks.

2. Place salmon on grill, cover and cook until just opaque throughout, about 4 minutes per side. Serve with lemon wedges. Makes 4 main-dish servings.

Each serving: About 403 calories, 40g protein, 4g carbohydrate, 24g total fat (5g saturated), 118mg cholesterol, 721mg sodium.

Miso-Glazed Salmon with Edamame Salad

Japanese flavors predominate in this very healthy, tasty meal.

Prep: 30 minutes   Grill: 10 minutes

Edamame Salad

- 1 bag (16 ounces) frozen shelled edamame (green soybeans) or frozen baby lima beans
- ¼ cup seasoned rice vinegar
- 1 tablespoon vegetable oil
- 1 teaspoon sugar
- ¾ teaspoon salt
- ⅛ teaspoon ground black pepper
- 1 bunch radishes (8 ounces), each cut in half and thinly sliced
- 1 cup loosely packed fresh cilantro leaves, chopped

Miso-Glazed Salmon

- 2 tablespoons red miso
- 1 green onion, minced
- 1 tablespoon grated, peeled fresh ginger
- 1 teaspoon brown sugar
- ⅛ teaspoon ground red pepper (cayenne)
- 1 salmon fillet (1½ pounds), with skin

1. Prepare outdoor grill for direct grilling over medium-low heat.

2. Prepare salad: Cook edamame as label directs; drain. Rinse edamame with cold running water to stop cooking and drain again.

3. In medium bowl, whisk vinegar, oil, sugar, salt, and pepper until blended. Add edamame, radishes, and cilantro and toss until evenly coated. Cover and refrigerate salad up to 1 day if not serving right away. Makes about 4 cups.

4. Prepare salmon: In small bowl, with spoon, mix miso, green onion, ginger, brown sugar, and ground red pepper. Use to rub on flesh side of salmon.

5. Place salmon, skin side down, on grill and cook until just opaque throughout, 10 to 12 minutes. Serve with edamame salad. Makes 4 main-dish servings.

Each serving salmon: About 280 calories, 29g protein, 3g carbohydrate, 16g total fat (3g saturated), 80mg cholesterol, 450mg sodium.

Each 1 cup salad: About 220 calories, 16g protein, 23g carbohydrate, 8g total fat (0g saturated), 0mg cholesterol, 1,020mg sodium.

Miso-Glazed Salmon with Edamame Salad

Salmon with Dill and Caper Sauce

Anchovy paste is available in tubes in the dairy section of many supermarkets. If you can't find anchovy paste, substitute two anchovy fillets. Mash the fillets with the flat side of a knife until they're the consistency of a smooth paste.

Prep: 10 minutes   Grill: 10 minutes

- ¼ cup drained capers, chopped
- 2 tablespoons chopped fresh dill
- 2 tablespoons fresh lemon juice
- 2 teaspoons sugar
- 2 teaspoons anchovy paste
- 1 salmon fillet (2 pounds), with skin
- ¼ teaspoon salt
  lemon wedges

1. Prepare outdoor grill for direct grilling over medium heat.

2. In small bowl, mix capers, dill, lemon juice, sugar, and anchovy paste.

3. With tweezers, remove any bones from salmon; sprinkle with salt. Place salmon in lightly oiled fish basket. Brush all of caper sauce on flesh side only.

4. Place fish basket on grill. Cook salmon, turning once, until just opaque throughout, about 10 minutes. Serve with lemon wedges. Makes 8 main-dish servings.

Each serving: About 210 calories, 22g protein, 2g carbohydrate, 12g total fat (2g saturated), 64mg cholesterol, 395mg sodium.

Swordfish with Balsamic Glaze

Balsamic vinegar blended with brown sugar and reduced to a syrup makes a rich, winelike glaze that is perfect with meaty swordfish. For a delicious variation, serve the fish atop a salad.

Prep: 15 minutes   Grill: 7 minutes

- 2 teaspoons olive oil
- ¼ cup finely chopped shallots
- ½ cup balsamic vinegar
- 2 teaspoons brown sugar
- 2 teaspoons tomato paste
- ¼ teaspoon dried thyme
- ¼ teaspoon salt
- ¼ teaspoon ground black pepper
- 4 swordfish steaks, 1 inch thick (6 ounces each)

1. Prepare outdoor grill for direct grilling over medium-high heat.

2. In 10-inch skillet, heat oil over medium-low heat. Add shallots and cook, stirring occasionally, until tender, about 4 minutes. Add vinegar and brown sugar; heat to boiling over high heat. Boil until liquid has thickened and is syrupy, about 5 minutes. Remove from heat and stir in tomato paste until blended.

3. Sprinkle thyme, salt, and pepper on swordfish. Place fish on grill and cook 4 minutes. Turn swordfish steaks and brush each with glaze; cook until just opaque throughout, 3 to 4 minutes longer. Makes 4 main-dish servings.

Each serving: About 226 calories, 30g protein, 5g carbohydrate, 8g total fat (2g saturated), 59mg cholesterol, 305mg sodium.

Balsamic-Glazed Swordfish with Greens

Prepare fish as directed above. In large bowl, whisk together **2 tablespoons balsamic vinegar, 2 tablespoons extra-virgin olive oil,** and **⅛ teaspoon salt.** Add **2 cups each washed, dried, and torn Bibb and Boston lettuce** and **2 cups sliced Belgian endive;** toss to coat. Arrange greens on dinner plates; top with fish.

Each serving: About 299 calories, 31g protein, 8g carbohydrate, 16g total fat (3g saturated), 59mg cholesterol, 388mg sodium.

Swordfish Kabobs

This is the method of choice for preparing swordfish along the coasts of Turkey. Serve it with steamed rice.

Prep: 25 minutes plus marinating   Grill: 5 minutes

- 1   pound boneless swordfish steak, 1 inch thick
- ½   cup chicken or vegetable broth
- 3   tablespoons fresh lemon juice
- 1   tablespoon olive oil
- 1   very small onion, thinly sliced
- 2   garlic cloves, thinly sliced
- 14   large bay leaves
- ½   teaspoon salt
- ½   teaspoon paprika
- ¼   teaspoon ground coriander
- ⅛   teaspoon ground black pepper
- 12   (7-inch) bamboo skewers
- 12   thin lemon slices, seeded and each cut in half
- 1   tablespoon chopped fresh parsley

1. Remove skin from swordfish and discard. Cut fish into 1-inch cubes.

2. In medium bowl, combine broth, lemon juice, oil, onion, garlic, 2 bay leaves, salt, paprika, coriander, and pepper. Add swordfish and toss to coat. Cover and refrigerate fish 3 hours to marinate, tossing occasionally.

3. Meanwhile, soak remaining 12 bay leaves and bamboo skewers 1 hour in enough *boiling water* to cover. Drain. With kitchen shears, snip each bay leaf crosswise in half.

4. Prepare outdoor grill for covered direct grilling over medium-high heat.

5. Remove swordfish from marinade, reserving marinade. Thread each skewer as follows: ½ bay leaf, 1 swordfish cube, ½ lemon slice, 1 swordfish cube; then repeat once, gently pressing bay leaves, lemon slices, and fish together.

6. Place kabobs on grill, cover and cook, turning kabobs and brushing with marinade during first half of cooking, until fish is just opaque throughout, 5 to 8 minutes.

7. Meanwhile, strain remaining marinade into small saucepan and heat to boiling; boil 3 minutes. Arrange kabobs on platter, drizzle with hot marinade, and sprinkle with parsley. Makes 4 main-dish servings.

Each serving: About 189 calories, 22g protein, 7g carbohydrate, 8g total fat (2g saturated), 42mg cholesterol, 514mg sodium.

Greek-Style Grilled Halibut

Greek cooks have long favored the clean, simple flavors of fresh lemon and oregano with fish. One bite of this, and you'll understand why.

Prep: 10 minutes plus marinating   Grill: 6 minutes

- 1   lemon
- 3   tablespoons olive oil
- 2   garlic cloves, finely chopped
- 2   teaspoons chopped fresh oregano
- ½   teaspoon salt
- 4   halibut steaks, ¾ inch thick (6 ounces each)

1. From lemon, grate 1 teaspoon peel and squeeze 2 tablespoons juice. In large bowl, with wire whisk, whisk lemon peel and juice, oil, garlic, oregano, and salt until mixed. Add halibut steaks, turning each to coat. Cover and refrigerate 1 hour to marinate, turning once or twice.

2. Meanwhile, prepare outdoor grill for covered direct grilling over medium heat.

3. Remove halibut from marinade; discard marinade. Place halibut on grill, cover and cook, brushing with marinade during first half of grilling, until halibut is just opaque throughout, 3 to 4 minutes per side. Makes 4 main-dish servings.

Each serving: About 199 calories, 29g protein, 1g carbohydrate, 8g total fat (1g saturated), 44mg cholesterol, 218mg sodium.

Shrimp Sonoma

Some of the sweetest dried tomatoes we've tried come from the Sonoma Valley in California. Choose dried tomatoes that are plump rather than dry and leathery. Serve shrimp on a bed of couscous seasoned with extra-virgin olive oil.

Prep: 25 minutes   Grill: 8 minutes

- 1 ounce dried tomatoes without salt
- 1 cup boiling water
- 1½ pounds large shrimp
- 2 tablespoons fresh lemon juice
- 2 tablespoons olive oil
- ½ teaspoon salt
- ½ teaspoon crushed red pepper
- 4 (12-inch) metal skewers

1. Place dried tomatoes in small bowl. Pour boiling water over tomatoes; let stand while preparing shrimp.

2. Meanwhile, pull off legs from shrimp. Insert tip of kitchen shears under shell of each shrimp and snip along back to tail, cutting about ¼ inch deep to expose dark vein. Leaving shell on, rinse shrimp to remove vein; pat dry with paper towels. Place shrimp in bowl.

3. Prepare outdoor grill for direct grilling over medium heat. Drain dried tomatoes, reserving ¼ cup soaking liquid.

4. In blender or in food processor with knife blade attached, puree tomatoes, reserved soaking liquid, lemon juice, oil, salt, and crushed red pepper until smooth. Pour mixture over shrimp; toss until shrimp are evenly coated.

5. Thread shrimp onto metal skewers. Place skewers on grill. Cook shrimp, turning skewers occasionally and basting with any remaining dried tomato mixture, until just opaque throughout, 8 to 10 minutes. Makes 6 main-dish servings.

Each serving: About 140 calories, 20g protein, 3g carbohydrate, 5g total fat (1g saturated), 140mg cholesterol, 290mg sodium.

Shrimp Sonoma

Cajun Shrimp with Rémoulade Sauce

This dish takes only four minutes on the fire! To streamline preparation, we added fresh lemon peel to store-bought Cajun seasoning (a blend of garlic, onion, chiles, peppers, and herbs). Seasoning mixes vary among manufacturers, especially with regard to salt content. Add salt to taste if necessary.

Prep: 25 minutes   Grill: 3 minutes

Rémoulade Sauce

- ½ cup light mayonnaise
- 2 tablespoons ketchup
- 2 tablespoons minced celery
- 1 tablespoon Dijon mustard with seeds
- 1 tablespoon minced fresh parsley
- 2 teaspoons fresh lemon juice
- ½ teaspoon Cajun seasoning
- 1 green onion, minced

Cajun Shrimp

- 1 tablespoon Cajun seasoning
- 1 tablespoon olive oil
- 2 teaspoons fresh lemon peel
- 1¼ pounds large shrimp, shelled and deveined, leaving tail part of shell on, if you like (page 193)
  lemon wedges

1. Prepare outdoor grill for direct grilling over medium-high heat.

2. Meanwhile, prepare sauce: In small bowl, mix mayonnaise, ketchup, celery, mustard, parsley, lemon juice, Cajun seasoning, and green onion. Cover and refrigerate up to 3 days if not serving right away. Makes about 1 cup.

3. Prepare shrimp: In medium bowl, mix Cajun seasoning, oil, and lemon peel. Add shrimp to spice mixture and toss until evenly coated.

4. Place shrimp on grill and cook, turning once, until just opaque throughout, 3 to 4 minutes.

5. Transfer shrimp to platter; serve with Rémoulade Sauce and lemon wedges. Makes 4 main-dish servings.

Each serving shrimp: About 155 calories, 24g protein, 2g carbohydrate, 5g total fat (1g saturated), 175mg cholesterol, 575mg sodium.

Each 1 tablespoon sauce: About 30 calories, 0g protein, 2g carbohydrate, 3g total fat (1g saturated), 3mg cholesterol, 95mg sodium.

Grilled Shrimp

Be sure to buy the freshest and most flavorful shrimp you can find for this simple preparation.

Prep: 10 minutes plus marinating   Grill: 5 minutes

- 1 lemon
- 1 tablespoon olive oil
- ¼ teaspoon salt
- ⅛ teaspoon freshly ground pepper
- 4 long metal skewers
- 1 pound large shrimp, shelled and deveined, leaving tail part of shell on, if desired (page 193)

1. Prepare outdoor grill for direct grilling over medium-high heat.

2. From lemon, grate ½ teaspoon peel and squeeze 1 tablespoon juice. In large bowl, whisk lemon peel and juice, oil, salt, and pepper. Add shrimp and toss to coat; let stand 10 minutes to marinate.

3. Thread shrimp on skewers. Place skewers on grill and cook, turning skewers occasionally, until shrimp are just opaque throughout, about 4 minutes. Makes 4 main-dish servings.

Each serving: About 129 calories, 19g protein, 1g carbohydrate, 5g total fat (1g saturated), 140mg cholesterol, 282mg sodium.

GUIDE TO GRILLED VEGETABLES

Preheat grill to medium-high

VEGETABLE (4 SERVINGS)	PREPARATION	SEASONING	GRILLING TIME
8 ears corn	Soak 15 minutes, then remove silk (leave husks on) or remove husks and silk.	Brush with 1 tablespoon oil.	45 minutes 20 minutes, turning occasionally
1½-pound eggplant	Cut crosswise into ½-inch-thick slices.	Brush with ¼ cup oil.	11 to 13 minutes per side
4 heads endive	Cut lengthwise in half.	Brush with 1 tablespoon oil.	10 to 12 minutes per side
2 medium fennel bulbs (1 pound each)	Cut lengthwise into ¼-inch-thick slices.	Brush with 4 teaspoons oil.	6 to 8 minutes per side
6 medium leeks	Remove dark green tops; blanch and cut lengthwise in half.	Toss with 1 tablespoon oil.	11 to 13 minutes per side
8 ounces large white mushrooms	Trim and thread onto skewers.	Brush with 2 teaspoons oil.	20 minutes, turning several times
4 large portobello mushrooms (about 1 pound)	Remove stems.	Brush with 4 teaspoons oil.	15 minutes per side
4 medium red or white onions	Cut crosswise into ½-inch-thick slices; secure with toothpicks.	Brush with 4 teaspoons oil.	12 to 14 minutes per side
2 bunches small green onions	Trim.	Toss with 4 teaspoons oil.	2 to 4 minutes, turning several times
4 red, green, or yellow peppers	Cut lengthwise into quarters.		10 to 12 minutes per side
2 heads radicchio (12 ounces each)	Cut lengthwise into quarters.	Brush with 2 tablespoons oil.	5 minutes per side
4 medium yellow squash or zucchini (8 ounces each)	Cut lengthwise into ¼-inch-thick slices.	Brush with 4 teaspoons oil.	5 minutes per side
4 medium tomatoes (8 ounces each)	Cut crosswise in half.	Brush cut sides with 2 tablespoons oil.	14 to 17 minutes per side
1 pint cherry tomatoes	Thread onto skewers.	Brush with 2 teaspoons oil.	5 to 7 minutes, turning several times

Lemon-Garlic Potato Packet

Whole cloves of garlic grill up butter-soft along with the potatoes. If you like, once the potatoes and garlic are cooked (and while they're still warm), toss them with your favorite vinaigrette for a grilled potato salad.

Prep: 15 minutes   Grill: 30 minutes

2½	pounds red potatoes, not peeled and cut into 1-inch chunks
12	garlic cloves, peeled
2	tablespoons olive oil
1½	teaspoons freshly grated lemon peel
1	teaspoon salt
¼	teaspoon coarsely ground black pepper

1. Prepare outdoor grill for covered direct grilling over medium heat.

2. In large bowl, toss potatoes, garlic, oil, lemon peel, salt, and pepper until potatoes are evenly coated.

3. Layer two 30" by 18" sheets heavy-duty foil to make double-thick sheet. Place potato mixture in center of stacked foil. Bring short ends of foil up and over potatoes; fold several times to seal. Fold remaining sides of foil several times to seal in juices.

4. Place packet on grill, cover and cook, turning packet once halfway through grilling, until potatoes are fork-tender, 30 minutes.

5. Before serving, with kitchen shears, cut an X in top of foil packet to let steam escape, then carefully pull back foil to open. Makes 8 accompaniment servings.

Each serving: About 140 calories, 3g protein, 25g carbohydrate, 4g total fat (1g saturated), 0mg cholesterol, 275mg sodium.

Shallot-and-Herb Potato Packet

Prepare as directed but omit garlic. Add **2 medium shallots,** thinly sliced, and **2 teaspoons minced fresh thyme or ½ teaspoon dried thyme.** Wrap and grill as directed. Sprinkle with ⅓ **cup chopped fresh parsley** before serving.

Each serving: About 140 calories, 3g protein, 25g carbohydrate, 4g total fat (1g saturated), 0mg cholesterol, 280mg sodium.

Grilled Vegetable Stacks

Perfect buffet fare, these colorful vegetable "napoleons" can be served hot, warm, or at room temperature. If you like, grate some Parmesan cheese over each stack before serving or set out in a bowl for self-serve.

Prep: 20 minutes   Grill: 8 minutes

	wooden toothpicks or bamboo skewers
1	medium red onion, cut into ½-inch-thick slices
2	medium zucchini and/or yellow summer squashes, cut diagonally into ½-inch-thick slices
1	large yellow or red pepper, cut lengthwise into quarters
1	medium eggplant, cut diagonally into eight ½-inch-thick slices
3	tablespoons olive oil
½	cup balsamic vinegar
½	teaspoon crushed red pepper
½	teaspoon salt
4	plum tomatoes, each cut lengthwise in half
8	large basil leaves
¾	pound fresh mozzarella cheese, thinly sliced basil sprigs for garnish

1. Prepare outdoor grill for covered direct grilling over medium heat.

2. Soak toothpicks in water for 10 minutes. Insert 2 toothpicks horizontally through center of each onion slice to hold rings together.

3. In large bowl, toss onion, zucchini, yellow pepper, and eggplant with oil; set aside.

4. In microwave-safe 2-cup liquid measuring cup, combine vinegar, crushed red pepper, and salt. Heat vinegar mixture in microwave oven on High 2 to 3 minutes or until reduced to ¼ cup.

5. Place onion, zucchini, yellow pepper, and eggplant on grill rack. Place tomatoes, cut sides down, on same rack. Cover grill and cook vegetables until grill marks appear and they begin to soften, 4 to 5 minutes. Turn vegetables; brush with vinegar mixture. Cook, covered, until tender, 4 to 8 minutes longer, transferring vegetables to platter as they are done.

6. Assemble vegetable stacks: Remove toothpicks from onion slices. In center of each of 4 dinner plates, place 1 eggplant slice. Top each with one-fourth of onion, zucchini, yellow pepper, tomatoes, basil, and mozzarella to make 4 equal stacks. Top stacks with eggplant slice. Drizzle any juices over and around stacks. Garnish with basil sprigs. Makes 4 main-dish servings.

Each serving: About 445 calories, 19g protein, 29g carbohydrate, 29g total fat (13g saturated), 66mg cholesterol, 370mg sodium.

Crumb-Topped Tomatoes

You can't get the bread crumbs crusty on the grill, so brown them ahead of time in a skillet. The crumbs may be prepared up to a day ahead and refrigerated. These tomatoes would be perfect as an accompaniment to Greek-Style Grilled Halibut (page 322) or Red Wine and Rosemary Porterhouse (page 293).

Prep: 15 minutes   Grill: 8 minutes

2 tablespoons butter or margarine
1 cup fresh bread crumbs (about 2 slices firm white bread)
1 garlic clove, crushed with garlic press
2 tablespoons chopped fresh parsley
½ teaspoon salt
½ teaspoon coarsely ground black pepper
8 large ripe plum tomatoes

1. Prepare outdoor grill for direct grilling over medium heat.

2. In 10-inch skillet, melt butter over low heat. Add bread crumbs and cook, stirring, until lightly browned. Stir in garlic; cook 30 seconds. Remove skillet from heat; stir in parsley, salt, and pepper.

3. Cut each tomato horizontally in half. Top each tomato half with some crumb mixture. Place tomatoes on grill and cook until hot but not mushy, 8 to 10 minutes. Makes 8 accompaniment servings.

Each serving: About 40 calories, 1g protein, 3g carbohydrate, 3g total fat (2g saturated), 8mg cholesterol, 191mg sodium.

Grilled Pizza

Quick-rise yeast gets mixed right in with the flour and salt and needs no proofing. Grilling pizza gives it a smoky flavor not unlike that from a wood-burning oven. If you like, grill onions, peppers, and sausages and let guests personalize their own pizzas.

Prep: 15 minutes plus dough resting   Grill: 5 minutes

2 cups all-purpose flour
1 package quick-rise yeast
¾ teaspoon salt
¾ cup hot water (120°F to 130°F)
2 teaspoons plus 2 tablespoons olive oil
8 ounces fresh mozzarella cheese, thinly sliced
12 fresh basil leaves
2 small ripe tomatoes, thinly sliced
   salt
   coarsely ground black pepper

1. Prepare outdoor grill for direct grilling over medium heat.

2. In large bowl, combine flour, yeast, and salt. Stir in hot water and 2 teaspoons oil until blended and dough comes away from side of bowl. Turn onto lightly floured surface; knead until smooth and elastic, about 5 minutes.

3. Shape pizza dough into two 10-inch rounds or four 6-inch rounds (do not form rims). Cover with greased plastic wrap; let rest 15 minutes.

4. Place dough rounds on grill over medium heat and grill until underside of dough turns golden and grill marks appear, 2 to 5 minutes. With tongs, turn rounds over. Brush lightly with some remaining oil. Top with mozzarella, basil, and tomato slices. Grill until cheese begins to melt, 3 to 5 minutes longer. Drizzle with remaining olive oil and sprinkle with salt and pepper. Makes 12 appetizer servings.

Each serving: About 170 calories, 7g protein, 17g carbohydrate, 8g total fat (3g saturated), 17mg cholesterol, 225mg sodium.

12

VEGETABLES

In kitchens across America, cooks are preparing lighter meals and are looking for ways to serve more vegetables as part of a well-balanced, healthful diet. Vegetables that were once considered exotic are now everyday fare. And what was old is new again, as farmers' markets offer intriguing and delicious heirloom varieties.

Vegetables are often grouped according to their family: onions, leafy greens, cruciferous (cabbage, broccoli, and cauliflower), fruits with seeds that aren't sweet and are therefore treated like vegetables (eggplants, peppers, and tomatoes), roots (carrots, turnips, and the like), stalks (asparagus and celery), tubers (starchy potatoes and sweet potatoes), and mushrooms. For easy reference, we present our recipes alphabetically by vegetable name.

BUYING AND STORING VEGETABLES

When buying vegetables, appearance is usually the best indication of freshness. Avoid bruised vegetables or those with soft spots. Leafy tops should be crisp and fresh looking. Prepackaged vegetables in bags aren't always a good choice because you can't inspect them thoroughly. Some vegetables are covered with a thin edible wax coating that seals in their moisture and gives them a fake sheen. Organic produce is available at natural-food stores and at most supermarkets. These vegetables and fruits have been grown without the use of chemical fertilizers or pesticides.

Refrigeration is the key to keeping most vegetables in prime condition. Store them in the coolest part of the refrigerator or in the crisper drawer. Don't store vegetables in zip-tight plastic bags, as the condensation that forms encourages rapid decay. The exception is leafy greens. Store them, loosely wrapped in paper towels, in a plastic bag, pressing out all the air. Mushrooms should be kept in a brown paper bag, and it is best to store potatoes, onions, garlic, and winter squash in a dark, well-ventilated place at cool room temperature.

PREPARING VEGETABLES

Wash vegetables briefly under cold running water just before using. If necessary, a gentle scrub with a soft vegetable brush will remove any surface dirt. When washing leafy greens, swish them around in a large bowl of cool water, changing the water several times. Cut or peel vegetables as close to serving time as possible. Once the skin on vegetables is broken, they begin to lose valuable nutrients. Some vegetables, such as artichokes, discolor when their cut surfaces are exposed to air. To prevent this, rub the cut surfaces with the cut side of a lemon half.

Not all vegetables require peeling, but you may want to peel certain types if their peel is tough or unpleasant tasting. It is important to remove as thin a layer of peel as possible; a vegetable peeler is the best choice. Vegetables should be cut into uniform pieces to ensure even cooking. If you are making soup or preparing a recipe for which evenly cut pieces aren't important, use a food processor to save time.

ARTICHOKES

Availability
Year-round

Peak Season
March, April, and May

Buying Tips
Buy compact, plump artichokes that are heavy for their size. The leaves should be thick, tightly closed, and evenly colored. Don't worry about brown spots or streaks; they are usually caused by frost. Avoid artichokes with dry, spreading, or hard-tipped leaves. An artichoke's size depends on where it grows on the plant. *Baby artichokes,* which are entirely edible, grow near the base between the leaves and the stalk, while larger ones grow higher up on the stalk.

To Store
Refrigerate in the crisper drawer up to three days.

To Prepare
Rinse the artichokes. Bend back the outer green leaves from around the base of an artichoke and snap them off. With kitchen shears, trim the thorny tops from the remaining outer leaves, rubbing all the cut surfaces with a lemon half to prevent browning. Lay the artichoke on its side and cut off the stem level with the bottom of the artichoke. Cut 1 inch off the top of the artichoke, then place in a bowl containing cold water and the juice of the remaining lemon half. Repeat with the remaining artichokes.

To Cook
Artichokes are often steamed or boiled, then served with a dip such as lemon butter. To steam artichokes, in a nonreactive 5-quart saucepot, heat 1 inch of water and 1 tablespoon lemon juice to boiling over high heat. Stand the artichokes in the boiling water. Reduce heat; cover and simmer until a knife inserted in bottom of an artichoke goes in easily, 30 to 40 minutes. Drain and cool. Cooked artichokes can also be stuffed and baked (remove the center leaves and choke).

To Eat
With your fingers, starting at the bottom, pluck off the leaves one by one until you reach leaves that are too thin to eat. Dip the base of each leaf in a dip or sauce, if using, then pull the leaf through your teeth, scraping off the pulp. Place the discarded leaves in a pile on your plate. Pull out all the remaining thin leaves from the artichoke to reveal the fuzzy choke. With the tip of a teaspoon, scrape out the choke and discard. Cut the solid heart into chunks and enjoy.

Braised Baby Artichokes with Olives

Cook baby artichokes the way Italians do: with garlic and olives.

Prep: 20 minutes   Cook: 15 minutes

2	pounds baby artichokes (about 16)
1	lemon, cut in half
¼	cup olive oil
3	garlic cloves, thinly sliced
1	cup water
½	teaspoon salt
½	teaspoon coarsely ground black pepper
⅓	cup oil-cured olives, pitted and coarsely chopped

1. Trim artichokes: Bend back outer green leaves and snap them off at base until remaining leaves are green on top and yellow at bottom. Cut off stem, level with bottom of artichoke. Cut off top half of each artichoke and discard. Rub cut surfaces with lemon half to prevent browning. Cut each artichoke lengthwise in half or into quarters if large, dropping them into bowl of cold water and juice of remaining lemon half.

2. In nonstick 12-inch skillet, heat *1 inch water* to boiling over high heat. Drain artichokes and add to skillet; cook 5 minutes, then drain. Wipe skillet dry with paper towels.

3. In same skillet, heat oil over medium-high heat. Add garlic and cook, stirring, until golden. Add artichokes; cook, turning once, until lightly browned, about 2 minutes. Stir in water, salt, and pepper; cover and cook until knife inserted in bottom of artichoke goes in easily, about 5 minutes longer. Stir in olives and heat through. Makes 8 first-course servings.

Each serving: About 103 calories, 2g protein, 6g carbohydrate, 9g total fat (1g saturated), 0mg cholesterol, 383mg sodium.

Baked Artichokes with Parmesan Stuffing

A simple bread stuffing, seasoned with Parmesan cheese, anchovies, and pine nuts, is a classic match for artichokes. If serving as a first course, use six small artichokes.

Prep: 1 hour   Bake: 15 minutes

- 4 large artichokes
- 1 lemon, cut in half
- 2 tablespoons fresh lemon juice
- 4 slices firm white bread, coarsely grated (right)
- 2 tablespoons olive oil
- 2 large garlic cloves, finely chopped
- 4 anchovy fillets, chopped
- ½ cup pine nuts (pignoli), lightly toasted (page 562), or walnuts, toasted and chopped
- ⅓ cup freshly grated Parmesan cheese
- 2 tablespoons chopped fresh parsley
- ¼ teaspoon salt
- ¾ cup chicken broth

1. Trim artichokes: From around base of artichoke, bend back outer green leaves and snap off. With kitchen shears, trim thorny tops from outer leaves, rubbing all cut surfaces with lemon half to prevent browning. Lay artichoke on its side and cut off stem, level with bottom of artichoke. Peel stem; place in bowl of cold water and juice of remaining lemon half. Cut 1 inch off top of artichoke; add artichoke to lemon water. Repeat with remaining artichokes.

2. In nonreactive 5-quart saucepot, heat *1 inch water* and 1 tablespoon lemon juice to boiling over high heat. Stand artichokes in boiling water; add stems and heat to boiling. Reduce heat; cover and simmer until knife inserted in bottom of artichoke goes in easily, 30 to 40 minutes. Drain. When cool enough to handle, pull out prickly center leaves from each

artichoke and, with teaspoon, scrape out fuzzy choke (without cutting into the heart) and discard. Finely chop stems.

3. Meanwhile, preheat oven to 400°F. Spread grated bread in jelly-roll pan. Place in oven and toast, stirring once, until golden, about 5 minutes.

4. In 1-quart saucepan, heat oil over medium heat. Add garlic and cook, stirring, 1 minute. Add anchovies and cook, stirring, until garlic is golden and anchovies have almost dissolved.

5. In medium bowl, combine toasted bread, pine nuts, Parmesan, parsley, chopped artichoke stems, garlic mixture, salt, ¼ cup broth, and remaining 1 tablespoon lemon juice.

6. Pour remaining ½ cup broth into 13" by 9" baking dish; stand artichokes in dish. Spoon bread mixture between artichoke leaves and into center cavities. Bake until stuffing is golden and artichokes are heated through, 15 to 20 minutes. Makes 4 main-dish servings.

Each serving: About 359 calories, 17g protein, 35g carbohydrate, 20g total fat (4g saturated), 9mg cholesterol, 934mg sodium.

GRATING FRESH BREAD CRUMBS

Grate firm day-old Italian or French bread on the large holes of a box grater. Or process the bread in a food processor with the knife blade attached to form coarse crumbs. One slice of bread yields about ½ cup crumbs.

For everyday meals, most green vegetables need little more than a drizzle of melted butter or olive oil or a squeeze of lemon juice. For more festive occcasions, it's nice to dress them up. Here are some suggestions for three popular vegetables that love being dipped in or slathered with sauce. All three are especially delicious with Hollandaise Sauce (page 432) or Béarnaise Sauce (page 433).

- Artichokes: Easy Aïoli (page 33), Mustard-Shallot Vinaigrette (page 428).
- Asparagus: Classic French Vinaigrette (page 428), Japanese Miso Dressing (page 429), Tahini Dressing (page 429), Olive Butter (page 434).
- Broccoli: Mornay Sauce (page 432), Cheese Sauce (page 432)

ASPARAGUS

Availability
Almost year-round

Peak Season
March, April, and May

Buying Tips
Look for bright green, firm, crisp stalks with compact tips and no trace of brown or rust. Buy evenly sized stalks for uniform cooking. White asparagus, imported from Europe, is an expensive delicacy.

To Store
Asparagus is very perishable. Stand the stalks in ½ inch of cold water in a container. Refrigerate up to two days.

To Prepare
Hold the base of each asparagus spear in one hand and bend back the stalk; the end will break off at the spot where the stalk becomes too tough to eat. Discard the tough portion. Rinse well to remove any sand. Some cooks like to peel asparagus, but this is a matter of personal choice. Leave asparagus whole or cut diagonally into 1- to 2-inch pieces.

To Cook
Asparagus can be boiled, steamed, stir-fried, roasted, or grilled. Serve hot, room temperature, or cold. To boil, in a 12-inch skillet, heat 1 inch of water to boiling over high heat. Add asparagus and ½ teaspoon salt; heat to boiling. Reduce heat to medium-high and cook, uncovered, until barely tender, 5 to 10 minutes (depending on the thickness of asparagus); drain. If serving cold, rinse under cold running water to stop cooking; drain again.

Roasted Asparagus

Easy and tasty, oven-roasting is sure to become a favorite way to enjoy this vegetable.

Prep: 12 minutes   Roast: 20 minutes

- 2 pounds asparagus, trimmed
- 1 tablespoon olive oil
- ½ teaspoon salt
- ¼ teaspoon coarsely ground black pepper
  freshly grated lemon peel (optional)
  lemon wedges

1. Preheat oven to 450°F.
2. In large roasting pan (17" by 11½"), toss asparagus, oil, salt, and pepper until coated.
3. Roast asparagus, shaking pan occasionally, until tender and lightly browned, about 20 minutes. Sprinkle with grated lemon peel, if you like, and serve with lemon wedges. Makes 6 accompaniment servings.

Each serving: About 47 calories, 4g protein, 5g carbohydrate, 3g total fat (0g saturated), 0mg cholesterol, 195mg sodium.

Sesame Stir-Fried Asparagus

Thin asparagus, which cooks quickly and requires little advance preparation, is the ideal candidate for stir-frying.

Prep: 15 minutes   Cook: 5 minutes

- 1 tablespoon vegetable oil
- ½ teaspoon Asian sesame oil
- 1 pound thin asparagus, trimmed and cut on diagonal into 1-inch pieces
- ¼ teaspoon salt
- 1 tablespoon sesame seeds, toasted

In 10-inch skillet, heat vegetable and sesame oils over high heat until hot. Add asparagus and sprinkle with salt; cook, stirring frequently (stir-frying), until tender-crisp, about 5 minutes. Transfer to serving bowl and sprinkle with toasted sesame seeds. Makes 4 accompaniment servings.

Each serving: About 68 calories, 3g protein, 4g carbohydrate, 5g total fat (1g saturated), 0mg cholesterol, 145mg sodium.

AVOCADOS

Availability
Year-round, but less plentiful in early winter

Buying Tips
The avocado is really a fruit, but because it isn't sweet, we treat it like a vegetable. Avocados must be ripened until they yield to gentle pressure, or they will be flavorless. Buy avocados that are heavy for their size and free of bruises and soft spots. Don't buy very soft avocados; they are overripe. The most common avocado is the *Haas* variety: It has thick pebbled skin that turns dark purple when ripe. The *Fuerte* (also called Florida) avocado is somewhat larger than the Haas and has shiny green skin that doesn't change color when ripe.

To Store
Ripen firm avocados at room temperature. To speed up ripening, place in a closed paper bag (this traps the gases given off by the avocado). Refrigerate ripe avocados up to three or four days.

To Prepare
Cut the avocado lengthwise in half, cutting around the seed. Twist the two halves to separate. To remove the seed, give it a whack with the blade of a knife so it is slightly embedded in the seed. Twist and lift out. With your fingers, gently peel away the skin from the avocado and discard. Slice or cut up the avocado. Avocado flesh darkens quickly when exposed to air; toss with lemon or lime juice to discourage discoloration, or press plastic wrap onto the cut surfaces. Avocados lose their flavor when cooked, so they are almost always served raw in salads and sandwiches or in dips.

BEANS, GREEN AND WAX

Availability
Year-round

Peak Season
June, July, and August

Buying Tips
The term *bean* refers to an enormous category of plants with edible seeds, but in some cases the pods are edible, too. When buying fresh green beans or wax beans, look for crisp, firm pods without any brown spots. You can use the old-fashioned test of breaking a bean in half; it should snap, and beads of moisture should appear at the break. Look for uniformly green or yellow beans. *Purple wax beans* turn green when cooked. Small, thin *haricots verts* aren't as firm as regular green beans, so they cook quickly. Flat *Italian (Romano)* beans are larger and take a bit longer to cook.

To Store
Refrigerate fresh beans in the crisper drawer up to two or three days.

To Prepare
Rinse the beans under cold running water. Snap off or trim the ends. Leave the beans whole or cut into bite-size pieces.

To Cook

Green and wax beans are most often steamed or boiled, but they can also be roasted or stir-fried. To steam, in a 12-inch skillet, heat 1 inch of water and 1 teaspoon salt to boiling over medium-high heat. Add beans; cover and cook until tender-crisp, 5 to 10 minutes; drain.

Roasted Green Beans with Dill Vinaigrette

Instead of steaming green beans, roast them. Toss the beans in the quick and tasty vinaigrette dressing, and serve warm.

Prep: 20 minutes   Roast: 20 to 30 minutes

- 2 pounds green beans, trimmed
- 3 tablespoons olive oil
- ¾ teaspoon salt
- 2 tablespoons white wine vinegar
- 1½ teaspoons Dijon mustard
- ½ teaspoon sugar
- ½ teaspoon coarsely ground black pepper
- 2 tablespoons chopped fresh dill

1. Preheat oven to 450°F. In large roasting pan (17" by 11½"), toss green beans, 1 tablespoon oil, and ½ teaspoon salt until coated. Roast, stirring twice, until tender and lightly browned, 20 to 30 minutes.

2. Meanwhile, prepare vinaigrette: In small bowl, with wire whisk, mix vinegar, mustard, sugar, remaining ¼ teaspoon salt, and pepper until blended. In thin, steady stream, whisk in remaining 2 tablespoons oil until blended; stir in dill.

3. When green beans are done, transfer to serving bowl. Drizzle vinaigrette over green beans; toss until coated. Makes 8 accompaniment servings.

Each serving: About 79 calories, 2g protein, 8g carbohydrate, 5g total fat (1g saturated), 0mg cholesterol, 247mg sodium.

Green Beans with Hazelnuts

Green beans are always popular at large holiday get-togethers. Here's a special way to serve them: with a hint of lemon and lots of crunchy toasted nuts.

Prep: 20 minutes   Cook: 15 minutes

- 1½ teaspoons salt
- 2 pounds green beans, trimmed
- 2 tablespoons butter or margarine
- ½ cup hazelnuts (filberts), toasted and skinned (page 562), chopped
- 1 teaspoon freshly grated lemon peel
- ¼ teaspoon ground black pepper

1. In 12-inch skillet, heat *1 inch water* and 1 teaspoon salt to boiling over high heat. Add green beans and heat to boiling. Cover and cook until tender-crisp, 6 to 8 minutes. Drain; wipe skillet dry with paper towels.

2. In same skillet, melt butter over medium heat. Add hazelnuts and cook, stirring, until butter just begins to brown, about 3 minutes. Add green beans, lemon peel, remaining ½ teaspoon salt, and pepper. Cook, stirring, until heated through, about 5 minutes. Makes 8 accompaniment servings.

Each serving: About 143 calories, 3g protein, 9g carbohydrate, 12g total fat (4g saturated), 16mg cholesterol, 356mg sodium.

Green Beans Amandine

Prepare as directed above but substitute ⅔ **cup slivered almonds,** toasted, for hazelnuts.

Lemony Green Beans

Prepare as directed above but omit hazelnuts in Step 2. Instead, add ¼ **teaspoon ground coriander,** ¼ **cup chopped fresh mint, 1 tablespoon fresh lemon juice,** and ½ **teaspoon lemon peel.** Toss until beans are evenly coated.

BEETS

Availability
Year-round

Peak Season
June through October

Buying Tips
Choose smooth, deeply colored beets without ridges and blemishes; soft spots indicate decay. Buy evenly sized beets for uniform cooking. The green tops, if attached, should be fresh-looking. (They can be cooked separately like other greens; see Stir-Frying 101, page 351.) In addition to the familiar crimson-colored beets, *golden beets* and *striped beets* are often available at specialty food stores and farmers' markets.

To Store
If the tops are attached, trim them, leaving about 1 inch of stem attached (this prevents the beets from "bleeding" and losing color). Place the tops and beets in separate plastic bags. Refrigerate in the the crisper drawer: beets up to one week, tops up to two days (they wilt quickly).

To Prepare
Wash beet tops under cool running water to remove any hidden grit. Scrub beets well under cold running water.

To Cook
Beets can be boiled, but roasting enhances their natural sweetness. Cook beets unpeeled and uncut to retain their color.

HOW TO AVOID BEET STAINS

Here is a simple way to protect your hands from beet stains. Before trimming raw beets or before removing the skins from and cutting up cooked beets, slip on a pair of rubber kitchen gloves or disposable surgical gloves. They will keep your hands from turning an unsightly pink.

Roasted Beets and Onions

An easy sweet-and-sour skillet sauce transforms roasted beets and red onions into a luscious side dish.

Prep: 20 minutes plus cooling
Roast/Cook: 1 hour 40 minutes

- 2 bunches beets with tops (2 pounds)
- 3 small red onions (1 pound), not peeled
- 2 tablespoons extra-virgin olive oil
- ⅓ cup chicken broth
- ¼ cup balsamic vinegar
- 1 teaspoon brown sugar
- 1 teaspoon fresh thyme
- ¼ teaspoon salt
- ¼ teaspoon coarsely ground black pepper
- 1 tablespoon chopped fresh parsley

1. Preheat oven to 400°F.

2. Trim all but 1 inch of top stems from beets. Place beets and onions in nonstick oven-safe 10-inch skillet (if skillet is not oven-safe, wrap handle with double layer of foil) or in 13" by 9" baking pan; drizzle with oil. Roast, shaking skillet occasionally, until onions have softened and beets are tender, about 1 hour 30 minutes, transferring vegetables to plate as they are done.

3. In same skillet, combine broth, vinegar, brown sugar, and thyme; heat to boiling over medium-high heat. Boil, stirring and scraping bottom of skillet, until vinegar mixture is dark brown and syrupy and has reduced to about ¼ cup, 5 to 7 minutes. Stir in salt and pepper. Remove from heat.

4. When cool enough to handle, peel beets and onions. Cut beets into ¼-inch-wide matchstick strips and onions into thin rounds; place in serving bowl. Pour vinegar mixture over vegetables and toss until coated. Sprinkle with parsley. Makes 6 accompaniment servings.

Each serving: About 103 calories, 2g protein, 14g carbohydrate, 5g total fat (1g saturated), 0mg cholesterol, 203mg sodium.

BOK CHOY

Availability
Year-round

Buying Tips
Look for bok choy in Asian markets and large supermarkets. Select heads with crisp white stalks and bright green leaves, which may be slightly wilted. Avoid bok choy that has any brown spots.

To Store
Refrigerate in the the crisper drawer up to three days.

To Prepare
Separate the stalks from their leafy tops; cut both into ½-inch-thick slices.

To Cook
Bok choy is almost always stir-fried with Asian seasonings to enhance its mild flavor. Cook the stalks first, then add the tender tops at the end.

BROCCOFLOWER

Availability
October through February

Buying Tips
Even though its fluorescent-green color is reminiscent of broccoli, this brightly colored vegetable is related to cauliflower. Look for firm heads with tightly packed flowerets and no browning. The leaves should look crisp.

To Store
Place in a plastic bag with a few holes poked in it. Refrigerate in the crisper drawer up to two days.

To Prepare
Discard the leaves; cut into bite-size flowerets or keep whole.

To Cook
Cook like cauliflower (boil, steam, or roast). When cooked, broccoflower turns deep green.

BROCCOLI

Availability
Year-round

Peak Season
October through February

Buying Tips
Look for firm stalks with tightly closed dark green flowerets. Avoid stalks with yellowing or blooming flowerets. Purple broccoli turns dark green when cooked.

To Store
Place in a plastic bag with a few holes poked in it. Refrigerate in the crisper drawer up to two days.

To Prepare
Remove the large leaves and trim the ends of the stalks if woody. Cut the broccoli tops into 2-inch flowerets. Peel the stalks and cut into ¼- to ½-inch-thick slices.

To Cook
Broccoli can be stir-fried, steamed or boiled. To cook, in a skillet, heat 1 inch of water to boiling over high heat; add broccoli stalks and heat to boiling. Cook 1 minute. Add flowerets and heat to boiling. Reduce heat to medium-low; cover and cook until broccoli is tender-crisp, about 5 minutes. Drain.

BROCCOLI RABE

Availability
Year-round

Buying Tips
This slightly bitter green is also called *broccoli raab, broccoli rape*, and *broccoli di rape*. The leaves should be perky, with thin green stalks and small, tight bud clusters. Avoid stalks with yellowish leaves.

Place in a plastic bag with a few holes poked in it. Refrigerate in the crisper drawer up to two days.

To Prepare

Trim stems and discard any tough leaves. Wash in several changes of cold water to remove any grit.

To Cook

Broccoli rabe is cooked like other leafy greens. In a large skillet, heat ½ inch of water to boiling; add broccoli rabe and heat to boiling. Reduce heat to medium-high and cook until stems are almost tender, about 5 minutes; drain well. Wipe skillet dry. In same skillet, cook some chopped garlic in olive oil until golden. Stir in broccoli rabe; cook, stirring, until heated through. Season with salt and pepper.

Broccoli Rabe with Garbanzo Beans

For a quick and flavorful weeknight supper, toss these tasty bitter greens with a hearty pasta, such as penne, rotelle, or bow ties, and sprinkle with Parmesan cheese.

Prep: 10 minutes   Cook: 18 minutes

2	bunches broccoli rabe (1¼ pounds each), trimmed
2½	teaspoons salt
2	tablespoons olive oil
3	garlic cloves, crushed with side of chef's knife
¼	teaspoon crushed red pepper
1	can (15 to 19 ounces) garbanzo beans, rinsed and drained

1. In 8-quart saucepot, heat *4 quarts water* to boiling over high heat. Add broccoli rabe and 2 teaspoons salt; heat to boiling. Cook until thickest part of stems is tender, about 3 minutes. Drain, reserving ¼ cup cooking water. Cool slightly, then cut into 1½-inch pieces.

2. Wipe saucepot dry with paper towels; add oil and heat over medium heat. Add garlic and cook, stirring, until golden. Add crushed red pepper and cook 15 seconds. Add broccoli rabe, garbanzo beans, reserved cooking water, and remaining ½ teaspoon salt. Cook, stirring, until heated through, about 3 minutes. Makes 8 accompaniment servings.

Each serving: About 93 calories, 5g protein, 10g carbohydrate, 4g total fat (0g saturated), 0mg cholesterol, 378mg sodium.

BRUSSELS SPROUTS

Availability

Year-round, except June and July

Peak Season

October through January

Buying Tips

Purchase firm, bright green sprouts with tight outer leaves. Avoid soft sprouts or any with black spots. Brussels sprouts are usually available in 10-ounce boxes, but some farmers' markets sell them still attached to their long stalks.

To Store

Refrigerate in the crisper drawer up to two days.

To Prepare

Trim off any yellow or wilted leaves, and trim the stem end. Cut a shallow X in the stem end to shorten the cooking time. Rinse well under cold running water.

To Cook

Brussels sprouts are usually boiled, but for a delicious change of pace, thinly slice and sauté until tender. For steamed Brussels sprouts with the freshest flavor, cook the sprouts just until tender-crisp; long cooking brings out their strong flavor and an unappealing sulfurous aroma. In a large saucepan, heat 1 inch of water to boiling over high heat; add Brussels sprouts and heat to boiling. Reduce heat to medium-high. Cover and cook until tender-crisp, about 10 minutes (or a little longer if you prefer very tender sprouts); drain.

Brussels Sprouts with Bacon

For many families, Brussels sprouts are a given at the Thanksgiving table. If you wish, prepare ahead through Step 2; then finish cooking at the last minute.

Prep: 15 minutes   Cook: 25 minutes

- 3 containers (10 ounces each) Brussels sprouts, trimmed and cut lengthwise in half
- 6 slices bacon
- 1 tablespoon olive oil
- 2 garlic cloves, finely chopped
- ½ teaspoon salt
- ¼ teaspoon coarsely ground black pepper
- ¼ cup pine nuts (pignoli), toasted (page 562)

1. In 4-quart saucepan, heat *2 quarts water* to boiling over high heat. Add Brussels sprouts and heat to boiling. Cook until tender-crisp, about 5 minutes; drain.

2. In 12-inch skillet, cook bacon over medium heat until browned. With tongs, transfer bacon to paper towels to drain; crumble.

3. Discard all but 1 tablespoon bacon drippings from skillet. Add oil and heat over medium-high heat. Add Brussels sprouts, garlic, salt, and pepper. Cook, stirring frequently, until Brussels sprouts are lightly browned, about 5 minutes. To serve, sprinkle with pine nuts and bacon. Makes 10 accompaniment servings.

Each serving: About 96 calories, 5g protein, 8g carbohydrate, 6g total fat (1g saturated), 4mg cholesterol, 202mg sodium.

Brussels Sprouts with Bacon and Chestnuts

Prepare as directed but substitute **Roasted Chestnuts** (page 344) for pine nuts. Cut chestnuts into quarters; add to Brussels sprouts with garlic, salt, and pepper.

NAPA (CHINESE) CABBAGE

Availability
Year-round

Buying Tips
Although Chinese cabbage is cylindrical and napa cabbage is roundish, they can be used interchangeably in most recipes. Look for crisp, fresh-looking cabbage, free from blemishes. Tiny brown freckles are to be expected.

To Store
Place in a plastic bag with a few holes poked in it. Refrigerate in the crisper drawer up to three days.

To Prepare
Remove any wilted leaves and cut cabbage lengthwise in half or into quarters. Rinse well. Cut out most of the core and thinly slice or prepare as directed.

GREEN AND RED CABBAGE

Availability
Year-round

Buying Tips
Buy heavy, firm, blemish-free heads with tightly packed crinkly leaves; the outer leaves of summer-harvested cabbage will be loosely packed and should be crisp and brightly colored. *Savoy* cabbage is considered the best-tasting green variety.

To Store
Place in a plastic bag with a few holes poked in it. Refrigerate in the crisper drawer up to one week.

To Prepare
Discard any tough outer leaves. Cut the head into wedges and cut away most of the tough core from each wedge, leaving just enough to hold the cabbage together. With a large knife, thinly slice, or shred in a food processor with the knife blade attached.

To Cook

Cabbage can be boiled, stir-fried, sautéed, braised, or served raw. To retain the color of red cabbage, add a little vinegar or lemon juice while it is cooking.

Braised Sweet-and-Sour Red Cabbage

Not your usual sweet-and-sour treatment: For sweet, we use fresh pear, apple juice, and brown sugar; for sour, cider vinegar. Then we add a hint of allspice for balance.

Prep: 20 minutes   Cook: 1 hour 30 minutes

- 3 tablespoons vegetable oil
- 2 medium onions, chopped
- 1 pear, peeled, cored, and chopped
- 2 medium heads red cabbage (2 pounds each), cut into quarters, cored, and thinly sliced
- 1 can (14½ ounces) beef broth or 1¾ cups Brown Beef Stock (page 61)
- 1 cup apple juice
- ⅓ cup cider vinegar
- ¼ cup packed brown sugar
- 2 small bay leaves
- ¾ teaspoon salt
- ¼ teaspoon coarsely ground black pepper
- ⅛ teaspoon ground allspice

1. In nonreactive 8-quart saucepot, heat oil over medium heat. Add onions and pear; cook, stirring frequently, until tender, 10 minutes.

2. Stir in cabbage, broth, apple juice, vinegar, brown sugar, bay leaves, salt, pepper, and allspice; heat to boiling over high heat. Reduce heat; cover and simmer, stirring occasionally, until cabbage is very tender, about 1 hour. Remove cover and cook over medium-high heat, stirring occasionally, until most of liquid has evaporated, about 15 minutes longer. Remove and discard bay leaves. Makes 10 accompaniment servings.

Each serving: About 136 calories, 3g protein, 23g carbohydrate, 5g total fat (1g saturated), 1mg cholesterol, 335mg sodium.

Braised Cabbage with Ginger and Cumin

Adding fresh ginger and cumin—spices typical of Indian cuisine—to braised cabbage turns an ordinary vegetable into an exotic taste experience.

Prep: 10 minutes   Cook: 20 minutes

- 1 tablespoon butter or margarine
- 1 tablespoon vegetable oil
- 1 medium onion, chopped
- 2 tablespoons minced, peeled fresh ginger
- 2 garlic cloves, finely chopped
- 1 medium head green cabbage (2 pounds), cut into quarters, cored, and very thinly sliced
- ½ teaspoon cumin seeds, crushed
- ½ teaspoon salt
- 1 cup water

In 12-inch skillet, melt butter with oil over medium heat. Add onion and cook until tender, about 5 minutes. Stir in ginger and garlic; cook, stirring, 30 seconds. Stir in cabbage, cumin seeds, and salt; increase heat to medium-high and cook, stirring frequently, until cabbage begins to wilt, about 5 minutes (do not let garlic burn). Add water and cook, stirring occasionally, until cabbage is very tender and water has evaporated, about 10 minutes. Makes 6 accompaniment servings.

Each serving: About 80 calories, 2g protein, 10g carbohydrate, 4g total fat (1g saturated), 5mg cholesterol, 236mg sodium.

THE VINEGAR CONNECTION

Test Kitchen Tip

Recipes for cooked cabbage often include a bit of vinegar. Here's why: If cut cabbage is exposed to even slightly alkaline conditions, such as hard water, the cabbage will turn blue. Adding a small amount of acid (fruit or fruit juice, vinegar, or wine) will prevent this from happening.

CARDOON

Availability
October through February

Buying Tips
Also called *cardoni*. Look for cardoons in Italian markets, especially around Christmas. Buy large, thick, ivory-colored stalks with prickly leaves.

To Store
Refrigerate in the crisper drawer up to five days.

To Prepare
Cardoons discolor when their cut surfaces are exposed to air. To discourage browning, rub the cut surfaces with lemon halves (but even if the surfaces brown, they will turn grayish white when cooked). Separate the stalks, discarding the tough outer ones. Using a vegetable peeler, remove the outer strings.

To Cook
Cardoons are always eaten cooked. In a medium saucepan, heat 1 inch of water to boiling over high heat; add cardoons and heat to boiling. Reduce heat to medium-high and cook until tender, about 20 minutes; drain.

CARROTS

Availability
Year-round

Buying Tips
Buy firm bright-colored carrots. Avoid any with yellowish greens or signs of sprouting on the carrots. Baby carrots are often available in bunches. Cut or shredded carrots, sold in plastic bags, should show no sign of moisture.

To Store
Cut off the greens, leaving about 2 inches of stem. Place in a plastic bag. Refrigerate in the crisper drawer up to five days.

To Prepare
Scrub under cold running water or peel. Leave carrots whole or slice, shred, or cut them into pieces.

To Cook
No longer are carrots simply boiled: They are glazed, candied, stir-fried, roasted, shredded, or served as slaw. To serve them the old-fashioned way, in a saucepan, heat 1 inch of water to boiling over high heat; add carrots and heat to boiling. Reduce heat to medium-high; cover and cook until tender-crisp, whole carrots about 15 minutes, cut-up carrots, 5 to 10 minutes.

Candied Carrots

These delicately sweetened carrots are sure to please both children and adults alike.

Prep: 15 minutes   Cook: 25 minutes

- 1 bag (16 ounces) carrots, peeled
- 1 lemon
- 2 tablespoons butter or margarine
- 3 tablespoons brown sugar

1. Cut each carrot crosswise in half. Cut thick portion lengthwise in half. In 4-quart saucepan, heat *1 inch water* to boiling over medium heat. Add carrots and heat to boiling. Cover and simmer until tender, about 15 minutes. Drain and return to saucepan.

2. Meanwhile, from lemon, grate ½ teaspoon peel and squeeze 1 teaspoon juice.

3. Add butter, brown sugar, and lemon juice to carrots; cook over medium heat, stirring gently, until sugar has dissolved and carrots are glazed, about 5 minutes.

4. Stir in peel. Makes 4 accompaniment servings.

Each serving: About 133 calories, 1g protein, 20g carbohydrate, 6g total fat (4g saturated), 16mg cholesterol, 98mg sodium.

Ginger Candied Carrots
Prepare as directed above but add **1 teaspoon grated, peeled fresh ginger** with butter.

Candied Parsnips
Prepare as directed above but substitute **1 pound parsnips,** peeled, for carrots.

Shredded Carrots

This is the fastest way to cook carrots and also one of the best. Add a pinch each of cloves and ginger for a spicier dish, if you like.

Prep: 5 minutes   Cook: 5 minutes

- 4 carrots, peeled and shredded (2 cups)
- 2 tablespoons water
- 2 tablespoons butter or margarine
- 1 teaspoon sugar
- ½ teaspoon salt

In small saucepan, combine carrots, water, butter, sugar, and salt; heat to boiling over high heat. Reduce heat; cover and simmer, stirring occasionally, until carrots are tender, 3 to 4 minutes. Makes 4 accompaniment servings.

Each serving: About 78 calories, 1g protein, 7g carbohydrate, 6g total fat (4g saturated), 16mg cholesterol, 367mg sodium.

CAULIFLOWER

Availability
Year-round

Peak Season
October through January

Buying Tips
Heads should be firm and creamy white with granular-looking flowerets. The leaves

should be fresh-looking. Do not buy heads with brown spots or flowering buds. Purple or green cauliflower occasionally shows up at farmers' markets.

To Store
Place in a plastic bag with a few holes poked in it. Refrigerate in the crisper drawer up to five days.

To Prepare
Remove the leaves and cut out the core. Separate the head into flowerets or leave whole. Rinse under cold running water.

To Cook
Cauliflower is frequently steamed, but it's also delicious roasted (see below). To steam, in a large saucepan, heat 1 inch of water to boiling over high heat; add cauliflower and heat to boiling. Reduce heat to medium-high. Cover and cook whole cauliflower until tender, 10 to 15 minutes, or flowerets until tender-crisp, about 5 minutes; drain well.

Roasted Cauliflower

Roasting cauliflower until it caramelizes turns its starch to sugar and gives it a delicious nutty flavor.

Prep: 10 minutes   Roast: 23 minutes

- 1 medium head cauliflower (2 pounds), cut into 1½-inch flowerets
- 1 tablespoon olive oil
- ½ teaspoon salt
- ¼ teaspoon coarsely ground black pepper
- 2 tablespoons chopped fresh parsley
- 1 garlic clove, finely chopped

1. Preheat oven to 450°F. In jelly-roll pan, toss cauliflower, oil, salt, and pepper until evenly coated. Roast until cauliflower is tender, about 20 minutes, stirring halfway through roasting.

2. In small cup, combine parsley and garlic. Sprinkle over cauliflower and stir to mix evenly. Roast 3 minutes longer. Spoon into serving dish. Makes 6 accompaniment servings.

Each serving: About 35 calories, 1g protein, 3g carbohydrate, 2g total fat (0g saturated), 0mg cholesterol, 202mg sodium.

Curry-Roasted Cauliflower

Prepare as directed above but substitute **2 tablespoons chopped fresh cilantro** for parsley and add **1 teaspoon curry powder** to garlic mixture.

Cauliflower with Golden Raisins and Pine Nuts

In Sicily, anchovies are used as a seasoning. If you prefer, omit the anchovy paste, and add a little more salt.

Prep: 20 minutes   Cook: 18 minutes

1	large head cauliflower (2½ pounds), cut into 1½-inch flowerets
2¼	teaspoons salt
2	tablespoons olive oil
2	garlic cloves, crushed with side of chef's knife
1	teaspoon anchovy paste (optional)
¼	teaspoon crushed red pepper
¼	cup golden raisins
2	tablespoons pine nuts (pignoli), lightly toasted (page 562)
1	tablespoon chopped fresh parsley

1. In 5-quart Dutch oven, heat *2 quarts water* to boiling over high heat. Add cauliflower and 2 teaspoons salt; heat to boiling. Cook until tender, 5 to 7 minutes; drain. Wipe Dutch oven dry.

2. In same Dutch oven, heat oil over medium heat. Add garlic and cook, stirring, until golden. Add anchovy paste, if using, and crushed red pepper; cook 15 seconds. Add cauliflower, raisins, pine nuts, and remaining ¼ teaspoon salt; cook, stirring, until heated through, about 2 minutes. To serve, sprinkle with parsley. Makes 6 accompaniment servings.

Each serving: About 93 calories, 2g protein, 9g carbohydrate, 6g total fat (1g saturated), 0mg cholesterol, 401mg sodium.

PINE NUTS

These tasty little nuts are the seeds of a particular variety of pine tree and have been cultivated for over 6,000 years. They contain about 31 grams of protein per 100 grams, the highest amount of any nut or seed. Pine nuts are called *piñones* in Spanish and *pignoli* in Italian.

CELERY

Availability
Year-round

Buying Tips
Choose a compact bunch of light-colored, crisp stalks with fresh-looking leaves. (Thin, dark-colored stalks can be bitter and stringy.)

To Store
Refrigerate in the crisper drawer up to five days.

To Prepare
Remove the leaves (use in soups or stews) and trim the root end. Rinse the stalks under cold running water. Use the outer stalks for cooking or cut up for salads. Serve the tender inner stalks raw in salads or with dips.

To Cook
To braise as a side dish, cut stalks into 4- to 6-inch pieces and place in shallow baking dish. Add enough chicken broth to come halfway up celery; sprinkle with pepper. Bake at 375°F, basting frequently, until very tender, about 30 minutes.

CELERY ROOT (CELERIAC)

Availability
Year-round

Peak Season
October through March

Buying Tips
Choose firm, small (less than 4 inches in diameter) celery root knobs that are well shaped (the smoother the knob, the easier it is to peel). If only large celery root is available, remove the center if soft and woody.

To Store
Refrigerate in the crisper drawer up to five days.

To Prepare
Scrub under cold running water. Use a small knife to cut away the peel and root end. Cut as directed. The flesh of

celery root discolors when exposed to air. If preparing ahead, place the cut celery root in a bowl containing 4 cups cold water and 2 tablespoons lemon juice or vinegar; set aside until ready to cook. Drain well.

To Cook

Celery root can be served raw (as a salad), boiled, mashed (alone or with potatoes), or braised.

Celery Root Rémoulade

Although rémoulade is usually paired with cold seafood salads, it is also excellent with crunchy raw vegetables.

Prep: 25 minutes plus chilling

2	tablespoons fresh lemon juice
1½	pounds celery root (celeriac), trimmed and peeled
½	cup mayonnaise
2	tablespoons Dijon mustard
1	tablespoon chopped fresh parsley
¼	teaspoon ground black pepper

1. Pour lemon juice into large bowl. With adjustable-blade slicer or very sharp knife, cut celery root into ⅛-inch-thick matchstick strips. Immediately place celery root in lemon juice as it is cut, tossing to coat completely to prevent celery root from browning.

2. In small bowl, combine mayonnaise, mustard, parsley, and pepper. Add to celery root and toss to coat. Cover and refrigerate at least 1 hour to blend flavors or up to overnight. Makes 6 accompaniment servings.

Each serving: About 176 calories, 2g protein, 10g carbohydrate, 15g total fat (2g saturated), 11mg cholesterol, 322mg sodium.

CHAYOTE

Availability

Year-round

Buying Tips

Also called *mirliton* and *christophene*, this ridged, pear-shaped dark green squash tastes like summer squash. When buying, choose firm chayote.

To Store

Refrigerate in the crisper drawer up to one week.

To Prepare

Small chayotes have thin skins that do not require peeling. Otherwise, remove the peel with a vegetable peeler or knife. Cut in half and discard the hard central seed; cut as directed.

To Cook

Chayote can be steamed, sautéed, or braised just like summer squash. To roast, brush the cut sides of chayote halves with some fruity olive oil and bake in a preheated 375°F oven until tender, 30 to 40 minutes.

CHESTNUTS

Availability

November through January, but most plentiful in November

Buying Tips

Chestnuts are always imported (usually from Italy), so buy them from a store with good turnover to ensure freshness. Buy chestnuts with firm, shiny shells; avoid any with tiny holes. Vacuum-packed chestnuts are acceptable in stuffings, but canned chestnuts don't have much flavor. One pound of fresh chestnuts yields about 2 cups peeled.

To Store

Refrigerate in a brown paper bag up to two weeks.

To Prepare

Chestnuts are always cooked and peeled before eating. The recipe on page 344 is the traditional method.

Roasted Chestnuts

Chestnuts can be presented in many guises: in almost any stuffing, added to your favorite vegetable medley, or pureed with sugar and vanilla and served with whipped cream for a special dessert.

Prep: 30 minutes   Roast: 20 minutes

1 pound fresh chestnuts

1. Preheat oven to 400°F. With sharp knife, cut an X in flat side of shell of each chestnut. Place in jelly-roll pan and roast chestnuts until shells open, about 20 minutes.

2. Cover chestnuts with a clean kitchen towel. When cool enough to handle, with paring knife, peel hot chestnuts, keeping unpeeled chestnuts warm for easier peeling. Makes 2 cups.

Each 1/2 cup: About 179 calories, 2g protein, 38g carbohydrate, 2g total fat (0g saturated), 0mg cholesterol, 3mg sodium.

CHICORY

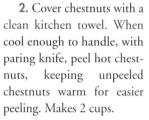

Availability
Year-round

Buying Tips
Chicory is sometimes called curly endive. Buy heads with curly, spiky, fresh-looking leaves that have dark green tops and pale green ribs.

To Store
Wrap loosely in paper towels and place in a plastic bag. Refrigerate in the crisper drawer up to five days.

To Prepare
Trim the stems. Wash leaves well in several changes of cold water to remove grit. Tear into bite-size pieces.

To Cook
Serve raw in salads combined with sweet-tasting greens, or cook like other bitter greens (page 350).

CORN

Availability
Year-round

Peak Season
July through September

Buying Tips
Buy ears that are firm and well shaped under fresh-looking husks with shiny, moist silk. (Unshucked corn stays fresh longer.) Pick ears that look plump, with kernels running to the tops of the ears. Tiny kernels indicate immaturity, but very large deep yellow kernels can be chewy. The fresher the corn, the sweeter the kernels: With age, the sugar in corn converts to starch. Frozen and canned corn kernels are good substitutes for fresh. Canned baby corn is used in Asian stir-fries. One medium ear of corn yields about 1/2 cup corn kernels.

To Store
Cook and eat corn as soon as possible after picking. If you must, refrigerate in the crisper drawer up to one or two days.

To Prepare

Shuck the corn and remove the silk just before cooking. (An exception is corn grilled with the husks intact.) To remove the kernels, trim the tip so you can stand the ear on end, then slice down to cut off the kernels, cutting close to the cob.

To Cook

Corn is one of the most versatile vegetables. Sauté the kernels alone or with other vegetables; stir into puddings, fritters, or other batters; or roast, microwave, or boil on the cob. To boil, in a large saucepot, heat 3 inches of water to boiling over high heat; add shucked corn and heat to boiling. Do not add salt; it toughens corn. Reduce heat to low. Cover and simmer 5 minutes; drain.

Creamy Corn Pudding

This savory pudding goes exceptionally well with baked ham. Perfect for a late summer feast.

Prep: 30 minutes   Bake: 1 hour 15 minutes

- 2 tablespoons butter or margarine
- 1 small onion, chopped
- ¼ cup all-purpose flour
- 2 cups half-and-half or light cream, warmed
- 1 cup milk, warmed
- 2 cups corn kernels cut from cobs (4 ears)
- 1 teaspoon salt
- ¼ teaspoon coarsely ground black pepper
- 4 large eggs

1. Preheat oven to 325°F. In 2-quart saucepan, melt butter over medium heat. Add onion and cook, stirring frequently, until tender and golden, about 10 minutes. Add flour and cook, stirring, 1 minute. With wire whisk, gradually whisk in warm half-and-half and warm milk; heat to boiling, whisking constantly. Reduce heat and simmer, stirring occasionally, until sauce has thickened and boils, about 5 minutes. Remove from heat; stir in corn, salt, and pepper.

2. In 2-quart casserole, with wire whisk, beat eggs lightly. Slowly add corn mixture, beating constantly.

3. Set casserole in 13" by 9" baking pan; place pan on oven rack. Pour enough *boiling water* into pan to come halfway up sides of casserole. Bake until knife inserted in center comes out clean, about 1 hour 15 minutes. Makes 10 accompaniment servings.

Each serving: About 168 calories, 6g protein, 13g carbohydrate, 11g total fat (6g saturated), 112mg cholesterol, 315mg sodium.

Sautéed Fresh Corn

While this is a fine way to cook raw corn, it's also a very clever way to heat up kernels cut from leftover corn on the cob.

Prep: 15 minutes   Cook: 5 minutes

- 2 tablespoons butter or margarine
- 4 cups corn kernels cut from cobs (about 6 ears)
- ½ teaspoon salt
- ¼ teaspoon coarsely ground black pepper
- ¼ cup snipped fresh chives or thinly sliced green onions

In 10-inch skillet, melt butter over medium-high heat. Add corn, salt, and pepper and cook, stirring frequently, until tender, about 4 minutes. Remove from heat and stir in chives. Makes 4 accompaniment servings.

Each serving: About 238 calories, 7g protein, 41g carbohydrate, 8g total fat (4g saturated), 16mg cholesterol, 381mg sodium.

CUCUMBERS

Availability
Year-round

Peak Season
June through September

Buying Tips
Pick firm, uniformly slender cucumbers. Overmature cu-

cumbers, which are generally seedy, are dull or yellowish and have an overgrown, puffy look. Smaller varieties, such as Kirbys, are preferred for pickling. English (seedless) cucumbers are long and slender and have very small seeds that do not have to be removed.

To Store
Refrigerate in the crisper drawer up to one week.

To Prepare

Rinse cukes under cold running water; scrub Kirbys with a vegetable brush. If the skin is tender and un-waxed (Kirbys and seedless varieties), cucumbers do not have to be peeled. Simply trim the ends and cut the cucumber as desired. To remove the seeds, cut the cucumber lengthwise in half and scoop out the seeds with a spoon.

To Cook

Cucumbers are well known as a salad ingredient, but they can also be sautéed alone or with other vegetables. When cooked, they have a mild squashlike flavor.

EGGPLANT

Availability
Year-round

Peak Season
July through October

Buying Tips
Eggplant should be firm and shiny with a bright green cap and no scars, cuts, or bruises. It should feel heavy for its size. Varieties include the familiar plump oval dark purple *Mediterranean*, the slender light purple *Japanese*, and the round green *Thai* eggplant.

To Store

Refrigerate in the crisper drawer up to one week.

To Prepare

Rinse under cold running water. Do not peel eggplant unless the skin seems tough. Some recipes call for salting eggplant, which draws out the water and any bitter juices. Slice or cut eggplant as desired just before cooking; it discolors quickly.

To Cook

Braise, grill, bake, sauté, or roast eggplant. It is often combined with tomato, zucchini, or roasted peppers.

Caponata

Caponata (which gets its name from the capers that accent it) has an intriguing sweet-and-sour flavor. Serve it as part of a cold antipasto, spread it on bruschetta, or offer it as a first course.

Prep: 30 minutes plus cooling   Roast/Cook: 55 minutes

2	small eggplants (1 pound each), ends trimmed, cut into ¾-inch pieces
½	cup extra-virgin olive oil
¼	teaspoon salt
3	small red onions, thinly sliced
1½	pounds ripe tomatoes (4 medium), peeled, seeded, and chopped
1	cup olives, such as Gaeta, green Sicilian, or Kalamata, pitted and chopped
3	tablespoons capers, drained
3	tablespoons golden raisins
¼	teaspoon coarsely ground black pepper
4	stalks celery with leaves, thinly sliced
⅓	cup red wine vinegar
2	teaspoons sugar
¼	cup chopped fresh flat-leaf parsley

1. Preheat oven to 450°F. In two jelly-roll pans, place eggplant, dividing evenly. Drizzle with ¼ cup oil and sprinkle with salt; toss to coat. Roast eggplant 10 minutes; stir, then roast until browned, about 10 minutes longer.

2. Meanwhile, in nonstick 12-inch skillet, heat remaining ¼ cup oil over medium heat. Add onions and cook, stirring, until tender and golden, about 10 minutes. Add tomatoes, olives, capers, raisins, and pepper. Reduce heat; cover and simmer 15 minutes.

3. Add eggplant and celery to skillet and cook, uncovered, over medium heat, stirring frequently, until celery is just tender, 8 to 10 minutes. Stir in vinegar and sugar and cook 1 minute longer. Cool to room temperature, or cover and refrigerate up to overnight. To serve, sprinkle with parsley. Makes about 5 cups.

Each ¼ cup: About 106 calories, 1g protein, 9g carbohydrate, 8g total fat (1g saturated), 0mg cholesterol, 336mg sodium.

Roasted Eggplant Parmesan

Eggplant Parmesan usually involves lots of frying, but for our version, the eggplant is roasted, requiring much less oil and much less time.

Prep: 35 minutes plus cooling   Roast/Cook: 60 minutes

- 2 small eggplants (1¼ pounds each), ends trimmed, cut into ½-inch-thick slices
- ¼ cup olive oil
- ½ teaspoon salt
- 1 can (28 ounces) plum tomatoes, drained and chopped
- ¼ teaspoon ground black pepper
- ⅓ cup chopped fresh parsley
- 4 ounces mozzarella cheese, shredded (1 cup)
- ½ cup freshly grated Parmesan cheese

1. Preheat oven to 450°F. Place eggplant slices on two large cookie sheets. Brush oil on both sides and sprinkle with ¼ teaspoon salt. Roast 15 minutes; turn slices and roast until browned and tender, 20 to 25 minutes longer.

2. Meanwhile, in nonstick 12-inch skillet, combine tomatoes, remaining ¼ teaspoon salt, and pepper; heat to boiling over medium heat. Reduce heat to low; cook, stirring occasionally, until tomatoes have thickened, about 20 minutes. Stir in parsley.

3. Turn oven control to 400°F. In shallow 2½-quart casserole, layer half of eggplant and top with half of tomato sauce; sprinkle with half of mozzarella. Repeat layers; top with grated Parmesan.

4. Cover loosely with foil. Bake until bubbling, about 10 minutes. Remove casserole from oven and let stand at least 10 minutes before serving. Serve hot or at room temperature. Makes 6 main-dish servings.

Each serving: About 248 calories, 11g protein, 19g carbohydrate, 16g total fat (5g saturated), 21mg cholesterol, 693mg sodium.

BELGIAN ENDIVE

Availability
Year-round

Peak Season
September through May

Buying Tips
Choose small compact heads with white leaves and pale yellow or deep red tips. Avoid wilted, brown-tipped, or green outer leaves or totally pale green heads. (Belgian endive is grown in the dark; light turns the leaves green and bitter.)

To Store
Wrap in paper towels. Refrigerate in the crisper drawer up to one week.

To Prepare
Trim away any bruised leaves. Rinse briefly under cold running water; Belgian endive is usually quite clean. If using for salad, cut out the tough inner core.

To Cook
Serve Belgian endive raw in salads, with dips, or braise.

Butter-Braised Belgian Endive

This meltingly tender endive is deliciously luxurious.

Prep: 5 minutes   Cook: 25 minutes

- 4 tablespoons butter or margarine
- ½ teaspoon sugar
- ¼ teaspoon salt
- 6 large heads Belgian endive, each halved lengthwise

In 12-inch skillet, melt butter with sugar and salt over medium-low heat. Arrange endive in skillet in one layer. Cover and cook, turning occasionally, until tender and lightly browned, about 15 minutes. Remove cover; cook until half of liquid has evaporated, about 5 minutes longer. Makes 6 accompaniment servings.

Each serving: About 79 calories, 1g protein, 2g carbohydrate, 8g total fat (5g saturated), 21mg cholesterol, 178mg sodium.

ESCAROLE

Availability
Year-round

Peak of Season
October through April

Buying Tips
Like chicory and Belgian endive, escarole's bitterness is its attraction. Look for broad heads of escarole with dark green leaves. If the leaves have white ribs, it indicates that the heads were blanched during cultivation, which is similar to the technique used to keep endive white.

To Store
Refrigerate in open plastic bag up to five days.

To Prepare
Trim stems. Wash well in several changes of cool water to remove any grit. Tear into bite-size pieces.

To Cook
Serve raw in salad combined with sweet-tasting greens, or cook like other bitter greens (See Stir-Frying 101, on page 351).

FENNEL

Availability
September through April

Buying Tips
Fennel is also called *finocchio*. Buy firm, compact, unblemished bulbs. The fronds, if attached, should be bright green and sprightly.

To Store
Refrigerate in the crisper drawer up to three days.

To Prepare
Trim off the fronds, if attached. Rinse fennel under cold running water. Trim the root end and remove the stalks. Cut the bulb lengthwise into wedges or slices; trim the central core.

To Cook
The mild licorice flavor and celerylike texture of fennel is accentuated by roasting. Layer with potatoes in a gratin, or braise.

Oven-Braised Fennel with Parmesan Crust

Fennel, with its subtle licorice flavor, takes nicely to being braised. The Parmesan–bread crumb topping is a classic way to finish the dish.

Prep: 15 minutes   Bake: 45 minutes

- 3 medium fennel bulbs (about 1¼ pounds each)
- 1 cup chicken broth, heated
- ½ teaspoon salt
- ¼ teaspoon ground black pepper
- ¾ cup plain dried bread crumbs
- ¾ cup freshly grated Parmesan cheese
- 3 tablespoons extra-virgin olive oil

1. Preheat oven to 400°F. Trim root ends and remove stalks from fennel bulbs. Cut each fennel bulb lengthwise in half. Cut each half into 6 wedges. Arrange wedges in 13" by 9" baking dish.

2. Pour hot broth over fennel; sprinkle with salt and pepper. Cover tightly with foil and bake 30 minutes.

3. In small bowl, combine bread crumbs, Parmesan, and oil.

4. Remove foil from baking dish. Sprinkle breadcrumb mixture over fennel. Bake, uncovered, until top browns and fennel is tender, 15 minutes longer. Makes 8 accompaniment servings.

Each serving: About 170 calories, 7g protein, 19g carbohydrate, 8g total fat (2g saturated), 5g fiber, 6mg cholesterol, 575mg sodium.

GARLIC

Availability
Year-round

Buying Tips
A garlic head should be firm, heavy for its size, and enclosed in dry, papery layers. Do not buy heads that have soft spots or are sprouting. Store-bought chopped garlic is a nice convenience, but nothing beats the flavor of freshly chopped garlic.

To Store
Store at cool room temperature in a well-ventilated area; it will keep for several months. Do not refrigerate.

To Prepare
Separate the garlic cloves from the head as needed. To peel, place a clove on the work surface and place the flat side of a large knife on top. Press down on the knife to lightly crush the garlic; remove the peel.

To Cook
Garlic is an indispensable seasoning, enhancing everything from soups to sauces. It is often used raw. Whole peeled garlic cloves can also be cooked in oil until golden and then removed, once their flavor has permeated the oil. When cooking garlic, take care not to let it brown, or it could turn bitter. Roasting a whole head of garlic (right) mellows its flavor.

Roasted Garlic

When garlic is roasted, it turns into a soft, spreadable paste with a tantalizingly sweet, mellow flavor. Try it the classic way: spread on grilled or toasted country-style bread. Or toss some of the garlic with cooked vegetables or hot pasta. Tightly covered, the paste will keep for a week in the refrigerator.

Prep: 10 minutes plus cooling   Roast: 1 hour

- 4 **heads garlic**
- 2 **tablespoons extra-virgin olive oil**
- 1/8 **teaspoon salt**
- 1/8 **teaspoon coarsely ground black pepper**
- 4 **thyme sprigs**

1. Preheat oven to 350°F. Remove any loose papery skin from garlic, leaving heads intact. Place garlic on sheet of heavy-duty foil; drizzle with oil and sprinkle with salt and pepper. Place 1 thyme sprig on top of each head.

2. Loosely wrap foil around garlic, folding foil edges securely to keep in oil. Roast until garlic has softened, about 1 hour. Transfer packet to plate. Open carefully and discard foil and herb sprigs.

3. When cool enough to handle, separate garlic into cloves. Squeeze soft garlic from each clove into small bowl and stir until smooth. Makes about 1¼ cups.

Each tablespoon: About 25 calories, 1g protein, 3g carbohydrate, 1g total fat (0g saturated), 0mg cholesterol, 16mg sodium.

ROASTED GARLIC — TASTY AND VERSATILE

Test Kitchen Tip

Here are some flavorful ways to enjoy roasted garlic:
- Mash roasted garlic with softened unsalted butter. Pack into a small crock and serve as a spread for sliced bread.
- When mashing potatoes, toss in some roasted garlic cloves.
- Whisk roasted garlic into the pan juices after roasting a chicken. Add a squeeze of fresh lemon juice, and you have a fabulous sauce.
- Whisk some roasted garlic into homemade or canned minestrone soup for rich flavor.

- Add roasted garlic to your favorite salad dressing, pesto, or stuffing.
- Dot a homemade pizza or focaccia with bits of roasted garlic for extra flavor.
- After steaming green beans, heat oil in a skillet and sauté some halved cherry tomatoes and roasted garlic. Add the beans, season with salt and pepper, and toss until heated through.
- When making quesadillas, spread a thin layer of mashed roasted garlic over half of each tortilla. Top as desired, then fold each tortilla in half and pan-fry.

GREENS

Also see beet greens (page 335), bok choy (page 336), broccoli rabe (page 336), chicory (page 344), escarole (page 348), napa (Chinese) cabbage (page 338), and spinach (page 370).

Availability
Year-round

Buying Tips
Buy clean, crisp (or tender) leaves, free of decay and dirt. Coarse stems or bruised, dried, or yellowing leaves indicate poor quality. Some greens are quite strongly flavored, even spicy. Popular greens for cooking include the following:

Collard greens Wide dark green leaves with thick stems and a pronounced spiciness.

Dandelion greens Spiky green leaves with a slight lemon flavor. Sometimes served raw in salads.

Kale Curly dark green leaves with a mildly bitter taste. Some purple or variegated kales are grown as ornamentals, but they are edible and have a milder flavor than regular kale. Varieties include *Tuscan kale* and *black kale* (*cavolo nero*).

Mustard greens Spicy and bitter, with large coarse leaves.

Swiss chard Delicately flavored greens with wide curly leaves. The stems are edible and should be cut off and prepared separately. Red Swiss chard has thin red stems and veins.

To Store
Wrap loosely in paper towels and place in a plastic bag. Refrigerate in the crisper drawer up to two days.

To Prepare
Rinse in several changes of cool water to remove all the grit. Drain but do not shake dry. Trim tough stems or ribs. Leave whole, or stack and cut into ½- to 1-inch-wide slices.

To Cook
See Stir-Frying 101, opposite.

Southern-Style Greens

This classic recipe makes a big batch, but it can easily be halved. Be traditional and do what Southerners do: drink the flavorful cooking liquid (pot liquor) or dunk chunks of corn bread into it.

Prep: 30 minutes   Cook: 1 hour 15 minutes

5	pounds assorted greens, such as kale, collard greens, and mustard greens
1½	pounds smoked ham hocks
1	medium onion, quartered
8	cups water
1	teaspoon salt
	hot pepper sauce

1. Trim and discard stems and tough ribs from greens; rinse well with cool running water. Cut into ½-inch pieces.

2. In 8-quart saucepot, combine ham hocks, onion, water, and salt; heat to boiling over high heat. Add greens in batches, stirring to wilt. Heat to boiling. Reduce heat; cover and simmer until very tender, about 1 hour. Discard ham hocks. Serve with hot pepper sauce. Makes 10 accompaniment servings.

Each serving: About 82 calories, 5g protein, 13g carbohydrate, 3g total fat (1g saturated), 2mg cholesterol, 560mg sodium.

One of the best ways to serve nutritious greens is to stir-fry them, which cooks them just enough to mellow their flavor but retain their bright color. Tough, bitter greens, such as broccoli rabe and collard greens, should be blanched first to tenderize them and to remove some of their bitterness.

PREPARATION

Discard discolored leaves and trim thick stem ends; slice or tear leaves, if necessary. To blanch (if recommended), add greens to *6 quarts boiling water;* cook, uncovered, as directed (begin timing as soon as greens are added), then drain. Now you're ready to let things sizzle.

STIR-FRYING

In nonstick 12-inch skillet or wok, heat 1 tablespoon olive oil over high heat until hot. Add 2 garlic cloves, crushed with flat side of chef's knife. Cook, stirring frequently (stir-frying), until golden. Add $1/8$ teaspoon salt and stir-fry as directed below. Discard garlic, if desired.

TYPE OF GREENS (1 POUND)	PREPARATION	BLANCH	STIR-FRY
Beet greens	Wash.	No	5 minutes
Bok choy (pak choi, pak choy, Chinese mustard cabbage)	Wash and thinly slice stems. Cut leaves into 1-inch-wide slices.	No	5 minutes
Broccoli rabe (rape, rapini, broccoli di rape)	Wash; trim stems.	5 minutes	5 minutes
Chicory (curly endive)	Wash; tear leaves into bite-size pieces.	No	5 minutes
Collard greens	Wash. Discard stems; cut leaves into 1-inch pieces.	3 minutes	5 minutes
Dandelion greens	Wash.	3 minutes	5 minutes
Escarole (broad-leaf endive)	Wash; tear leaves.	No	5 minutes
Kale, dinosaur kale (lacinato kale, Tuscan kale, black kale)	Wash; discard stems and center ribs. Cut leaves into 1-inch-wide slices.	5 minutes	5 minutes
Mustard greens	Wash.	5 minutes	5 minutes
Napa (Chinese) cabbage, celery cabbage	Wash and thinly slice.	No	3 minutes
Spinach	Wash thoroughly.	No	3 minutes
Swiss chard	Wash and thinly slice stems. Cut leaves into 1-inch-wide slices.	No	3 minutes
Watercress	Wash.	No	3 minutes

JICAMA

Availability
Year-round

Buying Tips
Turnip-shaped jicama has thin brown skin and white flesh. It tastes like water chestnuts and ranges in size from one to six pounds. Choose smaller jicama to avoid any woodiness.

To Store
Refrigerate in the crisper drawer up to two weeks.

To Prepare
Scrub under cold running water. Peel and slice to serve raw in salads or with dips, or cut into bite-size pieces; substitute for water chestnuts in stir-fries.

KOHLRABI

Availability
Year-round

Peak Season
May and June

Buying Tips
Bulbs should be pale green or purple, smooth and un-blemished, with fresh-looking tops and tender skin.

To Store
Discard leafy tops. Refrigerate bulbs in the crisper drawer up to one week.

To Prepare
Cut off the stems, then peel the bulb with a vegetable peeler or small knife, being sure to remove the fibrous layer just under the skin. Slice, quarter, shred, or cut into matchstick strips.

To Cook
Kohlrabi can be served raw in salads, sautéed, or simmered. In a medium saucepan, heat 1 inch of water to boiling over high heat; add sliced kohlrabi and heat to boiling. Reduce heat to medium-low; cover and cook until tender, 15 to 30 minutes; drain. Toss with butter.

LEEKS

Availability
Year-round

Peak Season
April through September

Buying Tips
Buy leeks that are straight, with firm white roots and leafy green tops. Avoid leeks with wilted or yellowish tops or cracked roots.

To Store
Refrigerate in the crisper drawer up to three days.

To Prepare
Cut off the roots and trim the dark green tops, leaving about 1 inch of the pale green area. Leeks have sand hidden between their layers and should be washed carefully. Cut the leeks lengthwise, almost halfway through, leaving 2 to 3 inches of the root ends uncut. Rinse the leeks in a large bowl of cold water, swishing to remove all the sand. Or chop the trimmed leeks and swish in a bowl of cold water. With a slotted spoon, transfer to a colander to drain.

Braised Leeks

Chopped leeks braised with a bit of butter make a divine side dish for mild-flavored fish.

Prep: 10 minutes   Cook: 15 minutes

1	bunch leeks (about 1½ pounds)
1	tablespoon butter or margarine
⅛	teaspoon salt
¼	cup water

1. Cut off roots and trim dark green tops from leeks; cut each leek lengthwise in half, then crosswise into ½-inch-thick slices. Rinse leeks in large bowl of cold water, swishing to remove sand. Transfer to colander to drain, leaving sand in bottom of bowl.

Leeks Vinaigrette

2. In 2-quart saucepan, combine leeks, butter, salt, and water; heat to boiling over high heat. Reduce heat; cover and simmer until just tender, about 5 minutes. Remove cover; cook until water has evaporated, about 5 minutes longer. Makes 4 accompaniment servings.

Each serving: About 68 calories, 1g protein, 10g carbohydrate, 3g total fat (2g saturated), 8mg cholesterol, 116mg sodium.

Leeks Vinaigrette

If you can find only large leeks, use just four. Cook them until tender (they'll take a bit longer), then cut lengthwise in half to serve.

Prep: 25 minutes   Cook: 10 minutes

8	slender leeks (2½ pounds)
2⅛	teaspoons salt
1	tablespoon red wine vinegar
1	teaspoon Dijon mustard
	pinch ground black pepper
2	tablespoons olive oil
1	tablespoon chopped fresh parsley

1. In 5-quart Dutch oven, heat *3 quarts water* to boiling over high heat. Meanwhile, cut off roots from leeks and trim leeks to 6 inches; discard green tops. Beginning at green end, make 4-inch-long slit in each leek, cutting almost halfway through, leaving 2 inches of root end uncut. Rinse leeks in large bowl of cold water, swishing to remove sand. Transfer to colander to drain, leaving sand in bottom of bowl.

2. Add leeks and 2 teaspoons salt to boiling water in Dutch oven; cook until tender, about 10 minutes. Transfer leeks to colander; rinse with cold running water. Drain; pat dry.

3. Prepare vinaigrette: In small bowl, with wire whisk, mix vinegar, mustard, remaining ⅛ teaspoon salt, and pepper until blended. In thin, steady stream, whisk in oil until blended, then whisk in parsley.

4. Arrange leeks on serving platter in single layer. Spoon vinaigrette over. Makes 4 first-course servings.

Each serving: About 146 calories, 2g protein, 20g carbohydrate, 7g total fat (1g saturated), 0mg cholesterol, 424mg sodium.

MUSHROOMS

Availability
Year-round

Buying Tips
Mushrooms generally fall into three categories: *common, wild,* and *exotic.* Common mushrooms are the familiar *white button* variety. Wild mushrooms are foraged from forests and are strictly seasonal: They include the

chanterelle, morel, and *porcini.* Wild mushrooms are always expensive. Exotic mushrooms are sometimes called wild mushrooms, but they are really just unusual cultivated varieties. Some exotic mushrooms include *shiitake* (meaty-tasting and often used in stir-fries), *oyster* (mild-flavored and smooth-textured), *enoki* (long thin white stems with tiny caps), *portobello* (very large with somewhat flat caps and a rich meaty flavor), and *cremini* (small portobellos with dark brown caps). Buy firm mushrooms with tightly closed gills (dark undersides). Mushrooms should never be withered, wrinkled, or show any sign of moisture.

To Store

Place mushrooms (unwashed) in a brown paper bag. Refrigerate up to three days.

To Prepare

Do not peel mushrooms. Rinse them briefly under cold running water and drain well on paper towels. The tough stems of shiitake mushrooms must be removed; trim the stem ends of other varieties. Leave mushrooms whole or prepare as the recipe directs.

Sautéed Mixed Mushrooms

This classic French preparation brings out the meaty texture and earthy flavor of mushrooms. Use just one variety, if you prefer.

Prep: 15 minutes   Cook: 10 minutes

2	tablespoons butter or margarine
¼	cup minced shallots
8	ounces white mushrooms, trimmed and quartered
4	ounces shiitake mushrooms, stems removed and caps cut into 1-inch-thick slices
4	ounces oyster mushrooms, cut in half if large
¼	teaspoon salt
⅛	teaspoon ground black pepper
⅛	teaspoon dried thyme
1	small garlic clove, finely chopped
1	tablespoon chopped fresh parsley

In 12-inch skillet, melt butter over medium-high heat. Add shallots and cook, stirring, 1 minute. Stir in white, shiitake, and oyster mushrooms. Sprinkle with salt, pepper, and thyme and cook, stirring frequently, until mushrooms are tender and liquid has evaporated, about 8 minutes. Stir in garlic and parsley and cook 1 minute longer. Makes 4 accompaniment servings.

Each serving: About 86 calories, 3g protein, 7g carbohydrate, 6g total fat (4g saturated), 16mg cholesterol, 207mg sodium.

Lemon-Marinated Mushrooms

A generous addition of shallots and a hit of fresh lemon juice bring out the flavor of the mushrooms.

Prep: 15 minutes plus standing

1	pound small mushrooms, trimmed and cut into quarters
¼	cup minced shallots
¼	cup chopped fresh parsley
5	tablespoons olive oil
1	tablespoon plus 1 teaspoon fresh lemon juice
½	teaspoon salt
¼	teaspoon ground black pepper

In large bowl, combine mushrooms, shallots, parsley, oil, lemon juice, salt, and pepper until mixed. Let stand at room temperature 1 hour, stirring occasionally. Serve, or refrigerate up to 6 hours. Makes 6 accompaniment servings.

Each serving: About 124 calories, 2g protein, 5g carbohydrate, 12g total fat (2g saturated), 0mg cholesterol, 198mg sodium.

MUSHROOM MEASUREMENTS

Test Kitchen Tip One pound of fresh white mushrooms equals approximately:

12 large (stuffing) mushrooms
20 medium mushrooms
30 to 40 small mushrooms
5 cups sliced mushrooms
2 cups cooked sliced mushrooms
½ cup cooked finely chopped mushrooms

OKRA

Availability
Year-round

Peak Season
July through September

Buying Tips
Buy tender, young pods less than 4½ inches long, without any brown spots.

To Store
Place in a brown paper bag. Refrigerate in the crisper drawer up to two days.

To Prepare
Rinse okra under cold running water and cut off the stem ends. Leave whole or slice.

Fried Okra

In this down-home favorite, okra gets a classic cornmeal coating. If pods are small, there is no need to cut them.

Prep: 15 minutes   Cook: 3 minutes per batch

1	large egg
12	ounces okra, cut crosswise into 1-inch pieces
½	cup cornmeal
½	teaspoon salt
⅛	teaspoon ground red pepper (cayenne)
	vegetable oil for frying

1. In medium bowl, lightly beat egg; add okra and toss to coat. On waxed paper, combine cornmeal, salt, and ground red pepper. Add okra and toss to coat.

2. Meanwhile, in heavy 10-inch skillet, heat ¼ inch oil over medium-high heat until hot. In small batches, fry okra until golden, 2 to 3 minutes. With slotted spoon, transfer to paper towels to drain. Makes 4 accompaniment servings.

Each serving: About 205 calories, 5g protein, 20g carbohydrate, 12g total fat (2g saturated), 53mg cholesterol, 313mg sodium.

ONIONS

Availability
Year-round

Buying Tips
Onions should be firm and clean, with dry, papery skin. Do not buy onions that have sprouted. Yellow *cooking onions* (also called *Spanish* onions) range from small to very large and have a sharp flavor that sweetens and mellows when cooked. *Red onions* have a stronger flavor than yellow onions, and although some people like to cook with them, they are probably best when sliced and served raw in salads. *White onions* are quite mild; they are the preferred cooking onion of many Latino cooks. Sweet onions, often named for the location of their harvest, are the ultimate salad onion: *Maui, Walla Walla,* and *Vidalia* are three of the most well known. Most are available in the late spring. Small white onions are often called *boiling onions;* they are braised until tender and often mixed with cream sauce. *Pearl onions* are smaller than boiling onions and can be red, white, or yellow.

To Store
Store onions in a cool (60°F or below) dark place (or in the refrigerator) in a container with good air circulation for up to several weeks.

To peel cooking, red, and sweet onions, trim the root and blossom ends, cutting off as little flesh as possible. With a small knife, peel off all the skin, along with the first layer of onion and the slippery membrane. To loosen the skins of small white boiling or pearl onions to make them easier to peel, in a large saucepan, heat 2 inches of water to boiling. Add onions and cook for 1 minute. Drain and rinse under cold running water.

Caramelized Onions

Sweet glazed onions are perfect with a holiday roast.

Prep: 15 minutes   Cook: 35 minutes

2   pounds small white onions
3   tablespoons butter or margarine
2   tablespoons sugar
½   teaspoon salt

1. Peel onions, leaving a little bit of the root end attached to help onions hold their shape.

2. In 12-inch skillet, combine onions and *3 cups water;* heat to boiling over high heat. Reduce heat; cover and simmer until tender, 10 to 15 minutes. Drain well.

3. In same skillet, melt butter over medium heat. Add onions, sugar, and salt; cook, shaking skillet occasionally, until onions

have browned, about 15 minutes. Makes 10 accompaniment servings.

Each serving: About 71 calories, 1g protein, 10g carbohydrate, 4g total fat (2g saturated), 9mg cholesterol, 159mg sodium.

Caramelized Onions with Raisins

Prepare as directed above but add ½ **cup golden raisins** at end of cooking; heat through.

Caramelized Shallots

Prepare as directed but substitute **shallots** for onions.

Creamed Pearl Onions

A traditional Thanksgiving side dish that is great year-round. For a classic look, be sure to use white—not purple—onions.

Prep: 20 minutes   Cook: 20 minutes

2   baskets (10 ounces each) pearl onions
3   tablespoons butter or margarine
3   tablespoons all-purpose flour
2   cups milk, warmed
¼   teaspoon salt
⅛   teaspoon ground black pepper
     pinch ground nutmeg

1. In 10-inch skillet, heat *1 inch water* to boiling over high heat. Add onions; heat to boiling. Reduce heat; cover and simmer until tender, 10 to 15 minutes. Drain.

2. When cool enough to handle, peel onions, leaving a little of root end attached to help onions hold their shape.

3. Meanwhile, prepare white sauce: In heavy 2-quart saucepan, melt butter over low heat. Add flour and cook, stirring, 1 minute. With wire whisk, gradually whisk in warm milk. Cook over medium heat, stirring constantly with wooden spoon, until sauce has thickened and boils. Reduce heat and simmer, stirring frequently, 3 minutes. Stir in salt, pepper, and nutmeg; remove from heat.

4. Return onions to skillet. Add white sauce and cook, stirring, until heated through. Makes 10 accompaniment servings.

Each serving: About 87 calories, 2g protein, 8g carbohydrate, 5g total fat (3g saturated), 16mg cholesterol, 121mg sodium.

Creamed Onions and Peas

Prepare as directed above but add **1 package (10 ounces) frozen peas,** thawed, to onions with sauce.

GREEN ONIONS, SCALLIONS, RAMPS, AND SHALLOTS

Availability
Green onions, scallions, and shallots, year-round; ramps, late March, April, and May

Buying Tips
Green onions are the shoots of any onion before the bulb has formed. *Scallions* are the shoots of white onions, although in some parts of the United States, the word *scallion* is used to mean any green onion. *Ramps* are tender wild onions that shoot up in the forests of West Virginia; they are very strong and should be used judiciously. *Shallots* are made up of bulbs containing two or three cloves each (similar to garlic). They have a complex flavor and are an integral part of French cooking.

Sautéed Green Onions

Try these as a light side dish or as a topping for fish.

Prep: 15 minutes   Cook: 8 minutes

1	tablespoon vegetable oil
5	bunches green onions, cut into 2-inch pieces (2½ cups)
½	teaspoon freshly grated lemon peel
¼	teaspoon salt
⅛	teaspoon coarsely ground black pepper
½	cup water

In 12-inch skillet, heat oil over medium-high heat. Add green onions, lemon peel, salt, and pepper and cook, stirring frequently, 2 minutes. Add water and cook, stirring, until green onions are tender and lightly browned and liquid has evaporated, 5 to 7 minutes longer. Makes 4 accompaniment servings.

Each serving: About 52 calories, 1g protein, 5g carbohydrate, 4g total fat (0g saturated), 0mg cholesterol, 154mg sodium.

PARSNIPS

Availability
Year-round, but less plentiful in April, May, and September

Buying Tips
Look for smooth, firm, well-shaped medium parsnips. Avoid large coarse roots and gray or soft spots.

To Store
Place in a plastic bag with a few holes poked in it. Refrigerate in the crisper drawer up to two weeks.

To Prepare
Scrub under cold running water. Trim the ends and peel. Leave whole, slice, cut lengthwise in half, or cut into quarters.

Pureed Parsnips

When pureed, parsnips may look like mashed potatoes, but that's where the similarity ends. They are one of the sweetest of all the root vegetables.

Prep: 15 minutes   Cook: 15 minutes

2½	pounds parsnips, peeled and cut into 1-inch pieces
1	cup milk, warmed
4	tablespoons butter or margarine, softened
1	teaspoon salt
2	tablespoons chopped fresh parsley (optional)

1. In 4-quart saucepan, combine parsnips and enough *water* to cover; heat to boiling over high heat. Reduce heat; cover and simmer until tender, about 15 minutes. Drain.

2. In food processor with knife blade attached, combine parsnips, warm milk, butter, and salt and puree until smooth. Serve hot, sprinkled with parsley, if desired. Makes 8 accompaniment servings.

Each serving: About 166 calories, 3g protein, 23g carbohydrate, 7g total fat (4g saturated), 20mg cholesterol, 377mg sodium.

PEAS

Availability
Year-round

Peak Season
April, May, and June

Buying Tips
The majority of peas are frozen or canned, so relatively few fresh peas ever make it to market. Frozen peas are a very good, reliable product, and we use them often in our recipes. When buying fresh peas, look for shiny light green pods that feel heavy, indicating they are full of plump medium peas. Large overmature peas tend to be starchy. *Petit pois* are small baby peas. One pound of peas in the pod yields about 1 cup shelled peas.

To Store
Place peas in their pods in a plastic bag. Refrigerate in the crisper drawer up to two days.

To Prepare
Remove the stem and string from each pod. Run your thumb along the length of the "seam" to open the pod and release the peas.

To Cook
To cook fresh peas, in a saucepan, heat 1 inch of water and 1 teaspoon salt to boiling over high heat; add peas and heat to boiling. Reduce heat to medium-high; cover saucepan and cook just until tender, 3 to 5 minutes; drain.

Peas with Green Onions and Mint

Fresh mint is a very good match for peas; the green onions add an extra touch of flavor.

Prep: 10 minutes Cook: 6 minutes

- 2 tablespoons butter or margarine
- ½ cup chopped green onions
- 1 bag (20 ounces) frozen peas, thawed
- ½ teaspoon salt
- ¼ teaspoon coarsely ground black pepper
- ¼ cup chopped fresh mint

1. In 10-inch skillet, melt butter over medium heat. Add green onions and cook, stirring frequently, until tender, about 2 minutes. Stir in peas, salt, and pepper and cook, stirring frequently, until heated through, about 3 minutes longer.

2. Remove skillet from heat; stir in mint. Makes 6 accompaniment servings.

Each serving: About 111 calories, 5g protein, 14g carbohydrate, 4g total fat (2g saturated), 10mg cholesterol, 340mg sodium.

SNOW PEAS AND SUGAR SNAP PEAS

Availability
Snow peas, year-round; sugar snap peas, May through August

Buying Tips
Snow peas (also called *Chinese pea pods*) should have fresh-looking, flat, bright green pods; the pods are so tender that they are eaten. *Sugar snap peas*, a variety of snow peas, should look plump, bright green, and crisp. Avoid wilted, mottled, or brown-tipped pods. The peas resemble regular green peas, but the pod is always eaten along with the peas.

To Store
Place in a plastic bag. Refrigerate in the crisper drawer up to two days.

To Prepare
Rinse under cold running water. Remove the stem and the string from each pod; do not shell.

Mixed Pea Pod Stir-Fry

This sweet and tender-crisp medley celebrates the glorious flavor of fresh green vegetables.

Prep: 15 minutes   Cook: 10 minutes

- 1 teaspoon salt
- 8 ounces green beans, trimmed
- 2 teaspoons vegetable oil
- 4 ounces snow peas, trimmed and strings removed
- 4 ounces sugar snap peas, trimmed and strings removed
- 1 garlic clove, finely chopped
- 1 tablespoon soy sauce

1. In 12-inch skillet, combine *4 cups water* and salt; heat to boiling over high heat. Add green beans and cook 3 minutes. Drain; wipe skillet dry with paper towels.

2. In same skillet, heat oil over high heat. Add green beans and cook, stirring frequently (stir-frying), until they begin to brown, 2 to 3 minutes Add snow peas, sugar snap peas, and garlic; stir-fry until snow peas and sugar snap peas are tender-crisp, about 1 minute longer. Stir in soy sauce and remove from heat. Makes 4 accompaniment servings.

Each serving: About 63 calories, 3g protein, 8g carbohydrate, 2g total fat (0g saturated), 0mg cholesterol, 844mg sodium.

Mixed Pea Pod Stir-Fry

PEPPERS, HOT

Availability
Year-round

Buying Tips
Purchase peppers that will provide the desired amount of heat to fit the recipe and to suit your taste. Depending on the variety of pepper, the degree of heat can range from relatively mild to fiery hot. *Anaheim peppers* are long and tapering, usually green, and among the mildest. *Poblano peppers* are large tapered dark green peppers that are moderately hot and are usually stuffed. The ever-popular *jalapeño pepper* is the workhorse of the well-spiced kitchen. It can be dark green or red and is often quite hot. Long curved *cayenne peppers* can be green or red and are a staple of Indian cooking. *Serrano peppers* are thin and small, with tapered tips, and are hotter still. The hottest of them all are the *habanero* and *Scotch bonnets*: Yellow, red, orange, or green, they resemble deflated little bells, 1 to 2 inches in diameter. They have a distinctive vegetablelike flavor that manages to hold its own even through the incendiary heat.

To Store
Refrigerate in the crisper drawer up to one week.

To Prepare
Hot peppers contain capsaicin, a colorless substance that can seriously irritate your skin and eyes. Wear rubber gloves while preparing hot peppers, and avoid touching your face, eyes, or other areas with delicate skin. Wash the gloves and your hands thoroughly with hot soapy water after handling hot peppers.

Remove the stems, seeds, and membranes (ribs) from the peppers. (Most of the heat is in the membranes and seeds; don't remove them if you prefer more heat.) Rinse the peppers under cold running water. Roast and peel Anaheim or poblano peppers (Roasted Peppers Master Recipe, page 360) before using in recipes.

PEPPERS, SWEET

Availability
Year-round

Buying Tips
Buy peppers that are firm, shiny, and thick-fleshed. Avoid wilted or flabby peppers with cuts or soft spots. *Red peppers* are mature (ripe) *green peppers*, but *yellow* and *purple peppers* are different

varieties. Long pale green *Italian frying peppers* are mild flavored and a good substitute for green peppers. *Pimientos* are mild thick-fleshed red peppers that are almost always canned.

To Store
Refrigerate in the crisper drawer up to one week.

ROASTED PEPPERS MASTER RECIPE

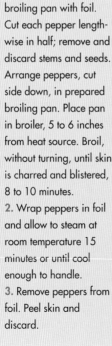

1. Preheat broiler. Line broiling pan with foil. Cut each pepper lengthwise in half; remove and discard stems and seeds. Arrange peppers, cut side down, in prepared broiling pan. Place pan in broiler, 5 to 6 inches from heat source. Broil, without turning, until skin is charred and blistered, 8 to 10 minutes.
2. Wrap peppers in foil and allow to steam at room temperature 15 minutes or until cool enough to handle.
3. Remove peppers from foil. Peel skin and discard.

To Prepare
Rinse peppers under cold running water. Trim the stem end and remove the seeds and white membranes (ribs). Use peppers whole, cut in half to stuff, or cut into strips, rings, or matchstick strips.

Roasted Peppers with Fresh Basil

Try these colorful peppers with any of our suggested toppings below, or mix a few together.

Prep: 35 minutes

2 large red peppers, roasted (left)
2 large yellow peppers, roasted (left)
1 tablespoon extra-virgin olive oil
¼ teaspoon salt or to taste
⅛ teaspoon ground black pepper
3 large fresh basil leaves, thinly sliced

1. Cut peppers lengthwise into ½-inch-wide strips. Pat dry with paper towels.
2. Place pepper strips on serving platter; drizzle with oil and sprinkle with salt and black pepper. To serve, top with basil leaves, or cover and refrigerate up to overnight. Makes 6 appetizer servings.

Each serving without additional toppings: About 38 calories, 1g protein, 4g carbohydrate, 2g total fat (0g saturated), 0mg cholesterol, 97mg sodium.

ADDITIONAL TOPPINGS

- Chopped fresh parsley, oregano, mint, chives, sage, marjoram, rosemary, savory, or a combination thereof
- Drained capers
- Finely chopped red onion
- Anchovy fillets, drained and chopped
- Minced garlic
- Crushed red pepper
- Chopped pitted olives, such as Kalamata or Gaeta
- Crumbled feta cheese

PLANTAINS

Availability
Year-round

Buying Tips
Plantains are related to the banana but they aren't as sweet. Unripe green plantains are very hard and starchy and are usually boiled. Ripe yellow plantains have a mild bananalike flavor. Very ripe plantains have dark brown to black skin and are slightly sweet.

To Store
Store plantains at room temperature, but refrigerate if they are very ripe.

To Prepare
Cut plantains crosswise into three or four pieces. Score the peel along the ridges, down to the flesh. Pull the peel away from the flesh and cut into pieces as directed.

Golden Sautéed Plantains

These are a great change of pace when you want an unusual side dish. Try them with roast pork or ham. If you can't find plantains, substitute very green unripe bananas; the cooking time may be slightly shorter.

Prep: 10 minutes   Cook: 20 minutes

- 4 tablespoons butter or margarine
- 4 very ripe plantains (2¼ pounds), peeled and cut on diagonal into ½-inch-thick slices
- ½ teaspoon salt or 1 tablespoon brown sugar

1. In 12-inch skillet, melt 2 tablespoons butter over medium-high heat. Add half of plantains and cook until lightly browned, about 5 minutes per side. Transfer to warm platter; sprinkle lightly with half of salt or brown sugar. Keep warm.

2. Repeat with remaining plantains, butter, and salt or brown sugar. Makes 8 accompaniment servings.

Each serving: About 152 calories, 1g protein, 26g carbohydrate, 6g total fat (4g saturated), 16mg cholesterol, 207mg sodium.

POTATOES

Availability
Year-round

Peak Season
October through December; new potatoes, April through June

Buying Tips
Buy potatoes that are well shaped and firm, without any blemishes or sprouts. Large cuts or bruises only mean you will have a lot of waste when peeling. Avoid potatoes with a greenish cast. Potatoes are categorized by the amount of starch in the flesh. *Baking potatoes,* such as russet, Idaho, and Burbank, are quite starchy: when baked, their flesh becomes fluffy and dry. *Waxy potatoes,* such as the red-skinned variety, hold their shape after cooking and are preferred for salads and boiling. When time is short, don't bother to peel them. *All-purpose potatoes,* such as Yukon Gold, have the qualities of both varieties and are, therefore, quite versatile. Not all small potatoes are new potatoes. True *new potatoes* are baby potatoes that have been harvested before they are fully grown; they are a seasonal delicacy worth waiting for.

Store in a cool (45° to 50°F) dark place with good air circulation, up to several weeks (don't refrigerate). In warmer weather, potatoes will keep up to one week.

To Prepare

If recipe directs, peel the potatoes and remove any "eyes" with the end of the vegetable peeler or the tip of a small knife. Otherwise, scrub the potatoes with a vegetable brush under cold running water.

Basic Mashed Potatoes

Here is our recipe for fluffy potatoes, plus five easy variations. To achieve a perfectly smooth texture, use a ricer or food mill.

Prep: 25 minutes   Cook: 30 minutes

- 3 **pounds all-purpose potatoes (9 medium), peeled and cut into 1-inch pieces**
- 4 **tablespoons butter or margarine, cut into pieces**
- 1½ **teaspoons salt**
- 1 **cup milk, warmed**

1. In 4-quart saucepan, combine potatoes and enough *water* to cover; heat to boiling over high heat. Reduce heat; cover and simmer until tender, about 15 minutes. Drain.

2. Return potatoes to saucepan. Mash potatoes with butter and salt. Gradually add warm milk; continue to mash until smooth and well blended. Keep warm. Makes 8 accompaniment servings.

Each serving: About 204 calories, 4g protein, 32g carbohydrate, 7g total fat (4g saturated), 20mg cholesterol, 516mg sodium.

Mashed Potatoes with Garlic and Lemon

Prepare as directed above in Step 1. Meanwhile, with garlic press, press **2 garlic cloves** into 1-quart saucepan with butter and salt. Cook, stirring, over low heat until butter has melted and garlic is golden, 2 to 3 minutes. Add garlic mixture to mashed potatoes with milk; mash. Stir in **2 tablespoons finely chopped parsley** and **1 teaspoon freshly grated lemon peel.**

Mashed Potatoes with Horseradish

Prepare as directed (left) but add **2 tablespoons bottled white horseradish** with milk.

Mashed Potatoes with Parsnips

Prepare as directed (left) but substitute **1 pound parsnips,** peeled and cut into 1-inch pieces, for 1 pound potatoes and use only ¾ **cup milk.**

Mashed Potatoes with Caramelized Onions

Prepare as directed (left) in Step 1. Meanwhile, heat ¼ **cup olive oil** in 12-inch skillet over medium heat. Add **4 large red onions** (about 3 pounds), thinly sliced, and ¼ **teaspoon salt.** Cook, stirring occasionally, until very tender and deep golden brown, about 30 minutes. In Step 2, omit butter and use only ½ **cup milk;** coarsely mash potatoes. Stir all but 3 tablespoons caramelized onions into potatoes; heat through. Top with remaining caramelized onions.

Lowfat Mashed Potatoes

Prepare as directed (left) but use Yukon Gold potatoes. Omit butter and substitute **3 tablespoons olive oil;** use only **1 teaspoon salt** and use **lowfat (1%) milk.** Mash potatoes.

ACCORDION POTATOES

Test Kitchen Tip

Accordion Potatoes (right), only look like they were prepared by a professional chef. Here's the trick: Place a chopstick along each long side of potato, then, using a chef's knife, cut crosswise (making even slices) until the knife meets the chopsticks. The chopsticks will stop you when the knife is about seven eighths of the way through, leaving the bottom of the potato intact. For easy slicing, we chose thin-skinned red potatoes.

Accordion Potatoes

Bake this festive dish in the same oven with a holiday ham or Sunday roast. Cut whole potatoes almost all the way through in a series of close vertical slices so they fan out as they cook. Choose potatoes that weigh no more than 6 ounces each; they won't cook in time if too large.

Prep: 20 minutes   Bake/Broil: 1 hour 22 minutes

- 8 medium red potatoes (about 6 ounces each)
- 32 (3-inch) thyme sprigs
- 4 tablespoons butter or margarine, melted
- ½ teaspoon salt
- ½ teaspoon coarsely ground black pepper
- 1 tablespoon chopped fresh parsley
- 1 tablespoon snipped fresh chives

1. Preheat oven to 325°F and grease 13" by 9" baking pan.

2. Set 1 potato on cutting board. With large knife, starting at one end of potato, cut a series of vertical slices about ⅛ inch apart, making sure not to cut all the way through (Accordian Potatoes, left). Repeat with remaining potatoes.

3. Insert a thyme sprig into 4 of the cuts in each potato. Arrange potatoes in prepared pan, cut side up; drizzle butter over the tops. Sprinkle potatoes with salt and pepper; cover baking pan tightly with foil.

4. Place pan in oven on lowest oven rack and bake potatoes 1 hour and 15 minutes or until fork-tender. Remove pan from oven and remove foil.

5. Turn oven control to broil. Place pan with potatoes on rack in broiler at closest position to heat source. Broil until browned on top, 5 to 7 minutes. Sprinkle with parsley and chives. Makes 8 accompaniment servings.

Each serving: About 206 calories, 3g protein, 35g carbohydrate, 16g total fat (4g saturated) 16mg cholesterol, 219mg sodium.

Accordion Potatoes

Baby Potatoes with Rosemary

For the best golden brown potatoes, roast them with olive oil and herbs in a hot oven. Instead of baby potatoes, you can also use larger potatoes cut into bite-size pieces.

Prep: 20 minutes   Roast: 30 to 40 minutes

- 5 pounds assorted small potatoes, such as red, white, purple, or golden, cut in half
- ¼ cup olive oil
- 2 tablespoons chopped fresh rosemary or thyme or 1 teaspoon dried rosemary or thyme
- 1½ teaspoons salt
- ½ teaspoon coarsely ground black pepper

Preheat oven to 425°F. In large roasting pan (17" by 11½"), toss potatoes, oil, rosemary, salt, and pepper to coat. Roast potatoes, turning occasionally, until golden and tender, 30 to 40 minutes. Makes 10 accompaniment servings.

Each serving: About 232 calories, 4g protein, 41g carbohydrate, 6g total fat (1g saturated), 0mg cholesterol, 366mg sodium.

Herbed Roasted Potatoes

Potato chunks tossed with parsley and butter cook into tender morsels when wrapped in foil.

Prep: 15 minutes   Bake: 30 minutes

2   tablespoons butter or margarine
1   tablespoon chopped fresh parsley
½   teaspoon freshly grated lemon peel
½   teaspoon salt
⅛   teaspoon coarsely ground black pepper
1½   pounds small red potatoes, cut in half

1. Preheat oven to 450°F. In 3-quart saucepan, melt butter with parsley, lemon peel, salt, and pepper over medium-low heat. Remove saucepan from heat; add potatoes and toss well to coat.

2. Place potato mixture in center of 24" by 18" sheet of heavy-duty foil. Fold edges over and pinch to seal tightly.

3. Place package in jelly-roll pan and bake until potatoes are tender when they are pierced (through foil) with knife, about 30 minutes. Makes 6 accompaniment servings.

Each serving: About 126 calories, 2g protein, 20g carbohydrate, 4g total fat (2g saturated), 10mg cholesterol, 241mg sodium.

Oven Fries

A quick way to make crispy "fries" without frying. Just don't crowd them in the pan, or they won't crisp.

Prep: 10 minutes   Bake: 45 minutes

3   medium baking potatoes or sweet potatoes (8 ounces each), not peeled
1   tablespoon vegetable oil
½   teaspoon salt
⅛   teaspoon ground black pepper

1. Preheat oven to 425°F. Cut each potato lengthwise into quarters, then cut each quarter lengthwise into 3 wedges.

2. In jelly-roll pan, toss potatoes, oil, salt, and pepper to coat. Bake, turning occasionally, until tender, about 45 minutes. Makes 4 accompaniment servings.

Each serving: About 156 calories, 4g protein, 28g carbohydrate, 4g total fat (0g saturated), 0mg cholesterol, 301mg sodium.

Baked Potatoes

Utterly simple and always satisfying.

Prep: 5 minutes   Bake: 45 minutes

6   medium baking potatoes (8 ounces each), not peeled
    choice of toppings: sour cream, butter or margarine, shredded Cheddar cheese, snipped fresh chives, crumbled cooked bacon (optional)

Preheat oven to 450°F. Wash potatoes and dry with paper towels; pierce with fork. Place directly on oven rack and bake until tender, about 45 minutes. If desired, slash top of potatoes; serve with choice of toppings. Makes 6 accompaniment servings.

Each serving without topping: About 166 calories, 3g protein, 38g carbohydrate, 0g total fat (0g saturated), 0mg cholesterol, 12mg sodium.

Twice-Baked Potatoes

Bake potatoes as directed. Cut them lengthwise in half. Scoop potato flesh into bowl; reserve shells. Mash potatoes with **4 tablespoons butter or margarine,** cut into pieces. Stir in **2 cups ricotta or cottage cheese, 1 cup shredded sharp Cheddar cheese, ½ teaspoon salt,** and ¼ **teaspoon coarsely ground black pepper.** Spoon into reserved potato shells, mounding slightly. Place in jelly-roll pan; sprinkle with ½ **cup shredded sharp Cheddar cheese.** Bake in 450°F oven 10 minutes longer. Makes 12 servings.

Each serving: About 245 calories, 10g protein, 21g carbohydrate, 14g total fat (9g saturated), 46mg cholesterol, 263mg sodium.

Scalloped Potatoes

Elegant and easy scalloped potatoes make a great family or company dish. For a variation, 30 minutes before the potatoes are done, generously sprinkle with shredded Gruyère cheese—a classic French treatment.

Prep: 30 minutes   Bake: 1 hour 30 minutes

- 3 tablespoons butter or margarine
- 1 small onion, chopped
- 3 tablespoons all-purpose flour
- 1½ cups milk, warmed
- 1 teaspoon salt
- ⅛ teaspoon ground black pepper
- 2 pounds all-purpose potatoes (6 medium), peeled and thinly sliced

1. Preheat oven to 375°F. In heavy 2-quart saucepan, melt butter over low heat. Add onion and cook until tender, about 5 minutes. Add flour and cook, stirring, 1 minute. With wire whisk, gradually whisk in warm milk. Cook over medium heat, stirring constantly with wooden spoon, until sauce has thickened and boils. Reduce heat and simmer, stirring frequently, 1 minute. Stir in salt and pepper; remove from heat.

2. Grease 9-inch square baking dish or shallow 2-quart casserole. Arrange half of potatoes in single layer in prepared dish; pour half of sauce on top. Repeat layers. Cover and bake 1 hour. Remove cover and bake until potatoes are tender and top is golden, about 30 minutes longer. Makes 6 accompaniment servings.

Each serving: About 199 calories, 5g protein, 28g carbohydrate, 8g total fat (5g saturated), 24mg cholesterol, 484mg sodium.

Potatoes Anna

This potato cake gets its distinctive appearance from weighting the concentric circles of layered sliced potatoes during baking so they stick together. A nonstick skillet makes unmolding a snap.

Prep: 25 minutes   Cook/Bake: 45 minutes

- 4 medium baking potatoes (8 ounces each)
- 3 tablespoons butter or margarine
- ½ teaspoon salt
- ⅛ teaspoon ground black pepper

1. Preheat oven to 425°F. Peel potatoes and cut into paper-thin slices. In nonstick oven-safe 10-inch skillet (if skillet is not oven-safe, wrap handle with double layer of foil), melt butter over low heat. Remove skillet from heat. Beginning at outside edge of skillet, arrange one layer of potatoes in circles of slightly overlapping slices. Sprinkle with some salt and pepper. Continue layering potatoes in concentric circles to make two or three more layers, sprinkling each layer with salt and pepper.

2. Lightly grease sheet of foil; place foil, greased side down, on top of potatoes. Place heavy 10-inch skillet on top of foil to weight down potatoes and cook over medium-high heat until underside is lightly browned, 5 to 10 minutes.

3. Place skillet in oven and bake 15 minutes. Uncover and bake until potatoes are tender, about 10 minutes more. Invert skillet onto serving plate. To serve, cut potato cake into wedges. Makes 8 accompaniment servings.

Each serving: About 110 calories, 2g protein, 15g carbohydrate, 5g total fat (3g saturated), 12mg cholesterol, 194mg sodium.

Parmesan Potatoes

Melted Parmesan cheese makes these roasted red potatoes absolutely irresistible.

Prep: 10 minutes   Bake: 30 minutes

- 4 medium red potatoes (5 ounces each)
- ½ cup freshly grated Parmesan cheese
- 1 tablespoon butter or margarine, melted
- ¼ teaspoon coarsely ground black pepper

1. Preheat oven to 450°F. Line jelly-roll pan with foil; lightly grease foil. Cut potatoes lengthwise in half and place, cut side down, on foil. Bake until tender, about 25 minutes.

2. Spread Parmesan on waxed paper. Turn potatoes. Brush cut side of each potato with melted butter, then dip in Parmesan. Return potatoes, Parmesan side up, to jelly-roll pan. Sprinkle with pepper. Bake until Parmesan melts, 5 to 7 minutes longer. Makes 4 accompaniment servings.

Each serving: About 196 calories, 8g protein, 26g carbohydrate, 7g total fat (4g saturated), 17mg cholesterol, 267mg sodium.

Potato Latkes

These potatoes, a must for Hanukkah, are best enjoyed right out of the skillet, but they can be kept warm in a 250°F oven until ready to serve. If you are preparing a large batch several hours ahead, to reheat them, place on a rack set over a cookie sheet in a 375°F oven for about 10 minutes or until piping hot.

Prep: 35 minutes   Cook: 8 to 10 minutes per batch

- 2½ pounds baking potatoes (4 large), peeled
- 1 medium onion, peeled
- 1 large egg
- 2 tablespoons matzoh meal or all-purpose flour
- 1 tablespoon chopped fresh parsley or dill
- 1 tablespoon fresh lemon juice
- ½ teaspoon baking powder
- ½ teaspoon salt
- ¼ teaspoon coarsely ground black pepper
- ¾ cup vegetable oil for frying
  applesauce or sour cream

1. In food processor with shredding blade attached, or with coarse side of box grater, shred potatoes and onion. Place in colander. With hands, squeeze to press out as much liquid as possible. Place potato mixture in large bowl; stir in egg, matzoh meal, parsley, lemon juice, baking powder, salt, and pepper.

2. Preheat oven to 250°F. In 12-inch skillet, heat 3 tablespoons oil over medium heat until hot. Drop potato mixture by scant ¼ cups into hot oil to make 5 latkes. With back of spoon, flatten each latke into 3-inch round. Cook until underside is golden, 4 to 5 minutes. With slotted spatula, turn latkes and cook until second side is golden brown and crisp, 4 to 5 minutes longer. Transfer latkes to paper towel–lined cookie sheet to drain; keep warm in oven.

3. Repeat with remaining potato mixture, stirring the mixture before each batch and using 3 tablespoons more oil for each new batch. Serve latkes hot with applesauce or sour cream. Makes about 20 latkes or 10 accompaniment servings.

Each latke without applesauce or sour cream: About 208 calories, 3g protein, 18g carbohydrate, 14g total fat (2g saturated), 21mg cholesterol, 152mg sodium.

"Leftover" Mashed-Potato Pancakes

These pancakes are a great "second act" for leftover mashed potatoes. In fact, plan to make extra so you can enjoy this easy dish the following day.

Prep: 10 minutes   Cook: 6 minutes

- 1½ cups cold or room-temperature mashed potatoes
- 2 tablespoons plain dried bread crumbs
- 1 tablespoon freshly grated Parmesan cheese
- 1 tablespoon butter or margarine

1. With hands, shape potatoes into eight 2-inch patties. On waxed paper, combine bread crumbs and Parmesan. Coat patties with bread-crumb mixture, patting crumbs to cover.

2. In nonstick 10-inch skillet, melt butter over medium heat. Add patties and cook until golden and heated through, 2 to 3 minutes per side. Makes 4 accompaniment servings.

Each serving: About 129 calories, 3g protein, 16g carbohydrate, 7g total fat (3g saturated), 11mg cholesterol, 319mg sodium.

PUMPKIN

Availability
September through
December

Peak Season
October

Buying Tips
Buy firm, bright-colored pumpkins, free from cuts or nicks. *Mini pumpkins* have a rich, sweet flavor. Other cooking pumpkins include *sugar, cheese,* and *pie pumpkins.* They are often cooked and used for pie filling, but canned solid-pack pumpkin is a very convenient, high-quality product. *Jack-o'-lantern pumpkins* have stringy, watery flesh and are best reserved for Halloween decorations.

To Store
Store pumpkins in a cool dry place up to one month.

To Prepare
Cut pumpkin in half or into quarters; remove seeds and scrape out stringy portions. Cut into large pieces.

To Cook
To steam, in a saucepot, heat 1 inch of water to boiling over high heat; add pumpkin pieces and heat to boiling. Reduce heat to medium-high; cover and cook until tender, 25 to 30 minutes. Drain, cool, and peel. If desired, mash with butter, brown sugar, and cinnamon. Or, if using for pie filling, puree in a blender or food processor with knife blade attached. Do not add other ingredients. Place in a paper towel–lined sieve set over a bowl and let drain to remove excess liquid; puree should have the same thickness as solid-pack canned pumpkin. One pound of uncooked pumpkin yields about 1 cup puree.

RADISHES

Availability
Year-round

Peak Season
Round radishes, April and May; Asian varieties October

Buying Tips
Radishes should be uniformly shaped, free from blemishes, firm, and bright red (or white, if icicle radishes).

To Store
If not serving within one day, remove leaves and place radishes in a plastic bag. Refrigerate up to one week.

To Prepare
Trim the radish roots and tops, if necessary. Rinse well under cold running water. If using as a garnish or in a relish tray, cut as desired and store in ice water in the refrigerator.

To Cook
Radishes can be sautéed in butter and served as a side dish; their flavor will be reminiscent of turnips.

RUTABAGAS

Availability
Year-round

Peak Season
October through March

Buying Tips
Also called *yellow turnip, wax turnip*, and *Swede.* Rutabagas should be large, heavy, and without any decay or soft spots. Extremely large ones should be passed over, however. Rutabagas are usually coated with a thick protective wax, which isn't a problem, because they are always peeled.

To Store
Store at cool room temperature or in the refrigerator in the crisper drawer up to one month.

To Prepare
Cut rutabaga into quarters; peel using a small knife.

Mashed Rutabagas with Brown Butter

Mashed rutabagas have a silken texture and a slightly sweet flavor. If using older rutabagas, they will take longer to cook.

Prep: 10 minutes   Cook: 30 minutes

- 2 rutabagas (1¼ pounds each)
- 1¾ teaspoons salt
- 4 tablespoons butter or margarine
- ½ teaspoon sugar
- ¼ cup milk, warmed

1. Cut each rutabaga into quarters; peel, then cut into 1-inch pieces. In 4-quart saucepan, combine rutabagas, enough *water* to cover, and 1 teaspoon salt; heat to boiling over high heat. Reduce heat to medium; cover and cook until tender, about 15 minutes. Drain.

2. In food processor with knife blade attached, combine rutabagas, 2 tablespoons butter, sugar, and remaining ¾ teaspoon salt, and puree until smooth, occasionally scraping down side with rubber spatula. With processor running, gradually add warm milk until blended.

3. In small saucepan over medium heat, melt remaining 2 tablespoons butter; cook, stirring, until golden brown (do not let burn).

4. To serve, spoon rutabaga puree into warmed bowl and pour brown butter over. Makes 12 accompaniment servings.

Each serving: About 67 calories, 1g protein, 7g carbohydrate, 4g total fat (3g saturated), 11mg cholesterol, 299mg sodium.

SALSIFY

Availability
Year-round

Peak Season
October through March

Buying Tips
There are two types: a light brown, slender, parsnip-shaped root that is sometimes referred to as "true" salsify and a brownish-black skinned variety that is much larger and more regularly shaped. They are interchangeable in most recipes.

To Store
Place in a plastic bag. Refrigerate up to one week.

To Prepare
Scrub salsify under cold running water; cut off the tops. Peel and cut as directed. Salsify discolors easily; place peeled pieces into a bowl containing 8 cups of water and 1 tablespoon of lemon juice.

To Cook
Cut the salsify into 1-inch pieces. In a 3-quart saucepan, combine the salsify, 2 quarts water, 1 tablespoon fresh lemon juice, and 1 teaspoon salt. Heat to boiling over high heat. Boil until tender, 10 to 15 minutes. Drain and return the salsify to the saucepan. Add 1 tablespoon butter, ¼ teaspoon salt, and pinch of ground black pepper; cook, stirring frequently, until the butter begins to brown, about 2 minutes. Transfer to a serving dish and sprinkle with parsley.

SPINACH

Availability
Year-round

Peak Season
September and October, March and April

Buying Tips
Buy spinach with bright green leaves. Avoid spinach that is yellowish or wilted. Packaged *curly spinach* is more strongly flavored than *loose-leaf spinach.* Curly spinach is better for cooking than delicate flat-leaf spinach. *Baby spinach,* available in bags, has very tender, edible stems. Frozen spinach is a very handy and excellent-quality convenience product.

To Store
Place unwashed in a plastic bag. Refrigerate up to two days.

To Prepare
Trim tough stems. Wash spinach well in several changes of cool water, swishing to remove all the grit. Transfer to a colander to drain. To use spinach raw, dry in a salad spinner or pat dry with paper towels.

SPINACH BASICS:
STEAMING AND SAUTÉING

Steaming and sautéing are the easiest ways to prepare this nutritious green. For 4 accompaniment servings, trim and wash two 10-ounce bags or 2 pounds of loose spinach. To steam the spinach, bring ¼ cup water to boiling in a 12-inch skillet. Add the spinach; cover and cook until wilted, about 3 minutes. To sauté the spinach, heat 1 tablespoon oil and 1 or 2 cloves peeled garlic in 12-inch skillet. Cook until garlic begins to color. Add spinach and cover; cook 1 minute. Uncover; stir until spinach is wilted and water is evaporated.

Creamed Spinach

Parsley adds fresh flavor to frozen spinach, while cream cheese and sour cream add richness and a delicate tang.

Prep: 20 minutes   Cook: 15 minutes

- 2 tablespoons butter or margarine
- 3 large shallots, finely chopped (about ¾ cup)
- 2 tablespoons all-purpose flour
- ½ cup milk
- ¾ teaspoon salt
- ¼ teaspoon coarsely ground black pepper
- ⅛ teaspoon ground nutmeg
- 1 package (3 ounces) cream cheese, softened and cut into pieces
- 3 packages (10 ounces each) frozen chopped spinach, thawed and squeezed dry
- 1 cup loosely packed fresh parsley leaves
- ¼ cup sour cream

1. In 4-quart saucepan, melt butter over medium-low heat. Add shallots and cook, stirring frequently, until tender, about 3 minutes. Add flour and cook, stirring, 1 minute. With wire whisk, gradually whisk in milk; heat to boiling, whisking constantly. Reduce heat and simmer, stirring occasionally with wooden spoon, until sauce has thickened and boils, about 2 minutes. Stir in salt, pepper, and nutmeg.

2. Remove from heat; stir in cream cheese until smooth. Stir in spinach, parsley, and sour cream; heat through, stirring frequently (do not boil). Makes 6 accompaniment servings.

Each serving: About 180 calories, 7g protein, 14g carbohydrate, 12g total fat (7g saturated), 33mg cholesterol, 500mg sodium.

Indian-Style Creamed Spinach

Cook shallots as directed above but stir in **2½ teaspoons minced, peeled fresh ginger, 2 garlic cloves,** finely chopped, **¾ teaspoon each ground coriander and cumin,** and ⅛ **teaspoon ground red pepper (cayenne).** Cook, stirring, 1 minute. Omit flour, milk, nutmeg, and cream cheese. Stir in spinach and ¼ **cup heavy cream** and heat through. Stir in sour cream.

Each serving: About 122 calories, 4g protein, 9g carbohydrate, 9g total fat (5g saturated), 28mg cholesterol, 415mg sodium.

SQUASH, SUMMER

Availability
Year-round

Peak Season
June through August

Buying Tips
Summer squash are picked while very young, before their skins have had time to mature and harden. *Zucchini* is the most common summer squash; some farmers' markets carry *yellow zucchini*. *Crookneck* squash is another popular summer squash. *Pattypan* squash is round and squat with firm flesh. If squash is allowed to mature, the skin will harden and must be removed before cooking. Buy thin-skinned, shiny squash without blemishes or soft spots.

To Store
Refrigerate in the crisper drawer up to three days.

To Prepare
Scrub gently under cold running water. Trim both ends. Do not remove the seeds or skin unless the squash is mature.

Zucchini Ribbons with Mint

Making long paper-thin strips of zucchini is an out-of-the-ordinary way to prepare it. If you don't have fresh mint, use basil or parsley instead.

Prep: 10 minutes   Cook: 4 minutes

4	small zucchini (4 ounces each) or 2 medium zucchini (8 ounces each)
1	tablespoon olive oil
2	garlic cloves, crushed with side of chef's knife
½	teaspoon salt
2	tablespoons chopped fresh mint

1. Trim ends from zucchini. With vegetable peeler, peel long thin ribbons from each zucchini.

2. In 12-inch skillet, heat oil over medium heat. Add garlic and cook, stirring, until golden; discard. Increase heat to high. Add zucchini and salt and cook, stirring, just until zucchini wilts, about 2 minutes. Remove from heat and stir in mint. Makes 4 accompaniment servings.

Each serving: About 49 calories, 1g protein, 4g carbohydrate, 4g total fat (0g saturated), 0mg cholesterol, 294mg sodium.

Parmesan-Broiled Squash

Sure to please kids and grown-ups alike, this quick dish can be made with zucchini, yellow squash, or both.

Prep: 10 minutes   Broil: 7 minutes

2	medium zucchini or yellow squash (8 ounces each), each cut crosswise in half, then lengthwise into ½-inch-thick slices
1	teaspoon olive oil
⅛	teaspoon salt
⅛	teaspoon ground black pepper
¼	cup freshly grated Parmesan cheese

1. Preheat broiler. In broiling pan without rack, toss zucchini and oil to coat; arrange in single layer and sprinkle with salt and pepper.

2. Place pan in broiler, 5 inches from heat source. Broil until zucchini is tender and begins to brown, 3 to 5 minutes per side. Sprinkle evenly with Parmesan and broil until bubbling, 30 to 60 seconds longer. Makes 4 accompaniment servings.

Each serving: About 54 calories, 4g protein, 4g carbohydrate, 3g total fat (1g saturated), 5mg cholesterol, 190mg sodium.

Availability
Year-round, but less plentiful April through July

Peak Season
October through January

Buying Tips
Unlike summer squash, the skin of winter squash is thick and inedible, and the seeds are rarely eaten (except for pumpkin). *Butternut*

squash resembles an elongated pear and has orange-colored flesh. The skin can be removed with a vegetable peeler. *Buttercup* is similar, but turban-shaped with very hard skin. *Acorn* squash has ridges that makes peeling difficult, so it isn't peeled. It has delicious flesh that is enhanced by sweet flavors, such as brown sugar and maple syrup. *Spaghetti squash* has unusual flesh: It separates into pastalike strands when scraped out of the cooked shell. *Delicata* squash has beautiful markings on its skin and its taste is reminiscent of sweet potatoes. *Sweet Dumpling* squash is closely related to Delicata but is round. *Hubbard* squash is very large and has hard, dry, sweet flesh. Buy winter squash with thick, hard skin; tender (softish) skin indicates immaturity and poor quality. Harmless bumpy "warts" appear on some varieties.

To Store
Refrigerate or store at cool room temperature up to two weeks.

To Prepare
Rinse under cold running water. Cut in half, or as directed. Scoop out and discard the seeds and stringy portion.

Maple Butternut Squash

We've added a generous amount of maple syrup to liven up the flavor of this puree.

Prep: 20 minutes   Cook: 20 minutes

- 2 medium butternut squash (2 pounds each)
- ½ cup maple or maple-flavored syrup
- 4 tablespoons butter or margarine, cut into pieces
- ½ teaspoon salt
- ¼ teaspoon ground black pepper

1. Cut each squash lengthwise in half; discard seeds. With vegetable peeler, remove peel, then cut squash crosswise into 1-inch-thick slices.

2. In 5-quart saucepot, heat *1 inch water* to boiling over high heat; add squash. Reduce heat; cover and simmer until tender, about 15 minutes. Drain.

3. In large bowl, combine squash, maple syrup, butter, salt, and pepper. With mixer at low speed, beat until smooth. Spoon puree into serving bowl. Makes 10 accompaniment servings.

Each serving: About 151 calories, 2g protein, 28g carbohydrate, 5g total fat (3g saturated), 12mg cholesterol, 170mg sodium.

Baked Acorn Squash

To ensure that the squash sits flat, trim about ¼ inch off the bottom of each half.

Prep: 10 minutes   Bake: 35 minutes

- 2 small acorn squash or other winter squash (1 pound each), each cut lengthwise in half and seeded
- 2 tablespoons butter or margarine, cut into pieces
- ¼ cup packed brown sugar

Preheat oven to 350°F. Grease 13" by 9" baking dish. Place squash, cut side down, in baking pan; bake 30 minutes. Turn cut side up. Place one-fourth of butter and brown sugar in each cavity. Bake until squash is tender and butter and brown sugar have melted, about 5 minutes longer. Makes 4 accompaniment servings.

Each serving: About 181 calories, 1g protein, 31g carbohydrate, 7g total fat (4g saturated), 16mg cholesterol, 69mg sodium.

Spaghetti Squash with Tomatoes

Spaghetti Squash with Tomatoes

We love the flavor of oven-roasted spaghetti squash, but if you're in a hurry, you can use your microwave.

Prep: 10 minutes   Cook/Bake: 1 hour

- 1 medium spaghetti squash (2½ pounds), cut lengthwise in half and seeded
- 3 tablespoons butter or margarine
- 1 garlic clove, finely chopped
- 1 can (28 ounces) diced tomatoes, drained
- ½ teaspoon salt
- ¼ teaspoon ground black pepper
- 2 tablespoons chopped fresh parsley

1. Preheat oven to 400°F. Place squash, cut side down, in jelly-roll pan; pour ¼ *inch water* into pan. Bake 45 minutes. Turn squash cut side up, and bake until very tender, about 15 minutes longer.

2. Meanwhile, in nonstick 12-inch skillet, melt 2 tablespoons butter over medium heat. Add garlic and cook, stirring, 1 minute. Stir in tomatoes, ¼ teaspoon salt, and ⅛ teaspoon pepper and cook, stirring, until flavors blend, about 5 minutes. Remove from heat and stir in parsley.

3. Using two forks, from squash, scrape out pulp in long strands and place on serving platter. Add remaining 1 tablespoon butter, remaining ¼ teaspoon salt, and remaining ⅛ teaspoon pepper and toss to mix. Spoon tomato sauce over squash. Serve hot. Makes 6 accompaniment servings.

Each serving: About 127 calories, 2g protein, 16g carbohydrate, 7g total fat (4g saturated), 16mg cholesterol, 493mg sodium.

Sweet and Smoky Spaghetti Squash

Prepare as directed in Step 1 (left). Omit butter, garlic, tomatoes, salt, pepper, and parsley. In microwave-safe bowl, microwave **3 slices bacon,** chopped, and **1 onion,** chopped, on High, stirring once, until bacon is browned, about 4 minutes. Using 2 forks, scrape squash pulp onto serving platter. Add bacon mixture, **3 tablespoons maple or maple-flavored syrup,** and **⅛ teaspoon ground black pepper** and toss to mix.

Southwestern Spaghetti Squash

Prepare as directed in Step 1 (left). Omit butter, garlic, tomatoes, salt, pepper, and parsley. Using 2 forks, scrape squash pulp onto serving platter. Add ¾ **cup mild salsa** and toss to mix. Sprinkle with **crushed tortilla chips.**

Asian Spaghetti Squash

Prepare as directed in Step 1 (left). Omit butter, garlic, tomatoes, salt, pepper, and parsley. Using 2 forks, scrape squash pulp onto serving platter. Add ¼ **cup soy sauce, 1 tablespoon grated, peeled fresh ginger,** and **1 teaspoon Asian sesame oil** and toss to mix.

Roasting vegetables in the oven produces a rich caramelized flavor and a beautifully browned exterior. To roast, preheat oven to 450°F. In large bowl, toss 2 pounds of vegetables with 1 tablespoon olive oil, ½ teaspoon salt, and ¼ teaspoon pepper until coated. Spread vegetables in one layer in a shallow 15½" by 10½" roasting pan. Roast until tender and lightly browned, stirring once or twice during cooking.

You can roast different vegetables together as long as their cooking times are similar. If using a larger amount of vegetables, divide them between two pans. Overcrowding the vegetables will cause them to steam instead of roast. Rotate pans between upper and lower oven racks halfway through cooking.

SEASONINGS

If desired, you can add other flavorings to the vegetables. Fresh or dried herbs are a wonderful addition to any roasted vegetable. Toss hearty herbs like rosemary, sage, or thyme with the vegetables before they roast, but save more tender herbs like dill, parsley, mint, or oregano for sprinkling on at or near the end of cooking. Roast strips of orange or lemon peel along with the vegetables, or sprinkle on freshly grated peel right after they come out of the oven.

VEGETABLES	HOW TO CUT	ROAST TIME (450°F)	SEASONINGS
Beets 2 lbs. not including tops (about 10 small)	Whole, unpeeled, pricked with fork	1 hour	Peel, quarter, and sprinkle with salt, pepper, and 1 tsp. freshly grated orange peel after roasting.
Carrots 2 lbs.	1-inch pieces	30 to 40 minutes	Toss with ½ tsp. pumpkin pie spice before roasting.
Potatoes 2 lbs. unpeeled	2-inch pieces	45 minutes	Toss with 1 tbsp. chopped fresh thyme or 1 tsp. dried thyme before roasting.
Butternut Squash 2 lbs.	2-inch pieces	40 minutes	Toss with ½ tsp. dried rosemary, crumbled, before roasting.
Cauliflower 1 medium head (1½ lbs.)	1½-inch flowerets	20 to 30 minutes	Sprinkle with 2 tbsp. chopped fresh parsley after roasting.
Onions 2 jumbo (1 lb. each)	Each cut into 12 wedges	20 to 30 minutes	Brush with mixture of 1 tbsp. brown sugar, 1 tsp. cider vinegar; roast 5 minutes more.
Fennel 2 large bulbs (1 lb. each)	Trimmed and each cut into 12 wedges	35 to 40 minutes	Sprinkle with freshly grated orange peel after roasting.
Sweet Potatoes 2 lbs.	Peeled, cut crosswise in half, then lengthwise into 1-inch wedges	30 minutes	Toss with 2 tbsp. chopped fresh rosemary before roasting.
Sunchokes 2 lbs.	Whole, pricked with fork	20 to 30 minutes	Sprinkle with 2 tbsp. chopped fresh chives after roasting.
Eggplant 2 medium (1 lb. each)	½-inch-thick slices	20 to 25 minutes	Drizzle with 1 tbsp. extra-virgin olive oil after roasting.
Sweet Peppers 2 lbs.	1-inch-wide strips	30 minutes	Sprinkle with 3 large fresh basil leaves, thinly sliced, after roasting.
Asparagus 2 lbs.	Trimmed	10 to 15 minutes	Sprinkle with freshly grated lemon peel after roasting.
Green Beans 2 lbs.	Trimmed	20 to 30 minutes	Toss with favorite vinaigrette.

SUNCHOKES

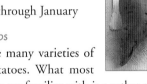

Availability
Year-round

Peak Season
September through March

Buying Tips
Also called *Jerusalem artichokes*. Buy firm, irregularly shaped sunchokes that are free from mold.

To Store
Place in a plastic bag with a few holes poked in it. Refrigerate in the crisper drawer up to two weeks.

To Prepare
Scrub under cold running water. Peel and drop into cold water to prevent discoloration.

SWEET POTATOES

Availability
Year-round

Peak Season
October through January

Buying Tips
There are many varieties of sweet potatoes. What most Americans are familiar with is a rather sweet, moist, orange-fleshed potato with very dark skin. When this variety was introduced in the 1930s, it was marketed as a Louisiana "yam," though it's not a yam at all. To make matters more confusing, in the rest of the world, sweet potatoes have rather dry, slightly sweet, white or yellow flesh. Look for sweet potatoes that feel heavy for their size and have no bruises, soft spots, or sign of sprouting. Handle them gently; they bruise easily.

To Store
Sweet potatoes are quite perishable. Store in a cool dark place up to one week. Do not refrigerate.

To Prepare
Scrub under cold running water.

To Cook
Sweet potatoes are often treated like their savory (white) cousins and mashed, sautéed, fried, or turned into pancakes. To bake, preheat oven to 450°F and bake on a cookie sheet until tender, 45 minutes to 1 hour.

Candied Sweet Potatoes

If you wish, sprinkle with toasted sliced almonds (page 562), chopped walnuts, or chopped pecans before serving. Or top with tiny marshmallows and broil until lightly browned.

Prep: 25 minutes   Cook/Bake: 1 hour 20 minutes

- 4 large sweet potatoes (12 ounces each), each peeled, cut crosswise in half, and each half cut lengthwise into 4 wedges
- 2½ teaspoons salt
- ⅓ cup packed brown sugar
- 3 tablespoons butter or margarine, cut into pieces
- ⅛ teaspoon ground red pepper (cayenne)
- 2 tablespoons dry sherry (optional)

1. Preheat oven to 375°F. In 5-quart Dutch oven, combine sweet potatoes, enough *water* to cover, and 2 teaspoons salt; heat to boiling over high heat. Boil until tender, about 10 minutes. Drain.

2. Meanwhile, in nonstick 10-inch skillet, combine brown sugar, butter, remaining ½ teaspoon salt, and ground red pepper; heat over medium heat, stirring, until butter melts, about 1 minute. Stir in sherry, if using. Cook, stirring occasionally, 2 minutes longer.

3. Transfer potatoes to shallow 13" by 9" baking dish and top with brown-sugar mixture. Cover with foil and bake 30 minutes, stirring halfway through baking. Remove foil and bake until syrup is dark and very thick, 30 to 40 minutes longer, stirring halfway through. Makes 8 accompaniment servings.

Each serving: About 201 calories, 2g protein, 39g carbohydrate, 5g total fat (3g saturated), 12mg cholesterol, 499mg sodium.

Praline Sweet Potatoes

These sweet potatoes are great for a crowd. You may prepare the praline up to one week ahead and the sweet potatoes up to one day ahead. When ready to serve, spread the potatoes in a 9-inch square baking dish. Cover with foil and reheat in a 350°F oven for 45 minutes; remove foil and bake 15 minutes longer, or until heated through. Sprinkle with the praline and serve.

Prep: 30 minutes   Cook: 40 minutes

- 5 **pounds sweet potatoes (8 medium), peeled and cut crosswise into thirds**
- ¼ **cup sugar**
- ¼ **cup water**
- 1 **cup chopped pecans (4 ounces)**
- 5 **tablespoons butter or margarine**
- ½ **cup milk**
- 1¼ **teaspoons salt**

1. In 8-quart saucepot, combine sweet potatoes and enough *water* to cover; heat to boiling over high heat. Reduce heat; cover and simmer until tender, about 25 minutes. Drain; return potatoes to saucepot.

2. Meanwhile, prepare praline: Grease cookie sheet. In 1-quart saucepan, combine sugar and water; heat over low heat, stirring gently, until sugar has dissolved, about 1 minute. Increase heat to medium-high and boil rapidly, without stirring, until syrup has turned light golden brown, about 7 minutes. Working quickly, stir in pecans and 1 tablespoon butter until combined and butter melts. Spread pecan mixture in thin layer on cookie sheet; cool.

3. To sweet potatoes in saucepot, add milk, remaining 4 tablespoons butter, and salt. With mixer at low speed, beat sweet potatoes until smooth, frequently scraping down side with rubber spatula. Increase speed to medium; beat until fluffy, about 2 minutes longer.

4. To serve, spoon potatoes into large bowl. Break praline into small pieces and sprinkle on top. Makes 12 accompaniment servings.

Each serving: About 329 calories, 4g protein, 47g carbohydrate, 15g total fat (5g saturated), 17mg cholesterol, 376mg sodium.

TOMATOES

Availability
Year-round

Peak Season
July through September

Buying Tips
Buy firm, plump, unblemished tomatoes. Size is not an indication of quality or flavor. Not so very long ago, only red tomatoes could be found in markets, but now there are orange, yellow, purple, green, and even striped varieties. Most tomatoes are picked unripe and allowed to ripen during shipping and storage. Vine-ripened tomatoes, usually locally grown and available mid-summer to early autumn, are picked as close to their flavorful peak as possible and have superior flavor.

Tomatoes are categorized by their shape. Round tomatoes range from the small *cherry tomatoes* to the large *beefsteak* variety. They are especially juicy and excellent in salads. *Plum tomatoes* are oval and have meatier flesh. *Roma tomatoes* are a popular West Coast plum tomato. They are best cooked into sauces. *Green tomatoes* have not been allowed to ripen; they have a nice lemonlike flavor.

To Store

Refrigeration dulls the flavor of tomatoes; only over-ripe tomatoes should be refrigerated. Store tomatoes, stem side up, at cool room temperature, out of direct sunlight, up to three or four days. As tomatoes ripen, their color deepens, but the amount of natural sugar remains the same.

To Prepare

Tomatoes do not usually have to be peeled before use. But if you wish to peel them, here's how: With a sharp knife, cut a small shallow X in the bottom of each tomato. Lower the tomatoes into a saucepot of boiling water for 1 minute. Remove with a slotted spoon and plunge into very cold water; drain and gently remove the skin with a knife. To seed tomatoes, cut them crosswise in half and gently squeeze to remove the seeds.

Cherry Tomato Gratin

Try using a pint each of red and yellow cherry tomatoes, or substitute grape tomatoes. Either way, this recipe is sure to be a winner.

Prep: 10 minutes   Bake: 20 minutes

- ¼ cup plain dried bread crumbs
- ¼ cup freshly grated Parmesan cheese
- 1 garlic clove, crushed with garlic press
- ¼ teaspoon coarsely ground black pepper
- 1 tablespoon olive oil
- 2 pints ripe cherry or grape tomatoes
- 2 tablespoons chopped fresh parsley

1. Preheat oven to 425°F. In small bowl, combine bread crumbs, Parmesan, garlic, pepper, and oil until blended.

2. Place cherry tomatoes in shallow 1½-quart casserole or 9-inch deep-dish pie plate. Top with breadcrumb mixture and sprinkle with parsley. Bake until heated through and crumbs have browned, about 20 minutes. Makes 6 accompaniment servings.

Each serving: About 72 calories, 3g protein, 7g carbohydrate, 4g total fat (1g saturated), 3mg cholesterol, 121mg sodium.

Savory Tomato Tart

(Pictured on page 328)

A show-stopping main dish. For the most color, include the yellow tomato, but it's equally delicious made with all red tomatoes.

Prep: 45 minutes   Bake/Broil: 31 minutes

- Pastry for 11-inch Tart (page 534)
- 1 tablespoon olive oil
- 3 medium onions, thinly sliced
- ½ teaspoon salt
- 1 package (3½ ounces) goat cheese
- 2 ripe medium red tomatoes (8 ounces each), cored and cut into ¼-inch-thick slices
- 1 ripe medium yellow tomato (8 ounces), cored and cut into ¼-inch-thick slices
- ½ teaspoon coarsely ground black pepper
- ¼ cup Kalamata olives, pitted and chopped

1. Preheat oven to 425°F. Prepare dough for 11-inch tart and use to line tart pan as directed. Line tart shell with foil; fill with pie weights or dry beans. Bake 15 minutes. Remove foil with weights and bake until golden, 5 to 10 minutes longer. If shell puffs up during baking, gently press it down with back of spoon.

2. Meanwhile, in nonstick 12-inch skillet, heat oil over medium heat. Add onions and ¼ teaspoon salt; cook, stirring frequently, until very tender, about 20 minutes.

3. Turn oven control to broil. Spread onions over bottom of tart shell and crumble half of goat cheese on top. Arrange red and yellow tomato slices, alternating colors, in concentric circles over onion-cheese mixture. Sprinkle with remaining ¼ teaspoon salt and the pepper. Crumble remaining goat cheese on top of tart.

4. Place tart on rack in broiling pan. Place pan in broiler about 7 inches from heat source. Broil until cheese has melted and tomatoes are heated through, 6 to 8 minutes. Sprinkle with olives. Carefully remove side of tart pan. Serve hot or at room temperature. Makes 6 main-dish servings.

Each serving: About 420 calories, 8g protein, 33g carbohydrate, 29g total fat (15g saturated), 54mg cholesterol, 753mg sodium.

Skillet Cherry Tomatoes

From start to finish, this cherry tomato side dish takes less than ten minutes.

Prep: 5 minutes   Cook: 3 minutes

1   tablespoon butter or margarine
1   pint ripe cherry or grape tomatoes
⅛ teaspoon salt
    chopped fresh parsley or basil

In 10-inch skillet, melt butter over medium-high heat. Add cherry tomatoes and salt and cook, shaking skillet frequently, just until heated through and skins split, about 2 minutes. Sprinkle with parsley. Makes 4 accompaniment servings.

Each serving: About 36 calories, 0g protein, 2g carbohydrate, 3g total fat (2g saturated), 8mg cholesterol, 107mg sodium.

Skillet Cherry Tomatoes with Garlic

Prepare as directed above but add **1 garlic clove,** finely chopped, to skillet with butter.

OVEN-DRIED TOMATOES

Preheat oven to 250°F. Peel 12 plum tomatoes (3 pounds; see page 377). Cut each lengthwise in half; scoop out seeds with small spoon. In large bowl, toss tomatoes with 2 tablespoons extra-virgin olive oil, ½ teaspoon dried basil, ½ teaspoon dried thyme, ½ teaspoon salt, and ¼ teaspoon coarsely ground black pepper. Arrange tomatoes, cut side down, on wire rack set over cookie sheet. Bake until tomatoes are shriveled and partially dried, about 5½ hours. Cool completely, then transfer to a zip-tight plastic bag. Refrigerate up to 2 months, or freeze up to 6 months. Makes 24 tomato halves.

Fried Green Tomatoes

Here's a classic Southern way to fry up green tomatoes. Serve as a side dish or use them in BLT sandwiches for a refreshing change of pace.

Prep: 20 minutes   Cook: 3 minutes per batch

6   slices bacon
1   large egg white
¼ teaspoon salt
½ cup cornmeal
¼ teaspoon coarsely ground black pepper
3   medium green tomatoes (1 pound), cut into scant
    ½-inch-thick slices

1. In 12-inch skillet, cook bacon over medium heat until browned. With tongs, transfer bacon to paper towels to drain; crumble. Set aside skillet with bacon drippings.

2. In pie plate, beat egg white and salt. On waxed paper, combine cornmeal and pepper. Dip tomatoes in egg mixture to coat both sides, then dip into cornmeal mixture, pressing so mixture adheres. Place on waxed paper.

3. Heat bacon drippings in skillet over medium-high heat. In batches, cook tomatoes until golden brown, about 1½ minutes per side, transferring to paper towels to drain.

4. Transfer tomatoes to platter and top with bacon. Makes 6 accompaniment servings.

Each serving: About 189 calories, 4g protein, 13g carbohydrate, 13g total fat (5g saturated), 15mg cholesterol, 270mg sodium.

Broiled Parmesan Tomatoes

These warm and juicy tomatoes are a guaranteed hit.

Prep: 10 minutes   Broil: 3 minutes

- 1 tablespoon butter or margarine
- 1 garlic clove, finely chopped
- ¼ cup freshly grated Parmesan cheese
- 4 small ripe plum tomatoes (3 ounces each), each cut lengthwise in half

1. Preheat broiler. In 1-quart saucepan, melt butter over low heat. Add garlic and cook, stirring, until golden; remove from heat.

2. Spread Parmesan on waxed paper. Dip cut side of each tomato in melted-butter mixture, then in Parmesan; place, cheese side up, on rack in broiling pan. Sprinkle any remaining Parmesan on top; drizzle with any remaining butter mixture.

3. Place pan in broiler at closest position to heat source. Broil until Parmesan is golden, 3 to 4 minutes. Makes 4 accompaniment servings.

Each serving: About 72 calories, 3g protein, 4g carbohydrate, 5g total fat (3g saturated), 13mg cholesterol, 151mg sodium.

Peppered Honey Turnips

The honey added to these turnips helps to bring out their full flavor by caramelizing them.

Prep: 15 minutes   Cook: 25 minutes

- ½ cup chicken broth
- ¼ cup white wine
- 2 tablespoons butter or margarine
- 1 teaspoon salt
- ½ teaspoon coarsely ground black pepper
- 3 pounds small turnips, peeled and each cut into 8 wedges
- ¼ cup honey

1. In nonstick 12-inch skillet, heat broth, wine, butter, salt, and pepper to boiling over medium-high heat.

2. Add turnips and cook, stirring occasionally, until most of liquid has evaporated, 10 to 12 minutes. Stir in honey; cook, stirring frequently, until turnips are very tender and browned, 13 to 15 minutes longer. Makes 12 accompaniment servings.

Each serving: About 66 calories, 1g protein, 12g carbohydrate, 2g total fat (1g saturated), 5mg cholesterol, 315mg sodium.

TURNIPS

Availability
Year-round

Peak Season
October through March

Buying Tips
Buy firm, unblemished turnips with fresh green tops, if attached. (Turnip greens can be cooked separately, just like beet greens. See Stir-Frying 101, page 351.)

To Store
Refrigerate the tops and turnips separately in plastic bags in the crisper drawer. Store turnips up to one week and the tops up to two days.

To Prepare
Rinse turnips under cold running water; peel. Leave whole, slice, or cut into pieces. Cook the turnips and the tops as directed in recipe.

FOUR-INGREDIENT CANDIED TURNIPS

In 12-inch skillet, combine 1½ pounds turnips, peeled and cut into 1-inch wedges, enough water to cover, and 1 teaspoon salt; heat to boiling over high heat. Reduce heat and simmer until tender, 7 to 10 minutes. Drain; wipe skillet dry.

In same skillet, melt 2 tablespoons butter or margarine over high heat. Add ⅓ cup sugar and cook, stirring, until sugar has turned amber, about 2 minutes. Add turnips and cook, stirring frequently, until well coated and golden, about 5 minutes. Makes 6 accompaniment servings.

Root Vegetable Gratin

A gratin is any dish that is topped with either cheese or bread crumbs and then heated until browned. Ours, made with a combination of root vegetables and topped with Gruyère, is a delicious example.

Prep: 25 minutes plus standing   Bake: 1 hour 10 minutes

½	cup chicken broth
2	tablespoons butter or margarine
1½	pounds baking potatoes (about 3 medium), peeled and thinly sliced
1½	pounds sweet potatoes (about 3 small), peeled and thinly sliced
1	pound celery root (celeriac), trimmed, peeled, and thinly sliced
1¼	teaspoons salt
½	teaspoon black pepper
⅔	cup heavy or whipping cream
6	ounces Gruyère cheese, shredded (1½ cups)

1. Preheat oven to 400°F. In 13" by 9" baking dish, combine broth and butter; place in oven to melt butter.

2. Meanwhile, in large bowl, toss baking and sweet potatoes, celery root, and parsnips with salt and pepper until well mixed.

3. Remove baking dish from oven; add vegetables and stir to coat with broth mixture. Cover dish with foil and bake vegetables 40 minutes.

4. Remove dish from oven. In 1-cup liquid measuring cup, heat cream in microwave oven on High, 45 seconds. Pour cream evenly over vegetables; sprinkle with Gruyère. Bake, uncovered, until top is golden and vegetables are fork-tender, about 30 minutes longer. Let stand 10 minutes before serving. Makes 12 accompaniment servings.

Each serving: About 218 calories, 6g protein, 23g carbohydrate, 12g total fat (7g saturated) 39mg cholesterol, 383mg sodium.

Ciambotta

You can vary the vegetables depending on what you have on hand and the flavors you prefer.

Prep: 30 minutes   Cook: 30 minutes

3	tablespoons olive oil
1	medium onion, chopped
2	garlic cloves, finely chopped
2	red peppers, cut into 1-inch pieces
1½	pounds zucchini (3 medium), cut lengthwise in half, then crosswise into ½-inch-thick pieces
1½	pounds ripe tomatoes, peeled, seeded, and chopped
¾	teaspoon salt
⅓	cup chopped fresh basil

1. In nonreactive 12-inch skillet, heat 2 tablespoons oil over medium heat. Add onion and garlic and cook, stirring frequently, until onion is tender, about 5 minutes. Add red peppers and cook, stirring frequently, until red peppers are tender-crisp, about 5 minutes longer.

2. Add remaining 1 tablespoon oil and zucchini; cook, stirring, until zucchini is tender-crisp, about 5 minutes. Add tomatoes and salt; heat to boiling. Reduce heat; cover and simmer until vegetables are very tender, about 10 minutes. Stir in basil. Makes 6 accompaniment servings.

Each serving: About 117 calories, 3g protein, 13g carbohydrate, 7g total fat (1g saturated), 0mg cholesterol, 305mg sodium.

Mashed Root Vegetables

Use just one of your favorite root vegetables or a combination of them for mashing with the potatoes.

Prep: 15 minutes   Cook: 25 minutes

2	pounds root vegetables, such as carrots, celery root, parsnips, white turnips, or rutabaga, peeled and cut into 1-inch pieces (5 cups)
1	pound all-purpose potatoes (3 medium), peeled and cut into 1-inch pieces
2½	teaspoons salt
3	tablespoons butter or margarine, cut into pieces
¼	teaspoon ground black pepper pinch ground nutmeg

1. In 4-quart saucepan, combine root vegetables, potatoes, enough *water* to cover, and 2 teaspoons salt; heat to boiling over high heat. Reduce heat; cover and simmer until vegetables are tender, about 15 minutes. Drain.

2. Return vegetables to saucepan. Add butter, remaining ½ teaspoon salt, pepper, and nutmeg; mash until smooth and well blended. Makes 8 accompaniment servings.

Each serving: About 118 calories, 2g protein, 18g carbohydrate, 5g total fat (3g saturated), 12mg cholesterol, 534mg sodium.

Succotash

We've added bacon to the traditional combo of corn and lima beans, two staples of Native American cooking. As a matter of fact, the name *succotash* comes from the Narraganset word for "ear of corn."

Prep: 10 minutes   Cook: 25 minutes

5	slices bacon
3	stalks celery, cut into ¼-inch-thick slices
1	medium onion, chopped
2	cans (15¼ to 16 ounces each) whole-kernel corn, drained
2	packages (10 ounces each) frozen baby lima beans
½	cup chicken broth
¾	teaspoon salt
¼	teaspoon coarsely ground black pepper
2	tablespoons chopped fresh parsley

1. In 12-inch skillet, cook bacon over medium-low heat until browned. With tongs, transfer to paper towels to drain; crumble.

2. Discard all but 2 tablespoons bacon drippings from skillet. Add celery and onion and cook over medium heat, stirring frequently, until vegetables are tender and golden, about 15 minutes. Stir in corn, lima beans, broth, salt, and pepper; heat to boiling over high heat. Reduce heat; cover and simmer until heated through, 5 to 10 minutes longer. Stir in parsley and sprinkle with bacon. Makes 10 accompaniment servings.

Each serving: About 171 calories, 7g protein, 27g carbohydrate, 5g total fat (1g saturated), 5mg cholesterol, 458mg sodium.

Ratatouille

This Provençal classic is very flexible: Serve it hot or cold, or as a first course, salad, or a side dish to accompany meat, poultry, or fish.

Prep: 20 minutes   Cook: 1 hour

2	tablespoons olive oil
1	medium onion, chopped
1	small eggplant (1 pound), ends trimmed, cut into 1-inch pieces
¾	teaspoon salt
¼	teaspoon ground black pepper
1	yellow or red pepper, cut into 1-inch pieces
1	medium zucchini (8 ounces), cut into 1-inch pieces
2	large garlic cloves, finely chopped
1	can (28 ounces) tomatoes, chopped
⅛	teaspoon dried thyme
¼	cup chopped fresh basil or parsley

In nonreactive 5-quart saucepot, heat oil over medium heat. Add onion; cook, stirring frequently, until tender and golden, about 10 minutes. Add eggplant, salt, and black pepper; cook, stirring frequently, until eggplant begins to brown, about 10 minutes. Stir in yellow pepper, zucchini, and garlic; cook, stirring, 1 minute. Stir in tomatoes with their juice and thyme; heat to boiling. Reduce heat; cover and simmer until eggplant is tender, about 30 minutes. Remove from heat; stir in basil. Makes 8 accompaniment servings.

Each serving: About 81 calories, 2g protein, 12g carbohydrate, 4g total fat (0g saturated), 0mg cholesterol, 384mg sodium.

13

FRUIT

Vitamin-packed, fiber-rich fruits are important components of a well-balanced diet: The USDA recommends two to four servings per day. There are many delicious ways to meet this goal. Enjoy a refreshing fruit salad for lunch, or top a green salad with orange or grapefruit sections. Serve juicy grapes or figs with cheese as a snack or dessert, or slip sliced fruit into a meat sandwich (try sliced peaches with baked ham and Dijon mustard). Toss dried apricots or prunes into braised chicken dishes and beef or lamb stews, or eat ripe fruit out of hand and savor every sweet bite.

BUYING AND STORING FRUIT

Over the years, more and more imported fruit (from Central America, South America, and New Zealand) has appeared in stores, making otherwise out-of-season fruit available. But practically every fruit has a season when it is at its flavorful peak and most reasonable price. Whenever possible, buy fruits in season from local farmers' markets; you will be rewarded with the most delicious produce possible.

Some fruits, such as apples, cherries, citrus fruits, pomegranates, and rhubarb, are purchased fully ripe and can be enjoyed immediately. Other fruits, especially those that have been shipped long distances, need further ripening. These include apricots, nectarines, peaches, pears, and plums. To ripen these fruits, place them in a closed paper (not plastic) bag or fruit-ripening bowl, and leave at room temperature for a few days. Some fruits, such as bananas, kiwifruit, mangoes, melons, papayas, and persimmons, ripen best at room temperature, away from direct sunlight. Refrigerate all ripened fruits to keep them from becoming overripe.

PREPARING FRUIT

All fruits with edible skins should be rinsed well before eating to remove any residual pesticides and surface bacteria. Some fruits, such as apples, are often covered with an edible wax coating to give them an attractive shine. Peel waxed fruit before eating, if you wish.

Nothing beats the flavor of fresh seasonal fruit, but canned fruit is a good pantry staple for a quick lunch or dessert. Some canned fruits are better than others; we are especially fond of pears and apricots. Keep in mind that fruits canned in light syrup have a fresher flavor than those in heavy syrup.

In this chapter, we offer tempting recipes that are easy and delicious for just about every fruit you will find in your supermarket, local produce market, or farmers' market. You'll learn how to choose each fruit, how to store it at home, how long it will keep, and the best way to prepare the fruit for eating out of hand or for cooking. Additional fruit recipes can be found in the Desserts chapter.

APPLES

Availability
Year-round

Peak Season
October through March

Buying Tips
Buy firm, crisp apples that are free of brown bruise spots. Apples range in color from yellow to bright green to deep red.

Choose a variety that will work well in your recipe. Use cooking apples for baking and pies. Some apples fall apart when cooked, so they make great applesauce.

Cortland A fine all-purpose apple, this large, round apple remains firm when baked. Cortland is good for fruit salads because the raw slices do not discolor.

Gala This New Zealand import is a cross between Kidd's Orange Red and Golden Delicious. Sweet, crisp, and juicy with red-streaked yellow skin, it is good for cooking.

Golden Delicious Another good all-purpose apple with yellow-gold skin and a sweet flavor. Excellent for eating out of hand, pies, applesauce, and salads.

Granny Smith Very crisp and slightly acidic, this green-skinned apple is named for its original cultivator, an Australian grandmother. Its slices hold their shape well during baking, so it's a good choice for pies.

Jonagold A crisp, yellow-fleshed apple that works well in pies, cobblers, and applesauce.

Macoun A cross between the McIntosh and Jersey Black, it has fragrant white flesh and is a good all-purpose apple.

McIntosh Round and juicy, this apple's flesh softens when cooked. Best for applesauce, eating out of hand, or in combination with firmer apples in pies.

Newtown Pippin A somewhat small apple with tart, firm flesh. Great in pies.

Red Delicious The most familiar red-skinned apple; best for eating out of hand.

Rome Beauty A large, aromatic apple that is excellent for baking whole.

Winesap A crisp pie apple with winelike juice.

To Store
Store apples in the crisper drawer in the refrigerator and use within two weeks.

To Prepare
Rinse apples and core. If the apples (except for Golden Delicious or Cortland) are to be peeled or sliced, sprinkle with lemon juice, vinegar, or a little vinaigrette (depending on their use) to prevent browning.

THE FASTEST BAKED APPLE

Our microwaved apples are ready in minutes. With a generous dollop of plain or vanilla yogurt, they make a nutritious breakfast or dessert.

Prep: 10 minutes   Microwave: 9 minutes

Remove cores from 4 large cooking apples (10 ounces each), such as Romes, but don't cut through to bottom. Peel one-third of way down. Stand apples in small individual bowls or 8-inch square baking dish. Spoon 1 teaspoon butter and 1 tablespoon brown sugar into cavity of each apple. Cover and cook on medium-high (70% power) until tender, about 9 minutes, turning halfway through. Cover and let stand 5 minutes.

Each apple: About 234 calories, 0g protein, 52g carbohydrate, 5g total fat (3g saturated), 10mg cholesterol, 44mg sodium.

McIntosh Applesauce

Cooking the apples with the cores and peels adds flavor and body to applesauce, and pressing the mixture through a sieve makes it silky smooth. If the apples you use are red-skinned, the sauce will turn a lovely pink.

Prep: 15 minutes   Cook: 15 minutes

- 1½ pounds cooking apples (6 small), preferably McIntosh
- ¼ cup water
- ⅓ cup sugar or more to taste
- 1 teaspoon fresh lemon juice

1. Cut apples into quarters but do not peel or remove cores. In 4-quart saucepan, combine apples and water; heat to boiling over high heat. Reduce heat; cover and simmer, stirring occasionally, until very tender, 10 to 15 minutes. Stir in sugar and lemon juice.

2. Press apple mixture through sieve or food mill set over large bowl; discard skins and seeds. Taste and add more sugar, if desired. Serve warm, or cover and refrigerate to serve chilled. Makes about 3½ cups.

Each ½ cup: About 84 calories, 0g protein, 22g carbohydrate, 0g total fat (0g saturated), 0mg cholesterol, 0mg sodium.

Ginger Applesauce

Prepare as directed above but add **1½ teaspoons grated, peeled fresh ginger** to apples.

Lemon Applesauce

Prepare as directed but add **2 strips (2" by 1" each) lemon peel** to apples.

Spiced Applesauce

Prepare as directed above but add **1 cinnamon stick (3 inches)** and **3 whole cloves** to apples. Remove and discard cinnamon stick before straining.

Horseradish Applesauce

Prepare as directed above but after straining, stir **2 tablespoons bottled white horseradish** into applesauce. (Serve with pork.)

Cranberry Applesauce

Prepare as directed (left) but increase sugar to **½ cup** and add **1½ cups fresh or frozen cranberries** to apples.

Vermont Baked Apples

Choose a sweet apple that holds its shape when baked, such as Rome Beauty or Cortland. If you like, serve with whipped cream.

Prep: 10 minutes   Bake: 1 hour

- 6 large cooking apples (7 to 8 ounces each)
- 3 tablespoons butter or margarine
- 1 cup maple syrup or maple-flavored syrup

1. Preheat oven to 350°F. Remove apple cores; beginning at stem end, peel apples one-third of way down. Stand apples in shallow 13" by 9" baking dish. Place 1½ teaspoons butter into cavity of each apple. Pour maple syrup over and around apples.

2. Bake apples, basting occasionally with syrup in baking dish, until tender, about 1 hour. Serve hot, or cover and refrigerate to serve chilled. Makes 6 servings.

Each serving: About 288 calories, 0g protein, 61g carbohydrate, 6g total fat (4g saturated), 16mg cholesterol, 63mg sodium.

Vermont Baked Apples

APRICOTS

Availability
June and July

Buying Tips
Select plump, juicy-looking, orange-yellow fruit; ripe apricots will yield to gentle pressure.

To Store
Handle carefully; apricots bruise easily. Ripen at room temperature, then refrigerate for up to three days.

To Prepare
Wash apricots and cut in half to remove the pit; peel if desired. If the apricots are not to be eaten immediately, sprinkle with lemon juice to prevent browning.

BANANAS

Availability
Year-round

Buying Tips
Yellow bananas are supermarket staples, but red and small yellow bananas are also available in some areas. Plantains (see Vegetables chapter) are considered cooking bananas because they are not sweet.

If you want to eat bananas right away, buy solid yellow bananas with some brown flecks. Bananas that are somewhat green will ripen within a few days at room temperature. To hasten ripening, store in a closed paper bag at room temperature.

To Store
After bananas ripen, they can be refrigerated for two or three days. (The skins will darken, but the fruit inside will remain ripe and fresh.) For longer storage, mash the fruit with a little lemon juice, pack into freezer containers (leaving ½-inch headspace), and freeze. Thaw in the refrigerator before using.

To Prepare
Peel and slice or cut bananas up, depending on their use. If they are not to be eaten immediately, sprinkle with a little lemon juice to prevent browning.

Flambéed Bananas

For our version of this classic dessert, we have added a touch of fresh lemon juice to balance the sweetness of the bananas.

Prep: 5 minutes   Cook: 8 minutes

3	tablespoons butter or margarine
¾	cup packed brown sugar
1	tablespoon fresh lemon juice
4	ripe medium bananas, each peeled, cut crosswise in half, and then lengthwise in half
⅓	cup dark Jamaican rum vanilla ice cream (optional)

1. In 12-inch skillet, melt butter over medium heat. Stir in brown sugar and lemon juice. Place bananas in single layer in skillet; cook until just slightly softened, about 2 minutes per side. Reduce heat to low.

2. In 1-quart saucepan, heat rum over low heat. With long match, carefully ignite rum; pour over bananas in skillet. Spoon pan juices over bananas until flames die. Serve warm, with ice cream, if you like. Makes 8 servings.

Each serving: About 179 calories, 1g protein, 34g carbohydrate, 5g total fat (3g saturated), 12mg cholesterol, 53mg sodium.

BERRIES

Availability
Year-round, depending on variety

Peak Season
June through October

Buying Tips
Berries should be plump, uniformly colored, and free of stems and leaves. Avoid bruised berries and cartons that are stained with berry juice. Beware of moldy and don't be tempted by the dewy-looking water-sprayed berries at the market; the moisture will only accelerate the decaying of the berries.

Blackberries
For the best flavor, buy deeply colored berries. Choose large maroon *boysenberries* for their rich, tart taste; deep red *loganberries,* which are long and tangy; medium to large purple *marionberries,* which have small seeds and an intense flavor; and large black *olallieberries,* whose flavor ranges from sweet to tart.

Blueberries
The silvery "bloom" on this berry is a natural protective coating and a sign of freshness. Only buy berries that still have their bloom. Blueberries range in color from purplish blue to almost black. Wild blueberries, also called *lowbush berries,* are pea-sized and quite tart; they hold their shape well in baked goods. Look for cultivated berries June through August; wild berries, most easily found along the coasts, in August and September. Refrigerate in their baskets for up to ten days.

Currants
Currants are red, white, and black. Red and white currants, found in farmers' markets in July and August, are sweet enough to eat out of hand and are often used in summer puddings. Black currants are made into liqueurs, syrups, and jams.

Dewberries
Dewberries resemble blackberries in appearance and flavor, but they grow on trailing ground-running vines.

Gooseberries
Ranging in color from green (the most common) to amber to red, tart gooseberries are usually cooked into jams, sauces, or pies. The *Chinese (Cape) gooseberry* is an entirely different species that is covered with a balloonlike papery husk (peel the shell back for a dramatic-looking dessert garnish). Gooseberries are available in June and July. You'll most likely find them in farmers' markets.

Raspberries
Red raspberries are the most common, but also look for sweet apricot-colored berries and sweet-tart black raspberries in produce or farmers' markets. If red raspberries have darkened to a dusky shade, they are past their prime. There are two peak seasons: June and July and September and October.

Strawberries
Choose bright red berries with fresh green stems still attached: Pale or yellowish white strawberries are unripe and sour. Strawberries do not ripen after they are picked. Local strawberries are available from April to July, but strawberries are found year-round.

To Store
Berries are very perishable and can deteriorate within twenty-four hours of purchase. You can store them in their baskets for a brief period, but to keep them for more than two days, place the (unwashed) berries in a paper towel–lined jelly-roll or baking pan, cover loosely with paper towels, and refrigerate.

To freeze berries, wash and drain, then spread in a single layer in a jelly-roll pan and place in the freezer. Once they're frozen, transfer to a heavy-duty zip-tight plastic bag and freeze for up to one year. Do not thaw or rinse frozen berries before using. Extend the cooking time ten to fifteen minutes for berry pies and five to ten minutes for muffins and quick breads.

To Prepare
Rinse fresh berries just before serving. Remove hulls from strawberries (with a huller or small knife) and any stems from the other berry varieties; drain well.

Raspberry-Lemonade Granita

Be sure to use a metal baking pan, not a glass baking dish, when making granita; it will freeze more efficiently. For a variation, layer the granita in wineglasses with fresh raspberries and top each with an emerald-green mint sprig just before serving.

Prep: 20 minutes plus freezing

- 2 to 3 lemons
- ¾ cup sugar
- 3 cups water
- 1 pint raspberries

1. From lemons, grate 1 teaspoon peel and squeeze ¼ cup juice.

2. In 1-quart saucepan, heat sugar, lemon peel, and 1½ cups water to boiling over high heat, stirring to dissolve sugar. Remove saucepan from heat; stir in raspberries. Cool sugar syrup to room temperature.

3. In food processor with knife blade attached, blend mixture until pureed. With back of spoon, press puree through sieve into bowl; discard seeds. Stir in lemon juice and remaining 1½ cups water. Pour into 13" by 9" metal baking pan.

4. Cover and freeze mixture about 1½ hours or until frozen around the edges. With fork, scrape ice, mixing it from the edge to the center. Repeat process about every 30 minutes or until mixture turns into ice shards, about 1½ hours.

5. Serve granita right away, spooning shards into chilled dessert dishes or wine goblets. Or, cover and freeze up to 1 month. To serve, let stand about 5 minutes at room temperature to soften slightly. Makes about 8 cups or 16 servings.

Each serving: About 45 calories, 0g protein, 11g carbohydrate, 0g total fat, 0mg cholesterol, 0mg sodium.

Fresh Fruit with Raspberry-Lime Dipping Sauce

(Pictured on page 382)

Greek-style yogurt has the rich texture of sour cream, making it perfect for sauces.

Prep: 20 minutes

- 1 cup raspberries
- 1 lime
- 1½ cups reduced-fat (2%) Greek (strained) yogurt
- ¼ cup packed light brown sugar
  assorted fresh fruit for dipping, such as strawberries, grapes, cut-up melon, banana or kiwifruit slices, and plum, peach, nectarine, pear, and/or apricot wedges

1. Place raspberries in sieve set over bowl. With back of spoon, mash and press raspberries through sieve into bowl; discard seeds. From lime, grate 1 teaspoon peel and squeeze 1 tablespoon juice.

2. Add lime peel and juice, yogurt, and brown sugar to raspberry puree and stir to combine. If not serving right away, cover and refrigerate up to 1 day.

3. To serve, spoon sauce into serving bowl and place on large platter. Arrange fruit on same platter. Makes about 2 cups sauce or enough for 8 servings.

Each ¼ cup sauce: About 55 calories, 3g protein, 10g carbohydrate, 1g total fat (1g saturated), 2mg cholesterol, 15mg sodium.

GREEK YOGURT

Test Kitchen Tip

Greek yogurt has recently gained in popularity in the U.S. It has a texture similar to that of sour cream but with the added health benefit of live bacteria, including *Lactobacillus bulgaricus* and *Streptococcus Thermophilus*. The yogurt is strained to remove the whey (milky liquid), which is how it gets its thick and creamy texture. Imported Greek yogurt is available in large supermarkets and in health-food stores in full-fat, light, 2%, and 0% fat versions. Unlike sour cream, Greek yogurt can be heated to high temperatures without curdling.

CACTUS PEARS

Availability
October through May

Peak Season
October and November

Buying Tips
Look for brightly colored cactus pears (also called *prickly pears*) minus their sharp spines (to be safe, pick up the fruit with a paper bag to protect your hands). When ripe, cactus pears yield to gentle pressure. Avoid shriveled or dried-out fruit.

To Store
Keep cactus pears at room temperature and use within two or three days.

To Prepare
Wearing rubber gloves or using a paper bag to protect your hands, peel a ripened cactus pear as you would an apple, being sure to cut away spines. Slice for salads, or eat out of hand with a squeeze of lime or lemon juice.

CHERIMOYAS

Availability
November through May

Buying Tips
Pick large, uniformly green cherimoyas (custard apples) without bruises or blackened skin. Because ripe cherimoyas are very fragile, it is best to choose firm fruit and ripen at home. When ripe, cherimoyas yield to gentle pressure.

To Store
Ripen at room temperature, then refrigerate and use within one or two days.

To Prepare
Wash, then cut lengthwise in half or into quarters. Serve as you would melon wedges. Discard the seeds when eating.

CHERRIES

Availability
Sweet cherries, May through July; tart (sour) cherries, late June to mid-July

Buying Tips
Look for plump, brightly colored cherries with fresh-looking stems still attached; stemless cherries are prone to mold. Avoid fruit that is soft, bruised, or moldy.

Sweet cherries, such as dark red *Bing* or golden *Rainier (Royal Anne)* varieties, make delicious summer eating. Fresh tart (sour) cherries, which can be found in farmers' markets, at roadside stands, and at some supermarkets are excellent in pies.

To Prepare
Wash and remove stems just before using. To use in desserts and salads, remove the pits.

Cherry Bruschetta

Serve this special bruschetta for afternoon tea or as part of a brunch menu.

Prep: 15 minutes plus standing

¾ pound dark, sweet fresh cherries, pitted and cut in half
1 tablespoon sugar
1 teaspoon fresh lemon juice
4 large slices rustic bread, about ¾ inch thick
½ cup Neufchâtel or mascarpone cheese or Greek (strained) yogurt

1. In medium bowl, toss cherries, sugar, and lemon juice. Let stand 15 minutes to allow juices to run.

2. Lightly toast bread; cool slightly. Spread bread with Neufchâtel. Cut slices in half; arrange on platter. Spoon cherries with juices on top. Makes 4 servings.

Each serving: About 255 calories, 7g protein, 38g carbohydrate, 9g total fat (5g saturated), 21mg cholesterol, 370mg sodium.

COCONUTS

Availability
Year-round

Peak Season
October through December

Buying Tips
Choose a coconut that is heavy for its size and sounds full of liquid when shaken. Avoid coconuts with moldy or wet eyes (the three indentations at one end).

To Store
Refrigerate and use whole coconut within one week. Shredded fresh coconut will keep in the refrigerator for one or two days.

To Prepare
Pierce two of the eyes using a clean screwdriver or an ice pick and hammer; drain the liquid (or strain and reserve for another use). Bake the coconut in a preheated 350°F oven for 15 minutes. Remove it from the oven and wrap in a kitchen towel. With the hammer, hit the coconut to break it into large pieces. With a knife, pry the coconut meat from the shell.

To shred With a vegetable peeler, remove the brown outer skin from the meat. Shred the meat on the coarse side of a box grater or in a food processor fitted with the fine shredding blade. One 1½-pound coconut yields 4 to 5 cups of shredded coconut.

To toast Preheat the oven to 350°F. Evenly spread the shredded coconut in a jelly-roll pan. Bake until delicately browned, 20 to 30 minutes, stirring occasionally to toast evenly.

CRANBERRIES

Availability
September through mid-December

Buying Tips
Berries should be plump and firm, from light to dark red, with a glossy sheen. Avoid shriveled, discolored, or moist berries.

To Store
Refrigerate and use within two weeks. To freeze, place cranberries in the freezer in their original bag.

To Prepare
Rinse the cranberries and remove any stems; discard any shriveled fruit and drain well. To use, do not thaw frozen cranberries, just rinse with cold water and drain.

DATES

Availability
Year-round

Buying Tips
The intensely sweet and moist *Deglet Noor* and *Medjool* dates are the most common. Choose dates that are shiny, plump, and rich golden brown. They are sold with and without pits and packaged or loose.

To Store
Wrap dates tightly in plastic wrap and refrigerate for up to several weeks.

To Prepare
Remove pits, if necessary.

FIGS

Availability
June through November

Buying Tips
Varieties range in color from greenish yellow (*Kadota*) to dark purple (*Black Mission*) to green (*Calimyrna*). Buy slightly firm fruit that yields to gentle pressure. Avoid bruised or very soft fruit, or fruit with a sour odor.

To Store
Figs are very perishable; refrigerate them and use within two days.

To Prepare
Wash figs and remove any stems.

To Serve

To Serve

Eat figs out of hand, serve them as a first course topped with thinly sliced prosciutto, alongside a salad of mixed greens, or for dessert with a soft, mild cheese.

Stuffed Fresh Figs

In addition to being delicious, figs are a good source of iron, calcium, and phosphorus. In this recipe, the figs are filled with a honey-sweetened ricotta-almond mixture for a lovely dessert. Use any variety of green or black figs.

Prep: 25 minutes

- 19 fresh ripe small figs (about 1¼ pounds)
- ¼ cup honey
- ½ cup part-skim ricotta cheese
- ¼ cup natural almonds, toasted and chopped

1. On plate, with fork, mash the ripest fig with honey; set aside.

2. With sharp knife, trim stems from remaining figs, then cut a deep X in the top of each, making sure not to cut all the way through to the bottom. With fingertips, gently spread each fig apart to make "petals."

3. In small bowl, combine ricotta and almonds. With back of spoon, press mashed fig mixture through sieve into 1-cup measure.

4. To serve, spoon ricotta mixture into figs. Arrange on platter. Drizzle with fig honey. Makes 6 servings.

Each serving: About 170 calories, 4g protein, 32g carbohydrate, 4g total fat (1g saturated), 4g fiber, 6mg cholesterol, 25mg sodium.

5-MINUTE FRUIT DESSERTS

No-Cook Raspberry Romanoff
In blender, combine 1 cup vanilla ice cream, ½ cup fresh raspberries, ½ cup sour cream, and 2 tablespoons orange-flavor liqueur or orange juice and blend until smooth. Spoon into champagne flutes or parfait glasses and top with additional raspberries.

Sangria-Steeped Berries
In medium bowl, combine 1 cup dry red wine, ¼ cup orange-flavor liqueur or orange juice, 2 tablespoons sugar, 1 teaspoon grated fresh lemon peel, and ½ teaspoon grated fresh orange peel. Add 4 cups assorted fresh berries, such as blackberries, blueberries, raspberries, and sliced strawberries. Cover and refrigerate 30 minutes or up to 4 hours to blend flavors.

Honey-Dipped Figs with Yogurt
Top individual dessert dishes of plain yogurt with figs that have been brushed with honey and coated with finely chopped walnuts.

Gingered Cream and Grapes
Serve halved red and green seedless grapes with a dollop of sour cream topped with coarsely chopped crystallized ginger or preserved ginger in syrup.

Honeydew Frappé
In blender, combine 4 cups cut-up ripe honeydew melon (about 2 pounds), 2 tablespoons fresh lime juice, ¼ cup loosely packed fresh mint leaves, and 1 to 2 tablespoons sugar (depending on sweetness of melon) and blend until smooth. Add 3 cups ice cubes and blend until thick and frothy.

Mint Melon Cups
Toss 1-inch chunks of honeydew and cantaloupe with fresh lime juice and honey. Spoon into wineglasses and garnish with a twist of lime peel.

Broiled Amaretti Plums
Place fresh plum halves, cut side up, in ungreased broiler-safe pan. Sprinkle with crushed amaretti (almond-flavored) cookies and broil just until crumbs have lightly browned and plums are tender. Great with peeled peaches, too.

GRAPEFRUIT

Availability
Year-round

Peak Season
January through April

Buying Tips
Grapefruit can have seeds or be seedless; they can be pink-, red-, or white-fleshed. Select well-shaped firm fruit that is heavy for its size. Brownish discolorations on the skin usually do not affect the eating quality. Avoid fruit that is soft or discolored at the stem end.

Pummelo (also called *pomelo* or *Chinese grapefruit*) looks like an overgrown grapefruit but is sweeter and firmer. Because it is seedy, it should be peeled, seeded, and sectioned like an orange (page 397) before eating.

To Store
Refrigerate grapefruit and use within one to two weeks.

To Prepare
Cut the fruit crosswise in half. With a knife, cut out the sections from between the membranes; leave the sections in place if serving the fruit in the shell. Remove any seeds.

Broiled Grapefruit

Serve this warm-and-juicy treat at breakfast or as a healthful dessert. Instead of sugar, spoon on 1 tablespoon of honey or orange marmalade.

Prep: 10 minutes   Broil: 10 minutes

- 1 medium ruby red or pink grapefruit, cut in half
- 1 tablespoon brown sugar
- 1 tablespoon butter or margarine, cut into pieces

1. Preheat broiler. Section grapefruit; remove seeds.
2. Line broiling pan with foil. Place grapefruit halves in pan, sprinkle with brown sugar, then dot with butter. Place pan in broiler, about 5 inches from heat source. Broil until golden on top and heated through, about 10 minutes. Serve hot. Makes 2 servings.

Each serving: About 115 calories, 1g protein, 16g carbohydrate, 6g total fat (4g saturated), 16mg cholesterol, 61mg sodium.

GRAPES

Availability
Year-round, depending on variety

Buying Tips
Bunches of grapes should be plump and fresh-looking, with individual grapes firmly attached to their stems. Avoid dry, brittle stems, shriveled grapes, or fruit that is leaking moisture.

Table grapes, which are for eating rather than winemaking (although a few varieties do double duty), are categorized as seedless or with seeds. Seedless grapes, derived from European varieties, include *Thompson, Perlette, Flame,* and *Ruby Seedless.* Grapes with seeds usually are indigenous American varieties and have a distinct musky flavor. Lambruscas, such as the purple *Concord,* pale red *Delaware,* and red-purple *Catawba,* are prized for their pectin-rich juice and make fine jellies. Muscadine grapes, which include the sweet-juiced southern *Scuppernong,* are also great for jellies.

To Store
Refrigerate grapes in their perforated plastic bags and use within one week.

To Prepare
Rinse grapes well and dry with paper towels.

Grapes with Sour Cream

Even if you are pressed for time, you can make this easy, delicious treat.

Prep: 10 minutes

- 2 cups seedless grapes
- ¼ cup sour cream
- 1 tablespoon brown sugar

In small bowl, gently stir grapes, sour cream, and brown sugar until well combined. Cover and refrigerate until ready to serve. Makes 4 servings.

Each serving: About 100 calories, 1g protein, 18g carbohydrate, 3g total fat (2g saturated), 6mg cholesterol, 11mg sodium.

GUAVAS

Availability
September through
November

Buying Tips
Depending on the variety, guavas have green to yellow-ish red skin. Ripe guavas yield to gentle pressure. As with other tropical fruits, it is best to buy firm, un-cracked guavas and ripen them at home.

To Store
Ripen fruit at room temperature in a brown paper bag. Refrigerate guavas after ripening and use within two or three days.

To Prepare
Wash guavas and remove the skin. Cut large guavas into pieces for eating out of hand. The tiny seeds are edible but can be cut out before serving, if you wish.

KIWIFRUIT

Availability
Year-round

Buying Tips
Kiwifruit should be slightly firm with very fuzzy skin. When fully ripe, they yield to gentle pressure.

To Store
Ripen kiwifruit at room temperature; refrigerate after ripening and use within one or two days. Firm, un-ripened, unwashed kiwifruit can be stored in a plastic bag in the refrigerator for up to several months.

To Prepare
With a sharp knife, peel off the skin, then cut into wedges or slices. Or cut unpeeled fruit crosswise in half and scoop out the pulp with a spoon.

KUMQUATS

Availability
November through April

Peak Season
November through
December

Buying Tips
Buy firm, glossy, bright orange kumquats. They are often sold with some stems and leaves still attached. Avoid soft, blemished, or shriveled fruit.

To Store
Keep kumquats at room temperature for up to two days, or refrigerate and use within two weeks.

To Prepare
Wash the fruit and remove the stems, then cut in half to remove the seeds.

To Serve
Eat the entire fruit, peel and all. Add cut-up kumquats to fruit salads or leave them whole as a garnish.

LEMONS AND LIMES

Availability
Year-round

Buying Tips
The fruits should be firm, brightly colored, and heavy for their size. Pale or green-ish yellow lemons usually indicate fruit that is more acidic. Limes should be glossy-skinned; irregular purplish brown marks on the skin do not affect the quality. Avoid soft, shriveled, or hard-skinned fruits.

In addition to the familiar supermarket varieties, two fragrant, distinctively flavored varieties can some-times be found in well-stocked produce markets. Thin-skinned *Meyer* lemons, more aromatic and sweeter than regular lemons, are favored by West Coast cooks. Small tart *key* limes (also known as *West Indian, bar-tender,* or *Mexican* limes) are so highly regarded that a pie was created for them. If you can't find fresh key limes, excellent bottled key lime juice is available.

To Store

Keep lemons and limes at room temperature for up to a few days, or refrigerate and use within two weeks.

To Prepare

When grating lemon or lime peel, be sure to grate only the zest (the thin colored part of the peel). The white pith underneath is very bitter. To get the most juice out of lemons or limes, press down on them while rolling them back and forth, or place them in hot tap water for several minutes.

LOQUATS

Availability
April through early May

Buying Tips
Look for fruit with deep, orange-yellow skin that yields to gentle pressure.

To Store
Refrigerate loquats and use within two or three days.

To Prepare
Pull off the peel, cut in half, and remove the large central seeds for eating out of hand, or cut up to use in salads.

LYCHEES

Availability
Late May through July

Buying Tips
Lychees are usually found in Asian markets. They have a bumpy, deep reddish brown shell that protects their slightly translucent soft white flesh. Choose blemish-free fruit.

To Store
Refrigerate lychees and use within one or two days.

To Prepare
With your thumb, beginning at the stem, pull off the skin as you would that of an orange; remove the seed (which clings tightly to the fruit) for eating lychees out of hand, or use in salads.

MANGOES

Availability
Year-round

Peak Season
May through August

Buying Tips
Purchase plump fruit with a fresh, sweet aroma. Some varieties are speckled, but tiny black spots indicate very ripe fruit. Ripe mangoes yield to gentle pressure. Avoid oversoft, shriveled, or bruised fruit.

To Store
Let mangoes ripen at room temperature, then refrigerate and use within two or three days.

Blueberry-Mango Compote

This lively dessert is a summer celebration of contrasts—appetizing primary colors and sweet versus acidic flavors—each balancing the other for a sweet, refreshing flavor.

Prep: 15 minutes

- 1 tablespoon dark Jamaican rum
- 1 tablespoon fresh lime juice
- 1 tablespoon sugar
- 2 large ripe mangoes, peeled and cut into ¾-inch pieces
- 1 pint blueberries

In medium bowl, combine rum, lime juice, and sugar. Add mangoes and blueberries; toss to coat. Cover and refrigerate if not serving right away. Makes 6 servings.

Each serving: About 97 calories, 1g protein, 24g carbohydrate, 0g total fat (0g saturated), 0mg cholesterol, 5mg sodium.

CUTTING A MANGO

With a sharp knife, cut a lengthwise slice from each side of the long flat seed, as close to the seed as possible. Peel seed section; cut off as much flesh as possible; discard seed.

Cut the mango pieces lengthwise into thick wedges. Use a sharp, thin knife to remove the peel from each wedge, cutting close to the peel.

For eating mango out of hand, score the flesh of each piece without cutting through the skin, and gently press on the skin to separate sections for eating.

MELONS

Availability
April through December, depending on variety

Buying Tips
Summer melons have a netted rind and thrive in hot climates. Winter melons, which are typically oblong in shape and can be grown in temperate climates, take longer to mature on the vine and appear later in produce markets.

Buy fully ripened melons for the most flavor and sweetness. (Only winter melons ripen after picking.) Melons should feel heavy for their size and exude a fruity aroma from the smooth (blossom) end. Avoid bruised or cracked melons or those with soft or damp spots. (See Watermelons, page 407.)

Canary
This winter melon is oval in shape and has a bright yellow rind. When ripe, it gives off a rich aroma. The sweet flesh tastes similar to honeydew. Look for canary melons from mid-June to mid-September.

Cantaloupe
Available June through September, this luscious melon has golden or greenish beige skin covered with thick netting. The scar at the stem end should be smooth, without any stem remaining. When ripe, cantaloupe has a sweet aroma and salmon-colored flesh. It should feel tender but not mushy at the blossom end.

Casaba

Chartreuse-yellow casaba is round with a point at one end. It has deep lengthwise furrows and cream-colored flesh. When ripe, the rind is a rich yellow (but the stem end may remain light green), and the blossom end will yield to gentle pressure.

Cranshaw (Crenshaw)

Globe-shaped, with shallow furrows and a point at the stem end, this winter melon has a gold-green rind that turns completely gold when the melon is ripe. The pink flesh has a rich aroma, and the blossom end yields to gentle pressure. These melons are at their peak from July through October.

Honeydew, Honeyball

These melons are similar except that the honeyball is smaller. The rind is cream-colored and covered with patches of netting. When the melon is ripe, the skin should feel velvety and the rind should give slightly. Look for honeyballs from July through November; honeydews year-round.

Although the flesh of the honeydew is usually green, there are several varieties that differ: These include the *Golden Honeydew,* the *Orange Honeydew,* and the *Temptation Honeydew.*

Persian

Resembling a large cantaloupe but with finer netting, the Persian melon has a dark green background that turns lighter green when ripe. The skin will yield to gentle pressure when ripe. The orange-pink flesh has a distinctive aroma. Persian melons are available from June through November.

Santa Claus

Available in December, this melon is large and oblong with yellow-green flesh and a lightly netted, green-gold rind that turns yellow when the melon is ripe. The blossom end will yield to gentle pressure.

To Store

Let melon ripen at room temperature, then refrigerate and use within two or three days. Keep the melon well wrapped after cutting to prevent it from absorbing odors from other foods.

NECTARINES

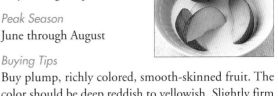

Availability
May through September

Peak Season
June through August

Buying Tips
Buy plump, richly colored, smooth-skinned fruit. The color should be deep reddish to yellowish. Slightly firm nectarines ripen well at room temperature. Avoid hard, soft, or shriveled nectarines or any with a large proportion of green skin.

To Store
Let nectarines ripen at room temperature, then refrigerate and use within two or three days.

To Prepare
Wash the fruit, cut in half along the seam line, and remove the pit. Nectarine skin is quite thin, so it does not need to be peeled. To prevent browning, sprinkle with lemon juice.

Nectarines in Red Wine

Top each serving with a dollop of sweetened sour cream or crème fraîche or with a scoop of strawberry sorbet.

Prep: 10 minutes plus chilling

   2 cups fruity red wine, such as Beaujolais, shiraz, or merlot

 ⅔ cup sugar

2½ pounds ripe nectarines (about 6 large), pitted and cut into ½-inch-thick wedges

In large bowl, stir wine and sugar until sugar dissolves. Add nectarines; cover and refrigerate at least 4 hours or up to 1 day to allow flavors to blend. Serve nectarines with wine in goblets or dessert bowls. Makes about 7 cups or 6 servings.

Each serving: About 225 calories, 2g protein, 43g carbohydrate, 1g total fat (0g saturated), 3g fiber, 0mg cholesterol, 5mg sodium.

ORANGES

Availability
Year-round

Peak Season
December through April

Buying Tips
Eating oranges, such as *Temple* and *navel,* are easily peeled and segmented. Other orange varieties, such as *Valencia, Pineapple,* and *Hamlin,* are valued for their abundant juice. Some specialty markets carry sweet, maroon-fleshed *Moro (blood)* oranges from late winter through early spring. Bitter oranges (also called Seville or sour oranges), which are used in Latino cooking and marmalades, have very thick skins and tart juice.

Oranges should be firm and heavy for their size. A slight greenish color or russeting on the skin does not affect the quality.

To Store
Keep at room temperature for a few days, or refrigerate and use within two weeks.

To Prepare
Peel oranges and separate into segments; slice or cut into pieces. When grating orange peel, be sure to grate only the zest (the thin colored part of the peel). The white pith underneath is very bitter.

CANDIED FRUITS

Test Kitchen Tip Candied fruits (fruits that have been preserved in sugar) are indispensable in many holiday recipes. They are sometimes crystallized (coated with granulated sugar) or glacéed (dipped into a glossy syrup). For the highest-quality candied fruits, shop at a store that specializes in European ingredients.

Most candied fruit is simply sweetened and artificially colored. Examples include cherries, citrus peel, pineapple, oranges, and apricots. A few edibles are cultivated almost exclusively so they can be candied. Citron is a large citrus fruit with thick skin; when candied it turns dull green. It is used in fruit cakes.

PREPARING CITRUS FRUITS

Using a vegetable peeler, remove the colored part of the citrus peel in strips. (Do not remove the bitter white pith.)

If directed, cut the citrus peel into thin slivers.

Cut a slice off the top and bottom of the fruit to steady it. Stand fruit upright on cutting board and cut off peel and white pith, turning the fruit as you cut.

Holding the fruit over a bowl to catch the juices, cut between the membranes to release the sections.

Oranges with Caramel

When these caramel-drizzled orange rounds are refrigerated, the caramel is transformed into a luscious golden syrup. Serve as a light and elegant finale to a rich meal.

Prep: 30 minutes plus chilling   Cook: 10 minutes

- 6 **large navel oranges**
- 2 **tablespoons brandy (optional)**
- 1 **cup sugar**

1. From oranges, with vegetable peeler, remove 6 strips (3" by ¾" each) peel. Cut strips lengthwise into slivers.

2. Cut remaining peel and white pith from oranges. Slice oranges into ¼-inch-thick rounds and place on deep platter, overlapping slices slightly. Sprinkle with brandy, if desired, and orange peel slivers.

3. In 1½-quart saucepan, cook sugar over medium heat, stirring to dissolve any lumps, until sugar has melted and turned deep amber. Drizzle caramel over orange slices. Cover and refrigerate until caramel melts, about 2 hours. Makes 6 servings.

Each serving: About 208 calories, 2g protein, 53g carbohydrate, 0g total fat (0g saturated), 0mg cholesterol, 2mg sodium.

Oranges with Caramel

ORANGES WITH CARAMEL

Cook the sugar over medium heat until melted, stirring constantly to dissolve any lumps.

Continue cooking until the syrup turns dark amber.

Carefully drizzle the caramel over the orange slices.

Ambrosia

Some ambrosias have gotten away from the pure simplicity of the original recipe—not ours.

Prep: 50 minutes   Bake: 15 minutes

- 1 fresh coconut
- 1 ripe pineapple
- 6 large navel oranges

1. Preheat oven to 350°F. Prepare coconut: Using hammer and screwdriver or large nail, puncture two of the three eyes (indentations) in coconut. Drain liquid. Bake coconut 15 minutes. Remove from oven and wrap in kitchen towel. With hammer, hit coconut to break it into large pieces. With knife, pry coconut meat from shell. With vegetable peeler, peel brown outer skin from coconut meat. With vegetable peeler or on large holes of grater, shred 1 cup coconut. (Wrap and refrigerate remaining coconut up to 2 days for another use.)

2. Prepare pineapple: Cut crown and stem end from pineapple. Stand pineapple on cutting board, cut off rind, and remove eyes. Cut pineapple lengthwise into quarters. Cut out core. Cut quarters lengthwise in half, then crosswise into pieces. Place in large bowl.

3. Prepare oranges: Cut ends off oranges; stand on cutting board and cut off peel and white pith. Holding oranges over bowl with pineapple, cut sections from between membranes, allowing sections to drop into bowl. Squeeze juice from membranes into bowl.

4. Add shredded coconut to bowl and toss gently to combine. Makes 10 servings.

Each serving: About 240 calories, 3g protein, 31g carbohydrate, 14g total fat (12g saturated), 0mg cholesterol, 10mg sodium.

PAPAYAS

Availability
Year-round

Buying Tips
Pick evenly colored gold-yellow fruit. Papayas are sometimes speckled with a few black spots; they do not affect the flavor or quality. The fruit should yield to gentle pressure. Fruit that is too hard will never fully ripen. Avoid oversoft, shriveled, or bruised fruit.

To Store
Ripen papayas at room temperature, then refrigerate and use within three or four days.

To Prepare
Cut papayas lengthwise in half and scoop out the black, peppery seeds. Peel and slice or simply cut up.

PASSION FRUIT

Availability
February through July

Buying Tips
Ripe passion fruit isn't very pretty (the skin is wrinkled and puckered), but the prize is the highly perfumed flesh inside. The skin is usually purple but may be yellow-gold.

To Store
Refrigerate ripe fruit and use within three days.

To Prepare
Cut the fruit crosswise in half and with a spoon, scoop out the pulp and seeds. If desired, strain the pulp through a fine sieve to remove the tiny edible seeds, pressing hard to extract all the juices. One passion fruit yields about 2 tablespoons pulp.

Test Kitchen Tip Dried fruits are great for snacking and stirring into cookies, muffins, and cakes. Sulfur dioxide is often used to preserve and enhance their color. If you have a sulfite allergy, look for sulfur-free dried fruits (they won't have the same bright color) at supermarkets and natural-food stores. Dried fruits can be stored in an airtight container in a dark, dry place at room temperature for up to one year.

Dried Apples Dried apple rings are often added to fruit compotes. Health-food store varieties are usually firmer and more flavorful than the packaged supermarket variety.

Dried Apricots Two types of dried apricots are sold in supermarkets and other food stores: apricot halves from California, which are deep orange and very flavorful, and smaller whole apricots from Turkey, which are pale orange and tart rather than sweet.

Dried Bananas Sold in strips, dried bananas can be cut up and used much like dried figs in cakes and muffins. Crisp banana chips are eaten as a snack, not used for cooking.

Dried Blueberries These berries sometimes lose a bit of flavor in the drying process, but they are a nice addition to muffins, scones, and quick breads. It's easy to dry your own: Spread blueberries in a single layer in a jelly-roll pan and place in a 200°F oven. Bake until leathery and all of the moisture has been removed, at least 5 hours. The drying time will depend on the size of the berries.

Dried Cherries Available tart or sweet. Dried sweet cherries are a delicious snack; dried tart cherries are excellent in baked goods. Dried cherries (sweet or tart) make a healthful and flavorful addition to homemade or store-bought granola and dried fruit compote.

Dried Cranberries Sometimes called Craisins®, they are sprayed with sugar syrup, which tames their characteristic tartness. Use them instead of raisins in oatmeal cookies and in bar cookies.

Dried Dates Use dried dates in small amounts because they are very sweet. They are also very sticky; cut them up with oiled kitchen scissors. Prechopped dates are very convenient but not as tasty.

Dried Figs Two types of figs are grown in the San Joaquin Valley in California: Mission and Calimyrna. Unlike other fruit trees, fig trees have no blossoms. The tiny flowers develop inside the figs and become crunchy seeds. Mission figs are small and black, while Calimyrnas are light golden and have a slightly nutty flavor. Choose dried figs that are plump and moist looking. Stuff them with herbed goat cheese or poach them in red wine just like fresh pears. Dried figs can be frozen for up to one year.

Dried Peaches and Pears Though mostly appreciated as an out-of-hand snack, these fruits can be turned into a lovely fruit compote when cooked up with dried plums, raisins, and sliced fresh lemon. Snipped into small pieces with oiled kitchen scissors, they can be added to quick breads, scones, or muffins for a nice flavor variation.

Dried Plums Formerly known as prunes, dried plums are sold pitted and unpitted. They are a quick source of energy and a good source of potassium, iron, and vitamins A and C. Organic dried plums, found in some supermarkets and in health-food stores, are very tasty and have a pleasant chewy texture.

Raisins Grapes have been sun-dried into raisins since 1490 BC, but it is believed that it wasn't until 1873 that California produced its first raisin crop. Even today raisins are made from sun-dried grapes. For optimum freshness, store raisins in an airtight container in the refrigerator or in a cool area in your kitchen. They also freeze well for up to one year and are quickly thawed at room temperature. To plump raisins, cover them with very hot tap water and soak for 3 to 5 minutes, then drain.

Golden Raisins Good in baking, these are seedless Thompson grapes that have been treated with sulfur dioxide to retain their light color.

Currants Also known as Zante currants, these are dried seedless grapes, totally unrelated to fresh currants. The name is derived from the grape variety's place of origin: Corinth, Greece.

PEACHES

Availability
May through September

Buying Tips
Peaches are classified as *freestone,* which means the fruit easily separates from the pit, or *clingstone,* where the fruit clings tightly to the pit.

Tree-ripened peaches have a sweet, fruity aroma, yield to gentle pressure, and have the best flavor. Underripe peaches will soften at room temperature but will not get sweeter than they were when purchased. Avoid green, shriveled, or bruised fruit.

To Store
Refrigerate ripe peaches and use within five days.

To Prepare
Peel the fruit, cut in half along the seam line, and remove the pit. To peel, dip whole peaches into rapidly boiling water for about 15 seconds, then plunge into a bowl of cold water; slip off the skins. Some peaches are almost impossible to peel; simply use a vegetable peeler. To prevent browning, sprinkle peeled fruit with lemon juice.

PEARS

Availability
Year-round

Buying Tips
Pears are picked unripe, then ripen during shipping and storage. Select well-shaped, fairly firm fruit; the color depends on the variety. Avoid shriveled, discolored, cut, or bruised fruit.

For cooking, *Bartlett, Anjou,* or *Bosc* pears are good choices. The elegant shape of the Bosc pear makes it especially appealing for poaching. Delicious eating pears include the *Comice, Seckel, Winter Nelis,* and *Kieffer* varieties. The *Asian* pear, a crisp and not very sweet relative of the common pear, is perfect for green salads or for use in combination with other fruits.

To Store
Knowing when a particular pear is ripe depends on the variety. Bartletts go from green to soft yellow; greenish brown Boscs turn the color of milk chocolate; and Anjous yield to gentle pressure. Let firm pears ripen at room temperature in a brown paper bag for a few days (it may even take up to a week), then refrigerate and use within three to five days. Never refrigerate pears in an airtight plastic bag; the centers will turn dark brown. Store pears away from strong-smelling foods, because they absorb odors easily. To prevent peeled or cut-up pears from browning, sprinkle with lemon juice.

To Prepare
Peel pears, if desired. Cut the fruit lengthwise in half and remove the core (use a small melon baller) and stem, if desired.

Roasted Pears with Marsala

Roasting pears at high heat intensifies their flavor, and the Marsala adds a sweet nuttiness. If you have some Ruby port on hand, use that instead.

Prep: 25 minutes Bake: 40 minutes

1	lemon
8	ripe medium Bosc pears with stems
2	teaspoons plus ⅓ cup sugar
½	cup sweet Marsala wine
⅓	cup water
2	tablespoons butter or margarine, melted

1. Preheat oven to 450°F. From lemon, with vegetable peeler, remove peel in strips (2½" by ½" each); squeeze juice.

2. With melon baller or small knife, remove cores from pears by cutting through blossom end (bottom) of unpeeled pears (do not remove stems). With pastry brush, brush cavity of each pear with lemon juice, then sprinkle each cavity with ¼ teaspoon sugar.

3. In shallow 1½- to 2-quart baking dish, combine lemon peel, wine, and water. Place remaining ⅓ cup sugar on waxed paper. With pastry brush, brush pears with melted butter, then roll in sugar to coat. Stand pears upright in baking dish. Sprinkle any remaining sugar into baking dish.

4. Bake pears, basting occasionally with syrup in dish, until tender, 40 to 45 minutes.

5. Cool slightly to serve warm, or cool completely and cover and refrigerate up to 1 day. Reheat to serve warm, if you like. Makes 8 servings.

Each serving: About 201 calories, 1g protein, 45g carbohydrate, 4g total fat (2g saturated), 8mg cholesterol, 31mg sodium.

Zinfandel-Poached Pears

Poaching is an easy way to cook the pears and to create a luscious, fat-free ruby-red syrup at the same time.

Prep: 20 minutes plus chilling   Cook: 45 minutes

1	bottle (750 ml) red zinfandel wine (about 3 cups)
2	cups cranberry-juice cocktail
1¼	cups sugar
1	cinnamon stick (3 inches)
2	whole cloves
½	teaspoon whole black peppercorns
8	ripe medium Bosc pears with stems

1. In nonreactive 5-quart Dutch oven, combine wine, cranberry-juice cocktail, sugar, cinnamon, cloves, and peppercorns; heat just to boiling over high heat, stirring occasionally, until sugar has dissolved.

2. Meanwhile, peel pears, leaving stems on. With melon baller or small knife, remove cores by cutting through blossom end (bottom).

3. Place pears in wine mixture; heat to boiling. Reduce heat; cover and simmer, turning pears occasionally, until tender but not soft, 15 to 25 minutes.

4. With slotted spoon, carefully transfer pears to platter. Strain wine mixture through sieve into bowl; pour back into Dutch oven. Heat to boiling over high heat. Cook, uncovered, until liquid has reduced to 1½ cups, 15 to 30 minutes.

5. Cover pears and syrup separately and refrigerate until well chilled, at least 6 hours. To serve, spoon syrup over pears. Makes 8 servings.

Each serving: About 352 calories, 1g protein, 76g carbohydrate, 1g total fat (0g saturated), 0mg cholesterol, 6mg sodium.

QUICK PEAR DESSERTS

Chocolate Pears
Microwave cored whole pears, covered, until tender; spoon hot fudge sauce over each.

Pear and Dried-Cherry Rice Pudding
Cook diced pears in nonstick skillet until tender. Stir into deli rice pudding along with some dried cherries.

Pear Smoothies
Peel very ripe pears; coarsely chop. Whirl in blender with milk, yogurt, honey, and ice until smooth.

PERSIMMONS

Availability
October through February

Buying Tips
The most common persim-
mon is the *Hachiya.* It is
deep orange, heart-shaped, and eaten raw or cooked.
This persimmon must be ripened until very soft and
almost translucent before using, or it will be inedibly
tannic. *Fuyu* persimmons are pale orange and squat
with a light bloom covering the skin. They are preferred for salads and are firm even when ripe.

Buy slightly firm, plump fruit with smooth, unbroken skin and the stem cap still attached; ripen at
home. If you buy soft-ripe fruit, transport it very carefully and use the same day. Avoid purchasing bruised or
cracked fruit.

To Store
Ripen Hachiya persimmons at room temperature in a
closed brown paper bag until very soft. Refrigerate and
use within one or two days. Hachiya pulp freezes very
well in an airtight container for up to two months.

To Prepare
Remove the stem cap. To use Hachiya pulp, cut persimmon in half and, with a spoon, scoop out the soft
flesh; discard the seeds. Puree in a blender or food
processor, or press through a fine sieve. To enjoy Fuyu
persimmons, simply peel and slice.

PINEAPPLES

Availability
Year round

Buying Tips
A pineapple's color depends
on the variety: It can range
from deep yellow to reddish
brown to green. Pineapple is
always picked ripe: It does not get sweeter with time, it
only softens. Pick a pineapple that is slightly soft with
a deep sweet fragrance. The leaves should be firm and
green. Avoid fruit with soft spots or dark areas.

To Store
If you like, chill pineapples before serving.

To Prepare
For rings or chunks, cut off the crown and stem end.
Stand the pineapple upright and slice off the rind and
eyes. Place the fruit on its side and cut crosswise into
¼- to 1-inch-thick slices. Core the pineapple with a
pineapple corer or knife and cut into chunks, if desired. For wedges, with a long serrated knife, cut fruit
lengthwise in half, then into quarters, cutting from the
crown to the stem. Slice off the core by cutting along
the top of the wedges, then slide a knife between the
rind and flesh, keeping the knife close to the rind.
Leave the flesh in the shell and cut each wedge into
¼- to ½-inch-thick slices.

PLUMS

Availability
June through September

Buying Tips
A plum's sweetness does not increase after it is picked,
so purchase ripe fruit. Color is determined by the variety. Ripe plums should be plump and evenly colored
and yield to gentle pressure. If the powdery bloom is
still on the skin, it's a sign they haven't been overhan-
dled. Avoid hard, shriveled, or cracked plums.

Greengage A round, very sweet, perfumed fruit
with greenish yellow skin. *Damson* and *Mirabelle*
plums are members of the same family.

Italian prune plums These are purplish black, oval, freestone plums. Because the flesh is somewhat dry, this plum is best cooked or dried. Look for them from late summer through early autumn.

Santa Rosa One of the most popular plum varieties. Grown primarily in California, this excellent all-purpose plum has juicy, sweet-tart flesh. *Friar* and *Queen Anne* plums are related to the Santa Rosa and have similar qualities.

Wild plums Although the name varies depending on the locale (from the *Sierra* plum in the West to the *beach* plum along the Atlantic Coast), these small plums grow in bunches and are used to make jams and jellies.

To Store

Refrigerate ripe plums and use within five days.

To Prepare

Wash plums, then cut into each center to remove the pit, if desired. For serving, slice or cut up the fruit, with or without the skin. When cooked, the amount of sugar needed will depend on the variety.

Roasted Almond– Crusted Plums

This quick and easy fruit crisp is perfect served warm with a scoop of vanilla ice cream.

Prep: 15 minutes   Bake: 25 minutes

6	large ripe plums (4 to 5 ounces each), each cut in half and pitted
3	tablespoons butter or margarine, softened
⅓	cup packed brown sugar
¼	cup all-purpose flour
⅓	cup sliced natural almonds

1. Preheat oven to 425°F. In shallow baking dish, arrange plums, cut side up, close together in one layer.

2. In medium bowl, beat butter and brown sugar until smooth. Stir in flour until blended. Stir in almonds. Sprinkle mixture evenly over plums. Bake until plums are tender, 25 to 35 minutes. Makes 6 servings.

Each serving: About 204 calories, 2g protein, 31g carbohydrate, 9g total fat (4g saturated), 16mg cholesterol, 64mg sodium.

POMEGRANATES

Availability

September through December but most plentiful in October

Buying Tips

Select fresh-looking fruit heavy for its size. Avoid shriveled fruit or any with broken peel or soft spots.

To Prepare

To eat out of hand, with a sharp knife held one inch from, and parallel to, the blossom end, make a shallow cut all around. With your fingers, pull off the top. Score the fruit (only cutting through the peel) into six wedges. Break the wedges apart.

To remove the seeds (which are very juicy and stain), immerse the wedges in a bowl of cold water; gently separate the seeds from the pith and peel, and let the seeds sink to the bottom of the bowl. Pomegranate seeds can be frozen in an airtight container for up to three months; rinse with cold water before serving.

To extract the juice, puree the seeds in a blender, then strain through a paper towel–lined sieve. (A medium pomegranate yields about ½ cup juice.)

To Serve

Use the juice in fruit drinks. Eat the seeds out of hand, add to fruit salads, or sprinkle on as a garnish.

POMEGRANATE POINTERS

Garnet-colored pomegranate seeds add a splash of color to foods. Sprinkle on Mixed Greens with Pears and Pecans (page 411), Citrus Salad with Sherry Dressing (page 411), or Curry-Grape Chicken Salad (page 426). Pomegranate juice has a tangy citruslike flavor that can substitute for some or all of the lime or lemon juice in your favorite pork or chicken marinades. It also adds a delicious zip to margaritas.

QUINCES

Availability
October and November

Buying Tips
Quinces are never eaten raw. Their hard flesh, tart flavor, and abundance of pectin, however, make them popular for jams and jellies. Buy fruit that is golden yellow with fuzzy skin. Depending on the variety, the fruit will be either round or pear-shaped. Avoid small, knotty, or bruised fruit.

To Store
Store for up to a few days at room temperature or refrigerate in a perforated plastic bag for up to two weeks.

To Prepare
First peel the fruit. Using a heavy knife, cut the fruit in half, remove all the seeds and every bit of core, and slice. In a saucepan, place the slices in 1 inch of boiling water over medium-high heat. Heat to boiling. Reduce heat; cover and simmer until tender and deep gold or rose-colored (the cooking time depends on the size of the slices). Add sugar to taste. (The cooked fruit will remain firm though tender.)

To Serve
The cooked fruit can be served as a sauce or dessert or used in puddings, pies, and tarts.

RHUBARB

Availability
April and May

Buying Tips
The stalks should be firm, crisp, and fairly thick. Rhubarb can range in color from pale pink to deep red. Avoid flabby stalks.

To Store
Refrigerate rhubarb and use within three to five days.

To Prepare
Wash and trim the stalks, then cut off and discard any leaves (which are toxic and should not be eaten).

TANGERINES, TANGELOS, AND OTHER MANDARIN ORANGES

Availability
November through May

Buying Tips
Tangerines, tangelos, clementines, satsumas, and *ugli fruit* are all members of the mandarin orange family. They are sweet and have loose-fitting, easy-to-peel skin and segments that come apart easily. No matter what type you purchase, buy fruit that is heavy for its size. Some popular varieties (with their seasons) include:

Tangerine Named for the city of Tangiers. Look for fruits with deep orange-red skin. They are in season from November through May.

Tangelo A cross between the tangerine and grapefruit, this fruit has a mild flavor and few seeds. The season runs from November through April.

Clementine Look for these sweet, seedless, compact mandarins from October through February.

Satsuma A super-juicy, virtually seedless favorite that's easy to peel and separate into segments. Available from mid-October through December.

RHUBARB-APPLE CRUMBLE

Test Kitchen Tip Preheat the oven to 375°F. In large bowl, combine ⅓ cup granulated sugar and 1 tablespoon cornstarch. Add 1¼ pounds rhubarb, cut into ½-inch pieces (4 cups) and 1¼ pounds Golden Delicious apples (3 medium), peeled, cored, and cut into 1-inch pieces; toss to coat. Spoon into 11" by 7" baking dish.

In medium bowl, with fingertips, mix ½ cup packed brown sugar, 2 tablespoons butter or margarine, and ¼ teaspoon cinnamon until blended. Stir in ⅓ cup old-fashioned or quick-cooking oats and ¼ cup all-purpose flour until combined; sprinkle over fruit.

Bake until filling is bubbling and topping has evenly browned, about 45 minutes. Makes 6 servings.

Ugli fruit This looks like a large greenish grapefruit (and has similar flesh) but is a bit sweeter. Dark spots on the skin are harmless, but don't buy fruit with a dried-out stem end. The season runs from December through May.

WATERMELONS

Availability
May through September

Buying Tips
Watermelons come in two sizes: icebox (around 8 pounds) and large (up to 20 pounds). The flesh can be red, the classic color, or yel-

low, and some varieties are seedless. Watermelons should be firm and symmetrically shaped, either oblong or round, depending on the variety. The side of the melon that touched the soil should be yellowish or cream-colored, not pale green or white. The rind should have a velvety bloom, giving it a dull, not shiny, appearance.

To test a whole melon for ripeness, slap the side of the melon with the open palm of your hand; the sound should be deep and resonant. A dull thud indicates an underripe melon, and a hollow sounds means it is over-ripe and mushy.

Cut watermelon should have firm, deep red flesh with dark brown or black seeds. Avoid melons with white streaks running through the flesh.

To Store
Refrigerate whole watermelon and use within one week. After cutting, cover the cut surface with waxed paper; use within one or two days.

To Serve
For wedges, with a large knife, cut the whole melon in half from stem to blossom end. Cut each piece lengthwise in half and cut crosswise into slices of desired thickness. Or, cut the melon flesh into bite-size chunks and discard the rind.

Watermelon Bowl

For a great presentation, serve this colorful mixture of sweet summer fruits and minty syrup in the hollowed-out watermelon. It makes a very large amount, so it's just right for casual summer get-togethers.

Prep: 1 hour plus chilling   Cook: 10 minutes

1½	cups water
1	cup sugar
1½	cups loosely packed fresh mint leaves and stems, chopped
3	tablespoons fresh lime juice
1	large watermelon (20 pounds), cut lengthwise in half
1	small ripe cantaloupe, cut crosswise in half
6	large ripe plums (about 1½ pounds)
4	large ripe nectarines (about 2 pounds)
1	pound seedless green grapes

1. In 2-quart saucepan, combine water and sugar; heat to boiling over medium heat, stirring occasionally, until sugar has dissolved. Cook 5 minutes. Stir in mint and lime juice and refrigerate until well chilled.

2. Meanwhile, cut watermelon flesh into bite-size pieces; discard seeds. Cut cantaloupe flesh into bite-size pieces. Cut plums and nectarines into wedges; discard pits. Combine cut-up fruit with grapes in very large bowl or in shell of watermelon. Hold sieve over fruit and pour chilled syrup through. Gently toss to mix well. Cover and refrigerate about 2 hours to blend flavors, stirring occasionally. Makes about 32 cups.

Each cup: About 111 calories, 2g protein, 26g carbohydrate, 1g total fat (0g saturated), 0mg cholesterol, 7mg sodium.

Anise Fruit Bowl

Prepare as directed above but substitute **2 tablespoons anise seeds** for mint.

14

SALADS & SALAD DRESSINGS

Salad, in its most familiar guise, is a cool, crisp, refreshing collection of greens tossed with a piquant dressing. The possibilities, however, don't end here. A salad can be created from a seemingly endless array of ingredients, each contributing different flavors and textures and sometimes even dictating different serving temperatures. Whether prepared with beans or bread, with grains or greens, or served chilled or warm, a salad is always welcome. It can also play a variety of roles. A salad can be an appetite-teasing first course or a tempting side dish, especially at summer barbecues and picnics, but, bolstered with meat, chicken, or seafood, a salad can also serve as a satisfying but light main dish for warm-weather meals.

BUYING, PREPARING, AND STORING SALAD GREENS

Choose crisp-looking greens with no bruised, yellowing, or brown-tipped leaves. Iceberg lettuce should be heavy for its size and feel firm when squeezed.

As soon as you get it home, wash, dry, and store the lettuce leaves. This will keep the greens fresh longer and provide a few days' worth of salad ready to be put together when you are. Even prewashed greens should be washed and dried to refresh them and to rinse off any bacteria from the surface of the leaves.

No one wants a gritty salad, so wash greens well. Separate the leaves, submerge them in a sinkful or large bowl of cold water, and gently agitate the greens to loosen the dirt. Lift the greens from the water, leaving the grit to sink to the bottom. Curly-leafed greens, as well as spinach and arugula, are especially sandy, and dirt often gets trapped in the crevices of the leaves. Wash these in cool water (the slightly warmer temperature loosens dirt better than cold water), and, if necessary, give the greens a second washing.

Dry salad greens thoroughly before using or storing. Not only do wet greens dilute the dressing and make for a less flavorful, soggy salad, but they won't keep well either. A salad spinner provides an efficient way to dry greens, but you can also pat greens dry with paper towels or clean kitchen towels. If you are washing spinach, arugula, or watercress, remove their tough stems after rinsing.

To store, wrap the rinsed and dried greens in a clean kitchen towel (or in a few paper towels), place in a plastic bag (pressing out all the excess air), and store in the vegetable crisper drawer of the refrigerator. Tender leaf lettuce will keep for two to three days; iceberg and other sturdy lettuces will keep for up to five days. Very delicate greens, such as arugula or watercress, will keep for only a day or so.

A GLOSSARY OF GREENS

Salad greens fall into either of two basic categories: delicate and tender or assertive and slightly bitter. Tender greens, such as lettuce, are served alone or combined with other vegetables. There are four types of lettuce: *crisphead* (iceberg) varieties are crisp and mild-flavored and stand up well to thicker dressings; *butterhead* (Bibb, Boston) is sweet-tasting and delicate and should be served with an appropriately light-bodied dressing; *loose-leaf* (oak leaf) is tender but has a slightly stronger flavor than butterhead; *long-leaf* (romaine) has long, firm, crisp leaves and is another candidate for rich, thick dressings.

Stronger-flavored greens (including members of the chicory family) are usually combined with sweeter lettuces for a well-balanced salad. Flavorwise, their mild bitterness contrasts nicely with the natural sweetness of the lettuces, but greens such as radicchio and Belgian endive are also invaluable as color elements in the salad palette.

Here are the basic characteristics of the different greens to help you make the right choice at the market.

Arugula Peppery arugula is also known as *rugula* or *rocket*. The older and larger the leaves, the more assertive the flavor. The leaves can be very gritty, so rinse them thoroughly.

Baby greens Available in bags or in bulk at many supermarkets, this combination of very young, tender salad greens is an Americanization of the French salad mix known as *mesclun*.

Belgian endive A member of the chicory family, Belgian endive is appreciated for its crisp texture and slightly bitter flavor. The leaves should be very white, graduating to pale yellow tips.

Bibb lettuce Also called *limestone* lettuce, has cup-shaped leaves and is best with mild vinaigrettes.

Boston lettuce A loose-leaf lettuce with tender floppy leaves, it is sometimes called *butterhead* lettuce.

Chicory Although chicory is an entire family of mildly bitter greens, Americans use the term to identify a dark green variety with fringed leaves. It is also known as *curly endive*.

Chinese cabbage A tightly formed head of white leaves with wide stalks.

Dandelion Tart greens that make a pungent addition to a salad. Some cooks gather the wild variety in the spring.

Escarole Sharp-tasting escarole should have curly leaves with firm stems that snap easily.

Frisée A delicate, pale green variety of chicory with curly, almost spiky leaves.

Iceberg lettuce A lettuce that is best appreciated for its refreshing crisp texture rather than for its mild flavor. Cut out the core before rinsing the leaves.

Mâche Also called *lamb's lettuce*, this green has a nutty taste and tiny tender leaves. Use within one day; it wilts easily.

Mesclun From the Provençal word for "mixture," true mesclun is made up of wild baby greens from the hillsides of southern France, and often includes herbs and edible flowers. Here, it is commonly a mix of sweet lettuces and bitter greens such as arugula, dandelion, frisée, mizuna, oak leaf, mâche, sorrel, and radicchio.

Mizuna A small, feathery, delicately flavored green of Japanese origin.

Napa cabbage Very similar to, and interchangeable with, Chinese cabbage, but shorter and rounder.

Oak leaf A variety of Boston lettuce with ruffled leaves. Green oak leaf is uniformly green, whereas red oak leaf has dark red tips.

Radicchio The most common radicchio is round with white-veined ruby-red leaves. *Radicchio di Treviso* has long, narrow red leaves that form a tapered head.

Radish sprouts Innocent-looking sprouts with tiny clover-shaped heads that pack a peppery punch.

Romaine Its long, crisp, dark green leaves and slightly nutty flavor make romaine the preferred lettuce for Caesar salad.

Spinach Whether dark green and crinkled or flat, spinach needs to be washed thoroughly to remove all the grit. Baby spinach has very tender edible stems.

Watercress Watercress adds crisp texture and a mildly spicy flavor to salads. It is very perishable, so use within one or two days of purchase.

Mixed Greens with Pears and Pecans

Sweet ripe pears and crunchy buttery pecans make this an irresistible holiday salad.

Prep: 45 minutes

- 3 tablespoons red wine vinegar
- 2 teaspoons Dijon mustard
- ½ teaspoon salt
- ½ teaspoon coarsely ground black pepper
- ⅓ cup olive oil
- 3 ripe medium pears, each peeled, cored, and cut into 16 wedges
- 1 wedge Parmesan cheese (4 ounces)
- 2 small heads radicchio, cored and torn into large pieces
- 2 small heads Belgian endive, separated into leaves
- 2 small bunches arugula (4 ounces each), tough stems trimmed, or 2 bags (5 ounces each) arugula
- ½ cup pecans, toasted (page 562) and coarsely chopped

1. Prepare dressing: In very large bowl, with wire whisk, mix vinegar, mustard, salt, and pepper. In thin, steady stream, whisk in oil until blended. Add pears, tossing to coat.

2. With vegetable peeler, remove enough shavings from wedge of Parmesan to measure 1 cup, loosely packed.

3. Add radicchio, endive, and arugula to pears; toss until mixed and coated with dressing. Top salad with Parmesan shavings and sprinkle with pecans. Makes 10 first-course servings.

Each serving: About 166 calories, 4g protein, 11g carbohydrate, 13g total fat (2g saturated), 4mg cholesterol, 244mg sodium.

Citrus Salad with Sherry Dressing

Spicy watercress is the perfect complement for this combination of tart apples, sweet oranges, and tangy grapefruit.

Prep: 30 minutes

- 2 tablespoons dry sherry
- 1 tablespoon red wine vinegar
- 1 teaspoon Dijon mustard
- ¼ teaspoon salt
- ⅛ teaspoon coarsely ground black pepper
- 2 tablespoons olive oil
- 1 large Granny Smith apple, cored and cut into paper-thin slices
- 2 large navel oranges
- 1 large pink grapefruit
- 1 bunch watercress (4 ounces), tough stems trimmed

1. Prepare dressing: In large bowl, with wire whisk, mix sherry, vinegar, mustard, salt, and pepper. In thin, steady stream, whisk in oil until blended.

2. Add apple slices to dressing in bowl and toss to coat. Cut peel and white pith from oranges and grapefruit. Holding oranges and grapefruit over small bowl to catch juice, cut sections from between membranes. (If you like, squeeze juice from membranes and reserve for another use.) Add orange and grapefruit sections to dressing in bowl; toss to coat.

3. Arrange watercress on platter. Spoon fruit mixture and dressing over watercress. Makes 6 accompaniment servings.

Each serving: About 109 calories, 2g protein, 16g carbohydrate, 5g total fat (1g saturated), 0mg cholesterol, 127mg sodium.

Frisée Salad with Warm Bacon Vinaigrette

If you don't find frisée in your grocery store, this salad works well with curly endive, frisée's less delicate cousin (also called chicory). Trim away the outer leaves and use only the pale center leaves for the salad.

Prep: 20 minutes   Bake: 10 minutes

- 2 tablespoons olive oil
- ¼ teaspoon salt
- 4 ounces country-style bread or French bread, cut into ½-inch cubes
- 4 slices thick-sliced bacon, cut into ½-inch pieces
- 2 tablespoons red wine vinegar
- 1 tablespoon Dijon mustard
- ⅛ teaspoon coarsely ground black pepper
- 1 pound frisée, ends trimmed
- 6 large eggs, poached (optional)

1. Preheat oven to 400°F. In large serving bowl, combine oil and salt. Add bread cubes to oil mixture and toss to coat. Transfer bread to jelly-roll pan and bake, stirring once, until golden brown and crisp, about 10 minutes. Cool in pan on wire rack.

2. Meanwhile, in 2-quart saucepan, cook bacon over medium heat, stirring frequently, until browned, about 8 minutes. Remove saucepan from heat. With slotted spoon, transfer bacon to paper towels to drain. Discard all but 3 tablespoons bacon drippings from saucepan.

3. With wire whisk, mix vinegar, mustard, pepper, and *2 tablespoons water* into bacon drippings in saucepan.

4. To serve, in same serving bowl, tear frisée into bite-size pieces. Toss frisée with warm bacon vinaigrette until coated. Arrange frisée on 6 dinner plates. Top each with croutons, bacon, and a poached egg, if you like. Makes 6 first-course servings.

Each serving without egg: About 210 calories, 6g protein, 13g carbohydrate, 15g total fat (4g saturated), 13mg cholesterol, 425mg sodium.

Each serving with egg: About 285 calories, 12g protein, 14g carbohydrate, 20g total fat (6g saturated), 224mg cholesterol, 565mg sodium.

Warm Arugula and Mushroom Salad

Peppery arugula leaves are coated with a warm mushroom dressing infused with rosemary, then topped with Parmesan cheese shavings.

Prep: 25 minutes   Cook: 12 to 14 minutes

- ¼ cup chicken broth
- 3 tablespoons olive oil
- 2 tablespoons balsamic vinegar
- 2 tablespoons dry vermouth
- ½ teaspoon sugar
- ½ teaspoon salt
- ½ teaspoon coarsely ground black pepper
- 3 small bunches arugula (4 ounces each), tough stems trimmed, or 3 bags (5 ounces each) arugula
- 1 wedge Parmesan cheese (4 ounces)
- 3 garlic cloves, crushed with side of chef's knife
- 8 ounces shiitake mushrooms, stems removed and caps cut into quarters
- 8 ounces white mushrooms, trimmed and sliced
- 1 teaspoon chopped fresh rosemary or ¼ teaspoon dried rosemary, crumbled

1. In small bowl, mix broth, 2 tablespoons oil, vinegar, vermouth, sugar, salt, and pepper. Arrange arugula on large serving platter.

2. With vegetable peeler, remove enough shavings from wedge of Parmesan to measure 1 cup, loosely packed.

3. In nonstick 12-inch skillet, heat remaining 1 tablespoon oil over medium heat. Add garlic and cook, stirring, just until golden. Increase heat to medium-high. Add shiitake and white mushrooms and rosemary; cook, stirring frequently, until mushrooms are browned and liquid has evaporated, 8 to 10 minutes; discard garlic, if you like.

4. Add broth mixture to skillet; cook, stirring, 30 seconds. Immediately spoon mushrooms and pan juices over arugula; top with Parmesan shavings. Makes 4 first-course servings.

Each serving: About 197 calories, 9g protein, 8g carbohydrate, 14g total fat (4g saturated), 10mg cholesterol, 596mg sodium.

Warm Goat Cheese Salad

If you like, coat the goat cheese with the bread crumbs early in the day, then refrigerate for last-minute baking.

Prep: 15 minutes Bake: 8 minutes

- ¼ cup plain dried bread crumbs
- 1 tablespoon chopped fresh parsley
- 1 tablespoon olive oil
- ¼ teaspoon coarsely ground black pepper
- 1 log (5 to 6 ounces) mild goat cheese
- 8 ounces mixed baby salad greens
- 3 tablespoons Classic French Vinaigrette (page 428)

1. Preheat oven to 425°F. In small bowl, stir bread crumbs, parsley, oil, and pepper until well blended. Slice goat cheese crosswise into 6 equal disks. Place on waxed paper; use bread-crumb mixture to coat cheese disks, patting crumbs to cover evenly.

2. Place crumb-coated cheese disks on cookie sheet and bake until crumbs are golden, 8 to 10 minutes.

3. Meanwhile, in large bowl, toss salad greens with dressing to coat. Divide greens among 6 salad plates and top each serving with a warm goat-cheese disk. Makes 6 first-course servings.

Each serving: About 178 calories, 7g protein, 5g carbohydrate, 15g total fat (6g saturated), 20mg cholesterol, 264mg sodium.

New Caesar Salad

Our recipe uses mayonnaise instead of raw egg yolk to create the classic dressing, and baked bread cubes stand in for the more usual deep-fried croutons.

Prep: 15 minutes Bake: 7 minutes

- 6 slices (½ inch thick) Italian bread
- 2 garlic cloves, each peeled and cut in half
- 3 tablespoons olive oil
- ¼ cup mayonnaise
- ¼ cup freshly grated Parmesan cheese
- 3 tablespoons fresh lemon juice
- 2 tablespoons water
- 2 teaspoons anchovy paste
- 1 head romaine lettuce, torn into bite-size pieces

1. Preheat oven to 400°F. Rub bread slices with cut side of garlic. Brush both sides of bread with 2 tablespoons oil. Cut bread into ½-inch cubes and place in jelly-roll pan. Bake, stirring once, until golden brown and crisp, about 7 minutes.

2. Meanwhile, prepare dressing: In large bowl, with wire whisk, mix mayonnaise, Parmesan, lemon juice, water, remaining 1 tablespoon oil, and anchovy paste until blended. Add romaine and croutons; toss to coat. Makes 4 first-course servings.

Each serving: About 367 calories, 9g protein, 27g carbohydrate, 25g total fat (5g saturated), 14mg cholesterol, 604mg sodium.

Chopped Salad

A chopped salad can be prepared from your favorite salad ingredients. Here's a classic combination. If you have a mezzaluna—a chopper with crescent blades—it will make preparation a breeze.

Prep: 25 minutes

- 1 large head romaine lettuce (1¼ pounds), chopped into ½-inch pieces
- 1 bunch watercress (4 ounces), tough stems trimmed, coarsely chopped
- 1¼ pounds ripe tomatoes (2 large), cut into ½-inch pieces
- 1 medium cucumber (8 ounces), peeled, seeded, and cut into ½-inch pieces
- 1 cup radishes, cut into quarters
- ¼ cup Classic French Vinaigrette (page 428) or dressing of choice

In large bowl, combine romaine, watercress, tomatoes, cucumber, radishes, and dressing; toss to coat. Makes 8 accompaniment servings.

Each serving: About 67 calories, 2g protein, 5g carbohydrate, 5g total fat (1g saturated), 0mg cholesterol, 109mg sodium.

Waldorf Salad

Serve this chunky salad alongside your favorite grilled chicken for a sweet and savory meal.

Prep: 30 minutes

- ⅓ cup mayonnaise
- ¼ cup sour cream
- 1 tablespoon fresh lemon juice
- 1 teaspoon honey
- ¼ teaspoon salt
- 2 red apples, such as Braeburn, Cortland, or Red Delicious, each cored, cut into 8 wedges, then crosswise into ¼-inch pieces
- 1 Granny Smith apple, cored, cut into 8 wedges, then crosswise into ¼-inch pieces
- 2 stalks celery, each cut lengthwise in half, then thinly sliced (½ cup)
- ½ cup walnuts, toasted (page 562) and coarsely chopped
- ⅓ cup dark seedless raisins

Prepare dressing: In medium bowl, with wire whisk, mix mayonnaise, sour cream, lemon juice, honey, and salt until blended. Add red and Granny Smith apples, celery, walnuts, and raisins to dressing in bowl and toss until mixed and coated with dressing. Makes 8 accompaniment servings.

Each serving: About 181 calories, 2g protein, 16g carbohydrate, 14g total fat (2g saturated), 9mg cholesterol, 135mg sodium.

Mozzarella and Tomato Salad

For this simple combination to be at its best, use only fresh mozzarella and vine-ripened summer tomatoes.

Prep: 15 minutes

- 2 ripe medium tomatoes (8 ounces each), thinly sliced
- 10 ounces fresh mozzarella, thinly sliced
- 2 tablespoons extra-virgin olive oil
- ¼ teaspoon salt
- ¼ teaspoon ground black pepper
- 2 tablespoons thinly sliced fresh basil leaves

On large platter, arrange tomatoes and mozzarella in overlapping rows. Drizzle with oil and sprinkle with salt and pepper. Top with basil. Makes 4 accompaniment servings.

Each serving: About 285 calories, 14g protein, 8g carbohydrate, 22g total fat (1g saturated), 50mg cholesterol, 203mg sodium.

Three-Bean Salad

If you can't find wax beans, simply double the amount of green beans called for.

Prep: 25 minutes plus chilling   Cook: 13 minutes

- 8 ounces green beans, trimmed and cut into 1-inch pieces (2 cups)
- 8 ounces wax beans, trimmed and cut into 1-inch pieces (2 cups)
- 1½ teaspoons salt
- 3 tablespoons olive or vegetable oil
- 3 tablespoons cider vinegar
- 2 tablespoons sugar
- 1 can (15 to 19 ounces) red kidney beans, rinsed and drained
- ¼ cup chopped onion

1. In 4-quart saucepan, heat *3 inches water* to boiling over high heat. Add green and wax beans and ½ teaspoon salt; heat to boiling. Cook until tender-crisp, 6 to 8 minutes. Drain. Rinse beans with cold running water to cool slightly; drain.

2. Meanwhile, prepare dressing: In large bowl, with wire whisk, mix oil, vinegar, sugar, and remaining 1 teaspoon salt until well blended. Add green and wax beans, kidney beans, and onion; toss until mixed and coated with dressing. Cover and refrigerate salad at least 2 hours to blend flavors or up to 24 hours. Makes 8 accompaniment servings.

Each serving: About 118 calories, 4g protein, 14g carbohydrate, 5g total fat (1g saturated), 0mg cholesterol, 441mg sodium.

Greek Peasant Salad

Serve this cool Mediterranean-style dish alongside grilled chicken, fish, or pork, or on its own with crusty bread.

Prep: 25 minutes

- 4 kirby cucumbers (about 1 pound), not peeled
- 2 tablespoons fresh lemon juice
- 1 tablespoon olive oil
- ¼ teaspoon salt
- ⅛ teaspoon ground black pepper
- 2 pounds ripe red and/or yellow tomatoes (about 6 medium), cut into 1-inch chunks
- ½ cup loosely packed fresh mint leaves, chopped
- ⅓ cup Kalamata olives, pitted and coarsely chopped
- ¼ cup loosely packed fresh dill, chopped
- 2 ounces feta cheese, crumbled (½ cup)

1. With vegetable peeler, remove 3 or 4 evenly spaced lengthwise strips of peel from each cucumber. Cut each cucumber lengthwise into quarters, then crosswise into ½-inch pieces.

Greek Peasant Salad

2. In large bowl, with wire whisk, mix lemon juice, oil, salt, and pepper. Add cucumbers, tomatoes, mint, olives, and dill, and toss until evenly mixed and coated with dressing. Top with feta. Makes about 6½ cups or 6 accompaniment servings.

Each serving: About 100 calories, 3g protein, 11g carbohydrate, 6g total fat (2g saturated), 8mg cholesterol, 280mg sodium.

Summer Corn Salad

We've created this colorful salad from a mélange of farmstand-fresh summer vegetables.

Prep: 30 minutes   Cook: 10 minutes

- 12 medium ears corn, husks and silk removed
- 12 ounces green beans, trimmed and cut into ¼-inch pieces
- ½ cup cider vinegar
- ¼ cup olive oil
- ¼ cup chopped fresh parsley
- 1 teaspoon salt
- ½ teaspoon coarsely ground black pepper
- 1 red pepper, finely chopped
- 1 small sweet onion, such as Vidalia or Walla Walla, finely chopped

1. In 8-quart saucepot, heat *2 inches water* to boiling over high heat; add corn. Heat to boiling. Reduce heat; cover and simmer 5 minutes. Drain. When cool enough to handle, cut kernels from cobs.

2. Meanwhile, in 2-quart saucepan, heat *1 inch water* to boiling over high heat; add green beans and heat to boiling. Reduce heat; simmer until tender-crisp, 3 to 5 minutes. Drain green beans. Rinse with cold running water; drain.

3. Prepare dressing: In large bowl, with wire whisk, mix vinegar, oil, parsley, salt, and black pepper until thoroughly blended.

4. Add corn, green beans, red pepper, and onion to dressing in bowl; toss to coat. If not serving immediately, cover and refrigerate up to 2 hours. Makes 12 accompaniment servings.

Each serving: About 179 calories, 5g protein, 31g carbohydrate, 6g total fat (1g saturated), 0mg cholesterol, 219mg sodium.

Spiced Watermelon and Tomato Salad

The combination of watermelon and tomato makes a surprisingly tasty and refreshing salad. Seedless watermelon makes preparation easy. Choose one that is heavy for its size and makes a thud when tapped.

Prep: 20 minutes

---

3 ripe medium tomatoes (about 1 pound), cut into ¾-inch pieces

¼ cup fresh lime juice (2 to 3 limes)

½ teaspoon salt

1 piece watermelon (about 2½ pounds with rind)

2 tablespoons chopped fresh cilantro leaves

½ teaspoon ground cumin

½ teaspoon ground coriander

⅛ teaspoon ground red pepper (cayenne)

1. In large bowl, toss tomatoes with lime juice and salt; set aside.

2. Cut rind from watermelon; discard rind. Cut flesh into ½-inch pieces to equal 4 cups; discard seeds.

3. Add watermelon, cilantro, cumin, coriander, and ground red pepper to tomato mixture; toss well to combine. Serve at room temperature or cover and refrigerate to serve later. Makes about 6 cups or 10 accompaniment servings.

Each serving: About 30 calories, 1g protein, 7g carbohydrate, 0g total fat, 0mg cholesterol, 120mg sodium.

Kirby Cucumber Salad

The unwaxed skin of kirby cucumbers doesn't need to be peeled. If you can't find them, buy regular cucumbers and remove half the peel in strips, creating stripes.

Prep: 30 minutes plus standing and chilling

---

4 pounds kirby cucumbers, not peeled, thinly sliced

1 tablespoon salt

¾ cup distilled white vinegar

2 tablespoons sugar

2 tablespoons chopped fresh dill

1. In colander set over large bowl, toss cucumbers and salt; let stand 30 minutes at room temperature. Discard liquid in bowl. Pat cucumbers dry with paper towels.

2. In same clean bowl, combine vinegar, sugar, and dill. Add cucumbers and toss to coat. Cover and refrigerate, stirring occasionally, at least 1 hour to blend flavors or up to 4 hours. Makes 12 accompaniment servings.

Each serving: About 30 calories, 1g protein, 7g carbohydrate, 0g total fat, (0g saturated), 0mg cholesterol, 149mg sodium.

Creamy Cucumber and Dill Salad

On hot summer days, serve these thinly sliced cucumbers as a cool side dish with grilled salmon.

Prep: 15 minutes plus standing and chilling

---

2 English (seedless) cucumbers, not peeled, thinly sliced

2 teaspoons salt

½ cup sour cream

2 tablespoons chopped fresh dill

2 teaspoons chopped fresh mint

1 teaspoon distilled white vinegar

⅛ teaspoon ground black pepper

1. In colander set over large bowl, toss cucumbers and salt; let stand 30 minutes at room temperature to drain. Discard liquid in bowl. Pat cucumbers dry with paper towels.

2. In same clean bowl, combine sour cream, dill, mint, vinegar, and pepper. Add cucumbers, stirring to coat. Cover and refrigerate at least 1 hour to blend flavors or up to 4 hours. Makes 6 accompaniment servings.

Each serving: About 60 calories, 2g protein, 5g carbohydrate, 4g total fat (3g saturated), 8mg cholesterol, 203mg sodium.

Coleslaw with Vinaigrette

Flavored with caraway seeds, this tasty coleslaw is best when thoroughly chilled.

Prep: 20 minutes plus chilling

- 2 tablespoons olive or vegetable oil
- 2 tablespoons red wine vinegar
- 1 tablespoon sugar
- 1 teaspoon salt
- ½ teaspoon caraway seeds or ¼ teaspoon celery seeds, crushed
- 1 small head green cabbage (1½ pounds), quartered, cored, and thinly sliced, tough ribs discarded (6 cups)
- 1 large red pepper, cut into 2" by ¼" matchstick strips

Prepare dressing: In large bowl, with wire whisk, mix oil, vinegar, sugar, salt, and caraway seeds until blended. Add cabbage and red pepper; toss to coat well. Cover and refrigerate at least 1 hour to blend flavors or up to 6 hours. Makes 6 accompaniment servings.

Each serving: About 75 calories, 1g protein, 8g carbohydrate, 5g total fat (1g saturated), 0mg cholesterol, 405mg sodium.

Asian Coleslaw

Plan ahead: Prepare all the vegetables for the coleslaw, cover and refrigerate for up to 6 hours. Combine the dressing ingredients in a jar, cover tightly, and store at room temperature. When ready to serve, shake the dressing and toss with the vegetables.

Prep: 35 minutes

- ⅓ cup seasoned rice vinegar
- 2 tablespoons vegetable oil
- 2 teaspoons Asian sesame oil
- ¾ teaspoon salt
- 1 medium head savoy cabbage (2½ pounds), quartered, cored, and thinly sliced, tough ribs discarded
- 1 bag (16 ounces) carrots, peeled and shredded
- ½ cup chopped fresh cilantro
- 4 green onions, thinly sliced

1. Prepare dressing: In large bowl, with wire whisk, mix vinegar, vegetable and sesame oils, and salt until blended.

2. Add cabbage, carrots, cilantro, and green onions to dressing in bowl; toss until mixed and coated with dressing. If not serving right away, cover and refrigerate up to 2 hours. Makes 12 accompaniment servings.

Each serving: About 69 calories, 2g protein, 10g carbohydrate, 3g total fat (0g saturated), 0mg cholesterol, 310mg sodium.

Light and Lemony Slaw

A crisp complement to any barbecue and lower in fat than the typical deli slaw. Its subtle sweetness is also a nice change of pace.

Prep: 25 minutes

- 2 lemons
- ½ cup light mayonnaise
- ¼ cup reduced-fat sour cream
- 1 tablespoon sugar
- 1 teaspoon salt
- ½ teaspoon coarsely ground black pepper
- ¼ teaspoon celery seeds, crushed
- 1 large head green cabbage (3 pounds), quartered, cored, and thinly sliced, tough ribs discarded (12 cups)
- 4 carrots, peeled and shredded

1. From lemons, grate 1 teaspoon peel and squeeze ¼ cup juice. In large bowl, with wire whisk, mix lemon peel and juice, mayonnaise, sour cream, sugar, salt, pepper, and celery seeds until blended.

2. Add cabbage and carrots to dressing in bowl; toss to coat. Serve at room temperature, or cover and refrigerate up to 4 hours. Makes 12 accompaniment servings.

Each serving: About 80 calories, 2g protein, 10g carbohydrate, 4g total fat (1g saturated), 5mg cholesterol, 298mg sodium.

Red Potato Salad

In France, potato salad is prepared with a shallot vinaigrette and the freshest, smallest red potatoes available. A bit of crumbled bacon sprinkled over the top is a delicious counterpoint that brings out the sweetness of the potatoes.

Prep: 25 minutes plus cooling   Cook: 30 minutes

4	pounds small red potatoes, not peeled, cut into quarters or eighths if large
3½	teaspoons salt
4	slices bacon
3	large shallots, chopped (¾ cup)
⅓	cup cider vinegar
¼	cup olive oil
2	teaspoons sugar
2	teaspoons Dijon mustard
¼	teaspoon coarsely ground black pepper
2	green onions, chopped

1. In 5-quart saucepot, combine potatoes, enough *water* to cover, and 2 teaspoons salt; heat to boiling over high heat. Reduce heat; cover and simmer until tender, 10 to 12 minutes.

2. Meanwhile, in 10-inch skillet, cook bacon over medium-low heat until browned. With slotted spoon, transfer to paper towels to drain; crumble.

3. Discard all but 1 teaspoon bacon drippings from skillet. Reduce heat to low. Add shallots and cook, stirring, until tender, about 5 minutes. Remove from heat.

4. Prepare dressing: In large bowl, with wire whisk, mix shallots, vinegar, oil, sugar, mustard, remaining 1½ teaspoons salt, and pepper until blended.

5. Drain potatoes. Add hot potatoes to dressing in bowl. With rubber spatula, stir gently until potatoes absorb dressing. Let potatoes cool 30 minutes at room temperature, stirring occasionally. Stir in green onions.

6. If not serving right away, cover and refrigerate up to 4 hours. If chilled, let stand 30 minutes at room temperature before serving. To serve, sprinkle with crumbled bacon. Makes 12 accompaniment servings.

Each serving: About 185 calories, 4g protein, 29g carbohydrate, 6g total fat (1g saturated), 2mg cholesterol, 456mg sodium.

Dilled Red Potatoes with Mint

Prepare potatoes as directed in Step 1 (left); drain. Omit bacon, shallots, vinegar, sugar, and mustard. In large bowl, mix olive oil, remaining 1½ teaspoons salt, and pepper. Add **6 green onions,** chopped, **⅓ cup chopped fresh dill,** and **¼ cup chopped fresh mint.** Add hot potatoes to herb mixture in bowl and toss until mixed. Makes 8 accompaniment servings.

Each serving: About 124 calories, 2g protein, 21g carbohydrate, 4g total fat (0g saturated), 0mg cholesterol, 301mg sodium.

Creamy Potato Salad

As familiar as this classic recipe may be, it is always welcome. For a variation, add ¼ cup chopped smoked ham or 2 coarsely chopped hard-cooked eggs.

Prep: 20 minutes   Cook: 35 minutes

3	pounds all-purpose potatoes (9 medium), not peeled
½	cup mayonnaise
½	cup milk
2	tablespoons distilled white vinegar
2	tablespoons chopped green onion
1	teaspoon sugar
1	teaspoon salt
¼	teaspoon coarsely ground black pepper
2	large stalks celery, thinly sliced

1. In 4-quart saucepan, combine potatoes and enough *water* to cover; heat to boiling over high heat. Reduce heat; cover and simmer until tender, 25 to 30 minutes. Drain. When cool enough to handle, peel potatoes and cut into ¾-inch cubes.

2. Meanwhile, prepare dressing: In large bowl, with wire whisk, mix mayonnaise, milk, vinegar, green onion, sugar, salt, and pepper until blended. Add potatoes and celery to dressing; toss to coat. If not serving right away, cover and refrigerate up to 4 hours. Makes 10 accompaniment servings.

Each serving: About 198 calories, 3g protein, 27g carbohydrate, 9g total fat (2g saturated), 8mg cholesterol, 315mg sodium.

Two-Potato Salad

Tossing warm potatoes with dressing is a traditional French technique; it enables the potatoes to soak up all the flavor.

Prep: 15 minutes plus cooling   **Cook:** 15 minutes

- 2 pounds red potatoes (about 8 medium), cut into 1-inch chunks
- 1 pound sweet potatoes (2 small), peeled and cut into 1-inch chunks
- ¼ cup red wine vinegar
- 1 tablespoon spicy brown mustard
- 1¼ teaspoons salt
- ½ teaspoon coarsely ground black pepper
- ½ cup mayonnaise
- ¼ cup milk
- 2 medium celery stalks, chopped
- 1 small red onion, minced
- ⅓ cup loosely packed fresh flat-leaf parsley leaves, chopped

1. In 5- to 6-quart saucepot, place red potatoes and enough *water* to cover by 1 inch; heat to boiling over high heat. Reduce heat to low and simmer 2 minutes. Stir in sweet potatoes; heat to boiling over high heat. Reduce heat to low; cover and simmer until potatoes are just fork-tender, 8 to 10 minutes.

2. Meanwhile, prepare dressing. In large bowl, with wire whisk, mix vinegar, mustard, salt, and pepper.

3. Drain potatoes. Add hot potatoes to dressing in bowl; gently stir with rubber spatula until evenly coated. Let stand until cool.

4. In small bowl, whisk mayonnaise and milk until smooth. Add mayonnaise mixture, celery, onion, and parsley to potato mixture; gently stir with rubber spatula until potatoes are well coated. Serve while still warm, or cover and refrigerate until ready to serve. Makes 14 accompaniment servings.

Each serving: About 150 calories, 2g protein, 21g carbohydrate, 7g total fat (1g saturated), 5mg cholesterol, 280mg sodium.

Tubetti Macaroni Salad

Carrots and celery add crunch to this tangy salad. If, after chilling, the salad seems a little dry, stir in a tablespoon or two of milk.

Prep: 25 minutes   **Cook:** 25 minutes

- 1 package (16 ounces) tubetti or ditalini pasta
- 2¾ teaspoons salt
- 4 carrots, peeled and cut into 2" by ¼" matchstick strips
- 1 to 2 lemons
- ⅔ cup light mayonnaise
- ⅓ cup milk
- 2 stalks celery, cut into 2" by ¼" matchstick strips
- 2 green onions, thinly sliced

1. In large saucepot, cook pasta as label directs, using 2 teaspoons salt. After pasta has cooked 10 minutes, add carrots to pasta water and cook until carrots are just tender-crisp and pasta is done, 1 to 2 minutes longer.

2. Meanwhile, from lemon, grate 1 teaspoon peel and squeeze 3 tablespoons juice. Prepare dressing: In large bowl, with wire whisk, mix mayonnaise, milk, lemon peel and juice, and remaining ¾ teaspoon salt until blended.

3. Drain pasta and carrots and add to dressing in bowl along with celery and green onions; toss until mixed and coated with dressing. Serve at room temperature, or cover and refrigerate up to 4 hours. Makes 12 accompaniment servings.

Each serving: About 202 calories, 5g protein, 33g carbohydrate, 5g total fat (1g saturated), 5mg cholesterol, 463mg sodium.

MACARONI SALAD

Test Kitchen Tip

Though popularized in the 1950s in school cafeterias across America, this creamy crowd-pleaser has been around since at least 1917. One of the first printed recipes appeared in *Mrs. Allen's Cook Book*, which was written by Ida Bailey Allen. The salad contained four simple ingredients—macaroni, celery, stuffed olives, and mayonnaise—and was served chilled on a bed of lettuce.

White and Wild Rice Salad

When people hear the word salad, they don't usually think of grains. This festive combination of white and wild rice tossed with cranberries, grapes, and toasted pecans is perfect for a holiday buffet.

Prep: 25 minutes plus cooling   **Cook:** 50 to 60 minutes

- ½ cup wild rice
- 1½ teaspoons salt
- ¾ cup regular long-grain rice
- ⅓ cup dried cranberries or currants
- 2 tablespoons olive oil
- 2 tablespoons red wine vinegar
- ½ teaspoon freshly grated orange peel
- ¼ teaspoon ground black pepper
- 2 cups seedless red grapes, cut in half
- 2 stalks celery, thinly sliced (1 cup)
- 2 tablespoons chopped fresh parsley
- ½ cup pecans, toasted and coarsely chopped

1. Cook wild rice as label directs, using ½ teaspoon salt. Cook white rice as label directs, using ¼ teaspoon salt. Set aside.

2. In small bowl, combine cranberries with just enough *boiling water* to cover; let stand 5 minutes to soften. Drain.

3. Meanwhile, prepare dressing: In large bowl, with wire whisk, mix oil, vinegar, orange peel, remaining ¾ teaspoon salt, and pepper until blended. Add wild and white rice and cranberries; toss to coat. Let cool 30 minutes, tossing several times.

4. Add grapes, celery, and parsley to rice mixture; toss until thoroughly mixed and coated with dressing. Transfer to serving bowl. Sprinkle with pecans. Makes 8 accompaniment servings.

Each serving: About 220 calories, 4g protein, 34g carbohydrate, 8g total fat (1g saturated), 0mg cholesterol, 452mg sodium.

Mediterranean Rice Salad

For extra color and flavor, add some ripe, juicy chopped tomatoes to this fresh-tasting salad.

Prep: 25 minutes plus cooling   **Cook:** 30 minutes

- 2 cups water
- 1 cup regular long-grain rice
- 3 garlic cloves, finely chopped
- 1¼ teaspoons salt
- 3 tablespoons olive oil
- 1 small red onion, chopped
- 1 red pepper, chopped
- 1 medium zucchini (8 ounces), cut lengthwise into quarters, then crosswise into ½-inch-thick pieces
- 2 tablespoons fresh lemon juice
- ⅓ cup Kalamata olives, pitted and coarsely chopped

1. In 2-quart saucepan, heat water to boiling over high heat. Add rice, garlic, and ½ teaspoon salt. Reduce heat; cover and simmer until rice is tender, about 17 minutes.

2. Meanwhile, in 10-inch skillet, heat 1 tablespoon oil over medium heat. Add onion and cook, stirring, 2 minutes. Add red pepper, zucchini, and ¼ teaspoon salt and cook, stirring occasionally, until tender-crisp, about 4 minutes.

3. Prepare dressing: In large bowl, with wire whisk, mix lemon juice, remaining 2 tablespoons oil, and remaining ½ teaspoon salt until blended. Add rice, vegetable mixture, and olives; toss until mixed and coated with dressing. Cool to room temperature. Serve at room temperature, or cover and refrigerate up to 2 hours. Makes 6 accompaniment servings.

Each serving: About 214 calories, 3g protein, 30g carbohydrate, 9g total fat (1g saturated), 0mg cholesterol, 623mg sodium.

Barley Salad with Nectarines

Barley is another grain that makes a flavorful salad. You can use mangoes or peaches instead of the nectarines, if you prefer.

Prep: 30 minutes   Cook: 55 minutes

1	package (16 ounces) pearl barley
2¾	teaspoons salt
4	limes
⅓	cup olive oil
1	tablespoon sugar
¾	teaspoon coarsely ground black pepper
1½	pounds nectarines (4 medium), cut into ½-inch pieces
1	pound ripe tomatoes (2 large), halved, seeded, and cut into ½-inch pieces
4	green onions, thinly sliced
½	cup chopped fresh mint

1. In 4-quart saucepan, heat *6 cups water* to boiling over high heat. Add barley and 1½ teaspoons salt; heat to boiling. Reduce heat; cover and simmer until barley is tender and liquid has been absorbed, about 45 minutes. (Barley will have a creamy consistency.)

2. Meanwhile, from limes, grate 1 tablespoon peel and squeeze ½ cup juice. Prepare dressing: In large bowl, with wire whisk, mix lime peel and juice, oil, sugar, pepper, and remaining 1¼ teaspoons salt until blended.

3. Rinse barley with cold running water; drain. Add barley, nectarines, tomatoes, green onions, and mint to dressing in bowl; stir gently until mixed and coated with dressing. If not serving right away, cover and refrigerate up to 1 hour. Makes 16 accompaniment servings.

Each serving: About 172 calories, 4g protein, 30g carbohydrate, 5g total fat (1g saturated), 0mg cholesterol, 333mg sodium.

Tomato and Mint Tabbouleh

Tabbouleh, the popular bulgur wheat and vegetable salad, offers one of the best ways to enjoy tomatoes, cucumbers, and fresh herbs.

Prep: 20 minutes plus standing and chilling

1½	cups medium-grain bulgur wheat
¼	cup fresh lemon juice (2 to 3 lemons)
1½	cups boiling water
1	pound ripe tomatoes (3 medium), cut into ½-inch pieces
1	medium cucumber (8 ounces), peeled and cut into ½-inch pieces
3	green onions, chopped
¾	cup loosely packed fresh flat-leaf parsley leaves, chopped
½	cup loosely packed fresh mint leaves, chopped
1	tablespoon olive oil
¾	teaspoon salt
¼	teaspoon coarsely ground black pepper

1. In medium bowl, combine bulgur, lemon juice, and boiling water, stirring to mix. Let stand until liquid has been absorbed, about 30 minutes.

2. To bulgur mixture, add tomatoes, cucumber, green onions, parsley, mint, oil, salt, and pepper, stirring to mix. Cover and refrigerate at least 1 hour to blend flavors or up to 4 hours. Makes 12 accompaniment servings.

Each serving: About 87 calories, 3g protein, 17g carbohydrate, 2g total fat (0g saturated), 0mg cholesterol, 157mg sodium.

TABBOULEH

Test Kitchen Tip

Also spelled tabouli and tabouleh, this Lebanese bulgur-based salad is often served as part of a *meze* (spread of appetizers). Its primary ingredients are bulgur, lots of fresh chopped parsley and mint, chunks of tomato, green onions, and a fresh lemon dressing. Some tabboulehs are flavored with crushed red pepper or fresh chiles, while others contain a hint of cinnamon or allspice.

Cobb Salad

The California classic is a *composed* salad in which the ingredients are artfully arranged rather than tossed. Make one large salad or, if you prefer, arrange on individual serving plates.

Prep: 25 minutes   Broil/Cook: 8 minutes

- 12 ounces skinless, boneless chicken-breast halves
- ¼ teaspoon salt
- ⅛ teaspoon ground black pepper
- 6 slices bacon, coarsely chopped
- 1 large head iceberg lettuce, thinly sliced (12 cups)
- 3 large hard-cooked eggs, peeled and coarsely chopped
- 1 large ripe tomato (10 ounces), cut into ½-inch pieces
- 1 ripe avocado, pitted, peeled, and cut into ½-inch pieces
- 3 ounces Roquefort cheese, crumbled (¾ cup)
  Classic French Vinaigrette (page 428)

1. Preheat broiler. Place chicken on rack in broiling pan and sprinkle with salt and pepper. Place pan in broiler 6 inches from heat source. Broil until chicken loses its pink color throughout, about 4 minutes per side. When chicken is cool enough to handle, cut into ½-inch pieces.

2. Meanwhile, in 10-inch skillet, cook bacon over medium heat until browned. With slotted spoon, transfer bacon to paper towels to drain.

3. Line large platter with iceburg lettuce. Arrange eggs, tomato, avocado, Roquefort, chicken, and bacon in striped pattern over lettuce. Pass dressing separately. Makes 6 main-dish servings.

Each serving (without dressing): About 272 calories, 24g protein, 9g carbohydrate, 16g total fat (6g saturated), 157mg cholesterol, 537mg sodium.

Cobb Salad

BLUE CHEESE

Test Kitchen Tip — Cheeses in this category have been injected with the spores of special molds so that they develop blue or blue-green veins or spotting. Most blue cheeses are strongly flavored and have a soft, crumbly texture. Some can be easily sliced, but most are best spread or crumbled.

Danish Blue A cow's milk cheese with a creamy, moist texture and uncomplicated flavor.

Gorgonzola An ivory-colored cow's milk cheese from Italy with a deliciously complex flavor and a creamy texture. There are two kinds of gorgonzola: *dolce*, which is milder, and *naturale*, which is more pungent.

Maytag Blue An American-made blue with a pleasantly bold flavor and creamy texture.

Roquefort Known by many as the "king of cheeses," it is one of the oldest and best-known cheeses in the world. It is made from sheep's milk and is aged for at least three months in the limestone caverns of Mount Combalou near the town of Roquefort in France. It has a moist, crumbly texture, assertive flavor, and is somewhat salty.

Stilton A cow's milk cheese from England with a firm yet creamy texture and bold flavor.

Niçoise Salad

(Pictured on page 408)

As the story goes, the first Niçoise salad was created in eighteenth-century France, and it's been a hit ever since.

Prep: 35 minutes   Cook: 25 minutes

- 1 tablespoon white wine vinegar
- 1 tablespoon fresh lemon juice
- 1 tablespoon minced shallot
- 1 teaspoon Dijon mustard
- 1 teaspoon anchovy paste
- ¼ teaspoon sugar
- ¼ teaspoon coarsely ground black pepper
- 3 tablespoons extra-virgin olive oil
- 1 pound medium red potatoes, not peeled, cut into ¼-inch-thick slices
- 8 ounces French green beans (haricots verts) or regular green beans, trimmed
- 1 head Boston lettuce, leaves separated
- 12 cherry tomatoes, each cut in half
- 1 can (12 ounces) solid white tuna in water, drained and flaked
- 2 large hard-cooked eggs, peeled and each cut into quarters
- ½ cup Niçoise olives

1. Prepare dressing: In small bowl, with wire whisk, mix vinegar, lemon juice, shallot, mustard, anchovy paste, sugar, and pepper until blended. In thin, steady stream, whisk in oil until blended.

2. In 3-quart saucepan, combine potatoes and enough *water* to cover; heat to boiling over high heat. Reduce heat; cover and simmer until tender, about 10 minutes. Drain.

3. Meanwhile, in 10-inch skillet, heat *1 inch water* to boiling over high heat. Add green beans; heat to boiling. Reduce heat to low and cook until tender-crisp, 6 to 8 minutes. Drain; rinse with cold running water. Drain.

4. To serve, pour half of dressing into medium bowl. Add lettuce leaves and toss to coat. Line large platter with dressed lettuce leaves. Arrange potatoes, green beans, cherry tomatoes, tuna, eggs, and olives in separate piles on lettuce. Drizzle remaining dressing over salad. Makes 4 main-dish servings.

Each serving: About 440 calories, 30g protein, 30g carbohydrate, 23g total fat (4g saturated), 140mg cholesterol, 716mg sodium.

Italian Seafood Salad

Italians often serve this salad on Christmas Eve, but why not enjoy it throughout the year?

Prep: 50 minutes plus chilling   Cook: 15 minutes

- 1 pound sea scallops
- 2 pounds cleaned squid
- 1 small lemon, thinly sliced
- 2 pounds large shrimp, shelled and deveined (page 193)
- ⅔ cup fresh lemon juice (4 lemons)
- ½ cup olive oil
- 1 small garlic clove, minced
- ½ teaspoon salt
- ½ teaspoon coarsely ground black pepper
- 4 large stalks celery, cut into ½-inch pieces
- ½ cup Gaeta or Niçoise olives (optional)
- ¼ cup loosely packed fresh parsley leaves

1. Pull tough crescent-shaped muscle from side of each scallop; discard. Rinse squid; slice bodies crosswise into ¾-inch-thick rings. Cut tentacles into several pieces if large. In 5-quart saucepot, combine *2½ inches water* and lemon; heat to boiling over high heat. Add shrimp. Reduce heat to medium; cook until shrimp are opaque throughout, 1 to 2 minutes. With slotted spoon, transfer shrimp to colander to drain; transfer to large bowl.

2. To boiling water in saucepot, add scallops; cook just until opaque throughout, 2 to 3 minutes. With slotted spoon, transfer to colander to drain; add to shrimp in bowl.

3. To boiling water in saucepot, add squid; cook until tender and opaque, 30 seconds to 1 minute. Drain in colander; add to shrimp and scallops in bowl.

4. Prepare dressing: In small bowl, with wire whisk, mix lemon juice, oil, garlic, salt, and pepper until blended. Add celery, olives if using, and parsley to seafood in bowl; toss to mix. Add dressing and toss until salad is mixed and coated with dressing. Cover and refrigerate salad at least 3 hours to blend flavors or up to 8 hours. Makes 12 first-course servings.

Each serving: About 255 calories, 31g protein, 6g carbohydrate, 11g total fat (2g saturated), 282mg cholesterol, 200mg sodium.

Panzanella Salad

We flavored our version of this classic Italian bread salad with pancetta and arugula.

Prep: 25 minutes   Cook: 15 minutes

- 4 ounces pancetta or 4 slices thick-sliced bacon, cut into ¼-inch pieces
- ½ small loaf peasant bread, cut into ½-inch cubes (about 4 cups)
- 3 tablespoons red wine vinegar
- 2 tablespoons extra-virgin olive oil
- 1 medium shallot, minced (¼ cup)
- ¾ teaspoon salt
- ½ teaspoon sugar
- ¼ teaspoon ground black pepper
- 2 pounds ripe tomatoes (about 6 medium), cut into 1-inch pieces
- 2 small bunches arugula (about 4 ounces each), tough stems trimmed, or 2 bags (5 ounces each) arugula

1. In nonstick 12-inch skillet, cook pancetta over medium heat until lightly browned. With slotted spoon, transfer to paper towels to drain.

2. To pancetta drippings in skillet, add bread cubes and cook, stirring frequently, until lightly browned, 2 to 3 minutes.

3. Meanwhile, prepare dressing: In large bowl, with fork, mix vinegar, oil, shallot, salt, sugar, and pepper until blended.

4. Add tomatoes, arugula, bread cubes, and pancetta to dressing in bowl; toss to combine. Makes 4 main-dish servings.

Each serving: About 300 calories, 9g protein, 29g carbohydrate, 17g total fat (5g saturated), 11mg cholesterol, 735mg sodium.

Sopressata and Roma Bean Salad with Pecorino

Slightly sweeter than green beans, broad beans are the oldest beans in existence. Look for those that are pale green, soft, and tender. These beans are best eaten within a few days of purchase.

Prep: 10 minutes   Cook: 12 minutes

- 1¼ pounds Roma (broad) beans or green beans, trimmed
- 1 lemon
- 2 tablespoons extra-virgin olive oil
- ¼ teaspoon salt
- ⅛ teaspoon coarsely ground black pepper
- 4 ounces thinly sliced sopressata or Genoa salami, cut into ½-inch-wide strips
- 2 small bunches arugula (4 ounces each), tough stems trimmed, or 2 bags (5 ounces each) arugula
- 1 wedge Pecorino-Romano cheese (about 2 ounces)

1. If Roma beans are very long, cut crosswise into 2½-inch pieces. In 12-inch skillet, heat *1 inch water* to boiling over high heat. Add beans; heat to boiling. Reduce heat to low; simmer until beans are tender-crisp, 6 to 8 minutes. Drain beans. Rinse with cold running water to stop cooking; drain.

2. Meanwhile, from lemon, grate ½ teaspoon peel and squeeze 2 tablespoons juice. In large bowl, with wire whisk, mix lemon peel and juice, oil, salt, and pepper.

3. Add beans, sopressata, and arugula to dressing in bowl; toss to coat.

4. To serve, spoon salad onto serving platter. With vegetable peeler, shave thin strips from wedge of Pecorino onto salad. Makes 4 main-dish servings.

Each serving: About 280 calories, 14g protein, 14g carbohydrate, 21g total fat (7g saturated), 41mg cholesterol, 845mg sodium.

Thai Beef Salad

Thinly sliced carrots and red pepper add color and crunch to this tangy, herb-packed salad. Roast beef from the deli makes it especially easy to prepare. You could also use grilled flank steak, cooked shrimp, or rotisserie chicken.

Prep: 30 minutes

Thai Dressing

- ¼ cup seasoned rice vinegar
- ¼ cup fresh lime juice (2 to 3 limes)
- 3 tablespoons vegetable oil
- 2 tablespoons grated, peeled fresh ginger
- 1 tablespoon Asian fish sauce (nam pla, page 26)
- ⅛ teaspoon ground red pepper (cayenne)

Salad

- 8 ounces thinly sliced deli roast beef, cut into ½-inch-wide strips
- 2 medium carrots, cut into 2" by ¼" matchstick strips
- 1 small red pepper, cut into 2" by ¼" matchstick strips
- 2 green onions, thinly sliced diagonally
- 1 large head Boston lettuce (10 ounces)
- 1½ cups loosely packed fresh cilantro leaves
- 1½ cups loosely packed fresh basil leaves
- 1½ cups loosely packed fresh mint leaves

1. Prepare dressing: In large bowl, with wire whisk, mix vinegar, lime juice, oil, ginger, fish sauce, and ground red pepper.

2. Prepare salad: Add roast beef, carrots, red pepper, and green onions to dressing in bowl; toss to coat.

3. To serve, separate 4 large leaves from head of lettuce and reserve. Tear remaining lettuce into bite-size pieces. Add torn lettuce, cilantro, basil, and mint to bowl with beef; toss again. Place 1 reserved lettuce leaf on each of 4 dinner plates; fill with salad mixture. Makes 4 main-dish servings.

Each serving: About 275 calories, 19g protein, 17g carbohydrate, 15g total fat (2g saturated), 46mg cholesterol, 880mg sodium.

Classic Egg Salad

The perfect egg salad, like other old-fashioned dishes, is a matter of individual taste. Our recipe leaves room for lots of creativity (see the variations below).

Prep: 10 minutes   Cook: 10 minutes plus standing

- 6 large eggs
- ¼ cup mayonnaise
- 1½ teaspoons Dijon or spicy brown mustard
- ¼ teaspoon salt

1. In 3-quart saucepan, place eggs and enough *cold water* to cover by at least 1 inch; heat to boiling over high heat. Immediately remove saucepan from heat and cover tightly; let stand 15 minutes. Pour off hot water and run cold water over eggs to cool. Peel eggs.

2. Coarsely chop eggs and transfer to medium bowl. Add mayonnaise, mustard, and salt and stir to combine. If not serving right away, cover and refrigerate up to 4 hours. Makes 2 cups or 4 main-dish servings.

Each serving: About 217 calories, 10g protein, 1g carbohydrate, 19g total fat (4g saturated), 327mg cholesterol, 359mg sodium.

Curried Egg Salad

Prepare as directed but add **4 teaspoons chopped mango chutney** and **½ teaspoon curry powder** to egg mixture.

Caesar-Style Egg Salad

Prepare as directed but use only **⅛ teaspoon salt**. Add **2 tablespoons freshly grated Parmesan cheese** and **1 teaspoon anchovy paste** to egg mixture.

Mexican-Style Egg Salad

Prepare as directed but add **⅓ cup chopped fresh cilantro** and **½ teaspoon hot pepper sauce** to egg mixture.

Deli-Style Egg Salad

Prepare as directed but add **¼ cup chopped celery** and **¼ cup chopped red onion** to egg mixture.

Best Chicken Salad

Plain or fancy, chicken salad is always a treat. Here's a basic recipe plus three of our favorite ways to make it extra special. If you don't want to poach a whole chicken, substitute 3 cups of coarsely chopped deli-roasted chicken or leftover turkey.

Prep: 20 minutes plus cooling   Cook: 1 hour

- 1 chicken (3 pounds)
- 1½ teaspoons salt
- 3 stalks celery, finely chopped
- ¼ cup mayonnaise
- 2 teaspoons fresh lemon juice
- ¼ teaspoon ground black pepper

1. In 4-quart saucepan, combine chicken, 1 teaspoon salt, and enough *water* to cover; heat to boiling over high heat. Reduce heat; cover and simmer gently until chicken loses its pink color throughout, about 45 minutes. Let stand 30 minutes; drain (reserve broth for another use). When chicken is cool enough to handle, discard skin and bones; cut meat into bite-size pieces.

2. In large bowl, combine celery, mayonnaise, lemon juice, remaining ½ teaspoon salt, and pepper; stir until blended. Add chicken and toss to coat. Makes 4 main-dish servings.

Each serving: About 337 calories, 36g protein, 2g carbohydrate, 20g total fat (4g saturated), 117mg cholesterol, 779mg sodium.

Basil and Dried Tomato Chicken Salad

Prepare as directed but add ¼ **cup chopped fresh basil** and **2 tablespoons finely chopped oil-packed dried tomatoes,** drained, to mayonnaise mixture.

Curry-Grape Chicken Salad

Prepare as directed but add **2 cups red or green seedless grapes,** cut in half, **1 teaspoon curry powder,** and **1 teaspoon honey** to mayonnaise mixture.

Lemon-Pepper Chicken Salad

Prepare as directed but use **1 tablespoon fresh lemon juice** and ½ **teaspoon black pepper,** coarsely ground; add ½ **teaspoon freshly grated lemon peel** to mayonnaise mixture.

Classic Tuna Salad

There are other ways to serve tuna salad besides between two slices of bread. Have fun personalizing your salad ingredients, then serve as an open-faced tuna melt or on a bed of crispy greens.

Prep: 10 minutes

- 1 can (6 ounces) solid white tuna in water, drained and broken into pieces
- 2 stalks celery, finely chopped
- 3 tablespoons mayonnaise
- 2 teaspoons fresh lemon juice
- ¼ teaspoon ground black pepper

In small bowl, combine tuna, celery, mayonnaise, lemon juice, and pepper, flaking tuna with fork. If not serving right away, cover and refrigerate up to 4 hours. Makes 1⅓ cups or 2 main-dish servings.

Each serving: About 264 calories, 22g protein, 3g carbohydrate, 18g total fat (3g saturated), 45mg cholesterol, 462mg sodium.

Curried Tuna Salad

Prepare as directed but substitute ½ **Granny Smith apple,** finely chopped, for celery, and add **1 teaspoon curry powder** to tuna mixture.

Mexican-Style Tuna Salad

Prepare as directed but add **2 tablespoons chopped fresh cilantro** and **1 pickled jalapeño chile,** finely chopped, to tuna mixture.

Mediterranean Tuna Salad

Prepare as directed but omit celery and mayonnaise. Increase lemon juice to 2 tablespoons. Rinse and drain **1 can (15 to 19 ounces) white kidney beans (cannellini).** In large bowl, mash 1 cup beans. Stir in ½ **cup chopped fresh basil, 3 tablespoons minced red onion, 3 tablespoons capers,** drained and chopped, **2 tablespoons olive oil, lemon juice,** and **pepper.** Add tuna and remaining beans; toss to combine. Makes 4 main-dish servings.

Cranberry Port-Wine Mold

A side dish for grown-ups, this jewel-like mold is luscious with a beef rib roast or roast turkey.

Prep: 20 minutes plus chilling Cook: 15 minutes

- 1 lemon
- 3 cups cranberry-juice cocktail
- 1¼ cups sugar
- 4 whole allspice berries
- 1 cinnamon stick (3 inches), broken in half
- 2 envelopes unflavored gelatin
- 1 cup port wine
  pinch salt
  kumquats, lemon leaves, and frosted cranberries for garnish (optional)

1. From lemon, with vegetable peeler or sharp paring knife, remove 4 strips peel (3" by ¾" each); squeeze 3 tablespoons juice.

2. In nonreactive 2-quart saucepan, heat cranberry juice, sugar, allspice, cinnamon stick, and lemon peel to boiling over high heat; boil 10 minutes.

3. Meanwhile, in small bowl, evenly sprinkle gelatin over port wine; let stand 2 minutes to soften gelatin.

4. With slotted spoon, remove lemon peel and whole spices from cranberry juice and discard. Stir in gelatin mixture and cook over low heat, stirring frequently, until gelatin has completely dissolved, 1 to 2 minutes. Stir in lemon juice and salt.

5. Pour gelatin mixture into 5- to 6-cup decorative mold. Cover with plastic wrap and refrigerate 6 hours or overnight until firm.

6. To unmold, dip pan in large bowl of hot water for 10 seconds and invert onto large round platter. Garnish as desired. Cover and refrigerate up to 2 hours before serving. Makes 8 accompaniment servings.

Each serving: About 225 calories, 2g protein, 48g carbohydrate, 0g total fat, 0mg cholesterol, 25mg sodium.

Cranberry Port-Wine Mold

Tomato Vinaigrette

For this salad dressing, a ripe tomato is *de rigueuer*. It's perfect spooned over sliced tomatoes and feta cheese, spinach salad, or mixed greens.

Prep: 15 minutes

- 1 small tomato (4 ounces), peeled and coarsely chopped
- 1 small shallot, cut in half
- 2 tablespoons olive oil
- 1 tablespoon red wine vinegar
- 1 tablespoon balsamic vinegar
- 2 teaspoons Dijon mustard with seeds
- 1 teaspoon chopped fresh oregano
- 1 teaspoon sugar
- ¼ teaspoon salt
- ¼ teaspoon ground black pepper

In blender, combine tomato, shallot, oil, red wine and balsamic vinegars, mustard, oregano, sugar, salt, and pepper; puree just until smooth. Transfer to small bowl or jar. Cover and refrigerate up to 1 day. Makes about 1 cup.

Each tablespoon: About 19 calories, 0g protein, 1g carbohydrate, 2g total fat (0g saturated), 0mg cholesterol, 51mg sodium.

Classic French Vinaigrette

Dijon mustard gives this vinaigrette smoothness and just the right amount of zing.

Prep: 5 minutes

- ¼ cup red wine vinegar
- 1 tablespoon Dijon mustard
- ¾ teaspoon salt
- ½ teaspoon coarsely ground black pepper
- ½ cup olive oil

In medium bowl, with wire whisk, mix vinegar, mustard, salt, and pepper until blended. In thin, steady stream, whisk in oil until blended. Cover and refrigerate up to 1 week. Makes about ¾ cup.

Each tablespoon: About 82 calories, 0g protein, 0g carbohydrate, 9g total fat (1g saturated), 0mg cholesterol, 175mg sodium.

Blue Cheese Vinaigrette

Prepare as directed but add **2 ounces blue cheese,** crumbled (½ cup). Cover and refrigerate up to 2 days. Makes about 1 cup.

Mustard-Shallot Vinaigrette

Prepare as directed but add **1 tablespoon minced shallot.** Cover and refrigerate up to 1 day. Makes about ¾ cup.

Balsamic Vinaigrette

Prepare as directed but replace red wine vinegar with **balsamic vinegar** and reduce mustard to 1 teaspoon.

Creamy Blue Cheese Dressing

This versatile dressing can be served on mixed greens, lettuce and tomato wedges, chilled cooked vegetables, cold sliced roast beef, or even hard-cooked eggs.

Prep: 10 minutes

- 4 ounces blue cheese, crumbled (1 cup)
- 3 tablespoons half-and-half or light cream
- ½ cup reduced-fat mayonnaise
- 2 tablespoons white wine vinegar
- 1 teaspoon Dijon mustard
- ⅛ teaspoon salt
- ⅛ teaspoon ground black pepper

In small bowl, with fork, mash cheese with half-and-half until creamy; add mayonnaise, vinegar, mustard, salt, and pepper. With wire whisk, beat until well mixed. Cover and refrigerate up to 3 days. Makes about 1 cup.

Each tablespoon: About 55 calories, 2g protein, 1g carbohydrate, 5g total fat (2g saturated fat), 9mg cholesterol, 178mg sodium.

Honey-Lime Vinaigrette

Try this sweet and tangy fat-free dressing on sliced cucumbers or your favorite greens.

Prep: 5 minutes

- ⅓ cup fresh lime juice (2 to 3 limes)
- 4 teaspoons honey
- 1 tablespoon rice vinegar
- ⅛ teaspoon salt

In small bowl, with wire whisk, mix lime juice, honey, vinegar, and salt until blended. Cover and refrigerate up to 3 days. Makes about ½ cup.

Each tablespoon: About 13 calories, 0g protein, 4g carbohydrate, 0g total fat (0g saturated), 0mg cholesterol, 37mg sodium.

Ranch Dressing

Buttermilk gives ranch dressing its characteristic tang and creaminess. Use the large holes on a box grater to grate the onion.

Prep: 10 minutes

- ½ cup buttermilk
- ⅓ cup mayonnaise
- 1 tablespoon chopped fresh parsley
- ½ teaspoon grated onion
- ¼ teaspoon salt
- ¼ teaspoon ground black pepper
- 1 garlic clove, cut in half

In small bowl, with wire whisk, mix buttermilk, mayonnaise, parsley, onion, salt, and pepper until blended; stir in garlic. Cover and refrigerate up to 3 days. Remove garlic before serving. Makes about ¾ cup.

Each tablespoon: About 48 calories, 0g protein, 1g carbohydrate, 5g total fat (1g saturated), 4mg cholesterol, 93mg sodium.

Tahini Dressing

Try this sesame-paste dressing on sautéed or broiled chicken or vegetables, as well as on salads.

Prep: 10 minutes

- ⅓ cup tahini (sesame seed paste)
- 2 tablespoons fresh lemon juice
- 4 teaspoons soy sauce
- 1 tablespoon honey (optional)
- ½ small garlic clove, minced
- ½ teaspoon ground black pepper

In small bowl, with wire whisk, mix tahini, lemon juice, soy sauce, honey if using, garlic, and pepper until smooth. Cover and refrigerate up to 2 days. Makes about ¾ cup.

Each tablespoon: About 41 calories, 1g protein, 2g carbohydrate, 4g total fat (0g saturated), 0mg cholesterol, 122mg sodium.

Japanese Miso Vinaigrette

Miso comes in different colors and flavor variances, but any one will make a tasty dressing.

Prep: 10 minutes

- 2 tablespoons miso (fermented soybean paste)
- ½ cup rice vinegar
- ¼ cup olive oil
- 1 tablespoon minced, peeled fresh ginger
- 1 tablespoon sugar

In small bowl, with wire whisk, stir miso into vinegar until smooth. In blender, combine miso mixture, oil, ginger, and sugar; puree until smooth. Transfer to small bowl or jar. Cover and refrigerate up to 3 days. Makes about 1 cup.

Each tablespoon: About 38 calories, 0g protein, 1g carbohydrate, 4g total fat (0g saturated), 0mg cholesterol, 78mg sodium.

15

SAUCES, SALSAS & CONDIMENTS

In fashion, a beautiful necklace can turn a simple black dress into an exquisite outfit. And in cooking, a fine sauce can turn simple food into something fabulous.

Sauces are typically described as liquid or semi-liquid accompaniments to main courses or desserts. Most of the classic sauces are French, with the base sauces called mother sauces. Different ingredients are added to these mother sauces to make an almost endless number of variations. For example, when béchamel (white sauce) has Gruyère cheese added, it becomes Mornay sauce. Many of the traditional sauces are cooked, and most depend on butter and homemade stock for body and flavor.

But these days, the French dominance over the saucepot no longer exists. Today's sauces come from all around the world; many aren't cooked at all and don't contain any stock or butter. Salsa, that sprightly chile-kissed sauce from south of the border, can be made with vegetables or fruits and served with everything from grilled fish to tortilla chips. And some sauces, such as the Italian *salmoriglio* and the Argentinean *chimichurri*, are based on olive oil and a combination of fragrant fresh herbs. These sauces are ideal for simple grilled fish, poultry, pork, or beef. In fact, chimichurri is the classic accompaniment to grilled steak in Argentina.

Classic French butter sauces, such as hollandaise, béarnaise, and beurre blanc, are meant to be served warm. They cannot be reheated, or they will curdle. So keep them at serving temperature the way they do in restaurants. To hold a butter sauce warm for up to 20 minutes, place the bowl of sauce in a skillet of very hot—not simmering—water. Whisk well before serving to dissolve any thin skin that may have formed. To hold for up to one hour, transfer the sauce, as soon as it is prepared, to a wide-mouthed vacuum bottle (rinse the bottle first with hot water to warm it) and seal. When ready to serve, transfer the sauce to a serving dish.

Sometimes a thick sweet-and-tangy condiment is the preferred way to accent a main course. Intricately seasoned but easy to make Indian-inspired fruit chutneys are excellent with grilled meats. In this chapter, you'll also find an assortment of tasty condiments, perfect accompaniments for the holiday turkey, a favorite sandwich, or your grilled London broil.

Dessert sauces are for those times when you want to gild the lily. A piece of chocolate cake can be wonderful, but when served in a pool of jewel-colored raspberry sauce, it becomes sublime. These sauces are also delicious served over ice cream or spooned over waffles for a special breakfast treat.

Peach Salsa, Tomato Salsa, and Tomatillo Salsa

White Sauce (Béchamel)

This classic sauce is the foundation for many popular dishes, including moussaka and macaroni and cheese.

Prep: 2 minutes   Cook: 15 minutes

2 tablespoons butter or margarine
2 tablespoons all-purpose flour
1 cup milk, warmed
½ teaspoon salt
pinch ground nutmeg

In heavy 1-quart saucepan, melt butter over low heat. Add flour and cook, stirring, 1 minute. With wire whisk, gradually whisk in warm milk. Cook over

medium heat, stirring constantly with wooden spoon, until sauce has thickened and boils. Reduce heat and simmer, stirring frequently, 5 minutes. Remove from heat and stir in salt and nutmeg. Makes about 1 cup.

Each tablespoon: About 26 calories, 1g protein, 1g carbohydrate, 2g total fat (1g saturated), 6mg cholesterol, 94mg sodium.

Cheese Sauce

Prepare sauce as directed above. Remove saucepan from heat. Add **4 ounces sharp Cheddar cheese,** shredded (1 cup); stir until cheese has melted and sauce is smooth. Makes about 1 cup.

Each tablespoon: About 54 calories, 2g protein, 2g carbohydrate, 4g total fat (3g saturated), 13mg cholesterol, 138mg sodium.

Mornay Sauce

Prepare sauce as directed above. Remove saucepan from heat. Add **2 ounces Gruyère cheese,** shredded (½ cup); stir until cheese has melted and sauce is smooth. Makes about 1 cup.

Each tablespoon: About 40 calories, 2g protein, 1g carbohydrate, 3g total fat (2g saturated), 10mg cholesterol, 106mg sodium.

Hollandaise Sauce

An irresistible velvety sauce that's easier to make than you would expect. The traditional recipe uses undercooked eggs, but our updated version cooks them long enough to make them safe to eat.

Prep: 5 minutes   Cook: 10 minutes

3 large egg yolks
¼ cup water
2 tablespoons fresh lemon juice
½ cup cold butter (1 stick), cut into 8 pieces (do not use margarine)
¼ teaspoon salt

1. In heavy nonreactive 1-quart saucepan, with wire whisk, mix egg yolks, water, and lemon juice until well blended. Cook over medium-low heat, stirring constantly with wooden spoon or heat-safe rubber spatula, until egg-yolk mixture just begins to bubble at edge, 6 to 8 minutes.

2. Reduce heat to low. With wire whisk, whisk in butter, one piece at a time, until each addition is incorporated and sauce has thickened. Remove from heat and stir in salt. Strain through sieve, if you like. Makes scant 1 cup.

Each tablespoon: About 62 calories, 1g protein, 0g carbohydrate, 7g total fat (4g saturated), 55mg cholesterol, 96mg sodium.

HOLLANDAISE VARIATIONS

Caper Sauce Stir 1 tablespoon drained capers into the hollandaise. Serve with fish or chicken.

Maltese Sauce Substitute orange juice for the lemon juice and add 1½ teaspoons grated orange peel to the hollandaise after straining. Pair this with asparagus.

Hollandaise Sauce

Béarnaise Sauce

A rich yet tangy topping for steak, grilled chicken, vegetables, or poached eggs. If you don't have tarragon vinegar, use white wine vinegar and toss in an extra tablespoon of fresh tarragon.

Prep: 5 minutes   Cook: 30 minutes

- ½ cup tarragon vinegar
- ⅓ cup dry white wine
- 2 shallots, finely chopped
- 3 large egg yolks
- ¼ cup water
  pinch ground black pepper
- ½ cup cold butter (1 stick), cut into 8 pieces
  (do not use margarine)
- 1 tablespoon chopped fresh tarragon
- ¼ teaspoon salt

1. In nonreactive 1-quart saucepan, combine vinegar, wine, and shallots; heat to boiling over high heat. Boil until liquid has reduced to ¼ cup, about 7 minutes. With back of spoon, press mixture through fine sieve into medium bowl or top of double boiler.

2. With wire whisk, beat egg yolks, water, and pepper into vinegar mixture. Set bowl over saucepan of simmering water. Cook, whisking constantly, until egg-yolk mixture bubbles around edge and has thickened, about 10 minutes.

3. Reduce heat to very low. With wire whisk, whisk in butter, one piece at a time, until each addition is incorporated and sauce has thickened. Remove from heat and stir in tarragon and salt. Makes 1 cup.

Each tablespoon: About 68 calories, 1g protein, 1g carbohydrate, 7g total fat (4g saturated), 55mg cholesterol, 60mg sodium.

Sauce Rémoulade

This rich flavorful sauce is excellent with chilled shellfish or cooked vegetables. You can also spice it up Cajun style: Omit the tarragon and Dijon, and heat it up with some Creole mustard and ground red pepper.

Prep: 20 minutes

- ⅓ cup mayonnaise
- 2 tablespoons sour cream
- 3 tablespoons finely chopped dill pickle
- 1 tablespoon chopped fresh parsley
- ¾ teaspoon chopped fresh tarragon or ¼ teaspoon dried tarragon
- ½ teaspoon chopped fresh chives
- 1 anchovy fillet, finely chopped
- 1 teaspoon capers, drained and chopped
- 1 teaspoon Dijon mustard

In small bowl, combine mayonnaise, sour cream, pickle, parsley, tarragon, chives, anchovy, capers, and mustard until well blended. Serve, or cover and refrigerate up to 1 day. Makes about ⅔ cup.

Each tablespoon: About 61 calories, 0g protein, 0g carbohydrate, 6g total fat (1g saturated), 6mg cholesterol, 143mg sodium.

Flavored butters are ideal for dressing up panfried or grilled steak or fish when unexpected company drops by. Here are a few favorites, but you can stir in just about any flavoring that strikes your fancy. For strong-flavored ingredients like horseradish or capers, start with about 2 tablespoons per stick of butter. You can add up to ¼ cup of ingredients total, just be sure to drain wet items well. Prepare ahead and freeze to eliminate last-minute fussing.

Prep: 10 minutes

In medium bowl, beat ½ cup butter or margarine (1 stick), softened, with wooden spoon until creamy. Beat in your choice of flavor ingredients (right); blend well. Transfer flavored butter to waxed paper and shape into log about 6 inches long; wrap, twisting ends of waxed paper to seal. Overwrap in plastic or foil before chilling or freezing. Flavored butters can be refrigerated up to 2 days or frozen up to 1 month. To serve, cut into ½-inch-thick slices. Makes 12 servings each.

Maître d'Hôtel Butter
Very versatile; use on beef, veal, chicken, pork, and fish.
- 2 tablespoons chopped fresh parsley
- ¼ teaspoon freshly grated lemon peel
- 1 tablespoon fresh lemon juice

Olive Butter
Best on fish and chicken.
- ⅓ cup Kalamata olives, pitted and finely chopped
- 1 tablespoon chopped fresh parsley

Ginger-Cilantro Butter
Good on chicken and fish.
- 2 tablespoons finely chopped fresh cilantro
- 2 teaspoons fresh lime juice
- ½ teaspoon grated, peeled fresh ginger

Caper Butter
Good on beef, veal, pork, fish, and chicken.
- 2 tablespoons capers, drained and chopped
- 1 tablespoon chopped fresh parsley
- ½ teaspoon freshly grated lemon peel

Tartar Sauce

Serve this tasty sauce with Crab Cakes (pages 40–41), shrimp, and baked, broiled, or fried fish.

Prep: 15 minutes

- ½ cup mayonnaise
- ¼ cup finely chopped dill pickle
- 1 tablespoon chopped fresh parsley
- 2 teaspoons milk
- 2 teaspoons distilled white vinegar
- ½ teaspoon finely chopped onion
- ½ teaspoon Dijon mustard

In small bowl, combine mayonnaise, pickle, parsley, milk, vinegar, onion, and mustard until well blended. Serve, or cover and refrigerate up to 2 days. Makes about ¾ cup.

Each tablespoon: About 68 calories, 0g protein, 0g carbohydrate, 7g total fat (1g saturated), 6mg cholesterol, 125mg sodium.

Cilantro Sauce

As with many fresh herb–based sauces, this one is perfect with beef tenderloin, cold roast turkey, or poached salmon.

Prep: 10 minutes

- 1 cup tightly packed fresh cilantro leaves
- ¾ cup light mayonnaise
- ¾ cup reduced-fat sour cream
- 2 teaspoons fresh lime juice
- ¼ teaspoon hot pepper sauce

In blender or in food processor with knife blade attached, puree cilantro, mayonnaise, sour cream, lime juice, and hot pepper sauce until smooth. Serve, or cover and refrigerate up to 1 day. Makes 1⅔ cups.

Each tablespoon: About 35 calories, 1g protein, 1g carbohydrate, 3g total fat (1g saturated), 5mg cholesterol, 59mg sodium.

Salmoriglio Sauce

If you have oregano growing in your garden, chop enough to equal 1 tablespoon and use instead of dried oregano.

Prep: 10 minutes plus standing

- ¼ cup fresh lemon juice (1 to 2 lemons)
- 1 garlic clove, crushed with side of chef's knife
- 1 teaspoon dried oregano, crumbled
- ¼ teaspoon salt
- ¼ teaspoon coarsely ground black pepper
- ⅓ cup extra-virgin olive oil

1. In medium bowl, combine lemon juice, garlic, oregano, salt, and pepper. Let stand 30 minutes.

2. With wire whisk, in thin, steady stream, whisk in oil until blended. Serve, or let stand up to 4 hours at room temperature. Whisk just before serving. Makes scant ⅔ cup.

Each tablespoon: About 66 calories, 0g protein, 1g carbohydrate, 7g total fat (1g saturated), 0mg cholesterol, 57mg sodium.

Chimichurri Sauce

This Argentinean herb vinaigrette is the sauce served at Buenos Aires steakhouses. Drizzle it on sandwiches, or serve with grilled or roasted meats.

Prep: 20 minutes

- 1 large garlic clove, minced
- ½ teaspoon salt
- 1½ cups loosely packed fresh parsley leaves, chopped
- 1 cup loosely packed fresh cilantro leaves, chopped
- ¾ cup olive oil
- 2 tablespoons red wine vinegar
- ½ teaspoon crushed red pepper

1. With side of chef's knife, mash garlic and salt to a smooth paste.

2. In small bowl, combine garlic mixture, parsley, cilantro, oil, vinegar, and crushed red pepper until well blended. Serve, or cover and refrigerate up to 4 hours. Makes about 1 cup.

Each tablespoon: About 93 calories, 0g protein, 1g carbohydrate, 10g total fat (1g saturated), 0mg cholesterol, 76mg sodium.

Salsa Verde (Green Sauce)

Especially good with fish, this uncooked bright green Italian sauce goes with almost any savory food.

Prep: 20 minutes

- 1 large garlic clove, minced
- ¼ teaspoon salt
- 2 cups tightly packed fresh flat-leaf parsley leaves
- 8 anchovy fillets, drained and finely chopped (optional)
- 3 tablespoons capers, drained
- 1 teaspoon Dijon mustard
- ⅛ teaspoon ground black pepper
- ½ cup olive oil
- 3 tablespoons fresh lemon juice (1 lemon)

1. With side of chef's knife, mash garlic and salt to a smooth paste.

2. In blender or in food processor with knife blade attached, puree parsley, anchovies if using, capers, mustard, pepper, oil, lemon juice and garlic mixture, until almost smooth. Serve, or cover and refrigerate up to 4 hours. Makes about 1 cup.

Each tablespoon: About 69 calories, 1g protein, 2g carbohydrate, 7g total fat (1g saturated), 0mg cholesterol, 123mg sodium.

GARLIC GLOSSARY

American This variety is white-skinned and strongly flavored.

Italian A variety with purplish skin; it is slightly milder than white-skinned variety.

Mexican This variety has purplish skin and has a slightly milder taste than American garlic.

Elephant Not a true garlic but a member of the leek family, it has a relatively tame garlic flavor. With a bulb the size of a grapefruit, it is sometimes sold by the clove.

Garlic shoots These green shoots, which resemble chives, are the stems of an immature garlic plant. They have a mild garlic flavor and can be used raw or cooked.

Green garlic Garlic that is harvested just before it begins to form cloves.

Asian Peanut Sauce

Toss with linguine, along with slivers of green onion, thin strips of red bell peppers, and half-moon slices of seedless cucumber for a tasty summertime side dish.

Prep: 10 minutes

- ½ cup creamy peanut butter
- ½ cup water
- ¼ cup soy sauce
- 1 tablespoon grated, peeled fresh ginger
- 2 tablespoons distilled white vinegar
- 2 tablespoons Asian sesame oil
- 1 tablespoon packed brown sugar
- ¼ teaspoon hot pepper sauce

In a blender or food processor with knife blade attached, combine peanut butter, water, soy sauce, ginger, vinegar, sesame oil, brown sugar, and hot pepper sauce; puree until smooth. Serve, or cover and refrigerate up to 1 day. Makes 1½ cups.

Each tablespoon: About 47 calories, 2g protein, 2g carbohydrate, 4g total fat (1g saturated), 0mg cholesterol, 189mg sodium.

Sweet Corn Salsa

This deftly seasoned salsa tastes equally delicious made with frozen corn kernels as with fresh. It keeps well in the refrigerator.

Prep: 20 minutes plus chilling   Cook: 10 minutes

- 8 ears corn, husks and silk removed, or 1 bag (20 ounces) frozen whole-kernel corn, thawed
- 3 tablespoons fresh lime juice (about 2 limes)
- 2 tablespoons olive oil
- ¾ teaspoon ground cumin
- ¾ teaspoon ground coriander
- ¾ teaspoon salt
- ½ teaspoon chili powder
- 1 large red pepper, finely chopped

1. If using fresh corn, with sharp knife, cut kernels from cobs. Heat 6-quart saucepot of *water* to boiling over high heat. Add corn kernels and heat to boiling; boil 30 seconds. Drain. Rinse with cold running water and drain.

2. In medium bowl, whisk lime juice, oil, cumin, coriander, salt, and chili powder until blended. Add corn and red pepper; toss until mixed and coated with dressing. Cover and refrigerate until well chilled, about 2 hours or up to 2 weeks. Makes about 5 cups.

Each ¼ cup: About 41 calories, 1g protein, 6g carbohydrate, 2g total fat (0g saturated), 0mg cholesterol, 93mg sodium.

Olive and Lemon Salsa

The sweet citrus flavor of oranges and lemons is the perfect foil for the salty olives in this sauce.

Prep: 15 minutes

- 2 small navel oranges
- 2 lemons
- ¼ cup coarsely chopped pimiento-stuffed olives (salad olives)
- 2 tablespoons chopped shallots
- 2 tablespoons chopped fresh parsley
- ½ teaspoon sugar
- ¼ teaspoon coarsely ground black pepper

1. Cut peel and white pith from oranges and lemons. Cut fruit into ¼-inch-thick slices; discard seeds. Cut slices into ½-inch pieces.

2. In small bowl, gently stir orange and lemon pieces, olives, shallots, parsley, sugar, and pepper until well mixed. Serve, or cover and refrigerate up to 1 day. Makes about 2 cups.

Each ¼ cup: About 28 calories, 1g protein, 7g carbohydrate, 1g total fat (0g saturated), 0mg cholesterol, 104mg sodium.

GINGER

Test Kitchen Tip

Ginger is not a root—though it is often called gingerroot—but a rhizome (underground stem). It is widely used in Asian dishes as an essential aromatic ingredient. Its flavor is a combination of spicy and slightly sweet. Peeled and chopped, or grated, sliced and pounded, it adds loads of flavor. Ginger is also available crystallized, ground, and pickled.

Tomato Salsa

(Pictured on page 430)

As a topping for burgers, this flavor-packed salsa is stiff competition for plain old ketchup.

Prep: 20 minutes plus chilling

1	large lime
1½	pounds ripe tomatoes (3 large), chopped
½	small red onion, finely chopped
1	small jalapeño chile, seeded and minced
2	tablespoons chopped fresh cilantro
¾	teaspoon salt
¼	teaspoon coarsely ground black pepper

From lime, grate ½ teaspoon peel and squeeze 2 tablespoons juice. In medium bowl, gently stir lime peel and juice, tomatoes, onion, jalapeño, cilantro, salt, and pepper until well mixed. Cover and refrigerate at least 1 hour or up to 2 days. Makes about 3 cups.

Each ¼ cup: About 15 calories, 1g protein, 3g carbohydrate, 0g total fat (0g saturated), 0mg cholesterol, 151mg sodium.

Tomatillo Salsa

(Pictured on page 430)

The tomatillo, also called a Mexican green tomato, is actually related to the gooseberry. It has an acidic fruity flavor that is excellent with grilled meats and fish.

Prep: 25 minutes plus chilling

1	pound fresh tomatillos (about 10 medium), husked, washed well, and cut into quarters
¾	cup loosely packed fresh cilantro leaves, chopped
¼	cup finely chopped onion
1	or 2 serrano or jalapeño chiles, seeded and minced
1	garlic clove, minced
1	tablespoon olive oil
1	teaspoon sugar
½	teaspoon salt

1. In food processor with knife blade attached, coarsely chop tomatillos.

2. In medium bowl, gently stir tomatillos, cilantro, onion, serranos, garlic, oil, sugar, and salt until well mixed. Cover and refrigerate at least 1 hour to blend flavors or up to 3 days. Makes about 2 cups.

Each ¼ cup: About 34 calories, 1g protein, 3g carbohydrate, 2g total fat (0g saturated), 0mg cholesterol, 146mg sodium.

Orange-Fennel Salsa

Not your usual tomato-based salsa, this is sweet, spicy, and aromatic. It is excellent with grilled fish or pork.

Prep: 20 minutes

3	small navel oranges
1	large fennel bulb (1½ pounds), trimmed and chopped
½	small red onion, thinly sliced
¼	cup chopped fresh cilantro leaves
1	jalapeño chile, seeded and minced
¼	teaspoon salt

1. Cut peel and white pith from oranges. Holding oranges over medium bowl to catch juice, cut sections from between membranes, allowing sections to drop into bowl.

2. Add fennel, onion, cilantro, jalapeño, and salt; gently stir until well mixed. Serve, or cover and refrigerate up to 1 day. Makes about 3 cups.

Each ¼ cup: About 24 calories, 1g protein, 5g carbohydrate, 0g total fat (0g saturated), 0mg cholesterol, 94mg sodium.

SEEDING CHILES

Test Kitchen Tip

Recipes usually call for seeding chiles, which tones down the heat. To avoid irritation, wear surgical or rubber gloves and do not touch your eyes. To seed a chile, using a small knife, cut the chile lengthwise in half, then cut out the membranes (which hold a lot of heat) and seeds; discard. Cut off the stem and mince or cut up as directed.

Peach Salsa

(Pictured on page 430)

For the best flavor, wait until it is the height of peach season to make this salsa. Spoon it over grilled chicken breasts or pork chops.

Prep: 30 minutes plus chilling

1¾	pounds ripe peaches (5 medium), peeled, pitted, and chopped
2	tablespoons finely chopped red onion
1	tablespoon chopped fresh mint
1	teaspoon seeded, minced jalapeño chile
1	tablespoon fresh lime juice
⅛	teaspoon salt

In medium bowl, gently stir peaches, onion, mint, jalapeño, lime juice, and salt until well mixed. Cover and refrigerate 1 hour to blend flavors or up to 2 days. Makes about 3 cups.

Each ¼ cup: About 23 calories, 0g protein, 6g carbohydrate, 0g total fat (0g saturated), 0mg cholesterol, 25mg sodium.

Plum Salsa

Prepare as directed above but substitute **1½ pounds ripe plums,** pitted and chopped, for peaches. Use only **1 tablespoon red onion,** finely chopped. Omit mint, jalapeño, and lime juice. Add **2 tablespoons balsamic vinegar** and **1 tablespoon chopped fresh basil** with salt.

Each ¼ cup: About 30 calories, 0g protein, 7g carbohydrate, 0g total fat (0g saturated), 0mg cholesterol, 25mg sodium.

Watermelon Salsa

Prepare as directed above but substitute **2½ pounds watermelon,** seeded and chopped, for peaches. Use only **1 tablespoon red onion,** finely chopped. Omit mint. Add **2 teaspoons seeded and minced jalapeño chile,** and **2 tablespoons fresh lime juice** with salt.

Each ¼ cup: About 17 calories, 0g protein, 4g carbohydrate, 0g total fat (0g saturated), 0mg cholesterol, 26mg sodium.

No-Cook Kirby and Carrot Pickles

Kirbys are thin-skinned small cucumbers that make the best pickles.

Prep: 10 minutes plus chilling

1	garlic clove, cut in half
½	cup distilled white vinegar
½	cup sugar
¾	teaspoon salt
5	small kirby (pickling) cucumbers (about 3 ounces each), unpeeled and cut crosswise into ¼-inch-thick slices
2	large carrots, peeled and cut crosswise into ¼-inch-thick slices

1. In large zip-tight plastic bag, combine all ingredients; seal bag, pressing out excess air. Shake to mix ingredients. Place bag on plate; refrigerate overnight, turning bag occasionally.

2. To serve, drain pickles or, if you like, spoon pickles with their liquid into jars with tight-fitting lids and refrigerate up to 1 week. Makes about 3½ cups.

Each ¼ cup, drained: About 15 calories, 0g protein, 3g carbohydrate, 0g total fat, 0mg cholesterol, 90mg sodium.

No-Cook Cranberry-Orange Relish

An classic holiday recipe that's truly no-fuss.

Prep: 15 minutes plus chilling

1	bag (12 ounces) cranberries, picked over and rinsed
1	medium orange, cut into pieces, seeds discarded
⅔	cup sugar

In food processor with knife blade attached, combine cranberries, orange, and sugar; pulse until coarsely chopped. Transfer to bowl. Cover and refrigerate until well chilled, about 2 hours or up to 2 days. Makes about 3 cups.

Each ¼ cup: About 62 calories, 0g protein, 17g carbohydrate, 0g total fat (0g saturated), 0mg cholesterol, 1mg sodium.

Southwestern-Style Cranberry Relish

Finely chopped jalapeño pepper adds lots of unexpected, delicious heat to sweet-tart cranberries. This relish is the perfect accompaniment for a smoky grilled turkey at Thanksgiving.

Prep: 10 minutes plus chilling   Cook: 15 minutes

- 1 lemon
- 1 bag (12 ounces) cranberries, picked over and rinsed
- 1 pickled jalapeño chile, finely chopped
- ½ cup honey
- ¼ cup cider vinegar
- 1 teaspoon mustard seeds
- ½ teaspoon salt
- ½ teaspoon ground black pepper

1. From lemon, with vegetable peeler, remove peel in 1-inch-wide strips. Cut strips crosswise into slivers.

2. In nonreactive 2-quart saucepan, combine cranberries, lemon peel, pickled jalapeño, honey, vinegar, mustard seeds, salt, and pepper; heat to boiling over high heat, stirring occasionally. Reduce heat; simmer, stirring occasionally, until most cranberries have popped and mixture has thickened slightly, about 10 minutes.

3. Cover and refrigerate until well chilled, about 3 hours or up to 4 days. Makes about 2 cups.

Each ¼ cup: About 90 calories, 0g protein, 24g carbohydrate, 0g total fat, 0mg cholesterol, 174mg sodium.

Cranberry-Fig Chutney

This sweet-tart condiment will stand up to any spicy food, especially Indian, but it will also perk up less highly seasoned dishes.

Prep: 15 minutes plus chilling   Cook: 35 minutes

- 1 bag (12 ounces) cranberries, picked over and rinsed
- 1 package (8 ounces) dried Calimyrna figs, stemmed and sliced
- 1 cup packed brown sugar
- 1 cup water
- ⅓ cup red wine vinegar
- 1 small onion, chopped
- ½ small lemon, chopped, seeds discarded
- 2 tablespoons minced, peeled fresh ginger
- ½ teaspoon salt
- ¼ teaspoon coarsely ground black pepper

1. In nonreactive 3-quart saucepan, combine cranberries, figs, brown sugar, water, vinegar, onion, lemon, ginger, salt, and pepper; heat to boiling over high heat, stirring occasionally. Reduce heat and simmer, stirring occasionally, 30 minutes.

2. Cover and refrigerate until well chilled, about 4 hours or up to 2 days. Makes about 4 cups.

Each ¼ cup: About 103 calories, 1g protein, 27g carbohydrate, 0g total fat (0g saturated), 0mg cholesterol, 80mg sodium.

TASTY WAYS TO SERVE OUR CRANBERRY-FIG CHUTNEY

- Puree in a blender until smooth and use as a glaze for roast ham or chicken.
- Stir in a little Dijon mustard and use as a dipping sauce for shish kebabs or mini frankfurters.
- Swirl into softened cream cheese and serve with crackers or apple slices.
- Stir into mayonnaise for a delicious spread for ham or turkey sandwiches.
- Serve as an accompaniment for grilled Cheddar cheese sandwiches.

Tomato Chutney

Enjoy this deeply-red and richly flavored chutney with grilled meat or vegetables, or serve alongside a favorite cold meat sandwich to add both flavor and moistness.

Prep: 25 minutes plus chilling   Cook: 55 minutes

- 3 pounds ripe tomatoes (9 medium), peeled and chopped
- 1 medium Granny Smith apple, peeled, cored, and coarsely grated
- 1 small onion, chopped
- 2 tablespoons minced, peeled fresh ginger
- 2 garlic cloves, finely chopped
- ⅓ cup golden raisins
- ⅓ cup packed brown sugar
- ½ teaspoon salt
- ¼ teaspoon coarsely ground black pepper
- ½ cup cider vinegar

In heavy nonreactive 12-inch skillet, combine tomatoes, apple, onion, ginger, garlic, raisins, brown sugar, salt, pepper, and vinegar; heat to boiling over high heat, stirring occasionally. Reduce heat to medium; cook, stirring occasionally, until mixture has thickened, 45 to 50 minutes. Cover and refrigerate until well chilled, about 4 hours or up to 2 weeks. Makes about 3½ cups.

Each ¼ cup: About 59 calories, 1g protein, 15g carbohydrate, 0g total fat (0g saturated), 0mg cholesterol, 94mg sodium.

Best Berry Sauce

The versatility of this fresh berry sauce cannot be exaggerated. The acidity of the berries complements the sweetness of many desserts, such as vanilla ice cream and pound cake.

Prep: 5 minutes   Cook: 5 minutes

- 3 cups assorted fresh berries (blueberries, hulled, sliced strawberries, raspberries)
- ½ to ¾ cup confectioners' sugar
- 3 tablespoons water
- 1 to 2 teaspoons fresh lemon or lime juice

1. In nonreactive 2-quart saucepan, combine berries, ½ cup confectioners' sugar, and water. Cook over medium heat, stirring occasionally, until berries have softened and sauce has thickened slightly, 5 to 8 minutes.

2. Remove saucepan from heat; stir in 1 teaspoon lemon juice. Taste, and stir in additional sugar and lemon juice, if desired. Serve warm, or cover and refrigerate up to 1 day. Reheat to serve, if you like. Makes about 2 cups.

Each tablespoon: About 17 calories, 0g protein, 4g carbohydrate, 0g total fat (0g saturated), 0mg cholesterol, 1mg sodium.

Butterscotch Sauce

This old-fashioned favorite can be depended on to liven up a simple scoop of ice cream but it's also wonderful with apple pie.

Prep: 5 minutes   Cook: 5 minutes

- 1 cup packed brown sugar
- ½ cup heavy or whipping cream
- ⅓ cup light corn syrup
- 2 tablespoons butter or margarine
- 1 teaspoon distilled white vinegar
- ⅛ teaspoon salt
- 1 teaspoon vanilla extract

In heavy 3-quart saucepan, combine brown sugar, cream, corn syrup, butter, vinegar, and salt; heat to boiling over high heat, stirring occasionally. Reduce heat and simmer 2 minutes. Remove saucepan from heat; stir in vanilla. Serve warm, or cover and refrigerate up to 1 week. Makes 1⅓ cups.

Each tablespoon: About 84 calories, 0g protein, 14g carbohydrate, 3g total fat (2g saturated), 11mg cholesterol, 38mg sodium.

SKILLET JAMS

If using blackberries and/or raspberries, press ½ cup through sieve to remove seeds, if you like. In heavy nonstick 12-inch skillet, combine fruit, pectin, and butter. Heat to boiling over high heat, stirring constantly. Stir in sugar and heat to boiling, stirring constantly; boil 1 minute. Remove from heat. Quickly ladle hot jam into hot jars. Wipe jar rims and threads clean; cover with lids. Refrigerate until set, about 6 hours. Refrigerate up to 3 weeks. Each recipe makes two 8-ounce jars.

JAM	FRUIT MIXTURE	POWDERED FRUIT PECTIN	BUTTER OR MARGARINE	SUGAR
Blackberry-Blueberry Skillet Jam	2 cups each blackberries and blueberries, crushed	2 tablespoons	½ teaspoon	¾ cup
Three-Berry Skillet Jam	1 cup each blackberries, raspberries, and sliced strawberries, crushed	4 teaspoons	½ teaspoon	1 cup
Strawberry Skillet Jam	2 cups sliced strawberries, crushed	4 teaspoons	½ teaspoon	1 cup
Raspberry Skillet Jam	3 cups raspberries, crushed	4 teaspoons	½ teaspoon	1½ cups
Blueberry Skillet Jam	2 cups blueberries, crushed	2 tablespoons	½ teaspoon	1 cup
Peach Skillet Jam	1 pound peaches, peeled, pitted, and mashed with 2 teaspoons fresh lemon juice	2 tablespoons	½ teaspoon	1 cup
Apricot Jam	1 pound apricots, pitted and finely chopped, mixed with 2 tablespoons fresh lemon juice	2 tablespoons	½ teaspoon	1 cup

Our Sublime Chocolate Sauce

Some people think that you can't improve a classic. They obviously haven't tasted our sauce. You'll want to make a double batch!

Prep: 5 minutes   Cook: 10 minutes

- 4 squares (4 ounces) unsweetened chocolate, chopped
- 1 cup heavy or whipping cream
- ¾ cup sugar
- 2 tablespoons light corn syrup
- 2 tablespoons butter or margarine
- 2 teaspoons vanilla extract

1. In heavy 2-quart saucepan, combine chopped chocolate, cream, sugar, and corn syrup; heat to boiling over high heat, stirring constantly. Reduce heat to medium. Cook at a gentle boil, stirring constantly, until sauce has thickened slightly, about 5 minutes.

2. Remove from heat; stir in butter and vanilla until smooth and glossy. Serve hot, or cool completely, then cover and refrigerate up to 1 week. Gently reheat before using. Makes about 1¾ cups.

Each tablespoon: About 83 calories, 1g protein, 8g carbohydrate, 6g total fat (4g saturated), 14mg cholesterol, 14mg sodium.

Hot Fudge Sauce

Use this rich sauce as a topping for ice cream or other desserts. Unsweetened cocoa powder makes it quick and easy to prepare.

Prep: 5 minutes   Cook: 5 minutes

¾	cup sugar
½	cup unsweetened cocoa
½	cup heavy or whipping cream
4	tablespoons butter or margarine, cut into pieces
1	teaspoon vanilla extract

In heavy 1-quart saucepan, combine sugar, cocoa, cream, and butter; heat to boiling over high heat, stirring frequently. Remove saucepan from heat; stir in vanilla. Serve warm, or cool completely, then cover and refrigerate up to 2 weeks. Gently reheat before using. Makes about 1¼ cups.

Each tablespoon: About 75 calories, 1g protein, 9g carbohydrate, 5g total fat (3g saturated), 14mg cholesterol, 26mg sodium.

Hot Fudge Sauce

Lemon Sauce

Try this time-honored favorite the next time you bake gingerbread or applesauce cake.

Prep: 5 minutes   Cook: 5 minutes

1	to 2 large lemons
½	cup sugar
1	tablespoon cornstarch
⅔	cup water
1	tablespoon butter or margarine

1. From lemons, grate 1 teaspoon peel and squeeze ¼ cup juice.

2. In nonreactive 2-quart saucepan, combine sugar and cornstarch until well blended. With wire whisk, whisk in water, lemon peel and juice, and butter. Heat to boiling over high heat, stirring constantly; boil 1 minute. Serve warm or at room temperature. Makes about 1¼ cups.

Each tablespoon: About 27 calories, 0g protein, 6g carbohydrate, 1g total fat (0g saturated), 2mg cholesterol, 6mg sodium.

Raspberry Sauce

Use this lively red sauce to dress up chocolate cake or angel food cake, or drizzle over ice cream, frozen yogurt, or fresh fruit.

Prep: 5 minutes   Cook: 5 minutes

1	package (10 ounces) frozen raspberries in syrup, thawed
2	tablespoons red currant jelly
2	teaspoons cornstarch

Into nonreactive 2-quart saucepan, with back of spoon, press raspberries through fine sieve; discard seeds. Stir in jelly and cornstarch. Heat to boiling over high heat, stirring constantly; boil 1 minute. Serve at room temperature, or cover and refrigerate up to 2 days. Makes 1 cup.

Each tablespoon: About 26 calories, 0g protein, 7g carbohydrate, 0g total fat (0g saturated), 0mg cholesterol, 1mg sodium.

Custard Sauce

This classic dessert sauce, known as *crème anglaise,* goes beautifully with pies, tarts, simple cakes, and fruit. If you like, substitute 1 tablespoon of your favorite liqueur or brandy for the vanilla.

Prep: 5 minutes   Cook: 15 minutes

- 1¼ cups milk
- 4 large egg yolks
- ¼ cup sugar
- 1 teaspoon vanilla extract

1. In heavy 2-quart saucepan, heat milk to boiling over high heat.

2. Meanwhile, in medium bowl, with wire whisk, mix egg yolks and sugar until well blended. In thin, steady stream, whisk about ¼ cup hot milk into egg-yolk mixture. Gradually whisk remaining hot milk into egg-yolk mixture. Return mixture to saucepan; cook over medium heat, stirring constantly with wooden spoon, just until mixture has thickened slightly and coats back of spoon. Do not boil, or sauce will curdle.

3. Remove saucepan from heat; strain custard through sieve into clean bowl. Stir in vanilla. Serve warm, or cover and refrigerate up to 1 day. Makes about 1½ cups.

Each tablespoon: About 26 calories, 1g protein, 3g carbohydrate, 1g total fat (1g saturated), 37mg cholesterol, 7mg sodium.

Hard Sauce

The essential companion to any warm steamed pudding—especially Christmas plum pudding.

Prep: 10 minutes

- 1 cup butter (2 sticks), softened (do not use margarine)
- 2 cups confectioners' sugar
- ¼ cup dark rum or brandy
- 1 teaspoon vanilla extract

1. In small bowl, with mixer at medium speed, beat butter until creamy. Reduce speed to low and gradually beat in confectioners' sugar until light and fluffy. Beat in rum and vanilla.

2. Serve, or transfer to airtight container and refrigerate up to 1 month. Let stand at room temperature until soft enough to spread, about 30 minutes. Makes about 2 cups.

Each tablespoon: About 84 calories, 0g protein, 7g carbohydrate, 6g total fat (4g saturated), 16mg cholesterol, 59mg sodium.

Sweetened Whipped Cream

Feel free to flavor the cream with vanilla or with one of the other tasty suggestions.

Prep: 10 minutes

- 1 cup heavy or whipping cream (preferably not ultrapasteurized), well chilled
- 1 to 2 tablespoons sugar
- 1 teaspoon vanilla extract, ⅛ teaspoon almond extract, or 1 tablespoon brandy, rum, or orange-flavored liqueur

1. Chill medium bowl and beaters 20 minutes.

2. In chilled bowl, with mixer at medium speed, beat cream, sugar to taste, and vanilla or other flavoring, until soft, fluffy peaks form. Do not overbeat, or cream will separate. Makes about 2 cups.

Each tablespoon: About 28 calories, 0g protein, 1g carbohydrate, 3g total fat (2g saturated), 10mg cholesterol, 3mg sodium.

16

QUICK BREADS

As their name implies, quick breads are faster to prepare than their yeast-leavened "cousins." Thanks to fast-acting leavening agents, these simple breads don't require a rising period. Just mix them up and pop them into the oven. Favorite breads from this wide-ranging category include biscuits, muffins, coffee cakes, popovers, pancakes, and waffles.

RISING TO THE OCCASION

Most quick breads rely on chemical leavenings, such as baking powder or baking soda, to make them rise.

Baking soda is an alkali that forms carbon dioxide gas bubbles when combined with an acidic ingredient, such as buttermilk, yogurt, chocolate, brown sugar, or molasses. Store baking soda in an airtight container in a cool, dry place for up to one year.

Baking powder is a combination of baking soda and a dry acid, such as cream of tartar. Most commercial baking powders are double-acting: They start to produce gas bubbles as soon as they are moistened, then release more when heated in the oven. Baking powder can stay potent for up to six months if stored airtight in a cool, dry place.

Buttermilk was originally the liquid left over from churning butter, but it is now made from milk to which bacterial cultures have been added. It is a favorite baking ingredient; its acidity balances sugar's sweetness, and it reacts with baking soda to give baked goods a fine crumb. It's a good ingredient to have on hand in your refrigerator. Dehydrated buttermilk powder is also available. Reconstitute it according to the package directions. In a pinch, a good substitute for buttermilk is sour cream (not reduced-fat) or plain lowfat yogurt blended with an equal amount of whole milk. You can also use soured milk: Place 1 tablespoon fresh lemon juice or distilled white vinegar in a glass measuring cup, then pour in enough whole milk to equal 1 cup. Stir and let stand for five minutes to thicken.

MIXING IT RIGHT

Always mix quick breads with a light hand. Simply combine the dry ingredients, add the liquids, and stir. Before starting, be sure your baking powder or baking soda is active. To test soda or powder, stir 1 teaspoon into 1 cup of boiling water; it should bubble and foam vigorously. All-purpose flour makes tender quick breads. Except for recipes in which chilled butter or margarine is cut into the flour mixture, batters are easier to mix and bake better if all the ingredients are at room temperature. After adding the liquids to the flour mixture, stir just until the batter is blended. If any lumps remain, they will disappear during baking. Overmixing will cause the bread to be tough, dense, and full of tunnels. Biscuit dough is usually kneaded just a few times to blend the mixture together. Lastly, quick breads should be baked as soon as the batter is mixed, while the leavening still has its rising power.

BAKING SUCCESS

Bake quick breads in the center of the oven. And if baking two loaves at once, be sure there is enough space between them so the air can circulate freely.

Always use the correct size pan. Loaf pans come in two standard sizes, 8½" by 4½" and 9" by 5". The larger pans holds 2 cups more than the smaller one! Fill loaf pans about two-thirds full. Smooth the top with a rubber spatula so the bread bakes uniformly. Don't be concerned if a lengthwise crack appears along the top during baking; it's very typical.

Muffin pans come in various sizes. Standard muffin-pan cups are about 2½" by 1¼", with 12 cups to the pan. There are also giant (4" by 2") and mini (1⅞" by ¾") muffin-pan cups. Regardless of their size, fill muffin-pan cups two-thirds to three-quarters full (to allow room for rising). Fill any empty cups with water to prevent the pan from warping during baking.

To test quick breads for doneness, use the toothpick test: Insert a wooden toothpick into the center of the bread. It should come out clean without any moist crumbs clinging. If it does not, bake the bread a few minutes longer, then test again. The bread might be done even if the crack in the top looks moist.

COOLING, STORING, AND REHEATING QUICK BREADS

Immediately remove baked biscuits, scones, and muffins from their cookie sheets or pans to prevent them from sticking. Most fruit-filled quick breads should be cooled in their pans for ten minutes to allow them to set. Invert them onto wire racks, then turn right side up to cool completely.

In general, the richer the batter (those containing eggs, butter, or fruit), the longer the baked bread will stay moist. Dense fruit breads are even better if made a day ahead so their flavors can blend. They'll also be firmer and easier to slice. Most muffins, biscuits, scones, and corn breads are best eaten the day they are made, otherwise freeze to serve later.

To store fruit breads and muffins at room temperature, first cool them completely. Wrap them in plastic wrap and then in foil; they will keep for up to three days. To freeze fruit breads, wrap them tightly in plastic wrap and then in heavy-duty foil, pressing out the air. Freeze for up to three months. Smaller items like muffins and biscuits can be frozen for up to one month. Thaw them, still wrapped, at room temperature.

Waffles can be frozen, too. Cook them until lightly browned, then cool completely on wire racks. Place them on cookie sheets and freeze until firm, then seal in heavy-duty zip-tight plastic bags and return to the freezer. To reheat, toast the frozen waffles until golden.

To warm fruit breads, wrap in foil, and heat at 400°F. Muffins, scones, and biscuits will take about ten minutes, while loaves and coffee cakes will take about 20 minutes. Muffins also warm well in a microwave oven. Loosely wrap each muffin in a paper towel and microwave on High for about ten seconds. Be careful, though: If the muffins have sugary add-ins, such as chocolate chips or jam, they could get very hot, and if baked goods are reheated too long, they become tough.

REMOVING MUFFINS FROM PAN

Run a small metal spatula or knife around the inside of the muffin-pan cups. Turn the pan on its side and rap it on the counter to remove the muffins.

Baking Powder Biscuits

To cut out biscuits, press the cutter straight down. If you twist it, the biscuits may rise unevenly.

Prep: 15 minutes   Bake: 12 minutes

- 2 cups all-purpose flour
- 1 tablespoon baking powder
- ½ teaspoon salt
- ¼ cup vegetable shortening
- ¾ cup milk

1. Preheat oven to 450°F. In large bowl, with wire whisk, stir flour, baking powder, and salt. With pastry blender or two knives used scissor-fashion, cut in shortening until mixture re-  sembles coarse crumbs. Stir in milk, stirring just until mixture forms soft dough that leaves side of bowl.

2. Turn dough onto lightly floured surface; knead 6 to 8 times, just until smooth. With floured rolling pin, roll dough ½ inch thick for high, fluffy biscuits or ¼ inch thick for thin, crusty biscuits.

3. With floured 2-inch biscuit cutter, cut out rounds, without twisting cutter. Arrange biscuits on ungreased cookie sheet, 1 inch apart for crusty biscuits or nearly touching for soft-sided biscuits.

4. Press trimmings together; reroll and cut out more biscuits. Bake until golden, 12 to 15 minutes. Serve warm. Makes about 18 tall or 36 thin biscuits.

Each tall biscuit: About 86 calories, 2g protein, 12g carbohydrate, 3g total fat (1g saturated), 1mg cholesterol, 151mg sodium.

Buttermilk Biscuits

Prepare as directed above but substitute ¾ **cup buttermilk** for milk and use only **2½ teaspoons baking powder;** add ½ **teaspoon baking soda** to flour mixture. Makes about 18 biscuits.

Drop Biscuits

Prepare as directed above but use **1 cup milk.** Stir dough just until ingredients are blended. Drop heaping tablespoons of mixture, 1 inch apart, on ungreased cookie sheet. Makes about 20 biscuits.

Popovers

Popovers are crispy on the outside and hollow on the inside. Serve them fresh from the oven or make them ahead and reheat in a 400°F oven for 15 minutes.

Prep: 10 minutes   Bake: 1 hour

- 3 large eggs
- 1 cup milk
- 3 tablespoons butter or margarine, melted
- 1 cup all-purpose flour
- ½ teaspoon salt

1. Preheat oven to 375°F. Generously grease eight 6-ounce custard cups or twelve 2½" by 1¼" muffin-pan cups with butter or vegetable oil. Place custard cups in jelly-roll pan for easier handling.

2. In blender, combine eggs, milk, melted butter, flour, and salt; blend until smooth.

3. Pour about ⅓ cup batter into each prepared custard cup, or fill muffin-pan cups half full. Bake 50 minutes, then, with tip of knife, quickly cut small slit in top of each popover to release steam; bake 10 minutes longer. Immediately remove popovers from cups, loosening with spatula if necessary. Serve hot. Makes 8 medium or 12 small popovers.

Each medium popover: About 159 calories, 5g protein, 14g carbohydrate, 9g total fat (5g saturated), 101mg cholesterol, 247mg sodium.

Giant Popovers

Generously grease six deep 8-ounce ceramic custard cups; place in jelly-roll pan. Prepare popovers as directed above but use **6 eggs, 2 cups milk, 6 tablespoons butter or margarine,** melted, **2 cups flour,** and **1 teaspoon salt.** Bake 1 hour before cutting slit in top of popovers. Makes 6 giant popovers.

Each popover: About 394 calories, 13g protein, 36g carbohydrate, 22g total fat (12g saturated), 260mg cholesterol, 629mg sodium.

Scones

A traditional Scottish quick bread, scones are welcome as a treat for breakfast or as an afternoon snack with tea. For currant scones, stir 1 cup dried currants into the dry ingredients before adding the milk mixture.

Prep: 15 minutes   Bake: 22 minutes

- 2 cups all-purpose flour
- 2 tablespoons plus 2 teaspoons sugar
- 2½ teaspoons baking powder
- ¼ teaspoon salt
- ½ cup cold butter or margarine (1 stick), cut into pieces
- ¾ cup milk
- 1 large egg, separated

1. Preheat oven to 375°F. In large bowl, with wire whisk, stir flour, 2 tablespoons sugar, baking powder, and salt. With pastry blender or two knives used scissor-fashion, cut in butter until mixture resembles coarse crumbs.

2. In 1-cup measuring cup, with fork, mix milk and egg yolk until blended. Make well in center of flour mixture and pour in milk mixture. Stir just until combined.

3. Turn dough onto lightly floured surface and knead 5 to 6 times, just until smooth. With lightly floured hands, pat into 7½-inch round. Transfer to ungreased cookie sheet.

4. With lightly floured knife, cut dough into 8 wedges (do not separate wedges). In small cup, lightly beat egg white. Brush scones with egg white and sprinkle with remaining 2 teaspoons sugar. Bake until golden brown, 22 to 25 minutes. Separate wedges. Serve warm, or cool on wire rack to serve later. Makes 8 scones.

Each scone: About 259 calories, 5g protein, 30g carbohydrate, 13g total fat (8g saturated), 61mg cholesterol, 361mg sodium.

Buttermilk Scones

Prepare as directed (left) but use only **2 teaspoons baking powder.** Add ½ **teaspoon baking soda** to flour mixture. Substitute ¾ **cup buttermilk** for milk.

Rich Scones

Prepare as directed (left) but preheat oven to 400°F. Use **3½ cups all-purpose flour, ½ cup sugar, 2 tablespoons baking powder, ½ teaspoon salt,** and **6 tablespoons butter or margarine.** Substitute **1 cup half-and-half or light cream** for milk and blend with **2 eggs.** Turn dough onto greased large cookie sheet (dough will be sticky), and with lightly floured hands, pat dough into 9-inch round. Brush with **1 tablespoon half-and-half or light cream** and sprinkle with **1 tablespoon sugar.** With floured knife, cut dough into 8 wedges (do not separate). Bake until golden, 15 to 20 minutes.

Each scone: About 390 calories, 8g protein, 58g carbohydrate, 14g total fat (8g saturated), 88mg cholesterol, 628mg sodium.

Lemon-Walnut Scones

Prepare as directed above for Rich Scones but add **1 teaspoon freshly grated lemon peel** to flour mixture; add **1 cup chopped walnuts (4 ounces)** with half-and-half mixture.

Rich Scones

Basic Muffins

Easy, buttery muffins are a snap to prepare. To make chocolate chip muffins, stir ¾ cup chocolate chips into the batter before baking. For orange muffins, add 1 teaspoon freshly grated orange peel to the dry ingredients.

Prep: 10 minutes   Bake: 20 minutes

- 2½ cups all-purpose flour
- ½ cup sugar
- 1 tablespoon baking powder
- ½ teaspoon salt
- 1 cup milk
- ½ cup butter or margarine (1 stick), melted
- 1 large egg
- 1 teaspoon vanilla extract

1. Preheat oven to 400°F. Grease twelve 2½" by 1¼" muffin-pan cups.

2. In large bowl, with wire whisk, stir flour, sugar, baking powder, and salt. In medium bowl, with fork, beat milk, melted butter, egg, and vanilla until blended. Add liquid mixture to flour mixture; stir just until flour is moistened (batter will be lumpy).

3. Spoon batter into prepared muffin-pan cups. Bake until toothpick inserted in center of muffin comes out clean, 20 to 25 minutes. Immediately remove muffins from pan. Serve muffins warm, or cool on wire rack to serve later. Makes 12 muffins.

Each muffin: About 225 calories, 4g protein, 30g carbohydrate, 10g total fat (6g saturated), 41mg cholesterol, 312mg sodium.

Jam-Filled Muffins

Prepare as directed (left) but fill muffin-pan cups one-third full with batter. Drop **1 rounded teaspoon strawberry or raspberry preserves** in center of each cup batter; top with remaining batter. Bake as directed.

Blueberry or Raspberry Muffins

Prepare as directed (left) but stir **1 cup blueberries or raspberries** into batter.

Walnut or Pecan Muffins

Prepare as directed (left) but stir ½ **cup chopped toasted walnuts or pecans** into batter. Sprinkle with **2 tablespoons sugar** before baking.

Basic Muffins with Variations

Carrot-Bran Muffins

Deliciously hearty and filled with fiber, these muffins will tide you over to your next meal.

Prep: 15 minutes plus standing   Bake: 30 minutes

- 1 cup milk
- ¼ cup vegetable oil
- 1 large egg, lightly beaten
- 1½ cups whole-bran cereal (not bran flakes)
- 1 cup shredded carrots
- 1¼ cups all-purpose flour
- ⅓ cup sugar
- 1 tablespoon baking powder
- ½ teaspoon salt
- ¼ teaspoon ground cinnamon
- 1 cup dark seedless raisins

1. Preheat oven to 400°F. Grease twelve 2½" by 1¼" muffin-pan cups.

2. In medium bowl, with fork, beat milk, oil, egg, cereal, and carrots until blended; let stand 10 minutes.

3. Meanwhile, in large bowl, with wire whisk, stir flour, sugar, baking powder, salt, and cinnamon. Add cereal mixture to flour mixture; stir just until flour is moistened (batter will be lumpy). Stir in raisins.

4. Spoon batter into prepared muffin-pan cups. Bake until muffins begin to brown and toothpick inserted in center of muffin comes out clean, about 30 minutes. Immediately remove muffins from pan. Serve warm, or cool on wire rack. Makes 12 muffins.

Each muffin: About 198 calories, 4g protein, 33g carbohydrate, 7g total fat (1g saturated), 21mg cholesterol, 309mg sodium.

Nutty Carrot-Bran Muffins

Prepare as directed above but substitute **golden raisins or dried cranberries** for the dark seedless raisins, if you like, or use a combination. Add ½ **cup chopped walnuts or pecans** in Step 2.

Golden Corn Bread

This slightly sweet batter can be baked into a tender square, muffins, or corn sticks.

Prep: 10 minutes   Bake: 20 minutes

- 1 cup all-purpose flour
- ¾ cup cornmeal
- 3 tablespoons sugar
- 1 tablespoon baking powder
- ¾ teaspoon salt
- ⅔ cup milk
- 4 tablespoons butter or margarine, melted
- 1 large egg

1. Preheat oven to 425°F. Grease 8-inch square baking pan.

2. In medium bowl, with wire whisk, stir flour, cornmeal, sugar, baking powder, and salt. In small bowl, with fork, beat milk, melted butter, and egg until blended. Add egg mixture to flour mixture; stir just until flour is moistened (batter will be lumpy).

3. Spread batter evenly in prepared pan. Bake until golden and toothpick inserted in center comes out clean, 20 to 25 minutes. Cut corn bread into 9 squares; serve warm. Makes 9 servings.

Each serving: About 178 calories, 4g protein, 25g carbohydrate, 7g total fat (4g saturated), 40mg cholesterol, 425mg sodium.

Corn Muffins

Grease twelve 2½" by 1¼" muffin-pan cups. Prepare as directed above but use **1 cup milk.** Fill each muffin-pan cup two-thirds full. Bake until golden and toothpick inserted in center of muffin comes out clean, about 20 minutes. Immediately remove muffins from pans. Serve warm, or cool on wire rack. Makes 12 muffins.

Each muffin: About 144 calories, 3g protein, 19g carbohydrate, 6g total fat (3g saturated), 31mg cholesterol, 322mg sodium.

Corn Sticks

Grease 14 corn-stick molds with vegetable oil. Heat molds in oven until hot, about 15 minutes. Meanwhile, prepare batter as directed (left). Spoon batter into hot molds. Bake until toothpick inserted in center of corn stick comes out clean, 15 to 20 minutes. Cool in molds on wire rack 10 minutes. Remove corn sticks from molds; serve warm. Makes 14 corn sticks.

Each corn stick: About 121 calories, 2g protein, 16g carbohydrate, 5g total fat (3g saturated), 26mg cholesterol, 273mg sodium.

Southern Corn Bread

Prepare as directed (left) but place a 9- to 10-inch cast-iron skillet in oven while preheating. In Step 2 omit sugar, reduce baking powder to 1 teaspoon and salt to ½ teaspoon; add ¼ **teaspoon baking soda,** and substitute **1 cup buttermilk** for milk. Spray hot skillet with nonstick spray; pour batter into skillet and spread evenly. Bake until a toothpick inserted in center comes out clean, 15 to 20 minutes. Cut corn bread into 8 wedges; serve warm. Makes 8 wedges.

Each wedge: About 243 calories, 7g protein, 35g carbohydrate, 8g total fat (4g saturated), 71mg cholesterol, 584mg sodium.

Southern Corn Bread

Lemon Tea Bread

The combination of butter and sour cream makes this quick bread remarkably moist, and the lemon glaze helps to keep it that way.

Prep: 30 minutes   Bake: 55 minutes

Bread

- 2 cups all-purpose flour
- ½ teaspoon baking powder
- ¼ teaspoon baking soda
- ½ teaspoon salt
- 1¼ cups sugar
- 4 large eggs
- 1 container (8 ounces) sour cream
- ½ cup butter (1 stick), melted
- 1 tablespoon freshly grated lemon peel
- 2 tablespoons fresh lemon juice

Glaze

- ⅓ cup sugar
- ⅓ cup fresh lemon juice

1. Prepare bread: Preheat oven to 350°F. Grease 9" by 5" metal loaf pan. Dust with flour.

2. In large bowl, with wire whisk, stir flour, baking powder, baking soda, and salt. In medium bowl, whisk sugar and eggs until blended. Add sour cream, butter, lemon peel, and lemon juice; stir until well mixed. Add sour cream mixture to flour mixture and fold together just until blended and no streaks of flour remain.

3. Pour batter into prepared pan, smooth top. Bake until toothpick inserted in center comes out clean, 55 to 60 minutes. Place pan on wire rack.

4. Prepare glaze: In cup, stir sugar and lemon juice. With thin wooden skewer, poke holes in hot bread and brush bread with glaze. Let cool completely in pan. Makes 1 loaf, 16 slices.

Each slice: About 235 calories, 4g protein, 32g carbohydrate, 10g total fat (6g saturated), 76mg cholesterol, 191mg sodium.

Cranberry-Orange Bread

Bake this tasty bread a day ahead to allow the flavors to develop and to make it easier to cut neat slices.

Prep: 20 minutes   Bake: 55 minutes

- 1 large orange
- 2½ cups all-purpose flour
- 1 cup sugar
- 2 teaspoons baking powder
- ½ teaspoon baking soda
- ½ teaspoon salt
- 4 tablespoons butter or margarine, melted
- 2 large eggs
- 2 cups cranberries, coarsely chopped
- ¾ cup walnuts, chopped (optional)

1. Preheat oven to 375°F. Grease 9" by 5" metal loaf pan. From orange, grate 1 teaspoon peel and squeeze ½ cup juice.

2. In large bowl, with wire whisk, stir flour, sugar, baking powder, baking soda, and salt. In small bowl, beat orange peel and juice, melted butter, and eggs until blended. With wooden spoon, stir egg mixture into flour mixture just until blended (batter will be stiff). Stir in cranberries and walnuts, if using.

3. Pour batter into prepared pan. Bake until toothpick inserted in center comes out clean, 55 to 60 minutes. Cool loaf in pan on wire rack 10 minutes; remove from pan and cool completely on wire rack. Makes 1 loaf, 12 slices.

Each slice without walnuts: About 223 calories, 4g protein, 40g carbohydrate, 5g total fat (3g saturated), 46mg cholesterol, 281mg sodium.

Banana Bread

For the best flavor, wait until your bananas are completely ripe and spotted but not blackened and soft.

Prep: 20 minutes   Bake: 1 hour

- 2 cups all-purpose flour
- ¾ teaspoon baking soda
- ½ teaspoon salt
- ½ cup butter or margarine (1 stick), softened
- ½ cup granulated sugar
- ½ cup brown sugar
- 2 large eggs
- 1½ cups mashed very ripe bananas (4 medium)
- 1 teaspoon vanilla extract

1. Preheat oven to 325°F. Evenly grease 8½" by 4½" metal loaf pan.

2. In medium bowl, with wire whisk, stir flour, baking powder, salt, and baking soda.

3. In large bowl, with mixer at medium speed, beat butter and granulated and brown sugars until light and fluffy. Beat in eggs, one at a time. Reduce speed to low; alternately add flour mixture and banana mixture, beginning and ending with flour mixture, occasionally scraping side of bowl with rubber spatula. Beat just until blended.

4. Pour batter into prepared pan. Bake until toothpick inserted in center comes out clean, about 1 hour. Cool loaf in pan on wire rack 10 minutes; remove from pan and cool completely on wire rack. Makes 1 loaf, 16 slices.

Each slice: About 197 calories, 3g protein, 32g carbohydrate, 7g total fat (4g saturated), 43mg cholesterol, 205mg sodium.

Banana-Nut Bread
Prepare bread as directed above but fold **1 cup walnuts or pecans (4 ounces),** coarsely chopped, into batter before baking.

Date-Nut Bread

Date-Nut Bread

Serve slices of this dense, moist, old-fashioned favorite plain or slathered with cream cheese.

Prep: 20 minutes plus cooling   Bake: 1 hour 15 minutes

- 1½ cups chopped pitted dates
- 6 tablespoons butter or margarine, cut into pieces
- 1¼ cups boiling water
- 2 cups all-purpose flour
- ¾ cup sugar
- 1 teaspoon baking powder
- ½ teaspoon baking soda
- ½ teaspoon salt
- 1 large egg, lightly beaten
- 1 cup walnuts (4 ounces), coarsely chopped

1. In medium bowl, combine dates, butter, and boiling water; let stand until cool.

2. Preheat oven to 325°F and grease 9" by 5" metal loaf pan.

3. In large bowl, with wire whisk, stir flour, sugar, baking powder, baking soda, and salt. Stir egg into cooled date mixture. Stir date mixture into flour mixture just until flour is moistened. Stir in walnuts.

4. Pour batter into prepared pan. Bake until toothpick inserted in center comes out clean, about 1 hour 15 minutes. Cool in pan on wire rack 10 minutes; remove from pan and cool completely on rack. Makes 1 loaf, 16 slices.

Each slice: About 232 calories, 3g protein, 35g carbohydrate, 10g total fat (3g saturated), 25mg cholesterol, 192mg sodium.

Zucchini Bread

Everyone loves zucchini bread—especially the baker. It delivers lots of flavor with very little effort.

Prep: 20 minutes   Bake: 1 hour 10 minutes

- 1½ cups all-purpose flour
- ¾ cup sugar
- 2¼ teaspoons baking powder
- ½ teaspoon ground cinnamon
- ½ teaspoon salt
- ⅓ cup vegetable oil
- 2 large eggs
- 1½ cups shredded zucchini (1 medium)
- ½ cup walnuts (2 ounces), chopped
- ½ teaspoon freshly grated orange peel

1. Preheat oven to 350°F. Grease 8½" by 4½" metal loaf pan.

2. In large bowl, with wire whisk, stir flour, sugar, baking powder, cinnamon, and salt. In medium bowl, with fork, mix oil, eggs, zucchini, walnuts, and orange peel. Stir zucchini mixture into flour mixture just until flour is moistened.

3. Pour batter into prepared pan. Bake until toothpick inserted in center comes out clean, about 1 hour 10 minutes. Cool in pan on wire rack 10 minutes; remove from pan and cool completely on wire rack. Makes 1 loaf, 12 slices.

Each slice: About 209 calories, 4g protein, 26g carbohydrate, 10g total fat (1g saturated), 35mg cholesterol, 200mg sodium.

Traditional Irish Soda Bread

This bread is rich and tender thanks to a good amount of butter and lots of tangy buttermilk. It's best served warm, slathered with butter.

Prep: 15 minutes   Bake: 1 hour

- 4 cups all-purpose flour
- ¼ cup sugar
- 1 tablespoon baking powder
- 1½ teaspoons salt
- 1 teaspoon baking soda
- 6 tablespoons cold butter or margarine, cut into pieces
- 1½ cups buttermilk

1. Preheat oven to 350°F. Grease cookie sheet.

2. In large bowl, with wire whisk, stir flour, sugar, baking powder, salt, and baking soda. With pastry blender or two knives used scissor-fashion, cut in butter until mixture resembles coarse crumbs. Stir in buttermilk just until flour is moistened (dough will be sticky).

3. Turn dough onto well-floured surface; with lightly floured hands, knead 8 to 10 times to mix. (Do not overknead, or bread will be tough.) Shape into ball; place on prepared cookie sheet.

4. Dust dough lightly with flour. With serrated knife or single-edge razor blade, in center, cut an X 4 inches long and about ¼ inch deep. Bake until toothpick inserted in center comes out clean, about 1 hour. Transfer loaf to wire rack to cool. Makes 1 loaf, 12 slices.

Each slice: About 235 calories, 5g protein, 38g carbohydrate, 7g total fat (4g saturated), 17mg cholesterol, 609mg sodium.

Soda Bread with Currants and Caraway Seeds

Prepare as directed but after adding buttermilk in Step 2, stir in **1½ cups dried currants** and **2 teaspoons caraway seeds**.

The Perfect Coffee Cake

The name says it all. Three tempting layers of a tender sour cream batter cushion two layers of a brown sugar, pecan, and cinnamon filling.

Prep: 30 minutes   Bake: 55 minutes

- 1½ teaspoons baking powder
- 1 teaspoon baking soda
- ¾ teaspoon salt
- 3 cups plus 1 tablespoon all-purpose flour
- ¾ cup chopped pecans
- ⅓ cup packed brown sugar
- 1¼ teaspoons ground cinnamon
- 1½ cups granulated sugar
- ¾ cup butter or margarine (1½ sticks), softened
- 2½ teaspoons vanilla extract
- 3 large eggs
- 1 container (16 ounces) sour cream
- 1 cup confectioners' sugar
- 4 to 6 teaspoons milk

1. Preheat oven to 350°F. Grease 12-cup Bundt pan; dust with flour.

2. In medium bowl, with wire whisk, stir baking powder, baking soda, salt, and 3 cups flour. In small bowl, combine pecans, brown sugar, cinnamon, and remaining 1 tablespoon flour.

3. In large bowl, with mixer at medium speed, beat granulated sugar, butter, and 2 teaspoons vanilla until creamy. Beat in eggs, one at a time. Alternately beat in flour mixture and sour cream, beginning and ending with flour mixture. Beat just until blended, occasionally scraping bowl.

4. Evenly spread 2 cups batter in prepared pan; sprinkle with half of nut mixture. Top with 2 cups batter. Sprinkle with remaining nut mixture, then top with remaining batter. Bake cake until toothpick inserted in center comes out clean, 55 to 60 minutes. Cool cake in pan on wire rack 10 minutes. With small metal spatula, loosen cake from pan; invert onto rack to cool completely.

5. Prepare glaze: In small bowl, stir confectioners' sugar, milk, and remaining ½ teaspoon vanilla until smooth. Drizzle glaze over cake. Makes 16 servings.

Each serving: About 410 calories, 5g protein, 51g carbohydrate, 21g total fat (10g saturated), 77mg cholesterol, 550mg sodium.

Classic Crumb Cake

The thick cinnamon-rich crumb topping on this coffee cake is irresistible—even better than that from a bakery!

Prep: 40 minutes   Bake: 40 minutes

Crumb Topping

- 2 cups all-purpose flour
- ½ cup granulated sugar
- ½ cup packed brown sugar
- 1½ teaspoons ground cinnamon
- 1 cup butter or margarine (2 sticks), softened

Cake

- 2¼ cups all-purpose flour
- 2¼ teaspoons baking powder
- ½ teaspoon salt
- ½ cup butter or margarine (1 stick), softened
- 1¼ cups granulated sugar
- 3 large eggs
- ¾ cup milk
- 2 teaspoons vanilla extract

1. Prepare topping: In medium bowl, with wire whisk, stir flour, granulated and brown sugars, and cinnamon until well blended. With fingertips, blend in butter until mixture resembles coarse crumbs.

2. Prepare cake: Preheat oven to 350°F. Grease and flour two 9-inch round cake pans. In medium bowl, with wire whisk, stir flour, baking powder, and salt.

3. In large bowl, with mixer at low speed, beat butter and sugar until blended, frequently scraping bowl with rubber spatula. Increase speed to medium; beat until light and fluffy, about 2 minutes, occasionally scraping bowl. Reduce speed to low; add eggs, one at a time, beating well after each addition.

4. In cup, combine milk and vanilla. With mixer at low speed, alternately add flour mixture and milk mixture to butter mixture, beginning and ending with flour mixture, beating until smooth.

5. Divide batter evenly between prepared pans. With hand, press crumb topping to form ¾-inch chunks; sprinkle evenly over batter. Bake until toothpick inserted in center comes out clean, 40 to 45 minutes. Cool in pans on wire racks 15 minutes. With small metal spatula, loosen cakes from sides of pans. Invert onto plates, then invert, crumb side up, onto wire racks to cool completely. Makes 2 crumb cakes, each 10 servings.

Each serving: About 330 calories, 4g protein, 44g carbohydrate, 16g total fat (9g saturated), 70mg cholesterol, 270mg sodium.

Easy Christmas Stollen

Expect all the flavor and richness of a traditional holiday sweet bread without the bother of yeast dough.

Prep: 25 minutes   Bake: 1 hour

- 2¼ cups all-purpose flour
- ½ cup sugar
- 1½ teaspoons baking powder
- ¼ teaspoon salt
- 8 tablespoons butter or margarine (1 stick)
- 1 cup ricotta cheese
- ½ cup candied lemon peel or coarsely chopped red candied cherries
- ½ cup dark seedless raisins
- ⅓ cup slivered blanched almonds, toasted (page 562)
- 1 teaspoon vanilla extract
- ½ teaspoon freshly grated lemon peel
- 1 large egg, lightly beaten
- 1 large egg yolk

1. Preheat oven to 325°F. Grease large cookie sheet.

2. In large bowl, with wire whisk, stir flour, sugar, baking powder, and salt. With pastry blender or two knives used scissor-fashion, cut in 6 tablespoons butter until mixture resembles fine crumbs. With spoon, stir in ricotta until mixture is moistened. Stir in candied lemon peel, raisins, almonds, vanilla, grated lemon peel, egg, and egg yolk until well mixed.

3. Turn dough onto lightly floured surface; gently knead dough 2 or 3 times. With floured rolling pin, roll dough into 10" by 8" oval. Fold oval lengthwise almost in half, so that edges do not quite meet.

4. Place stollen on prepared cookie sheet. Bake until toothpick inserted in center comes out clean, about 1 hour. Transfer to wire rack. Melt remaining 2 tablespoons butter and brush over warm stollen. Cool completely. Makes 12 servings.

Each serving: About 298 calories, 7g protein, 38g carbohydrate, 14g total fat (7g saturated), 67mg cholesterol, 211mg sodium.

Fruit-Streusel Coffee Cake

This delectable coffee cake can be made year-round with almost any seasonal fruit.

Prep: 30 minutes   Bake: 50 minutes

Streusel Topping

- ¾ cup all-purpose flour
- ½ cup packed brown sugar
- 1 teaspoon ground cinnamon
- 4 tablespoons cold butter or margarine, cut into pieces

Cake

- 2¼ cups all-purpose flour
- 1½ teaspoons baking powder
- ½ teaspoon baking soda
- ½ teaspoon salt
- ¾ cup butter or margarine (1½ sticks), softened
- 1½ cups granulated sugar
- 3 large eggs
- 1 cup milk
- 1 teaspoon vanilla extract
- 1¼ pounds ripe pears, apples, or peaches, peeled and thinly sliced; or nectarines or plums, not peeled, thinly sliced (3 cups); or fresh or frozen rhubarb, cut into 1-inch pieces (4 cups); or 1 pint blueberries

1. Prepare topping: In medium bowl, with wire whisk, stir flour, brown sugar, and cinnamon. With fingertips, blend flour mixture and butter until mixture resembles coarse crumbs.

2. Prepare cake: Preheat oven to 350°F. Grease and flour 13" by 9" baking pan. In medium bowl, whisk flour, baking powder, baking soda, and salt.

3. In large bowl, with mixer at low speed, beat butter and sugar until blended, frequently scraping bowl with rubber spatula. Increase speed to high; beat until light and fluffy, about 2 minutes, occasionally scraping bowl. Reduce speed to low; add eggs, one at a time, beating well after each addition.

4. In cup, combine milk and vanilla. With mixer at low speed, alternately add flour mixture and milk mixture to butter mixture, beginning and ending with flour mixture, beating until smooth.

5. Spread batter evenly in prepared pan. Arrange fruit slices on top, overlapping them slightly. Evenly sprinkle streusel topping over fruit. Bake cake until toothpick inserted in center comes out clean, 50 to 55 minutes. Cool in pan on wire rack 10 minutes to serve warm, or cool completely in pan. Makes 15 servings.

Each serving: About 353 calories, 5g protein, 52g carbohydrate, 14g total fat (8g saturated), 78mg cholesterol, 317mg sodium.

Pancakes

For thinner pancakes, add a little more milk to the batter.

Prep: 15 minutes   Cook: 4 minutes per batch

- 1 cup all-purpose flour
- 2 tablespoons sugar
- 2½ teaspoons baking powder
- ½ teaspoon salt
- 1¼ cups milk
- 3 tablespoons butter or margarine, melted
- 1 large egg, lightly beaten
  vegetable oil for brushing pan

1. In bowl, with wire whisk, stir flour, sugar, baking powder, and salt. Add milk, butter, and egg and stir until flour is moistened.

2. Heat griddle or 12-inch skillet over medium heat until drop of water sizzles; brush lightly with oil. Pour batter by scant ¼ cups onto hot griddle, making a few pancakes at a time. Cook  until tops are bubbly, some bubbles burst, and edges look dry. With wide spatula, turn and cook until underside is golden. Transfer to platter; keep warm.

3. Repeat with remaining batter, brushing griddle with more oil if necessary. Makes 3 servings.

Each serving: About 388 calories, 10g protein, 46g carbohydrate, 19g total fat (10g saturated), 116mg cholesterol, 981mg sodium.

Blueberry Pancakes

Prepare as directed (left) but add **1 cup blueberries** to pancake batter.

Buckwheat Pancakes

Prepare as directed (left) but use **½ cup all-purpose flour** and **½ cup buckwheat flour.**

Banana Pancakes

Prepare as directed (left) but add **1 very ripe medium banana,** mashed (about ½ cup), and **¼ teaspoon baking soda;** use only **¾ cup milk.**

Cornmeal Pancakes

Prepare as directed (left) but add **¼ cup cornmeal** to flour mixture.

Buttermilk Pancakes

(Pictured on page 444)

Prepare as directed (left) but use only **2 teaspoons baking powder** and **½ teaspoon baking soda.** Substitute **1¼ cups buttermilk or 1 cup plain yogurt plus ¼ cup milk** for milk.

Sour Cream Pancakes

Prepare as directed but substitute **1 container (8 ounces) sour cream** and **¼ cup milk** for milk.

MAPLE SYRUP

Pure maple syrup is graded by color, which can range from pale brownish gold to an almost molasses hue. *Vermont Fancy* or *U.S. Grade A Light Amber* is mild and tastes best with foods that won't overpower its sweet, subtle flavor. *U.S. Grade A Medium Amber* and *U.S. Grade A Dark Amber* have a stronger taste and aroma and pair well with breakfast waffles and pancakes. *Grade A Medium* is the type most often found on store shelves. *U.S. Grade B* has an intense flavor that can stand up to the heat of cooking. Once opened, store pure maple syrup in glass in the refrigerator, and use within 6 months. Unopened, it will keep indefinitely. Maple syrup also freezes well.

Buttermilk Waffles

Crisp yet fluffy, these are worth getting out of bed for. Top with butter, syrup, or your favorite fresh fruit.

Prep: 15 minutes   Bake: 4 minutes per batch

- 1¾ cups all-purpose flour
- 1½ teaspoons baking powder
- 1 teaspoon baking soda
- ½ teaspoon salt
- 2 cups buttermilk
- 4 tablespoons butter or margarine, melted
- 2 large eggs, lightly beaten

1. Preheat waffle baker as manufacturer directs.

2. In large bowl, with wire whisk, stir flour, baking powder, baking soda, and salt. Add buttermilk, melted butter, and eggs; whisk until smooth.

3. When waffle baker is ready, pour batter into center until it spreads to within 1 inch of edges. Cover and bake as manufacturer directs; do not lift cover while waffle is baking.

4. When waffle is done, lift cover and loosen waffle with fork. Serve immediately or keep warm in oven (place waffle directly on oven rack to keep crisp). Reheat waffle baker before pouring in more batter. If batter becomes too thick upon standing, thin with a little more buttermilk. Makes eleven 4" by 4" waffles or 4 servings.

Each serving: About 388 calories, 13g protein, 48g carbohydrate, 16g total fat (9g saturated), 142mg cholesterol, 1,065mg sodium.

Pecan Waffles

Prepare as directed above but add **1 tablespoon sugar** and **1 cup pecans (4 ounces),** chopped, to batter. Stir batter for each waffle before pouring.

Sweet Milk Waffles

Prepare as directed above but omit baking soda; use **1 tablespoon baking powder.** Substitute **2 cups milk** for buttermilk.

17

YEAST BREADS & SANDWICHES

YEAST BREADS

There's something magical about mixing flour and yeast with liquid and witnessing the transformation of the ingredients into a tempting loaf. Whether you enjoy the ritual of hands-on kneading or prefer the convenience of using a bread machine, it's always satisfying to make bread at home. In this chapter, you'll find sweet buns for breakfast, firm loaves to slice for sandwiches or toast, rolls for serving alongside main courses, and pizzas that will make a meal.

TYPES OF YEAST

Yeast is the organism that makes bread rise. It reacts with the natural sugars in flour to create carbon dioxide gas, which is trapped in the dough and forces it to expand.

Dry yeast comes in ¼-ounce packages, jars, and in bulk. One ¼-ounce package of dry yeast equals 2¼ teaspoons of fresh yeast.

Fresh yeast is available in foil-wrapped 1-ounce cakes. It is very perishable; refrigerate and use within two weeks. Fresh and dry yeast become activated when mixed with warm water (105° to 115°F). Let the water-yeast mixture stand for about five minutes. It should look creamy, which indicates that the yeast is alive.

Quick-rise yeast cuts the rising time of traditional yeast doughs by about 50 percent. This yeast requires very hot tap water (120° to 130°F) to be activated.

KNOW YOUR FLOURS

A variety of flours can be used for bread making. Different flours contain varying amounts of gluten, which is what gives dough its strength and elasticity. Wheat flours milled from hard winter wheat are high in gluten and great for bread making.

Bread flour is made entirely from hard wheat and makes delicious, chewy, crusty loaves.

All-purpose flour is a blend of hard and soft wheats and yields a more tender bread. All-purpose flour is available unbleached and bleached. Bleaching somewhat reduces the amount of gluten. You can use either bread or unbleached all-purpose flour for bread, but you will need more all-purpose flour as it absorbs less liquid.

Whole-wheat flour and rye *flour* are usually combined with bread or all-purpose flour in yeast doughs.

MIXING THE DOUGH

When mixing bread dough, use a large glass or ceramic bowl and a sturdy wooden spoon, or a heavy-duty electric mixer. Use the paddle to make a soft dough, then switch to the dough hook to knead.

Flour and yeast are the basic ingredients in bread making, but other ingredients play a role. Salt slows the rising and enhances the flavor of bread. Fat (butter, oil, or eggs) adds richness, moistness, and softness to the crumb. Milk gives bread a tender, sweet crumb, and sugar promotes tenderness and a golden crust.

Because yeast works best in a warm environment, have all the ingredients at room temperature. The

Whole Wheat–Walnut Bread

YEAST BREADS & SANDWICHES **459**

amount of flour needed to make a dough will vary according to the type of flour and the amount of humidity in the air (on a humid day, a dough will require more flour).

KNEADING THE DOUGH

Kneading activates the gluten in flour, which strengthens the dough. Knead in just enough flour to prevent the dough from sticking to the work surface. Doughs that are sweet and rich or contain whole-grain flours should be somewhat sticky. If kneading in a heavy-duty mixer, take care not to overknead; six to eight minutes is usually sufficient.

Place the dough on a lightly floured surface. To knead, fold one-fourth of the dough back onto itself, then push it down and away from you with the heel of

your hand. Give the dough a quarter turn and repeat until the dough is smooth and elastic and tiny blisters appear on the surface, which will usually take from eight to ten minutes.

RISING AND SHAPING THE DOUGH

- Choose a bowl large enough to allow the dough to rise until doubled in volume. Grease the bowl lightly with butter, margarine, or oil. Gather the dough into a ball and place in the bowl; turn to coat the top. Cover the bowl with plastic wrap and place in a warm, draft-free spot.
- If you like, you can let the dough rise in the refrigerator for up to twelve hours. Before shaping the dough, let it stand at room temperature for about two hours, or until it loses its chill.

- The dough should rise until doubled. To test, press two fingers about $\frac{1}{2}$ inch deep into the center of the dough. If the indentation stays, the dough has risen sufficiently.
- To punch the dough down, gently push your fist into the center to deflate it.
- The bread is now ready to be shaped. Place the dough on a lightly floured work surface, cover with plastic wrap, and let rest for 15 minutes.
- Grease the pans as directed in the recipe, add the bread, and loosely cover with plastic wrap. Let stand in a warm place until doubled in volume.

BAKING THE BREAD

Position a rack in the center of the oven and preheat for at least ten minutes. If baking two loaves at once, allow at least two inches between the pans.

To prevent bread from bursting during baking, most loaves are slashed with a serrated knife or single-edge razor blade before baking. The tops of loaves can be brushed with beaten whole egg for a golden crust, egg yolk for a dark brown crust, or egg white for a shiny crust. Bread is done when it pulls away from the sides of the pan and is nicely browned. If tapped on the bottom with your knuckles, the bread will sound hollow, and the sides of the loaf should feel crisp and firm.

COOLING AND STORING

Remove the bread from the pan and place, right side up, on a wire rack, away from drafts. If you must have warm bread, let it rest for at least 20 minutes before slicing; hot rolls, however, can be served immediately.

Be sure bread is completely cool before wrapping or freezing. Store soft breads in plastic bags and crusty breads in paper bags at room temperature for up to five days. Most breads freeze well for up to three months. Place in a heavy-duty zip-tight plastic bag or tightly wrap in heavy-duty foil. To thaw, let stand at room temperature for about one hour, or wrap the frozen bread in foil (with an opening at the top so steam can escape) and heat in a 300°F oven for about 20 minutes.

White Bread

The all-American bread: beautiful tall loaves for toast and sandwiches.

Prep: 25 minutes plus rising   Bake: 30 minutes

½	cup warm water (105° to 115°F)
2	packages active dry yeast
1	teaspoon plus ¼ cup sugar
2¼	cups milk, heated to warm (105° to 115°F)
4	tablespoons butter or margarine, softened
1	tablespoon salt
	about 7½ cups all-purpose or bread flour

1. In large bowl, combine warm water, yeast, and 1 teaspoon sugar; stir to dissolve. Let stand until foamy, about 5 minutes. Add milk, butter, remaining ¼ cup sugar, salt, and 4 cups flour. Beat well with wooden spoon. Gradually stir in 3 cups flour to make soft dough.

2. Turn dough onto floured surface and knead until smooth and elastic, about 8 minutes, working in enough of remaining ½ cup flour just to keep dough from sticking.

3. Shape dough into ball; place in greased large bowl, turning dough to grease top. Cover bowl loosely with greased plastic wrap and let rise in warm place (80° to 85°F) until doubled in volume, about 1 hour.

4. Grease two 9" by 5" metal loaf pans. Punch down dough. Turn dough onto lightly floured surface and cut in half. Shape each half into rectangle about 12" by 7". Roll up from a short side. Pinch seam and ends to seal. Place dough, seam side down, in prepared pans. Cover pans loosely with greased plastic wrap and let rise in warm place until almost doubled, about 1 hour.

5. Meanwhile, preheat oven to 400°F. Bake until browned and loaves sound hollow when lightly tapped on bottom, 30 to 35 minutes. Remove loaves from pans; cool on wire racks. Makes 2 loaves, 12 slices each.

Each slice: About 187 calories, 5g protein, 34g carbohydrate, 3g total fat (2g saturated), 8mg cholesterol, 323mg sodium.

Cinnamon-Raisin Bread

Prepare as directed (left) but stir **2 cups dark seedless raisins** into yeast mixture with milk. Spread each rectangle with **2 tablespoons butter or margarine,** softened, leaving ½-inch border. In small cup, combine ⅓ **cup firmly packed brown sugar** and **1 tablespoon ground cinnamon;** sprinkle evenly over butter. Roll up each loaf from a short side. Pinch seam and ends to seal. Makes 2 loaves, 12 slices each.

Each slice: About 244 calories, 5g protein, 47g carbohydrate, 4g total fat (2g saturated), 11mg cholesterol, 335mg sodium.

TROUBLESHOOTING

- *Dough overrises in bowl:* To fix (otherwise, loaf could collapse in the oven or be heavy-textured), turn the dough onto a lightly floured work surface and knead for two to three minutes. Cover, let rest 15 minutes, then shape as directed.
- *Bread is too pale:* Place the loaf directly on the oven rack and bake for five to ten minutes longer.
- *Bread is dry and crumbly:* The dough contained too much flour or the dough overrose.
- *Bread collapses in oven:* The shaped dough overrose in the pan. Don't let dough rise above the pan's rim.
- *Bread has cracks:* The dough contained too much flour or the pan was not large enough.
- *Bread has holes:* The dough wasn't kneaded enough (it's almost impossible to overknead by hand), rising time was too long, or the dough rose in too warm a place.

Olive-Rosemary Loaves

This robust peasant loaf is flavored with Kalamata olives and fresh rosemary. Using high-gluten bread flour guarantees your baking success.

Prep: 30 minutes plus rising   Bake: 30 minutes

1½ cups warm water (105° to 115°F)
 4 tablespoons extra-virgin olive oil
 2 packages active dry yeast
 1 tablespoon sugar
 1 cup Kalamata or green olives, pitted and chopped
 2 tablespoons finely chopped fresh rosemary
 2 teaspoons salt
   about 5 cups bread flour
   or 5¼ cups all-purpose flour

1. In large bowl, combine ½ cup warm water, 3 tablespoons oil, yeast, and sugar; stir to dissolve. Let stand until foamy, about 5 minutes. Stir in remaining 1 cup warm water, olives, rosemary, salt, and 4 cups flour until combined.

2. Turn dough onto lightly floured surface and knead until dough is smooth and elastic, about 8 minutes, working in enough of remaining 1 cup bread flour or 1¼ cups all-purpose flour just to keep dough from sticking.

3. Shape dough into ball; place in greased large bowl, turning dough to grease top. Cover bowl loosely with plastic wrap and let dough rise in warm place (80° to 85°F) until doubled in volume, about 1 hour.

4. Punch down dough. Turn dough onto lightly floured surface and cut in half; cover and let rest 15 minutes for easier shaping. Grease large cookie sheet.

5. Shape each dough half into 7½" by 4" oval; place 3 inches apart on prepared cookie sheet. Cover and let rise in warm place until doubled, about 1 hour.

6. Meanwhile, preheat oven to 400°F. Brush tops of loaves with remaining 1 tablespoon oil. With serrated knife or single-edge razor blade, cut three parallel diagonal slashes across top of each loaf. Bake until golden and loaves sound hollow when tapped on bottom, about 30 minutes. Cool on wire rack. Makes 2 loaves, 12 slices each.

Each slice: About 148 calories, 4g protein, 23g carbohydrate, 4g total fat (1g saturated), 0mg cholesterol, 296mg sodium.

Whole Wheat–Oatmeal Bread

This recipe makes two slightly flat breads with a sweet nutty flavor and dense texture.

Prep: 42 minutes plus rising   Bake: 35 minutes

 2 cups warm water (105° to 115°F)
 2 packages active dry yeast
 ½ teaspoon sugar
 ½ cup honey
 4 tablespoons butter or margarine, softened
 1 cup quick-cooking or old-fashioned oats, uncooked
 1 tablespoon salt
 4 cups whole-wheat flour
 1 large egg
   about 2½ cups all-purpose flour
   or 2 cups bread flour

1. In large bowl, combine ½ cup warm water, yeast, and sugar; stir to dissolve. Let stand until foamy, about 5 minutes. Stir in remaining 1½ cups warm water, honey, butter, oats, salt, and 2 cups whole-wheat flour until smooth. Stir in egg. Gradually stir in remaining 2 cups whole-wheat flour, then 2 cups all-purpose flour or 1½ cups bread flour.

2. On lightly floured surface, knead dough until smooth, about 7 minutes, working in enough of remaining ½ cup flour just to keep dough from sticking.

3. Shape dough into ball; place in greased large bowl, turning dough to grease top. Cover bowl loosely with plastic wrap and let rise in warm place (80° to 85°F) until doubled in volume, about 1 hour.

4. Punch down dough. Turn dough onto lightly floured surface and cut in half; cover and let rest 15 minutes. Grease large cookie sheet.

5. Shape each dough half into 7" by 4" oval; place on prepared cookie sheet. Cover with damp kitchen towel; let rise in warm place until doubled, about 1 hour.

6. Meanwhile, preheat oven to 350°F. With serrated knife, cut three to five ¼-inch-deep crisscross slashes across top of each loaf. Lightly dust tops of loaves with all-purpose flour. Bake until loaves sound hollow when tapped on bottom, 35 to 40 minutes. Transfer to wire racks to cool. Makes 2 oval loaves, 12 slices each.

Each slice: About 177 calories, 5g protein, 33g carbohydrate, 3g total fat (1g saturated), 14mg cholesterol, 315mg sodium.

Whole Wheat–Walnut Bread
(Pictured on page 458)

Prepare as directed (left), **using ½ cup milk,** heated to warm (105° to 115°F), instead of water and only **1 package active dry yeast.** Stir in **1 cup warm water, 3 tablespoons butter or margarine,** softened, **2 tablespoons molasses, 1½ teaspoons salt, 2 cups whole-wheat flour,** and only **½ cup all-purpose or bread flour.** Then, gradually, stir in **¾ cup all-purpose or bread flour.** Proceed as directed, but after punching down dough in Step 4, knead in **2 cups walnuts,** toasted and coarsely chopped. In Step 5, reduce rising time to about 45 minutes. Preheat oven to 375°F. Just before baking, with sharp knife or single-edge razor blade, cut three 3-inch-long and ¼-inch-deep diagonal slashes across tops of loaves. Bake loaves about 30 minutes.

Each slice: About 155 calories, 4g protein, 17g carbohydrate, 9g total fat (2g saturated), 5mg cholesterol, 165mg sodium.

Bread-Machine Multigrain Loaf

Bread machines have become the favorite appliance of many home bakers. This recipe uses the setting for a 1½-pound whole-wheat loaf. Be sure to add the ingredients according to your machine's instructions.

Prep: 10 minutes   Bake: per bread machine's instructions

- 2 cups whole-wheat flour
- 1 cup all-purpose flour
- ¼ cup bulgur wheat
- ¼ cup old-fashioned oats, uncooked
- 2 tablespoons toasted wheat germ
- 1½ teaspoons salt
- 1¼ cups buttermilk
- ¼ cup honey
- 3 tablespoons vegetable oil
- 1 package active dry yeast

Prepare recipe according to your bread machine's instructions. Makes 1 loaf, 16 slices.

Each slice: About 143 calories, 4g protein, 25g carbohydrate, 3g total fat (0g saturated), 1mg cholesterol, 240mg sodium.

Brioche

Rich and buttery brioche, a classic in French bread making, rests overnight in the refrigerator and is put into a preheated oven the next morning in time for breakfast. A heavy-duty mixer is a must for the stiff, sticky dough. It makes excellent French toast and bread pudding.

**Prep: 25 minutes plus rising and overnight to refrigerate
Bake: 30 minutes**

- ¾ cup milk, heated to warm (105° to 115°F)
- 1 package active dry yeast
- 1 teaspoon plus ¼ cup sugar
- 4 cups bread flour or all-purpose flour
- 1 teaspoon salt
- 6 large eggs
- 1 cup butter (2 sticks), softened and cut into pieces (do not use margarine)

1. In large bowl of heavy-duty mixer, combine warm milk, yeast, and 1 teaspoon sugar; stir to dissolve. Let stand until foamy, about 5 minutes.

2. Stir in remaining ¼ cup sugar, 1 cup flour, and salt until blended. With mixer at low speed, beat in 1 egg. Continue beating, alternately adding remaining 3 cups flour and remaining 5 eggs until well incorporated. Gradually beat in butter until smooth.

3. Transfer dough to lightly buttered large bowl. Cover bowl with greased plastic wrap and let rise in warm place (80° to 85°F) until doubled in volume, about 2½ hours.

4. Meanwhile, lightly grease two 8½" by 4½" metal loaf pans. Punch down dough. Divide dough in half; place in prepared pans. Cover pans with lightly greased plastic wrap; refrigerate overnight.

5. Preheat oven to 350°F. Bake loaves until golden brown and toothpick inserted in center comes out clean, about 30 minutes. Removes loaves from pans; cool on wire racks. Makes 2 loaves, 12 slices each.

Each slice: About 188 calories, 5g protein, 19g carbohydrate, 10g total fat (6g saturated), 75mg cholesterol, 197mg sodium.

Quick-and-Easy Anadama Bread

We've streamlined this Early American cornmeal-molasses bread by turning it into a batter bread and using quick-rise yeast.

Prep: 25 minutes plus rising   Bake: 30 minutes

- 3 cups all-purpose flour
- ⅓ cup cornmeal
- 1 teaspoon salt
- 1 package quick-rise yeast
- 1 cup water
- ¼ cup light (mild) molasses
- 3 tablespoons butter or margarine, softened
- 1 large egg

1. In large bowl, with wire whisk, stir 1 cup flour, cornmeal, salt, and yeast. In 1-quart saucepan, heat water and molasses over low heat until very warm (120° to 130°F). Meanwhile, grease 2-quart soufflé dish or deep casserole.

2. With mixer at low speed, gradually beat molasses mixture and butter into flour mixture just until blended. Increase speed to medium; beat 2 minutes, occasionally scraping bowl with rubber spatula. Beat in egg and 1 cup flour to make thick batter; continue beating 2 minutes, frequently scraping bowl. With wooden spoon, stir in remaining 1 cup flour to make soft dough.

3. Place dough in prepared soufflé dish. Cover with plastic wrap and let rise in warm place (80° to 85°F) until doubled, about 1 hour.

4. Meanwhile, preheat oven to 375°F. Bake bread until browned and loaf sounds hollow when lightly tapped on bottom, 30 to 35 minutes. Remove loaf from soufflé dish; cool on wire rack. Makes 1 round loaf, 10 slices.

Each slice: About 219 calories, 5g protein, 38g carbohydrate, 5g total fat (2g saturated), 31mg cholesterol, 279mg sodium.

Double-Cheese Batter Bread

This simple batter bread gets its fabulous flavor from shredded cheddar and freshly grated Parmesan cheese. It makes terrific toast.

Prep: 25 minutes plus rising   Bake: 35 minutes

- ¾ cup warm water (105° to 115°F)
- 1 package active dry yeast
- 1 teaspoon plus 1 tablespoon sugar
- 6 ounces extrasharp Cheddar cheese, shredded (1½ cups)
- ¼ cup freshly grated Parmesan cheese
- ½ teaspoon salt
- 2½ cups all-purpose flour
- 2 large eggs

1. In large bowl, combine warm water, yeast, and 1 teaspoon sugar; stir to dissolve. Let stand until foamy, about 5 minutes. With wooden spoon or mixer at low speed, stir in Cheddar, Parmesan, remaining 1 tablespoon sugar, salt, and 1½ cups flour just until blended.

2. Separate 1 egg. Cover egg white and reserve in refrigerator. Beat remaining egg and remaining egg yolk into batter.

3. Stir batter vigorously or increase speed to medium and beat 3 minutes, frequently scraping bowl with rubber spatula. Stir in remaining 1 cup flour to make stiff batter that leaves side of bowl.

4. Cover bowl loosely with greased plastic wrap; let dough rise in warm place (80° to 85°F) until doubled in volume, about 1 hour.

5. Grease deep 1½-quart round casserole. Stir down batter; turn into prepared casserole. Cover loosely with greased plastic wrap; let rise in warm place until doubled in volume, about 45 minutes.

6. Meanwhile, preheat oven to 350°F. Beat reserved egg white; brush over top of loaf. Bake bread until browned and loaf sounds hollow when tapped on bottom, about 35 minutes. Remove loaf from casserole and cool on wire rack. Makes 1 loaf, 12 slices.

Each slice: About 185 calories, 8g protein, 22g carbohydrate, 7g total fat (4g saturated), 52mg cholesterol, 234mg sodium.

Breadsticks

3. Meanwhile, preheat oven to 375°F. Grease two large cookie sheets. Cut dough in half. Cover one half; cut remaining half into 32 equal pieces. Shape each piece into 12-inch-long rope; place 1 inch apart on prepared cookie sheets. If not using caraway seeds, sprinkle with sesame seeds, poppy seeds, or Parmesan.

4. Bake breadsticks until golden and crisp, about 20 minutes, rotating cookie sheets between upper and lower oven racks halfway through baking. Transfer to wire racks to cool. Repeat with remaining dough. Makes 64 breadsticks.

Each breadstick: About 52 calories, 1g protein, 7g carbohydrate, 2g total fat (0g saturated), 0mg cholesterol, 91mg sodium.

Rosemary-Fennel Breadsticks

Prepare as directed but omit caraway, sesame, or poppy seeds or Parmesan. In Step 1, stir **2 teaspoons fennel seeds,** crushed, **1 teaspoon dried rosemary leaves,** crumbled, and ½ **teaspoon coarsely ground black pepper** into dough. Proceed as directed.

Breadsticks

These breadsticks can be made well ahead. They keep perfectly for up to two weeks in an airtight container.

Prep: 40 minutes plus resting   Bake: 20 minutes per batch

> 2 **packages quick-rise yeast**
> 2½ **teaspoons salt**
>   **about 4¾ cups all-purpose flour**
> 1⅓ **cups very warm water (120° to 130°F)**
> ½ **cup olive oil**
> 3 **tablespoons caraway, sesame, or poppy seeds, or freshly grated Parmesan cheese**

1. In large bowl, combine yeast, salt, and 2 cups flour. With wooden spoon, stir in very warm water; beat vigorously 1 minute. Stir in oil. Gradually stir in 2¼ cups flour. Stir in caraway seeds, if using.

2. Turn dough onto lightly floured surface and knead until smooth and elastic, about 8 minutes, working in enough of remaining ½ cup flour just to keep dough from sticking. Cover dough loosely with plastic wrap; let rest 10 minutes.

SPECIAL BUTTERS FOR YEAST BREADS

Try these delicious butters on your freshly baked bread.

Marmalade or Strawberry Preserves Butter
In small bowl, with mixer at medium speed, beat 1 cup butter or margarine (2 sticks), softened, and ⅓ cup orange marmalade or strawberry preserves until blended. Cover and refrigerate up to one week. To use, let stand at room temperature 30 minutes for easier spreading. Makes about 1⅓ cups.

Whipped Honey Butter
Prepare as directed for Marmalade Butter but omit marmalade and beat in 2 tablespoons honey and ⅛ teaspoon ground cinnamon. Makes about 1¼ cups.

Fresh Strawberry Butter
Prepare as directed for Marmalade Butter but omit marmalade and beat in ½ pint strawberries, hulled and crushed, and 3 tablespoons confectioners' sugar. Cover and refrigerate up to 2 days. Makes about 2¼ cups.

Refrigerator Rolls

Be sure to offer a basket of these soft, buttery rolls at your next holiday feast. (The dough can be made ahead and refrigerated overnight.)

Prep: 35 minutes plus rising   Bake: 15 minutes

- 1½ cups warm water (105° to 115°F)
- 2 packages active dry yeast
- 1 teaspoon plus ½ cup sugar
- ½ cup (1 stick) plus 2 tablespoons butter or margarine, softened
- 2 teaspoons salt
  about 6 cups all-purpose flour
- 1 large egg
  vegetable oil for brushing

1. In large bowl, combine ½ cup warm water, yeast, and 1 teaspoon sugar; stir to dissolve. Let stand until foamy, about 5 minutes. Stir in remaining 1 cup warm water, ½ cup butter, remaining ½ cup sugar, salt, and 2¼ cups flour. With wooden spoon or mixer at low speed, gradually beat in egg and ¾ cup flour; continue beating 2 minutes, scraping bowl frequently with rubber spatula. Stir in 2½ cups flour to make soft dough.

2. Turn dough onto lightly floured surface and knead until smooth and elastic, about 10 minutes, working in enough of remaining ½ cup flour just to keep dough from sticking to surface.

3. Shape dough into ball; place in greased large bowl, turning dough to grease top. Cover bowl loosely with plastic wrap and let rise in warm place (80° to 85°F) until doubled in volume, about 1½ hours.

4. Punch down dough and turn; brush with oil. Cover bowl tightly with greased plastic wrap and refrigerate overnight or up to 24 hours. (Or, if you like, after punching down dough, shape into rolls as in Step 5. Cover and let rise until doubled, about 45 minutes, and bake as in Step 6.)

5. About 2½ hours before serving, remove dough from refrigerator. Grease 15½" by 10½" deep roasting pan. Cut dough into 30 equal pieces; shape into balls. Place balls in prepared pan; cover pan and let rise in warm place until doubled, about 1½ hours.

6. Meanwhile, preheat oven to 400°F. Bake until golden and rolls sound hollow when lightly tapped on bottom, 15 to 20 minutes. Melt remaining 2 tablespoons butter. With pastry brush, lightly brush melted butter over hot rolls. Serve warm. Makes 30 rolls.

Each roll: About 147 calories, 3g protein, 23g carbohydrate, 5g total fat (3g saturated), 17mg cholesterol, 197mg sodium.

Parker House Rolls

Prepare dough as directed in Steps 1 through 4 (left). About 2½ hours before serving, melt **½ cup (1 stick) butter or margarine** in large shallow baking pan. On lightly floured surface, with floured rolling pin, roll out dough ½ inch thick. With floured 2¾-inch round biscuit cutter, cut out as many rounds as possible. Knead trimmings together; reroll and cut out more rounds. Dip both sides of each dough round in melted butter; fold rounds in half and arrange in rows in prepared roasting pan, letting rolls touch each other. Cover and let rise in warm place until doubled, about 1½ hours. Bake rolls 18 to 20 minutes. Serve warm, or cool on wire racks to serve later. Makes about 40 rolls.

Each roll: About 127 calories, 2g protein, 17g carbohydrate, 5g total fat (3g saturated), 18mg cholesterol, 165mg sodium.

Oatmeal-Molasses Rolls

Topped with a butter-molasses glaze and sprinkled with oats, these light rolls look as good as they taste.

Prep: 1 hour plus rising   Bake: 45 minutes

- 1 cup boiling water
- 1 cup plus 2 tablespoons old-fashioned oats, uncooked
- ¾ cup warm water (105° to 115°F)
- 1 package active dry yeast
- 1 teaspoon sugar
- 5 tablespoons butter or margarine, softened
- ⅓ cup plus 2 teaspoons light (mild) molasses
- 1½ teaspoons salt
  about 4¼ cups all-purpose flour

1. In medium bowl, pour boiling water over 1 cup oats, stirring to combine. Let stand until oats have absorbed water and mixture has cooled to warm (105° to 115°F), about 10 minutes.

2. Meanwhile, in small bowl, combine warm water, yeast, and sugar; stir to dissolve. Let mixture stand until foamy, about 5 minutes.

3. In large bowl, with mixer at low speed, beat 4 tablespoons butter until creamy. Add $\frac{1}{3}$ cup molasses, beating until combined. Beat in oat mixture, yeast mixture, and salt just until blended. Gradually beat in 2 cups flour just until blended. With wooden spoon, stir in 2 cups more flour. Turn dough onto lightly floured surface and knead until smooth and elastic, about 5 minutes, working in enough of remaining $\frac{1}{4}$ cup flour just to keep dough from sticking.

4. Shape dough into ball; place in greased large bowl, turning dough to grease top. Cover bowl loosely with plastic wrap and let rise in warm place (80° to 85°F) until doubled in volume, about 1 hour. Grease 13" by 9" baking pan.

5. Punch down dough. On lightly floured surface, cut dough into 18 equal pieces. Shape each piece into ball and arrange in prepared pan in three rows of six balls each. Cover pan and let rise in warm place until doubled, about 1 hour.

6. Meanwhile, preheat oven to 350°F. Bake rolls until very lightly browned, about 30 minutes.

7. Melt remaining 1 tablespoon butter. Stir in remaining 2 teaspoons molasses.

8. After rolls have baked 30 minutes, remove from oven. Brush with molasses mixture and sprinkle with remaining 2 tablespoons oats. Bake rolls until golden, about 15 minutes longer. Serve warm, or cool on wire racks to serve later. Reheat if desired. Makes 18 rolls.

Each roll: About 183 calories, 4g protein, 32g carbohydrate, 4g total fat (2g saturated), 9mg cholesterol, 230mg sodium.

Basic Pizza Dough

Try making this dough the night before to save some time; double the recipe and freeze half to have on hand for another meal. All-purpose flour produces a light crust, and bread flour gives it a chewy texture.

Prep: 40 minutes plus rising   Bake: 15 minutes

1¼	cups warm water (105° to 115°F)
1	package active dry yeast
1	teaspoon sugar
2	tablespoons olive oil
2	teaspoons salt
	about 4 cups all-purpose flour
	or 3½ cups bread flour
	cornmeal for sprinkling

1. In large bowl, combine ¼ cup warm water, yeast, and sugar; stir to dissolve. Let stand until foamy, about 5 minutes.

2. With wooden spoon, stir in remaining 1 cup warm water, oil, salt, and 1½ cups flour until smooth. Gradually add 2 cups all-purpose flour or 1½ cups bread flour, stirring until dough leaves side of bowl. Turn dough onto lightly floured surface and knead until smooth and elastic, about 10 minutes, working in enough of remaining ½ cup flour just to keep dough from sticking.

3. Shape dough into ball; place in greased large bowl, turning dough to grease top. Cover bowl loosely with plastic wrap and let rise in warm place (80° to 85°F) until doubled in volume, about 1 hour.

4. Punch down dough. Turn onto lightly floured surface and cut in half; cover and let rest 15 minutes. Or, if not using right away, place dough in greased large bowl, cover loosely with greased plastic wrap, and refrigerate up to 24 hours.

5. Sprinkle two large cookie sheets with cornmeal. Shape each dough half into ball. On one prepared cookie sheet, with floured rolling pin, roll one ball into 14" by 10" rectangle. Fold edges in to form 1-inch rim. Repeat to make second pizza. Makes enough dough for 2 large pizzas, 4 main-dish servings each.

Each ⅛ dough: About 262 calories, 7g protein, 49g carbohydrate, 4g total fat (1g saturated), 0mg cholesterol, 584mg sodium.

Cheese Pizza

The champ of all pizzas. If you like, sprinkle the top with 1 teaspoon dried oregano or 2 to 3 tablespoons chopped fresh basil just before serving.

Prep: 40 minutes plus rising and resting   Bake: 15 minutes

Basic Pizza Dough (page 467)
1   cup Marinara Sauce (page 222)
2   tablespoons freshly grated Parmesan cheese
4   ounces mozzarella cheese, shredded (1 cup)

1. Prepare pizza dough (if using Basic Pizza Dough, reserve half of dough for separate pizza).

2. Meanwhile, prepare Marinara Sauce.

3. Shape pizza dough as directed. Sprinkle with Parmesan. Spread sauce over Parmesan and top with mozzarella.

4. Preheat oven to 450°F. Let pizza dough pizza rest 20 minutes. Bake until crust is golden, 15 to 20 minutes. Makes 4 main-dish servings.

Each serving: About 391 calories, 14g protein, 55g carbohydrate, 12g total fat (5g saturated), 25mg cholesterol, 899mg sodium.

MORE PIZZA TOPPINGS

To keep the crust crispy, scatter cheese over the dough before topping with other ingredients. Sprinkle fresh herbs over the pizza just before serving.
Try these delicious combinations:

- grilled radicchio, cooked crumbled pancetta or bacon, crumbled goat cheese, chopped fresh sage
- sautéed cremini mushrooms, cooked sweet Italian sausage, thinly sliced fresh mozzarella cheese, dried oregano
- coarsely chopped grilled eggplant, marinated artichoke hearts, chopped plum tomatoes, shredded mozzarella cheese, fresh basil leaves
- thinly sliced mozzarella, crumbled gorgonzola, spoonfuls of ricotta, freshly ground black pepper, fresh basil leaves

Focaccia

This bread's wonderfully chewy texture and fine crumb are the result of three risings. Sprinkle 2 tablespoons chopped fresh sage or 1 tablespoon chopped fresh rosemary over the focaccia just before baking, if you wish.

Prep: 25 minutes plus rising   Bake: 18 minutes

1½ cups warm water (105° to 115°F)
1   package active dry yeast
1   teaspoon sugar
5   tablespoons extra-virgin olive oil
1½ teaspoons table salt
3¾ cups all-purpose flour or 3½ cups bread flour
1   teaspoon kosher salt or coarse sea salt

1. In large bowl, combine ½ cup warm water, yeast, and sugar; stir to dissolve. Let stand until foamy, about 5 minutes. Add remaining 1 cup warm water, 2 tablespoons oil, table salt, and flour; stir to combine.

2. Turn dough onto floured surface and knead until smooth and elastic, about 7 minutes. Dough will be soft; do not add more flour.

3. Shape dough into ball; place in greased large bowl, turning dough to grease top. Cover bowl loosely with plastic wrap and let stand in warm place (80° to 85°F) until doubled in volume, about 1 hour.

4. Lightly oil 15½" by 10½" jelly-roll pan. Punch down dough and pat into prepared pan. Cover loosely with plastic wrap and let rise in warm place until doubled, about 45 minutes.

5. With fingertips, make deep indentations, 1 inch apart, over entire surface of dough, almost to bottom of pan. Drizzle with remaining 3 tablespoons oil; sprinkle with kosher salt. Cover  loosely with plastic wrap; let rise in warm place until doubled, about 45 minutes.

6. Meanwhile, preheat oven to 450°F. Bake focaccia on lowest oven rack until bottom is crusty and top is lightly browned, about 18 minutes. Transfer focaccia to wire rack to cool. Makes 12 servings.

Each serving: About 201 calories, 4g protein, 31g carbohydrate, 7g total fat (1g saturated), 0mg cholesterol, 537mg sodium.

Tomato Focaccia

Prepare as directed but drizzle with only **1 tablespoon olive oil.** Arrange **1 pound ripe plum tomatoes,** cut into ¼-inch-thick slices, over top; sprinkle with **1 tablespoon chopped fresh rosemary or 1 teaspoon dried rosemary,** crumbled, **½ teaspoon coarsely ground black pepper,** and **1 teaspoon kosher salt.** Bake as directed.

Red Pepper Focaccia

Prepare as directed but do not sprinkle with kosher salt. In 12-inch skillet, heat **1 tablespoon olive oil** over medium heat. Add **4 red peppers,** sliced, and **¼ teaspoon salt** and cook, stirring frequently, until tender, about 20 minutes. Cool to room temperature. Sprinkle over focaccia just before baking.

Dried Tomato and Olive Focaccia

Prepare as directed but do not sprinkle with kosher salt. Combine **½ cup Gaeta olives,** pitted, **¼ cup drained oil-packed dried tomatoes,** coarsely chopped, and **1½ teaspoons kosher salt.** Sprinkle over focaccia just before baking.

Onion Focaccia

Prepare as directed but do not sprinkle with kosher salt. In 12-inch skillet, heat **2 teaspoons olive oil** over medium heat. Add **2 medium onions,** sliced, **1 teaspoon sugar,** and **½ teaspoon salt** and cook, stirring frequently, until golden brown, about 20 minutes. Cool to room temperature. Spread over focaccia just before baking.

Focaccia

Pissaladière

A specialty of Nice, France, this pizzalike tart is usually served as a snack or appetizer, but it makes a nice supper or brunch dish too. You can prepare the dough in advance. Let it rise once, then freeze for up to three months. Defrost and follow the recipe.

Prep: 40 minutes plus rising   Cook/Bake: 55 minutes

- 1 cup warm water (105° to 115°F)
- 1 package active dry yeast
- 3 cups all-purpose flour
- 1¾ teaspoons salt
- 2 tablespoons olive oil
- 2 pounds onions, chopped
- 1 can (2 ounces) anchovy fillets, rinsed, drained, and coarsely chopped
- ⅓ cup pitted and halved Kalamata or Gaeta olives

1. In cup, combine ¼ cup warm water and yeast; stir to dissolve. Let stand until foamy, about 5 minutes.

2. In large bowl, with wire whisk, stir flour and 1½ teaspoons salt. Stir in yeast mixture, remaining ¾ cup warm water, and 1 tablespoon oil. Turn dough onto lightly floured surface and knead until smooth and elastic, about 8 minutes. Shape dough into ball; place in greased large bowl, turning to grease top. Cover bowl with plastic wrap and let rise in warm place (80° to 85°F) until doubled in volume, about 45 minutes.

3. Meanwhile, in 12-inch skillet, heat remaining 1 tablespoon oil over low heat. Add onions and remaining ¼ teaspoon salt and cook, stirring frequently, until onions are very soft and golden, about 30 minutes. Remove from heat; set aside to cool.

4. Grease 15½" by 10½" jelly-roll pan. Punch down dough and pat into prepared pan. Cover loosely with plastic wrap and let rise 30 minutes.

5. Meanwhile, preheat oven to 425°F. With fingertips, make shallow indentations over surface of dough. Toss onions and anchovies and spread mixture over top. Place olives on onion mixture at 2-inch intervals. Bake on lowest oven rack until crust is golden, about 25 minutes. Cut into 32 squares. Makes 32 appetizers.

Each square: About 73 calories, 2g protein, 12g carbohydrate, 2g total fat (0g saturated), 1mg cholesterol, 205mg sodium.

Soft Pretzels

These soft pretzels, a specialty of Pennsylvania Dutch country that has swept the nation, are best served warm with mustard. Freeze them after shaping, if you like. Let them thaw, then dip in the baking-soda mixture and bake as directed. The pretzels can be sprinkled with sesame or poppy seeds in addition to the salt.

Prep: 30 minutes plus rising   Bake: 16 minutes

- 2 cups warm water (105° to 115°F)
- 1 package active dry yeast
- 1 teaspoon sugar
- 1 teaspoon salt
- about 4 cups all-purpose flour
- 2 tablespoons baking soda
- 1 tablespoon kosher or coarse sea salt

1. In large bowl, combine 1½ cups warm water, yeast, and sugar; stir to dissolve. Let stand until foamy, about 5 minutes. Add salt and 2 cups flour; beat well with wooden spoon. Gradually stir in 1½ cups flour to make soft dough.

2. Turn dough onto floured surface and knead until smooth and elastic, about 6 minutes, kneading in enough of remaining ½ cup flour just to keep dough from sticking.

3. Shape dough into ball; place in greased large bowl, turning dough to grease top. Cover bowl with plastic wrap and let rise in warm place (80° to 85°F) until doubled in volume, about 30 minutes.

4. Meanwhile, preheat oven to 400°F. Grease two cookie sheets. Punch down dough and cut into 12 equal pieces. Roll each piece into 24-inch-long rope. Shape ropes into loop-shaped pretzels.

5. In small bowl, whisk remaining ½ cup warm water and baking soda until soda has dissolved.

6. Dip pretzels in baking-soda mixture and place 1½ inches apart on prepared cookie sheets; sprinkle with kosher salt. Bake, rotating cookie sheets between upper and lower oven racks halfway through baking, until browned, 16 to 18 minutes. Serve pretzels warm, or transfer to wire racks to cool. Makes 12 pretzels.

Each pretzel: About 167 calories, 5g protein, 33g carbohydrate, 1g total fat (0g saturated), 0mg cholesterol, 1,192mg sodium.

Overnight Sticky Buns

Make these rich, yummy rolls the night before serving. Let them rise overnight in the refrigerator, then bake and serve for breakfast. You can wrap any leftovers in foil and freeze; reheat, still wrapped, in a 350°F oven for 15 to 20 minutes.

Prep: 1 hour plus rising and overnight to refrigerate
Bake: 30 minutes

Dough

- ¼ cup warm water (105° to 115°F)
- 1 package active dry yeast
- 1 teaspoon plus ¼ cup granulated sugar
- ¾ cup milk
- 4 tablespoons butter or margarine, softened
- 3 large egg yolks
- 1 teaspoon salt
  about 4 cups all-purpose flour

Filling

- ½ cup packed brown sugar
- ¼ cup dried currants
- 1 tablespoon ground cinnamon
- 4 tablespoons butter or margarine, melted

Topping

- ⅔ cup packed brown sugar
- 3 tablespoons butter or margarine
- 2 tablespoons light corn syrup
- 2 tablespoons honey
- 1¼ cups pecans (5 ounces), coarsely chopped

1. Prepare dough: In cup, combine warm water, yeast, and 1 teaspoon granulated sugar; stir to dissolve. Let stand until foamy, about 5 minutes.

2. In large bowl, with mixer at low speed, blend yeast mixture with milk, butter, remaining ¼ cup granulated sugar, egg yolks, salt, and 3 cups flour until blended. With wooden spoon, stir in ¾ cup flour.

3. Turn dough onto lightly floured surface and knead until smooth and elastic, about 5 minutes, working in enough of remaining ¼ cup flour just to keep dough from sticking.

4. Shape dough into ball; place in greased large bowl, turning dough to grease top. Cover bowl loosely with plastic wrap and let rise in warm place (80° to 85°F) until doubled, about 1 hour.

5. Meanwhile, prepare filling: In small bowl, combine brown sugar, currants, and cinnamon; set aside. Reserve melted butter.

6. Prepare topping: In 1-quart saucepan, combine brown sugar, butter, corn syrup, and honey; heat over low heat, stirring occasionally, until brown sugar and butter have melted. Grease 13" by 9" baking pan; pour melted brown-sugar mixture into pan and sprinkle evenly with pecans.

7. Punch down dough. Turn dough onto lightly floured surface; cover and let rest 15 minutes. Roll dough into 18" by 12" rectangle. Brush dough with reserved melted butter and sprinkle with currant mixture. Starting at a long side, roll up dough jelly-roll fashion; place, seam side down, on surface. Cut dough crosswise into 20 slices.

8. Place slices, cut side down, on brown-sugar mixture in prepared pan in four rows of five slices each. Cover and refrigerate at least 12 hours or up to 15 hours.

9. Preheat oven to 375°F. Bake buns until golden, about 30 minutes. Remove from oven. Immediately place serving tray or jelly-roll pan over top of baking pan and invert; remove pan. Let buns cool slightly to serve warm, or cool on wire racks to serve later. Makes 20 buns.

Each bun: About 291 calories, 4g protein, 42g carbohydrate, 13g total fat (5g saturated), 50mg cholesterol, 195mg sodium.

ORIGINS OF STICKY BUNS

German-speaking immigrants brought with them their recipes for beloved foods, including sweets. These buns were made popular in the 19th century by the Pennsylvania Dutch, who settled in various parts of Pennsylvania, but especially around Philadelphia. Cinnamon buns, sticky buns, stickies, *schnecken*, and icing-topped sugar buns are all similar and all scrumptious.

SANDWICHES

The first sandwich, created in 1762, was a matter of necessity. The Earl of Sandwich, an enthusiastic gambler, requested bread and meat dishes that he could consume while continuing to gamble, and at that moment the sandwich was born. Every culture has its sandwich: The Italians relish their paninis and calzones, the Mexicans enjoy burritos, bagels and lox are a Jewish tradition, and the Croque Madame and Croque Monsieur are standard fare in Paris bistros. These days, you don't even need sliced bread to make a sandwich. It could just as easily be a filled and rolled-up flour tortilla. And the meat is optional too: No one thinks twice about eating a pita pocket filled with a crisp Greek salad or a vegetable frittata tucked between thin slabs of herbed focaccia.

You can perk up an old standard by adding a tasty new condiment like one of our flavored mayonnaises (try Ginger-Sesame Mayonnaise or Chipotle Mayonnaise), or by serving it on your own home-baked bread.

SAFE SANDWICHES

The brown-bag lunch is an American tradition, but it should be carefully packed to ensure that the contents remain tasty and safe to eat.

If you are making a lot of sandwiches, use this simple assembly-line technique: Line up the bread slices in rows, apply the spreads, top with the fillings, and cover with the remaining bread. Wrap the sandwiches tightly in waxed paper or foil, or place in zip-tight sandwich bags. Some ingredients, such as tomatoes, lettuce, and cucumbers, can make bread soggy, so it's best to wrap these items separately and to add them to the sandwich just before eating.

Sandwiches containing meat, poultry, fish, or eggs should not stand at room temperature for longer than two hours; warm temperatures encourage the growth of salmonella. Pack these sandwiches in insulated lunch boxes with portable ice packs to keep them at a safe cold temperature.

FLAVORED MAYONNAISE

It's easy to transform mayonnaise into a luscious condiment that will boost the flavor of any simple sandwich.

Roasted–Red Pepper Mayonnaise
1/2 cup mayonnaise, 1/4 cup finely chopped roasted red pepper, and 1 tablespoon chopped fresh parsley

Lemon Mayonnaise
1/2 cup mayonnaise, 1 1/2 teaspoons fresh lemon juice, 1 teaspoon freshly grated lemon peel, and pinch ground black pepper

Ginger-Sesame Mayonnaise
1/2 cup mayonnaise, 2 small green onions, finely chopped, 1 tablespoon chopped fresh cilantro, 1 teaspoon minced, peeled fresh ginger, and 1/4 teaspoon Asian sesame oil

Chutney Mayonnaise
1/2 cup mayonnaise, 1/4 cup mango chutney, finely chopped, and 1 tablespoon chopped fresh cilantro

Basil Mayonnaise
1/2 cup mayonnaise, 1/4 cup chopped fresh basil, and 1/8 teaspoon ground black pepper

Chipotle Mayonnaise
1/2 cup mayonnaise, 1 finely chopped chipotle chile in adobo, 1 teaspoon adobo sauce, and 1/4 teaspoon ground cumin

Pesto Mayonnaise
1/2 cup mayonnaise and 1 tablespoon plus 1 teaspoon pesto

Horseradish Mayonnaise
1/2 cup mayonnaise, 1 tablespoon bottled white horseradish, and 1 teaspoon fresh lemon juice

Pickled Jalapeño Mayonnaise
1/2 cup mayonnaise, 1/4 cup chopped fresh cilantro, and 1 to 2 pickled jalapeños, finely chopped

Health Club Sandwiches

This carrot-sprout-and-bean-spread combo will satisfy your palate and ease your conscience.

Prep: 25 minutes   Cook: 2 minutes

- 2 tablespoons olive oil
- 2 teaspoons plus 1 tablespoon fresh lemon juice
- 1 teaspoon honey
- 1/8 teaspoon ground black pepper
- 3 carrots, peeled and shredded (1 cup)
- 2 cups alfalfa sprouts
- 1 garlic clove, finely chopped
- 1/2 teaspoon ground cumin
- pinch ground red pepper (cayenne)
- 1 can (15 to 19 ounces) garbanzo beans, rinsed and drained
- 1 tablespoon water
- 12 slices multigrain bread, lightly toasted
- 1 large ripe tomato (12 ounces), thinly sliced
- 1 bunch watercress, tough stems trimmed

1. In medium bowl, stir 1 tablespoon oil, 2 teaspoons lemon juice, honey, and ground black pepper until mixed. Add carrots and alfalfa sprouts; toss until mixed and evenly coated with dressing.

2. In 2-quart saucepan, heat remaining 1 tablespoon oil over medium heat. Add garlic, cumin, and ground red pepper and cook until very fragrant. Stir in garbanzo beans and remove from heat. Add remaining 1 tablespoon lemon juice and water; mash beans to a coarse puree.

3. Spread garbanzo-bean mixture on 8 toast slices. Place tomato slices and watercress over 4 garbanzo-topped toast slices. Top remaining 4 garbanzo-topped slices with alfalfa-sprout mixture and place on watercress-topped bread. Cover with 4 remaining toast slices. Cut sandwiches in half. Makes 4 main-dish servings.

Each serving: About 379 calories, 14g protein, 57g carbohydrate, 12g total fat (2g saturated), 0mg cholesterol, 545mg sodium.

Health Club Sandwiches

SLIM SANDWICHES

Test Kitchen Tip
A sandwich doesn't have to be calorie- and fat-laden. Replace high-fat mayonnaise with one of the reduced-fat varieties (stir in some chopped fresh herbs for a flavor lift). Or hold the mayo and spread your bread with naturally lowfat mustard or try a spread of nonfat yogurt mixed with a bit of mustard. Chutney, delicious by itself or when blended with mayonnaise or mustard, adds a sweet-and-spicy dimension to a sandwich.

Many lunch meats are high in calories and sodium. Look for alternatives such as grilled vegetables or skinless chicken breast, freshly roasted turkey breast, shrimp in lowfat dressing, or water-packed tuna. Cheese is another high-fat sandwich ingredient that should be enjoyed in moderation.

Instead of ordering your sandwich at the deli counter, take a stroll by the salad bar. There are lots of candidates for a terrific sandwich just waiting to be piled onto bread (or into a pita) and drizzled with lowfat dressing: Artichoke hearts, roasted peppers, peperoncini, sprouts, shredded carrots, asparagus, sliced tomatoes, and tofu are all smart choices.

Perfectly Simple Tomato Sandwiches

These sandwiches are fabulous just the way they are, but we also like them with a few sprigs of watercress tucked in. Make them with absolutely ripe tomatoes.

Prep: 15 minutes

1	lemon
⅓	cup mayonnaise
¼	teaspoon ground coriander
¼	teaspoon salt
¼	teaspoon coarsely ground black pepper
1	large round or oval loaf (1 pound) sourdough or other crusty bread
2	pounds ripe tomatoes (3 large), thickly sliced

1. From lemon, grate ½ teaspoon peel and squeeze 1 teaspoon juice. In small bowl, combine mayonnaise, lemon peel and juice, coriander, salt, and pepper until well blended.

2. Cut eight ½-inch-thick slices from center of bread. (Reserve ends for another use.) Toast bread, if desired. Spread mayonnaise mixture on each bread slice. Arrange tomato slices on 4 bread slices; top with remaining bread slices. To serve, cut each sandwich in half. Makes 4 main-dish servings.

Each serving: About 392 calories, 9g protein, 52g carbohydrate, 18g total fat (3g saturated), 11mg cholesterol, 742mg sodium.

Smoked Salmon Sandwiches with Dill Cream Cheese

To turn this open-face sandwich into a heartier, more portable treat, top with an additional slice of pumpernickel that's been spread with cream cheese.

Prep: 15 minutes

1	package (3 ounces) cream cheese, softened
1	tablespoon minced shallot
1	tablespoon capers, drained and chopped
1	tablespoon chopped fresh dill plus additional sprigs
1	teaspoon fresh lemon juice
4	slices pumpernickel bread
6	ounces thinly sliced smoked salmon
	ground black pepper
4	teaspoons salmon caviar (optional)

In small bowl, stir cream cheese, shallot, capers, chopped dill, and lemon juice until well blended. Spread evenly on bread slices and arrange smoked salmon on top. Sprinkle lightly with pepper. Place 1 teaspoon caviar on each sandwich, if you like, and top with dill sprigs. Makes 4 main-dish servings.

Each serving: About 207 calories, 12g protein, 17g carbohydrate, 10g total fat (5g saturated), 33mg cholesterol, 1,224mg sodium.

"HEROES"

Whether you call it a sub, hero, wedge, hoagie, grinder, Italian sandwich, Po' Boy, torpedo, or zeppelin, each of these cheese, meat, and vegetable–filled oblong sandwiches reflects regional culinary traditions and ethnic preferences. There is one element, however, they all share: They're simply delicious. For our Double Tomato-Brie Heroes we use fresh as well as dried tomatoes that have been marinated in lightly salted oil with herbs. If you use the unseasoned variety, you may want to sprinkle them with some salt.

In small bowl, combine 1 jar (6½ ounces) oil-packed dried tomatoes, drained and finely chopped, 2 tablespoons extra-virgin olive oil, and 2 tablespoons white wine vinegar. Spread dried-tomato mixture evenly on cut sides of 2 long loaves (8 ounces each) Italian bread, each cut horizontally in half. Slice 1 pound Brie cheese with rind left on and arrange on bottom halves of bread. Divide 1 cup loosely packed fresh basil leaves and tomato slices from 2 ripe medium tomatoes (12 ounces). Replace tops of bread. To serve, cut each hero crosswise into 4 pieces. Makes 8 main-dish servings.

Pan Bagnat

Tuna salad sandwiches *á la française*! It's best to make this large sandwich a day ahead to allow the juices to soak into the bread.

Prep: 30 minutes plus chilling

- 1 round loaf (8 inches) country-style bread (12 ounces)
- 1 garlic clove, cut in half
- ¼ cup extravirgin olive oil
- 2 tablespoons red wine vinegar
- ¼ teaspoon salt
- ⅛ teaspoon ground black pepper
- 3 ripe medium tomatoes (1 pound), sliced
- ½ cup loosely packed small fresh basil leaves
- 1 tablespoon fresh mint leaves
- 1 can (6 ounces) tuna packed in olive oil, drained and flaked
- ⅓ cup Mediterranean olives, such as Gaeta or Kalamata, pitted and chopped
- 2 green onions, chopped
- 1 tablespoon capers, drained
- 1 large hard-cooked egg, peeled and sliced

1. Cut bread horizontally in half. Remove enough soft center from each half to make 1-inch shell. (Reserve soft bread for another use.)

2. Rub inside of bread halves with cut side of garlic. In cup, stir oil, vinegar, salt, and pepper until blended. Drizzle about one-fourth of oil mixture over garlic-rubbed bread.

3. On bottom half of bread, arrange one-third of tomato slices; drizzle with about half of remaining oil mixture, then top with half of basil and all of mint.

4. In small bowl, combine tuna, olives, green onions, and capers. Spoon tuna mixture over herbs; top with sliced egg. Arrange remaining tomato slices and remaining basil on top. Drizzle with remaining oil mixture. Replace top half of bread.

5. Wrap sandwich tightly in foil and refrigerate at least 4 hours or up to 24 hours before serving to blend flavors and let juices moisten bread. To serve, cut into 4 wedges. Makes 4 main-dish servings.

Each serving: About 396 calories, 16g protein, 31g carbohydrate, 25g total fat (3g saturated), 68mg cholesterol, 1,111mg sodium.

Turkey and Mango Roll-Ups

A lime-spiked curried chutney adds zip to this rolled sandwich. If you can't find lavash, divide the filling ingredients among four 8- to 10-inch flour tortillas.

Prep: 25 minutes plus chilling

- 1 large lime
- ¼ cup light mayonnaise
- 3 tablespoons mango chutney, chopped
- ½ teaspoon curry powder
- ⅛ teaspoon paprika
- 1 lavash flatbread (7 ounces)
- 1 medium cucumber (8 ounces), peeled and thinly sliced
- 8 ounces thinly sliced smoked turkey breast
- 1 medium mango, peeled and finely chopped
- 6 large green-leaf lettuce leaves

1. From lime, grate ¼ teaspoon peel and squeeze 1 tablespoon juice. In bowl, stir mayonnaise, chutney, lime peel and juice, curry powder, and paprika until blended.

2. Unfold lavash; spread evenly with mayonnaise mixture. Arrange cucumber slices over mayonnaise, then top with turkey, mango, and lettuce. From a short side, roll up lavash, jelly-roll fashion.

3. Wrap lavash roll in foil and refrigerate at least 2 hours or up to 4 hours to blend flavors and let bread soften. To serve, trim ends, then cut lavash roll into 4 pieces. Makes 4 main-dish servings.

Each serving: About 375 calories, 18g protein, 55g carbohydrate, 7g total fat (2g saturated), 29mg cholesterol, 939mg sodium.

Chicken Club Sandwiches

This is a great way to use leftover turkey or chicken—you'll need about 2 cups shredded or sliced meat.

Prep: 20 minutes   Cook: 15 minutes

- 4 small skinless, boneless chicken breast halves (1 pound)
- ¼ cup flavored mayonnaise (page 472) or plain mayonnaise
- 8 slices bacon, each cut crosswise in half
- 12 slices firm white or whole-wheat bread
- 2 ripe medium tomatoes (12 ounces), thinly sliced
- 8 small romaine lettuce leaves

1. In 10-inch skillet, combine chicken and enough *cold water* to cover; heat to boiling over high heat. Reduce heat; cover and simmer until chicken loses its pink color throughout, 8 to 10 minutes. Drain and cool to room temperature.

2. Meanwhile, prepare flavored mayonnaise.

3. In 12-inch skillet, cook bacon over medium heat until browned. Transfer bacon to paper towels to drain.

4. Spread about 1 teaspoon mayonnaise on each bread slice; top 4 bread slices with tomato slices and lettuce.

5. Cut chicken breasts on diagonal into thin slices. Place 4 more bread slices, mayonnaise side up, on top of lettuce. Arrange chicken and bacon on top and cover with remaining 4 bread slices.

6. To serve, cut each sandwich on diagonal into quarters. Use frilled toothpicks to hold slices together, if you like. Makes 4 main-dish servings.

Each serving: About 513 calories, 38g protein, 47g carbohydrate, 18g total fat (4g saturated), 83mg cholesterol, 800mg sodium.

Open-Faced Steak and Mushroom Sandwiches

Thin slices of juicy steak topped with onions and mushrooms sautéed in butter and red wine are served on crusty French bread for this classic.

Prep: 15 minutes   Cook: 30 minutes

- 2 tablespoons butter or margarine, softened
- 1 tablespoon plus 1 teaspoon chopped fresh tarragon
- ⅜ teaspoon ground black pepper
- 1 loaf (8 ounces) French bread, cut horizontally in half
- 3 teaspoons vegetable oil
- 1 beef flank steak (1¼ pounds)
- ¾ teaspoon salt
- 1 medium onion, thinly sliced
- 12 ounces mushrooms, trimmed and sliced
  pinch dried thyme
- ⅓ cup dry red wine

1. In small bowl, stir butter, 1 tablespoon tarragon, and ⅛ teaspoon pepper until well blended. Spread tarragon butter evenly on cut sides of bread. Cut each half into 4 pieces.

2. In heavy 12-inch skillet (preferably cast iron), heat 2 teaspoons oil over medium-high heat until very hot. Pat steak dry with paper towels and sprinkle with ¼ teaspoon salt and ⅛ teaspoon pepper. Add steak to skillet and cook 6 to 8 minutes per side for medium-rare or until desired doneness. Transfer steak to cutting board. Set aside.

3. Add remaining 1 teaspoon oil and onion to skillet; cook over medium heat, stirring frequently, until tender, about 5 minutes. Stir in mushrooms, thyme, remaining ½ teaspoon salt, and remaining ⅛ teaspoon pepper. Cook over medium-high heat until mushrooms are tender and liquid has evaporated, about 8 minutes. Stir in wine and boil 2 minutes. Remove from heat. Keep warm.

4. Holding knife almost parallel to cutting board, cut steak into thin slices across the grain; arrange on bread. Spoon mushroom mixture on top; sprinkle with remaining 1 teaspoon tarragon. Makes 4 main-dish servings.

Each serving: About 544 calories, 35g protein, 38g carbohydrate, 26g total fat (11g saturated), 89mg cholesterol, 946mg sodium.

Classic Italian Hero

If you feel the urge, build on the basic recipe by adding any of the ingredients listed below and/or whatever else you can think of.

Prep: 15 minutes

¼ cup vinaigrette of choice

1 large loaf (12 ounces) Italian bread

4 ounces thinly sliced hot and/or sweet capocollo, prosciutto, soppressata, and/or salami

4 ounces mozzarella cheese, preferably fresh, thinly sliced

shredded romaine lettuce or arugula, peperoncini, basil leaves, roasted red peppers, very thinly sliced red onions, pesto, olivada, and/or sliced ripe tomatoes

1. Prepare vinaigrette.

2. Cut bread horizontally in half. Remove enough soft center from each half to make 1-inch shell. (Reserve soft bread for another use.)

3. Brush vinaigrette evenly over cut sides of bread. Layer meats and cheese on bottom half of bread. Top with additional ingredients of your choice. Replace top half of bread. If not serving right away, wrap sandwich in foil and refrigerate up to 4 hours. Cut into 4 pieces. Makes 4 main-dish servings.

Each serving: About 430 calories, 20g protein, 36g carbohydrate, 23g total fat (7g saturated), 48mg cholesterol, 1,226mg sodium.

Classic Italian Hero

Muffuletta

This rich sandwich is a classic in New Orleans' French Quarter, where it's especially good at the Central Grocery. But you don't have to travel all that way; this recipe will "let the good times roll" at your house.

Prep: 25 minutes plus chilling

- 1¼ cups finely chopped celery with leaves
- 1 cup drained giardiniera (Italian mixed pickled vegetables), chopped
- ¾ cup green and black Mediterranean olives, such as Gaeta or Kalamata, pitted and chopped
- ⅓ cup chopped fresh parsley
- 1 garlic clove, minced
- ¼ cup olive oil
- ¼ teaspoon ground black pepper
- 1 round loaf (8 to 10 inches) soft French bread
- 4 ounces thinly sliced smoked ham
- 4 ounces thinly sliced Provolone cheese
- 4 ounces thinly sliced Genoa salami

1. In medium bowl, stir celery, giardiniera, olives, parsley, garlic, oil, and pepper until well mixed. Cover and refrigerate at least 4 hours or up to overnight to blend flavors.

2. Cut bread horizontally in half. Remove enough soft center from each half to make 1-inch shell. (Reserve soft bread for another use.) Onto bottom half of bread, spoon half of celery-olive mixture; layer ham, cheese, and salami on top. Spoon remaining celery-olive mixture over. Replace top half of bread.

3. Wrap sandwich in foil and refrigerate at least 4 hours or up to 24 hours to blend flavors and let juices soften bread. To serve, let stand at room temperature about 30 minutes, then cut into 6 wedges. Makes 6 main-dish servings.

Each serving: About 399 calories, 17g protein, 28g carbohydrate, 24g total fat (8g saturated), 41mg cholesterol, 1,615mg sodium.

Cucumber Tea Sandwiches

Utterly English and perfectly delicious, these classic sandwiches are a necessity at a tea party. A V-slicer or mandoline will make the thinnest cucumber slices.

Prep: 20 minutes plus chilling

- 1 English (seedless) cucumber
- ½ teaspoon salt
- 5 tablespoons butter or margarine, softened
- 16 very thin slices white or whole-wheat bread
- 32 fresh mint leaves (optional)

1. Cut cucumber lengthwise in half and remove soft seed area in center. Cut cucumber crosswise into paper-thin slices. In colander set over bowl, toss cucumber and salt. Cover and refrigerate 30 minutes, stirring occasionally. Discard liquid in bowl. Pat cucumber slices dry with paper towels.

2. Lightly spread butter on each bread slice. Arrange cucumber on 8 buttered slices; place 1 mint leaf, if using, in each corner of bread. Top with remaining bread slices. Trim crusts and cut each sandwich on diagonal into quarters. Makes 32 tea sandwiches.

Each sandwich: About 36 calories, 1g protein, 4g carbohydrate, 2g total fat (1g saturated), 5mg cholesterol, 74mg sodium.

MAKE-AHEAD TIP FOR TEA SANDWICHES

Test Kitchen Tip

To enjoy more time with your guests, make tea sandwiches ahead and store them as follows:

Line a jelly-roll pan with damp paper towels. Place sandwiches in the pan and cover with additional damp paper towels to keep the bread from drying out. Cover the pan tightly with plastic wrap and refrigerate up to four hours.

Watercress and Radish Tea Sandwiches

These tea sandwiches look demure but have a pleasant peppery kick.

Prep: 20 minutes

- 3 tablespoons butter or margarine, softened
- 8 very thin slices white or whole-wheat bread
  pinch salt
  pinch ground black pepper
- ½ bunch watercress, tough stems trimmed
- 3 radishes, very thinly sliced

Lightly spread butter on each bread slice and sprinkle with salt and pepper. Arrange only very tender watercress sprigs on 4 buttered slices and top with radishes. Cover with remaining bread slices. Trim crusts and cut each sandwich on diagonal into quarters. Makes 16 tea sandwiches.

Each sandwich: About 39 calories, 1g protein, 4g carbohydrate, 2g total fat (1g saturated), 6mg cholesterol, 71mg sodium.

Dilled-Egg Tea Sandwiches

Use this recipe for large-size sandwiches as well as delicate tea sandwiches. They're tasty either way.

Prep: 40 minutes

- 3 large hard-cooked eggs, peeled and finely shredded
- ¼ cup mayonnaise
- 2 tablespoons chopped fresh dill
- ¼ teaspoon freshly grated lemon peel
- ¼ teaspoon ground black pepper
- 12 very thin slices white or whole-wheat bread

In medium bowl, stir eggs, mayonnaise, dill, lemon peel, and pepper. Spread evenly on 6 bread slices; top with remaining bread slices. Trim crusts and cut each sandwich into 3 equal rectangles. Makes 18 tea sandwiches.

Each sandwich: About 68 calories, 2g protein, 6g carbohydrate, 4g total fat (1g saturated), 37mg cholesterol, 95mg sodium.

Cheddar and Chutney Tea Sandwiches

This sweet-and-savory combination is a treat with a cup of tea or even a cocktail.

Prep: 15 minutes

- 3 tablespoons butter or margarine, softened
- 3 tablespoons mango chutney, finely chopped
- 8 very thin slices white or whole-wheat bread
- 4 ounces Cheddar cheese, shredded (1 cup)

In small bowl, stir butter and chutney until well blended. Spread evenly on bread slices. Sprinkle Cheddar on buttered side of 4 bread slices. Top with remaining bread. Trim crusts and cut each sandwich into 4 squares or triangles. Makes 16 tea sandwiches.

Each sandwich: About 78 calories, 2g protein, 6g carbohydrate, 5g total fat (3g saturated), 13mg cholesterol, 136mg sodium.

Smoked Salmon Tea Sandwiches

Using two different breads for these sandwiches is a nice touch but not absolutely necessary.

Prep: 20 minutes

- 8 very thin slices white bread
- 8 very thin slices whole-wheat bread
- 6 tablespoons butter or margarine, softened, or whipped cream cheese
- 6 ounces very thinly sliced smoked salmon

Lightly spread butter on each bread slice. Arrange salmon on buttered side of white bread, trimming to fit. Top with whole-wheat bread. Trim crusts and cut each sandwich on diagonal into quarters. Makes 32 tea sandwiches.

Each sandwich: About 43 calories, 2g protein, 3g carbohydrate, 3g total fat (1g saturated), 7mg cholesterol, 166mg sodium.

18

DESSERTS

Our collection of scrumptious desserts is sure to tempt you: soufflés, meringues, custards, puff pastry desserts, pudding cakes, and other earthly delights. Many of the desserts rely on eggs for their distinctive textures, so here are some tips to help you with some basic techniques.

CUSTARDS

Custard, a cooked milk or cream mixture thickened with eggs and sweetened with sugar, can be baked for a dessert or cooked on top of the stove for a silky dessert sauce (called a stirred custard).

A moderate cooking temperature is necessary for baked custards, so they are cooked in a water bath (a roasting pan filled with hot water to come halfway up the sides of the cups), which insulates them from the oven's heat. For stirred custards, the yolks are gradually heated. A small amount of the hot liquid is stirred into the yolks, then the yolk mixture is stirred back into the hot liquid. This prevents the custard from curdling.

The center of a properly cooked custard will jiggle, as it will continue to cook as it cools. Insert the tip of a knife into the custard about 1 inch from the center; it should come out clean.

Custard sauces must be stirred constantly over low heat to prevent scorching and overcooking. The custard is cooked until thick enough to coat a spoon. Strain the custard into a bowl, then press a piece of plastic wrap directly onto the surface.

HIGH-RISING SOUFFLÉS

The secret to a beautifully risen soufflé isn't really that secret. It's all about perfectly beaten eggs whites. Separate the eggs while cold, then let them sit at room temperature until warm, so they will beat to their highest volume.

Beat the egg whites just until stiff—not dry. Fold about one-third of the whites into the batter to lighten it, then fold in the remaining whites.

Because soufflés need a blast of hot air to rise properly, be sure the oven is preheated thoroughly. A soufflé is done when puffed and golden brown, with a somewhat soft, barely set center. Once exposed to the air, a soufflé will keep its puff for only three to five minutes.

MAGICAL MERINGUES

Meringues are nothing more complicated than a beaten mixture of egg whites and sugar. There are two types of meringue, soft and hard, which simply depend on the proportion of sugar to egg whites. Soft meringue contains less sugar while hard meringue contains more sugar.

Never make meringue on a humid or rainy day, because it will absorb the moisture from the air and end up soggy or "weep." Beat room-temperature egg whites at high speed until soft peaks form. Then add the sugar, two tablespoons at a time, beating just until stiff, glossy peaks form. Check that the sugar has dissolved by rubbing a bit of the meringue between your fingers.

Meringue Shells

Fill these versatile shells with whipped cream or Lemon Filling (page 528) and berries or with ice cream and chocolate sauce. Do not make meringues in humid weather: They will get soggy.

Prep: 15 minutes plus cooling   Bake: 2 hours

3   large egg whites
$1/8$ teaspoon cream of tartar
$3/4$ cup sugar
$1/2$ teaspoon vanilla extract

1. Preheat oven to 200°F. Line large cookie sheet with foil or parchment paper. In small bowl, with mixer at high speed, beat egg whites and cream of tartar until soft peaks form when beaters are lifted. Sprinkle in sugar, 2 tablespoons at a time, beating until sugar has dissolved. Add vanilla; continue beating until egg whites stand in stiff, glossy peaks when beaters are lifted.

2. Spoon meringue into 6 equal mounds on prepared cookie sheet, 4 inches apart. With back of tablespoon, spread each mound into 4-inch round. Make well in center of each round to form "nest."

3. Bake until meringues are firm and just begin to color, about 2 hours. Turn off oven; leave meringues in oven 1 hour or up to overnight to dry. If not leaving overnight, cool completely on cookie sheet on wire rack. Store meringue shells in airtight container. Makes 6 servings.

Each serving: About 106 calories, 2g protein, 25g carbohydrate, 0g total fat (0g saturated), 0mg cholesterol, 28mg sodium.

Miniature Meringue Shells

Preheat oven to 200°F. Line two cookie sheets with foil or parchment paper. Prepare as directed in Step 1 above. Drop meringue by rounded teaspoons, 2 inches apart, on prepared cookie sheets. With back of teaspoon, make well in center of each to form "nest" about $1/2$ inches across. Bake until meringues are firm and just begin to color, about 1 hour. Turn off oven; leave meringues in oven 1 hour or up to overnight to dry. If not leaving overnight, cool completely on cookie sheet on wire rack. Store as directed. Makes 20 miniature shells.

Each serving: About 32 calories, 0g protein, 8g carbohydrate, 0g total fat (0g saturated), 0mg cholesterol, 8mg sodium.

PERFECT MERINGUE SHELLS

For symmetrically shaped meringue shells, mark circles on the foil with a toothpick. Use a saucer as a guide for large shells or a $1/2$-inch jar cap or cookie cutter for miniature shells.

PAVLOVA

This Australian favorite was created to honor prima ballerina Anna Pavlova, who was renowned for her leading role in *Swan Lake*. Swanlike in its delicacy and pristine whiteness, it always gets rave reviews.

Preheat oven to 275°F. Line large cookie sheet with foil. Grease foil; dust with flour. Using a 9-inch round cake pan as a guide, with toothpick, trace a circle in center of foil. In small bowl, whisk $2/3$ cup sugar and 1 tablespoon cornstarch. In large bowl, with mixer at medium speed, beat 4 large egg whites and $1/4$ teaspoon salt until foamy. Beat in sugar mixture, 1 tablespoon at a time, beating well after each addition, until sugar has completely dissolved and whites stand in stiff, glossy peaks when beaters are lifted. Beat in 2 teaspoons distilled white vinegar and 1 teaspoon vanilla extract. Spoon meringue into circle on foil. With back of spoon, spread meringue to edge of circle, forming a "nest" with a 2-inch-high rim all around.

Bake until set, about 2 hours. Turn off oven; leave meringue in oven 2 hours. Cool completely on cookie sheet on wire rack.

In small bowl, with mixer at medium speed, beat 1 cup heavy cream and 2 tablespoons sugar to soft peaks. Beat in $1/2$ teaspoon vanilla. To serve, spoon whipped cream into center of meringue and top with peeled, thickly sliced kiwifruit and sliced strawberries.

Raspberry Jam Soufflé

This impressive fat-free dessert is easier to make than you think—just fold store-bought fruit spread into beaten egg whites and bake. To do ahead, prepare and refrigerate soufflé mixture in soufflé dish up to three hours, then bake as directed just before serving.

Prep: 20 minutes   Bake: 15 minutes

- 2/3 cup seedless raspberry spreadable fruit (no-sugar-added jam)
- 1 tablespoon fresh lemon juice
- 4 large egg whites
- 1/2 teaspoon cream of tartar
- 2 tablespoons sugar
- 1 teaspoon vanilla extract

1. Preheat oven to 375°F. In large bowl, with wire whisk, beat fruit spread with lemon juice; set aside.

2. In medium bowl, with mixer at high speed, beat egg whites and cream of tartar until soft peaks form when beaters are lifted. Sprinkle in sugar, 1 tablespoon at a time, beating until sugar has dissolved. Add vanilla; continue beating until egg whites stand in stiff peaks when beaters are lifted.

3. With rubber spatula, gently fold one-third of beaten egg whites into raspberry mixture. Fold in remaining whites, just until blended. Spoon mixture into 1½-quart soufflé dish; gently spread evenly.

4. Bake until soufflé has puffed and is lightly browned, and knife inserted 1 inch from edge comes out clean, 15 to 18 minutes. Serve immediately. Makes 6 servings.

Each serving: About 75 calories, 3g protein, 16g carbohydrate, 0g total fat, 1g fiber, 0mg cholesterol, 35mg sodium.

Banana Soufflé

Prepare soufflé as directed but prepare banana puree instead of spreadable fruit. In blender or in food processor with knife blade attached, puree **2 very ripe medium bananas,** cut into large pieces, with **2 tablespoons sugar, 1 tablespoon fresh lemon juice** and **¼ teaspoon ground cinnamon** until smooth. Fold beaten egg whites into banana puree and bake as directed.

Chocolate Soufflés

Soufflés always make an impression. They are irresistible as individual soufflés and spectacular baked as one large dessert.

Prep: 20 minutes plus cooling   Bake: 25 minutes

- 1¼ cups plus 3 tablespoons granulated sugar
- ¼ cup all-purpose flour
- 1 teaspoon instant espresso-coffee powder
- 1 cup milk
- 5 squares (5 ounces) unsweetened chocolate, chopped
- 3 tablespoons butter or margarine, softened
- 4 large eggs, separated, plus 2 large egg whites
- 2 teaspoons vanilla extract
- ¼ teaspoon salt
  confectioners' sugar

1. In heavy 3-quart saucepan, combine 1¼ cups granulated sugar, flour, and espresso powder. With wire whisk, gradually stir in milk until blended. Cook over medium heat, stirring constantly, until mixture has thickened and boils; boil, stirring, 1 minute. Remove from heat.

2. Stir in chocolate and butter until melted and smooth. With whisk, beat in egg yolks until well blended; stir in vanilla. Cool to lukewarm.

3. Meanwhile, preheat oven to 350°F. Grease eight 6-ounce custard cups or ramekins or 2-quart soufflé dish; sprinkle lightly with remaining 3 tablespoons granulated sugar.

4. In large bowl, with mixer at high speed, beat egg whites and salt just until stiff peaks form when beaters are lifted. With rubber spatula, gently fold one-third of beaten egg whites into chocolate mixture; fold back into remaining egg whites just until blended.

5. Spoon into prepared custard cups. (If using custard cups, place in jelly-roll pan for easier handling.) Bake until soufflés have puffed and centers are glossy, 25 to 30 minutes for individual soufflés, 35 to 40 minutes for large soufflé. Dust with confectioners' sugar. Serve immediately. Makes 8 servings.

Each serving: About 356 calories, 7g protein, 44g carbohydrate, 19g total fat (10g saturated), 122mg cholesterol, 178mg sodium.

Orange Liqueur Soufflé

This is perhaps the most popular and elegant of all soufflés. Infuse it with your favorite orange liqueur: Grand Marnier, curaçao, or triple sec.

Prep: 20 minutes plus cooling   Bake: 30 minutes

- 4 tablespoons butter or margarine
- ⅓ cup all-purpose flour
- 1⅛ teaspoon salt
- 1½ cups milk, warmed
- ½ cup plus 2 tablespoons granulated sugar
- 4 large egg yolks
- ⅓ cup orange-flavored liqueur
- 1 tablespoon freshly grated orange peel
- 6 large egg whites
  confectioners' sugar
  whipped cream (optional)

1. In heavy 2-quart saucepan, melt butter over low heat. Add flour and salt; cook, stirring, 1 minute. With wire whisk, gradually whisk in warm milk. Cook over medium heat, stirring with wooden spoon, until mixture has thickened and boils. Reduce heat and simmer 1 minute. Remove from heat.

2. With wire whisk, stir ½ cup granulated sugar into milk mixture. Gradually whisk in egg yolks, whisking rapidly to prevent curdling. Cool egg-yolk mixture to lukewarm, stirring occasionally. Stir in orange liqueur and orange peel.

3. Preheat oven to 375°F. Grease 2-quart soufflé dish with butter and evenly sprinkle with remaining 2 tablespoons granulated sugar.

4. In large bowl, with mixer at high speed, beat egg whites until stiff peaks form when beaters are lifted. With rubber spatula, gently fold one-third of beaten egg whites into egg-yolk mixture; fold mixture back into remaining egg whites just until blended.

5. Spoon mixture into prepared soufflé dish. To create top-hat effect (center will rise higher than edge), with back of spoon, make 1-inch-deep indentation all around top of soufflé about 1 inch from edge  of dish. Bake until soufflé has puffed, is golden, and knife inserted 1 inch from edge comes out clean, 30 to 35 minutes. Dust with confectioners' sugar. Serve immediately. If desired, pass whipped cream to spoon onto each serving. Makes 8 servings.

Each serving: About 214 calories, 6g protein, 26g carbohydrate, 10g total fat (5g saturated), 128mg cholesterol, 162mg sodium.

Orange Liqueur Soufflé

Raspberry-Banana Trifle

This beautiful dessert is easier to make than you think—store-bought pound cake and jam are the secret ingredients.

Prep: 1 hour plus chilling   Cook: 15 minutes

Cake

- 1 frozen pound cake (1 pound), thawed
- 6 tablespoons seedless red-raspberry jam

Custard

- 6 large eggs
- ¾ cup sugar
- ⅓ cup cornstarch
- 4 cups milk
- 4 tablespoons margarine or butter
- 2 tablespoons vanilla extract

- 3 large ripe bananas (1½ pounds), sliced

Topping

- 1 cup heavy or whipping cream
- 2 tablespoons sugar
  Fresh raspberries and fresh mint leaves for garnish

1. Prepare cake: With serrated knife, cut crust from pound cake. Place cake on 1 long side; cut lengthwise into 4 equal slices. With small spatula, spread 2 tablespoons jam on top of 1 cake slice; top with another cake slice. Repeat with remaining jam and cake, ending with cake. Slice jam-layered cake crosswise into ¼-inch slices, keeping slices together, then cut cake lengthwise in half down center. (You should have about 26 slices jam-layered cake cut in half to make 52 half slices.)

2. Prepare custard: In medium bowl, with wire whisk, beat eggs, sugar, and cornstarch; set aside. In 4-quart saucepan, heat milk just to boiling. While constantly beating with whisk, gradually pour about half of hot milk into egg mixture. Pour egg mixture back into milk in saucepan, and cook over medium-low heat, whisking constantly, until mixture thickens and begins to bubble around edge of pan; mixture will not boil vigorously. Simmer custard 1 minute, whisking constantly; it must reach at least 160°F. Remove saucepan from heat; stir in margarine or butter with vanilla.

3. Assemble trifle: In 4-quart glass trifle dish or deep glass bowl, place 2 rows of cake slices around side of bowl, alternating horizontal and vertical placement of cake slices to make a checkerboard design. Place some cake slices in a layer to cover bottom of bowl; top with one-third of sliced bananas. Spoon one-third of warm custard on top of bananas. Top with half of remaining bananas and half of remaining custard. Top with remaining cake, then bananas and custard. Cover surface of custard with plastic wrap to prevent skin from forming. Refrigerate trifle 6 hours or overnight.

4. Before serving, prepare topping: In small bowl, with mixer at medium speed, beat cream with sugar until stiff peaks form. Remove plastic wrap from trifle; top trifle with whipped cream and garnish with raspberries and mint. Makes 24 servings.

Each serving: About 240 calories, 4g protein, 28g carbohydrate, 12g total fat (5g saturated), 72mg cholesterol, 120mg sodium.

VARIATIONS ON A TRIFLE

Though there are many, many recipes for trifles, they probably have three elements in common: strips or cubes of cake for their base, a rich custard sauce for pouring between the layers, and fresh fruit. After that, whipped cream, sliced or slivered nuts, candied fruit, jam, and brandy or fruit-flavored liqueur are all popular add-ins. Here are some ways to vary our delectable trifle:

- Use plain or chocolate sponge cake or a fruit-flavored pound cake instead of the store-bought pound cake.
- Try orange, apricot, or strawberry jam instead of the raspberry jam.
- Substitute 3 cups of whole, sliced, or diced fresh fruit—strawberries, blackberries peaches, apricots, plums—for the banana.
- Drizzle the cake with a little brandy or orange-flavored liquer before brushing it with jam.

Tiramisù

Rich and moist but light-as-a-feather, this classic sweet is a favorite afternoon treat in Italy where its name literally means "pick me up."

Prep: 35 minutes plus chilling

1	cup hot espresso or very strong brewed coffee
3	tablespoons brandy
2	tablespoons plus ½ cup sugar
18	crisp Italian ladyfingers (savoiardi; 5 ounces)
½	cup milk
1	container (16 to 17½ ounces) mascarpone cheese
¾	cup heavy or whipping cream
	unsweetened cocoa
	Chocolate Curls (page 529)

1. In 9-inch pie plate, stir coffee, brandy, and 2 tablespoons sugar until sugar has dissolved; cool to room temperature. Dip both sides of 9 ladyfingers into coffee mixture, one at a time, to soak completely; arrange in single layer in 8-inch square baking dish.

2. In large bowl, stir milk and remaining ½ cup sugar until sugar has dissolved. Stir in mascarpone until blended.

3. In small bowl, with mixer at high speed, beat cream until soft peaks form. With rubber spatula, gently fold whipped cream into mascarpone mixture until blended. Spread half of mixture over ladyfingers in baking dish.

4. Dip remaining 9 ladyfingers into coffee mixture and arrange on top of mascarpone mixture. Spread with remaining mascarpone mixture. Refrigerate 3 hours or up to overnight.

5. Meanwhile, prepare Chocolate Curls.

6. Just before serving, dust with cocoa. Cut into squares and spoon into goblets or dessert dishes. Garnish with chocolate curls. Makes 12 servings.

Each serving: About 323 calories, 4g protein, 22g carbohydrate, 23g total fat (15g saturated), 55mg cholesterol, 59mg sodium.

Crème Caramel

A masterpiece of French dessert making: individual custards in their own caramel sauce.

Prep: 15 minutes plus cooling and chilling
Bake: 50 minutes

¼	plus ⅓ cup sugar
4	large eggs
2	cups milk
1½	teaspoons vanilla extract
¼	teaspoon salt

1. Preheat oven to 325°F. In heavy 1-quart saucepan, heat ¼ cup sugar over medium heat, swirling pan occasionally, until sugar has melted and is amber in color. Immediately pour into six 6-ounce custard cups or ramekins.

2. In large bowl, with wire whisk, beat eggs and remaining ⅓ cup sugar until blended. Whisk in milk, vanilla, and salt until well combined; pour mixture through fine mesh sieve into prepared custard cups.

3. Place custard cups in small baking pan; place on rack in oven. Carefully pour enough *very hot water* into pan to come halfway up sides of cups. Bake just until knife inserted 1 inch from center of custards comes out clean, 50 to 55 minutes. Transfer custard cups to wire rack to cool. Cover and refrigerate until well chilled, 3 hours or up to overnight.

4. To serve, run tip of small knife around edge of custards. Invert cups onto dessert plates, shaking cups gently until custards slip out, allowing caramel syrup to drip onto custards. Makes 6 servings.

Each serving: About 177 calories, 7g protein, 24g carbohydrate, 6g total fat (3g saturated), 153mg cholesterol, 177mg sodium.

CARAMEL

Always, immediately pour caramel into custard cups. Otherwise, it will overcook and harden.

Crème Brûlée

Its brittle caramelized top and velvety custard make this an ultimate indulgence.

Prep: 20 minutes plus cooling and chilling
Bake/Broil: 38 minutes

- ½ **vanilla bean or 2 teaspoons vanilla extract**
- 1½ **cups heavy or whipping cream**
- 1½ **cups half-and-half or light cream**
- 8 **large egg yolks**
- ⅔ **cup granulated sugar**
- ⅓ **to ½ cup packed brown sugar**

1. Preheat oven to 325°F. With knife, cut vanilla bean lengthwise in half; scrape out seeds. Into heavy 3-quart saucepan, add cream, half-and-half, and vanilla bean. Heat over medium heat until bubbles form around edge. Remove from heat. Remove vanilla bean.

2. Meanwhile, in large bowl, with wire whisk, beat egg yolks and granulated sugar until well blended. Slowly stir in hot cream mixture until well combined. Pour cream mixture into ten 4- to 5-ounce broiler-proof ramekins or shallow 2½-quart casserole.

3. Place ramekins or casserole in large roasting pan; place pan on rack in oven. Carefully pour enough *very hot water* into pan to come halfway up sides of ramekins. Bake just until set (mixture will still be slightly soft in center), 35 to 40 minutes. Transfer ramekins to wire rack to cool to room temperature. Cover and refrigerate, at least 3 hours or up to overnight.

4. Up to 2 hours before serving, preheat broiler. Place brown sugar in small sieve; with spoon, press sugar through sieve to cover tops of chilled custards.

5. Place ramekins in jelly-roll pan for easier handling. With broiler rack at closest position to heat source, broil custard just until sugar melts, 3 to 4 minutes. Serve, or refrigerate up to 2 hours. The melted brown sugar will form a delicious brittle crust. Makes 10 servings.

Each serving: About 307 calories, 4g protein, 25g carbohydrate, 21g total fat (12g saturated), 232mg cholesterol, 38mg sodium.

BAIN MARIE

A *bain marie* (hot water bath) is the best way to ensure that delicate custard mixtures cook evenly. Here's how to do it: Place custard cups or baking dish in a baking or roasting pan. Place the pan on the oven rack. Pour in enough very hot water (not boiling) to come halfway up the sides of the dish. This method is sometimes used for cheesecakes and other egg-based dishes.

GETTING TO KNOW GELATIN

Test Kitchen Tip

Odorless, tasteless, and colorless, gelatin is used as a thickening agent in desserts. The most common form is powdered gelatin, which comes in individual envelopes. One envelope equals about 2½ teaspoons (¼ ounce) and will set about 2 cups of liquid.

Gelatin must always be dissolved. Sprinkle it over a small amount of cold liquid and allow to stand until it has softened and soaked up the liquid, about 5 minutes. Add the softened gelatin to the recipe's liquid; stir constantly over low heat until completely dissolved. To check that the gelatin has fully dissolved, lift a little into a spoon: There should be no visible crystals. Or, rub a bit of the gelatin between your fingers.

Panna Cotta with Raspberry Sauce

Panna cotta, which means "cooked cream" in Italian, is a custard that is served cold with a sauce. If you prefer, you can serve it with Best Berry Sauce (page 440) instead of Raspberry Sauce.

Prep: 20 minutes plus chilling   Cook: 15 minutes

- 1 envelope unflavored gelatin
- 1 cup milk
- ½ vanilla bean or 1½ teaspoons vanilla extract
- 1¾ cups heavy or whipping cream
- ¼ cup sugar
- 1 strip (3" by 1") lemon peel
- 1 cinnamon stick (3 inches)
    Raspberry Sauce (page 442)
    fresh raspberries

1. In 2-cup measuring cup, evenly sprinkle gelatin over milk; let stand 2 minutes to soften gelatin slightly. With knife, cut vanilla bean lengthwise in half; scrape out seeds and reserve.

2. In heavy 1-quart saucepan, combine cream, sugar, lemon peel, cinnamon stick, and vanilla bean halves and seeds (do not add vanilla extract); heat to boiling over high heat, stirring occasionally. Reduce heat and simmer, stirring occasionally, 5 minutes. Stir in milk mixture; cook over low heat, stirring frequently, until gelatin has dissolved, 2 to 3 minutes.

3. Discard lemon peel, cinnamon stick, and vanilla bean from cream mixture. (Stir in vanilla extract, if using.) Pour cream mixture into medium bowl set in large bowl of ice water. With rubber spatula, stir mixture until it just begins to set, 10 to 12 minutes. Pour cream mixture into eight 4-ounce ramekins. Place ramekins in jelly-roll pan for easier handling. Cover and refrigerate panna cotta until well chilled and set, 4 hours or up to overnight.

4. Meanwhile, prepare Raspberry Sauce.

5. To unmold panna cotta, run tip of knife around edges. Tap side of each ramekin sharply to break seal. Invert onto dessert plates. Spoon raspberry sauce around each panna cotta and sprinkle with raspberries. Makes 8 servings.

Each serving without Raspberry Sauce: About 228 calories, 3g protein, 9g carbohydrate, 20g total fat (13g saturated), 76mg cholesterol, 37mg sodium.

Panna Cotta with Raspberry Sauce

Pumpkin Cheesecake Crème Caramel

This is a wonderful do-ahead alternative to pumpkin pie. Use a thin-bladed knife to make slicing easier.

Prep: 30 minutes plus chilling Bake: 1 hour 10 minutes

water
1 orange
1¼ cups sugar
1 package (8 ounces) cream cheese, softened
1 cup can solid-pack pumpkin (not pumpkin-pie mix)
6 large eggs
1 can (12 ounces) evaporated milk
½ cup heavy or whipping cream
¼ cup orange-flavored liqueur
1 teaspoon vanilla extract
1 teaspoon ground cinnamon
pinch ground nutmeg
salt

1. Preheat oven to 350°F. Fill kettle or covered 4-quart saucepan with water; heat to boiling over high heat.

2. Meanwhile, from orange, with vegetable peeler, remove 6 strips peel, about 3" by 1" each. With knife, trim off as much white pith as possible from peel. In 1-quart saucepan, heat orange peel, ¾ cup sugar, and ¼ cup water to boiling over medium heat; cover and cook 5 minutes. Remove cover and cook until sugar mixture is amber in color, 1 to 2 minutes longer. Pour hot caramel into 9" by 5" metal loaf pan. With fork, remove and discard orange peel. (Hold loaf pan with pot holder to protect hands from heat of caramel.) Set pan aside.

3. In large bowl, with mixer on medium speed, beat cream cheese and remaining ½ cup sugar 2 minutes, occasionally scraping bowl with rubber spatula. Beat in pumpkin, then eggs, one at a time. Reduce speed to low; beat in evaporated milk, cream, liqueur, vanilla, cinnamon, nutmeg, and pinch salt just until well mixed.

4. Pour pumpkin mixture through medium-mesh sieve over caramel in loaf pan, pressing it through with rubber spatula. Place loaf pan in 13" by 9" baking pan; place in oven. Carefully pour boiling water into baking pan to come three-quarters up sides of loaf pan.

5. Bake until knife inserted 1 inch from edge of custard comes out clean (center will jiggle), 1 hour 10 to 15 minutes. Remove loaf pan from baking pan to cool on wire rack 1 hour. Cover and refrigerate crème caramel at least 8 hours or overnight.

6. To unmold, run small metal spatula or knife around sides of loaf pan; invert crème caramel onto serving plate. Leave loaf pan in place several minutes, allowing caramel syrup to drip from pan onto loaf. (Don't worry if some caramel remains in loaf pan.) Makes 12 servings.

Each serving: About 280 calories, 7g protein, 28g carbohydrate, 15g total fat (9g saturated), 150mg cholesterol, 135mg sodium.

Bread Pudding

The combination of dark raisins, just a touch of cinnamon and nutmeg, and a splash of dark rum makes this pudding a classic. For best texture, be sure to use day-old bread.

Prep: 20 minutes plus standing and cooling
Bake: 45 minutes

½ cup dark seedless raisins
3 tablespoons dark rum or bourbon
½ cup sugar
¼ teaspoon ground cinnamon
⅛ teaspoon ground nutmeg
4 large eggs
2 teaspoons vanilla extract
3 cups milk
3 cups day-old French bread cubes (½ inch)

1. In cup, combine raisins and rum; let stand 15 minutes. Grease 8" by 8" glass or ceramic baking dish.

2. In large bowl, whisk sugar, cinnamon, and nutmeg. Whisk in eggs and vanilla until combined. Add milk to egg mixture and whisk until well blended. Stir in bread cubes. Let stand 15 minutes, stirring occasionally. Stir in raisin mixture.

3. Preheat oven to 325°F. Pour bread mixture into prepared dish. Bake 45 to 50 minutes, or until a knife inserted near center of pudding comes out clean. Let cool on wire rack. Serve warm or refrigerate and serve cold. Makes 8 servings.

Each serving: About 213 calories, 8g protein, 31g carbohydrate, 6g total fat (3g saturated), 119mg cholesterol, 164mg sodium.

Brownie Pudding Cake

Two desserts for the price of one! The batter separates during baking into a fudgy brownie with a silky smooth chocolate pudding base.

Prep: 20 minutes   Bake: 30 minutes

- 2 teaspoons instant-coffee powder (optional)
- 2 tablespoons plus 1¾ cups boiling water
- 1 cup all-purpose flour
- ¾ cup unsweetened cocoa
- ½ cup granulated sugar
- 2 teaspoons baking powder
- ¼ teaspoon salt
- ½ cup milk
- 4 tablespoons butter or margarine, melted
- 1 teaspoon vanilla extract
- ½ cup packed brown sugar
  whipped cream or vanilla ice cream (optional)

1. Preheat oven to 350°F. In cup, dissolve coffee powder in 2 tablespoons boiling water, if using.

2. In large bowl, combine flour, ½ cup cocoa, granulated sugar, baking powder, and salt. In 2-cup measuring cup, combine milk, melted butter, vanilla, and coffee mixture, if using. With wooden spoon, stir milk mixture into flour mixture until just blended. Pour into ungreased 8-inch square baking dish.

3. In small bowl, thoroughly combine brown sugar and remaining ¼ cup cocoa; sprinkle evenly over batter. Carefully pour remaining 1¾ cups boiling water evenly over mixture in baking dish; do not stir.

4. Bake 30 minutes (batter will separate into cake and pudding layers). Cool in pan on wire rack 10 minutes. Serve hot with whipped cream, if you like. Makes 8 servings.

Each serving: About 238 calories, 4g protein, 43g carbohydrate, 7g total fat (5g saturated), 18mg cholesterol, 267mg sodium.

Brownie Pudding Cake

Lemon Pudding Cake

A tried-and-true dessert that is just plain wonderful served from the baking dish while steaming hot. Try the orange version too.

Prep: 20 minutes   Bake: 40 minutes

- 3 lemons
- ¾ cup sugar
- ¼ cup all-purpose flour
- 3 large eggs, separated
- 1 cup milk
- 4 tablespoons butter or margarine, melted
- ⅛ teaspoon salt

1. Preheat oven to 350°F. Grease 8-inch square baking dish. From lemons, grate 1 tablespoon peel and squeeze ⅓ cup juice. In large bowl, combine sugar and flour. With wire whisk, beat in egg yolks, milk, melted butter, and lemon peel and juice.

2. In small bowl, with mixer at high speed, beat egg whites and salt until soft peaks form when beaters are lifted. With rubber spatula, gently fold one-third of beaten egg whites into lemon mixture. Fold in remaining whites, just until blended. Pour batter into prepared baking dish.

3. Set baking dish in medium roasting pan; place on rack in oven. Carefully pour enough *very hot water* into roasting pan to come halfway up sides of baking dish. Bake until top is golden and set, about 40 minutes (batter will separate into cake and pudding layers). Cool in pan on wire rack 10 minutes. Serve hot. Makes 6 servings.

Each serving: About 256 calories, 5g protein, 32g carbohydrate, 12g total fat (7g saturated), 133mg cholesterol, 179mg sodium.

Orange Pudding Cake

Prepare as directed above but in Step 1 use **¼ cup fresh lemon juice, ¼ cup fresh orange juice,** and **2 teaspoons freshly grated orange peel.**

Rice Pudding

Cooking the rice very slowly in lots of milk makes this pudding especially creamy. Serve with fresh berries.

Prep: 10 minutes   Cook: 1 hour 15 minutes

- 4 cups milk
- ½ cup regular long-grain rice
- ½ cup sugar
- ¼ teaspoon salt
- 1 large egg
- 1 teaspoon vanilla extract

1. In heavy 4-quart saucepan, combine milk, rice, sugar, and salt; heat to boiling over medium-high heat stirring frequently. Reduce heat; cover and simmer mixture, stirring occasionally, until rice is very tender, about 1 hour.

2. In small bowl, with fork, lightly beat egg; stir in ½ cup hot rice mixture. Slowly pour egg mixture back into rice mixture, stirring rapidly to prevent curdling. Cook, stirring constantly, until rice mixture has thickened, about 5 minutes (do not boil, or mixture will curdle). Remove from heat; stir in vanilla. Serve warm, or spoon into medium bowl and refrigerate until well chilled, about 3 hours. Makes 4 cups or 6 servings.

Each serving: About 234 calories, 7g protein, 37g carbohydrate, 6g total fat (4g saturated), 58mg cholesterol, 187mg sodium.

Rich Rice Pudding

Prepare as directed above and refrigerate. In small bowl, with mixer at medium speed, beat **½ cup heavy or whipping cream** until soft peaks form. With rubber spatula, gently fold into rice pudding. Refrigerate until ready to serve, up to 4 hours. Makes 8 servings.

Sticky Toffee Pudding

Long a British holiday tradition, this pudding, with its sticky caramel topping, is outstanding whatever the occasion. Serve it warm with whipped cream.

Prep: 20 minutes plus standing and cooling
Bake/Broil: 31 minutes

- 1 cup chopped pitted dates
- 1 teaspoon baking soda
- 1½ cups boiling water
- 10 tablespoons butter or margarine (1¼ sticks), softened
- 1 cup granulated sugar
- 1 large egg
- 1 teaspoon vanilla extract
- 2 cups all-purpose flour
- 1 teaspoon baking powder
- 1 cup packed brown sugar
- ¼ cup heavy or whipping cream
  whipped cream (optional)

1. Preheat oven to 350°F. Grease 13" by 9" baking pan. In medium bowl, combine dates, baking soda, and boiling water; let stand 15 minutes.

2. In large bowl, with mixer at medium speed, beat 6 tablespoons butter until creamy. Beat in granulated sugar until light and fluffy. Add egg and vanilla; beat until blended. Reduce speed to low; add flour and baking powder, beating to combine. Add date mixture and beat until well combined (batter will be very thin). Pour batter into prepared pan. Bake until golden and toothpick inserted in center of pudding comes out clean, about 30 minutes.

3. Meanwhile, in heavy 2-quart saucepan, combine brown sugar, cream, and remaining 4 tablespoons butter; heat to boiling over medium-high heat, stirring frequently. Boil 1 minute; remove saucepan from heat.

4. Turn oven control to broil. Spread brown-sugar mixture evenly over top of hot pudding. Broil at position closest to heat source until bubbling, about 30 seconds. Cool in pan on wire rack 15 minutes. Serve warm with whipped cream, if you like. Makes 12 servings.

Each serving: About 362 calories, 3g protein, 62g carbohydrate, 12g total fat (7g saturated), 50mg cholesterol, 259mg sodium.

Vanilla Pastry Cream

This versatile cream is used to fill many classic desserts, such as Cream Puffs (opposite). Be sure to cook the cream for the full two minutes, or it may not set up.

Prep: 5 minutes plus chilling   Cook: 10 minutes

- 2¼ cups milk
- 4 large egg yolks
- ⅔ cup sugar
- ¼ cup all-purpose flour
- ¼ cup cornstarch
- 1 tablespoon vanilla extract

1. In heavy 3-quart saucepan, heat 2 cups milk over medium-high heat until bubbles form around edge. Meanwhile, in large bowl, with wire whisk, beat egg yolks, remaining ¼ cup milk, and sugar until combined; whisk in flour and cornstarch until blended. Gradually whisk hot milk into egg-yolk mixture.

2. Return milk mixture to saucepan; cook over medium-high heat, whisking constantly, until mixture has thickened and boils. Reduce heat to low and cook, stirring, with wooden spoon, 2 minutes.

3. Remove from heat and stir in vanilla. Pour pastry cream into shallow dish. Press plastic wrap onto surface of pastry cream. Refrigerate at least 2 hours or up to overnight. Makes 2¾ cups.

Each tablespoon: About 31 calories, 1g protein, 5g carbohydrate, 1g total fat (0g saturated), 21mg cholesterol, 7mg sodium.

Chocolate Pastry Cream

Prepare pastry cream as directed above but add **3 squares (3 ounces) semisweet chocolate** and **1 square (1 ounce) unsweetened chocolate,** chopped and melted, with vanilla. Makes about 3 cups.

Each tablespoon: About 44 calories, 1g protein, 3g carbohydrate, 3g total fat (2g saturated), 23mg cholesterol, 37mg sodium.

Choux Pastry

This light, airy pastry is the basis for many glorious desserts, such as éclairs and cream puffs. Use the batter while it is still warm to get the highest puff possible.

Prep: 10 minutes Cook: 5 minutes

½ cup butter or margarine (1 stick), cut into pieces
1 cup water
¼ teaspoon salt
1 cup all-purpose flour
4 large eggs

In 3-quart saucepan, combine butter, water, and salt; heat over medium-high heat until butter melts and mixture boils. Remove from heat. Add flour all at once and, with wooden spoon, vigorously stir until mixture leaves side of pan and forms a ball. Add eggs to flour mixture, one at a time, beating well after each addition, until mixture is smooth and satiny. Shape and bake warm dough as directed in following recipes.

One recipe: About 1,566 calories, 39g protein, 98g carbohydrate, 113g total fat (64g saturated), 1,098mg cholesterol, 1,763mg sodium.

Cream Puffs

If you like, fill these cream puffs with Vanilla Pastry Cream (opposite) instead of vanilla ice cream.

Prep: 30 minutes plus standing and cooling
Bake: 40 minutes

Choux Pastry (left)
Hot Fudge Sauce (page 442)
1 quart vanilla ice cream

1. Preheat oven to 400°F. Grease and flour large cookie sheet. Prepare Choux Pastry. Drop slightly rounded ¼ cups batter in 8 large mounds, 3 inches apart, on prepared cookie sheet. With moistened finger, gently smooth tops.

2. Bake until golden, 40 to 45 minutes. Remove puffs from oven; with tip of knife, make small slit in side of each puff to release steam. Turn off oven. Return puffs to oven and let stand 10 minutes. Transfer puffs to wire rack to cool completely. With serrated knife, cut each cooled puff horizontally in half; remove and discard any moist dough inside puffs.

3. Prepare Hot Fudge Sauce. To serve, place ½-cup scoop vanilla ice cream in bottom half of each cream puff; replace tops. Spoon Hot Fudge Sauce over puffs. Makes 8 servings.

Each serving: About 525 calories, 9g protein, 51g carbohydrate, 34g total fat (20g saturated), 202mg cholesterol, 339mg sodium.

CHOUX PASTRY

Test Kitchen Tip

Choux pastry dough is unique because it is cooked twice: first on the stove and then in the oven. (Its original name was *chaud*, or "hot pastry," which eventually became *choux*.) The dough makes a light, airy, hollow pastry that is perfect for filling with ice cream, whipped cream, or pastry cream.

• When cooking the dough, be sure the butter is completely melted by the time the water comes to a full boil. If too much water evaporates, the dough will be dry.

• For the best results, use room-temperature eggs. Add them to the batter, one at a time, mixing well after each addition.

• For the highest puff, always shape and bake choux pastry dough while it is still warm.

• Bake the pastries until golden brown: Pale, undercooked pastries collapse when removed from the oven.

• Choux dough creates a lot of steam when baked: This steam needs to be released or the pastries will become soggy. As soon as the pastries are removed from the oven, use the tip of a small knife to cut a slit into the side of each one.

• Unfilled choux dough pastries can be frozen in heavy-duty ziptight plastic bags for up to one month; simply recrisp in a 400°F oven for a few minutes before serving.

Praline Cream Puff Wreath

Also known as Paris-Brest (named in honor of the bicycle race between Paris and the city of Brest in Brittany), this is cream-puff dough baked in the shape of a bicycle wheel. It makes a festive dessert at Christmas.

Prep: 50 minutes plus chilling and cooling
Bake: 55 minutes

- 2 cups milk
- 3 large egg yolks
- ⅔ cup granulated sugar
- 3 tablespoons cornstarch
- 2 teaspoons vanilla extract
- Choux Pastry (page 493)
- ¼ cup water
- ⅓ cup sliced natural almonds, toasted
- 1 cup heavy or whipping cream
- 1 tablespoon confectioners' sugar, plus additional for dusting

1. Prepare pastry cream: In heavy 3-quart saucepan, heat milk over medium-high heat until bubbles form around edge. Meanwhile, in medium bowl, with wire whisk, beat egg yolks, ⅓ cup granulated sugar, and cornstarch until well blended. Gradually whisk about half of hot milk into egg-yolk mixture. Whisk egg mixture into milk in saucepan and cook over medium heat, whisking constantly, until mixture has thickened and boils. Reduce heat to low and cook, stirring with a wooden spoon, 2 minutes.

2. Remove saucepan from heat; stir in vanilla. Pour pastry cream into medium bowl; press plastic wrap onto surface. Refrigerate until well chilled, 2 hours or up to overnight.

3. Meanwhile, prepare wreath: Preheat oven to 425°F. Grease and flour large cookie sheet. Using 8-inch cake pan or plate as guide, with toothpick, trace circle in flour on prepared cookie sheet. Prepare Choux Pastry.

4. Spoon dough into pastry bag fitted with ½-inch plain tip. Using tracing as guide, pipe dough in 1-inch-thick ring just inside circle. Pipe second ring outside of first, making sure dough rings touch. With remaining dough, pipe third ring on top of center seam of first two rings. With moistened finger, gently smooth dough rings where ends meet.

5. Bake wreath 20 minutes. Turn oven control to 375°F and bake until golden, about 25 minutes longer. Remove wreath from oven; with tip of knife, make several small slits in sides to release steam. Bake 10 minutes longer. Transfer wreath to wire rack and cool completely.

6. While wreath is baking, prepare almond praline: Lightly grease cookie sheet. In heavy 1-quart saucepan, combine remaining ⅓ cup granulated sugar and water; heat to boiling over medium-high heat, swirling pan occasionally, until sugar has dissolved. Boil mixture, without stirring, until amber in color, 5 to 7 minutes. Remove from heat and stir in almonds. Stir mixture over low heat just until it reliquifies. Immediately pour praline mixture onto prepared cookie sheet; spread with back of spoon to ½-inch thickness. Let praline stand on cookie sheet on wire rack until completely cool, about 10 minutes.

7. Break praline into small pieces. In food processor with knife blade attached, process praline to fine powder. With rubber spatula, gently fold praline into chilled pastry cream.

8. In small bowl, with mixer at medium speed, beat cream and 1 tablespoon confectioners' sugar just until stiff peaks form.

9. With long serrated knife, slice cooled wreath horizontally in half; remove and discard moist dough from inside. Spoon or pipe pastry cream into bottom of wreath; top with whipped cream. Replace top of wreath. Refrigerate up to 2 hours if not serving right away. To serve, dust with confectioners' sugar. Makes 12 servings.

Each serving: About 326 calories, 7g protein, 26g carbohydrate, 22g total fat (11g saturated), 178mg cholesterol, 177mg sodium.

Nectarine and Cherry Crisp

Two favorite summertime fruits become the perfect foil for the cookie-like topping.

Prep: 30 minutes   Bake: 1 hour to 1 hour 15 minutes

Nectarine and Cherry Filling

- ½ cup granulated sugar
- 3 tablespoons cornstarch
- 10 ripe medium nectarines (3 pounds), each cut in half, pitted, and cut into 6 wedges
- 1½ pounds dark sweet cherries, pitted
- 2 tablespoons fresh lemon juice
- 2 tablespoons cold butter or margarine, cut into small pieces

Oatmeal Topping

- 6 tablespoons butter or margarine, softened
- ⅔ cup packed brown sugar
- 1 large egg
- 2 teaspoons vanilla extract
- 1½ cups old-fashioned oats, uncooked
- ¾ cup all-purpose flour
- ¼ teaspoon baking soda
- ¼ teaspoon salt

1. Preheat oven to 375°F. Prepare filling: In large bowl, combine granulated sugar and cornstarch. Add nectarines, cherries, and lemon juice; toss until coated.

2. Spoon mixture into 13" by 9" baking dish; dot with butter. Place baking dish on foil-lined cookie sheet to catch any overflow during baking. Cover with foil and bake until mixture is gently bubbling, 40 to 50 minutes.

3. Meanwhile, prepare topping: In large bowl, with mixer at medium-high speed, beat butter and brown sugar until smooth. Add egg and vanilla; beat until fluffy. With spoon, stir in oats, flour, baking soda, and salt until mixed.

4. Drop topping by scant ¼ cups over bubbling fruit. Bake, uncovered, until topping has browned, 20 to 25 minutes. Cool slightly on wire rack to serve warm. Makes 12 servings.

Each serving: About 317 calories, 5g protein, 56g carbohydrate, 10g total fat (5g saturated), 38mg cholesterol, 162mg sodium.

Fruit Crisp

We love the flavor of pecans in the crisp topping, but you can use walnuts, hazelnuts, or almonds, if you like.

Prep: 20 minutes plus cooling   Bake: 40 minutes

- 1 lemon
- 2 pounds nectarines (about 6 medium), pitted and cut into thick wedges
- ½ pint (1 cup) raspberries
- 1 cup blueberries
- ¼ cup granulated sugar
- ⅔ cup packed brown sugar
- ½ cup all-purpose flour
- ½ teaspoon ground nutmeg
- 6 tablespoons cold butter or margarine, cut into pieces
- ½ cup old-fashioned oats, uncooked
- ⅓ cup chopped pecans
  vanilla ice cream (optional)

1. Preheat oven to 400°F. From lemon, grate ½ teaspoon peel and squeeze 2 teaspoons juice. In shallow 2-quart casserole or 8-inch baking dish, toss nectarines, raspberries, blueberries, granulated sugar, and lemon peel and juice until fruit is evenly coated.

2. In medium bowl, combine brown sugar, flour, and nutmeg. With pastry blender or 2 knives used scissor-fashion, cut in butter until mixture resembles coarse crumbs. Stir in oats and pecans; sprinkle evenly over fruit.

3. Bake crisp until top is golden and fruit is hot and bubbly, 40 to 45 minutes. Cool crisp slightly on wire rack. Serve warm with vanilla ice cream if you like. Makes 8 servings.

Each serving without ice cream: About 300 calories, 3g protein, 51g carbohydrate, 14g total fat (6g saturated), 4g fiber, 25mg cholesterol, 100mg sodium.

The Perfect Strawberry Shortcake

It just wouldn't be summer without this classic dessert.

Prep: 30 minutes plus cooling   Bake: about 15 minutes

Shortcake Biscuits
- 2½ cups all-purpose flour
- 1 tablespoon baking powder
- ½ teaspoon baking soda
- ½ teaspoon salt
- ⅓ cup plus 1 tablespoon sugar
- ½ cup (1 stick) cold butter or margarine, cut into pieces
- 1 large egg, separated
- 1 cup buttermilk

Sugared Strawberries
- 2½ pounds strawberries (8 cups)
- 2 tablespoons sugar

Whipped Cream
- 1 cup heavy or whipping cream
- 2 tablespoons sugar
- 1 teaspoon vanilla extract

The Perfect Strawberry Shortcake

1. Preheat oven to 425°F. Prepare shortcakes: In large bowl, combine flour, baking powder, baking soda, salt, and ⅓ cup sugar. Cut in butter.

2. In small bowl, with fork, beat eggyolk with buttermilk; stir into flour mixture just until mixture forms soft dough that leaves side of bowl.

3. On floured surface, with floured hands, knead dough 6 to 8 times to combine; pat dough to ¾-inch thickness.

4. Cut out shortcakes; place 1 inch apart on ungreased large cookie sheet. Press trimmings together; cut to make 8 biscuits in all.

5. In another small bowl, with fork, lightly beat egg white; brush on shortcakes. Sprinkle with remaining 1 tablespoon sugar. Bake 15 to 20 minutes or until golden. Cool on wire rack.

6. Hull strawberries, then slice. In large bowl, stir strawberries, sugar, and 1 tablespoon water. Let stand 15 minutes or refrigerate up to 4 hours.

7. Prepare whipped cream: In medium bowl, with mixer at medium speed, beat cream, sugar, and vanilla until stiff peaks form.

8. Split each shortcake horizontally. Place bottom halves on 8 dessert plates. Layer berries and cream over shortcake bottoms; replace tops. Dollop with cream and berries.

Each serving: 480 calories, 7g protein, 58g carbohydrate, 25g total fat (15g saturated), 4g fiber, 102mg cholesterol, 550mg sodium.

Peach Cobbler

A true summer treat, bursting with the flavor of ripe peaches and topped with lemon-scented biscuits. Serve with rich vanilla ice cream or softly whipped cream.

Prep: 45 minutes   Bake: 45 minutes

Peach Filling

- 6 pounds ripe medium peaches (16 to 18), peeled, pitted, and sliced (13 cups)
- ¼ cup fresh lemon juice
- ⅔ cup granulated sugar
- ½ cup packed brown sugar
- ¼ cup cornstarch

Lemon Biscuits

- 2 cups all-purpose flour
- ½ cup plus 1 teaspoon granulated sugar
- 2½ teaspoons baking powder
- ¼ teaspoon salt
- 1 teaspoon freshly grated lemon peel
- 4 tablespoons cold butter or margarine, cut into pieces
- ⅔ cup plus 1 tablespoon half-and-half or light cream

1. Prepare Peach Filling: Preheat oven to 425°F. In nonreactive 8-quart saucepot, toss peaches with lemon juice; add granulated and brown sugars and cornstarch, tossing to coat. Heat over medium heat, stirring occasionally, until bubbling; boil 1 minute. Spoon hot peach mixture into 13" by 9" baking dish. Place baking dish on foil-lined cookie sheet to catch any overflow during baking. Bake 10 minutes.

2. Prepare biscuits: In medium bowl, combine flour, ½ cup granulated sugar, baking powder, salt, and lemon peel. With pastry blender or two knives used scissor-fashion, cut in butter until mixture resembles coarse crumbs. Stir in ⅔ cup half-and-half just until mixture forms soft dough that leaves side of bowl.

3. Turn dough onto lightly floured surface. With lightly floured hands, pat into 10" by 6" rectangle. With floured knife, cut rectangle lengthwise in half, then cut each half crosswise into 6 pieces.

4. Remove baking dish from oven. Arrange biscuits on top of fruit. Brush biscuits with remaining 1 tablespoon half-and-half and sprinkle with remaining 1 teaspoon granulated sugar. Return cobbler to oven and bake until filling is hot and bubbling and biscuits are golden, about 35 minutes longer. To serve warm, cool cobbler on wire rack about 1 hour. Makes 12 servings.

Each serving: About 331 calories, 4g protein, 69g carbohydrate, 6g total fat (3g saturated), 16mg cholesterol, 199mg sodium.

Plum Kuchen

The word *kuchen*, which is German for "cake," is used to describe any number of fruit-topped or custard-filled desserts that have a yeast-batter or cake-batter base.

Prep: 30 minutes   Bake: 35 to 40 minutes

- 5 large plums or 10 prune plums
- 1 cup all-purpose flour
- 1 teaspoon baking powder
- ¼ teaspoon salt
- 6 tablespoons butter, softened
- ⅔ cup plus 2 tablespoons sugar
- 2 large eggs
- ½ teaspoon vanilla extract
- ½ teaspoon ground cinnamon

1. Cut large plums into quarters and remove pits. If using prune plums, cut in half and remove pits. Preheat oven to 350°F. Grease a 9-inch square baking pan.

2. Whisk flour, baking powder, and salt in a small bowl. In large bowl, with electric mixer on medium speed, beat butter and ⅔ cup sugar until creamy, about 2 minutes. Beat in eggs one at a time until well blended. Beat in vanilla. With mixer on low speed, beat in flour mixture just until blended.

3. Spoon batter into prepared pan and spread evenly. Arrange plums, skin side down on batter. Combine remaining 2 tablespoons sugar and cinnamon in a small bowl; sprinkle over plums. Bake until toothpick inserted in center comes out clean, 35 to 40 minutes. Cool in pan on wire rack and serve warm or room temperature. Makes 8 servings.

Each serving: About 261 calories, 4g protein, 38g carbohydrate, 11g total fat (6g saturated), 78mg cholesterol, 231mg sodium.

Berry-Lemon Tiramisù

A summer alternative to traditional tiramisù, this rendition is light, fruity, and refreshing. If time is short, use 1½ cups good-quality store-bought lemon curd.

Prep: 1 hour plus chilling

Lemon Curd

- 2 large lemons
- 3 large egg yolks
- 2 large eggs
- ⅓ cup sugar
- 6 tablespoons butter or margarine, cut into pieces

Tiramisù

- double recipe Best Berry Sauce (page 440)
- 1 lemon
- ¼ cup sugar
- ¼ cup water
- 1 package (7 ounces) crisp Italian-style ladyfingers (savoiardi)
- 1 container (8 ounces) mascarpone cheese
- ½ cup heavy or whipping cream

1. Prepare lemon curd: From 2 lemons, finely grate 1 tablespoon peel and squeeze ⅓ cup juice. In heavy nonreactive 2-quart saucepan, with wire whisk, beat grated lemon peel and juice, egg yolks, whole eggs, and sugar just until mixed. Add butter and cook over low heat, stirring constantly with a wooden spoon, until mixture coats back of spoon (do not boil, or mixture will curdle). Pour lemon curd through sieve into small bowl; press plastic wrap onto surface and refrigerate until cool, about 45 minutes.

2. Meanwhile, prepare Best Berry Sauce; cool to room temperature. From lemon, with vegetable peeler, remove 3 strips (3" by ¾" each) peel. In nonreactive, 1-quart saucepan, combine lemon peel, sugar, and water; heat over medium heat, stirring occasionally, until sugar has dissolved and syrup boils. Pour syrup into small bowl; cool to room temperature.

3. Line bottom and short sides of 13" by 9" baking dish with ladyfingers. Discard lemon peel from syrup. Brush ladyfingers with syrup. Spread berry sauce over ladyfingers in bottom of dish.

4. In large bowl, with wire whisk, mix cooled lemon curd, mascarpone, and cream until smooth. Spoon mascarpone mixture evenly over berry sauce, spreading to cover completely. Cover and refrigerate until well chilled, at least 6 hours or up to overnight. Makes 12 servings.

Each serving: About 386 calories, 5g protein, 47g carbohydrate, 21g total fat (12g saturated), 133mg cholesterol, 129mg sodium.

Red Fruit Napoleons

(Pictured on page 480)

Store-bought butter-wafer cookies make preparing this tempting dessert easy.

Prep: 15 minutes plus standing   Microwave: 1½ minutes

- 1 pound strawberries
- 1 cup raspberries
- 2 tablespoons granulated sugar
- 3 ounces white chocolate, chopped
- ½ cup heavy or whipping cream
- 3 tablespoons sour cream
- 24 very thin oval waffle-shaped butter wafer cookies
  confectioners' sugar (optional)

1. Reserve 8 small strawberries for garnish. Hull and slice remaining strawberries. In medium bowl, combine sliced strawberries, raspberries, and granulated sugar. Let stand 15 minutes, stirring occasionally to allow juices to run.

2. Meanwhile, in microwave-safe medium bowl, heat chocolate in microwave oven on High 1½ minutes; stir until melted and smooth. Cool slightly.

3. In small bowl, with mixer at medium speed, beat heavy cream and sour cream until stiff peaks form when beaters are lifted. With rubber spatula, fold mixture into white chocolate just until combined.

4. To serve, place 1 cookie on each of 8 dessert plates; top with half of cream and fruit mixtures. Repeat layering. Top with remaining cookies; sprinkle with confectioners' sugar, if you like. Garnish with strawberries. Makes 8 servings.

Each serving: About 380 calories, 5g protein, 42g carbohydrate, 22g total fat (15g saturated), 2g fiber, 62mg cholesterol, 185mg sodium.

Apple-Calvados Crepes

These crepes can be filled with almost any seasonal fruit. If you can't find Calvados, French apple brandy, use applejack. If you prefer, you can substitute apple juice.

Prep: 50 minutes plus chilling   Bake: 5 minutes

12 Basic Crepes (page 206)

Apple Filling

  5 tablespoons butter or margarine
  3 pounds Golden Delicious apples (6 large), peeled, cored, and finely chopped
  ½ cup plus 1 tablespoon sugar
  ¼ cup Calvados or applejack brandy

1. Prepare Basic Crepes. Preheat oven to 400°F. In 12-inch skillet, melt 4 tablespoons butter over medium-high heat. Stir in apples and ½ cup sugar; cover and cook until apples are soft, about 10 minutes. Remove cover and cook, stirring occasionally, until apples begin to caramelize, about 10 minutes. Stir in Calvados and remove from heat.

2. Spread scant ¼ cup apple mixture down center of each crepe and roll up jelly-roll fashion. Arrange rolled crepes in single layer, seam side down, in shallow 3½- to 4-quart baking dish. Dot with remaining 1 tablespoon butter and sprinkle with remaining 1 tablespoon sugar. Bake until heated through, about 5 minutes. Makes 6 servings.

Each serving: About 488 calories, 7g protein, 64g carbohydrate, 22g total fat (13g saturated), 161mg cholesterol, 430mg sodium.

Plum Filling

In 12-inch skillet, melt 3 tablespoons butter or margarine over medium-high heat. Add **2½ pounds ripe plums (10 large), quartered and pitted, ⅔ cup granulated sugar,** and **pinch ground cloves.** Cook, stirring occasionally, until plums are tender, 15 to 20 minutes. Fill crepes and bake as directed. in Step 2, above

Mixed Berry Filling

In medium bowl, toss **1½ cups hulled and halved strawberries, 1½ cups blueberries, 1½ cups raspberries,** and **⅔ cup granulated sugar.** Fill crepes and bake as directed in Step 2 above.

Banana Filling

In medium bowl, toss **2 large ripe bananas, sliced, with ¼ cup packed brown sugar.** Fill crepes and bake as directed in Step 2 (left).

Autumn Fruit Compote

Poach a combination of dried fruits and fresh apples with just a touch of citrus and cinnamon for a satisfying compote. Serve after a rich entrée, such as pork or roast goose.

Prep: 20 minutes plus chilling   Cook: 25 minutes

  1 orange
  1 lemon
  4 medium Golden Delicious or Jonagold apples, each peeled, cored, and cut into 16 wedges
  1 package (8 ounces) mixed dried fruit (with dried plums)
  1 cup dried Calimyrna figs (6 ounces)
  ½ cup sugar
  1 cinnamon stick (3 inches)
  3 cups water

1. From orange and lemon, with vegetable peeler, remove peel in 1-inch-wide strips. From lemon, squeeze 2 tablespoons juice (reserve orange for another use).

2. In nonreactive 4-quart saucepan, combine apples, mixed dried fruit, figs, orange and lemon peels, lemon juice, sugar, cinnamon stick, and water; heat to boiling over high heat, stirring frequently. Reduce heat; cover and simmer, stirring occasionally, until apples are tender, 15 to 20 minutes.

3. Pour fruit mixture into serving bowl; cover and refrigerate at least 4 hours to blend flavors. Serve chilled. Store in refrigerator up to 4 days. Makes 8 servings.

Each serving: About 211 calories, 1g protein, 55g carbohydrate, 1g total fat (0g saturated), 0mg cholesterol, 8mg sodium.

Chocolate Fondue with Fruit

A fun ending to any meal.

Prep: 15 minutes   Cook: 5 minutes

- 6 squares (6 ounces) semisweet chocolate, coarsely chopped
- ½ cup half-and-half or light cream
- ½ teaspoon vanilla extract
- 4 small bananas, each peeled and cut into ½-inch-thick slices
- 2 to 3 small pears, not peeled, each cored and cut into ½-inch-thick wedges
- 1 pint strawberries
- ½ cup finely chopped almonds, toasted

1. In heavy 1-quart saucepan, heat chocolate and half-and-half over low heat, stirring frequently, until chocolate has melted and mixture is smooth, about 5 minutes. Stir in vanilla; keep warm.

2. To serve, arrange bananas, pears, and strawberries on large platter. Spoon sauce into small bowl; place nuts in separate small bowl. With forks or toothpicks, have guests dip fruit into chocolate sauce, then into nuts. Makes 8 servings.

Each serving: About 249 calories, 4g protein, 36g carbohydrate, 13g total fat (5g saturated), 6mg cholesterol, 10mg sodium.

FROZEN DESSERTS

5-Minute Frozen Peach Yogurt

A food processor makes quick work of this dessert. Try it with strawberries, blueberries, or your favorite combination of flavorful frozen fruits.

Prep: 15 minutes plus standing

- 1 bag (20 ounces) frozen unsweetened peach slices
- 1 container (8 ounces) plain lowfat yogurt
- 1 cup confectioners' sugar
- 1 tablespoon fresh lemon juice
- ⅛ teaspoon almond extract

1. Let frozen peaches stand at room temperature 10 minutes. In food processor with knife blade attached, process peaches until fruit resembles finely shaved ice, occasionally scraping down side with rubber spatula.

2. With processor running, add yogurt, confectioners' sugar, lemon juice, and almond extract; process until mixture is smooth and creamy, occasionally scraping down side. Serve immediately. Makes about 4 cups or 8 servings.

Each serving: About 107 calories, 2g protein, 25g carbohydrate, 1g total fat (0g saturated), 2mg cholesterol, 20mg sodium.

ICE CREAM AND OTHER FROZEN DESSERTS

Ice cream Dairy-rich ice cream is one of life's sweet indulgences. Most are prepared with an egg-custard base, which gives ice cream its incomparable texture. These ice creams may also be called frozen custard, French ice cream, or gelato. Philadelphia-style ice cream, which doesn't contain egg yolks, has a slightly icy texture that emphasizes the flavor of the cream.

Frozen Yogurt Made from either lowfat or fat-free yogurt along with fruit or flavorings; it has the creaminess of ice cream but without all the fat.

Sherbet A frozen combination of fruit juice (usually citrus), sugar, and milk, cream, or egg whites.

Sorbet Smooth-textured sorbet is usually made from a sweetened fruit puree with no dairy products.

Ices Made from sweetened fruit purees or juices, ices are beaten with a mixer after an initial freezing to incorporate air and produce a lighter texture and then frozen again until firm.

Granita Italian in origin, granita has the same ingredients as sorbet, but it is chilled in a (baking) pan and stirred frequently during freezing to achieve a granular, icy texture (*granita* comes from the Latin word for "grain").

Berry Granita

We love using raspberries or blackberries in this granita, but you can use blueberries or a combination of berries, if you like.

Prep: 15 minutes plus cooling and freezing
Cook: 5 minutes

- 1 cup sugar
- 1¼ cups water
- 6 cups raspberries or blackberries
- 2 tablespoons fresh lime juice

1. In 2-quart saucepan, combine sugar and water; heat to boiling over high heat, stirring until sugar has dissolved. Reduce heat to medium and cook 1 minute. Set saucepan in bowl of ice water until syrup is cool.

2. Meanwhile, in blender or in food processor with knife blade attached, puree raspberries until smooth. With spoon, press puree through sieve into medium bowl; discard seeds.

3. Stir sugar syrup and lime juice into puree; pour into 9-inch square metal baking pan. Cover, freeze, and scrape as directed for granitas (opposite). Makes about 8 cups or 16 servings.

Each serving: About 71 calories, 0g protein, 18g carbohydrate, 0g total fat (0g saturated), 0mg cholesterol, 0mg sodium.

Strawberry Granita

Prepare syrup as directed in Step 1 above, but use ½ **cup sugar** and **1 cup water.** In blender or in food processor with knife blade attached, puree **2 pints strawberries,** hulled. Stir strawberry puree and **1 tablespoon fresh lemon juice** into syrup. Freeze as directed. Makes about 6 cups or 12 servings.

Each serving: About 49 calories, 0g protein, 12g carbohydrate, 0g total fat (0g saturated), 0mg cholesterol, 1mg sodium.

Watermelon Granita

Prepare syrup as directed in Step 1 (left), but use ¾ **cup water.** Remove rind and seeds from **1 piece (5½ pounds) watermelon;** cut fruit into bite-size pieces (9 cups). In blender or in food processor with knife blade attached, in batches, puree watermelon until smooth. Press through sieve into large bowl; discard fibers. Stir sugar syrup and lime juice into watermelon puree. Freeze as directed. Makes about 9 cups or 18 servings.

Each serving: About 69 calories, 0g protein, 17g carbohydrate, 0g total fat (0g saturated), 0mg cholesterol, 2mg sodium.

Coffee Granita

This granita is a Neapolitan tradition. If you prefer, use decaffeinated espresso.

Prep: 10 minutes plus cooling and freezing

- ⅔ cup sugar
- 2 cups hot espresso coffee
  unsweetened whipped cream (optional)

In medium bowl, stir sugar and espresso until sugar has completely dissolved. Pour into 9-inch square metal baking pan; cool. Cover, freeze, and scrape as directed for granitas (opposite). Serve granita with whipped cream, if you like. Makes about 5 cups or 10 servings.

Each serving without whipped cream: About 53 calories, 0g protein, 14g carbohydrate, 0g total fat (0g saturated), 0mg cholesterol, 1mg sodium.

 Test Kitchen Tip If you do not have an espresso coffeemaker, use 3 cups water and 1⅓ cups ground espresso coffee in an automatic drip coffeemaker.

Lemon Granita

This simple, zesty granita has an invigorating tang.

Prep: 10 minutes plus cooling and freezing
Cook: 10 minutes

- 1 cup sugar
- 2 cups water
- 4 large lemons

1. In 2-quart saucepan, combine sugar and water; heat to boiling over high heat, stirring until sugar has dissolved. Reduce heat to medium and cook 5 minutes. Set saucepan in bowl of ice water until syrup is cool.

2. Meanwhile, from lemons, grate 2 teaspoons peel and squeeze ¾ cup juice.

3. Stir lemon peel and juice into sugar syrup; pour into 9-inch square metal baking pan. Cover, freeze, and scrape as directed for granitas (below). Makes about 4 cups or 8 servings.

Each serving: About 103 calories, 0g protein, 27g carbohydrate, 0g total fat (0g saturated), 0mg cholesterol, 1mg sodium.

GRANITAS

Cover and freeze the granita mixture until partially frozen, about 2 hours. Stir with a fork to break up the chunks. Cover and freeze until completely frozen, at least 3 hours or up to overnight. To serve, let the granita stand at room temperature until slightly softened, about 15 minutes. Use a metal spoon to scrape across the surface of the granita, transferring the ice shards to chilled dessert dishes or wine goblets without packing them.

Tartufo

These chocolate-coated ice-cream balls are intended to resemble truffles (*tartufo* means "truffle" in Italian).

Prep: 30 minutes plus freezing

- 1 pint chocolate or vanilla ice cream
- 2 tablespoons brandy
- 6 maraschino cherries, stems removed
- 1 cup fine amaretti cookie crumbs (20 cookies)
- 1½ cups semisweet chocolate chips
- 4 tablespoons butter or margarine, cut into pieces
- 2 tablespoons light corn syrup

1. Place ice cream in refrigerator to soften slightly, about 30 minutes. Line small cookie sheet with waxed paper and place in freezer. In cup, pour brandy over cherries. Place amaretti crumbs on waxed paper.

2. Working quickly, with large ice-cream scoop (⅓ cup), scoop ball of ice cream. With ice cream still in scoop, gently press 1 cherry deep into center of ball; reshape ice cream around cherry. Release ice-cream ball on top of amaretti crumbs and roll to coat well. Place on prepared cookie sheet in freezer. Repeat to make 6 ice-cream balls. Freeze until firm, at least 1½ hours.

3. In medium bowl set over saucepan of simmering water, heat chocolate chips with butter and corn syrup, stirring occasionally, until chocolate and butter have melted and mixture is smooth. Remove pan from heat, but leave bowl in place to keep chocolate warm for easier coating.

4. Remove 1 ice-cream ball from freezer; place in slotted spoon and slip ice-cream ball into melted chocolate, turning quickly to coat thoroughly. Return to cookie sheet. Repeat with remaining ice-cream balls. Freeze until chocolate is firm, about 1 hour. If not serving right away, wrap in foil and freeze up to 1 day.

5. To serve, let tartufo stand at room temperature until slightly softened, about 10 minutes. Makes 6 servings.

Each serving: About 476 calories, 5g protein, 59g carbohydrate, 27g total fat (15g saturated), 36mg cholesterol, 133mg sodium.

Tulipes

For an elegant presentation at a dinner party or other special occasion, serve your favorite ice cream or sorbet in these delicate cookie shells.

Prep: 30 minutes   Bake: 5 minutes per batch

- 3 large egg whites
- ¾ cup confectioners' sugar
- ½ cup all-purpose flour
- 6 tablespoons butter, melted (do not use margarine)
- ½ teaspoon vanilla extract
- ¼ teaspoon salt
- 1 quart ice cream or sorbet

1. Preheat oven to 350°F. Grease large cookie sheet. In large bowl, with wire whisk, beat egg whites, confectioners' sugar, and flour until well blended. Beat in melted butter, vanilla, and salt.

2. Make 2 cookies by dropping batter by heaping tablespoons, 4 inches apart, on prepared cookie sheet. With narrow metal spatula, spread batter to form 4-inch rounds. Bake cookies until golden around edges, 5 to 7 minutes.

3. Place two 2-inch-diameter glasses upside down on work surface. With spatula, quickly lift 1 hot cookie and gently shape over bottom of glass. Shape second cookie. When cookies are  cool, transfer to wire rack. (If cookies become too firm to shape, return them to cookie sheet and place in oven to soften slightly.)

4. Repeat Steps 2 and 3 with remaining batter. (Batter will become slightly thicker upon standing.) Store tulipes in single layer in airtight container at room temperature. To serve, place on dessert plates and fill with ice cream. Makes about 12 tulipes.

Each serving with ice cream: About 192 calories, 3g protein, 22g carbohydrate, 11g total fat (7g saturated), 35mg cholesterol, 155mg sodium.

Sorbet-and-Cream Cake

Here's a colorful dessert for a festive meal. Substitute raspberry and passion fruit sorbets, or your favorite flavors, for the strawberry and mango, if you prefer.

**Prep: 30 minutes plus freezing and chilling
Bake: 10 minutes**

- 1 cup vanilla wafer crumbs (30 cookies)
- 4 tablespoons butter or margarine, melted
- ½ teaspoon freshly grated lime peel
- 2 pints vanilla ice cream
- 1 pint strawberry sorbet
- 1 pint mango sorbet
- 1 pint lemon sorbet
- 1 ripe mango, peeled and sliced
  fresh raspberries

1. Preheat oven to 375°F. In 9" by 3" springform pan, with fork, stir wafer crumbs, melted butter, and lime peel until crumbs are evenly moistened. With hand, press mixture firmly onto bottom of pan. Bake crust 10 minutes. Place in freezer until well chilled, about 30 minutes.

2. Meanwhile, place 1 pint vanilla ice cream and strawberry, mango, and lemon sorbets in refrigerator to soften slightly, about 30 minutes.

3. Arrange alternating scoops of vanilla ice cream and strawberry, mango, and lemon sorbets over crust in two layers; with rubber spatula, press down to eliminate air pockets. Place in freezer until ice cream is firm, about 30 minutes.

4. Meanwhile, place remaining 1 pint vanilla ice cream in refrigerator to soften slightly. With narrow metal spatula, evenly spread vanilla ice cream over ice-cream and sorbet layers. Cover and freeze until firm, at least 4 hours or up to 1 day.

5. To serve, dip small knife in hot water, shaking off excess; run knife around edge of pan to loosen cake. Remove side of pan; place cake on platter. Let stand about 15 minutes at room temperature for easier slicing. Decorate top of cake with mango slices and raspberries. Makes 20 servings.

Each serving: About 161 calories, 1g protein, 27g carbohydrate, 6g total fat (3g saturated), 18mg cholesterol, 63mg sodium.

Raspberry Baked-Alaska Pie

A showstopping dessert that is sure to win you applause.

Prep: 40 minutes plus freezing   Bake: 2 minutes

- 3 pints vanilla ice cream
- 2 packages (3 ounces each) soft ladyfingers, split in half
- ⅓ cup orange-flavored liqueur
- 1 package (10 ounces) frozen raspberries in syrup, slightly thawed
- 4 large egg whites
- ¾ cup sugar
- 4 teaspoons water
- ¼ teaspoon cream of tartar
- ¼ teaspoon salt

ICE CREAM TREATS

Mini Ice Cream Sandwiches
Spread flat side of 2 chocolate- or vanilla-wafer cookies with thin layer of creamy peanut butter. Sandwich a small scoop of your favorite (slightly softened) ice cream between two peanut butter–coated sides.

Waffles and Ice Cream
Lightly toast 1 frozen Belgian waffle. Top with vanilla ice cream or frozen yogurt and frozen (thawed) strawberries or raspberries in syrup.

Ice Cream Parfaits
Pour some almond-flavored liqueur over 1 scoop coffee ice cream. Top with whipped cream and crushed amaretti cookies.

Ice Cream Drink
In blender, combine 2 tablespoons orange-flavored liqueur with 2 scoops peach or vanilla ice cream; blend until smooth. Pour into tall glass and top with whipped cream.

S'more Sundae
Spoon 1 tablespoon fudge sauce over graham cracker. Top with 1 scoop chocolate ice cream and marshmallow topping.

1. Transfer ice cream to large bowl and place in refrigerator to soften slightly, about 30 minutes. Line bottom and side of 9-inch deep-dish pie plate with about two-thirds of ladyfingers, rounded side down, allowing ends to extend beyond pie plate rim. Drizzle with half of liqueur.

2. In medium bowl, crush raspberries. Drop dollops of raspberries over ice cream in large bowl; with knife, cut through raspberries and ice cream once or twice to create marbled effect. With large serving spoon, carefully transfer half of ice cream into pie plate, keeping marbled effect; place bowl of remaining ice cream in freezer. Arrange remaining ladyfingers on top of ice cream in pie plate; drizzle with remaining liqueur. Spoon remaining ice cream evenly over ladyfingers. Cover and freeze until firm, at least 4 hours.

3. In medium bowl set over saucepan of simmering water, with mixer at medium speed, beat egg whites, sugar, water, cream of tartar, and salt until soft peaks form when beaters are lifted or until temperature on thermometer reaches 160°F, 10 to 14 minutes. Place bowl on work surface; continue to beat egg whites until stiff peaks form when beaters are lifted, 8 to 10 minutes longer. With spoon, quickly spread meringue over top of pie, sealing meringue to edge and making decorative swirls with back of spoon. Freeze, uncovered, up to 6 hours.

4. To serve, preheat oven to 500°F. Bake pie until meringue is lightly browned, 2 to 3 minutes. Serve immediately. Makes 12 servings.

Each serving: About 281 calories, 5g protein, 45g carbohydrate, 9g total fat (5g saturated), 81mg cholesterol, 140mg sodium.

19

CAKES & FROSTINGS

This all-American dessert may be one of the most enduring images in the world of desserts. So, to satisfy everyone's sweet cravings, we offer cakes for every appetite and every occasion: gingerbread for the holidays, luscious cheesecakes for parties, tempting butter cakes for family suppers, and some of the most delectable chocolate cakes ever.

PERFECT CAKES EVERY TIME

The ingredients in cake recipes are carefully balanced, so it is essential that you precisely measure the ingredients and make sure that they are at room-temperature.

Butter You can usually use either butter or stick margarine, but butter has superior flavor. Soften the butter just until malleable.

Eggs We use large eggs to make our cakes. Chilled eggs don't beat to their maximum volume, so leave them out at room temperature after separating them.

Flour Although most of our recipes call for all-purpose flour, some use cake flour, which produces tender cakes. If you don't have cake flour, for every cup of cake flour, spoon 2 tablespoons of cornstarch into a 1-cup measure. Spoon in enough all-purpose flour to fill the cup, then level it off. When measuring flour, use the spoon-and-sweep method (see Basics, page 11).

Pans Always use the recommended pan size. Measure the pan if necessary. To line a pan, place it on a piece of waxed paper. Use a pencil to trace around the bottom edge and cut out the shape.

Greasing and Flouring If the recipe directs you, grease or grease and flour the pan(s). (Pans for foam cakes are not greased because these batters need to cling to the side of the pan as they rise.) Apply a film of vegetable shortening using a folded piece of paper towel. When greasing a Bundt pan, be sure to get into all the crevices, or use nonstick cooking spray. To flour a greased pan, sprinkle a tablespoon or so of flour into the pan, tilting it to coat the bottom and side. Invert the pan and tap out the excess.

Oven Know-How Position the oven racks as directed, then thoroughly preheat the oven. When baking two cakes, place a rack in the center of the oven. If baking more cakes, place the racks in the center and upper third of the oven. Stagger the pans so they are not directly above one another. Cake pans should never touch the sides of the oven or each other. For cakes baked in tube pans, position the oven rack in the lower third of the oven.

Vanilla Chiffon Cake

STORING CAKES

Always refrigerate cakes that contain fillings or frostings made with whipped cream, cream cheese, sour cream, yogurt, or eggs. Because of their high fat content, unfrosted butter cakes stay moist for two or three days at room temperature. Foam cakes contain little or no fat and dry out quickly; store at room temperature for up to two days.

To freeze butter cakes, place them, unwrapped, in the freezer until firm; wrap in plastic and then in heavy-duty foil. Frosted cakes can be frozen for up to two months; unfrosted cakes for up to six months. Do not freeze cakes with whipped-cream frostings or egg-based fillings. Foam cakes can be frozen in heavy-duty zip-tight plastic bags for up to three months.

BUTTER CAKES

These cakes rely on fat for moistness and richness. The fat must be beaten well with the sugar to provide an aerated base. Beat the butter-and-sugar mixture with an electric mixer on medium speed until light and fluffy, scraping down the side of the bowl as directed. Beat in the eggs, one a time, beating well after each addition.

Pour the batter into the prepared pan(s) and gently tap the pan(s) on a counter to break any large air bubbles. The cake is done when a toothpick inserted into the center comes out clean. Some cakes also pull away slightly from the side of the pan. Or lightly press the center of the cake with your finger; the top should spring back.

Cool the cake on a wire rack for ten minutes. Run a knife around the inside of the pan. Invert a second rack on top of the pan. Invert both racks along with the pan. Remove the top rack and the cake pan. Replace the top rack and invert the cake again, so it is right side up.

Yellow Cake

Make this versatile cake with shortening (for delicate flavor and crumb) or butter (for rich flavor). Either way, it will have the taste of old-fashioned goodness.

Prep: 45 minutes plus cooling   Bake: 30 minutes

- 2 **cups all-purpose flour**
- 2 **teaspoons baking powder**
- 1 **teaspoon salt**
- ½ **cup vegetable shortening or ½ cup butter or margarine (1 stick), softened**
- 1¼ **cups sugar**
- 3 **large eggs**
- 1 **teaspoon vanilla extract**
- 1 **cup milk**
  Chocolate Butter Frosting (page 526)

1. Preheat oven to 350°F. Grease and flour two 8-inch round cake pans or one 9-inch square baking pan, or line twenty-four 2½-inch muffin-pan cups with paper baking liners. (Preheat oven to 325°F if using 9-inch square pan.)

2. In medium bowl, with wire whisk, stir flour, baking powder, and salt. In large bowl, with mixer at medium speed, beat shortening and sugar until light and fluffy, about 5 minutes. Add eggs, one at a time, beating well after each addition. Beat in vanilla. Reduce speed to low; add flour mixture alternately with milk, beginning and ending with flour mixture. Beat just until smooth, frequently scraping bowl with rubber spatula.

3. Divide batter between prepared pans; spread evenly. Bake until toothpick inserted in center comes out clean, about 30 minutes for 8-inch layers, 40 to 45 minutes for 9-inch square cake, or 20 to 25 minutes for cupcakes. Cool in pans on wire racks 10 minutes. Run thin knife around layers to loosen from sides of pans; invert onto racks to cool completely.

4. Prepare Chocolate Butter Frosting. Place one layer, rounded side down, on cake plate. With narrow metal spatula, spread ⅔ cup frosting over layer. Top with second layer, rounded side up. Spread remaining frosting over side and top of cake. Makes 12 servings.

Each serving with Chocolate Butter Frosting: About 526 calories, 5g protein, 66g carbohydrate, 28g total fat (13g saturated), 87mg cholesterol, 421mg sodium.

Orange Cake

Prepare cake as directed but add **1 teaspoon freshly grated orange peel** with vanilla. Frost with Fluffy White Frosting (page 528) or Orange Butter Frosting (page 526).

Each serving with Fluffy White Frosting: About 345 calories, 5g protein, 56g carbohydrate, 11g total fat (3g saturated), 56mg cholesterol, 312mg sodium.

Each serving with Orange Butter Frosting: About 494 calories, 5g protein, 77g carbohydrate, 19g total fat (8g saturated), 77mg cholesterol, 383mg sodium.

Silver White Cake

Made without egg yolks, this cake has a pristine ivory color that can be accented by a variety of frostings. Try Peppermint Whipped Cream Frosting (page 527), or fill with Lemon Filling (page 528), then frost with Fluffy White Frosting (page 528).

Prep: 50 minutes plus cooling   Bake: 30 minutes

- 2 cups cake flour (not self-rising)
- 2 teaspoons baking powder
- 1 teaspoon salt
- 4 large egg whites
- 1¼ cups sugar
- ½ cup vegetable shortening
- 1 teaspoon vanilla extract
- ¼ teaspoon almond extract
- 1 cup milk
- Chocolate Butter Frosting (page 526)

1. Preheat oven to 350°F. Grease and flour two 8-inch round cake pans.

2. In medium bowl, with wire whisk, stir flour, baking powder, and salt. In medium bowl, with mixer at high speed, beat egg whites until soft peaks form when beaters are lifted. Sprinkle in ¼ cup sugar, 1 tablespoon at a time, beating until sugar has dissolved and egg whites stand in stiff, glossy peaks when beaters are lifted.

3. In large bowl, with mixer at low speed, beat shortening and remaining 1 cup sugar until blended. Increase speed to medium. Beat in vanilla and almond extracts. Reduce speed to low; add flour mixture alter-

nately with milk, beginning and ending with flour mixture. Beat just until smooth, occasionally scraping bowl with rubber spatula. Gently fold in beaten egg whites, one-third at a time, just until blended.

4. Divide batter between prepared pans; spread evenly. Bake until toothpick inserted in center comes out clean, about 30 minutes. Cool in pans on wire racks 10 minutes. Run thin knife around layers to loosen from sides of pans. Invert onto racks to cool completely.

5. Prepare Chocolate Butter Frosting. Place one layer, rounded side down, on cake plate. With narrow metal spatula, spread ⅔ cup frosting over layer. Top with second layer, rounded side up. Spread remaining frosting over side and top of cake. Makes 12 servings.

Each serving with Chocolate Butter Frosting: About 492 calories, 4g protein, 63g carbohydrate, 26g total fat (13g saturated), 34mg cholesterol, 423mg sodium.

FROSTING LAYER CAKES

Use a narrow metal spatula to spread frosting. It is easiest to frost a cake if it is elevated and can be turned. If you don't have a cake decorating stand, place the cake on a serving plate set on a large coffee can or inverted bowl.

Simply brush off any crumbs and use a serrated knife to trim away any crisp edges. Place the first layer, rounded side down, on the serving plate. To keep the plate clean, tuck strips of waxed paper under the cake, covering the plate edge. Spread the cake layer with ½ to ⅔ cup frosting, spreading it almost to the edge. Top with the second cake layer, rounded side up. Thinly frost the cake to set the crumbs and keep them in place; first coat the top of the cake, then the side. Finish the cake with a thicker layer of frosting. Where the top and side of the frosting meet, smooth it by sweeping and swirling the edge of the frosting toward the center of the cake. Then slip out the waxed paper strips and discard.

Golden Butter Cake

This classic layer cake is a good candidate for frosting, but it is so moist that it can also be baked in a tube pan, dusted with confectioners' sugar, and enjoyed.

Prep: 45 minutes plus cooling   Bake: 23 minutes

- 3 cups cake flour (not self-rising)
- 1 tablespoon baking powder
- ½ teaspoon salt
- 1 cup butter or margarine (2 sticks), softened
- 2 cups sugar
- 4 large eggs
- 2 teaspoons vanilla extract
- 1 cup milk
- Orange Butter Frosting (page 526)

1. Preheat oven to 350°F. Grease three 8-inch round cake pans. Line bottoms with waxed paper; grease and flour paper. Or grease and flour 9-inch fluted tube pan.

2. In medium bowl, with wire whisk, stir flour, baking powder, and salt. In large bowl, with mixer at medium-high speed, beat butter and sugar until light and fluffy, about 5 minutes. Add eggs, one at a time, beating well after each addition. Beat in vanilla. Reduce speed to low; add flour mixture alternately with milk, beginning and ending with flour mixture. Beat just until smooth, scraping bowl with rubber spatula.

Spice Layer Cake with Brown Butter Frosting

3. Divide batter among prepared cake pans; spread evenly. Place two pans on upper oven rack and one pan on lower oven rack so that pans are not directly above one another. Bake until toothpick inserted in center comes out clean, 23 to 28 minutes for 8-inch layers, or 50 to 55 minutes for tube pan. Cool in pans on wire racks 10 minutes. Run thin knife around layers to loosen from sides of pans. Or, if using fluted tube pan, run tip of knife around edge of cake to loosen. Invert onto racks. Remove waxed paper; cool completely.

4. Prepare Orange Butter Frosting. Place one layer, rounded side down, on cake plate. With narrow metal spatula, spread ⅔ cup frosting over layer. Top with second layer, rounded side up, and spread with ⅔ cup frosting. Place remaining layer, rounded side up, on top. Spread remaining frosting over side and top of cake. Makes 16 servings.

Each serving with Orange Butter Frosting: About 472 calories, 4g protein, 70g carbohydrate, 20g total fat (12g saturated) 105mg cholesterol, 359mg sodium.

Each serving without frosting: About 315 calories, 4g protein, 43g carbohydrate, 14g total fat (8g saturated), 86mg cholesterol, 305mg sodium.

Spice Layer Cake

Prepare as directed but use **2⅔ cups all-purpose flour, 2½ teaspoons baking powder,** and **1 teaspoon salt.** Add **2 teaspoons ground cinnamon, 1 teaspoon ground ginger, ½ teaspoon ground ginger,** and **¼ teaspoon ground cloves;** with wire whisk, stir until blended. In Step 2, use **1 cup granulated** and **1 cup dark brown sugar** and **5 eggs.** Omit vanilla. Bake 25 to 30 minutes. Proceed as directed, using Brown Butter Frosting (page 526). Makes 16 servings.

Each serving with Brown Butter Frosting: About 490 calories, 5g protein, 73g carbohydrate, 20g total fat (12g saturated), 116mg cholesterol, 360mg sodium.

Peanut Butter Cupcakes

These cupcakes are great for kids' parties. If you prefer, omit the chocolate topping and use your favorite frosting.

Prep: 10 minutes Bake: 18 minutes

1¾ cups all-purpose flour
 1 tablespoon baking powder
 ½ teaspoon salt
 ½ cup creamy or chunky peanut butter
 ¼ cup vegetable shortening
 ¾ cup sugar
 2 large eggs
 ¾ teaspoon vanilla extract
 1 cup milk
 1 bar (4 ounces) semisweet or milk chocolate, cut into 18 pieces

1. Preheat oven to 350°F. Line eighteen 2½-inch muffin-pan cups with paper baking liners.

2. In small bowl, with wire whisk, stir flour, baking powder, and salt.

3. In large bowl, with mixer at medium speed, beat peanut butter and shortening until combined. Add sugar and beat until light and fluffy, about 3 minutes. Add eggs, one at a time, beating well after each addition. Beat in vanilla. Reduce speed to low. Add flour mixture alternately with milk, beginning and ending with flour mixture, occasionally scraping bowl with rubber spatula.

4. Divide batter evenly among cups. Bake until toothpick inserted in center of cupcake comes out clean, about 18 minutes. Place 1 piece of chocolate on top of each cupcake; return to oven until chocolate melts, about 1 minute. With small metal spatula, spread chocolate over tops of cupcakes. Remove from pans and cool on wire rack. Makes 18 cupcakes.

Each cupcake: About 192 calories, 5g protein, 23g carbohydrate, 10g total fat (3g saturated), 26mg cholesterol, 193mg sodium.

Applesauce Spice Cake

For a quick snack, make this easy cake. You may already have all of the ingredients on hand.

Prep: 20 minutes Bake: 40 minutes

 2 cups all-purpose flour
1½ teaspoons ground cinnamon
 1 teaspoon baking powder
 ½ teaspoon baking soda
 ½ teaspoon ground ginger
 ¼ teaspoon ground nutmeg
 ½ teaspoon salt
 ½ cup butter or margarine (1 stick), softened
 ¼ cup granulated sugar
 1 cup packed dark brown sugar
 2 large eggs
1¼ cups unsweetened applesauce
 ½ cup dark seedless raisins
 confectioners' sugar

1. Preheat oven to 350°F. Grease and flour 9-inch square baking pan.

2. In medium bowl, with wire whisk, stir flour, cinnamon, baking powder, baking soda, ginger, nutmeg, and salt.

3. In large bowl, with mixer at low speed, beat butter and granulated and brown sugars until blended. Increase speed to medium-high; beat until light and fluffy, about 3 minutes. Add eggs, one at a time, beating well after each addition. Reduce speed to low; beat in applesauce. Mixture may appear curdled. Beat in flour mixture until smooth, occasionally scraping bowl with rubber spatula. Stir in raisins.

4. Scrape batter into prepared pan; spread evenly. Bake cake until toothpick inserted in center comes out clean, about 40 minutes. Cool completely in pan on wire rack. To serve, dust with confectioners' sugar. Makes 9 servings.

Each serving: About 369 calories, 5g protein, 62g carbohydrate, 12g total fat (7g saturated), 75mg cholesterol, 383mg sodium.

Pineapple Upside-Down Cake

We cut the pineapple slices in half to fit more fruit into the pan. Plums or apples make delicious variations (you won't need the pineapple juice).

Prep: 30 minutes   Bake: 40 minutes

- 2 cans (8 ounces each) pineapple slices in juice
- 1/3 cup packed brown sugar
- 8 tablespoons butter or margarine (1 stick), softened
- 1 cup cake flour (not self-rising)
- 1 teaspoon baking powder
- 1/4 teaspoon salt
- 2/3 cup granulated sugar
- 1 large egg
- 1 teaspoon vanilla extract
- 1/3 cup milk

1. Preheat oven to 325°F. Drain pineapple slices in sieve set over bowl. Reserve 2 tablespoons juice. Cut 8 pineapple slices in half and drain on paper towels. Refrigerate remaining slices for another use.

2. In 10-inch oven-safe skillet (if skillet is not oven-safe, wrap handle with double layer of foil), heat brown sugar and 2 tablespoons butter over medium heat until melted. Stir in reserved pineapple juice and heat to boiling; boil 1 minute. Remove skillet from heat. Decoratively arrange pineapple in skillet, overlapping slices slightly to fit.

3. In small bowl, with wire whisk, stir flour, baking powder, and salt. In large bowl, with mixer at high speed, beat remaining 6 tablespoons butter and granulated sugar until fluffy, frequently scraping bowl with rubber spatula. Reduce speed to low; beat in egg and vanilla until well blended. Add flour mixture alternately with milk, beginning and ending with flour mixture. Beat just until blended.

4. Spoon batter over pineapple; spread evenly with rubber spatula. Bake until toothpick inserted in center comes out clean, 40 to 45 minutes. Run thin knife around cake to loosen from side of skillet; invert onto serving plate. (If any pineapple slices stick to skillet, place on cake.) Serve warm or at room temperature. Makes 8 servings.

Each serving: About 302 calories, 3g protein, 46g carbohydrate, 13g total fat (8g saturated), 59mg cholesterol, 267mg sodium.

Plum Upside-Down Cake

Prepare as directed but substitute **1 pound plums** for pineapple. Cut plums into 1/2-inch-thick wedges. Heat brown sugar and 2 tablespoons butter in oven-safe skillet over medium heat until melted. Add plums and increase heat to high. Cook, stirring, until plums are glazed with brown-sugar mixture, about 1 minute.

Apple Upside-Down Cake

Prepare as directed but substitute **3 large Golden Delicious apples (1 1/2 pounds)** for pineapple. Peel, core, and cut apples into 1/4-inch-thick wedges. Heat brown sugar and 2 tablespoons butter in oven-safe skillet over medium heat until melted. Add apple wedges and cook over high heat until apples are fork-tender and begin to brown, 7 to 8 minutes.

Gingerbread

Because it's mixed by hand, this gingerbread has a dense, chewy texture. For a more cakelike consistency, beat the batter with an electric mixer for two full minutes. (One important tip: Measure the water *after* it comes to a boil.)

Prep: 15 minutes   Bake: 45 minutes

- 2 cups all-purpose flour
- 1/2 cup sugar
- 2 teaspoons ground ginger
- 1 teaspoon ground cinnamon
- 1/2 teaspoon baking soda
- 1/2 teaspoon salt
- 1 cup light (mild) molasses
- 1/2 cup butter or margarine (1 stick), cut into 4 pieces
- 3/4 cup boiling water
- 1 large egg, lightly beaten

1. Preheat oven to 350°F. Grease and flour 9-inch square baking pan.

2. In large bowl, with wire whisk, stir flour, sugar, ginger, cinnamon, baking soda, and salt until blended.

3. In small bowl, combine molasses and butter. Add boiling water and stir until butter melts. Add molasses mixture and beaten egg to flour mixture; whisk until smooth.

4. With rubber spatula, scrape batter into prepared pan. Bake gingerbread until toothpick inserted in center comes out clean, 45 to 50 minutes. Cool in pan on wire rack. Serve gingerbread warm or at room temperature. Makes 9 servings.

Each serving: About 349 calories, 4g protein, 59g carbohydrate, 12g total fat (7g saturated), 51mg cholesterol, 324mg sodium.

Carrot Cake

Legend has it that George Washington enjoyed some carrot tea bread in 1783, and it remains one of America's favorite desserts.

Prep: 40 minutes plus cooling   Bake: 55 minutes

2½	cups all-purpose flour
2	teaspoons baking soda
2	teaspoons ground cinnamon
1	teaspoon baking powder
1	teaspoon salt
½	teaspoon ground nutmeg
4	large eggs
1	cup granulated sugar
¾	cup packed light brown sugar
½	cup vegetable oil
¼	cup milk
1	tablespoon vanilla extract
3	cups loosely packed shredded carrots (about 6 medium)
1	cup walnuts (4 ounces), chopped
¾	cup dark seedless raisins
	Cream Cheese Frosting (page 528)

1. Preheat oven to 350°F. Grease 13" by 9" baking pan. Line bottom with waxed paper; grease paper. Dust pan with flour. Or grease and flour 10-inch Bundt pan.

2. In medium bowl, with wire whisk, stir flour, baking soda, cinnamon, baking powder, salt, and nutmeg.

3. In large bowl, with mixer at medium-high speed, beat eggs and granulated and brown sugars until blended, about 2 minutes, frequently scraping bowl with rubber spatula. Beat in oil, milk, and vanilla. Reduce speed to low; add flour mixture and beat until smooth, about 1 minute, scraping bowl. Fold in carrots, walnuts, and raisins.

4. Spoon batter into prepared pan; spread evenly. Bake until toothpick inserted in center comes out almost clean, 55 to 60 minutes for 13" by 9" cake or about 1 hour for Bundt cake. Cool in pan on wire rack 10 minutes. Run thin knife around cake to loosen from sides of pan. Or, if using Bundt pan, run tip of knife around edge of cake to loosen. Invert onto rack. Remove waxed paper; cool completely.

5. Meanwhile, prepare Cream Cheese Frosting. Transfer cooled cake to cake plate. With narrow metal spatula, spread frosting over sides and top of cake. Makes 16 servings.

Each serving with Cream Cheese Frosting: About 486 calories, 6g protein, 70g carbohydrate, 22g total fat (7g saturated) 78mg cholesterol, 436mg sodium.

Deluxe Carrot Cake

Prepare as directed but omit milk; fold in **1 can (8 to 8¼ ounces) crushed pineapple in unsweetened juice** with walnuts and raisins.

Carrot Cake with Cream Cheese Frosting

Apricot-Pecan Fruitcake

This light fruitcake has a mellow brandy flavor and is studded with chunks of tangy apricots and buttery pecans. You can make it up to one week ahead, but it's best to glaze it the day it's served.

Prep: 20 minutes plus cooling
Bake: 1 hour 10 minutes

1	pound dried apricot halves (2½ cups), cut into ½-inch pieces
2	cups pecans (8 ounces), coarsely chopped, plus ⅔ cup pecan halves
1	tablespoon plus 2 cups all-purpose flour
2	teaspoons baking powder
1	teaspoon salt
1	cup butter or margarine (2 sticks), softened
1¼	cups sugar
5	large eggs
½	cup brandy
1	tablespoon vanilla extract
⅓	cup apricot preserves

1. Preheat oven to 325°F and grease 9- to 10-inch tube pan.

2. In medium bowl, toss apricots and coarsely chopped pecans with 1 tablespoon flour. In separate medium bowl, with wire whisk, stir remaining 2 cups flour, baking powder, and salt.

3. In large bowl, with mixer at low speed, beat butter and sugar until blended. Increase speed to high; beat until light and fluffy, about 5 minutes, occasionally scraping bowl with rubber spatula. Reduce speed to low. Add eggs, brandy, vanilla, and flour mixture; beat until well blended, frequently scraping bowl. Stir apricot mixture into flour mixture.

4. Spoon batter into prepared pan; spread evenly. Arrange pecan halves on top of batter in two concentric circles. Bake until toothpick inserted in center comes out clean, 1 hour 10 to 20 minutes. Cool in pan on wire rack 10 minutes. Run thin knife around cake to loosen from side and center tube of pan; lift tube to separate cake from pan side. Slide knife under cake to separate from bottom of pan. Invert cake onto wire rack and remove center tube. Turn cake, right side up, onto rack to cool completely.

5. In 1-quart saucepan, heat apricot preserves over medium-high heat, stirring constantly, until melted and bubbling. Strain through sieve set over small bowl. With pastry brush, brush cooled cake with preserves. Or wrap cake and refrigerate up to 1 week, then brush with preserves before serving. Makes 24 servings.

Each serving: About 300 calories, 4g protein, 35g carbohydrate, 17g total fat (6g saturated), 65mg cholesterol, 233mg sodium.

Cranberry-Raisin Fruitcake

Prepare as directed but substitute **2 cups walnuts (8 ounces),** toasted and coarsely chopped, plus **⅔ cup walnut halves** for pecans and **1½ cups golden raisins plus 1 cup dried cranberries** for apricots.

Molten Chocolate Cakes

Molten Chocolate Cakes

When you cut into these warm cakes, their delectable molten centers flow out. You can assemble them up to 24 hours ahead and refrigerate, or freeze up to two weeks. If you refrigerate the cakes, bake them for ten minutes; if they are frozen, bake for 16 minutes. Serve with whipped cream or vanilla ice cream.

Prep: 20 minutes Bake: 8 minutes

- 4 squares (4 ounces) semisweet chocolate, chopped
- ½ cup butter or margarine (1 stick), cut into pieces
- ¼ cup heavy or whipping cream
- ½ teaspoon vanilla extract
- ¼ cup all-purpose flour
- ¼ cup sugar
- 2 large eggs
- 2 large egg yolks
  whipped cream or vanilla ice cream (optional)

1. Preheat oven to 400°F. Grease eight 6-ounce custard cups. Dust with sugar.

2. In heavy 3-quart saucepan, combine chocolate, butter, and cream; heat over low heat, stirring occasionally, until butter and chocolate melt and mixture is smooth. Remove from heat. Add vanilla; with wire whisk, stir in flour just until mixture is smooth.

3. In medium bowl, with mixer at high speed, beat sugar, eggs, and yolks until thick and lemon-colored, about 10 minutes. Fold egg mixture, one-third at a time, into chocolate mixture until blended.

4. Divide batter evenly among prepared custard cups. Place cups in jelly-roll pan. Bake until edge of cakes is set but center still jiggles, 8 to 9 minutes. Cool in pan on wire rack 3 minutes. Run thin knife around cakes to loosen from sides of cups; invert onto dessert plates. Serve immediately with whipped cream or ice cream, if desired. Makes 8 servings.

Each serving: About 281 calories, 4g protein, 20g carbohydrate, 22g total fat (12g saturated), 148mg cholesterol, 139mg sodium.

Apple-Walnut Bundt Cake

This easy-to-make, dense cake is filled with lots of apple chunks for flavor and moistness as well as tasty golden raisins (substitute dark raisins or dried cranberries, if you like), and a generous amount of walnuts.

Prep: 25 minutes plus cooling Bake: 1 hour 15 minutes

- 3 cups all-purpose flour
- 1¾ cups granulated sugar
- 1 teaspoon baking soda
- 1 teaspoon ground cinnamon
- ¾ teaspoon salt
- ¼ teaspoon ground nutmeg
- 1 cup vegetable oil
- ½ cup apple juice
- 2 teaspoons vanilla extract
- 3 large eggs
- 1 pound Golden Delicious or Granny Smith apples (3 medium), peeled, cored, and coarsely chopped
- 1 cup walnuts (4 ounces), coarsely chopped
- 1 cup golden raisins
  confectioners' sugar

1. Preheat oven to 350°F. Grease and flour 10-inch Bundt pan.

2. In large bowl, combine flour, granulated sugar, baking soda, cinnamon, salt, nutmeg, oil, apple juice, vanilla, and eggs. With mixer at low speed, beat until well blended, frequently scraping bowl with rubber spatula. Increase speed to medium; beat 2 minutes, scraping bowl. With wooden spoon, stir in apples, walnuts, and raisins.

3. Spoon batter into prepared pan; spread evenly. Bake until cake pulls away from side of pan and toothpick inserted in center comes out clean, about 1 hour 15 minutes. Cool in pan on wire rack 10 minutes. Run tip of thin knife around edge of cake to loosen. Invert cake onto rack; cool completely. Dust with confectioners' sugar. Makes 16 servings.

Each serving: About 408 calories, 5g protein, 54g carbohydrate, 20g total fat (3g saturated), 40mg cholesterol, 202mg sodium.

Chocolate Buttermilk Cake

The deep chocolate flavor comes from unsweetened cocoa and the tender crumb from buttermilk.

Prep: 45 minutes plus cooling   Bake: 30 minutes

- 2 cups all-purpose flour
- 1 cup unsweetened cocoa
- 1½ teaspoons baking soda
- ¾ teaspoon salt
- 1½ cups buttermilk
- 2 teaspoons vanilla extract
- 1¾ cups sugar
- ¾ cup butter or margarine (1½ sticks), softened
- 3 large eggs
  Classic Butter Frosting (page 526)

1. Preheat oven to 350°F. Grease two 9-inch round cake pans. Line bottom of pans with waxed paper; grease waxed paper. Dust with cocoa, shaking out excess.

2. In medium bowl, with wire whisk, stir flour, cocoa, baking soda, and salt. In 2-cup liquid measuring cup, mix buttermilk and vanilla; set aside.

3. In large bowl, with mixer at low speed, beat sugar and butter until blended. Increase speed to high; beat until creamy, about 3 minutes, occasionally scraping bowl with rubber spatula. Reduce speed to low; add eggs, one at a time, beating well after each addition. Add flour mixture alternately with buttermilk mixture beginning and ending with flour mixture. Beat just until blended, scraping bowl occasionally.

5. Divide batter between prepared pans; spread evenly. Bake until toothpick inserted in center of cake comes out clean, 30 to 35 minutes. Cool in pans on wire racks 10 minutes. Run thin knife around layers to loosen from sides of pans. Invert cakes onto racks to cool completely. Carefully remove and discard waxed paper.

6. Prepare Classic Butter Frosting.

7. Place one layer, rounded side down, on cake plate. With narrow metal spatula, spread ⅔ cup frosting over layer. Top with second layer, rounded side up. Spread remaining frosting over side and top of cake. Makes 16 servings.

Each serving without frosting: About 255 calories, 5g protein, 37g carbohydrate, 11g total fat (7g saturated), 65mg cholesterol, 360mg sodium.

Chocolate Truffle Cake

This exceptionally sinful chocolate dessert is easy to make, but it must be refrigerated for twenty-four hours before serving for the best flavor and texture. For the neatest slices, dip the knife into hot water before cutting each one.

Prep: 1 hour plus overnight to chill   Bake: 35 minutes

- 14 squares (14 ounces) semisweet chocolate, chopped
- 2 squares (2 ounces) unsweetened chocolate, chopped
- 1 cup butter (2 sticks; do not use margarine)
- 8 large eggs, separated
- ½ cup granulated sugar
- ¼ teaspoon cream of tartar
  confectioners' sugar

1. Preheat oven to 300°F. Remove bottom from 9" by 3" springform pan and cover with foil; wrap foil around back. Replace pan bottom. Grease and flour foil bottom and side of pan.

2. In heavy 2-quart saucepan, combine semisweet and unsweetened chocolates and butter; heat over low heat, stirring frequently, until melted and smooth. Pour chocolate mixture into large bowl.

3. In small bowl, with mixer at high speed, beat egg yolks and granulated sugar until very thick and lemon-colored, about 5 minutes. With rubber spatula, stir egg-yolk mixture into chocolate mixture until blended.

4. In separate large bowl, with clean beaters and with mixer at high speed, beat egg whites and cream of tartar until soft peaks form when beaters are lifted. With rubber spatula, gently fold beaten egg whites, one-third at a time, into chocolate mixture just until blended.

5. Scrape batter into prepared pan; spread evenly. Bake 35 minutes. (Do not overbake; cake will firm upon standing and chilling.) Cool completely in pan on wire rack; refrigerate overnight in pan.

6. Run thin knife, rinsed under very hot water and dried, around cake to loosen from side of pan; remove side of pan. Invert cake onto serving plate; unwrap foil from pan bottom and lift off pan. Carefully peel foil away from cake.

7. To serve, let cake stand 1 hour at room temperature. Dust with confectioners' sugar. Or dust heavily with confectioners' sugar over paper doily or stencil. Makes 20 servings.

Each serving: About 251 calories, 4g protein, 19g carbohydrate, 20g total fat (12g saturated) 113mg cholesterol, 126mg sodium.

Light Chocolate Bundt Cake

Satisfy your chocolate cravings with this lowfat treat. Skip the Mocha Glaze and save 45 calories and 11 carbs per serving.

Prep: 30 minutes plus cooling Bake: 45 minutes

2¼ cups all-purpose flour
1½ teaspoons baking soda
½ teaspoon baking powder
½ teaspoon salt
¾ cup unsweetened cocoa
1 teaspoon instant espresso-coffee powder
¾ cup hot water
2 cups sugar
⅓ cup vegetable oil
2 large egg whites
1 large egg
1 square (1 ounce) unsweetened chocolate, melted
2 teaspoons vanilla extract
½ cup buttermilk
   Mocha Glaze

1. Preheat oven to 350°F and grease 10-inch Bundt pan.

2. In medium bowl, with wire whisk, stir flour, baking soda, baking powder, and salt.

3. In 2-cup measuring cup, stir cocoa, espresso-coffee powder, and hot water until blended.

4. In large bowl, with mixer at low speed, beat sugar, oil, egg whites, and egg until blended. Increase speed to high; beat until creamy, about 2 minutes. Reduce speed to low; beat in cocoa mixture, melted chocolate, and vanilla. Add flour mixture alternately with buttermilk, beginning and ending with flour mixture. Beat just until blended, occasionally scraping bowl with rubber spatula.

5. Scrape batter into prepared pan; spread evenly with rubber spatula. Bake until toothpick inserted in center comes out clean, about 45 minutes. Cool in pan on wire rack 10 minutes. Run tip of thin knife around edge of cake to loosen from side of pan. Invert onto rack to cool completely.

6. Prepare Mocha Glaze. Place cake on cake plate; pour glaze over cooled cake. Makes 16 servings.

Mocha Glaze

In medium bowl, combine **¼ teaspoon instant espresso-coffee powder** and **2 tablespoons hot water;** stir until blended. Stir in **3 tablespoons unsweetened cocoa, 3 tablespoons dark corn syrup,** and **1 tablespoon coffee-flavored liqueur** until blended. Add **1 cup confectioners' sugar;** stir until smooth.

Each serving with Mocha Glaze: About 280 calories, 4g protein, 53g carbohydrate, 7g total fat (2g saturated), 14mg cholesterol, 232mg sodium.

TYPES OF COCOA

 Not all cocoas are created equal. There is a difference between natural and Dutch-process cocoas. Don't swap cocoa types and do not use mixes for hot chocolate drinks; use what is recommended in the recipe. Both type of cocoa have rich chocolate flavor, are equally delicious, and contain between 8 and 24 percent fat.

In our kitchens, we usually use natural cocoa because it is readily available. Its acidity works in tandem with the baking soda in a batter to create carbon dioxide bubbles, which leaven cakes. Dutch-process cocoa is treated with an alkali agent that neutralizes and removes some of the cocoa's acidity. The process was developed in the Netherlands in the mid-1800s, hence the name. This procedure changes the cocoa's chemical composition, so it doesn't need to be combined with baking soda. You'll find Dutch-process cocoa at specialty food stores and most supermarkets. Look closely at the label; some cocoas are alkalized even if the label doesn't clearly state it.

Vanilla Pound Cake

This delicate, finely textured pound cake is not as sweet as some. It's perfect with an afternoon cup of tea.

Prep: 20 minutes plus cooling   Bake: 1 hour

1½   cups butter or margarine (3 sticks), softened
2¼   cups granulated sugar
6   large eggs
1   tablespoon vanilla extract
¾   teaspoon salt
3   cups cake flour (not self-rising)
    confectioners' sugar

1. Preheat oven to 325°F. Grease and flour 10-inch Bundt pan.

2. In large bowl, with mixer at low speed, beat butter and granulated sugar just until blended. Increase speed to high; beat until light and fluffy, about 5 minutes, frequently scraping bowl with rubber spatula. Reduce speed to medium. Add eggs, one at a time, beating well after each addition. Add vanilla and salt. Increase speed to high; beat 3 minutes, scraping bowl. With wire whisk, stir in flour just until smooth.

3. Spoon batter into prepared pan; spread evenly. Bake until toothpick inserted near center comes out clean, 1 hour to 1 hour 10 minutes. Cool in pan on wire rack 10 minutes. Run tip of thin knife around edge of cake to loosen. Invert onto rack to cool completely. Dust with confectioners' sugar. Makes 20 servings.

Each serving: About 299 calories, 3g protein, 36g carbohydrate, 16g total fat (9g saturated), 101mg cholesterol, 247mg sodium.

Lemon–Poppy Seed Pound Cake

This tangy-sweet cake keeps well. Store poppy seeds in the refrigerator; they turn rancid quickly if stored at room temperature.

Prep: 25 minutes plus cooling   Bake: 1 hour 20 minutes

2   cups all-purpose flour
2   tablespoons poppy seeds
½   teaspoon baking powder
¼   teaspoon baking soda
¼   teaspoon salt
2   large lemons
¾   cup butter or margarine (1½ sticks), softened
1½   plus ⅓ cups sugar
4   large eggs
1   teaspoon vanilla extract
½   cup sour cream

1. Preheat oven to 325°F. Grease and flour 9" by 5" metal loaf pan.

2. In medium bowl, with wire whisk, stir flour, poppy seeds, baking powder, baking soda, and salt until combined. From lemons, grate 1 tablespoon peel and squeeze 3 tablespoons juice.

3. In large bowl, with mixer at low speed, beat butter and 1½ cups sugar until blended. Increase speed to high; beat until light and fluffy, about 5 minutes. Add eggs, one at a time, beating well after each addition, frequently scraping bowl with rubber spatula. Beat in lemon peel and vanilla. Reduce speed to low. Add flour mixture alternately with sour cream, beginning and ending with flour mixture; beat just until smooth.

4. Spoon batter into prepared pan; spread evenly. Bake until toothpick inserted in center comes out clean, about 1 hour 20 minutes. Cool in pan on wire rack 10 minutes. Run thin knife around cake to loosen from sides of pan. Remove from pan; place on rack set over waxed paper.

5. In small bowl, combine lemon juice and remaining ⅓ cup sugar. With pastry brush, brush mixture over top and sides of warm cake. Cool completely. Makes 16 servings.

Each serving: About 267 calories, 4g protein, 36g carbohydrate, 12g total fat (7g saturated), 80mg cholesterol, 178mg sodium.

FOAM CAKES

Foam cakes depend on whole eggs or egg whites for their airy texture. Angel food cake is light because it doesn't contain any fat; it gets its height from a large amount of beaten whites. Chiffon and sponge cakes contain beaten whole eggs or egg yolks, along with vegetable oil or melted butter. Patience is the key to success with foam cakes. If a recipe calls for the eggs to be beaten until thick and lemon colored, expect it to take from three to ten minutes. When the beaters are lifted, the egg mixture should form a thick ribbon.

How to Mix When combining the ingredients for these batters, fold them in with a rubber spatula. Cut down through the center of the batter, then draw the spatula across the bottom of the batter and up the side of the bowl. Flip the spatula over and draw it across the top. Give the bowl a quarter turn, and repeat until ingredients are blended.

How to Bake Bake the cake for the minimum recommended time, then check often for doneness.

How to Cool Cakes baked in tube pans are cooled upside down so they keep their shape. Invert the pan and insert it over the neck of a tall bottle or funnel (some pans have small feet), and cool completely. Sponge layer cakes are cooled just like butter cakes. Jelly-roll cakes are removed from the pan and rolled up with a towel.

BEATING EGG WHITES

The secret to light, "heavenly" angel food cakes is properly beaten egg whites. Start with room-temperature egg whites to get the fullest volume. For "stiff glossy peaks" beat the whites until they form peaks that hold their shape when the beaters are lifted but are still moist. Overbeaten whites look lumpy and watery; there is no way to salvage them. Begin again with new egg whites.

Angel Food Cake

Angel food cake, beloved for its clean flavor and light texture, has an added attraction—it's lowfat.

Prep: 30 minutes   Bake: 35 minutes

- 1 cup cake flour (not self-rising)
- ½ cup confectioners' sugar
- 1⅔ cups egg whites (12 to 14 large egg whites)
- 1½ teaspoons cream of tartar
- ½ teaspoon salt
- 1¼ cups granulated sugar
- 2 teaspoons vanilla extract
- ½ teaspoon almond extract

1. Preheat oven to 375°F. Sift flour and confectioners' sugar through sieve set over small bowl.

2. In large bowl, with mixer at medium speed, beat egg whites, cream of tartar, and salt until foamy. Increase speed to medium-high; beat until soft peaks form when beaters are lifted. Sprinkle in granulated sugar, 2 tablespoons at a time, beating until sugar has dissolved and egg whites stand in stiff, glossy peaks when beaters are lifted. Beat in vanilla and almond extracts.

3. Transfer egg-white mixture to larger bowl. Sift flour mixture, one-third at a time, over beaten egg whites; fold in with rubber spatula just until flour mixture is no longer visible. Do not overmix.

4. Scrape batter into ungreased 9- to 10-inch tube pan; spread evenly. Bake until cake springs back when lightly pressed, 35 to 40 minutes. Invert cake in pan onto large metal funnel or bottle; cool completely in pan. Run thin knife around cake to loosen from side and center tube of pan. Remove from pan and place on cake plate. Makes 16 servings.

Each serving: About 115 calories, 3g protein, 25g carbohydrate, 0g total fat (0g saturated), 0mg cholesterol, 114mg sodium.

Cappuccino Angel Food Cake

Prepare as directed but add **4 teaspoons instant espresso-coffee powder** and ½ **teaspoon ground cinnamon** to egg whites before beating; use **1½ teaspoons vanilla extract** and omit almond extract. In cup, **mix 1 tablespoon confectioners' sugar** with ⅛ **teaspoon ground cinnamon;** sprinkle evenly over cooled cake.

Vanilla Chiffon Cake

(Pictured on page 506)

All this tall, handsome cake needs is a dusting of confectioners' sugar and some fresh berries served on the side.

Prep: 20 minutes   Bake: 1 hour 15 minutes

- 2¼ cups cake flour (not self-rising)
- 1½ cups granulated sugar
- 1 tablespoon baking powder
- 1 teaspoon salt
- ¾ cup cold water
- ½ cup vegetable oil
- 5 large eggs, separated, plus 2 large egg whites
- 1 tablespoon vanilla extract
- ½ teaspoon cream of tartar
  confectioners' sugar

1. Preheat oven to 325°F. In large bowl, with wire whisk, stir flour, 1 cup granulated sugar, baking powder, and salt. Make a well in center; add cold water, oil, egg yolks, and vanilla to well. With wire whisk, stir until smooth.

2. In separate large bowl, with mixer at high speed, beat egg whites and cream of tartar until soft peaks form when beaters are lifted. Sprinkle in remaining ½ cup granulated sugar, 2 tablespoons at a time, beating until sugar has dissolved and egg whites stand in stiff, glossy peaks when beaters are lifted. With rubber spatula, gently fold one-third of beaten egg whites into egg-yolk mixture, then fold in remaining egg whites until blended.

3. Scrape batter into ungreased 9- to 10-inch tube pan; spread evenly. Bake until cake springs back when lightly pressed, about 1 hour 15 minutes. Invert cake in pan onto large metal funnel or bottle; cool completely. Run thin knife around cake to loosen from side and tube of pan. Remove from pan and place on cake plate. Dust with confectioners' sugar. Makes 16 servings.

Each serving: About 217 calories, 4g protein, 31g carbohydrate, 9g total fat (1g saturated), 66mg cholesterol, 264mg sodium.

Citrus Chiffon Cake

Prepare as directed (left) but substitute **1 tablespoon freshly grated orange peel** and **1 teaspoon freshly grated lemon peel** for vanilla, and substitute ½ **cup fresh orange juice** and ¼ **cup fresh lemon juice** for cold water. In small bowl, combine **1 cup confectioners' sugar, 1 teaspoon freshly grated lemon peel,** ¼ **teaspoon vanilla extract,** and about **5 teaspoons orange juice** to make smooth glaze. Spoon over cooled cake.

Golden Sponge Cake

This cake is just perfect for soaking up fruit juices. Serve it with fresh fruit, or use it as a base for a shortcake or trifle.

Prep: 20 minutes   Bake: 15 minutes

- ¾ cup all-purpose flour
- 2 tablespoons cornstarch
- 3 large eggs
- ½ cup sugar
- 1 tablespoon butter or margarine, melted

1. Preheat oven to 375°F. Grease and flour 9-inch square baking pan.

2. In small bowl, with wire whisk, stir flour and cornstarch.

3. In large bowl, with mixer at high speed, beat eggs and sugar until thick and lemon colored and mixture forms ribbon when beaters are lifted, about 10 minutes, occasionally scraping bowl with rubber spatula. Fold in flour mixture until well blended, then fold in melted butter.

4. Scrape batter into prepared pan; spread evenly. Bake until cake is golden and springs back when lightly pressed, 15 to 20 minutes. Cool in pan on wire rack 10 minutes. Run thin knife around cake to loosen from sides of pan; invert onto rack to cool completely. Makes 8 servings.

Each serving: About 148 calories, 4g protein, 24g carbohydrate, 4g total fat (2g saturated), 84mg cholesterol, 39mg sodium.

Jelly Roll

Jelly rolls are easy to make and look sensational on a decorative platter. Fill the roll with your favorite jam or tangy Lemon Filling (page 528).

Prep: 20 minutes plus cooling   Bake: 10 minutes

- 5 **large eggs, separated**
- ½ **cup granulated sugar**
- 1 **teaspoon vanilla extract**
- ½ **cup all-purpose flour**
  confectioners' sugar
- ⅔ **cup strawberry jam**

1. Preheat oven to 350°F. Grease 15½" by 10½" jelly-roll pan. Line with waxed paper; grease paper.

2. In large bowl, with mixer at high speed, beat egg whites until soft peaks form when beaters are lifted. Sprinkle in ¼ cup granulated sugar, 1 tablespoon at a time, beating until egg whites stand in stiff, glossy peaks when beaters are lifted. Do not overbeat.

3. In small bowl, with mixer at high speed, beat egg yolks, remaining ¼ cup granulated sugar, and vanilla until very thick and lemon colored, 8 to 10 minutes. Reduce speed to low; beat in flour until blended. With rubber spatula, gently fold egg-yolk mixture into beaten egg whites just until blended.

4. Scrape batter into prepared pan; spread evenly. Bake until cake springs back when lightly pressed, 10 to 15 minutes.

5. Meanwhile, sift confectioners' sugar onto clean kitchen towel. Run thin knife around edges of cake to loosen from sides of pan; invert onto towel. Carefully remove waxed paper. Trim ¼ inch from edges of cake. From a short side, roll cake up with towel jelly-roll fashion. Place rolled cake, seam side down, on wire rack; cool completely.

6. Unroll cooled cake. With narrow metal spatula, spread evenly with jam. Starting from same short side, roll up cake (without towel). Place rolled cake, seam side down, on platter and dust with confectioners' sugar. Makes 10 servings.

Each serving: About 163 calories, 4g protein, 30g carbohydrate, 3g total fat (1g saturated), 106mg cholesterol, 40mg sodium.

Jelly Roll

CHEESECAKES

There are two types of cheesecake: cream cheese and curd cheese. Some have a crust, which can be made of pastry dough, graham crackers, or cookies. The filling can be plain or flavored with citrus, chocolate, or pumpkin. To bake perfect cheesecakes, the cream cheese must be well softened. Let it stand for at least one hour at room temperature.

How to Bake To prevent the butter in the crust from leaking or to waterproof the cake if placed in a water bath, the outside of the pan is often wrapped with heavy-duty foil. Cheesecake should be baked until the center barely jiggles; it will firm up during cooling and chilling.

How to Cool To help prevent cracking during cooling, run a thin knife around the edge of the cheesecake as soon as the cheesecake comes out of the oven.

Deluxe Cheesecake

This is the classic New York–style cheesecake: very dense, rich, and baked in a pastry crust. Baking it at a low temperature and slowly cooling it in the oven are the keys to its perfect texture.

Prep: 45 minutes plus cooling and chilling
Bake: 50 minutes plus standing

½ **cup butter or margarine (1 stick), softened**
1½ **cups sugar**
3 **large egg yolks**
1¼ **cups plus 3 tablespoons all-purpose flour**
5 **packages (8 ounces each) cream cheese, softened**
5 **large eggs**
¼ **cup milk**
1 **teaspoon freshly grated lemon peel**

1. Preheat oven to 400°F. In small bowl, with mixer at low speed, beat butter and ¼ cup sugar until blended. Add 1 egg yolk and beat until well combined. Beat in 1¼ cups flour just until combined. Divide dough into almost equal parts; wrap slightly larger piece in plastic wrap and refrigerate.

2. With hand, press smaller piece of dough onto bottom of 10" by 2½" springform pan. Bake until golden, about 8 minutes; cool completely in pan on wire rack.

3. Turn oven control to 475°F. In large bowl, with mixer at medium speed, beat cream cheese just until smooth; gradually beat in remaining 1¼ cups sugar. Reduce speed to low. Beat in eggs, remaining 2 egg yolks, milk, remaining 3 tablespoons flour, and lemon peel just until blended, occasionally scraping bowl with rubber spatula.

4. Press remaining piece of dough around side of pan 1 inch from rim (do not bake). Scrape cream-cheese mixture into crust. Bake 12 minutes. Turn oven control to 300°F; bake 30 minutes longer. Edge will be set, but center will still jiggle. Turn off oven; let cheesecake remain in oven 30 minutes.

5. Remove cheesecake from oven and place on wire rack. Run thin knife around edge of cheesecake to prevent cracking during cooling. Cool completely in pan on wire rack. Cover and refrigerate until well chilled, at least 4 hours or up to overnight. Remove side of pan to serve. Makes 20 servings.

Each serving: About 359 calories, 7g protein, 24g carbohydrate, 27g total fat (16g saturated), 160mg cholesterol, 233mg sodium.

CHEESECAKE TOPPINGS

Sometimes a delectable slice of plain cheesecake hits the spot, but there are also times when a bit of "gilding the lily" is called for. It is easy to dress up a cream cheese cheesecake without a lot of fuss. Here are some of our favorite ways:

- Top chilled cheesecake with hulled whole, halved, or sliced strawberries. Brush with ½ cup melted red currant jelly.
- Serve slices of cheesecake accompanied by a sauceboat of Sublime Chocolate Sauce (page 441). For a very special occasion, cover the top of the cheesecake with chocolate curls (page 529).
- Top chilled cheesecake with fresh raspberries or concentric circles of raspberries and blackberries. Serve with Best Berry Sauce (page 440).
- Top chilled cheesecake with ½-inch wedges of peeled ripe peaches. Serve with sauceboat of Raspberry Sauce (page 442).

Lemon-Ricotta Cheesecake

Lemon-Ricotta Cheesecake

Serving this cake with fresh raspberries and thin strips of lemon zest is both beautiful and tasty.

Prep: 20 minutes plus cooling and chilling
Bake: 1 hour 25 minutes plus standing

- 4 large lemons
- 1 cup vanilla wafer crumbs (about 30 cookies)
- 4 tablespoons butter or margarine, melted
- 1¼ cups sugar
- ¼ cup cornstarch
- 2 packages (8 ounces each) cream cheese, softened
- 1 container (15 ounces) ricotta cheese
- 4 large eggs
- 2 cups half-and-half or light cream
- 2 teaspoons vanilla extract

1. Preheat oven to 375°F. Tightly wrap outside of 9" by 3" springform pan with heavy-duty foil. From lemons, grate 4 teaspoons peel and squeeze ⅓ cup juice. In pan, combine cookie crumbs, melted butter, and 1 teaspoon lemon peel; stir with fork until evenly moistened. With hand, press mixture firmly onto bottom of pan. Bake until crust is deep golden, about 10 minutes. Cool completely in pan on wire rack.

2. Turn oven control to 325°F. In small bowl, stir sugar and cornstarch until blended. In large bowl, with mixer at medium speed, beat cream cheese and ricotta until very smooth, about 5 minutes; slowly beat in sugar mixture. Reduce speed to low. Beat in eggs, half-and-half, lemon juice, vanilla, and remaining 3 teaspoons lemon peel just until blended, frequently scraping bowl with rubber spatula.

3. Pour cream-cheese mixture into cooled crust. Bake 1 hour 15 minutes. Turn off oven; let cheesecake remain in oven 1 hour longer.

4. Remove cheesecake from oven and transfer to wire rack; remove foil. Run thin knife around edge of cheesecake to prevent cracking during cooling. Cool completely in pan on wire rack. Cover and refrigerate until well chilled, at least 6 hours or up to overnight. Remove side of pan to serve. Makes 16 servings.

Each serving: About 324 calories, 8g protein, 25g carbohydrate, 22g total fat (13g saturated), 117mg cholesterol, 182mg sodium.

Pumpkin Cheesecake

Pumpkin pie, move over. Here's a deliciously creamy dessert that is bound to become a new tradition at your next Thanksgiving dinner.

**Prep: 30 minutes plus cooling and chilling
Bake: 1 hour 25 minutes**

Crumb Crust

- 1 cup graham cracker crumbs
  (8 rectangular crackers)
- 3 tablespoons butter or margarine, melted
- 2 tablespoons sugar

Pumpkin Filling

- 2 packages (8 ounces each) cream cheese, softened
- 1¼ cups sugar
- 1 can (15 ounces) solid-pack pumpkin
  (not pumpkin-pie mix)
- ¾ cup sour cream
- 2 tablespoons bourbon or
  2 teaspoons vanilla extract
- 1 teaspoon ground cinnamon
- ½ teaspoon ground allspice
- ¼ teaspoon salt
- 4 large eggs

Sour Cream Topping

- 1 cup sour cream
- 3 tablespoons sugar
- 1 teaspoon vanilla extract

1. Preheat oven to 350°F. Tightly wrap outside of 9" by 3" springform pan with heavy-duty foil. In pan, combine graham-cracker crumbs, melted butter, and sugar; stir with fork until evenly moistened. With hand, press mixture firmly onto bottom of pan. Bake 10 minutes. Cool completely in pan on wire rack.

2. Prepare pumpkin filling: In large bowl, with mixer at medium speed, beat cream cheese until smooth. Slowly beat in sugar until blended, about 1 minute, frequently scraping bowl with rubber spatula. Reduce speed to low. Beat in pumpkin, sour cream, bourbon, cinnamon, allspice, and salt. Add eggs, one at time, beating after each addition, just until blended.

3. Pour pumpkin mixture into crust and place in large roasting pan. Place pan on oven rack. Carefully pour enough very hot water into roasting pan to come 1 inch up side of springform pan. Bake until center of cake barely jiggles, about 1 hour 10 minutes.

4. Prepare topping: In small bowl, with wire whisk, beat sour cream, sugar, and vanilla until smooth. Remove cheesecake from water bath (leave water bath in oven); spread sour-cream mixture evenly over top. Return cake to water bath and bake 5 minutes longer.

5. Remove cheesecake from water bath and transfer to wire rack; remove foil. Run thin knife around edge of cheesecake to prevent cracking during cooling. Cool completely in pan on wire rack. Cover and refrigerate until well chilled, at least 6 hours or up to overnight. Remove side of pan to serve. Makes 16 servings.

Each serving: About 307 calories, 5g protein, 29g carbohydrate, 19g total fat (11g saturated), 101mg cholesterol, 217mg sodium.

Margarita Cheesecake

Lots of fresh lime juice and zest and a generous amount of orange-flavored liqueur make this cheesecake special. To prevent a thick bottom edge of crust, first press crumbs onto the bottom of the pan, then pack crumbs against the side of the pan.

Prep: 35 minutes plus chilling   Bake: 1 hour plus standing

- 4 to 5 limes
- 1 orange
- 8 ounces vanilla wafer cookies (65 wafers)
- 7 tablespoons butter or margarine, melted
- 4 packages (8 ounces each) cream cheese, softened
- 1¼ cups sugar
- ¼ teaspoon salt
- 4 large eggs
- 1 container (8 ounces) sour cream
- ¼ cup orange-flavor liqueur or orange juice
  orange and lime slices for garnish (optional)

1. Preheat oven to 350°F. From limes, grate 1 tablespoon plus 2 teaspoons peel and squeeze ½ cup juice. From orange, grate ½ teaspoon peel. In food processor with knife blade attached, pulse vanilla wafers and 2 teaspoons lime peel to make fine crumbs (you should have about 2½ cups crumbs). In 9" by 3" springform pan, combine cookie crumbs and melted butter; stir with fork until evenly moistened. With hand, press mixture firmly onto bottom and 2 inches up side of pan. Tightly wrap outside of pan with heavy-duty foil. Bake crust 15 minutes. Cool completely in pan on wire rack.

2. In large bowl, with mixer at medium speed, beat cream cheese until smooth, occasionally scraping bowl with rubber spatula. Gradually beat in sugar and salt until blended. Reduce speed to low; beat in eggs, one at a time, sour cream, liqueur, orange peel, lime juice, and remaining 1 tablespoon lime peel just until blended and smooth.

3. Pour cream-cheese mixture into crust, making sure to scrape any peel on beaters into batter. Bake until cheesecake is set 2 inches from edge but center still jiggles, about 45 minutes. Turn off oven; let cheesecake remain in oven 1 hour longer.

4. Remove cheesecake from oven and cool completely in pan on wire rack. Cover and refrigerate cheesecake until well chilled, at least 6 hours or up to 2 days.

5. To serve, carefully remove side of springform pan. Let cheesecake stand at room temperature 30 minutes for better flavor. If you like, arrange orange and lime slices on top of cake for garnish. Makes 20 servings.

Each serving: About 335 calories, 6g protein, 23g carbohydrate, 25g total fat (15g saturated), 111mg cholesterol, 265mg sodium.

Milk Chocolate Cheesecake

To ensure a creamy smooth texture, make sure that the cream cheese, eggs, and sour cream are at room temperature. About 30 minutes on the counter is all it takes.

Prep: 25 minutes plus cooling and chilling   Bake: 1 hour

- 1 package (9 ounces) chocolate wafer cookies
- 6 tablespoons butter or margarine, melted
- 2 packages (8 ounces each) cream cheese, softened
- ½ cup plus 2 tablespoons sugar
- ¼ teaspoon salt
- 3 large eggs, lightly beaten
- ¼ cup whole milk
- 2 teaspoons vanilla extract
- 1 bag (11½ ounces) milk chocolate chips, melted
- 1½ cups sour cream

1. Preheat oven to 350°F. In food processor with knife blade attached, pulse chocolate cookies until fine crumbs form. Add butter to crumbs and pulse several times to combine. Transfer cookie mixture to 9-inch springform pan. With hand, press firmly onto bottom and about 2 inches up side of pan. Bake 10 minutes. Cool completely in pan on wire rack.

2. In large bowl, with mixer at medium speed, beat cream cheese, ½ cup sugar, and ¼ teaspoon salt until smooth, about 2 minutes, scraping bowl with rubber spatula. Reduce speed to low. Add eggs, milk, and vanilla; beat just until blended, occasionally scraping bowl. Add chocolate and beat until combined.

3. Pour cream-cheese mixture into crust. Bake until cheesecake is set 2 inches from edge but center still jiggles, about 45 minutes.

4. In small bowl, stir sour cream and remaining 2 tablespoons sugar until sugar dissolves; set aside.

5. Remove cheesecake from oven. Gently spread sour-cream mixture evenly over top. Return cheesecake to oven and bake 5 minutes longer to set sour cream. Remove from oven and cool completely in pan on wire rack. Cover and refrigerate until well chilled, at least 6 hours or up to 3 days.

Each serving: About 315 calories, 5g protein, 27g carbohydrate, 22g total fat (12g saturated), 74mg cholesterol, 755mg sodium.

Classic Butter Frosting

This may be the simplest frosting to prepare but you'd never suspect so from its rich flavor.

Prep: 10 minutes

- ½ cup butter or margarine (1 stick), softened
- 1 package (16 ounces) confectioners' sugar
- 4 to 6 tablespoons milk, half-and-half, or light cream
- 1½ teaspoons vanilla extract

In large bowl, with mixer at medium-low speed, beat butter, confectioners' sugar, 3 tablespoons milk, and vanilla until smooth and blended. Beat in additional milk as needed for easy spreading consistency. Increase speed to medium-high; beat frosting until light and fluffy, about 1 minute. Makes about 2⅓ cups.

Each tablespoon: About 71 calories, 0g protein, 12g carbohydrate, 3g total fat (2g saturated), 7mg cholesterol, 26mg sodium.

Lemon Butter Frosting

Prepare as directed but omit vanilla and use **2 tablespoons fresh lemon juice, 2 tablespoons milk,** and **1 teaspoon freshly grated lemon peel.** Use only **1 to 2 tablespoons milk** as needed for easy spreading.

Orange Butter Frosting

Prepare as directed for Lemon Butter Frosting but substitute **orange juice** for lemon juice and **orange peel** for lemon peel.

Brown Butter Frosting

In small skillet, over medium heat, cook butter until lightly browned; let cool. Prepare as directed.

White Chocolate Butter Frosting

Use this sweet frosting on your favorite chocolate cake.

Prep: 15 minutes

- 1 cup butter (2 sticks), softened
- 2 cups confectioners' sugar
- 6 ounces white chocolate, Swiss confectionery bars, or white baking bars, melted and cooled
- 3 tablespoons milk

In large bowl, with mixer at low speed, beat butter, confectioners' sugar, white chocolate, and milk just until combined. Increase speed to high; beat until light and fluffy, about 2 minutes, frequently scraping bowl with rubber spatula. Makes about 3½ cups.

Each tablespoon: About 62 calories, 0g protein, 6g carbohydrate, 4g total fat (3g saturated), 9mg cholesterol, 37mg sodium.

Chocolate Butter Frosting

The combination of semisweet and unsweetened chocolates gives this frosting its perfect flavor balance.

Prep: 15 minutes

- ¾ cup butter (1½ sticks), softened
- 2 cups confectioners' sugar
- 1 teaspoon vanilla extract
- 4 squares (4 ounces) semisweet chocolate, melted and cooled
- 2 squares (2 ounces) unsweetened chocolate, melted and cooled

In large bowl, with mixer at low speed, beat butter, confectioners' sugar, and vanilla until almost combined. Add semisweet and unsweetened chocolates. Increase speed to high; beat frosting until light and fluffy, about 1 minute. Makes about 2½ cups.

Each tablespoon: About 75 calories, 0g protein, 8g carbohydrate, 5g total fat (3g saturated), 9mg cholesterol, 36mg sodium.

Silky Vanilla Butter Frosting

Butter is beaten into a flour-thickened base to make an exquisitely light and creamy frosting. Make sure the frosting base is completely cooled before beating in the butter.

Prep: 10 minutes plus cooling Cook: 8 minutes

- 1 cup sugar
- ½ cup all-purpose flour
- 1⅓ cups milk
- 1 cup butter or margarine (2 sticks), softened
- 1 tablespoon vanilla extract

1. In 2-quart saucepan, thoroughly combine sugar and flour. With wire whisk, gradually stir in milk until smooth. Cook over medium-high heat, stirring frequently, until mixture has thickened and boils. Reduce heat to low; cook 2 minutes, stirring constantly. Remove from heat; cool completely.

2. In medium bowl, with mixer at medium speed, beat butter until light and fluffy. Gradually beat in milk mixture; beat in vanilla. Makes about 3¼ cups.

Each tablespoon: About 55 calories, 0g protein, 5g carbohydrate, 4g total fat (2g saturated), 10mg cholesterol, 39mg sodium.

Silky Lemon Butter Frosting

Prepare as directed but substitute **1 tablespoon freshly grated lemon peel** for vanilla extract.

Silky Orange Butter Frosting

Prepare as directed but substitute **1 teaspoon freshly grated orange peel** for vanilla extract.

Silky Chocolate Butter Frosting

Prepare as directed but use **¾ cup sugar, ¼ cup all-purpose flour,** and **3 tablespoons unsweetened cocoa.** Gradually whisk in **1 cup milk** until smooth. Continue as directed but in Step 2 beat in **4 squares (4 ounces) semisweet chocolate, melted and cooled** with milk mixture and vanilla. Makes 3 cups.

Each tablespoon: About 64 calories, 0g protein, 6g carbohydrate, 5g total fat (3g saturated), 11mg cholesterol, 42mg sodium.

Whipped Cream Frosting

For the occasions when a cake needs no other embellishment than some freshly whipped cream.

Prep: 5 minutes

- 2 cups heavy or whipping cream
- ¼ cup confectioners' sugar
- 1 teaspoon vanilla extract or
  2 tablespoons brandy or fruit liqueur

In small bowl, with mixer at medium speed, beat cream, confectioners' sugar, and vanilla until stiff peaks form. Makes about 4 cups.

Each tablespoon: About 28 calories, 0g protein, 1g carbohydrate, 3g total fat (2g saturated), 10mg cholesterol, 3mg sodium.

Coffee Whipped Cream Frosting

Prepare as directed but dissolve **2 teaspoons instant-coffee powder** in **2 teaspoons hot water;** add to cream.

Peppermint Whipped Cream Frosting

Beat cream as directed but omit sugar and vanilla extract. Fold in **¼ cup crushed peppermint candy.**

Cocoa Whipped Cream Frosting

Prepare as directed but use **½ cup confectioners' sugar** and add **½ cup unsweetened cocoa.**

Chocolate Glaze

Pour or spread the warm, never hot, glaze over cakes, cream puffs, or other desserts. The glaze will thicken and set as it cools.

- 3 squares (3 ounces) semisweet chocolate, coarsely chopped
- 3 tablespoons butter
- 1 tablespoon light corn syrup
- 1 tablespoon milk

In heavy 1-quart saucepan, heat chocolate, butter, corn syrup, and milk over low heat, stirring occasionally, until smooth. Makes about ½ cup.

Each tablespoon: About 100 calories, 1g protein, 9g carbohydrate, 8g total fat (5g saturated), 12mg cholesterol, 50mg sodium.

Fluffy White Frosting

This irresistible marshmallowlike frosting is at its best the day it is made. If you're planning on frosting a chocolate cake, omit the lemon juice.

Prep: 15 minutes Cook: 7 minutes

2	large egg whites
1	cup sugar
¼	cup water
2	teaspoons fresh lemon juice (optional)
1	teaspoon light corn syrup
¼	teaspoon cream of tartar

1. In medium bowl set over 3- to 4-quart saucepan filled with *1 inch simmering water* (bowl should sit about 2 inches above water), with hand-held mixer at high speed, beat egg whites, sugar, water, lemon juice if using, corn syrup, and cream of tartar until soft peaks form and mixture reaches 160°F on candy thermometer, about 7 minutes.

2. Remove bowl from pan; beat egg-white mixture until stiff, glossy peaks form, 5 to 10 minutes longer. Makes about 3 cups.

Each tablespoon: About 17 calories, 0g protein, 4g carbohydrate, 0g total fat (0g saturated), 0mg cholesterol, 2mg sodium.

Fluffy Harvest Moon Frosting

Prepare as directed but use **1 cup packed dark brown sugar** for granulated sugar and omit lemon juice.

Cream Cheese Frosting

This is the classic frosting for carrot cake but do try it with banana or spice layer cakes, too.

Prep: 10 minutes

2	packages (3 ounces each) cream cheese, slightly softened
6	tablespoons butter or margarine, softened
3	cups confectioners' sugar
1½	teaspoons vanilla extract

In large bowl, with mixer at low speed, beat cream cheese, butter, confectioners' sugar, and vanilla just until blended. Increase speed to medium. Beat until smooth and fluffy, about 1 minute, frequently scraping bowl with rubber spatula. Makes about 2½ cups.

Each tablespoon: About 66 calories, 0g protein, 9g carbohydrate, 3g total fat (2g saturated), 9mg cholesterol, 30mg sodium.

Lemon Filling

This vibrant pucker-producing filling is always popular. It makes enough to fill two or three cake layers.

Prep: 15 minutes plus chilling Cook: 8 minutes

3	large lemons
1	tablespoon cornstarch
6	tablespoons butter, cut into pieces (do not use margarine)
¾	cup sugar
4	large egg yolks

1. From lemons, grate 1 tablespoon peel and squeeze ½ cup juice. In 2-quart saucepan, with wire whisk, mix cornstarch and lemon peel and juice until blended. Add butter and sugar. Heat to boiling over medium-high heat, stirring constantly; boil 1 minute.

2. In small bowl, lightly beat egg yolks. Into egg yolks, beat ¼ cup hot lemon mixture; pour egg mixture back into lemon mixture in saucepan, beating rapidly to prevent curdling. Reduce heat to low; cook, stirring constantly, until mixture has thickened (do not boil), about 5 minutes. Pour into medium bowl. Press plastic wrap onto surface. Refrigerate until chilled, at least 3 hours or up to 3 days. Makes about 1 cup.

Each tablespoon: About 93 calories, 1g protein, 11g carbohydrate, 6g total fat (3g saturated), 65mg cholesterol, 46mg sodium.

Ganache

Ganache is a thick, creamy chocolate filling meant to be slathered between layers of your favorite cake.

Prep: 15 minutes plus chilling

1	cup heavy or whipping cream
2	tablespoons sugar
2	teaspoons butter or margarine
10	squares (10 ounces) semisweet chocolate, chopped
1	teaspoon vanilla extract
1	to 2 tablespoons brandy or orange- or almond-flavored liqueur (optional)

1. In 2-quart saucepan, combine cream, sugar, and butter; heat to boiling over medium-high heat. Remove saucepan from heat.

2. Add chocolate to cream mixture and with wire whisk, whisk until chocolate melts and mixture is smooth. Stir in vanilla and brandy, if using. Pour into jelly-roll pan and refrigerate until spreadable, at least 30 minutes. Makes 2 cups.

Each tablespoon: About 74 calories, 1g protein, 6g carbohydrate, 6g total fat (3g saturated), 11mg cholesterol, 6mg sodium.

CHOCOLATE GARNISHES

Chocolate Curls

Use these curls to garnish ice cream, cakes, and pies.

Prep: 15 minutes plus chilling

1	package (6 ounces) semisweet chocolate chips
2	tablespoons vegetable shortening

1. In heavy 1-quart saucepan, combine chocolate chips and shortening; heat over low heat, stirring frequently, until melted and smooth.

2. Pour chocolate mixture into foil-lined or disposable 5¾" by 3¼" loaf pan. Refrigerate until chocolate is set, about 2 hours.

3. Remove chocolate from pan. Using vegetable peeler and working over waxed paper, draw blade across surface of chocolate to make large curls. If chocolate is too cold and curls break, let chocolate stand about 30 minutes at room temperature until slightly softened. To avoid breaking curls, use toothpick or wooden skewer to transfer.

Chocolate Leaves

Use only nontoxic leaves, such as lemon, gardenia, grape, magnolia, nasturtium, rose, and violet, which are available at some florist shops.

Prep: 30 minutes plus chilling

12	lemon leaves
1	package (6 ounces) semisweet chocolate chips
¼	cup vegetable shortening

1. Wash leaves in warm soapy water; pat thoroughly dry with paper towels.

2. In heavy 1-quart saucepan, combine chocolate chips and shortening; heat over low heat, stirring frequently, until melted and smooth.

3. With pastry brush or small metal spatula, spread layer of melted chocolate mixture on underside (back) of each leaf (underside will give more distinct leaf design). Place chocolate-coated leaves, chocolate side up, on waxed paper–lined cookie sheet. Refrigerate until chocolate is firm, about 30 minutes.

4. With cool hands, carefully and gently peel each leaf away from chocolate.

TOXIC LEAVES

Do not allow these leaves to come in contact with chocolate or any other foods: amaryllis, azalea, caladium, daffodil, delphinium, dieffenbachia, English ivy, hydrangea, jonquil, larkspur, laurel, lily of the valley, mistletoe, narcissus, oleander, rhododendron.

20

PIES & TARTS

Whether a pie is bursting with seasonal fruit, filled with creamy custard, or crowned with meringue, you can always count on one thing: It will be delicious. Of course, a tender, flaky crust is one of the most important elements. There's no mystery to making a fine crust: Just follow our easy mixing and rolling techniques, and you'll find that it's as . . . easy as pie.

INGREDIENTS

The flavor and texture of a baked piecrust depend on two main ingredients: flour and fat. For the tenderest crust, use all-purpose flour.

The single most important factor in the quest for tender pastry is the fat. Butter gives a dough rich flavor, crispness, and color; vegetable shortening makes it flaky. We use butter and shortening to give piecrust the best qualities of each. To keep the fat in the dough chilled and firm, use ice water to bring the ingredients together. And be sure both the butter and shortening are well chilled. The pieces of fat should hold their shape. The kitchen should be cool, too. If you must make pie on a hot day, chill the flour.

MIXING THE DOUGH

- A pastry blender is the best utensil for blending fat and flour. But you can also use two dinner knives, scissor-fashion, to cut in the fat until the mixture resembles coarse crumbs. Using a fork to toss, combine the mixture, then sprinkle in the water, 1 tablespoon at a time, mixing lightly after each addition,

just until the dough is moist enough to hold together.
- Shape the dough into one or more disks, depending on the recipe. Wrap each disk in waxed paper or plastic wrap and chill for at least 30 minutes or up to overnight. If it's been chilled overnight, allow the dough to stand at room temperature for about 30 minutes to soften it slightly or it will crack when rolled out.

ROLLING OUT THE DOUGH

To prevent sticking, dust the work surface lightly with flour. Rub the rolling pin with flour, too. If you wish, sprinkle a little flour on top of the dough. Start in the center and roll out the dough, rolling up to—but not over—the edge. Give the dough a quarter turn. Repeat until you have an even round. If the dough tears, just moisten the edges and press them together.

THE PERFECT FIT

Use a glass pie plate or a dull metal one. We use a standard 9-inch pie plate for most of our pies. Some fruit pies call for a deep-dish pie plate (9 inches wide by $1\frac{1}{2}$ to 2 inches deep). For tarts, use a fluted pan with a removable bottom.

There are two ways to transfer rolled-out dough to a pie plate or tart pan: Loosely roll the dough onto the rolling pin, position the pin at one side of the pie plate, and unroll the dough. Alternatively, fold the rolled-out dough into quarters, set it into the pie plate, and unfold.

Deep-Dish Peach-Berry Pie

Fit the dough into the pie plate by gently easing it onto the bottom and against the sides with your fingertips. Never stretch the dough to fit, or the crust may shrink during baking. To help reduce shrinkage in single-crust pies, chill the piecrust for 10 to 15 minutes before baking.

DECORATIVE PIE EDGES

These borders are the perfect way to add a professional finish to homemade pies.

Forked Edge Trim the dough edge even with the rim of the pie plate. With floured fork tines, press the dough edge at even intervals.

Fluted Edge Trim the dough edge, leaving a 1-inch overhang. Fold the overhang under; form a stand-up edge. Place the thumb and forefinger of one hand, 1/2 inch apart, on the outside of the pastry edge; pinch the dough into a V shape. With the forefinger of your other hand on the inner side of the pastry edge, push the dough to define the shape. Repeat.

Turret Edge Trim the dough edge, leaving a 1-inch overhang. Fold the overhang under; form a stand-up edge. With a knife, cut the dough at 1/2-inch intervals. Fold the dough pieces down, alternating toward and away from the rim.

Appliqué Edge Prepare Pastry Dough for 2-Crust Pie (opposite). Roll out the dough for the bottom crust and place in the pie plate as directed; trim the edge even with the rim of the plate. Roll out the remaining disk of dough 1/8 inch thick. With a floured small knife or small cookie cutter, cut out small leaves or hearts. Lightly brush the dough edge with water. Gently press the shapes, slightly overlapping them, onto the dough edge to adhere.

Crimped Edge Trim the dough edge, leaving a 1-inch overhang. Fold the overhang under; form a stand-up edge. Push one index finger against the inside edge of the rim; with the index finger and thumb of the other hand, pinch dough to flute. Repeat all around the edge, leaving 1/4 inch between each flute.

PIE TOPS

Prepare Pastry Dough for 2-Crust Pie (right). Roll out the dough for the bottom crust and place in the pie plate as directed; fill. Roll out the remaining disk into a 12-inch round; proceed as directed below.

Window Center the dough round over the filling. Trim the edge, leaving a 1-inch overhang. Form a stand-up edge and make a decorative edge. Cut a 4-inch X in the center of the top crust; gently fold back the points to make a square opening.

Lattice With a pastry wheel or small knife, cut the dough round into 1/2-inch-wide strips. Moisten the edge of the bottom crust with water. Evenly space half of the pastry strips across the top of the pie; press at both ends to seal. Place an equal number of strips on top at a right angle. Trim the edge, leaving a 1-inch overhang, then moisten and press the strips. Turn the overhang over the ends of the strips. Form a high stand-up edge and make a decorative edge.

Appliqué Center the dough round over the filling. Trim the edge, leaving a 1-inch overhang. Form a stand-up edge and make a decorative edge. Roll out the trimmings. Use a small knife dipped in flour to cut free-form shapes. Brush the undersides of the dough shapes with water; place, moistened-side down, on top of the pie.

BAKING IT RIGHT

To catch any overflow, bake the pie on a sheet of foil with the edges crimped, or place on a foil-lined cookie sheet. Bake the pie in the lower third of the oven so the bottom crust crisps and the top doesn't overbrown (if the top is browning too fast, cover it loosely with foil, opposite).

Before serving, always cool fruit pies on a wire rack so the filling can set.

STORING PIES

Fruit pies can be covered and stored overnight at room temperature. For longer storage, refrigerate. Meringue pies are best the day they are made. Pies with cream or custard fillings should be refrigerated as soon as they are cool. Refrigerate leftovers.

Pastry Dough for 2-Crust Pie

Every cook should know how to make a from-scratch piecrust. Our perfect recipe gets its flavor from butter and its flakiness from vegetable shortening.

Prep: 15 minutes plus chilling

- 2¼ cups all-purpose flour
- ½ teaspoon salt
- ½ cup cold butter or margarine (1 stick), cut into pieces
- ¼ cup vegetable shortening
- 4 to 6 tablespoons ice water

1. In large bowl, with wire whisk, stir flour and salt. With pastry blender or two knives used scissor-fashion, cut in butter and shortening until mixture resembles coarse crumbs.

2. Sprinkle in ice water, 1 tablespoon at a time, mixing lightly with fork after each addition, until dough is just moist enough to hold together.

3. Shape dough into two disks, one slightly larger than the other. Wrap each disk in plastic wrap and refrigerate 30 minutes or up to overnight. (If chilled overnight, let stand 30 minutes at room temperature before rolling.)

4. On lightly floured surface, with floured rolling pin, roll larger disk into 12-inch round. Roll dough round onto rolling pin and ease into pie plate, pressing dough against side of plate. Trim edge, leaving 1-inch overhang. Reserve trimmings for decorating pie, if you like. Spoon filling into crust.

5. Roll remaining disk of dough into 12-inch round. Cut ¾-inch circle out of center and cut 1-inch slits to allow steam to escape during baking; center dough over filling. Or make desired pie top (opposite). Fold overhang under; make decorative edge (opposite). Bake as directed in recipe. Makes enough dough for one 9-inch 2-crust pie.

Each ⅒th pastry: About 235 calories, 3g protein, 23g carbohydrate, 15g total fat (7g saturated), 25mg cholesterol, 210mg sodium.

Food Processor Pastry Dough

In food processor with knife blade attached, pulse flour and salt to mix. Evenly distribute butter and shortening on top of flour mixture; pulse just until mixture resembles coarse crumbs. With processor running, pour ¼ **cup ice water** through feed tube. Immediately stop motor and pinch dough; it should be just moist enough to hold together. If not, with fork, stir in up to **2 tablespoons additional ice water.** Refrigerate and roll as directed.

Shortening Pastry Dough

Prepare as directed but use ¾ **cup vegetable shortening** and omit butter; use **1 teaspoon salt.**

Vinegar Pastry Dough

Prepare as directed but substitute **1 tablespoon distilled white vinegar** for 1 tablespoon ice water.

PROTECTING EDGES OF PIECRUST

Fold a 12-inch square of foil into quarters. With scissors, cut out an 8-inch round from middle. Unfold foil and place over pie, folding foil edges around piecrust to cover it.

Place a 12-inch square of foil over pie. Fold foil edges around piecrust to cover it.

Pastry Dough for 1-Crust Pie

Chilling a piecrust before baking helps it retain its shape.

Prep: 15 minutes plus chilling

- 1¼ **cups all-purpose flour**
- ¼ **teaspoon salt**
- 4 **tablespoons cold butter or margarine, cut into pieces**
- 2 **tablespoons vegetable shortening**
- 3 **to 5 tablespoons ice water**

1. In large bowl, with wire whisk, stir flour and salt. With pastry blender or two knives used scissor-fashion, cut in butter and shortening until mixture resembles coarse crumbs.

2. Sprinkle in ice water, 1 tablespoon at a time, mixing lightly with fork after each addition, until dough is just moist enough to hold together.

3. Shape dough into disk; wrap in plastic wrap. Refrigerate 30 minutes or up to overnight. (If chilled overnight, let stand 30 minutes at room temperature before rolling.)

4. On lightly floured surface, with floured rolling pin, roll dough into 12-inch round. Ease into pie plate, gently pressing dough against side of plate.

5. Make decorative edge (page 532) as desired. Refrigerate or freeze until firm, 10 to 15 minutes. Fill and bake as directed in recipe. Makes enough dough for one 9-inch crust.

Each ¹/₁₀th pastry: About 123 calories, 2g protein, 13g carbohydrate, 7g total fat (4g saturated), 12mg cholesterol, 104mg sodium.

Pastry for 9-Inch Tart

Prepare as directed but use **1 cup all-purpose flour, ¼ teaspoon salt, 6 tablespoons cold butter or margarine,** cut into pieces, **1 tablespoon vegetable shortening,** and **2 to 3 tablespoons ice water.** In Step 4, roll dough into 11-inch round. Ease dough into 9-inch tart pan with removable bottom. Fold overhang in and press dough against side of pan so it extends ⅛ inch above rim. Proceed as directed. Makes enough pastry for one 9-inch tart shell.

Each ⅛ pastry: About 151 calories, 2g protein, 13g carbohydrate, 10g total fat (6g saturated), 23mg cholesterol, 160mg sodium.

Pastry for 11-Inch Tart

Prepare as directed but use **1½ cups all-purpose flour, ½ teaspoon salt, ½ cup cold butter or margarine** (1 stick), cut into pieces, **2 tablespoons vegetable shortening,** and **3 to 4 tablespoons ice water.** In Step 4, roll dough into 14-inch round. Ease dough into 11-inch tart pan with removable bottom. Fold overhang in and press dough against side of pan so it extends ⅛ inch above rim. Proceed as directed. Makes enough pastry for one 11-inch tart shell.

Each ¹/₁₂ pastry: About 148 calories, 2g protein, 13g carbohydrate, 10g total fat (5g saturated), 21mg cholesterol, 175mg sodium.

Prebaked Piecrust or Tart Shell

For the best flavor and texture, be sure to bake the piecrust until evenly golden.

Prep: 15 minutes plus chilling   Bake: 20 minutes

Pastry Dough for 1-Crust Pie, Pastry for 9-Inch Tart, or Pastry for 11-Inch Tart

1. Prepare pastry dough as directed through chilling.

2. Preheat oven to 425°F. Use dough to line 9-inch pie plate, 9-inch tart pan with removable bottom, or 11-inch tart pan with removable bottom. If using pie plate, make decorative edge. If using tart pan, finish edge as directed in recipe. Refrigerate or freeze until firm, 10 to 15 minutes.

3. Line pie or tart shell with foil; fill with pie weights or dry beans. Bake 15 minutes. Remove foil with weights; bake until golden, 5 to 10 minutes longer. If shell puffs up during baking, gently press it down with back of spoon. Cool on wire rack. Fill (and bake) as directed in recipe. Makes 1 piecrust or tart shell.

Graham Cracker–Crumb Crust

For the freshest flavor, make your own cookie crumbs.

Prep: 10 minutes   Bake: 10 minutes

- 1¼ cups graham-cracker crumbs (9 rectangular graham crackers)
- 4 tablespoons butter or margarine, melted
- 1 tablespoon sugar

1. Preheat oven to 375°F. In 9-inch pie plate, with fork, mix crumbs, melted butter, and sugar until crumbs are evenly moistened. Press mixture firmly onto bottom and up side of pie plate, making small rim.

2. Bake 10 minutes; cool on wire rack. Fill as recipe directs. Makes one 9-inch crust.

Each 1/10th crust: About 105 calories, 1g protein, 12g carbohydrate, 6g total fat (3g saturated), 12mg cholesterol, 137mg sodium.

Chocolate Wafer–Crumb Crust

Prepare as directed but substitute **1¼ cups chocolate-wafer crumbs (24 cookies)** for graham-cracker crumbs.

Each 1/10th crust: About 108 calories, 1g protein, 12g carbohydrate, 7g total fat (3g saturated), 13mg cholesterol, 130mg sodium.

Vanilla Wafer–Crumb Crust

Prepare as directed but substitute **1¼ cups vanilla-wafer crumbs (35 cookies)** for graham-cracker crumbs.

Each 1/10th crust: About 92 calories, 1g protein, 9g carbohydrate, 6g total fat (3g saturated), 12mg cholesterol, 80mg sodium.

MAKING COOKIE CRUMBS

 Test Kitchen Tip
To make cookie crumbs, place the cookies in a heavy-duty zip-tight plastic bag and crush them with a rolling pin or meat mallet. You can also use a food processor or blender. For about 1 cup crushed cookie crumbs, use twenty 2¼-inch chocolate wafers, 14 gingersnaps, 22 vanilla wafers, or 7 rectangular plain or chocolate graham crackers.

Apple Pie

For the best flavor, fill this pie with a combination of apples, such as Gala, Granny Smith, and Golden Delicious. You can also use half brown sugar and half granulated sugar.

Prep: 45 minutes plus chilling   Bake: 1 hour 20 minutes

- Pastry Dough for 2-Crust Pie (page 533)
- ⅔ cup sugar
- 2 tablespoons all-purpose flour
- ½ teaspoon ground cinnamon
- ⅛ teaspoon salt
- 3 pounds cooking apples (9 medium), peeled, cored, and thinly sliced
- 1 tablespoon fresh lemon juice
- 1 tablespoon butter or margarine, cut into pieces

1. Prepare pastry dough as directed through chilling.

2. In large bowl, with wire whisk, stir sugar, flour, cinnamon, and salt. Add apples and lemon juice; gently toss to combine.

3. Preheat oven to 425°F. Use larger disk of dough to line 9-inch pie plate. Spoon apple filling into crust; dot with butter. Roll out remaining disk of dough; cut center circle and 1-inch slits to allow steam to escape during baking. Place over filling and make decorative edge.

4. Place pie on foil-lined cookie sheet to catch any overflow during baking. Bake 20 minutes. Turn oven control to 375°F; bake until filling bubbles in center, about 1 hour longer. If necessary, cover pie loosely with foil during last 20 minutes of baking to prevent over-browning. Cool on wire rack 1 hour to serve warm, or cool completely to serve later. Makes 10 servings.

Each serving: About 369 calories, 3g protein, 55g carbohydrate, 16g total fat (8g saturated), 28mg cholesterol, 251mg sodium.

Very Blueberry Pie

Prepare as directed above but use **¾ cup sugar, ¼ cup cornstarch,** and a **pinch salt,** and substitute **6 cups blueberries (about 3 pints)** for apples. In Step 3, dot filling with **2 tablespoons butter or margarine,** cut into pieces. Bake and cool as directed.

Each serving: About 374 calories, 4g protein, 53g carbohydrate, 17g total fat (8g saturated), 31mg cholesterol, 253mg sodium.

Peach Pie

Double Blueberry Pie

In our version of this old New England recipe, we maximize the blueberry flavor by stirring raw berries into the cooked filling. To make it easy for casual summer entertaining, we've paired it with a simple gingersnap crust.

Prep: 30 minutes plus chilling   Bake: 8 minutes

1²/₃ cups gingersnap cookie crumbs
(about 25 cookies)
5 tablespoons butter or margarine, melted
2 tablespoons plus ½ cup sugar
2 tablespoons cornstarch
2 tablespoons cold water
3 pints blueberries
whipped cream (optional)

1. Preheat oven to 375°F. In 9-inch pie plate, with fork, mix cookie crumbs, melted butter, and 2 tablespoons sugar until moistened. With hand, press mixture firmly onto bottom and up side of pie plate. Bake 8 minutes. Cool on wire rack.

2. Meanwhile, in 2-quart saucepan, blend cornstarch and water until smooth. Add half of blueberries and remaining ½ cup sugar to cornstarch mixture; heat to boiling over medium-high heat, pressing blueberries against side of saucepan with back of spoon. Boil, stirring constantly, 1 minute. Remove from heat; stir in remaining blueberries.

3. Pour blueberry filling into cooled crust. Press plastic wrap onto surface and refrigerate until thoroughly chilled, about 5 hours. Serve with whipped cream, if desired. Makes 10 servings.

Each serving: About 241 calories, 2g protein, 42g carbohydrate, 8g total fat (4g saturated), 16mg cholesterol, 201mg sodium.

Peach Pie

Prepare as directed for Apple Pie (page 535) but use ³/₄ **cup sugar, ¼ cup cornstarch,** and a **pinch salt,** and substitute **3 pounds ripe peaches (9 large),** pitted, peeled, and sliced (7 cups), for apples. In Step 3, dot filling with **2 tablespoons butter or margarine,** cut into pieces. Bake and cool as directed.

Each serving: About 360 calories, 4g protein, 52g carbohydrate, 16g total fat (8g saturated), 28mg cholesterol, 236mg sodium.

Rhubarb Pie

Prepare as directed for Apple Pie (page 535) but use 1½ **cups sugar, ¼ cup cornstarch,** and a **pinch salt,** and substitute **2 pounds rhubarb,** trimmed and cut into ½-inch pieces (7 cups), for apples. In Step 3, dot filling with **2 tablespoons butter or margarine,** cut into pieces. Bake and cool as directed.

Each serving: About 387 calories, 4g protein, 59g carbohydrate, 16g total fat (8g saturated), 28mg cholesterol, 239mg sodium.

Deluxe Cheese Pie

This is like a scrumptious classic cheesecake, but it's made in a fraction of the time.

Prep: 20 minutes plus cooling and chilling
Bake: 45 minutes

Graham Cracker–Crumb Crust (page 535)
1½ packages (8 ounces each) cream cheese, softened
½ cup plus 2 tablespoons sugar
2 large eggs
½ teaspoon vanilla extract
1 container (8 ounces) sour cream

1. Preheat oven to 350°F. Prepare crust as directed. Cool on wire rack.

2. In medium bowl, with mixer at low speed, beat cream cheese and ½ cup sugar until smooth, occasionally scraping side of bowl with rubber spatula. Add eggs and vanilla; beat just until combined.

3. Pour cheese filling into cooled crust. Bake until set, about 30 minutes.

4. Blend sour cream and remaining 2 tablespoons sugar. Spread evenly over hot pie. Bake until set, about 5 minutes. Cool pie on wire rack. Refrigerate at least 2 hours for easier slicing or up to overnight. Makes 10 servings.

Each serving: About 337 calories, 6g protein, 27g carbohydrate, 23g total fat (14g saturated), 102mg cholesterol, 262mg sodium.

Strawberry Cheese Pie

Prepare as directed but omit sour-cream mixture; cool pie completely. Arrange **1½ pints strawberries,** hulled and cut in half, on top of pie. In small saucepan, heat **⅓ cup red currant jelly** over medium-low heat until melted and bubbling; brush over strawberries.

Strawberry Cheese Pie

Tart Cherry Pie

If you see tart (sour) cherries in your farmers' market, buy enough to make several desserts and freeze the extra cherries for later use.

Prep: 1 hour plus chilling
Bake: 1 hour 20 minutes

Pastry Dough for 2-Crust Pie (page 533)
1 cup sugar
¼ cup cornstarch
pinch salt
2¼ pounds tart (sour) cherries, pitted (4½ cups)
1 tablespoon butter or margarine, cut into pieces

1. Prepare pastry dough as directed through chilling.
2. Preheat oven to 425°F. In large bowl, with wire whisk, stir sugar, cornstarch, and salt. Add cherries and toss to combine.
3. Use larger disk of dough to line 9-inch pie plate. Spoon cherry filling into crust; dot with butter. Roll out remaining disk of dough; cut out center circle and 1-inch slits to allow steam to escape during baking. Place dough over filling; make decorative edge.
4. Place pie on foil-lined cookie sheet to catch any overflow during baking. Bake 20 minutes. Turn oven control to 375°F; bake until filling bubbles in center, 1 hour to 1 hour 10 minutes longer. Cover pie loosely with foil during last 20 minutes of baking to prevent overbrowning. Cool on wire rack 1 hour to serve warm, or cool completely to serve later. Makes 10 servings.

Each serving: About 381 calories, 4g protein, 57g carbohydrate, 16g total fat (8g saturated), 28mg cholesterol, 239mg sodium.

Frozen Tart Cherry Pie

Prepare as directed above but use **1¼ cups sugar, 1 bag (20 ounces) frozen tart cherries,** thawed (with their juice), and **⅓ cup cornstarch.**

Canned Cherry Pie

Prepare as directed but use **2 cans (16 ounces each) pitted tart (sour) cherries packed in water.** Drain; reserve ½ cup cherry juice. In medium bowl, combine **¾ cup sugar, ¼ cup cornstarch, ⅛ teaspoon ground cinnamon,** and **pinch salt.** Add reserved cherry juice, cherries, and ½ **teaspoon vanilla;** toss to combine.

Lemon Meringue Pie

Here is our favorite recipe for this all-time classic lemon masterpiece, crowned with billowing meringue.

Prep: 45 minutes plus chilling and cooling
Bake: 30 minutes

Pastry Dough for 1-Crust Pie (page 534)
4 to 6 lemons
1½ cups sugar
⅓ cup cornstarch
¼ teaspoon plus pinch salt
1½ cups water
3 large eggs, separated, plus 1 large egg white
2 tablespoons butter or margarine, cut into pieces
¼ teaspoon cream of tartar

1. Prepare pastry dough as directed through chilling.
2. Preheat oven to 425°F. Use dough to line 9-inch pie plate; make decorative edge. Refrigerate or freeze until firm, 10 to 15 minutes.
3. Line pie shell with foil; fill with pie weights or dry beans. Bake 15 minutes. Remove foil with weights; bake until golden, 5 to 10 minutes longer. If pastry puffs up during baking, press it down with back of spoon. Cool on wire rack.
4. Meanwhile, from lemons, grate 1 tablespoon peel and squeeze ¾ cup juice; set aside.
5. In 2-quart saucepan, combine 1 cup sugar, cornstarch, and ¼ teaspoon salt; stir in water. Cook over medium heat, stirring constantly, until mixture has thickened and boils; boil 1 minute. Remove from heat.
6. In small bowl, whisk egg yolks. Stir in ⅓ cup hot cornstarch mixture until blended; slowly pour yolk mixture back into in saucepan, stirring rapidly to prevent curdling. Place pan over low heat; cook, stirring constantly, until filling is very thick, about 4 minutes. Remove from heat; stir in butter, then gradually stir in lemon peel and juice until blended. Pour into cooled pie shell.
7. Turn oven control to 400°F. In small bowl, with mixer at high speed, beat egg whites, cream of tartar, and pinch salt until soft peaks form when beaters are lifted. Sprinkle in ½ cup sugar, 2 tablespoons at a time, beating until sugar has dissolved and egg whites stand in stiff, glossy peaks when beaters are lifted.

8. Spread meringue over filling to edge of pie shell. Decoratively swirl meringue with back of spoon. Bake until meringue is golden, about 10 minutes. Cool on wire rack away from drafts. Refrigerate at least 3 hours for easier slicing or up to 2 days. Makes 10 servings.

Each serving: About 321 calories, 4g protein, 52g carbohydrate, 11g total fat (5g saturated), 82mg cholesterol, 224mg sodium.

Pilgrim Pumpkin Pie

For those who prefer a spicy pie, add ⅛ teaspoon ground white pepper, or serve with softly whipped cream flavored with ground ginger, if you like.

Prep: 25 minutes plus chilling   Bake: 1 hour 10 minutes

Pastry Dough for 1-Crust Pie (page 534)
1   can (15 ounces) solid-pack pumpkin (not pumpkin-pie mix) or 2 cups mashed cooked pumpkin
1   can (12 ounces) evaporated milk
¾   cup packed brown sugar
2   large eggs
1   teaspoon ground cinnamon
½   teaspoon ground ginger
½   teaspoon salt
¼   teaspoon ground nutmeg

1. Prepare pastry dough as directed through chilling.
2. Preheat oven to 425°F. Use dough to line 9-inch pie plate; make high stand-up edge. Refrigerate or freeze until firm, 10 to 15 minutes.
3. Line pie shell with foil; fill with pie weights or dry beans. Bake 15 minutes. Remove foil with weights; bake until golden, 5 to 10 minutes longer. If shell puffs up during baking, gently press it down with back of spoon. Turn oven control to 375°F.
4. In large bowl, with wire whisk, mix pumpkin, evaporated milk, brown sugar, eggs, cinnamon, ginger, salt, and nutmeg until well combined. Place piecrust-lined pie plate on oven rack; carefully pour in pumpkin filling. Bake until knife inserted 1 inch from edge comes out clean, about 50 minutes. Cool on wire rack at least 1 hour or up to 6 hours. Makes 10 servings.

Each serving: About 267 calories, 6g protein, 36g carbohydrate, 11g total fat (6g saturated), 66mg cholesterol, 282mg sodium.

Frozen Key Lime Pie

Quick, refreshing, and light—what more could you ask for in a summer dessert?

Prep: 20 minutes plus cooling and freezing
Bake: 10 minutes

Graham Cracker–Crumb Crust (page 535)
4   limes
1   can (14 ounces) sweetened condensed milk
1   cup heavy or whipping cream

1. Prepare crust as directed. Cool completely.
2. From limes, grate 1 tablespoon peel and squeeze ½ cup juice. In large bowl, with wire whisk, stir condensed milk and lime peel and juice until well blended.
3. In large bowl, with mixer at medium speed, beat cream until stiff peaks form. Fold whipped cream, one-third at a time, into lime mixture just until blended.
4. Pour mixture into cooled crust. Cover and freeze at least 3 hours or up to 1 month. Before serving, let pie stand 10 minutes at room temperature for easier slicing. Makes 10 servings.

Each serving: About 319 calories, 5g protein, 36g carbohydrate, 18g total fat (11g saturated), 59mg cholesterol, 196mg sodium.

Frozen Key Lime Pie

Deep-Dish Peach-Berry Pie

(Pictured on page 530)

We love to prepare this pie with a mix of berries, but it is equally delicious with only one or two types of berries.

Prep: 40 minutes plus chilling Bake: 35 minutes

Crust

1	cup all-purpose flour
1½	teaspoons baking powder
¼	cup plus 1 tablespoon sugar
3	tablespoons cold butter or margarine, cut into pieces
½	cup plus 1 tablespoon heavy or whipping cream
⅛	teaspoon ground cinnamon

Fruit Filling

½	cup sugar
¼	cup cold water
2	tablespoons cornstarch
2	pounds ripe peaches (about 5 medium), pitted and cut into 1-inch pieces
3	cups assorted berries (1 cup each blueberries, blackberries, and raspberries)

1. Prepare crust: In medium bowl, combine flour, baking powder, and ¼ cup sugar. With pastry blender or two knives used scissor-fashion, cut in butter until mixture resembles fine crumbs. Add ½ cup cream and stir with fork until dough comes together. Gather dough into ball and place on lightly floured sheet of waxed paper. With floured rolling pin, roll into 9-inch round. Slide waxed paper onto cookie sheet; refrigerate dough. Mix cinnamon and remaining 1 tablespoon sugar.

2. Prepare filling: Preheat oven to 400°F. Place cookie sheet lined with foil in oven. In 4-quart saucepan, stir sugar, water, and cornstarch until cornstarch dissolves. Add peaches; heat to boiling over medium-high heat, stirring often. Reduce heat to low; simmer, stirring often, 2 minutes. Remove from heat; stir in berries. Pour filling into 9½-inch deep-dish pie plate.

3. Immediately remove dough from refrigerator and, using waxed paper, invert over fruit. Peel off paper. Cut 4-inch X in center of round; fold back points to make square opening. Brush dough with remaining 1 tablespoon cream; sprinkle with cinnamon sugar.

4. Place pie on foil-lined cookie sheet to catch any overflow. Bake until fruit is bubbly in center, 35 to 40 minutes. If necessary, cover pie loosely with foil during last 10 minutes of baking to prevent overbrowning. Cool pie on wire rack. Makes 8 servings.

Each serving: About 310 calories, 3g protein, 51g carbohydrate, 11g total fat (7g saturated), 35mg cholesterol, 130mg sodium.

Pecan Pie

This southern classic couldn't be richer or more delicious.

Prep: 25 minutes plus chilling and cooling
Bake: 1 hour 5 minutes

	Pastry Dough for 1-Crust Pie (page 534)
1¾	cups pecan halves (7 ounces)
¾	cup dark corn syrup
½	cup packed brown sugar
4	tablespoons butter or margarine, melted
1	teaspoon vanilla extract
3	large eggs

1. Prepare pastry dough as directed through chilling.

2. Preheat oven to 425°F. Use dough to line 9-inch pie plate; make decorative edge. Refrigerate or freeze until firm, 10 to 15 minutes.

3. Line pie shell with foil; fill with pie weights or dry beans. Bake 15 minutes. Remove foil with weights; bake until golden, 5 to 10 minutes longer. If shell puffs up during baking, gently press it down with back of spoon. Cool on wire rack. Turn oven control to 350°F.

4. Coarsely chop 1 cup pecans. In large bowl, with wire whisk, mix corn syrup, brown sugar, melted butter, vanilla, and eggs until blended. Stir in chopped pecans and remaining ¾ cup pecan halves.

5. Pour pecan filling into cooled pie shell. Bake until filling is set around edges but center jiggles slightly, 45 to 50 minutes. Cool on wire rack at least 1 hour for easier slicing. Makes 12 servings.

Each serving: About 353 calories, 4g protein, 38g carbohydrate, 22g total fat (7g saturated), 74mg cholesterol, 177mg sodium.

Chocolate Pecan Pie

Prepare as directed for Pecan Pie but use ¾ **cup packed dark brown sugar** and add **2 squares (2 ounces) unsweetened chocolate,** melted, to filling with butter.

Banana Cream Pie

A vanilla wafer–crumb crust is our favorite for this pie, but if you love the combination of chocolate and bananas, use the Chocolate Wafer–Crumb Crust, page 535.

Prep: 30 minutes plus cooling and chilling
Bake: 10 minutes

Vanilla Wafer–Crumb Crust (page 535)
¾ cup sugar
⅓ cup cornstarch
¼ teaspoon salt
3¾ cups milk
5 large egg yolks
2 tablespoons butter or margarine, cut into pieces
1¾ teaspoons vanilla extract
3 ripe medium bananas
¾ cup heavy or whipping cream

1. Prepare crust as directed. Cool completely.

2. Meanwhile, prepare filling: In 3-quart saucepan, combine sugar, cornstarch, and salt; stir in milk. Cook over medium heat, stirring constantly, until mixture has thickened and boils; boil 1 minute.

3. In small bowl, with wire whisk, lightly beat egg yolks; beat in ½ cup hot milk mixture. Slowly pour egg-yolk mixture back into milk mixture, stirring rapidly to prevent curdling. Cook over low heat, stirring constantly, until mixture has thickened, about 2 minutes.

4. Remove saucepan from heat. Add butter and 1½ teaspoons vanilla; stir until butter melts. Transfer mixture to medium bowl. Press plastic wrap onto surface. Refrigerate, stirring occasionally, until cool, about 1 hour.

5. Slice 2 bananas. Spoon half of filling into crust. Arrange sliced bananas on top; spoon remaining filling evenly over bananas. Press plastic wrap onto surface; refrigerate at least 4 hours or up to overnight.

6. To serve, prepare topping: In small bowl, with mixer at medium speed, beat cream and remaining ¼ teaspoon vanilla until stiff peaks form; spread over filling. Slice remaining banana; arrange around edge of pie. Makes 10 servings.

Each serving: About 367 calories, 6g protein, 41g carbohydrate, 21g total fat (12g saturated), 162mg cholesterol, 216mg sodium.

Coconut Cream Pie

Prepare as directed but omit bananas; fold ¾ **cup sweetened flaked coconut** into filling before spooning into crust. Refrigerate and top with whipped cream as directed. To serve, sprinkle with ¼ **cup sweetened flaked coconut,** toasted.

Easy Eggnog Pumpkin Pie

For a special finish, top each serving with a dollop of whipped cream sprinkled with pumpkin-pie spice.

Prep: 20 minutes plus chilling and cooling   Bake: 1 hour

Pastry Dough for 1-Crust Pie (page 534)
1 can (15 ounces) pure pumpkin (not pumpkin-pie mix)
1¼ cups prepared eggnog
⅔ cup sugar
1½ teaspoons pumpkin-pie spice
¼ teaspoon salt
3 large eggs

1. Prepare pastry dough as directed through chilling.

2. 2. Preheat oven to 375°F. Use dough to line 9-inch pie plate; place on foil-lined cookie sheet.

3. In large bowl, with wire whisk, mix pumpkin, eggnog, sugar, pumpkin-pie spice, salt, and eggs until combined. Pour pumpkin mixture into piecrust (mixture will come up to almost top of crust).

4. Bake until filling puffs up around edges and center is just set but not puffed, about 1 hour. Cool completely on wire rack. Refrigerate until ready to serve. Makes 12 servings.

Each serving: About 165 calories, 3g protein, 23g carbohydrate, 7g total fat (3g saturated), 69mg cholesterol, 150mg sodium.

Chocolate Cream Pie

Dessert doesn't get better than a traditional chocolate cream pie.

Prep: 35 minutes plus cooling and chilling
Bake: 10 minutes

Chocolate Wafer–Crumb Crust (page 535)
¾ cup sugar
⅓ cup cornstarch
½ teaspoon salt
3¾ cups milk
5 large egg yolks
3 squares (3 ounces) unsweetened chocolate, melted
2 tablespoons butter or margarine, cut into pieces
2 teaspoons vanilla extract
Chocolate Curls (page 529; optional)
1 cup heavy or whipping cream

1. Prepare crust as directed. Cool completely.

2. Meanwhile, in heavy 3-quart saucepan, combine sugar, cornstarch, and salt; whisk in milk until smooth. Cook over medium heat, stirring constantly, until mixture has thickened and boils; boil 1 minute.

3. In small bowl, with wire whisk, lightly beat egg yolks. Beat ½ cup hot milk mixture into beaten egg yolks. Slowly pour egg-yolk mixture back into milk mixture, stirring rapidly to prevent curdling. Cook over low heat, stirring constantly, until mixture is very thick or until temperature on thermometer reaches 160°F.

4. Remove saucepan from heat and stir in melted chocolate, butter, and vanilla until butter melts and mixture is smooth. Pour hot chocolate filling into cooled crust; press plastic wrap onto surface. Refrigerate until filling is set, about 4 hours.

5. Meanwhile, make Chocolate Curls, if using.

6. To serve, in small bowl, with mixer at medium speed, beat cream until stiff peaks form; spoon over chocolate filling. Top with chocolate curls, if desired. Makes 10 servings.

Each serving: About 417 calories, 7g protein, 38g carbohydrate, 28g total fat (16g saturated), 171mg cholesterol, 329mg sodium.

Chocolate Cream Pie

Apple Crumb Squares

A tender butter crust; a generous filling of cooked apples, raisins, and brown sugar; and a walnut and brown sugar topping make this dessert irresistible.

Prep: 1 hour plus cooling   Bake: 1 hour

Crumb Topping

1 cup all-purpose flour
1 cup pecans or walnuts, coarsely chopped
½ cup butter or margarine (1 stick), slightly softened
½ cup light or dark brown sugar
1 tablespoon vanilla extract
1 teaspoon ground cinnamon

Crust

3 cups all-purpose flour
⅓ cup granulated sugar
¼ teaspoon salt
¾ cup cold butter or margarine (1½ sticks)

Apple Filling

- 4 pounds green cooking apples, such as Granny Smith, peeled, cored, and cut into ½-inch pieces
- 4 tablespoons butter or margarine
- ¾ cup raisins or dried currants
- ½ cup packed light or dark brown sugar
- ¾ teaspoon ground cinnamon
- 1 tablespoon plus 2 teaspoons cornstarch
- 3 tablespoons fresh lemon juice

1. Prepare topping: In medium bowl, with fingertips, mix flour, pecans, butter, brown sugar, vanilla, and cinnamon until mixture comes together. Shape into a ball; wrap in plastic wrap and refrigerate.

2. Preheat oven to 375°F. Lightly grease sides of 15½" by 10½" jelly-roll pan.

3. Prepare crust: In large bowl, with fork, mix flour, granulated sugar, and salt. With pastry blender or two knives used scissor-fashion, cut in butter until mixture resembles fine crumbs. With hand, press crumb mixture evenly onto bottom of prepared pan.

4. Bake crust until golden brown (crust may crack slightly), 20 to 24 minutes.

5. Meanwhile, prepare filling: In nonstick 12-inch skillet, cook apples, butter, raisins, brown sugar, and cinnamon over medium heat, stirring occasionally, until apples are very tender and most of liquid from apples has evaporated, 25 to 30 minutes. In cup, mix cornstarch and lemon juice. Stir lemon-juice mixture into apple mixture and cook, stirring, until mixture thickens. Remove skillet from heat.

6. Spread apple mixture over hot crust. Break crumb topping into chunks and scatter over apple mixture. Bake until topping browns, about 40 minutes. Cool completely in pan on wire rack.

7. To serve, cut lengthwise into 4 strips, then cut each strip crosswise into 6 squares. Makes 24 squares.

Each square: About 315 calories, 3g protein, 42g carbohydrate, 16g total fat (8g saturated), 33mg cholesterol, 155mg sodium.

Chocolate-Caramel Walnut Tart

The pastry for this luscious tart can be prepared, baked, and frozen up to one week ahead of time. Thaw it at room temperature before filling.

Prep: 40 minutes plus chilling and cooling
Bake: 30 minutes

- Pastry for 11-Inch Tart (page 534)
- 1 cup sugar
- ¼ cup water
- ¾ cup plus 1 cup heavy or whipping cream
- 2 bars (4 ounces each) bittersweet chocolate, chopped
- 2 tablespoons butter or margarine
- 2 cup walnuts (8 ounces), lightly toasted and chopped
- 2 teaspoons vanilla extract
- walnut halves

1. Prepare pastry dough as directed through baking and cooling.

2. Prepare filling: In heavy 3-quart saucepan, heat sugar and water over medium-high heat, swirling pan occasionally, until sugar is melted and amber in color, about 10 minutes. Remove from heat. Stir in cream until a smooth caramel forms. Stir in chocolate and butter until melted. Add chopped walnuts and vanilla and stir to combine.

3. Pour warm filling into cooled tart shell. Refrigerate until set, at least 3 hours.

4. To serve, remove side of pan. In small bowl, with mixer at medium speed, beat remaining 1 cup cream until stiff peaks form. Garnish tart with whipped cream and walnut halves. If not serving right away, refrigerate up to one day. Makes 12 servings.

Each serving: About 505 calories, 6g protein, 42g carbohydrate, 38g total fat (16g saturated), 48mg cholesterol, 160mg sodium.

Chocolate Truffle Tart

So unbelievably decadent, all you'll need is one thin slice!

Prep: 20 minutes plus chilling and cooling
Bake: 40 minutes

Pastry for 9-Inch Tart (page 534)
6 squares (6 ounces) semisweet chocolate, coarsely chopped
½ cup butter or margarine (1 stick)
¼ cup sugar
1 teaspoon vanilla extract
3 large eggs
½ cup heavy or whipping cream
softly whipped cream (optional)

1. Prepare pastry dough as directed through chilling.

2. Preheat oven to 425°F. Use dough to line 9-inch tart pan with removable bottom. Trim edge even with rim of pan. Refrigerate or freeze until firm, 10 to 15 minutes.

3. Line tart shell with foil; fill with pie weights or dry beans. Bake 15 minutes. Remove foil with weights; bake until golden, 5 to 10 minutes longer. If shell puffs up, gently press it down with back of spoon. Cool in pan on wire rack. Turn oven control to 350°F.

4. Meanwhile, in heavy 2-quart saucepan, melt chocolate and butter over very low heat, stirring frequently, until smooth. Add sugar and vanilla; stir until sugar has dissolved. In small bowl, with wire whisk, lightly beat eggs and cream. Whisk ⅓ cup warm chocolate mixture into egg mixture; stir egg mixture back into chocolate mixture in saucepan until blended.

5. Pour warm chocolate filling into cooled tart shell. Bake until custard is set but center still jiggles slightly, about 20 minutes.

6. Cool in pan on wire rack. When cool, remove side of pan. Refrigerate until chilled, about 4 hours. Serve with a dollop of whipped cream, if desired. Makes 12 servings.

Each serving: About 306 calories, 4g protein, 22g carbohydrate, 24g total fat (14g saturated), 103mg cholesterol, 206mg sodium.

Apple Tarte Tatin

This caramelized apple tart—a classic French dessert—is baked in a skillet. Serve it warm with ice cream.

Prep: 1 hour 10 minutes plus chilling   Bake: 25 minutes

Pastry for 9-Inch Tart (page 534)
6 tablespoons butter or margarine
1 cup sugar
1 tablespoon fresh lemon juice
3¾ pounds Golden Delicious apples (9 medium), peeled, cored, and each cut in half

1. Prepare pastry dough as directed but roll into 12-inch round. Transfer to cookie sheet; refrigerate.

2. Preheat oven to 425°F. In heavy 10-inch skillet with oven-safe handle (if skillet is not oven-safe, wrap handle in double layer of foil), combine butter, sugar, and lemon juice; cook over medium-high heat until butter melts and mixture bubbles. Place apples in skillet, overlapping them. Cook 10 minutes, turning apples to cook evenly. Carefully turn apples rounded side down; cook until syrup has thickened and is amber in color, 8 to 12 minutes longer. Remove from heat.

3. Place chilled dough on top of apples in skillet; fold edge of dough under to form rim around apples. With knife, cut six ¼-inch slits in dough to allow steam to escape during baking. Bake until crust is golden, about 25 minutes.

4. When tart is done, place large platter on top. Wearing oven mitts to protect your hands, quickly turn skillet upside down to unmold tart. Cool 30 minutes to serve warm, or cool completely to serve later. Makes 10 servings.

Each serving: About 342 calories, 2g protein, 52g carbohydrate, 16g total fat (9g saturated), 37mg cholesterol, 198mg sodium.

Peach Tarte Tatin

Prepare as directed above but substitute **3¾ pounds ripe-firm peaches (11 medium),** peeled, halved, and pitted, for apples. Bake and cool as directed.

Pear Tarte Tatin

Prepare as directed but substitute **3¾ pounds ripe-firm Bosc pears (about 7),** peeled, cored, and cut lengthwise in half, for apples. Bake and cool as directed.

Buttery Apricot Tart

The pastry for this spectacular tart can also be prepared in a food processor with the knife blade attached: Combine all of the sweet pastry dough ingredients and pulse just until the dough comes together.

**Prep: 20 minutes plus cooling
Bake: 1 hour 10 minutes**

Sweet Pastry Dough

1¼ cups all-purpose flour
¼ cup sugar
¼ teaspoon salt
7 tablespoons butter or margarine, cut up

Apricot Filling

¼ cup sugar
1½ teaspoons all-purpose flour
1½ pounds apricots (8 to 10 large), each cut in half and pitted
2 tablespoons plain dried bread crumbs
2 tablespoons chopped shelled pistachios

1. Preheat oven to 375°F.

2. Prepare pastry dough: In medium bowl, with wire whisk, stir flour, sugar, and salt. With pastry blender or two knives used scissor-fashion, cut in butter until mixture resembles coarse crumbs. With hand, press dough together in bowl.

3. Transfer dough to 11-inch fluted tart pan with removable bottom. Press dough onto bottom and up side of pan. Trim edge even with rim of pan. Bake shell 20 minutes.

4. Meanwhile, prepare filling: In medium bowl, stir sugar and flour; add apricots and toss to coat.

5. Sprinkle hot tart shell with bread crumbs. Arrange apricot halves, cut sides down, in shell. Bake tart until shell is golden and apricots are tender, 50 to 55 minutes. Cool tart in pan on wire rack.

6. To serve, carefully remove side of pan. Sprinkle tart with pistachios. Makes 8 servings.

Each serving: About 265 calories, 4g protein, 37g carbohydrate, 12g total fat (7g saturated), 29mg cholesterol, 200mg sodium.

Warm Banana-Pecan Tart

To minimize last-minute preparation, bake the crust up to two days ahead. Prepare the toasted-pecan cream up to one day in advance and refrigerate. Then simply assemble the tart just before serving.

Prep: 1 hour plus chilling   Bake/Broil: 32 minutes

Pastry for 11-Inch Tart (page 534)
½ cup pecans, toasted
½ cup plus 1 tablespoon sugar
3 large egg yolks
1 tablespoon cornstarch
¾ cup half-and-half or light cream
2 tablespoons butter or margarine, cut into pieces
1 teaspoon vanilla extract
5 ripe medium bananas (about 2 pounds)

1. Prepare pastry dough as directed through chilling.

2. Prepare pecan cream: In blender or in food processor with knife blade attached, process pecans and ¼ cup sugar until pecans are very finely ground.

3. In small bowl, stir ¼ cup sugar, egg yolks, and cornstarch until blended. In 2-quart saucepan, heat half-and-half to simmering over medium-high heat. While whisking constantly, gradually pour about half of half-and-half into egg-yolk mixture. Return egg-yolk mixture to saucepan and cook over low heat, stirring constantly, until mixture has thickened (do not boil), 4 to 5 minutes. Stir in pecan mixture, butter, and vanilla until butter melts. Transfer pecan cream to medium bowl. Press plastic wrap onto surface and refrigerate at least 30 minutes or up to overnight.

4. Meanwhile, preheat oven to 425°F. Use dough to line 11-inch tart pan with removable bottom. Trim edge even with rim of pan. Refrigerate or freeze until firm, 10 to 15 minutes.

5. Line tart shell with foil; fill with pie weights or dry beans. Bake 15 minutes. Remove foil with weights; bake until golden, 5 to 10 minutes longer. If shell puffs up during baking, gently press it down with back of spoon. Turn oven control to broil.

6. Cut bananas on diagonal into thin slices. Arrange slices, overlapping slightly, in tart shell. Spoon chilled pecan cream over bananas and sprinkle with remaining 1 tablespoon sugar. Cover edge of shell with foil. Place at position closest to heat source and broil until top is

lightly caramelized, 1 to 2 minutes. Carefully remove side of pan. Serve warm. Makes 12 servings.

Each serving: About 315 calories, 4g protein, 36g carbohydrate, 18g total fat (8g saturated), 85mg cholesterol, 203mg sodium.

Double Berry Linzer Tart

To give this fine Austrian tart holiday flair, we've added fresh cranberries to the traditional raspberry jam.

Prep: 30 minutes plus chilling **Bake:** 40 minutes

- 1 cup cranberries
- ¼ plus ⅓ cup packed brown sugar
- ¼ cup cranberry-juice cocktail
  pinch plus ¼ teaspoon salt
- ¾ cup seedless raspberry jam
- ⅔ cup hazelnuts (filberts), toasted and skinned (page 562)
- 1¼ cups all-purpose flour
- 6 tablespoons butter or margarine, softened
- 1 large egg
- ½ teaspoon vanilla extract
- ¼ teaspoon baking powder
- ¼ teaspoon ground cinnamon
  confectioners' sugar (optional)

1. In nonreactive 1-quart saucepan, combine cranberries, ¼ cup brown sugar, cranberry-juice cocktail, and pinch salt; heat to boiling over medium-high heat. Reduce heat to medium; cook, stirring occasionally, until cranberries pop and mixture has thickened slightly, about 6 minutes. Stir in raspberry jam; refrigerate until cool, about 30 minutes.

2. Meanwhile, in blender or in food processor with knife blade attached, process hazelnuts and ¼ cup flour until nuts are very finely ground.

3. In large bowl, with mixer at low speed, beat butter and remaining ⅓ cup brown sugar until blended. Increase speed to medium-high; beat until light and fluffy, about 3 minutes. With mixer at medium speed, beat in egg and vanilla until smooth, about 1 minute. Reduce speed to low. Add hazelnut mixture, remaining 1 cup flour, baking powder, cinnamon, and remaining ¼ teaspoon salt; beat just until combined.

4. With floured hands, press two-thirds of dough onto bottom and up side of 9-inch tart pan with removable bottom. Trim edge even with rim of pan. Wrap tart shell and remaining dough in plastic wrap and refrigerate until disk of dough is firm enough to shape, about 30 minutes.

5. Preheat oven to 400°F. Spoon cooled filling into tart shell. On lightly floured surface, divide remaining dough into 10 equal pieces. With floured hands, roll each piece into 8½-inch-long rope. Place 5 ropes, 1½ inches apart, across top of tart. Place remaining 5 ropes at right angle to first ropes to make lattice pattern. Or, if desired, weave dough ropes to create "fancy" lattice pattern. Trim ends of ropes even with edge of tart and press ends to seal. With hands, roll any dough trimmings into ¼-inch-thick ropes. Press ropes around edge of tart to make finished edge. If ropes break, press pieces together.

6. Bake until filling bubbles and crust is lightly browned, about 40 minutes. Cool in pan on wire rack at least 1 hour. When cool, carefully remove side of pan. Dust with confectioners' sugar, if desired. Makes 10 servings.

Each serving: About 290 calories, 4g protein, 43g carbohydrate, 12g total fat (5g saturated), 40mg cholesterol, 175mg sodium.

Double Berry Linzer Tart

Lemon Tart

This tangy French-style tart can be served on its own or accented with fresh berries. Be sure to make a high pastry rim to contain all the delicious filling.

Prep: 25 minutes plus chilling and cooling
Bake: 50 minutes

Pastry for 9-Inch Tart (page 534)
4 to 6 lemons
4 large eggs
1 cup granulated sugar
⅓ cup heavy or whipping cream
  confectioners' sugar

1. Prepare pastry dough as directed through chilling.
2. Preheat oven to 425°F. Use dough to line 9-inch tart pan with removable bottom; press dough up side so it extends ¼ inch above rim of pan. Refrigerate or freeze until firm, 10 to 15 minutes.
3. Line tart shell with foil; fill with pie weights or dry beans. Bake 15 minutes. Remove foil with weights; bake until golden, 5 to 10 minutes longer. If shell puffs up during baking, gently press it down with back of spoon. Cool tart shell in pan on wire rack. Turn oven control to 350°F.
4. From lemons, grate 1½ teaspoons peel and squeeze ⅔ cup juice. In medium bowl, with wire whisk, beat eggs, granulated sugar, and lemon peel and juice until well combined. Whisk in cream.
5. Carefully pour lemon filling into cooled tart shell. Place tart on foil-lined cookie sheet to catch any overflow during baking. Bake until filling is set but center still jiggles slightly, about 30 minutes. Cool completely on wire rack. Just before serving, dust with confectioners' sugar. Makes 8 servings.

Each serving: About 324 calories, 5g protein, 40g carbohydrate, 17g total fat (9g saturated), 143mg cholesterol, 195mg sodium.

Peach-Raspberry Galette

A galette is a little more casual than a pie but just as tasty. The combination of sweet and juicy fresh peaches and flavorful raspberries is a perfect match.

Prep: 30 minutes plus chilling   Bake: 45 minutes

Pastry Dough

1½ cups all-purpose flour
¼ teaspoon salt
½ cup cold butter (1 stick), cut into pieces
4 to 6 tablespoons ice water

Peach-Raspberry Filling

3 tablespoons cornstarch
¾ cup plus 1 tablespoon sugar
1½ pounds peaches (4 to 5 medium), peeled and cut into thick wedges
½ pint raspberries
2 tablespoons butter, cut into small pieces
1 large egg white, lightly beaten

1. Preheat oven to 425°F.
2. Prepare pastry dough: In medium bowl, with wire whisk, stir flour and salt. With pastry blender or two knives used scissor-fashion, cut in butter until mixture resembles coarse crumbs. Sprinkle in ice water, 1 tablespoon at a time, mixing with hands after each addition until dough is just moist enough to hold together (it will feel dry at first). Shape dough into a disk. Wrap in plastic wrap and refrigerate 30 minutes.
3. Line large cookie sheet with parchment paper. On floured surface, roll dough into 13-inch round (edge may be uneven). Transfer dough round to prepared cookie sheet.
4. Prepare filling: In large bowl, with wire whisk, stir cornstarch and ¾ cup sugar. Add peaches and raspberries; gently toss until fruit is evenly coated.
5. Spoon filling onto dough, leaving 2½-inch border; dot with butter. Fold border of dough over filling, pleating edges and leaving an opening in center. Pinch dough to seal any cracks. Brush dough with egg white; sprinkle with remaining 1 tablespoon sugar.

6. Place two sheets of foil under cookie sheet; crimp foil to form rim to catch any overflow during baking. Bake until crust is golden brown and filling is gently bubbling, 45 to 50 minutes. As soon as galette is done, use long metal spatula to loosen it from parchment to prevent sticking. Cool 15 minutes on cookie sheet, then slide galette onto rack to cool completely. Makes 8 servings.

Each serving: About 345 calories, 4g protein, 49g carbohydrate, 16g total fat (10g saturated), 41mg cholesterol, 235mg sodium.

Plum Frangipane Tart

Use either red or black plums for this tart. Frangipane, a rich almond, butter, and sugar mixture is a classic partner for plums.

Prep: 30 minutes plus chilling   Bake: 1 hour 10 minutes

Pastry for 11-Inch Tart (page 534)

- 1 tube or can (7 to 8 ounces) almond paste, crumbled
- 4 tablespoons butter or margarine, softened
- ½ cup sugar
- ¼ teaspoon salt
- 2 large eggs
- 2 teaspoons vanilla extract
- ¼ cup all-purpose flour
- 1¼ pounds ripe plums (5 large), pitted and each cut into 6 wedges

1. Prepare pastry dough as directed through chilling.

2. Preheat oven to 425°F. Use dough to line 11-inch tart pan with removable bottom. Trim edge even with rim of pan. Refrigerate or freeze until firm, 10 to 15 minutes.

3. Line tart shell with foil; fill with pie weights or dry beans. Bake 15 minutes. Remove foil with weights; bake until golden, 5 to 10 minutes longer. If shell puffs up during baking, gently press it down with back of spoon.

4. Meanwhile, in large bowl, with mixer at low speed, beat almond paste, butter, sugar, and salt until almond paste is crumbly. Increase speed to medium-high and beat until well blended, about 3 minutes, frequently scraping bowl with rubber spatula. (There may be some tiny lumps.) Add eggs and vanilla; beat until smooth. With wooden spoon, stir in flour.

5. Pour almond-paste mixture into warm tart shell; spread evenly. Arrange plums in concentric circles over filling. Bake until golden, 50 to 60 minutes. Cool in pan on wire rack. When cool, carefully remove side of pan. Makes 12 servings.

Each serving: About 342 calories, 6g protein, 37g carbohydrate, 20g total fat (8g saturated), 66mg cholesterol, 274mg sodium.

Cranberry-Almond Tart

Prepare as directed but omit plums. Bake almond filling until golden, about 20 minutes. Cool in pan on wire rack. In 2-quart saucepan, combine **1 cup cranberries, ¾ cup sugar, ⅓ cup water,** and **½ teaspoon freshly grated orange peel;** heat to boiling over high heat. Reduce heat; simmer until cranberries pop and mixture has thickened slightly, about 5 minutes. Stir in additional **2 cups cranberries;** set aside until cool. When cool, carefully remove side of pan; spoon cranberry topping over almond filling.

PEELING PEACHES

Test Kitchen Tip

Our favorite method for peeling peaches is to submerge them, a few at a time, in boiling water for about 20 seconds (no longer or they will start to cook). With a slotted spoon, immediately transfer them to a large bowl of ice water. One at a time, lift out the peaches and slip the skin off. Here's a good method to use if the peaches are perfectly ripe: Put the tip of a paring knife into the stem end and peel away the skin in strips. Whatever you do, don't peel a ripe peach with a vegetable peeler; you'll bruise the delicate flesh.

21

COOKIES & CONFECTIONS

Cookies are one of the simplest and most delicious treats you can make. Here is our collection of favorite recipes and tips to help guarantee your baking success.

TYPES OF COOKIES

- Bar cookies couldn't be easier. Mix up some dough, spread it in a pan, then bake, cool, and cut.
- Drop cookies are made by dropping spoonfuls of soft dough onto cookie sheets.
- Molded cookies are made from a stiff dough that is formed into balls, logs, pretzels, or other shapes or baked in individual molds.
- Pressed cookies are made from a stiff dough that is squeezed through a cookie press or pastry bag.
- Refrigerator cookies (also called icebox cookies) begin with a chilled stiff dough that is sliced and baked.
- Rolled cookies are made from a stiff dough that is rolled out into a thin layer, then cut into shapes.

COOKIE SHEET SAVVY

Good-quality cookie sheets are one of the secrets to perfect cookies. Heavy-gauge metal cookie sheets that have a dull finish turn out the most evenly browned cookies; aluminum is ideal. Double-thick insulated cookie sheets discourage overbaking and are a good investment. Dark cookie sheets can overbrown the bottoms of cookies. If your cookie sheets are old and discolored, line them with foil. Better still, purchase new ones.

The air in your oven should circulate freely around the cookie sheet(s), which should be at least 2 inches smaller in length and width than your oven. Cookie sheets should be rimless (or have only one or two turned-up edges) for the best air circulation.

Grease cookie sheets only when a recipe directs you to. Some cookies have a high fat content, so greasing isn't necessary. Vegetable shortening is better than butter for greasing cookie sheets because butter sometimes browns as it melts in the oven. Nonstick cookie sheets and silcone nonstick baking liners are good alternatives to greasing and flouring.

For an even coat when greasing is required, use a crumpled piece of paper towel. To flour a cookie sheet, sprinkle the greased sheet evenly with a little flour, then tap off the excess. For easy cleanup, line cookie sheets with foil (dull side up).

Never place cookie dough on a hot cookie sheet; always let cookie sheets cool between batches. A hot cookie sheet will melt the dough before it has a chance to set. If the recipe calls for greased sheets, regrease for each batch.

BAKING SUCCESS

- While butter and margarine are interchangeable in some cookie recipes, for the best flavor and texture, use butter.
- If you prefer margarine, make sure it contains 80 percent fat. Spreads (diet, whipped, liquid, or soft) have a high water content, which produces tough cookies that lack flavor.

Chocolate Wows

- For the tenderest cookies, once the flour has been added, mix the dough just until blended.
- Use a measuring spoon to scoop up equal portions of dough to make consistently shaped cookies that will bake in the same amount of time.
- For drop cookies, place spoonfuls of dough 2 inches apart unless the recipe directs otherwise.
- Dust the work surface lightly and evenly with flour before rolling out dough. Rub the rolling pin well with flour to keep it from sticking to the dough, or lightly dust the top of the dough with flour.
- When rolling out chilled dough, roll out one portion at a time; keep the remaining dough covered in the refrigerator.
- If a chilled dough cracks when rolled, let it stand at room temperature to soften slightly, then try again.
- For evenly baked cookies, bake one sheet of cookies at a time in the center of the oven. If you want to bake two sheets at a time, position the racks in the upper and lower thirds of the oven. Then, halfway through baking, rotate the cookie sheets between the upper and lower oven racks (unless directed otherwise) and also rotate them front to back.
- Bake cookies for the minimum suggested baking time, then check for doneness. If not done, watch them carefully for the remainder of the time to avoid overbaking.
- Unless a recipe directs otherwise, cool cookies briefly on the cookie sheet to firm slightly, then transfer to wire racks to cool completely; hot cookies are too soft to be moved immediately to racks. Cool bar cookies completely in the pan before cutting.

STORING COOKIES

Store soft and crisp cookies in separate containers with tight-fitting covers. Crisp cookies that soften can be recrisped in a 300°F oven for three to five minutes. Soft cookies can be kept soft by adding a piece of apple or bread to the container; change it every other day or so. (This technique also works for soft cookies that have hardened.) Store bar cookies in the pan they were baked in, tightly covered with foil or plastic wrap.

To freeze baked cookies, cool them thoroughly. Place them in airtight containers, cushioned with crumpled waxed paper, if necessary. If the cookies have been decorated, freeze them until hard in a single layer on a cookie sheet, then pack for storage, separating the layers with waxed paper. To thaw, unwrap the cookies and let stand for about ten minutes at room temperature.

To freeze unbaked cookie dough, wrap tightly in heavy-duty foil and store in a container. For refrigerator cookies, wrap the logs of dough in heavy-duty foil. Freeze for up to six months; thaw in the refrigerator. Remember to label and date each package.

CHOCOLATE AND COCOA

Because of its unique flavor and smooth texture, chocolate is an essential component in all kinds of sweets, including candies. There are many different kinds of chocolates, and they are rarely interchangeable. See Chocolate and Cocoa Powder, page 558.

Chocolate has two enemies: water and high heat. If a single drop of water gets into chocolate while it's melting, the chocolate can "seize" (form a dull, thick paste). Chocolate melted over heat that is too high clumps and becomes grainy, so melt it over low heat.

To chop chocolate, use a sharp, heavy knife and a dry, clean cutting board. Chop into ¼-inch pieces.

To melt chocolate, place the chopped chocolate in a heavy-bottomed saucepan; stir frequently over low heat until melted, watching carefully to avoid scorching. Or place the chocolate in the top of a double boiler over very hot, not simmering, water and stir until melted. Or place it in a microwave-safe bowl and microwave at 50 percent power, stirring at intervals.

Store chocolate and cocoa powder in a cool, dry place. "Blooms" or pale streaks that may appear will not affect the chocolate's performance or taste.

Good Housekeeping's Fudgy Brownies

Ultrarich with lots of deep, dark chocolate flavor, these brownies are fabulous with or without our praline icing. For a moist, fudgy texture, do not overbake.

Prep: 10 minutes   Bake: 30 minutes

- 1¼ cups all-purpose flour
- ½ teaspoon salt
- ¾ cup butter or margarine (1½ sticks)
- 4 squares (4 ounces) unsweetened chocolate, chopped
- 4 squares (4 ounces) semisweet chocolate, chopped
- 2 cups sugar
- 1 tablespoon vanilla extract
- 5 large eggs, beaten

1. Preheat oven to 350°F. Grease 13" by 9" baking pan. In small bowl, with wire whisk, stir flour and salt.

2. In heavy 4-quart saucepan, melt butter and unsweetened and semisweet chocolates over low heat, stirring frequently, until smooth. Remove from heat. With wooden spoon, stir in sugar and vanilla. Add eggs; stir until well mixed. Stir flour mixture into chocolate mixture just until blended. Spread batter evenly in prepared pan.

3. Bake until toothpick inserted 1 inch from edge comes out clean, about 30 minutes. Cool completely in pan on wire rack. When cool, cut lengthwise into 4 strips, then cut each strip crosswise into 6 pieces. Makes 24 brownies.

Each brownie: About 206 calories, 3g protein, 26g carbohydrate, 11g total fat (6g saturated), 60mg cholesterol, 121mg sodium.

Praline-Iced Brownies

Prepare brownies as directed; cool. In 2-quart saucepan, heat **5 tablespoons butter or margarine** and **⅓ cup packed brown sugar** over medium-low heat until mixture has melted and bubbles, about 5 minutes. Remove from heat. With wire whisk, beat in **3 tablespoons bourbon or 1 tablespoon vanilla extract plus 2 tablespoons water;** stir in **2 cups confectioners' sugar** until smooth. With small metal spatula, spread topping over room-temperature brownies; sprinkle ½ **cup pecans,** toasted and coarsely chopped, evenly over topping. Cut brownies lengthwise into 8 strips, then cut each strip crosswise into 8 pieces. Makes 64 brownies.

Each brownie: About 297 calories, 3g protein, 39g carbohydrate, 15g total fat (8g saturated), 66mg cholesterol, 147mg sodium.

Praline-Iced Brownies

Cocoa Brownies

Whenever you get a chocolate craving, you can whip up these easy saucepan brownies on the spur of the moment.

Prep: 10 minutes   Bake: 25 minutes

- ½ cup all-purpose flour
- ½ cup unsweetened cocoa
- ¼ teaspoon baking powder
- ¼ teaspoon salt
- ½ cup butter or margarine (1 stick)
- 1 cup sugar
- 2 large eggs
- 1 teaspoon vanilla extract
- 1 cup walnuts (4 ounces), coarsely chopped (optional)

1. Preheat oven to 350°F. Grease 9-inch square baking pan. In small bowl, with wire whisk, stir flour, cocoa, baking powder, and salt.

2. In 3-quart saucepan, melt butter over low heat. Remove from heat and stir in sugar. Stir in eggs, one at a time, until well blended; add vanilla. Stir flour mixture into sugar mixture until blended. Stir in walnuts, if using. Spread batter evenly in prepared pan.

3. Bake until toothpick inserted 2 inches from center comes out almost clean, about 25 minutes. Cool completely in pan on wire rack.

4. When cool, cut into 4 strips, then cut each strip crosswise into 4 pieces. Makes 16 brownies.

Each brownie: About 132 calories, 2g protein, 17g carbohydrate, 7g total fat (4g saturated), 42mg cholesterol, 110mg sodium.

Fudgy Lowfat Brownies

Moist, chocolaty, and low-fat. Need we say more? Serve with cold skim milk for a delicious treat that won't overload your daily calorie count.

Prep: 15 minutes   Bake: 18 minutes

- 1 teaspoon instant espresso-coffee powder
- 1 teaspoon hot water
- ¾ cup all-purpose flour
- ½ cup unsweetened cocoa
- ½ teaspoon baking powder
- ¼ teaspoon salt
- 3 tablespoons butter or margarine
- ¾ cup sugar
- 2 large egg whites
- ¼ cup dark corn syrup
- 1 teaspoon vanilla extract

1. Preheat oven to 350°F. Grease 8-inch square baking pan. In cup, dissolve espresso powder in hot water; set aside. In large bowl, with wire whisk, stir flour, cocoa, baking powder, and salt.

2. In 2-quart saucepan, melt butter over low heat. Remove from heat. With wooden spoon, stir in sugar, egg whites, corn syrup, vanilla, and espresso until blended. Stir sugar mixture into flour mixture just until blended (do not overmix). Pour batter into prepared pan.

3. Bake until toothpick inserted in center comes out almost clean, 18 to 22 minutes. Cool completely in pan on wire rack.

4. When cool, cut into 4 strips, then cut each strip crosswise into 4 pieces. If brownies are difficult to cut, use knife dipped in hot water and dried; repeat as necessary. Makes 16 brownies.

Each brownie: About 103 calories, 2g protein, 19g carbohydrate, 3g total fat (2g saturated), 6mg cholesterol, 88mg sodium.

Blondies

These scrumptious bars, sometimes known as butterscotch brownies, are a pecan lover's dream.

Prep: 10 minutes   Bake: 30 minutes

- 1 cup all-purpose flour
- 2 teaspoons baking powder
- 1 teaspoon salt
- 6 tablespoons butter or margarine
- 1¾ cups packed light brown sugar
- 2 teaspoons vanilla extract
- 2 large eggs
- 1½ cups pecans (6 ounces), coarsely chopped

1. Preheat oven to 350°F. Grease 13" by 9" baking pan. In small bowl, with wire whisk, stir flour, baking powder, and salt.

2. In 3-quart saucepan, melt butter over low heat. Remove from heat. With wooden spoon, stir in brown sugar and vanilla; add eggs, stirring until well blended. Stir flour mixture into sugar mixture just until blended. Stir in pecans. Spread batter evenly in prepared pan.

3. Bake until toothpick inserted 2 inches from edge of pan comes out clean, about 30 minutes. Do not overbake; blondies will firm as they cool. Cool completely in pan on wire rack.

4. When cool, cut lengthwise into 4 strips, then cut each strip crosswise into 6 pieces. Makes 24 blondies.

Each blondie: About 159 calories, 2g protein, 21g carbohydrate, 8g total fat (2g saturated), 25mg cholesterol, 179mg sodium.

Coconut Blondies

Prepare as directed above, stirring in ¾ **cup flaked sweetened coconut** with pecans.

Chocolate Chip Blondies

Prepare as directed through Step 2 above; let batter stand 15 minutes. Stir in **1 package (6 ounces) semisweet chocolate chips.** Proceed as directed.

Lemon-Cranberry Shortbread

Not your grandmother's shortbread, these glazed melt-in-your-mouth bars are festive enough for the holidays and pretty enough for afternoon tea.

Prep: 30 minutes plus standing   Bake: 35 minutes

- 2 to 3 lemons
- ¾ cup cold butter (1½ sticks), cut into pieces (do not use margarine)
- ¼ cup granulated sugar
- 1½ cups confectioners' sugar
- 2 cups all-purpose flour
- ½ cup dried cranberries

1. Preheat oven to 300°F. Line 13" by 9" metal baking pan with foil, extending foil over rim.

2. From lemons, grate 2 tablespoons plus ½ teaspoon peel and squeeze 2 tablespoons plus 1 teaspoon juice.

3. In food processor with knife blade attached, blend butter, granulated sugar, ½ cup confectioners' sugar, 2 tablespoons lemon peel, and 1 tablespoon lemon juice until creamy. Reserve remaining lemon peel and juice for glaze. Add flour and pulse until dough begins to come together. Add cranberries and pulse until evenly mixed into dough (most cranberries will be chopped, a few will remain whole). With hand, press dough evenly onto bottom of prepared pan.

4. Bake until edges are lightly browned and top is pale golden, 35 to 40 minutes. Cool completely in pan on wire rack.

5. When shortbread is cool, in small bowl, with spoon, stir remaining 1 cup confectioners' sugar, 1 tablespoon lemon juice, and ½ teaspoon lemon peel until smooth, adding some of remaining 1 teaspoon juice, if necessary, to obtain a good spreading consistency. Spread glaze over shortbread. Let stand until glaze sets, about 30 minutes.

6. Remove shortbread from pan by lifting edges of foil; transfer to cutting board. Cut lengthwise into 3 strips, then cut each strip crosswise into 12 bars. Makes 36 bars.

Each bar: About 90 calories, 1g protein, 13g carbohydrate, 4g total fat (3g saturated), 11mg cholesterol, 40mg sodium.

Caramel-Pecan Bars

These easy-to-make bar cookies were inspired by the popular bite-size candies that resemble little turtles.

Prep: 1 hour plus cooling and chilling
Bake: 25 minutes

Cookie Crust

- ¾ cup cold butter (1½ sticks), softened (do not use margarine)
- ¾ cup confectioners' sugar
- 1½ teaspoons vanilla extract
- 2¼ cups all-purpose flour

Caramel-Pecan Filling

- 1 cup packed light or dark brown sugar
- ½ cup honey
- ½ cup butter (1 stick), cut into pieces (do not use margarine)
- ⅓ cup granulated sugar
- ¼ cup heavy or whipping cream
- 2 teaspoons vanilla extract
- 1½ cups pecans, toasted and coarsely chopped

Topping

- 2 ounces semisweet chocolate, melted

1. Preheat oven to 350°F. Grease 13" by 9" metal baking pan; line pan with foil, extending foil over rim.

2. Prepare crust: In large bowl, with mixer at medium speed, beat butter, confectioners' sugar, and vanilla until creamy, about 2 minutes. Reduce speed to low, gradually beat in flour until evenly moistened (mixture will resemble fine crumbs). With hand, firmly pat crumbs evenly onto bottom of prepared pan.

3. Bake until lightly browned, 25 to 30 minutes. Transfer pan to wire rack.

4. Prepare filling: In 2-quart saucepan, combine brown sugar, honey, butter, granulated sugar, cream, and vanilla; heat to full rolling boil over high heat, stirring frequently. Reduce heat to medium-high; set candy thermometer in place and continue cooking, without stirring, until temperature reaches 248°F or firm-ball stage (when small amount of mixture dropped into very cold water forms a firm ball that does not flatten upon removal from water).

5. Sprinkle pecans evenly over warm crust. Pour hot caramel over nuts. Cool in pan on wire rack 1 hour or until caramel is room temperature and has formed a skin on top.

6. With fork, drizzle melted chocolate over caramel layer. Cover and refrigerate until cold and chocolate has set, at least 1 hour.

7. When cold, remove from pan by lifting edges of foil; transfer to cutting board. Cut lengthwise into 6 strips, then cut each strip crosswise into 8 bars. Let stand at room temperature to soften slightly before serving. Makes 48 bars.

Each bar: About 140 calories, 1g protein, 16g carbohydrate, 8g total fat (4g saturated), 15mg cholesterol, 55mg sodium.

LINING PAN WITH FOIL

Invert the baking pan so it is bottom side up. Mold a length of foil, shiny side facing out, over the pan, pressing the foil firmly to set the shape. Lift up the foil.

Turn the pan right side up. Lower the foil "pan" into the baking pan; smooth it out to create a tight fit.

The Perfect Lemon Bar

A tender cookie crust and a silky smooth fresh lemon filling makes these bars perfect.

Prep: 25 minutes plus cooling   Bake: 40 minutes

- ¾ cup butter (1½ sticks), softened (do not use margarine)
- 2¼ cups all-purpose flour
- ⅔ cup plus 1 tablespoon confectioners' sugar
- 3 to 4 large lemons
- 6 large eggs
- 2 cups granulated sugar
- 1 teaspoon baking powder
- ¾ teaspoon salt

1. Preheat oven to 350°F. Grease 13" by 9" baking pan. Line pan with foil, extending foil over rim; lightly grease foil.

2. In food processor with knife blade attached, pulse butter, 2 cups flour, and ⅔ cup confectioners' sugar until mixture is moist but crumbly. Dough should hold together when pressed between two fingers. Sprinkle mixture evenly into prepared pan. Bake until lightly browned, 20 to 25 minutes.

3. Meanwhile, prepare filling: From lemons, grate 2½ teaspoons peel and squeeze ⅔ cup juice. In large bowl, with wire whisk, beat eggs. Add lemon peel and juice, granulated sugar, baking powder, salt and remaining ¼ cup flour; whisk until well blended.

4. Whisk filling again and pour over hot crust. Bake until filling is just set and golden around edges, 18 to 22 minutes. Transfer pan to wire rack. Sift remaining 1 tablespoon confectioners' sugar over warm filling. Cool completely in pan on wire rack.

5. When cool, remove from pan by lifting edges of foil; transfer with foil to cutting board. If you like, trim edges. Cut lengthwise into 4 strips, then cut each strip crosswise into 8 pieces. Makes 32 bars.

Each bar: About 145 calories, 2g protein, 22g carbohydrate, 6g total fat (3g saturated), 52mg cholesterol, 126mg sodium.

Honey Granola Breakfast Bars

Instead of eating overly sweet and high-fat store-bought granola bars, we highly recommend making your own. These are quickly mixed in one bowl.

Prep: 15 minutes   Bake: 30 minutes

- 2 cups old-fashioned oats, uncooked
- 1 cup all-purpose flour
- ¾ cup packed light brown sugar
- ¾ cup dark seedless raisins
- ½ cup toasted wheat germ
- ¾ teaspoon ground cinnamon
- ¾ teaspoon salt
- ½ cup vegetable oil
- ½ cup honey
- 1 large egg
- 2 teaspoons vanilla extract

1. Preheat oven to 350°F and grease 13" by 9" baking pan.

2. In large bowl, with wooden spoon, stir oats, flour, brown sugar, raisins, wheat germ, cinnamon, and salt until blended. Stir in oil, honey, egg, and vanilla until well combined. With wet hand, pat oat mixture evenly onto bottom of prepared pan.

3. Bake until light golden around edges, 30 to 35 minutes. Cool completely in pan on wire rack.

4. When cool, cut lengthwise into 4 strips, then cut each strip crosswise into 4 pieces. Makes 16 bars.

Each bar: About 242 calories, 4g protein, 39g carbohydrate, 9g total fat (1g saturated), 13mg cholesterol, 119mg sodium.

Chewy Oatmeal-Chocolate-Cherry Cookies

For chewy cookies, bake the minimum time; for a crispy treat, bake a few minutes longer.

Prep: 35 minutes plus cooling
Bake: 12 minutes per batch

- 1½ cups all-purpose flour
- 2 teaspoons baking soda
- ½ teaspoon salt
- ¾ cup granulated sugar
- ¾ cup packed brown sugar
- ¾ cup butter or margarine (1½ sticks), softened
- 2 large eggs
- 2 teaspoons vanilla extract
- 3 cups old-fashioned oats, uncooked
- 1 cup dried tart cherries or raisins
- 1 package (6 ounces) semisweet chocolate chips (1 cup)

1. Preheat oven to 350°F. Grease large cookie sheet. In small bowl, with wire whisk, stir flour, baking soda, and salt.

2. In large bowl, with mixer at medium speed, beat granulated and brown sugars and butter until creamy, occasionally scraping bowl with rubber spatula. Beat in eggs, one at a time, beating well after each addition. Beat in vanilla. Reduce speed, to low; gradually beat in flour mixture just until blended, occasionally scraping bowl. With wooden spoon, stir in oats, dried cherries, and chocolate chips.

3. Drop dough by rounded measuring tablespoons, 2 inches apart, onto prepared cookie sheet. Bake until tops are golden, 12 to 14 minutes. With wide spatula, transfer cookies to wire racks to cool. Repeat with remaining dough. Makes about 54 cookies.

Each cookie: About 100 calories, 1g protein, 15g carbohydrate, 4g total fat (2g saturated), 15mg cholesterol, 100mg sodium.

CHOCOLATE AND COCOA POWDER

We always use pure chocolate products and avoid artificially flavored compound (summer) coatings or premelted chocolate, all of which include large amounts of vegetable fats.

Unsweetened chocolate is simply ground cocoa beans. Professionals call it chocolate liquor. It's not very tasty on its own, so it is combined with sugar and other ingredients in recipes.

Bittersweet chocolate has been sweetened, but the amount of sugar varies greatly from brand to brand. Some list the percentage of chocolate liquor on the label. A brand with 70 percent will be more bitter than one with 64 percent. Most European chocolate bars are bittersweet, and some bittersweet chocolate is now produced in the U.S.

Semisweet chocolate is similar to bittersweet chocolate, although it is usually a bit sweeter. It is available in individually wrapped one-ounce squares and in bulk. It can be used instead of bittersweet chocolate.

Sweet chocolate is usually sold under a brand name (and used to make German chocolate cake). Do not confuse it with bitter- or semisweet chocolate.

Milk chocolate contains dried milk powder and a high proportion of sugar. It is essentially an eating chocolate—it is not usually used for baking.

White chocolate is not really a chocolate but rather vanilla-flavored, sweetened cocoa butter (a by-product of chocolate processing), although some brands substitute vegetable fat for the cocoa butter.

Unsweetened cocoa powder provides the rich chocolate flavor in many desserts. There are two kinds: *natural* and *Dutch-processed*; check the label. In baking, they are not interchangeable. They react differently when mixed with baking soda or baking powder. However, for a cup of hot cocoa, use your favorite.

Natural cocoa powder is the most common cocoa in American kitchens. Unless stated otherwise, it is the one we used for the recipes in this book.

Dutch-processed cocoa powder has been treated with an alkali to mellow cocoa's natural bitterness and to give baked goods a darker color.

Chocolate Wows

(Pictured on page 550)

After one bite of these decadent cookies, you will understand why we call them "Wows."

Prep: 20 minutes   Bake: 13 minutes per batch

⅓ cup all-purpose flour
¼ cup unsweetened cocoa
1 teaspoon baking powder
¼ teaspoon salt
6 squares (6 ounces) semisweet chocolate, chopped
½ cup butter or margarine (1 stick)
2 large eggs
¾ cup sugar
1½ teaspoons vanilla extract
2 cups pecans (8 ounces), chopped
1 package (6 ounces) semisweet chocolate chips (1 cup)

1. Preheat oven to 325°F. Grease two large cookie sheets. In small bowl, with wire whisk, stir flour, cocoa, baking powder, and salt.

2. In heavy 2-quart saucepan, melt chopped chocolate and butter over low heat, stirring frequently, until smooth. Remove from heat and cool.

3. In large bowl, with mixer at medium speed, beat eggs and sugar until light, about 2 minutes, frequently scraping bowl with rubber spatula. Reduce speed to low. Add cooled chocolate mixture, flour mixture, and vanilla; beat just until blended. Increase speed to medium; beat 2 minutes. Stir in pecans and chocolate chips.

4. Drop batter by rounded teaspoons, 2 inches apart, on cookie sheets. With small metal spatula, spread batter into 2-inch rounds. Bake until tops are shiny and cracked, about 13 minutes, rotating cookie sheets

between upper and lower oven racks halfway through baking. Cool 10 minutes on cookie sheet. With wide spatula, transfer cookies to wire racks to cool completely.

5. Repeat with remaining batter. Makes about 48 cookies.

Each cookie: About 102 calories, 1g protein, 9g carbohydrate, 7g total fat (3g saturated), 14mg cholesterol, 45mg sodium.

Chocolate Chip Cookies

Who can say no to this classic cookie?

Prep: 15 minutes   Bake: 10 minutes per batch

1¼ cups all-purpose flour
½ teaspoon baking soda
½ teaspoon salt
½ cup butter or margarine (1 stick), softened
½ cup packed brown sugar
¼ cup granulated sugar
1 large egg
1 teaspoon vanilla extract
1 package (6 ounces) semisweet chocolate chips (1 cup)
½ cup walnuts, chopped (optional)

1. Preheat oven to 375°F. In small bowl, with wire whisk, stir flour, baking soda, and salt.

2. In large bowl, with mixer at medium speed, beat butter and brown and granulated sugars until light and fluffy. Beat in egg and vanilla until well combined. Reduce speed to low; beat in flour mixture just until blended. With wooden spoon, stir in chocolate chips and walnuts, if using.

3. Drop dough by rounded tablespoons, 2 inches apart, on two ungreased cookie sheets. Bake until golden around edges, 10 to 12 minutes, rotating cookie sheets between upper and lower oven racks halfway through baking. With wide spatula, transfer cookies to wire racks to cool completely. Repeat with remaining dough. Makes about 36 cookies.

Each cookie: About 80 calories, 1g protein, 11g carbohydrate, 4g total fat (2g saturated), 13mg cholesterol, 79mg sodium.

White Chocolate–Macadamia Cookies

Prepare as directed but substitute ¾ **cup white baking chips** for semisweet chocolate chips and **1 cup chopped macadamia nuts (4 ounces)** for walnuts, if you like.

Each cookie: About 110 calories, 1g protein, 11g carbohydrate, 7g total fat (3g saturated), 13mg cholesterol, 84mg sodium.

Peanut Butter Cookies

Great as an afternoon snack or as a special treat to sneak into a brown-bag lunch. If you like, instead of cross-hatching the cookies with a fork, lightly press mini non-melting chocolate-covered candies into the top of each cookie before baking.

Prep: 15 minutes   Bake: 15 minutes per batch

1¼ cups all-purpose flour
 1 teaspoon baking soda
¼ teaspoon salt
 1 cup creamy peanut butter
½ cup butter or margarine (1 stick), softened
½ cup packed brown sugar
¼ cup granulated sugar
 1 large egg
½ teaspoon vanilla extract

1. Preheat oven to 350°F. In small bowl, with wire whisk, stir flour, baking soda, and salt.

2. In large bowl, with mixer at medium speed, beat peanut butter, butter, brown and granulated sugars, egg, and vanilla until combined, occasionally scraping bowl with rubber spatula. Reduce speed to low. Add flour mixture and beat just until blended.

3. Drop dough by heaping tablespoons, 2 inches apart, on two ungreased large cookie sheets. With fork, press crisscross pattern into top of each cookie.

4. Bake until lightly browned, 15 to 20 minutes, rotating cookie sheets between upper and lower oven racks halfway through baking. With wide spatula, transfer cookies to wire racks to cool completely.

5. Repeat forming and baking with remaining dough. Makes about 36 cookies.

Each cookie: About 100 calories, 3g protein, 9g carbohydrate, 6g total fat (2g saturated), 13mg cholesterol, 114mg sodium.

Sour Cream Cookies

Fresh lemon peel brings out the richness of these cookies.

Prep: 15 minutes   Bake: 10 minutes per batch

 1 cup all-purpose flour
¼ teaspoon baking soda
¼ teaspoon salt
 6 tablespoons butter or margarine, softened
½ cup sugar
½ cup sour cream
 1 teaspoon freshly grated lemon peel
½ teaspoon vanilla extract

1. Preheat oven to 350°F. Grease two cookie sheets. In small bowl, stir flour, baking soda, and salt.

2. In large bowl, with mixer at medium speed, beat butter until creamy. Gradually add sugar and beat until light and fluffy. Beat in sour cream, lemon peel, and vanilla. Reduce speed to low; beat in flour mixture just until blended.

3. Drop dough by rounded teaspoons, 1 inch apart, on prepared cookie sheets. Bake until set and golden around edges, 10 to 12 minutes, rotating cookie sheets between upper and lower oven racks halfway through baking. Cool 1 minute on cookie sheets; with wide spatula, transfer cookies to wire racks to cool completely. Repeat with remaining dough. Makes about 36 cookies.

Each cookie: About 49 calories, 0g protein, 6g carbohydrate, 3g total fat (2g saturated), 7mg cholesterol, 46mg sodium.

Coconut Cookies

Adding flaked coconut to the rich dough adds texture as well as flavor to these melt-in-your-mouth gems.

Prep: 20 minutes   Bake: 15 minutes per batch

2¾ cups all-purpose flour
 1 teaspoon baking powder
½ teaspoon salt
 1 cup butter or margarine (2 sticks), softened
 1 cup sugar
 1 large egg
 2 tablespoons milk
 1 teaspoon vanilla extract
1½ cups flaked sweetened coconut

1. Preheat oven to 325°F. In medium bowl, with wire whisk, stir flour, baking powder, and salt.

2. In large bowl, with mixer at medium speed, beat butter and sugar until light and fluffy. Beat in egg, milk, and vanilla. Reduce speed to low; beat in flour mixture just until blended. Stir in coconut (dough will be crumbly). With hands, press dough together.

3. Drop dough by rounded teaspoons, 2 inches apart, on two ungreased cookie sheets. With fork, press crosshatch into each cookie, flattening to ¼-inch thickness. Bake until edges are lightly browned, 15 to 17 minutes, rotating cookie sheets between upper and lower oven racks halfway through baking. With wide spatula, transfer cookies to wire racks to cool.

4. Repeat shaping and baking with remaining dough. Makes about 72 cookies.

Each cookie: About 45 calories, 0g protein, 5g carbohydrate, 2g total fat (2g saturated), 7mg cholesterol, 41mg sodium.

Almond Macaroons

We've rolled classic macaroons in sliced almonds for extra texture and an elegant presentation.

Prep: 20 minutes   Bake: 18 minutes

 1 tube or can (7 to 8 ounces) almond paste,
    cut into 1-inch pieces
 ⅓ cup confectioners' sugar
 1 large egg white
 ½ cup sliced natural almonds

1. Preheat oven to 325°F. Evenly grease and flour large cookie sheet.

2. In small bowl, with mixer at low speed, beat almond paste until crumbly. Add confectioners' sugar and egg white; beat until well blended (dough will be wet and sticky).

3. Place almonds on waxed paper. With lightly floured hands, roll dough into 1-inch balls. Roll balls in almonds, gently pressing to coat. Place balls, 1 inch apart, on prepared cookie sheet. Bake until golden, 18 to 20 minutes. With wide spatula, transfer cookies to wire racks to cool completely. Makes about 30 cookies.

Each cookie: About 50 calories, 1g protein, 5g carbohydrate, 3g total fat (0g saturated), 0mg cholesterol, 3mg sodium.

Coconut Macaroons

These chewy flourless cookies, a traditional Passover dessert, are good any time of the year.

Prep: 10 minutes   Bake: 25 minutes

 3 cups flaked sweetened coconut
 ¾ cup sugar
 4 large egg whites
 ¼ teaspoon salt
 1 teaspoon vanilla extract
 ⅛ teaspoon almond extract

1. Preheat oven to 325°F. Line two cookie sheets with parchment paper or foil.

2. In large bowl, stir coconut, sugar, egg whites, salt, vanilla, and almond extract until well combined.

3. Drop batter by rounded teaspoons, 1 inch apart, on prepared cookie sheets. Bake until set and lightly golden, about 25 minutes, rotating cookie sheets between upper and lower oven racks halfway through baking. Cool 1 minute on cookie sheets; with wide spatula, transfer cookies to wire racks to cool completely. Makes about 42 cookies.

Each cookie: About 41 calories, 1g protein, 6g carbohydrate, 2g total fat (2g saturated), 0mg cholesterol, 32mg sodium.

Chocolate Coconut Macaroons
Prepare as directed, stirring **2 tablespoons unsweetened cocoa** and **1 square (1 ounce) semisweet chocolate,** grated, into coconut mixture.

CONFECTIONERS' SUGAR

Test Kitchen Tip

Confectioners' sugar is a blend of very finely ground sugar and some cornstarch to prevent lumps. The addition of cornstarch notwithstanding, confectioners' sugar often contains small lumps. We recommend sifting it after measuring.

Almond Crescents

These classic holiday favorites are great for gift giving. Butter is essential to the exquisite texture and flavor.

Prep: 45 minutes plus chilling **Bake:** 20 minutes per batch

- 1 cup blanched whole almonds (4 ounces), lightly toasted (right)
- ½ cup granulated sugar
- ¼ teaspoon salt
- 1 cup butter (2 sticks), softened (do not use margarine)
- 2 cups all-purpose flour
- 1 teaspoon almond extract
- ½ teaspoon vanilla extract
- ¾ cup confectioners' sugar

1. In food processor with knife blade attached, process almonds, ¼ cup granulated sugar, and salt until almonds are very finely ground.

2. In large bowl, with mixer at low speed, beat butter and remaining ¼ cup granulated sugar until blended, occasionally scraping bowl with rubber spatula. Increase speed to high; beat until light and fluffy, about 3 minutes. Reduce speed to low. Gradually add flour, ground-almond mixture, almond extract, and vanilla and beat until blended. Divide dough in half; wrap each piece with plastic wrap and refrigerate until dough is firm enough to handle, about 1 hour, or freeze about 30 minutes.

3. Preheat oven to 325°F. Working with one piece of dough at a time, with lightly floured hands, shape rounded teaspoons of dough into 2" by ½" crescents. Place, 1 inch apart, on two ungreased cookie sheets.

4. Bake until lightly browned around edges, about 20 minutes, rotating cookie sheets between upper and lower oven racks halfway through baking. With spatula, transfer cookies to wire racks set over waxed paper. Immediately dust confectioners' sugar over cookies until well coated; cool completely. Repeat with remaining dough. Makes about 72 cookies.

Each cookie: About 58 calories, 1g protein, 6g carbohydrate, 4g total fat (2g saturated), 7mg cholesterol, 34mg sodium.

Walnut or Pecan Crescents

Prepare crescents as directed but substitute **1 cup walnuts or pecans** (not toasted) for almonds and omit almond extract.

Hazelnut Crescents

Prepare crescents as directed but substitute **1 cup toasted, skinned hazelnuts (filberts)** for almonds and omit almond extract.

Almond Crescents

TOASTING NUTS

Test Kitchen Tip

Toasting nuts brings out their flavor and in the case of nuts such as hazelnuts, facilitates removal of the skins.

To toast almonds, pecans, walnuts, or hazelnuts, preheat the oven to 350°F. Spread the shelled nuts in a single layer on a cookie sheet. Bake, stirring occasionally, until lightly browned and fragrant, about 10 minutes. Toast hazelnuts until the skins begin to peel away. Let the nuts cool completely before chopping.

To skin hazelnuts, wrap the still-warm toasted nuts in a clean kitchen towel and let stand for about 10 minutes. Using the towel, rub off as much of the skins as possible (all of the skin may not come off).

Jumbo Gingersnaps

The ginger-molasses flavor in these crackle-top cookies is just perfect. Their generous size makes them especially festive, but you can also make smaller cookies.

Prep: 20 minutes Bake: 15 minutes

- 2 cups all-purpose flour
- 2 teaspoons ground ginger
- 1 teaspoon baking soda
- ½ teaspoon ground cinnamon
- ½ teaspoon salt
- ¼ teaspoon ground black pepper (optional)
- ¾ cup vegetable shortening
- ½ cup plus 2 tablespoons sugar
- 1 large egg
- ½ cup dark molasses

1. Preheat oven to 350°F. In medium bowl, with wire whisk, stir flour, ginger, baking soda, cinnamon, salt, and pepper if using.

2. In large bowl, with mixer at medium speed, beat shortening and ½ cup sugar until light and fluffy. Beat in egg until blended, then beat in molasses. Reduce speed to low; beat in flour mixture just until blended.

3. Place remaining 2 tablespoons sugar on waxed paper. Roll ¼ cup dough into ball; roll in sugar to coat evenly. Repeat with remaining dough to make 10 balls in all. Place balls, 3 inches apart, on ungreased large cookie sheet. Or, for small cookies, roll dough into balls by slightly rounded tablespoons and place 2 inches apart on two ungreased cookie sheets.

4. Bake until set, about 15 minutes for large cookies or 9 to 11 minutes for smaller cookies, rotating cookie sheets between upper and lower oven racks halfway through baking. Cookies will be very soft and may appear moist in cracks. Cool 1 minute on cookie sheets on wire racks; with wide spatula, transfer cookies to wire racks to cool completely. Makes 10 giant cookies or about 30 small cookies.

Each giant cookie: About 323 calories, 3g protein, 42g carbohydrate, 16g total fat (4g saturated), 21mg cholesterol, 258mg sodium.

Raspberry Linzer Thumbprints

These cookies have all the flavor and texture of a classic Austrian linzer torte: a nutty crust and a raspberry jam filling.

Prep: 45 minutes plus cooling Bake: 20 minutes per batch

- 1 cup hazelnuts (filberts), toasted and skinned (opposite) plus ⅓ cup (not toasted)
- ½ cup sugar
- ¾ cup butter or margarine (1½ sticks), cut into pieces
- 1 teaspoon vanilla extract
- ¼ teaspoon salt
- 1¾ cups all-purpose flour
- ¼ cup seedless raspberry jam

1. Preheat oven to 350°F.

2. In food processor with knife blade attached, process 1 cup toasted hazelnuts and sugar until nuts are finely ground. Add butter, vanilla, and salt and process until blended. Add flour and process just until evenly combined. Remove knife blade and press dough together with hands.

3. Finely chop remaining ⅓ cup hazelnuts; spread on waxed paper. Roll dough into 1-inch balls (dough may be slightly crumbly). Roll balls in nuts, gently pressing to coat. Place balls, 1½ inches apart, on two ungreased large cookie sheets. With thumb, make small indentation in center of each ball. Fill each indentation with ¼ teaspoon jam.

4. Bake until lightly golden around edges, about 20 minutes, rotating cookie sheets between upper and lower oven racks halfway through baking. With wide spatula, transfer cookies to wire racks to cool completely.

5. Repeat with remaining balls and raspberry jam. Makes about 48 cookies.

Each cookie: About 74 calories, 1g protein, 7g carbohydrate, 5g total fat (2g saturated), 8mg cholesterol, 42mg sodium.

Lemon Icebox Cookies

This dough is wonderful to have on hand in the freezer so you can bake fresh cookies whenever you wish. It's also the base for three delicious variations.

Prep: 20 minutes plus chilling   **Bake:** 10 minutes per batch

1⅔ cups all-purpose flour
1 teaspoon baking powder
¼ teaspoon baking soda
⅛ teaspoon salt
3 lemons
½ cup butter or margarine (1 stick), softened
¾ cup sugar
1 large egg yolk

1. In medium bowl, with wire whisk, stir flour, baking powder, baking soda, and salt. From lemons, grate 1 tablespoon peel and squeeze 2 tablespoons juice.

2. In large bowl, with mixer at medium speed, beat butter and sugar until light and fluffy. Beat in egg yolk and lemon peel and juice until combined. Reduce speed to low; beat in flour mixture just until blended.

3. Divide dough in half. On waxed paper, form one piece of dough into 12-inch log. Repeat with remaining dough. Wrap each log and refrigerate overnight, or freeze until very firm, at least 2 hours.

4. Preheat oven to 375°F. Grease and flour two large cookie sheets or line with parchment paper or foil. Cut 1 log crosswise into ¼-inch-thick slices. Place slices, 1 inch apart, on prepared cookie sheets.

5. Bake until set and golden brown around edges, 10 to 12 minutes, rotating cookie sheets between upper and lower oven racks halfway through baking. With wide spatula, transfer cookies to wire racks to cool completely. Repeat with remaining dough. Makes about 96 cookies.

Each cookie: About 25 calories, 0g protein, 3g carbohydrate, 1g total fat (1g saturated), 5mg cholesterol, 21mg sodium.

Lemon-Walnut Icebox Cookies

Prepare as directed, stirring **1 cup walnuts (4 ounces)**, finely chopped, into dough after adding flour.

Each cookie: About 33 calories, 0g protein, 4g carbohydrate, 2g total fat (1g saturated), 5mg cholesterol, 21mg sodium.

Lemon-Anise Icebox Cookies

Prepare as directed, beating **2 teaspoons anise seeds** into dough with lemon peel.

Orange Icebox Cookies

Prepare as directed but substitute **1 tablespoon freshly grated orange peel** and **2 tablespoons fresh orange juice** for lemon peel and lemon juice.

Lemon Icebox Cookies

Hermits

These spicy fruit bars date back to New England's clipper-ship days and got their name from their long-keeping quality. Sailors would stow them away "like hermits" for snacking on during their extended voyages.

Prep: 20 minutes plus cooling Bake: 13 minutes

- 2 cups all-purpose flour
- 1 teaspoon ground cinnamon
- ½ teaspoon baking powder
- ½ teaspoon baking soda
- ½ teaspoon ground ginger
- ¼ teaspoon ground nutmeg
- ¼ teaspoon salt
- ⅛ teaspoon ground cloves
- 1 cup packed brown sugar
- ½ cup butter or margarine (1 stick), softened
- ⅓ cup dark molasses
- 1 large egg
- 1 cup dark raisins
- 1 cup pecans, toasted (page 562) and coarsely chopped (optional)

1. Preheat oven to 350°F. Grease and flour two large cookie sheets.

2. In medium bowl, with wire whisk, stir flour, cinnamon, baking powder, baking soda, ginger, nutmeg, salt, and cloves.

3. In large bowl, with mixer at medium speed, beat sugar and butter until light and fluffy. Beat in molasses until blended. Beat in egg. Reduce speed to low; beat in flour mixture just until blended, occasionally scraping bowl with rubber spatula. With wooden spoon, stir in raisins and pecans, if using, just until combined.

4. Divide dough into quarters. With lightly floured hands, shape each quarter into 12" by 1½" log. Place 2 logs, about 3 inches apart, on each cookie sheet.

5. Bake until logs flatten and edges are firm, 13 to 15 minutes, rotating cookie sheets between upper and lower racks halfway through baking. Cool logs on cookie sheets on wire racks 15 minutes. Transfer logs to cutting board. Slice each log crosswise into 8 cookies. Transfer cookies to wire racks to cool completely. Makes 32 cookies.

Each cookie: About 105 calories, 1g protein, 19g carbohydrate, 3g total fat (2g saturated), 15mg cholesterol, 80mg sodium.

Butterscotch Fingers

When butter and brown sugar are combined, there's an almost magical transformation into the flavor we know as butterscotch. Here, pecans are added for texture.

Prep: 30 minutes plus chilling and cooling Bake: 12 minutes per batch

- 2⅓ cups all-purpose flour
- 1½ teaspoons baking powder
- ½ teaspoon salt
- 1 cup butter or margarine (2 sticks), softened
- 1 cup packed dark brown sugar
- 1 large egg
- 1 teaspoon vanilla extract
- ¾ cup pecans, chopped

1. In medium bowl, with wire whisk, stir flour, baking powder, and salt.

2. In large bowl, with mixer at medium speed, beat butter and sugar until creamy, occasionally scraping bowl with rubber spatula. Beat in egg and vanilla. Reduce speed to low; beat in flour mixture just until blended, occasionally scraping bowl. With wooden spoon, stir in pecans.

3. Shape dough into 12" by 3¾" by 1" brick. Wrap brick in plastic wrap and refrigerate until firm enough to slice, at least 6 hours or overnight. Or freeze about 2 hours. (If using margarine, freeze brick overnight.)

4. Preheat oven to 350°F. Grease large cookie sheet.

5. With sharp knife, cut brick crosswise into ⅛-inch-thick slices. Place slices, 1 inch apart, on prepared cookie sheet. Bake until edges are lightly browned, 12 to 14 minutes. Transfer cookies to wire rack to cool.

6. Repeat with remaining dough. Makes about 96 cookies.

Each cookie: About 65 calories, 1g protein, 7g carbohydrate, 4g total fat (2g saturated), 11mg cholesterol, 55mg sodium.

Cookie Jigsaw

If you want to make the puzzle ahead of time, it's best to wrap and freeze undecorated pieces, then unwrap, thaw completely, and follow decorating directions.

Prep: 1 hour 15 minutes plus cooling and decorating
Bake: 30 minutes

lightweight cardboard or sturdy paper
for pattern template
2½ cups all-purpose flour
1½ teaspoons baking powder
¼ teaspoon salt
¾ cup butter or margarine (1½ sticks), softened
¾ cup sugar
1 large egg
1 tablespoon milk
2 teaspoons vanilla extract
¾ cup light corn syrup
assorted decorations: green, red, white, yellow, and blue sugar crystals; chocolate sprinkles; multicolor, white, and star-shaped candy décors; and small round yellow candies

1. On cardboard or paper, draw a Christmas-tree template 10 inches high (from tip of tree to top of trunk) and 10½ inches wide (at base of tree above trunk), with a 1-inch high by 2-inch wide trunk. Cut out template and set aside.

2. Preheat oven to 325°F. Grease and flour large cookie sheet. In medium bowl, with wire whisk, stir flour, baking powder, and salt.

3. In large bowl, with mixer at medium speed, beat butter and sugar until creamy. Beat in egg, milk, and vanilla until well blended (mixture may look curdled). Reduce speed to low; beat in flour mixture just until blended. Pat dough into small rectangle.

4. Place dough in center of cookie sheet. With floured rolling pin, roll dough into 13" by 11" rectangle. Bake 15 minutes.

5. Transfer cookie sheet to wire rack. Center tree template lengthwise on warm cookie. With knife, cut around template into cookie; remove template, leaving tree outline. Press floured 1½-inch star-shaped cookie cutter into cookie at top of tree; remove cutter, leaving star outline. Press floured 1-inch round cookie cutters into tree in several places, leaving ornament outlines. Press 2½-inch star cutter into remaining cookie around tree, leaving star outlines.

6. Cut tree into various geometrically shaped puzzle pieces, being careful not to cut into ornament outlines. Cut remaining cookie around tree into puzzle pieces, being careful not to cut into star outlines.

7. Return cookie sheet to oven and bake until cookie is light brown, 12 to 14 minutes longer. Transfer cookie sheet to wire rack; cut through all designs and pieces. Cool cookie puzzle on cookie sheet 10 minutes. Carefully slide puzzle, in one piece, onto wire rack; cool completely.

8. To decorate: In 1-quart saucepan, heat corn syrup to boiling over medium heat, stirring frequently. Boil, stirring, 1 minute. Remove round ornament pieces from tree; brush tree and trunk with corn syrup. Sprinkle tree with green sugar crystals to coat, then attach small round yellow candies as desired. Sprinkle with or dip trunk into chocolate sprinkles. Brush ornament pieces with corn syrup; sprinkle with or dip into choice of colored sugar crystals or décors. Remove star decorations from around tree; brush with corn syrup and sprinkle with or dip into yellow sugar crystals. Brush puzzle pieces around tree with corn syrup; sprinkle with blue sugar crystals, then sprinkle lightly with white and star-shaped décors. Reheat corn syrup if it becomes too thick.

9. Allow puzzle pieces to dry completely, about 1 hour. When pieces are dry, reassemble puzzle on large tray to serve, or store puzzle in tightly covered container at room temperature up to 1 week. Makes about 42 cookies.

Each cookie: About 95 calories, 1g protein, 15g carbohydrate, 4g total fat (2g saturated), 15mg cholesterol, 80mg sodium.

Classic Sugar Cookies

Our tender, delicate butter cookie is sure to become a favorite in your house. Decorate with colored sugar or Ornamental Frosting (right), if you like.

Prep: 1 hour 30 minutes plus chilling
Bake: 12 minutes per batch

- 3 cups all-purpose flour
- ½ teaspoon baking powder
- ½ teaspoon salt
- 1 cup butter (2 sticks), softened (do not use margarine)
- 1½ cups sugar
- 2 large eggs
- 1 teaspoon vanilla extract

1. In large bowl, with wire whisk, stir flour, baking powder, and salt. In separate large bowl, with mixer at low speed, beat butter and sugar until blended. Increase speed to high; beat until light and fluffy, about 5 minutes. Reduce speed to low; beat in eggs and vanilla until mixed, then beat in flour mixture just until blended, occasionally scraping bowl with rubber spatula. Shape dough into four equal disks; wrap each disk and refrigerate overnight, or freeze until firm enough to roll, at least 2 hours.

2. Preheat oven to 350°F. On lightly floured surface, with floured rolling pin, roll one piece of dough until slightly less than ¼ inch thick; keep remaining dough refrigerated. With floured 3- to 4-inch cookie cutters, cut dough into as many cookies as possible; reserve trimmings for rerolling. Place cookies, 1 inch apart, on two ungreased large cookie sheets.

3. Bake until golden around edges, 12 to 15 minutes, rotating cookie sheets between upper and lower oven racks halfway through baking. With wide spatula, transfer cookies to wire racks to cool completely.

4. Repeat with remaining dough and trimmings. Makes about 72 cookies.

Each cookie: About 61 calories, 1g protein, 8g carbohydrate, 3g total fat (2g saturated), 13mg cholesterol, 47mg sodium.

Jam-Filled Sugar Cookies

Prepare, chill, and roll dough as directed (left). With 2½-inch fluted round or other decorative cutter, cut dough into rounds; with smaller cutter (1 to 1¼ inches), cut out and remove centers from half of rounds. Reserve centers for rerolling. Bake as directed; cool completely. Using **1 cup seedless raspberry jam,** warmed, spread whole rounds with thin layer of jam. Top with cutout rounds. Makes 36 cookies.

Each cookie: About 144 calories, 2g protein, 23g carbohydrate, 5g total fat (3g saturated), 26mg cholesterol, 98mg sodium.

Ornamental Frosting

This glossy, hard-drying frosting is often made with raw egg whites, but we prefer meringue powder, which is available at supermarkets and baking supply stores.

Prep: 5 minutes

- 1 package (16 ounces) confectioners' sugar
- 3 tablespoons meringue powder
- ⅓ cup warm water
  assorted food colorings (optional)

1. In large bowl, with mixer at medium speed, beat confectioners' sugar, meringue powder, and water until stiff and knife drawn through mixture leaves path, about 5 minutes.

2. If desired, tint frosting with food colorings. Keep tightly covered to prevent drying out. With small metal spatula, artists' paintbrushes, or decorating bags with small plain tips, decorate cookies with frosting. (You may need to thin frosting with a little warm water to obtain good spreading or piping consistency.) Makes about 3 cups.

Each tablespoon: About 39 calories, 0g protein, 10g carbohydrate, 0g total fat (0g saturated), 0mg cholesterol, 2mg sodium.

Gingerbread Cutouts

For tree decorations, before baking, make a hole in each cookie with a drinking straw. After baking, tie a loop of nylon fishing line through the hole of each cookie for easy hanging.

**Prep: 45 minutes plus cooling and decorating
Bake: 12 minutes per batch**

- ½ cup sugar
- ½ cup light (mild) molasses
- 1½ teaspoons ground ginger
- 1 teaspoon ground allspice
- 1 teaspoon ground cinnamon
- 1 teaspoon ground cloves
- 2 teaspoons baking soda
- ½ cup butter or margarine (1 stick), cut into pieces
- 1 large egg, beaten
- 3½ cups all-purpose flour
- Ornamental Frosting (left)

1. In 3-quart saucepan, combine sugar, molasses, ginger, allspice, cinnamon, and cloves; heat to boiling over medium heat, stirring occasionally with wooden spoon. Remove from heat; stir in baking soda (mixture will foam up). Stir in butter until melted. Stir in egg, then flour.

2. On floured surface, knead dough until thoroughly blended. Divide dough in half; wrap one piece in plastic wrap and set aside.

3. Preheat oven to 325°F. With floured rolling pin, roll remaining piece of dough slightly less than ¼ inch thick. With floured 3- to 4-inch cookie cutters, cut dough into as many cookies as possible; reserve trimmings. Place cookies, 1 inch apart, on two ungreased large cookie sheets. If desired, with drinking straw or skewer, make ¼-inch hole in each cookie for hanging.

4. Bake until brown around edges, about 12 minutes, rotating cookie sheets between upper and lower oven racks halfway through baking. With wide spatula, transfer cookies to wire racks to cool completely. Repeat with remaining dough and trimmings.

5. When cookies are cool, prepare Ornamental Frosting; use to decorate cookies as desired. Allow frosting to dry completely, about 1 hour. Makes about 36 cookies.

Each cookie without frosting: About 93 calories, 1g protein, 15g carbohydrate, 3g total fat (2g saturated), 13mg cholesterol, 100mg sodium.

Meringue Fingers

These ethereal meringue cookies are dipped into chocolate, which gives them fabulous flavor.

Prep: 25 minutes plus cooling   Bake: 1 hour

- 3 large egg whites
- ¼ teaspoon cream of tartar
- ⅛ teaspoon salt
- ½ cup sugar
- 1 teaspoon vanilla extract
- 2 squares (2 ounces) semisweet chocolate, chopped
- 1 teaspoon vegetable shortening

1. Preheat oven to 200°F. Line two large cookie sheets with foil or parchment paper.

2. In small bowl, with mixer at high speed, beat egg whites, cream of tartar, and salt until soft peaks form when beaters are lifted. Beating at high speed, gradually sprinkle in sugar, 2 tablespoons at a time; beat until sugar has dissolved. Add vanilla; continue beating until meringue stands in stiff, glossy peaks when beaters are lifted.

3. Spoon meringue into pastry bag fitted with ½-inch star tip. Pipe meringue in 3-inch lengths, 1 inch apart, on prepared cookie sheets.

4. Bake cookies until set, about 1 hour, rotating cookie sheets between upper and lower oven racks halfway through baking. Cool 10 minutes on cookie sheets on wire racks; then, with spatula, transfer cookies to wire racks to cool completely.

5. When cookies have cooled, in heavy 1-quart saucepan, melt chocolate and shortening over low heat, stirring frequently, until smooth; remove from heat. Dip one end of each cookie into melted chocolate; let dry on wire racks set over waxed paper. Makes about 48 cookies.

Each cookie: About 16 calories, 0g protein, 3g carbohydrate, 0g total fat (0g saturated), 0mg cholesterol, 10mg sodium.

Apricot-Raspberry Rugelach

A tender cream cheese–dough gives these rugelach traditional taste and texture.

Prep: 1 hour plus chilling Bake: 35 minutes

- 1 cup butter or margarine (2 sticks), softened
- 1 package (8 ounces) cream cheese, softened
- ¾ cup granulated sugar
- 1 teaspoon vanilla extract
- ¼ teaspoon salt
- 2 cups all-purpose flour
- 1 cup walnuts (4 ounces), chopped
- ¾ cup dried apricots, chopped
- ¼ cup packed brown sugar
- 1½ teaspoons ground cinnamon
- ½ cup seedless raspberry preserves
- 1 tablespoon milk

1. In large bowl, with mixer at low speed, beat butter and cream cheese until creamy. Beat in ¼ cup granulated sugar, vanilla, and salt. Beat in 1 cup flour. Stir in remaining 1 cup flour just until blended. Divide dough into four equal disks. Wrap each disk and refrigerate until firm, at least 2 hours or up to overnight.

2. Prepare filling: In medium bowl, combine walnuts, apricots, brown sugar, ¼ cup plus 2 tablespoons granulated sugar, and ½ teaspoon cinnamon until well mixed. Line two large cookie sheets with foil; grease foil.

3. On lightly floured surface, with floured rolling pin, roll one disk of dough into 9-inch round; keep remaining dough refrigerated. Spread 2 tablespoons preserves over dough. Sprinkle with ½ cup walnut mixture, gently pressing to adhere. With pastry wheel or sharp knife, cut dough into 12 equal wedges. Starting at curved edge, roll up each wedge. Place, point side down, ½ inch apart, on prepared cookie sheet. Repeat with remaining dough, one disk at a time.

4. Preheat oven to 325°F. In cup, with fork, stir remaining 2 tablespoons granulated sugar and remaining 1 teaspoon cinnamon. With pastry brush, brush rugelach with milk. Evenly sprinkle cinnamon-sugar on top.

5. Bake until golden, 35 to 40 minutes, rotating cookie sheets between upper and lower oven racks halfway through baking. With wide spatula, immediately transfer rugelach to wire racks to cool completely. Makes 48 rugelach.

Each rugelach: About 116 calories, 1g protein, 12g carbohydrate, 7g total fat (4g saturated), 16mg cholesterol, 67mg sodium.

MOLASSES

Test Kitchen Tip

During the sugar refining process, the juice that is extracted from sugarcane or sugar beets is boiled down to a syrupy mixture from which sugar crystals are removed. The syrup that remains is molasses.

Light molasses comes from the first boiling of sugar syrup. It has a light color and flavor and is often used as a pancake/waffle syrup as well as for baking.

Dark molasses comes from the second boiling and is darker, not as sweet, and thicker than light molasses. It is the molasses used to flavor baked goods such as gingerbread and for Indian pudding and baked beans.

Blackstrap molasses comes from the third boiling of sugar syrup. It is very dark, a bit bitter, and rather thick.

Whether or not molasses is sulphured or unsulphured simply depends on whether sulphur dioxide was used in the processing of the molasses. Unsulphured molasses has a milder, cleaner flavor. Store molasses in a dark, cool place for up to one year.

Brandy Snaps

Brandy Snaps

Make these elegant lacy cookies in dry weather, otherwise they will be sticky.

Prep: 25 minutes   Bake: 5 minutes per batch

½ **cup butter (1 stick) (do not use margarine)**
3 **tablespoons light (mild) molasses**
½ **cup all-purpose flour**
½ **cup sugar**
1 **teaspoon ground ginger**
¼ **teaspoon salt**
2 **tablespoons brandy**

1. Preheat oven to 350°F. Grease large cookie sheet.

2. In 2-quart saucepan, melt butter with molasses over medium-low heat, stirring occasionally, until smooth. Remove from heat. With wooden spoon, stir in flour, sugar, ginger, and salt until blended and smooth; stir in brandy. Set saucepan in bowl of hot water to keep warm.

3. Drop 1 teaspoon batter on cookie sheet; with small metal spatula, spread in circular motion to make 4-inch round (during baking, batter will spread and fill in any thin areas). Repeat three times more, placing rounds 2 inches apart. (Do not place more than 4 cookies on sheet.)

4. Bake until golden brown, about 5 minutes. Cool 30 to 60 seconds on cookie sheet on wire rack, just until edges have set; then, quickly flip cookies over.

5. Working as quickly as possible, roll each cookie around handle (½-inch diameter) of wooden spoon. If cookies become too hard to roll, return to oven briefly to soften. As each cookie is  shaped, slip off spoon handle and cool completely on wire racks. Repeat with remaining batter. Makes about 24 cookies.

Each cookie: About 72 calories, 0g protein, 8g carbohydrate, 4g total fat (2g saturated), 10mg cholesterol, 64mg sodium.

Almond-Anise Biscotti

Soaking the anise seeds in liqueur softens them and releases their delicious flavor.

Prep: 25 minutes plus cooling Bake: 55 minutes

- 1 tablespoon anise seeds, crushed
- 1 tablespoon anise-flavored apéritif or liqueur
- 2 cups all-purpose flour
- 1 cup sugar
- 1 cup whole almonds (4 ounces), toasted (page 562) and coarsely chopped
- 1 teaspoon baking powder
- ⅛ teaspoon salt
- 3 large eggs

1. Preheat oven to 325°F. In medium bowl, combine anise seeds and anise-flavored apéritif; let stand 10 minutes.

2. Meanwhile, grease large cookie sheet.

3. In large bowl, with wire whisk, stir flour, sugar, chopped almonds, baking powder, and salt. With wire whisk, beat eggs into anise mixture. With wooden spoon, stir egg mixture into flour mixture until blended. Divide dough in half. On prepared cookie sheet, with floured hands, shape each half into 15-inch log, placing them 3 inches apart (dough will be sticky).

4. Bake until golden and toothpick inserted in center comes out clean, about 40 minutes. Cool 10 minutes on cookie sheet on wire rack, then transfer logs to cutting board.

5. With serrated knife, cut each log crosswise on diagonal into ¼-inch-thick slices. Place slices, cut side down, on two ungreased cookie sheets. Bake 15 minutes, turning slices over once and rotating cookie sheets between upper and lower oven racks halfway through baking. With spatula, transfer biscotti to wire racks to cool completely. Makes about 84 biscotti.

Each biscotto: About 33 calories, 1g protein, 5g carbohydrate, 1g total fat (0g saturated), 8mg cholesterol, 12mg sodium.

Chocolate and Hazelnut Truffles

Use the best chocolate you can find to give these truffles European flair. If you wish, add 2 tablespoons of coffee-, orange-, or almond-flavored liqueur to the melted-chocolate mixture.

Prep: 25 minutes plus chilling

- 8 ounces bittersweet chocolate or 6 squares (6 ounces) semisweet chocolate plus 2 squares (2 ounces) unsweetened chocolate, coarsely chopped
- ½ cup heavy or whipping cream
- 3 tablespoons butter, cut into pieces and softened (do not use margarine)
- ⅓ cup hazelnuts (filberts), toasted and skinned (page 562), finely chopped
- 3 tablespoons unsweetened cocoa

1. Line 8½" by 4½" loaf pan with plastic wrap; smooth out wrinkles. In food processor with knife blade attached, process chocolate until finely ground.

2. In 1-quart saucepan, heat cream to simmering over medium-high heat. Add to chocolate in food processor and puree until smooth. Add butter and process until smooth.

3. Pour chocolate mixture into prepared pan; spread evenly. Refrigerate until cool and firm enough to handle, about 3 hours.

4. Remove chocolate mixture from pan by lifting edges of plastic wrap. Invert chocolate block onto cutting board; discard plastic wrap. Cut chocolate lengthwise into 4 strips, then cut each strip crosswise into 8 pieces. (To cut chocolate easily, dip knife in hot water and wipe dry; repeat as needed.) With cool hands, quickly roll each square into ball. Roll 16 truffles in chopped hazelnuts and remaining 16 truffles in cocoa. Place in single layer in waxed paper–lined airtight container. Refrigerate up to 1 week, or freeze up to 1 month. Remove from freezer 5 minutes before serving. Makes 32 truffles.

Each truffle: About 66 calories, 1g protein, 5g carbohydrate, 6g total fat (3g saturated), 8mg cholesterol, 13mg sodium.

Chocolate-Walnut Fudge

A rich and creamy fudge that couldn't be easier to make.

Prep: 25 minutes plus chilling

- 1 pound bittersweet chocolate or 16 squares (16 ounces) semisweet chocolate, chopped
- 1 can (14 ounces) sweetened condensed milk
- 1 cup walnuts (4 ounces), coarsely chopped
- 1 teaspoon vanilla extract
- ⅛ teaspoon salt

1. Line 8-inch square baking pan with plastic wrap; smooth out wrinkles. In heavy 2-quart saucepan, melt chocolate with condensed milk over medium-low heat, stirring constantly, until smooth. Remove from heat.

2. Stir in walnuts, vanilla, and salt. Scrape chocolate mixture into prepared pan; spread evenly. Refrigerate until firm, about 3 hours.

3. Remove fudge from pan by lifting edges of plastic wrap. Invert fudge onto cutting board; discard plastic wrap. Cut fudge into 8 strips, then cut each strip crosswise into 8 pieces. Layer between waxed paper in airtight container. Store at room temperature up to 1 week, or refrigerate up to 1 month. Makes 64 pieces.

Each piece: About 67 calories, 1g protein, 8g carbohydrate, 4g total fat (2g saturated), 2mg cholesterol, 13mg sodium.

SUGAR SYRUP TEMPERATURES

Test Kitchen Tip

Many candies are made with sugar syrup. Measuring the temperature of sugar syrup accurately is crucial in candy making. For the best results, always use a candy thermometer. When attaching the thermometer to the pan, be sure the tip of the thermometer doesn't touch the bottom of the pan.

When cooking a sugar syrup, crystals form on the side of the saucepan. They must be dissolved, otherwise the candy may be grainy. Rub a pastry brush that's been dipped into cold water against the sugar crystals to wash them into the syrup. Repeat all around the inside of the saucepan until no sugar crystals remain.

Butter-Nut Toffee Crunch

This classic candy is perfect for gift-giving during the holidays. You can purchase festive packaging at your local "party" store.

Prep: 15 minutes plus cooling   Cook: 25 minutes

- 1¾ cups sugar
- ⅓ cup light corn syrup
- ¼ cup water
- 1 cup butter or margarine (2 sticks)
- 2 cups walnuts (8 ounces), lightly toasted (page 562)
- 2 squares (2 ounces) unsweetened chocolate, chopped
- 2 squares (2 ounces) ounces semisweet chocolate, chopped
- 1 teaspoon vegetable shortening

1. In heavy 2-quart saucepan, combine sugar, corn syrup, and water; heat to boiling over medium heat, stirring occasionally. Stir in butter. Set candy thermometer in place and continue cooking, stirring frequently, about 20 minutes or until temperature reaches 300°F (hard-crack stage).

2. Meanwhile, lightly grease 15½" by 10½" jelly-roll pan. Finely chop walnuts.

3. Remove saucepan from heat. Reserve ⅓ cup walnuts; stir remaining walnuts into hot syrup. Immediately pour mixture into prepared jelly-roll pan. Working quickly, spread evenly with spatula. Cool candy completely in pan on wire rack.

4. Prepare chocolate glaze: In small saucepan, melt chocolates and shortening over low heat, stirring until smooth. Remove saucepan from heat; cool slightly.

5. Lift out candy in one piece and place on cutting board. With metal spatula, spread warm chocolate evenly over candy; sprinkle with reserved walnuts. Let stand until chocolate sets, about 1 hour.

6. With knife, break toffee crunch into serving-size pieces. Layer between waxed paper in airtight container. Store at room temperature up to 2 weeks. Makes about 1¾ pounds candy.

Each ounce: About 195 calories, 2g protein, 18g carbohydrate, 14g total fat (6g saturated), 19mg cholesterol, 75mg sodium.

INDEX

ACKNOWLEDGMENTS

A book of this scope takes the efforts of many people to make it a reality. Along with those who worked on this edition, I'd also like to thank the people who brought the first edition of this book to life. Frank Bennack and Ellen Levine for the green light to do it right—and in color! Lisa Brainerd Burge and Rick Rodgers, shapers of chapters; Sandy Gluck, Lori Longbotham, Gina Miraglia, Fraya Berg, Wendy Kalen, Maryanne Marinelli, Marianne Svec, food lovers who all produce delicious recipes that work.

TO COLLEAGUES AT GOOD HOUSEKEEPING: Rosemary Ellis, Sarah Scrymser, Richard Eisenberg.

TO OUR BOOK TEAM who approached every word, recipe, taste, photo, and query with enthusiasm and a fresh eye, you have our eternal admiration and appreciation. Deborah Mintcheff, writer and tweaker par excellence; Debby Goldsmith, Sharon Franke, Delia Hammock, Cathy Lo, Allison Dewine, Rosanne Toroian, Sarah Reynolds, Carol Prager, Paul Picciuto, who added new ideas and recipes to make any occasion delicious; Maryanne Bannon, managing editor, guardian angel, traffic cop, counselor.

TO OUR FRIENDS IN THE FOOD INDUSTRY: National Cattleman's Beef Association, National Pork Producer's Council, National Chicken Council, American Egg Board, California Fig Advisory Board; California Tree Fruit Agreement. Thank you for all your help in clarifying product information, cooking techniques, and food safety practices.

FOR ADVICE ON TABLE ETIQUETTE: Cardel Ltd. and Tiffany & Company.

Many thanks to everyone who gave so generously of their time and talent to make this book a reality.

IT WAS A JOY TO WORK WITH SO MANY GIFTED PEOPLE.

—SUSAN WESTMORELAND
Food Director, *Good Housekeeping*

PHOTOGRAPHY CREDITS

METRIC EQUIVALENT CHARTS

The recipes that appear in this cookbook use the standard United States method for measuring liquid and dry or solid ingredients (teaspoons, tablespoons, and cups). The information on this chart is provided to help cooks outside the U.S. successfully use these recipes. All equivalents are approximate.

METRIC EQUIVALENTS FOR DIFFERENT TYPES OF INGREDIENTS

A standard cup measure of a dry or solid ingredient will vary in weight depending on the type of ingredient. A standard cup of liquid is the same volume for any type of liquid. Use the following chart when converting standard cup measures to grams (weight) or milliliters (volume).

Standard Cup	Fine Powder (e.g., flour)	Grain (e.g., rice)	Granular (e.g., sugar)	Liquid Solids (e.g., butter)	Liquid (e.g., milk)
1	140 g	150 g	190 g	200 g	240 ml
3/4	105 g	113 g	143 g	150 g	180 ml
2/3	93 g	100 g	125 g	133 g	160 ml
1/2	70 g	75 g	95 g	100 g	120 ml
1/3	47 g	50 g	63 g	67 g	80 ml
1/4	35 g	38 g	48 g	50 g	60 ml
1/8	18 g	19 g	24 g	25 g	30 ml

USEFUL EQUIVALENTS FOR LIQUID INGREDIENTS BY VOLUME

1/4 tsp	=				1 ml
1/2 tsp	=				2 ml
1 tsp	=				5 ml
3 tsp	=	1 tbls	=		1/2 fl oz =	15 ml
		2 tbls	=	1/8 cup =	1 fl oz =	30 ml
		4 tbls	=	1/4 cup =	2 fl oz =	60 ml
		5 1/3 tbls	=	1/3 cup =	3 fl oz =	80 ml
		8 tbls	=	1/2 cup =	4 fl oz =	120 ml
		10 2/3 tbls	=	2/3 cup =	5 fl oz =	160 ml
		12 tbls	=	3/4 cup =	6 fl oz =	180 ml
		16 tbls	=	1 cup =	8 fl oz =	240 ml
		1 pt	=	2 cups =	16 fl oz =	480 ml
		1 qt	=	4 cups =	32 fl oz =	960 ml
					33 fl oz =	1000 ml = 1l

USEFUL EQUIVALENTS FOR DRY INGREDIENTS BY WEIGHT

(To convert ounces to grams, multiply the number of ounces by 30.)

1 oz	=	1/16 lb	=	30 g
4 oz	=	1/4 lb	=	120 g
8 oz	=	1/2 lb	=	240 g
12 oz	=	3/4 lb	=	360 g
16 oz	=	1 lb	=	480 g

USEFUL EQUIVALENTS FOR COOKING/OVEN TEMPERATURES

	Fahrenheit	Celsius	Gas Mark
Freeze Water	32° F	0° C	
Room Temperature	68° F	20° C	
Boil Water	212° F	100° C	
Bake	325° F	160° C	3
	350° F	180° C	4
	375° F	190° C	5
	400° F	200° C	6
	425° F	220° C	7
	450° F	230° C	8
Broil			Grill

USEFUL EQUIVALENTS FOR LENGTH

(To convert inches to centimeters, multiply the number of inches by 2.5.)

1 in =		2.5 cm
6 in = 1/2 ft =		15 cm
12 in = 1 ft =		30 cm
36 in = 3 ft = 1 yd =	90 cm
40 in =		100 cm = 1 m

Bacon, 16-ounce package, diced, cooked	$1\frac{1}{2}$ cups pieces	Cottage cheese, 8 ounces	1 cup

Beans, dry
  1 pound
  1 cup
	
	2 cups
	2 to $2\frac{1}{2}$ cups cooked
		Couscous, 1 cup	about $2\frac{1}{2}$ cups cooked

Berries	See individual varieties.	Crackers, crushed
		  graham, 7
		  5" by $2\frac{1}{2}$" crackers
			
			about 1 cup fine crumbs

Blackberries, 1 pint	about 2 cups	saltine, 28	about 1 cup fine crumbs
Blueberries, 1 pint	about 3 cups	Cranberries, 12-ounce bag	3 cups
Bread crumbs, dried 8-ounce package	$2\frac{1}{4}$ cups	Cream, heavy or whipping, 1 cup	about 2 cups whipped cream

Bread crumbs, fresh 1 slice bread	$\frac{1}{2}$ cup bread crumbs	Cream cheese
		  3-ounce package
		  8-ounce package
			
			6 tablespoons
			1 cup

Butter or margarine $\frac{1}{4}$-pound stick	 $\frac{1}{2}$ cup or 8 tablespoons	Currants, dried, 5 ounces	about 1 cup
1 pound	4 sticks or 2 cups	Dates, dry, pitted, 10-ounce container	about 2 cups

Cabbage, 1 pound coarsely sliced	about 4 to 5 cups	Egg whites, large
		  1
		  1 cup
			about
			2 tablespoons
			8 to 10 egg whites

Celery, 1 medium bunch sliced/diced	about 4 cups	Egg yolks, large, 1 cup	12 to 14 egg yolks
Cheddar cheese, 4 ounces	1 cup shredded	Flour, 1 pound all-purpose	 about $3\frac{1}{2}$ cups
Cherries, 1 pound	about 2 cups pitted	cake	about 4 cups
Chicken, cooked $2\frac{1}{2}$-pound to 3-pound chicken, diced meat	about $2\frac{1}{2}$ cups	whole-wheat	about $3\frac{3}{4}$ cups
Cocoa, unsweetened, 8-ounce can	2 cups	Gelatin, unflavored, to gel 2 cups liquid	1 envelope
Coconut, flaked, $3\frac{1}{2}$ ounces	$1\frac{1}{3}$ cups	Green or red bell pepper, 1 large	about 1 cup chopped
Cookies, crushed chocolate wafers, 20 $2\frac{1}{4}$-inch	 about 1 cup fine crumbs	Hominy grits, 1 cup	about $4\frac{1}{2}$ cups cooked
gingersnaps, 15	about 1 cup fine crumbs	Honey, liquid, 16 ounces	$1\frac{1}{3}$ cups
vanilla wafers, 22	about 1 cup fine crumbs		